OBJECTIVE

English 18 Days Wonder

OBJECTIVE

English 18 Days Wonder

FOR ALL COMPETITIVE EXAMS

- 1st time introducing a day to day result oriented and fully solved course for sure success.
- Covers Concepts/Tricks/Strategy for various Exams/Practice Exercises
- Covers all the topics from entrance point of view
- Contains Advance Grammar topics are Modifiers, Parallelism etc.
- Includes 30 latest competitive exam papers (2007-2009) for self evaluation

Must for : MBA (CAT), CDS, NDA, BANKING, SSC, RAILWAYS, HOTEL Mgt., NIFT Entrance, IAS & all other Competitive Exams.

By

KHURANA KJS

MARKANDAY R

S. CHAND & COMPANY LTD.

(An ISO 9001 : 2000 Company)

RAM NAGAR, NEW DELHI - 110 055

S. CHAND & COMPANY LTD.

(An ISO 9001 : 2000 Company)

Head Office: 7361, RAM NAGAR, NEW DELHI - 110 055
Phone: 23672080-81-82, 9899107446, 9911310888
Fax: 91-11-23677446
Shop at: **schandgroup.com;** e-mail: **info@schandgroup.com**

Branches :

AHMEDABAD : 1st Floor, Heritage, Near Gujarat Vidhyapeeth, Ashram Road, **Ahmedabad** - 380 014, Ph: 27541965, 27542369, ahmedabad@schandgroup.com
BENGALURU : No. 6, Ahuja Chambers, 1st Cross, Kumara Krupa Road, **Bengaluru** - 560 001, Ph: 22268048, 22354008, bangalore@schandgroup.com
BHOPAL : 238-A, M.P. Nagar, Zone 1, **Bhopal** - 462 011, Ph: 4274723. bhopal@schandgroup.com
CHANDIGARH : S.C.O. 2419-20, First Floor, Sector - 22-C (Near Aroma Hotel), **Chandigarh** -160 022, Ph: 2725443, 2725446, chandigarh@schandgroup.com
CHENNAI : 152, Anna Salai, **Chennai** - 600 002, Ph: 28460026, 28460027, chennai@schandgroup.com
COIMBATORE : Plot No. 5, Rajalakshmi Nagar, Peelamedu, **Coimbatore** -641 004, (M) 09444228242, coimbatore@schandgroup.com
CUTTACK : 1st Floor, Bhartia Tower, Badambadi, **Cuttack** - 753 009, Ph: 2332580; 2332581, cuttack@schandgroup.com
DEHRADUN : 1st Floor, 20, New Road, Near Dwarka Store, **Dehradun** - 248 001, Ph: 2711101, 2710861, dehradun@schandgroup.com
GUWAHATI : Pan Bazar, **Guwahati** - 781 001, Ph: 2738811, 2735640 guwahati@schandgroup.com
HYDERABAD : Padma Plaza, H.No. 3-4-630, Opp. Ratna College, Narayanaguda, **Hyderabad** - 500 029, Ph: 24651135, 24744815, hyderabad@schandgroup.com
JAIPUR : A-14, Janta Store Shopping Complex, University Marg, Bapu Nagar, **Jaipur** - 302 015, Ph: 2719126, jaipur@schandgroup.com
JALANDHAR : Mai Hiran Gate, **Jalandhar** - 144 008, Ph: 2401630, 5000630, jalandhar@schandgroup.com
JAMMU : 67/B, B-Block, Gandhi Nagar, **Jammu** - 180 004, (M) 09878651464
KOCHI : Kachapilly Square, Mullassery Canal Road, Ernakulam, **Kochi** - 682 011, Ph: 2378207, cochin@schandgroup.com
KOLKATA : 285/J, Bipin Bihari Ganguli Street, **Kolkata** - 700 012, Ph: 22367459, 22373914, kolkata@schandgroup.com
LUCKNOW : Mahabeer Market, 25 Gwynne Road, Aminabad, **Lucknow** - 226 018, Ph: 2626801, 2284815, lucknow@schandgroup.com
MUMBAI : Blackie House, 103/5, Walchand Hirachand Marg, Opp. G.P.O., **Mumbai** - 400 001, Ph: 22690881, 22610885, mumbai@schandgroup.com
NAGPUR : Karnal Bag, Model Mill Chowk, Umrer Road, **Nagpur** - 440 032, Ph: 2723901, 2777666 nagpur@schandgroup.com
PATNA : 104, Citicentre Ashok, Govind Mitra Road, **Patna** - 800 004, Ph: 2300489, 2302100, patna@schandgroup.com
PUNE : 291/1, Ganesh Gayatri Complex, 1st Floor, Somwarpeth, Near Jain Mandir, **Pune** - 411 011, Ph: 64017298, pune@schandgroup.com
RAIPUR : Kailash Residency, Plot No. 4B, Bottle House Road, Shankar Nagar, **Raipur** - 492 007, Ph: 09981200834, raipur@schandgroup.com
RANCHI : Flat No. 104, Sri Draupadi Smriti Apartments, East of Jaipal Singh Stadium, Neel Ratan Street, Upper Bazar, **Ranchi** - 834 001, Ph: 2208761, ranchi@schandgroup.com
VISAKHAPATNAM: Plot No. 7, 1st Floor, Allipuram Extension, Opp. Radhakrishna Towers, Seethammadhara North Extn., **Visakhapatnam** - 530 013, (M) 09347580841, visakhapatnam@schandgroup.com

First Edition 2010

ISBN : 81-219-3564-4 **Code** : 06 181

PRINTED IN INDIA
By Rajendra Ravindra Printers Pvt. Ltd., 7361, Ram Nagar, New Delhi -110 055 and published by S. Chand & Company Ltd., 7361, Ram Nagar, New Delhi -110 055.

PREFACE

It gives us immense pleasure to present this English 18 Days Wonder course. English has been an important part of every competition. A large number of aspirants are weak at English. The reason is that their foundations are weak which is a manifestation of their inability to feel at home. A need was felt to have a book in simple language to which an average student can understand and a brilliant can brush up his knowledge fast. To bridge this gap this course is prepared. It took years to complete this course and thousands of students were interacted before putting this course into final shape. Care has been taken to ensure that even a minor concept should not go unexplained. It is hoped that this course will serve the purpose for which it is made. Errors might have crept in despite at the efforts. Suggestions will be received with gratitude. For suggestions and feed back feel free to write at kanwar003@gmail.com or rmarkanday@gmail.com

AUTHORS

ACKNOWLEDGEMENTS

At the very outset, we fail to find adequate words, with limited words at our command, to express our indebtedness to the Almighty, whose eternal blessing, sublime presence, and erudite guidance gave shape to our efforts. So, it is with deepest sense of gratitude that we are attempting to reciprocate magnanimity He bestowed on us.

Least definable but most sincerely left is our loving indebtedness to all our family members, friends and colleagues whose love and unfailing encouragement proved precious in our academic ministry.

We shall always remain obliged to all the readers who appreciated our intentions manifested in the form of this book. Overwhelming response around the country has been most helpful in the formation of this course. A sense of obligation beckons us to mention our students who remained a constant source of inspiration all the time during these years.

At last but not the least we are thankful to S. Chand & Company Ltd. for the faith they have shown in us.

AUTHORS

CONTENT

Day 1.	Introduction	1–15
Day 2.	Vocabulary Building	16–24
Day 3.	Nouns	25–35
Day 4.	Pronouns	36–49
Day 5.	Adjective	50–63
Day 6.	Verbs & Tenses	64–77
Day 7.	Adverbs	78–86
Day 8.	Conjunctions	87–95
Day 9.	Articles	96–103
Day 10.	Prepositions	104–110
Day 11.	Modifiers and Parallelism	111–125
Day 12.	Common – Errors	126–136
Day 13.	Sentence Rearrangement	137–156
Day 14.	Reading Comprehension	157–181
Day 15.	Fill in the Blanks	182–199
Day 16.	Idioms and Phrases	200–209
Day 17.	Idioms and Phrases	210–220
Day 18.	Evaluation	221–229
Test Yourself Section –I (Easy Level Papers)		**231–314**
1.	Dena Bank P.O. 2008	233–238
2.	ALLAHABAD BANK CLERK 2008	239–242
3.	BANK OF BARODA CLERK 2009	243–247
4.	ANDHRA BANK P.O. 2007	248–253
5.	BANK OF MAHARASHTRA P.O. 2007	254–260
6.	B.O.I. CLERK 2008	261–266
7.	CORPORATION BANK P.O. 2007	267–273
8.	MAHARASHTRA CET 2009	274–282
9.	NMAT 2008	283–289

10. PNB TRAINEE MANAGEMENT 2008 290–297
11. SBI CLERK 2008 – 1ST Shift 298–301
12. SBI CLERK 2008 – 2nd Shift 302–306
13. SNAP 2008 307–314

Test Yourself Section – II (Medium Difficulty Level Papers) 315–406

1. ATMA 2009 317–332
2. IBSAT 2007 333–345
3. IRMA 2007 346–351
4. JMET 2007 352–361
5. JMET 2008 362–367
6. MAT – Feb. 2007 368–378
7. MAT – MAY 2009 379–392
8. MAT –Sept. 2007 393–406

Test Yourself Section – III (Tough Level Papers) 407–541

1. ATMA 2008 409–425
2. CAT 2008 426–439
3. CAT 2007 440–452
4. FMS 2008 453–473
5. FMS 2009 474–484
6. IIFT 2007 485–501
7. IIFT 2008 502–514
8. XAT 2007 515–528
9. XAT 2009 529–541

Day

1

Introduction

Dear Student,

The ***English 18 days wonder*** package is in your hand. It is your first day of 18 day wonder course. Before starting this course, let us discuss a few facts about **English**. In your day-to-day life you might have met people who are very good at **English**. **Have you ever thought why these people are very good at English** ?

These people are very good at English because :

1. They have good **vocabulary** or **knowledge of words.**
2. They have excellent knowledge of **English grammar** like **tenses, nouns, adjectives,** etc.
3. The most important reason is that they take **sincere interest in reading any matter written in English.**

The basic approach of this course is to **increase your knowledge of English grammar as well as to increase your word power simultaneously.** It will help you in attempting grammar section in English Language Paper easily. Also you can attempt and score well in other areas like **reading comprehensions, antonyms, synonyms, one word substitutions, spellings, jumble re-arrangement, cloze test etc.**

This method has been developed after seeing its effectiveness on more than **thousand of students**. Therefore you can call it a **research product** that will make you fully confident in attempting English language paper in any entrance examination.

So this is not just an English book for preparing competitions. This has been brilliantly written, very carefully and scientifically planned course to deliver more than you expect . Now before starting chapters in this book, we will like you to know a few of the **basic terms (definitions)** of **English language** which will help you in understanding English language and also to cover this book effectively.But before doing a few basics of English language. We would like you to have an idea or style of English language paper that comes in most of competitive exams.

Generally we have following types of questions asked in English language paper.

1. **Locate the Error/Errors in given sentence.**
2. **Questions based on Reading comprehensions.**
3. **Antonyms/Synonyms of words.**
4. **Fill in the Blanks**
5. **Rearrangement of Sentences.**
6. **One word substitutions and idiom/phrases.**
7. **Analogies, spellings etc.**

Now we will explain each of the above one by one.

1. **Locate the Error/Errors in given sentence.**

We will explain it with following example.

I like	**the poeteries**	**of**	**Tagore**
(a)	**(b)**	**(c)**	**(d)**

Here the error is in **part (b)** of the above sentence.

As **poeteries** should be replaced with **poetry or poems**. Now to find errors in sentences you should have proper knowledge of **grammar**. For this we will cover each topic of **English grammar** in this course.

2. **Questions based on comprehensions.**

In this section paragraphs are given and questions based on paragraphs are asked. An example is given below.

Directions : (Question 1 - 5)

Read the Passage carefully and answer the questions given below it.

PASSAGE

A well-dressed young man entered a big textile shop one evening. He was able to draw the attention of the salesmen who thought him rich and likely to make heavy purchases. He was shown the superior varieties of suit lengths, and sarees. But after casually examining them, he kept moving to the next section where readymade goods were being sold and further onto the hosiery section. By then, the salesmen had begun to doubt his intentions, and drew the attention of the manager. The manager asked him what exactly he wanted, and he replied that he wanted courteous treatment. He explained that he had come to the same shop in casual dress that morning and drawn little attention. His pride was hurt and he wanted to assert himself. He had come in good dress only to get decent treatment, not for getting any textiles. He left without making any purchase.

1. The youngman was well-dressed because
   (a) it was his habit to dress well.
   (b) it was his wedding day.
   (c) he wanted to meet the manager of the shop.
   (d) he wanted to impress the salesmen.
2. The salesmen in the shop are described as people who pay attention to
   (a) only young men and women.
   (b) pretty women.
   (c) only rich customers.
   (d) regular customers.
3. The young man moved away to the hosiery section because he
   (a) was not interested in purchasing anything now.
   (b) did not like the readymade clothes.
   (c) wanted better clothes.
   (d) was restless.
4. The manager asked the young man what he wanted because
   (a) he would give him exactly what he was looking for.

(b) the salesmen had drawn his attention to the indifferent attitude of the young man.

(c) he thought they could do more business with him that way.

(d) he thought the visitor was dissatisfied.

5. The young man left without making purchases because he

(a) did not have money.

(b) could not find any item of his choice.

(c) had come only to make a point about the indifferent attitude of the salesmen towards casually dressed customers.

(d) decided to come to make the purchases later on.

Answers :

1 (a) 2. (b) 3. (c) 4. (d) 5. (e)

This part of the paper is **usually very easy** but some paragraphs are **tough** as words used in them are **difficult to understand**. To attempt this section you have to read a paragraph **very carefully**. Only then you can give the answers to the questions asked. For the difficult paragraphs you should have the **word power** (**vocabulary**) otherwise you will not be able to understand the paragraph.

But do not worry, we will tell you a very effective method to increase your word power on Day 2.

3. Antonyms/Synonyms of words.

Antonyms means opposite.

For example Antonym or opposite of **LOVE** is **HATE**.

Synonym mean same.

For example Synonym of **POLITE** is **GENTLE**.

4. Fill in the blanks.

There are two types of fill in the blanks.

A. Single Line Fill in the Blanks.

B. Fill in the Blanks in paragraph or Cloze Test.

We will explain each of them one by one.

A. Single Line Paragraph.

(i) I am coming directly ____________ my office.

(a) since (b) from

(c) of (d) none

The answer to the above is **(b)**.

(ii) Justice should be ____________ evenhandedly.

(a) Discharged (b) Performed

(c) Declared (d) Administered

The answer to the above is **(d)**.

B. Cloze Test.

An Example is given below.

Directions:

In the following passage, there are blanks each of which has been numbered these numbers are printed below the passage and against each, four words, are suggested. One of which fits into the blank appropriately. Find out the appropriate word.

In this section some fill the blanks are given in the form of paragraph.

The law of virtue implies ___1___ observance of discipline. But once ___2___ keen to uphold ___3___ rules governingh good conduct, starts ___4___ he will ultimately ___5___ a stage when he will refrain from treading the path of evil.

1. (a) hard (b) rigid
   (c) routine (d) temporary.
2. (a) the person (b) any
   (c) some (d) a
3. (a) many (b) several
   (c) the (d) those
4. (a) abiding by them (b) obeying
   (c) flouting (d) ignoring
5. (a) cross (b) achieve
   (c) arrive (d) reach

Answers: 1 (a) 2 (a) 3 (c) 4 (a) 5 (d)

5. Rearrangement of Sentences.

This can be clearly understood by the following examples.

Directions. :

In each of the items given below, there is a sentence, of which some parts have been jumbled up. You are required to re-arrange these parts which are labelled P, Q, R and S to produce the correct sentence. Choose the proper sequence.

1. One of the earliest attempts

P was the Dover House

Q designed

R by two American scientists

S at solar heating

The proper sequence should be ...

(a) QRPS

(b) QSPR

(c) SPRQ

(d) SPQR

2. At the intersection

P the highway robber

Q snatched away his wallet

R threatening the scooter driver

S with his knife.

The proper sequence should be

(a) PRSQ

(b) RSPQ

(c) PSQR

(d) RPQS

Answers : 1 (d) 2 (a)

6. One word substitutions and idiom/phrases.

This can also be understood by following example.

(i) One word substitution :

Those who eat only flesh : Carnivorous

Present everywhere : Omnipresent

(ii) Idioms

A snake in grass : It means the danger which cannot be seen or hidden danger.

(iii) Phrase

My friend **got the sack from** his first job.

Here **got the sack** from means **was dismissed from**

7. Analogies, spellings etc.

i. **Analogies:** In this we have to find that answer from the choices which is having the same relationship as given in question.

Examples are given below.

a. 'Hospital' is related to 'Nurse' in the same way as 'Court' is related to ...

1. Justice
2. Lawyer
3. Judgement
4. Trial
5. None of these

Answer: **(2)**

b. 'Bouquet' is related to 'Flowers' in the same way as 'Sentence' is related to ......

1. Letters
2. Paragraph
3. Content
4. Words
5. Construction

Answer: **(2)**

Again some relationships are easy to understand and some are difficult. This is because either the words used or relationships given are difficult.

So this is basic format of an **English paper** that comes in most of the **entrance exams**. Also you have observed that in order to attempt the paper successfully, you should have **proper knowledge of grammar** and should have excellent **vocabulary**. As the **error finding** is based on knowledge of **grammar** and the rest of paper is based on your **knowledge of words, idioms, phrase,one word etc.** Thatswhy we have been trying to insist that we will do **each topic of grammar** and word-meanings on each day as we move forward.

As we will be doing grammar topic on each day so it is must for us to clear the basic terminology on day 1. It will help you to understand the course better.

Now we will do some basic terms used in English language.

BASIC TERMS USED IN ENGLISH

The English language, which we speak or write, consists of many words. Each word is used as per situation and time in which we are speaking or writing that sentence.

So each word is to be used as per certain rules.

Also each word can be classified into certain groups as nouns, pronouns, verbs, helping verbs etc.

This classification or putting each word as nouns, pronouns,adverbs, adjectives etc is known as **Parts of speech.** We will discuss each part of speech one by one

PARTS OF SPEECH

1. NOUN :

Word which is used to name a person, a place or a thing.

Examples of Nouns are given below :

Person	-	**Ram, Sham** etc.
Place	-	**Delhi, Ambala** etc.
Things	-	**Table, Chair** etc.

2. Pronoun :

Word used in place of noun is called pronoun.

Examples of Pronouns are given below :

I, We, You, He, She, It, They etc. are some of the pronouns.

3. Verb :

Any word used to represent an action done by noun or pronoun is called verb.

Examples of Verbs are given below :

Running, Eating, Dancing, etc.

Whereas there are certain words which help the main verbs to express themselves. These are known as **helping verbs.**

is, am, are, was, were, has, have etc. are a few **helping verbs**.

4. Adjectives :

Any word which is used to represent the **quality or characterstics** or any thing about noun or pronoun is called an **adjective.**

This can be clearly understood by following Examples:

Ex. 1 : **Manu** is an **intelligent** person.

Ex. 2 : **Deepu** is **good** girl.

In Ex.1 **Manu** is a **noun** And **intelligent** is an **adjective** because this word is showing the quality of the person. Similiraly in Ex. 2 **Deepu** is a **Noun** and **Good** is an **adjective**.

5. Adverb :

Words which are used to **qualify verbs/adverbs/adjectives** or which tell us anything about **verbs/adverbs/adjectives** are known as **adverbs**. These words tell us **how, when, where** the **action is done**.

This can be clearly understood by following Examples:

Ex. 1 : He ran **fast.**

Ex. 2 : He turned **quickly.**

Ex. 3: He speaks too slowly

Ex. 4 : This is a very sweet Mango.

In Ex. 1 fastly is an **adverb** because it is showing that person (He) has done the **action** of running **fastly**. Similiraly in Ex. 2 **quickly** is an **adverb**.

In Ex. 3 too is qualifying in adverb (slowly). Therefore too is an adverb.

In Ex. 4 very is qualifying the adjective (sweet) therefore very is an adverb.

6. **Preposition :**

It is the word which shows the relationship or connection between :

(a) **Noun** and **Pronoun**

(b) **Verb** and **Noun/pronoun**

(c) **Adjective** and **Noun/pronoun**

Examples :

(i) She is suffering **from** fever.

(ii) I am waiting **for** my friend.

(iii) He failed **in** the examination.

In above examples **from, for** and **in** are preposotions.

Some of Prepositions are **in, on, before, after, under, across, along, through, about, up** etc.

7. **Conjunction :**

It is a word used to join any two sentences or any two words. Some conjunctions are **but, or, it, before, after, since, untill, unless, because etc.**

Ex. 1 : You can visit Dehli **or** Jaipur.

Ex. 2 : She is gentle **and** helps poor.

In above examples **or, and** are **conjunctions.**

8. **Articles :**

These are words used to denote a single number, a small or a large number of any common noun. There are three articles in English language.

These are

(i) **A**

(ii) **An**

(iii) **The**

A and **An** are known as indefinite aritcles. **The** is called definite aritcle.

9. **Interjection :**

These are the words which are used to express sudden feeling of **joy, sorrow, surprise** and **shock.**

Ex. 1 : Alas! we lost the match.

Ex. 2 : Oh! what a sad story.

In above examples **alas** and **oh** are **interjections.**

Till now we have seen that how each word in English language is classified and is known by the names like noun, pronoun etc.

Now we will do different types of sentences and some of basic terms related to sentences.

First we will define, what is a sentence.

Sentence : A group of words complete in meaning or sense.

Let us consider a few examples :

Ex. 1 : **Some of the girls** **are playing.**

Ex. 2 : **Lata** **sings a song.**

Ex. 3 : **Ram** **is shouting.**

We see that every sentence written above shows person or noun or a group of persons is doing something.

As in Ex. 1 some girls are playing and in Ex. 2 Lata sings.

Therefore in English language every sentence can be divided into two parts.

(i) Subject

(ii) Predicate

For Example again in above sentences.

(i) **Lata** is **subject** and **sings a song** is **predicate.**

(ii) **Ram** is **subject** and is **shouting** is **predicate.**

So now we can define subject and predicate.

1. **Subject :** It is usually a **noun** or **a pronuon** or gerund in sentence which is saying or doing something or **about which** something is said.

For Example :

In Ram is shouting **Ram** is **subject.**

Swimming is a good exercise

In above example Swimming (gerund) is subject.

2. **Predicate :** In a sentence what has been said by subject or what is being described by the subject or **about the subject** is known as **predicate.**

3. **Object:-** It is either what has been done by doer or whatever has been said about the subject.

For Example :

In Ram is playing **is playing** is **predicate.**

In **Swimming is a good exercise** **good exercise** is the object.

Now we will study different types of sentences.

These are as follows :-

(i) Assertive sentence

(ii) Interrogative sentence

(iii) Imperative sentence

(iv) Exclamatory sentence

(v) Optative sentence

We will explain each of the above one by one.

(i) Assertive sentence :

The sentence which has some information or it is any simple statement.

These are of two types.

(a) positive or affirmative

(b) negative

positive	:	Ram is playing
negative	:	Ram is not playing.

(ii) Interrogative sentence :

In this type questions are asked.

For Example :

who are you ? where are you ?.

are interrogative sentences.

(iii) Imperative sentence :

In this type of sentence an order, a request, an advice or a prohibition is given.

For Example :

(a)	Be quiet.	(order)
(b)	Never tell a lie.	(advice).
(c)	Please take your seat.	(request).
(d)	Do not go there.	(prohibition)

(iv) Exclamatory sentence :

In this sudden feeling of joy sorrow, shock, or surprise is expressed.

For Example :

(a) What a pity. !

(b) Oh! What a terrible sight.

(v) Optative sentence :

In this type of sentence we express wishes.

For Example :

(a) May you Live long

(b) God bless you.

The above classification of sentences is as per situation in which we are either speaking or writing sentences.

Also there is classification of the sentence as per structure like simple, compound and complex sentence but from entrance examination point of view, this classification is not important.

Always keep in mind that in **competitive exams** we **don't have much time** to answer the questions. So you have to be very **precise, fast and accurate** and for that you must have proper knowledge of **basic grammar** and generally used **vocabulary (word power)**.

Now it is hoped that you have understood the purpose of this course and some of the basic definitions of English Language. So if you are ready, shall we take your test about what we have studied so far.

• TEST - 1 •

Q1. Identify the parts of speech in the following sentences (In Italics).

(i) ***Ali*** sat on wall.

(ii) How are ***you***?

(iii) Sheela has ***good*** Memory.

(iv) He has thrown the ball ***into*** the air.

(v) Ravi ***jumped*** out from running train.

(vi) ***Hurrah!*** we won the match.

(vii) We should ***have*** gone there.

(viii) He said the ***truth.***

(ix) Gold ***and*** Diamond are costly.

Q2. In the following sentences identify subject and predicate.

(i) A black man ran.

(ii) Birds fly.

(iii) My younger brother is in Delhi.

(iv) Walking is good exercise.

(v) To see is to Believe.

Answers to above test are given in the solutions at the end of this chapter.

Now we will give you a sample paper, so that you may have an idea of English language paper which comes in most of competitive exams. We also know that till now you are not prepared to face such a paper and if you attempt it, you may not be able to score much. But do not worry, this is just to give you an idea of paper from competitive exam's point of view. Also after attempting it honestly you will be able to know your weaknesses in various areas of the English Language.

Therfore dear students it is our sincere wish that you will read and understand each word of this course very sincerly and honestly. Hence for proper evaluation of yourself, try to attempt this paper honestly and in single sitting.

The paper is as follows :

- ALL THE BEST -

TEST

Directions (Questions I - 5) :

Read the passage carefully to answer these questions given below it.

PASSAGE

The greatest enemy of mankind, as people have discovered, is not science, but war. science merely reflects the social forces by which it is surrounded. It is found that when there is peace, science is constructive; when there is war, science is perverted to destructive ends. The weapons which science gives us do not necessarily create war, these make war increasingly more terrible. Until now it has brought us to the doorstep of dooni. Our main problem, therefore, is not to curb science, but to stop war. This is a job in which everybody must participate, including tile scientists. But the bomb of Hiroshima suddenly woke us to the fact that we have very little time. The hour is late and our work has scarcely begun. Now we are face to face with this urgent question : "Can education and tolerance, understanding and creative intelligence run fast enough to keep us abreast with our own mounting capacity to destroy ?" That is the question which we will have to answer one way or the other in this generation. Science must help us in finding the answer, but ultimately the main decision lies within ourselves.

1. The phrase 'our work has scarcely begun' implies that our work
 (A) Has only just begun
 (B) Has not yet begun
 (C) Has begun but not yet finished
 (D) Is not likely to begin

2. Our mounting capacity to destroy can be kept under control by
 (A) Encouraging social forces
 (B) Education for all
 (C) Creativity and intelligence
 (D) Education, liberal thinking and creativity

3. According to the author, the real enemy of mankind is not science but war, because
 (A) Science during wars is very destructive
 (B) Science merely invents the weapons with which war is fought
 (C) The weapons that science invents necessarily lead to war
 (D) The weapons invented by science do not cause war, though they make it more destructive

4. According to the author, the solution lies in
 (A) Preventing scientists from participating in destructive activities
 (B) Abolishing war
 (C) Stopping scientific activities everywhere
 (D) Stopping science from reflecting social forces

5. The expression "bring to the doorstep of doom" means
 (A) Lead us to the threshold of a new destiny
 (B) Introduce us to an unpredictable future
 (C) Carry us close to death and destruction
 (D) Take us step by step to ruin

Directions (Questions 6 to 15) :

In the following passage, there are blanks, each of which has been numbered. These numbers are printed below the passage and against each, four words are suggested, one of which fits into the blank appropriately. Find out the appropriate word.

There is no ... (6)... about the fact that travelling broadens the mind. It is a ... (7)... of education. People who have not travelled may be ... (8)... to frogs living in a well. just like frogs, they begin to ... (9)... that their village, or town, or city is the... (10)... world. This way of thinking makes them ... (11)... and parochial. Those people who read books, magazines and newspapers come to ... (12)... something about the world outside, but this is not the same thing as seeing the outside world with one's own eyes. To see the beautiful Taj Mahal ...(13)... moonlight is an experience and a lesson in ...(14)... beauty that no ...(15)... book or magazine can provide.

6. (A) Proof (B) Hesitation
(C) Doubt (D) Claim

7. (A) Site (B) Way
(C) Method (D) Means

8. (A) Similar (B) Compared
(C) Matched (D) Like

9. (A) Believe (B) Realise
(C) Remember (D) Recall

10. (A) Complete (B) Entire
(C) Enormous (D) Full

11. (A) Narrow (B) Contained
(C) Constrained (D) Restrained

12. (A) Believe (B) Imagine
(C) Know (D) Think

13. (A) From (B) Witli
(C) Of (D) By

14. (A) Admirable (B) Aesthetic
(C) Commendable (D) Remarkable

15. (A) Knowledgable (B) Coloured
(C) Illustrated (D) Entertaining

Directions (Questions 16 - 30):

In each of these questions in the given sentence below there is a blank. ~_'hoose the word or phrase which best completes the sentence.

16. A special committee was set up to ____________ on the problem of football hooliganism.
(A) Investigate (B) Inform
(C) Research (D) Report

17. I'm afraid I can't tell vou what he said. It would be a __________ of confidence.
(A) Rapture (B) Break
(C) Rift (D) Breach

18. The hotel room was __________ furnished with only a bed, a wardrobe and an ancient arm chair.
(A) Sparely (B) Sparsely
(C) Scarcely (D) Sketchily

19. Our hosts had prepared a meal with five courses to celebrate our arrival.
(A) Generous (B) Profuse
(C) Lavish (D) Spendthrift

20. Don't thank me for helping in the garden. It was ______ pleasure to be working outdoors.

(A) Plain (B) Mere
(C) Simple (D) Sheer

21. She _______ which kept her alert and well-informed even in old age.

(A) An examining (B) A demanding
(C) An enquiring (D) A querying

22. The police decided to _____ the department store after they had received a bomb warning.

(A) Abandon (B) Evacuate
(C) Evict (D) Expel

23. The school authorities _____ the child's unruly behaviour on his parents' lack of discipline.

(A) Attribute (B) Accuse
(C) Blame (D) Ascribe

24. He was a hardened criminal without a scrap of _____ for his crimes.

(A) Pity (B) Reproach
(C) Remorse (D) Penance

25. Doctor prescribed tablets to _____the pain.

(A) Lighten (B) Calm
(C) Relieve (D) Rid

26. After the robbery, the shop installed a alarm system as an insurance _____further losses.

(A) For (B) From
(C) Towards (D) Against

27. If you _____ in arriving late, I shall have to report you to the Manager.

(A) Persist (B) Persevere
(C) Insist (D) Prevail

28. Far from finding the job too demanding, she seems to ______ the challenges it presents.

(A) Savour (B) Relish
(C) Cherish (D) Regard

29. In the hands of a reckless driver a car becomes a _____ weapon.

(A) Lethal (B) Fatal
(C) Mortal (D) Killer

30. She took up so many hobbies when she _____ retired that she had hardly any time

(A) On her hands (B) In hand
(C) At her hand (D) At hand

Directions (Questions 31 to 40) :

In these questions, fill in the blanks in the sentence with the correct option.

31. They still think that women are inferior ______ men.

(A) To (B) Than

(C) From (D) With

32. The teacher was angry ______ me.

(A) Upon (B) To

(C) Against (D) At

33. A word processor is ______ a typewriter.

(A) More easier to use than

(B) Easier to use as

(C) As easy to use as

(D) Not as easy to use than

34. If you ______ ice in warm water, 'it soon melts.

(A) Will place (B) Would place

(C) Place (D) Placed

35. How many copies ______ with the order ?

(A) Did we sent

(B) Have we sended

(C) Sent we

(D) Did we send

Directions (Questions 36–40) :

In each of these questions, a sentence divided into 3 parts A, B, C. If there is some error in any of the parts A, B or C, then this is your answer, otherwise answer is D.

36. I advised (A)/ to him (B)/ to do his work properly (C)/ No error. (D)

37. The teacher called Ravi (A)/ and asked him (B) / to describe about, the incident (C)/ No error. (D)

38. This pen writes (A)/ very well (B)/ but it costed me 100 rupees (Q/ No error. (D)

39. The bomb caused (A)/ extensive damages (B)/ of the surrounding buildings. (C)/ No error. (D)

40. There were (A)/ hardly no trees left (B)/ just bare rocky land. (C)/ No error. (D)

Solutions :
Answer Test 1

Q1. (i) **Ali** Noun (as it a name of person.)

(ii) **you** Pronoun (as it used to refer a person.)

(iii) **Good** It is an adjective (as it is saying the quality of noun (sheela) and it is also qualifying the word memory.)

(iv) **into** into is a preposition (as it is showing or connecting the noun (ball) with another noun (air))

(v)	**jumped**	Here jumped and running are verbs (as as both of these words are showing some kind of action).
(vi)	**Hurrah !**	it is (an interjection as the word is showing the anticipatory happiness of team menbers after wining the match).
(vii)	**Have**	It is (helping or auxillary verb).
(viii)	**Truth**	Is an (abstract noun of quality or a characterstic in any person).
(ix)	**And**	Is a (conjunction as it is joining two words Gold and diamond.)

Q2.	(i)	**A black man**	Subject
		ran	Predicate.
	(ii)	**Birds**	Subject
		fly	Predicate.
	(iii)	**My younger brother**	Subject
		is in Dehli	Predicate.
	(iv)	**Walking**	Subject
		is good exercise	Predicate.
	(v)	**To see**	Subject
		is to believe	Predicate.

Solutions : Answer Test 2

1. (B)	2. (C)	3. (D)	4. (A)	5. (C)	6. (C)	7. (D)
8. (B)	9. (A)	10. (B)	11. (A)	12. (C)	13. (D)	14. (B)
15. (A)	16. (D)	17. (D)	18. (B)	19. (C)	20. (D)	21. (C)
22. (B)	23. (C)	24. (C)	25. (C)	26. (D)	27. (A)	28. (B)
29. (A)	30. (D)	31. (A)	32. (D)	33. (C)	34. (C)	35. (D)

36. (B) Part 'B' should be 'him'.
37. (C) Part 'C' should be 'to describe the incident'.
38. (C) Part 'C' should be 'but it cost me 100 rupees'.
39. (C) Part 'C' should be 'to the surrounding buildings'.
40. (B) Part 'B' should be 'hardly any trees left'.

Day 2

Vocabulary Building

On **day 1** we gave you an idea of English language paper that comes in most of the competitive exams. Now it is clear to you that two essential requirements to attempt English paper accurately are :

1. **Grammar**
2. **Vocabulary**

For **Grammar section** we will do each of the grammar topic from day 3 onwards. But today *i.e.* on **day 2** we will teach you a way to develop your **vocabulary** ? As **vocabulary development** is a **gradual process** that is why we are starting it from today so that at the end of course you may have an excellent **vocabulary**. Simultaneously it will help you to attempt comprehension section more effectively. Now before going further let us discuss something about vocabulary section.

Why vocabulary is difficult to develop or improve

1. Problem of Retention of words.
2. How many words?

The problem of retention is because we donot use these so called difficult words while speaking. But we cannot and we should not use these words while speaking as it will kill the purpose of communication. In communication, all the participants/ members should be able to express themselves clearly and should also make other people/participants understand what they are trying to convey. Now how to overcome this problem of retention. The answer is Revison. But How it is to be done ? As far as the number of words are concerned, on an average vocabulary of 1000-1500 good words is sufficient.

As already discussed that in Reading Comprehension section paragraphs are given to you and you have to answer the questions based on the given paragraph. Normally this section is very easy. But if tough words are being used in paragraphs then it will be difficult to understand. But we will use these tough paragraphs to our advantage and **how we do that is a surprise** ? You will also know about this as we move forward. Let us do a few comprehensions to remove your doubts.

Passage I

Directions (Questions No. 1-4) :

In this section, you have one short passage. After the passage you will find several questions based on the passage. First, read passage and answer the questions based on it.

When you buy a car, examine carefully the important features of the model you are considering. Many a buyer of the latest models has got into trouble by buying a car too broad or too long for his garage. Furthermore, a long car is much harder to manoeuvre in traffic and much more difficult to park. Another feature is the comfort afforded. Are the seats nice and durably upholstered ? Is there enough glass area to -gjve the driver a good view in all directions, particularly to the rear ? It should be remembered that the heavier and more powerful a car is, the more expensive it will be-to operate. High powered motors require expensive high-octane petrol. The greater weight means greater tyre wear and enlarged brakes. The old cliche is still true; it is not the initial cost but the upkeep which matters !

1. According to this passage, the two factors that the buyer of a new car should keep in mind are

(A) its price and size.

(B) its model and upholstery.

(C) its size and the comfort it offers.

(D) its upholstery and glass area.

2. The size of the car should be in accordance with

(A) the money one can afford to pay.

(B) the size of the garage the buyer has.

(C) the width of the road where the buyer lives.

(D) the volume of traffic on the mad.

3. The writer favours a car with a wide glass area so that the driver can

(A) enjoy the scene outside while driving.

(B) have a good view of the rear.

(C) roll down the glasspanes to get enough fresh air.

(D) display his beautiful upholstery with pride.

4\. It is very expensive to maintain a large car because it

(A) is heavy.

(B) requires more space for parking

(C) needs changing its tyres more

(D) Brakes

After reading the passage it seems that passage is not very difficult to understand.

What is in the passage ?

The writer is explaining the advantages of buying small car over big cars. He is saying that it is easy to maintain, control and keep small cars in comparison to big cars. He has mentioned some of qualities that buyer must check before buying a new car. i.e. is there enough glass area to give driver a good view in all directions particularly the rear or back. Whether it is easy to control while driving. About big cars, he says that these cars are heavy therefore tyres may finish in lesser period of time. These big cars require high quality petrol. There maintenance is tough. These cars require larger area for parking and more garage space etc.

So overall the passage is not difficult to understand except few difficult words. These words are :

(a) Manoeuver

(b) Upholstered

(c) Rear

(d) Upkeep

The meanings of above said words are as follows:-

(a) **Manoeuver** to control

(b) **Upholstered** material used to cover chair etc.

(c) **rear** back
(d) **upkeep** care needed to keep something in good condition.

Answers of the passage 1 are as follow:

Answer :

1. c **2. b** **3. b** **4. c**

Now to understand the process of vocabulary development attempt the passage II honestly.

Passage II

What's wrong with having a vision; a **futuristic peg to hang** the country's hopes and aspirations on especially since we can now **finesse** them with our rapidly increasing advances along cutting edge technologies? Back in the early 1960s Vikram Sarabhai too had a dream of satellites. This was at a time when the only things we were capable of launching were **puny** American-made Nike-Apache rockets from thumba which barely made it past the atmosphere. But thereafter Dr Sarabhai **scoured** the east coast till Sriharikota was identified from where today we've already launched an **array** of space-based **remote** sensing satellites which are one of the biggest **constellations** of such satellites in the world. They not only provide data for applications ranging from agriculture, forestry and groundwater **harvesting** to **urban** planning, land use and ocean resources survey, the information can also be sold to other countries.

Sure, we may not be able to orbit an **unmanned probe** around the Moon; we may not even make it to the Moon at all by that date, but if the **gauntlet** is picked up and there is a **concerted follow-through**, it would be a **courageous** move in the right direction. For one thing, it would mean a jointly **orchestrated** effort by governmental, **autonomous** and private agencies **pooling** their **resources** towards a common national Coal-For another, the **spin-offs** from such a programme would be directly -and **immensely beneficial** to such **diverse** fields as **meteorology geology**, materials research and knowlede-based systems like information technology and communications, We have the labour base, the finest computer software people in the world and a proven track record which includes placing a satellite in **geo synchronous** orbit using an **indigenous** launch vehicle when previously only five other countries had managed to do the same. So if we do manage to pull it off it would be another example of our **self-reliance** at work. It would also leave a lot of people with **silly grins** on their faces.

Q.1 What is vision that author is talking about
(1) to develop self-reliance is space-technology
(2) to be able to launch more advanced Amarican satellites
(3) to send an unmanned probe around the moon
(4) to show other developed countries that we too can launch satellites.

Q.2 In author's view what can be possible ways to realise his vision ?
(1) That we should went for miracle to happen in space science.
(2) We should take help from other developed countries.
(3) These should be joint effort by government, autonomous bodies and to contribute in every possible manner to realse his vision.
(4) None of these.

Q.3 Why author is so hopeful that his country/ countrymen can make his vision realised ?
(1) His countrymen are supermen.
(2) His countrymen known magic by which they can do anything.

(3) Because his country has labour base of finest computer savvy men in the world know how to launch satellites. Using indigenous launch vehicle.

(4) None of these.

Q.4 How the advanced technological advancement can help mankind ?

(1) This developement will remove all pain and sufferings of mankind.

(2) With the help of these developements, every one will be able to know his/her future so that he/she can correct it accordingly.

(3) With the advancement we would be able to increase our knowledge in the field of meterology, geology, material research, information technology and communications.

(4) Everyone will be able to perform miracles on the earth.

Now this passage is not as simple as the previous one. There are a few words in this passage which are making the given paragraph difficult to understand. We have highlighted these words.

After knowing the meaning of underlined words, we can understand the passage. Before attempting the questions based on passage II Just try to find out the meaning of underlined words from dictionary. After finding the meaning of these word, read the passage again to understand it. For your convenience we have given you the meanings of highlighted words this time, but from next time you have to find the meaning of underlined words yourself. This is for your own benefit.

The meaning of underline words are as follows :

1.	Futuristic	:	What may happen in future
2.	Peg to Hang	:	Something that is use as reason.
3.	Finesse	:	Tact
4.	Puny	:	Very Small
5.	Scoured	:	Search
6.	Array	:	To put in order
7.	Remote	:	Distant
8.	Constellations	:	Group of Stars
9.	Harvesting	:	Season for Reaping
10.	Urban	:	Town
11.	Unmanned	:	Without Man
12.	Probe	:	Exploring
13.	Gauntlet	:	To accept invitation to fight
14.	Cocerted	:	Collective
15.	Courageous	:	Brave
16.	Orchestrated	:	To Organise
17.	Autonomus	:	Under Self-Governent
18.	Pooling	:	Combining
19.	Resources	:	Means of raising money
20.	Spin offs	:	Unexpected but useful results
21.	Immensely	:	Very Much

22. Beneficial : Useful
23. Diverse : Different
24. Meteorology : Related to Weather
25. Geology : Related to Earth
26. Geosynchronous : Moving around the earth at the same speed of earth itself
27. Indigenious : Self Grown
28. Self Reliance : Without Depending on others.
29. Silly : Not Sensible
30. Grins : Stupid Smile

After the above excercise read the passage again and we hope that you will find it easier to answer the questions asked on the basis of above paragraph.

And the answers are as follows :

Answer :

1. a **2.** c **3.** c **4.** c

In the start of this chapter we have told you about a trick to improve your word power marvelously. This trick is very simple yet powerful.

Trick: As you have seen in the passage II some of the words are difficult to understand. We have found the meaning of these words from dictionary. Now the trick is to write these words on plain cards or empty visiting cards (Normally you can have these cards from any stationery shop or you can make these cards by cutting a chart paper).

So the cards will look as follows :

Why Cards :

There are many reasons for using the cards and a few of them are given below.

1. These cards are easier to carry. You can revise words while travelling in a bus/train etc.
2. You can add any new word anytime and anywhere as soon as you find word.
3. These cards are longlasting and unending treasure.

Card -1

1. Futuristic :	What may happen in future
2. Peg to Hang :	Something that is use as reason.
3. Finesse :	Tact
4. Puny :	Very Small
5. Scoured :	Search
6. Array :	To put in order
7. Remote :	Distant
8. Constellations :	Group of Stars
9. Harvesting :	Season for Reaping
10. Urban :	Town
11. Unmanned :	Without Man
12. Probe :	Exploring
13. Gauntlet :	To accept invitation to fight
14. Cocerted :	Collective
15. Courageous :	Brave

Card -2

16. Orchestrated :	To Organise
17. Autonomus :	Under Self-Governent
18. Pooling :	Combining
19. Resources :	Means of raising money
20. Spin offs :	Unexpected but useful results
21. Immensely :	Very Much
22. Beneficial :	Useful
23. Diverse :	Different
24. Meteorology :	Related to Weather
25. Geology :	Related to Earth
26. Geosynchronous :	Moving around the earth at the same speed of earth itself
27. Indigenious :	Self Grown
28. Self Reliance:	Without Depending on others.
29. Silly :	Not Sensible
30. Grins :	Stupid Smile

4. You will never forget the words on cards as you have put honest labour in finding the meaning of these words.

5. Last but not least this method has been implemented by thousands of students and believe us that they have been immensely benefitted by this method.

Sources for New Words :

There are many sources like Articles from General Magazines like India Today, Frontline, Outlook etc. but the best source is any newspaper's editorial. As not only you can find new words but it will also increase your general knowledge side by side.

Now as you have started this course so to your benefit, we are giving you a collection of 800 words which have been searched by the above said method. Believe us these words will cover more than 90% vocab section of any entrance exam. But it is very difficult rather impossible to learn or cram all the words in a day so we have given you a list of 50 words daily. So that by the end of course you have these very important words on your fingertips. In this way you will have a very good vocabulary by the end of this course. The list of today's word is given below and after learning the words you have to attempt a self evaluation test.

All the Best

Vocab List

Sr.	***Words***	***Meanings***
1.	Whim	Fancy, Imagination
2.	Dissolute	Immoral, Licentious
3.	Niggard	Miser, Covetous, Stingy
4.	Placate	Appease, To Please somebody
5.	Supervene	Interfere, To come extraneously
6.	Sanguine	Hopeful, Ardent, Confident, Bright
7.	Affluent	Prosperous, Copious, Wealthy
8.	Belittle	Disparage, To Degrade Someone
9.	Penchant	Liking (for)
10.	Barter	Exchange
11.	Bounty	Gift
12.	Divvy	Slang, A stupid person
13.	Abstruse	Profound, Deep, Difficult to understand
14.	Yob	Aggressive, Rude, Violent
15.	Morose	Gloomy, Sullen, Austere, Sad
16.	Candid	Frank, Honest, Sincere, Impartial
17.	Ephemeral	Short living, Transitory
18.	Inanition	Emptiness
19.	Impeccable	Faultless, sinless
20.	Internecine	Deadly, destructive

21.	Umpteen	A great many, a large no. of
22.	Covetous	Grasping, greedy, desirous
23.	Simon-pure	Genuine
24.	Vilify	Defame
25.	Yammer	Lament
26.	Stridency	Harshness
27.	Lissome	Quick, nimble, agile
28.	Gaffe	Blunder
29.	Denounce	Rap publicly
30.	Rap	Criticize
31.	Abstemious	Moderate
32.	Specious	Insincere, Plausible
33.	Mellifluous	Sweet, smooth
34.	Debilitate	Weaken, enfeeble
35.	Restitute	Wanting, devoid of
36.	Wan	Tired, repair
37.	Foray	Raid, incursion
38.	Hanker	Desire, long for
39.	Edify	Instruct, to build spiritually
40.	Accentuated	Projected, pronounce with an accent
41.	Sumptuous	Lavish, magnifies, costly
42.	Latent	Concealed, hidden
43.	Numinous	Inspiring
44.	Inexplicable	Unaccountable
45.	Jest	Joke, Fun
46.	Ingenuous	Frank, innocent, generous
47.	Chimerical	Imaginary
48.	Muffle	Wrap
49.	Scour	Search, cleanse
50.	Forage	Search for food

...

BREAK FOR WORDS REVISION

REVISE THE VOCAB

TEST No- 1
(Words 1-50)

Choose the correct meaning of the given words from amongst their alternatives :

(1) Divvy
(a) gloomy (b) immoral
(c) slang (d) miser

(2) Whim
(a) appear (b) fancy
(c) aggressive (d) desire

(3) Ephemeral
(a) transitory (b) long-lived
(c) prosperous (d) hoped for

(4) Umpteen
(a) a small no. of (b) a large no. of
(c) empty (d) none

(5) Denounce
(a) to leave (b) rap publicly
(c) interfere (d) sullen

(6) Yammer
(a) honest (b) disparage
(c) moderate (d) lament

(7) Inanition
(a) emptiness (b) fullness
(c) quickness (d) dullness

(8) Abstemious
(a) harsh (b) moderate
(c) precious (d) obscure

(9) Inexplicable
(a) unaccountable (b) unaffordable
(c) unlike (d) untouchable

(10) Jest
(a) criticism (b) joke
(c) deadly (d) faulty

(11) Wan
(a) tired (b) slept
(c) dead (d) needy

(12) Latent
(a) open (b) concealed
(c) protected (d) produced

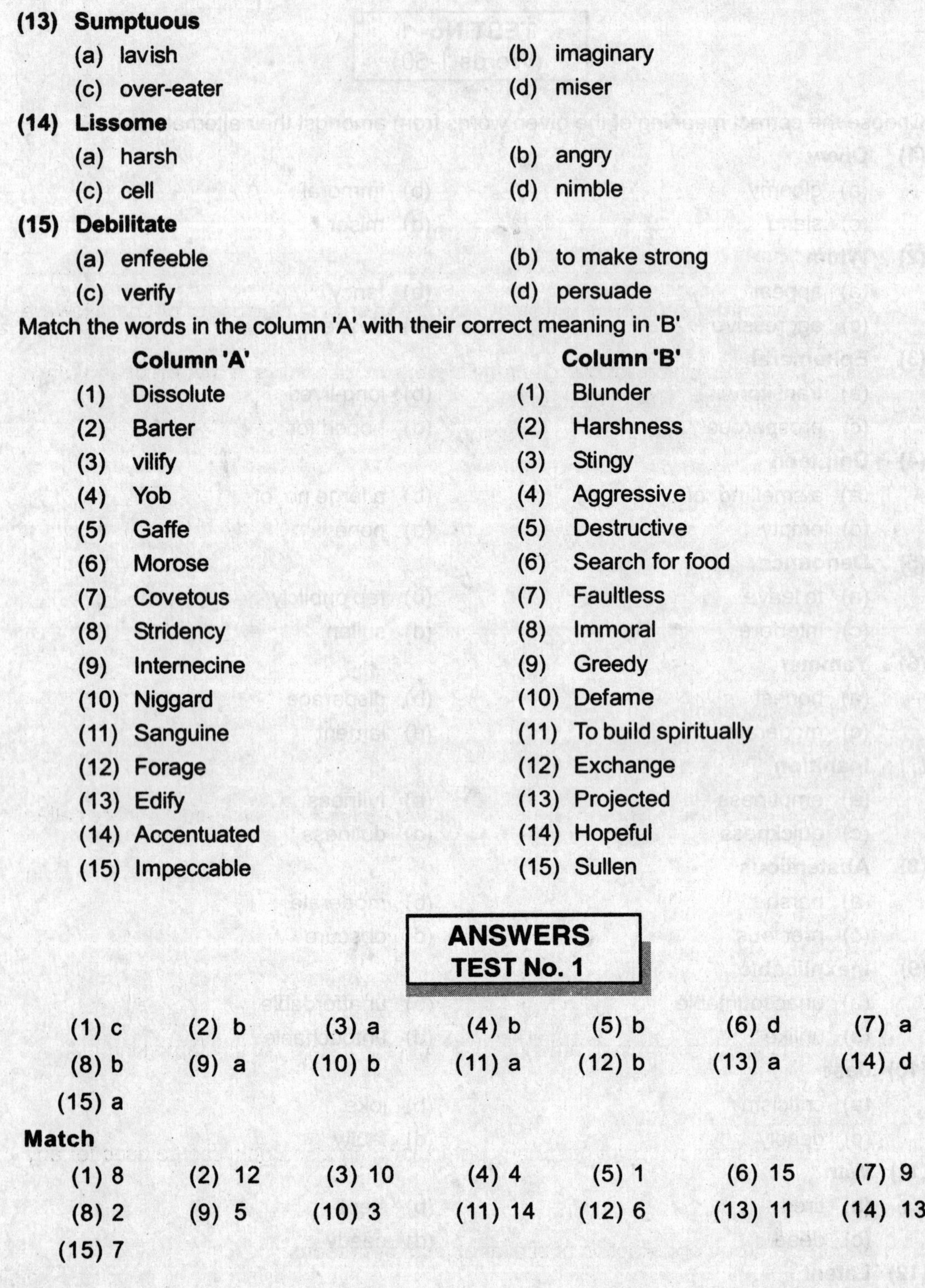

(13) Sumptuous

(a) lavish (b) imaginary
(c) over-eater (d) miser

(14) Lissome

(a) harsh (b) angry
(c) cell (d) nimble

(15) Debilitate

(a) enfeeble (b) to make strong
(c) verify (d) persuade

Match the words in the column 'A' with their correct meaning in 'B'

Column 'A'	Column 'B'
(1) Dissolute	(1) Blunder
(2) Barter	(2) Harshness
(3) vilify	(3) Stingy
(4) Yob	(4) Aggressive
(5) Gaffe	(5) Destructive
(6) Morose	(6) Search for food
(7) Covetous	(7) Faultless
(8) Stridency	(8) Immoral
(9) Internecine	(9) Greedy
(10) Niggard	(10) Defame
(11) Sanguine	(11) To build spiritually
(12) Forage	(12) Exchange
(13) Edify	(13) Projected
(14) Accentuated	(14) Hopeful
(15) Impeccable	(15) Sullen

ANSWERS
TEST No. 1

(1) c (2) b (3) a (4) b (5) b (6) d (7) a
(8) b (9) a (10) b (11) a (12) b (13) a (14) d
(15) a

Match

(1) 8 (2) 12 (3) 10 (4) 4 (5) 1 (6) 15 (7) 9
(8) 2 (9) 5 (10) 3 (11) 14 (12) 6 (13) 11 (14) 13
(15) 7

Day

3

Nouns

Today in grammar section we will study nouns and errors in the use of nouns. Now we start with nouns.

Nouns : Words which denote the name of **person**, or a **thing** or **an object** and which are distinct from each other.

For Example : Ram, Shyam - Persons.

Delhi, Agra - Places.

Table, Pen - Objects.

In English Language there are five types of nouns.

1. **Proper noun.**
2. **Common noun.**
3. **Collective noun.**
4. **Material noun.**
5. **Abstract noun.**

We will explain each of the noun one by one.

1. **Proper noun :**

   Words used to denote Name, a Person, or an Object or a Place in particular are called Proper Nouns.

   For example :

   Thomas (a person).

   Haridwar (a place).

   Black pen (a object).

2. **Common noun :**

   Words which are common to any and every person or thing of the same kind.

   For example

   Man, Book, Country, River.

   As here Man does not point out to any particular man also Book can be used for any or every book.

3. **Collective Noun :**

   Denotes a group or collection of similar objects or persons.

   For example :

   Team, Crowd, Army.

4. Material Noun :

Words which denote matter or substance of which things are made of or made from.

For example :

Gold, Silver, Wood, Paper, etc.

5. Abstract noun

Words which define any quality, a state, or an action. And these things can not be seen, touched, heard etc.

Quality - Cleverness.

State - Youth, Poverty, Sorrow, Slavery.

Action - Laugther, Fight, Revenge.

•••

Now we will discuss Gender.

Gender : Nouns which are used to denote, Male or Female of any animal species. Sometime a single word is used to denote both the sexes. As per use we have following kinds of Genders.

1. Masculine :

Noun denoting Male, Animals.

2. Feminine :

Nouns denoting Female Animals.

3. Common :

Noun denoting Animals of either sex.

4. Neuter :

Noun denoting neither of sexes.

Collective noun, Material noun and abstrtact noun are considered as Neuter Gender.

Young children and lower animals are also considered as Neuter Gender.

Generally we use

i. Masculine Gender :

It is used to show the strength of that object or person and to show some sort of violence (Negativity) associated with them.

For example : summer, sun, winter, time, death.

ii. Feminine Gender :

It is used to represent the female members or the beauty, gentleness and gracefulness in a person or in an object.

For example : moon, earth, spring, nature, liberty etc. are considered Feminine.

Note: *Ship is always considered as Feminine.*

For example : The ship lost her way.

Also railway train, motor-car and other Machines are considered as Feminines in use.

Following nouns are used as common gender.

Friend, cousin, pupil, servent, person, enemy, orphan, student, baby, neighbour, relation, parent, etc.

Now we will discuss the rules to form plural nouns from singular nouns.

i. Generally plural of noun is formed by adding 's' to singular.

For example :

	Singular	**Plural**
(a)	Boy	Boys
(b)	Eye	Eyes
(c)	House	Houses

ii. If the noun ends in s, sh, x, or, ch, the plural is formed by adding es to ch singular.

For example :

	Singular	**Plural**
(a)	Glass	Glasses
(b)	Brush	Brushes
(c)	Box	Boxes

iii. If the noun ends in 'y' and the 'y' is preceeded by consonant, the plural is formed by changing the 'y' into 'ies'.

For example :

	Singular	**Plural**
(a)	Army	Armies
(b)	Lady	Ladies
(c)	Fly	Flies

But if the 'y' at the end is preceded by vowel (as in ay, ey or oy) the plural is formed by simply adding s to the singular.

For example :

	Singular	**Plural**
(a)	Day	Days
(b)	Boy	Boys
(c)	Key	Keys

(iv) If the noun ends in O and the O is preceeded by consonant, the plural is formed by adding 'es' to singular.

For example :

	Singular	**Plural**
(a)	Mango	Mangoes
(b)	Potato	Potatoes
(c)	Mosquito	Mosquitoes

But if the singular noun ends at (o, io, eo, yo) then plural are formed by adding 's' at the end of word.

For example :

	Singular	**Plural**
(a)	Bamboo	Bamboos
(b)	Piano	Pianos
(c)	Solo	Solos

(v) If noun ends in 'f' or 'fe' then plurals are formed by changing 'f' or 'fe' into 'ves'.

For example :

	Singular	**Plural**
(a)	Wife	Wives
(b)	Thief	Thieves
(c)	Myself	Ourselves.

But sometimes no change is made, only 's' is attached to the words.

For example :

	Singular	**Plural**
(a)	Belief	Beliefs
(b)	Roof	Roofs
(c)	Dwarf	Dwarfs

In English language usually when the subject (which is usually noun or pronoun) is singular/plural, we have to use singular/plural, helping verb i.e. with

He, she it 'Is' is used in **present tense.**
'Was' is used in **past tense.**
'Will' is used in **future tense.**

Likewise if subject is
we, you, they, then.

'Are' is used in **present tense.**
'Were' is used in **past tense.**
'Shall' is used in **future tense.**

Mostly, error in the use of nouns in the sentences occur when the Singular noun is used in place of Plural or vice-versa. To make you understand the rules properly, we have written the **incorrect sentences on the left side** and **correct sentences, on the right side.** After a few examples, we have given the rules i.e. what is wrong in the sentences and why. The rules with solved examples are as follow:

Errors in the use of nouns

Rule 1

Certain nouns like **Scenery, Furniture, Information, Language, Poetry, Abuse, Damaged, Machinery, Expenditure, Advice, Mischief work etc.** are used as singular nouns instead of plural nouns. This can be clearly understood by the following examples.

	Incorrect	**Correct**
(a)	The sceneries in Switzerland are charming.	The scenes in Switzerland are charming or The scenery in Switzerland is charming.
(b)	I have sold old furnitures.	I have sold old furniture.
(c)	Ram gave me many advices.	Ram gave me much advice or many pieces of advice.

(d)	Tilak has many works to do.	Tilak has lots of work to do or much work to do.
(e)	He has bought new machineries.	He has bought new machines or machinery.
(f)	The recent earthquake has done much damages in Japan.	The recent earthquake has done much damage in Japan.
(g)	The old man gave him many abuses.	The old man gave him many words of abuse or lots of abuse.
(h)	His younger brother has no male issues.	His younger brother has no male issue.
(i)	She has brown hairs.	She has brown hair.
(j)	She gave money to the blinds.	She gave money to the blind or blind persons.

Note: Advices is not plural for advise as advices means information and advice is to give or receive suggestion.

Rule 2: Some nouns like vegetables, trousers, scissors, spectacles, proceeds, remain, thanks, circumstances, alms, ashes etc. are used only in plural therefore helping verbs used in sentences given below are plural on correct sides.

	Incorrect	**Correct**
(a)	What is the content of this letter.	What is the contents of this letter.

Contents means matter (in written). So here contents is not plural for content. Also content means satisfied and happy, Therefore to use content instead of contents is incorrect.

(b)	This scissor is blunt.	This scissors are blunt.
(c)	He does not like vegetable.	He does not like vegetables.
(d)	My trousers is clean.	My trousers are clean.
(e)	His thank is due to my his principals.	His thanks are due to his principal.

In (e) we mean to say, that till now he has not thanked his principal so sometimes you should properly understand the meaning of given sentence as a whole, only then you can find an error.

Rule 3 :

Some nouns like Mathematics, riches, Politics, Innings, Odds, Means etc. are used as singular though in appearance they seem to be plural as the each of the above said noun ends at **s** in spellings. Therefore in sentences (a to c) given below, the plural helping verbs have been changed to singular helping verbs. like in each sentence **'are'** has been changed into **'is'**.

	Incorrect	**Correct**
(a)	Mathematics are a difficult subjects.	Mathemathics is a difficult subject.

	Incorrect	Correct
(b)	Politics are a dirty game.	Politics is a dirty game.
(c)	These news are sad.	This news is sad.

Rule 4 :

Nouns indicating measure or number do not change into plural especially when used after numerals.

For example In sentence (a) When **five** is used before **dozen** then there is no need to use dozens. This rule can be understood by the examples given below.

	Incorrect	Correct
(a)	I bought five dozens mangoes.	I bought five dozen mangoes.
(b)	Our five years plan will suceed.	Our five year plan will succeed.
(c)	He has joined three years computer course.	He has joined three year computer course.

Rule 5 :

A few nouns like cattle, people, Gentry, Sheep, Deer, Public, Peasentry seem to be singular in from but actually are plural in meaning. Therefore they require plural verbs.

For example

Cattle means group of animals so there is no need to write cattles to show group of animals. Hence after cattle, plural helping verb **are** is used. This rule is explained below.

	Incorrect	Correct
(a)	The cattles are grazing.	The cattle are grazing.
(b)	Sheeps are grazing.	Sheep are grazing.

Rules 6 :

When material nouns are used to denote a mass of matter, they are not used as plurals. This rule is explained below with the help of a few examples.

	Incorrect	Correct
(a)	The house is built of bricks.	The house is built of brick.
(b)	The Taj is built of white marbles.	The Taj is built of white marble.

Rules 7 :

Some nouns like house, church, school, shop are not used after **apostrophe**. This rule is also explained below.

	Incorrect	Correct
(a)	Today I will dine at my uncle's house.	Today I will dine at my uncle's.

In the sentences given below (a - e) singular noun is used instead of plural.

	Incorrect	Correct
(a)	Have you taken your meal.	Have you taken your meals.

(b)	The judge has issused order for his arrest.	The judge has issused orders for his arrest.
(c)	His friend has discontinued his study.	His friend has discontinued his studies.
(d)	Yesterday I was feeling out of sort.	Yesterday I was feeling out of sorts.
(e)	His brother is man of small mean.	His brother is man of small means.

In the sentence given below (a to e) Plural noun has been used in place of Singular.

	Incorrect	**Correct**
(a)	I want some blotting.	I want a piece of blotting.
(b)	lam fond of fruits.	I am fond of fruit.
(c)	He discussed the answer in details.	He discussed the answer in detail.

Some more sentences with errors are given below.

	Incorrect	Correct
(a)	He saw a Theatre.	He saw a play or movie or drama.
(b)	He is my cousin brother.	He is my cousin.
(c)	He will not put his sign there	He will not put his signature there or he will not sign there.

So till now we have studied the errors in the use of nouns. We have seen that how singular nouns were used in place of plural noun and vice-versa.

As stated earlier for good hold on English language you should have a sound grammar base and for that today we have covered the topic of noun. So you should have all the rules discussed on your fingertips. It is advised that before starting the test on nouns, you should learn these rules by heart and should devote at least 15-20 minutes to revise the rules.

It is hoped that you have gone through all the rules.

Let us have a simple test to check your understanding of nouns.

TEST

Directions (Questions 1 - 10) :

In each of these questions, a sentence is divided into 3 parts A, B, C. If there is an error in any of the parts A, B or C, then this is your answer, otherwise answer is D.

1. They have got (A)/ no information (B)/ about this matter(C)/No Error /D.
2. I feel that (A)/ the circumstances (B)/ here is quite bad (C)/ /No Error /D.
3. Vegetable (A)/ is very much (B) / liked by me (C)/(No Error) /D.
4. Hers hairs (A)/ are glossy and lustrously (B)/ black/C)/ /No Error /D.
5. His (A)/ house is (B)/ built of stones (C)/. /No Error-D/
6. She says that (A)/ she has given you (B)/ twenty rupees note (C)/. /(No Error-D).

7. The girls /(A)/ made many /(B)/ mischiefs/(C)/. /No Error-D.
8. The cattles and sheep /(A)/ are grazing /(B)/ in the meadow /(C)/. /No Error-D.
9. The poetries /(A)/ of Shakespeare /(B)/ are quite alluring /(C) /No Error/ (D).
10. These /(A)/ news are hair /(B)/ raising /(C)/. /No Error / (D).
11. His advices were /(A)/ quite /(B)/ effective /(C)/. /No Error (D).
12. The First Innings /(A)/ were lost by /(B)/ Indians /(C). /No Error(D).
13. Good News /(A)/ spread quite /(B)/ gradually /(C)/./No Error(D).
14. I have /(A)/ some business /(B)/ to attend/(C)/. /No Error(D).
15. This road /(A)/ is under /(B)/ repair /(C)/. /No Error (D).

Answers to the above test are given at the end of this chapter.

This was all about grammar part today. As discussed on day 2 we will do 50 words daily to improve our vocabulary now here the vocab list is given on next page. You have to learn these words by heart and solve the test based on vocab given after the vocab list.

Sr.	Words	Meanings
51.	Ulterior	Remote, situated beyond
52.	Wary	Cautious
53.	Delibrate	To taste, to sip
54.	Caveat	Warning
55.	Delirious	Insane
56.	Amicable	Friendly
57.	Quell	Suppress
58.	Ambit	Scope
59.	Ominous	Forbidding, inauspicious
60.	Lug	Drag
61.	Levitate	Float
62.	Subside	Subdue, Disappear
63.	Gainsay	Contradict, oppose
64.	Sporadic	Soothing
65.	Foster	Nurture, cherish
66.	Ecstatic	Enraptured, rapturous
67.	Wallow	Luxuriate
68.	Innate	Inborn, natural
69.	Furtive	Stealthy, thievish
70.	Accolade	Award
71.	Requite	Repay
72.	Overstrung	Too sensitive
73.	Fraternize	Associate

74. Nugatory Worthless
75. Deride Mock
76. Commiserate Sympathize
77. Rein Control
78. Gooey Sentimental
79. Absolute Limitless
80. Glitzy Glamorous
81. Morbid Diseased, sickly, unwholesome
82. Insolvent Bankrupt
83. Paradigm Example
84. Augur Signify, predict
85. Maunder Wander
86. Jink Dodge
87. Reluctant Hesitating
88. Dowdy Unstylish, untidy
89. Assuage Ease, calm
90. Contemplative Thoughtful
91. Brook Tolerate
92. Deference Respect, regard
93. Nepotism Favoritism
94. Waft Odour
95. Sullen Silent
96. Purge Purify, clean
97. Narked Annoyed, angry
98. Elam Vivacity, verve
99. Irascible Easily made angry, hot-tempered
100. Putrid Rotten, noxious

. . .

BREAK FOR WORDS REVISION

TEST
Words 51 - 100

Choose the correct meaning of the given words from amongst their alternatives:

(1) Wary
(a) cautious (b) lazy
(c) tired (d) joyous

(2) Amicable
(a) negligible (b) moderate
(c) friendly (d) instructing

(3) Ominous
(a) inauspicious (b) auspicious
(c) stealthy (d) worthless

(4) Levitate
(a) sunk (b) drunken
(c) dead (d) float

(5) Gainsay
(a) support (b) leading to gain
(c) contradict (d) none

(6) Sporadic
(a) soothing (b) infectious
(c) harmful (d) healthy

(7) Purge
(a) dive (b) wander
(c) purify (d) worship

(8) Deride
(a) limitless (b) repay
(c) silent (d) mock

(9) Gooey
(a) happy (b) sentimental
(c) friendly (d) instructing

(10) Nepotism
(a) favouritism (b) opposition
(c) criticism (d) association

(11) Maunder
(a) sleep (b) wander
(c) study (d) sing

(12) Reluctant
(a) annoy (b) hesitating
(c) cheerful (d) moderate

(13) Commiserate
(a) scold (b) sympathize
(c) rap (d) warn

(14) Foster
(a) nurture (b) hesitate
(c) force to do (d) speedy

(15) Morbid
(a) healthy (b) sick
(c) tired (d) slept

Match the words in the column 'A' with their correct meaning in 'B'

	Column 'A'		Column 'B'
(1)	Ulterior	(1)	Noxious
(2)	Quell	(2)	Purify
(3)	Putrid	(3)	Scope
(4)	Dowdy	(4)	Remote
(5)	Purge	(5)	Dodge
(6)	Glitzy	(6)	Glamorous
(7)	Ambit	(7)	Example
(8)	Furtive	(8)	Suppress
(9)	Jink	(9)	Thoughtful
(10)	Requite	(10)	Warning
(11)	Paradigm	(11)	Unstylish
(12)	Contemplative	(12)	Odour
(13)	Waft	(13)	Vivacity
(14)	Elam	(14)	Thievish
(15)	Caveat	(15)	Repay

ANSWERS GRAMMAR

1. (b) Informations
2. (c) **are** in place of **is**
3. (a) it should be vegetables.
4. (a) **hair** in place of **hairs**
5. (c) **stone** in place of **stones**
6. (c) **rupee** in place of **rupees**
7. (c) it should be **many acts of mischief**
8. (a) **cattle** in place of **cattles**
9. (a) **poems or poetry** in place of **poetries**
10. (d)
11. (a) **was** in place of **were**
12. (b) **was** in place of **were**
13. (d)
14. (b) **urgent piece** of in place of **some**
15. (c) **repairs** in place of **repair**

ANSWER VOCAB
TEST NO.2

(1) a (2) c (3) a (4) d (5) c (6) a (7) c
(8) d (9) b (10) a (11) b (12) b (13) b (14) a
(15) b

Match

(1) 4 (2) 8 (3) 1 (4) 4 (5) 2 (6) 6 (7) 3
(8) 14 (9) 5 (10) 15 (11) 7 (12) 9 (13) 12 (14) 13
(15) 10

Day

4

Pronouns

Let us consider an example by which you will be able to understand the importance of pronouns. **"While going to college, I saw Ram. Ram is a nice person. Ram has a car. Ram is an engineer. Ram lives in Ganga Colony."**

The above said passage can be put in a way as follows. While going to college, I saw Ram. He is a nice person. He has a car. He is an engineer. He lives in Ganga Colony.

Here 'He' is a pronoun and is being used instead of Noun (Ram). So we see that the basic purpose of a pronoun is to avoid the repetition of noun. Now we can define pronouns.

Pronoun: Words used instead of Nouns are called Pronouns.

For example He, the, it we, which, when, how, you, they theirs etc.

Types of Pronouns.

We have nine types of pronouns in English language.

These are as follow:

(1) **Personal pronouns.**

(2) **Reflexive Pronoun.**

(3) **Emphatic Pronoun.**

(4) **Demonstrative Pronoun.**

(5) **Reciprocal Pronouns.**

(6) **Interrogative Pronouns.**

(7) **Indefinite Pronouns.**

(8) **Relative Pronouns.**

(9) **Distributive Pronouns.**

Now we will define the above said types of Pronouns one by one.

1. **Personal Pronouns** :

Words which are used to denote only persons. These are of three types.

i. **First person :**

I, we and words formed by them like **me, my, mine, us, our** etc.

ii. **Second person :**

Words used to refer the persons to whom we are speaking and these words are **you, yours**.

iii. **Third person :**

Words which represent another person, when two persons are talking. These are **He, she, it, him, her, has, its, them, their**.

2. Reflexive Pronouns :

These words show that the Action done by the subject turns back upon it.

For example i. I did it myself.

ii. The boys did it themselves.

iii. You can do it yourself.

So it is clear that Reflexive Pronouns are formed by adding **self or selves** after, my, our, him, her, them it. For example some of Reflexive Pronouns are **Myself, ourselves, himself, yourself, herself, yourselves.**

Remember, Reflexive Pronouns are never used as subject .

For example It is wrong to say that **Myself will go there** instead of this the correct use will be **I will go there myself.**

3. Emphatic Pronouns :

These Pronouns are used for the sake of Emphasis only. To emphasise, we use same pronouns which are used as Reflexive Pronouns but they are placed immediately after the subject.

For example

i He himself said it.

ii It was told by the teacher himself.

4. Demonstrative Pronouns :

Pronouns which point out Nouns.

In this category, Pronouns are **this, that, these, those.**

For example

i **This** is a book.

ii **That** is a house.

iii **These** are pencils.

In **i** **This** is used to point book.

In **ii** **That** is used to point house.

5. Reciprocal Pronouns :

These pronouns are used to show mutual relationship or mutual give and take.

These Pronouns are formed by joining two pronouns. We have only two Pronouns in this type and these are **Each other, One another.**

For example

i The two friends love each other.

ii The three sisters helped one another.

In **i** There is Mutual relationship.

In **ii** There is Mutual give and take.

6. Interrogative Pronouns :

Pronouns used to ask questions. In this type we have **what, which, who, whose, whom** as Interrogative Pronouns :

For example

i Who are you ?

ii Whom do you want to see ?

7. Indefinite Pronouns :

Pronouns used to refer persons or things in general.

In this type we have **All, some, many, everyone, everybody** etc. as indefinite pronouns.

For example

i **Some** of my friends are Rich.

ii **Everyone** of you is smart

iii **Many** persons are invited.

So in

i We are not talking about any particular friend.

In ii We are referring to all persons who are siting or standing in front of Speaker in that sentence.

8. Relative Pronouns:

Words which represent the relationships to the Nouns used in the sentence or sometimes which join the Noun to the rest of sentence are called Relative pronouns. In this category we have who, what, whom, whose, which, that.

For example

i This is the man who gave me money.

ii This a bag **which** I bought yesterday. Here again **which** is showing relationship to Noun **Bag** used in above sentence or you can say that pronoun 'which' is related to the Noun Bag only, and not to any other word in above sentence.

9. Distributive Pronouns :

These pronoun refer to one person or thing at a time or words used to represent every person or thing in group about which we are talking at that time.

In this category we have Each,either,neither,none .

For example

i **Each** boy was given a prize.

Here Pronoun **each** is showing that every boy (which were present there) got a prize. So **Each** here represents every boy.

ii None can solve this problem.

Here **None** means that nobody present there can solve the problem.

So again **None** is referred to every person present there.

So this is all about pronouns and the types of Pronouns. Before going further we would like to tell you about the **'Cases'.** We will discuss this type (cases) only from competitive point of view.

What is CASE?

Sometimes a word is subject or sometimes a word can be object in a given sentence. So CASE is a situation or rule by which we can find how we have to use pronouns in a given sentence. We have three type of **cases** & we have cases only for personal pronouns. These cases are as follow:

1. Subjective case :

When Pronouns are used as subjects it is subjective case.

For example :

i. **I** am Raj.

You are Mohan.

Here **I** and **You** are subjects.

2. Objective Case :

When Pronouns are used as object to the verbs

for example :

i. The teacher shouted at **me**.

Here **Teacher** is subject, **shouted**, being an action is verb and **Me** which is used as object to the verb **shouted** i.e. An objective case.

ii. He ran after me.

Here also:

He is subject

ran is verb

Me, which is a pronoun is an object to verb after.

So here **Me** is an objective case.

3. Possessive Case:

When Pronouns show some kind of right or Possession or claim on any object or person or place by the subject .

For example

1. This is my house.

In above sentence **my** is showing that this House belongs to me.

So **my** is showing the Speaker's right on that house.

So it is hoped that you would have understood **cases**. Below we have given you the table which will show you that how each pronoun is used in different cases :

Table of different cases for Personal pronouns :

	Pronoun	Nominative /subjective case	Objective case	Possessive Case
1.	I	I	Me	My, Mine
2.	we	we	us	our, ours
3.	you	you	you	your, yours
4.	He	He	him	his
5.	She	She	her	her,hers
6.	it	it	it	its
7.	They	they	them	Their

***** The basic principle in using cases. or different forms of pronouns.**

(A) If pronouns are used before the verbs then pronouns should always be in subjective forms.

(B) If Pronouns are to be to be used after verbs then pronouns should be in objective forms. For example.

1. They have invited you and I / **me**.
2. You **and I** / me are invited there.

In Ex. 1 me(objective) is correct because it is used after the verb invited. In Ex. 2 I (subjective) is correct because it is used before the verb.

Now we will study the errors in the use of **Pronouns**.

Rule 1 : When first person, second person and third person pronouns are used then the order of their use is second, third and first respectively in positive situations. But if the context is negative then the order is 1, 2, 3 i.e. first person, second person, third person.

	INCORRECT	CORRECT
a	I and you are friends.	You and I are friends.
b	I, he and you went to Delhi.	You,he and I went to Delhi.

Rule 2 : **Each other** is used for two persons and **one another** is used for more than two persons. This is shown below.

	INCORRECT	CORRECT
a.	The two sister help one another.	The two sisters help each other.
b.	The four friends love each other.	The four friends love one another.

Rule 3 : Each, everyone, everybody, anybody, Nobody must be followed by verbs, pronouns and adjectives in singular. As below in sentence (a), we have changed pronoun **their** into **his**. Similarly in sentence (b). This is shown below.

	INCORRECT	CORRECT
a.	Everyone of them did their work.	Everyone of them did his work.
b.	He advised everybody to perform their duty.	He advised everybody to perform his duty.

Rule 4 : If pronouns are used before the verbs then pronouns should always be in subjective forms.

If Pronouns are to be used after verbs then pronouns should be in objective forms. If any sentence starts with **let or between then following pronouns are always used in objective form.**

	INCORRECT	CORRECT
a.	These presents are for you and I.	These presents are for you and me.
b.	Let you and I go there.	Let you and me go there.

Rule 5 : After **Such** we have to use **as**. An example is given below and if **such** is use to show consequence then **such** ..... **that** is used.

	INCORRECT	CORRECT
a.	Life is such a problem that cannot be solved.	Life is such a problem as cannot be solved.

Rule 6 : Either and neither are used for two objects or persons. Any or None is used for more than two persons or objects. Also either and Any,are used in positive sense. Neither or None is used in Negative Sense.

	INCORRECT	CORRECT
a.	Any of these two houses will serve our purpose.	Either of these two houses will serve our purpose.
b.	He is poorer than either of his four friends.	He is poorer than any of his four friends.
c.	None of these two pens are yours.	Neither of these two pens is yours.

Rule 7 : The Role of **it**.

While speaking **"it** is not necessary". But in written English **it** is used to emphasise the noun or pronoun we are using for example in below sentence **it** is used to show a glass of water only. And in sentence (b), the person is refusing to take a cup of tea only.

	INCORRECT	CORRECT
a.	Please give me a glass of water.I am giving.	Please give me a glass of water. I am giving it.
b.	Please take a cup of tea. Thanks I don't need.	Please take a cup of tea. Thanks I don't need it.

Rule 8 : After one, one's is used i.e. if one is in subjective case, then one's should be used in objective case. So after one, one's or onself is used. This is shown below.

	INCORRECT	CORRECT
a.	One should serve his Country	One should serve one's Country.

Rule 9 : Generally who is used as subjective case and whom is used as objective case.

Now we will discuss a shortcut to learn the use of who or whom. Let us consider two example.

(1) The person (who/whom) we thought [he] was an actor proved to be a soldier.

(2) The person (who/whom) we feared we had shot [him] proved to be unharmed.

Trick:- Where ever in any sentence, if we are able to insert/fit in (**he/she**) then **who** is used and if we are able to insert **(him or her)** then **whom** is used.

In Ex. 1 after **we thought, he** can come **so who** in the sentence will be correct. Similarly in Ex. 2 We can insert **him after we had shot so whom** will be correct in the sentence.

	INCORRECT	CORRECT
a.	Who did you saw yesterday ?	Whom did you saw yesterday ?
b.	Whom do you think will be leader of our party ?	Who do you think will be leader of our party.

Rule 10 : If two singular Nouns are joined by or,either-or,Neither-nor then pronoun used must be in singular.

As below in sentence **(a)** when two singular Nouns are Ram and Shyam joined by 'or' the pronoun **their** is changed into **his.**

	INCORRECT	CORRECT
a.	Ram or Shyam gave me their share	Ram or Shyam gave me his share.
b.	Either Sita or Gita must do their work.	Either Sita or gita must do her work.
c.	Neither Mohan nor Sohan did their work	Neither Mohan nor Sohan did his work.

Rule 11 : The possesive pronouns **yours, ours, hers, their** and **its** are written without apostrophe. This is shown below.

	INCORRECT	CORRECT
a.	Your's	Yours
b.	Our's	ours
c.	her's	hers

d. their's — theirs

e. it's — its

Rule 12 : When a personal pronoun is used as a complement to the verb **to be**, the pronoun must be in subjective case or it + any helping verb is followed by subjective pronoun.

As in **(a)** after **'was' he** should be used, here verb is **was** and after verb, the pronoun him should be subjective case which is **he.** This is shown below.

	INCORRECT	**CORRECT**
a.	It was him who did it	It was he who did it.
b.	It was her who did it.	It was she who did it .
c.	It is me.	It is I

Rule 13 : When the sentence starts with **Let,** the pronoun must be in objective case.

As in sentence **(a)** the objective case of **he** is **him**. (See the table of cases). This is shown by following examples.

	INCORRECT	**CORRECT**
a.	Let he do the question.	Let him do the question.
b.	Let I go there.	Let me go there.

Rule 14 : When comparison is made using **as or than** the pronoun used should be of same case. For example in **(a)** the pronouns are He, and me on incorrect side. But here He is in Subjective case, so instead of me (which is objective) I (subjective case) is used. This is shown below by examples.

	INCORRECT	**CORRECT**
a.	He is faster than me.	He is faster than I (am).
b.	You are stronger than him.	You are stronger than he.
c.	You are as small as me.	You are as small as I.

Rule 15 : We use **that** after **all, some, any, none, anyone**. **That** is also used after superlative. Examples are given below.

	INCORRECT	**CORRECT**
a.	All which glitter is not gold.	All that glitter is not gold.
b.	It is the same picture. which I saw yesterday.	It is the same picture. that I saw yesterday.
c.	It is only the dog who barks.	It is only the dog that barks.

Rule 16 : A relative pronoun **'that'** can never take place of **who** or **which**. Example is given below.

	INCORRECT	**CORRECT**
a.	My wife that is an actress is very smart.	My wife who is an actress is very smart.

Rule 17 : Certain verbs like **avail, enjoy, absent, exert, distinguish, resign etc.** are always followed by reflexive pronouns like **himself, herself, yourself etc.** i.e. when the subject is the object of any sentence. This is shown below by examples.

	INCORRECT	CORRECT
a.	He availed the opportunity.	He availed himself of the opportunity.
b.	I covered me with a blanket.	I covered myself with a blanket.
c.	He enjoyed during the shows.	He enjoyed himself during the show.
d.	He has resigned to almighty.	He has resigned himself to almighty.

MISCELLANEOUS RULES

Rule 18 : **None** is used as both singular as well as in plural as per the sense and requirement of sentence.

Rule 19 : Emphatic pronouns are never used as subject or you cannot start sentences with emphatic pronouns like myself, yourself, himself etc. For example

INCORRECT	CORRECT
myself will do this.	I myself will do this.

Rule 20 : The relative pronoun **who** is always placed near the noun for which it is used.

For example The man, **who** came to me is an actor.

In above sentence we have placed who near the noun **Man** as **who** is used for this man only.

Rule 21 : **That** or **those** is used to avoid the repetition of a noun already used in the given sentence.

For example. The streets of Delhi are wider than that of Hardwar.

So here **that** is used in place of **streets**

Rule 22 : **Who, Whom, Whose** are used for persons.

Who is used as subjective case.

Whom is used as objective case.

Whose is used as possessive case.

What is used for objective.

Which s used for selection of person or objects or anmal out of given objects or persons or animals.

So till now, we have learnt the ways to find errors in the use of pronouns.

BREAK FOR WORDS REVISION

REVISE THE VOCAB

TEST

Find out the errors in following sentences :

No.	a	b	c	d	e
(1)	Ram is	more	intelligent	than me.	no error
(2)	Ajay and	Kajol	love	one another.	no error
(3)	Who do	you	went	to see.	No error
(4)	Everybody	should perform	their duty	sincerely.	No error
(5)	Both	of them	did	not go	No error
(6)	She	enjoyed	during	the show.	No error
(7)	Is there	anybody ?	Yes	it is me.	No error
(8)	This the same	man whom you	met yesterday	in the market	No error
(9)	I am	not weak	as	him.	No error
(10)	This pen	is superior	to	your.	No error
(11)	He will	not object to	me going	there.	No error
(12)	What is it	which causes	you so	much trouble.	No error
(13)	This is the	tree	whose fruits	you like.	so much
(14)	One must	not be	dishonest to his	society.	No error
(15)	It was him	who	did	it	No error

VOCAB LIST

Sr.	*Words*	*Meanings*
101.	Adipose	Fatty
102.	Distribe	Criticize
103.	Traipse	Walk weanily
104.	Miasma	Obnoxious fume
105.	Meliorate	Improve
106.	Equanimity	Composure
107.	Incinerated	To destroy by burning
108.	Nippy	Quick in movement
109.	Incessant	Constant
110.	Disdain	Hate
111.	Jibe	Taunts
112.	Credible	Believable
113.	Waver	Hesitate, Unsteady
114.	Congenial	Pleasing
115.	Outset	Beginning
116.	Gullet	Throat
117.	Renaissance	Revival
118.	Abortive	Not successful/Failing
119.	Fecund	Fruitful
120.	Privation	Hardship/a life of misery
121.	Puerile	Childish
122.	Lampoon	Ridicule
123.	Discreet	Prudent
124.	Imminent	Impending
125.	Homilies	Sermons
126.	Salubrious	Healthful/Pleasant
127.	Genial	Friendly/Cheerful
128.	Mendacious	False/Lying

129.	Odious	Hateful/Unpleasant
130.	Fulminate	Protest
131.	Sham	Pretender
132.	Hobnobbing	Associating
133.	Behest	Orders
134.	Tenacious	Strong
135.	Consummation	Completion
136.	Expostulate	Protest
137.	Memoirs	Life
138.	Fictitious	Imaginative
139.	Persuasive	Convincing
140.	Quirk	Strange habit
141.	Implicate	Involve oneself
142.	Weird	Unnatural/Strange
143.	Ransacked	Searched
144.	Exemplary	Admirable
145.	Sheer	Complete/Nothing more than
146.	Fluke	Accident
147.	Lay	Ordinary
148.	Proselytize	Persuade to accept one's own beliefs
149.	Execrable	Very bad/Terrible
150.	Eye	Aim

...

BREAK FOR WORDS REVISION

REVISE THE VOCAB

TEST No- 3
(Words 101-150)

Choose the correct meaning of the given words from amongst their alternatives :

(1) Adipose

(a) thin (b) thick
(c) fatty (d) round

(2) Miasma

(a) obnoxious fame (b) hot fire
(c) water (d) lava

(3) Disdain

(a) love (b) hate
(c) praise (d) to talk low of

(4) Outset

(a) end (b) middle
(c) beginning (d) none

(5) Abortive

(a) successful (b) not successful
(c) interrupted (d) not started

(6) Puerile

(a) elderly (b) childish
(c) manly (d) of woman

(7) Genial

(a) friendly (b) genious
(c) faulty (d) healthy

(8) Expostulate

(a) accept (b) support
(c) protest (d) praise

(9) Quirk

(a) strange talk (b) strange walk
(c) strange habit (d) quick

(10) Ransacked

(a) loot (b) destroyed
(c) built (d) searched

(11) Lampoon

(a) serious (b) ridicule
(c) lazy (d) drunken

(12) Eye

(a) fame (b) name
(c) aim (d) claim

(13) Homilies

(a) sermons (b) songs of Holy

(c) sad songs (d) songs of sympathy

(14) Implicate

(a) indicate (b) involve oneself

(c) order (d) protest

(15) Discreet

(a) prudent (b) greedy

(c) shameless (d) precious

Match the words in the column 'A' with their correct meaning in 'B'

Column 'A'	Column 'B'
(1) Jibe	(1) Quick in movement
(2) Nippy	(2) Imaginative
(3) Congenial	(3) Accident
(4) Execrable	(4) Persuade to accept one's own
(5) Fictitious	(5) Unnatural
(6) sham	(6) Unsteady
(7) Fluke	(7) Taunts
(8) Tenacious	(8) Hate
(9) Proselytize	(9) Revival
(10) Waver	(10) Strong
(11) Weird	(11) Admirable
(12) Disdain	(12) Terrible
(13) Renairsance	(13) Pretender
(14) Hobnobbing	(14) Associating
(15) Exemplary	(15) Pleasing

Answers Grammar

(1) **(d)** I should be used (Rule 14)

(2) **(d)** In place of **one another** it should I be **each other** (Rule2)

(3) **(a)** **Whom** in place of **who** (Rule 9)

(4) **(c)** It should be **his** in place of **their** (Rule 3)

(5) **(a)** Replace Both with Neither (Rule 6)

(6) **(b)** Add herself after enjoyed and before during (Rule 17)

(7) **(d)** It should be I in place of me (Rule 12)

(8) **(b)** Use that in place of whom
Rule - The same is followed by that

(9) **(b)** He in place of him

Rule : If we have to use pronoun after the conjuction of comparison as or than, the the **case** of pronoun used after as or than is same as that of first pronoun in that sentence. For example in (9)

First pronoun **'i'** is nominative case, so the pronoun after **as** must be in nominative case i.e. him is objective case of He (third person pronoun) and the nominative case of He is He itself.

(10) **(d)** Yours in place of your.

As yours mean your pen or simply say your pen. Also comparison should be made between same objects or same qualities.

(11) **(c)** my in place of me

(12) **(b)** **that** in place of **which**. As **which** is used for selecting some objects or persons out of given objects of person. Also which cannot take place of that (Rule 16)

(13) **(c)** **'The fruit of which'** should be used in place of **'whose fruits'**. The sentence will become This is the tree, the fruit of which you like so much (Rule 16).

(14) **(c)** **One's** in place of **his** (Rule 15)

(15) **(b)** **he** in place of **him** (Rule 12)

ANSWERS Vocab TEST NO. 3

(1) c (2) a (3) b (4) d (5) b (6) b (7) a
(9) c (10) d (11) b (12) c (13) a (14) b (15) a
(8) c

Match

(1) 7 (2) 1 (3) 15 (4) 12 (5) 2 (6) 13 (7) 3
(8) 10 (9) 4 (10) 6 (11) 5 (12) 8 (13) 9 (14) 14
(15) 11

Day 5

Adjective

Today we will study adjectives. Before going into detail of this topic, read the following sentences.

(i) Ram is a **good** boy.

(ii) He is **my** brother.

(iii) She is wearing **black** shirt.

(iv) Sachin is the **best** batsman.

(v) You are a **wise** man.

We observe that in all the above sentences we are saying some thing about noun or pronoun in the sentences.

For example :

In **(i)** We are saying that is Ram (noun) is good.

In **(ii)** We are saying something about pronoun (He) that the person (He) is my brother.

In **(iii)** Also we are saying about shirt (noun) that it is black.

So in all the five sentences the words **good, my, black, best, wise** are describing the qualities of noun or pronoun.

Therefore

Adjectives are the words used to qualify nouns or pronouns.

or

Adjectives are the words to show the qualities of nouns or pronouns.

or

Adjectives are the words which tell us anything about noun or pronouns.

So, now it is hoped that you have understood the definition of adjective.

Now we will discuss the types of Adjectives.

In English Language we have following types of adjectives.

1. **Adjectives of quality.**
2. **Adjectives of quantity.**
3. **Adjectives of numbers.**
4. **Demonstrative adjectives.**
5. **Distributive adjectives.**
6. **Interrogative adjectives.**

Now we will discuss each type of **Adjective one by one.**

1. **Adjectives of Quality :**

Words which show the quality of noun or pronoun.

For example :

(i) He is a good boy.

(ii) He is a bad boy.

In **(i)** adjective is good and is telling the quality of **noun** (boy).

In **(ii)** the word **bad** is also telling about a **boy (noun).**

So here **good and bad** are adjectives of quality.

2. **Adjectives of quantity :**

Words which tell us the quantity of noun or pronoun.

For example :

(i) I need **a little** sugar for tea.

(ii) He lost **all** his moeny.

(iii) He ate **some** food.

Here **a little, all, some** are showing the quantity or how much of that object.

3. **Adjectives of number :**

Words which tell us the number of objects or persons in the sentence.

For example :

One, Two, Three, a few, many, most, some are some of adjectives of numbers.

For example :

(i) There are **four** persons in this room.

(ii) **Many** persons come here.

Adjectives of number are of two types :

(a) Cardinal : One, Two, Three etc.

(b) Ordinal : First, Second, Third etc.

4. **Demonstrative Adjectives :**

Words which point out to some noun.

In this category we have **This, That, There, Those etc.**

For example :

(i) **This** pen is good.

(ii) **That** place is beautiful.

In **(i)** **'This'** is demonstrative adjective and it is pointing to pen (Noun).

5. **Distributive Adjectives :**

Words which refer to persons or things taken separtelely or in separate groups.

In this category **we have Each, Every, Either, Neither, etc. as Distributive Adjectives.**

For example :

(i) Each boy got a prize.

(ii) Every person has done his duty.

(iii) Either of two boys wiil get the prize.

(iv) Neither of you were there.

6. Interrogative Adjectives :

Words used to ask questions regarding nouns.These Adjectives are placed near nouns. In this category **we have What, Which, Whose etc.**

For example :

(i) What is the price of this table?

(ii) Which shirt do you like?.

(iii) Whose pen is this?.

7. Possesive Adjectives :

Word used to show possession or relationship with noun.

In this category **we have My, His, This, One's, Its, Our, Your Their etc.**

For example :

(i) This is my room.

Here **'my'** is possesive adjective showing some kind of authority on the room.

Degrees of comparison of adjectives

The forms of adjectives used for comparison in English Language are called degrees of comparision. We have three degrees of comparision.

These are :

1. **Positive**
2. **Comparative**
3. **Superlative**

1. Positive :

In this words are used to tell simple things or something about nouns. These kinds of sentences are simple.

For example :

(i) Ram is good boy.

(ii) He is an intelligent person.

2. Comparative degree :

When two things or objects are compared we use comparative degree.

or

When one person or object or quality of person or object is compared with another person or object or with group of persons or objects then we have to use this degree. The main feature of these sentences are that the use of word **'than'** is always there But when one subject is compared rest of the subjects then we use

than.... any ..... other

For example :

(i) Ram is better than his brother.

(ii) Shyam is weaker than any other boy in his class.

So In **(i)** we are compairing Ram with his brother.

In **(ii)** we are comparing Shyam with rest of boys in his class.

3. **Superlative degree :**

When, we want to show that the subject is superior to all or if it is to be compared with more than two subjects.

For example :

(i) Ram is **the richest** person in India.

(ii) Sachin is **the best** batsman.

Here **best** and **richest** are superlative.

Now we will do the rules for making three degrees of comparision. These are as follow:

Rules :

For formation of comparative & superlative degree.

Rule 1 :

When **'-er-'** is added after postitive degree we get comparetive degree. And when **'-est-'** is added after positive we get superlative degree.

For example :

	Positive	Comparative	Superlative
(a)	Great	Greater	Greatest
(b)	Tall	Taller	Tallest.
(c)	Poor	Poorer	Poorest.

Rule 2 :

If an adjective ends at **'e'** then **'r'** is added to get compartive degree and **'st'** is added to get superlative degree.

For example :

	Positive	Comparative	Superlative
(a).	Wise	Wiser	Wisest
(b).	Large	Larger	Largest.
(c).	Fine	Finer	Finest.

Rule 3 :

If an adjective ends at any consonant and before consonant there is vowel then **'er'** is added to get comparative degree and **'est'** is added to get superlative.

For example :

	Positive	Comparative	Superlative
(a)	Big	Bigger	Biggest.
(b)	Red	Redder	Reddest.
(c)	Wet	Wetter	Westest.

Rule 4 :

There are certain adjectives for which no rule is applicable. These we have to learn as they are.

For example :

	Positive	Comparative	Superlative
(a)	Good	Better	Best.
(b).	Many	More	Most.
(c)	Well	Better	Best.

Rule 5 :

For a few adjectives more or most are used before them to form comparative or superlative degree.

For example :

	Positive	Comparative	Superlative
(a).	Beautiful	More beautiful	Most beautiful.
(b)	Useful	More useful	Most useful.

Now we will study the errors in the use of adjectives.

ERRORS IN THE USE OF ADJECTIVES

Rule 1 :

In any sentence the use of two comparatives together should be avoided.

In **(a)** more and happier should not be used together

This is explained below by some examples :

	Incorrect	Correct
(a)	Ram is more happier than you.	Ram is happier than you.
(b)	This pen is more better than that.	This pen is better than that.

Rule 2 :

In a sentence the use of two superlatives together, should be avoided.

For example In **(a)** the use of most and ablest together is wrong, as most and ablest are superlatives.

This is explained below with a few examples.

	Incorrect	Correct
(a)	She is most ablest girl.	She is the ablest girl.
(b)	Hari is most tallest of his four friends.	Hari is the tallest of his four friends.

Rule 3 :

When the two objects or persons are compared, we have to use comparative degree using **than**.

For example In **(b)** we are comparing sita with other person, therefore the adjective **'tall'** has been changed into comparative degree **(taller).**

This is explained below by some examples :

	Incorrect	Correct
(a)	This pen is useful than that.	This pen is more useful than that.
(b)	Sita is tall than you.	Sita is taller than you.

Rule 4 :

If a person or a object is to be shown superior to all person or object in that group by using comparative degree then, (than, any,other) is used.

For example In (a) we have shown that Gita is abler than rest of girls in her class and if we use comparative degree to say this then we have to use (than any other)

This is explained below by some examples :

	Incorrect	Correct
(a)	Gita is abler than any girl in her class.	Gita is abler than any other girl in her class.
(b)	Raju is stronger than any boy in his class.	Raju is stronger than any other boy in his class.

Rule 5 :

If 'All' is used {as in (a)} then, the use of 'other' is uneccessary.

And In (b) when we are comparaing one person with more than we have to use superlative degree.

This is explained below by some examples :

	Incorrect	Correct
(a)	Ram is richest of all other friends.	Ram is the richest of all friends.
(b)	He is stronger of his four brothers.	He is the strongest of his four brothers.

Rule 6 :

Definite article "THE' is used before any superlative.

This is explained below by an example :

	Incorrect	Correct
(a)	Sachin is best batsman.	Sachin is the best batsman.

Rule 7 :

With word 'comparatively' no comparative degree is used.

This is explained below by an example :

	Incorrect	Correct
(a)	Ram is comparatively weaker in maths.	Ram is comparatively weak in maths.

Rule 8 :

After the words prefer, preferrable, senior, junior, superior, inferior, prior etc. 'To' is used instead of **than**.

This is explained below by some examples :

	Incorrect	Correct
(a)	I prefer tea than coffee.	I prefer tea to coffee.
(b)	Ram prefers health than wealth.	Ram prefers health to wealth.
(c)	He is junior than me.	He is junior to me.

Rule 9 :

When ages of persons other than family or outside family are compared, we use older or oldest.

And elder or eldest is used when ages of the members of family are compared.Elder is used only for persons and older can be used for both persons and animals.

This is explained below by some examples :

	Incorrect	Correct
(a)	He is the eldest man in the town.	He is the oldest man in town.
(b)	Hari is my oldest son.	Hari is my eldest son.

Rule 10 :

Some adjectives like 'Ideal', 'Unique', 'Complete', 'Perfect', 'Full', 'Cheap', 'Entire', 'Impossible', ' Preferrable', 'Extreme' etc are used as such. We cannot change them into comparatives or superlatives.

This is explained below by some examples :

	Incorrect	Correct
(a)	Sachin is the most ideal batsman.	Sachin is an ideal batsman.
(b)	This pen is the most unique.	This pen is unique.

Rule 11 :

Few, Little, mean no body, nothing respectively.

A few, A little mean somebody, something, respectively.

Little is used for quantity (uncountable nouns) and few is used to count number persons or objects (countable nouns).

This is explained below by some examples :

	Incorrect	Correct
(a)	Few boys were present in the class.	A few boys were present in the class.
(b)	Little happiness is better than none.	A little happiness is better than none.
(c)	He wants little salt for soup.	He wants a little salt for soup.

Rule 12 :

'Many a' is always follwed by noun and verb in the singular.

This is explained below by example :

	Incorrect	Correct
(a)	Many a girls were absent.	Many girls were absent or many a girl was absent.

Rule 13 :

Other is always follwed by 'Than' not by But.

This is explained below by an example :

	Incorrect	Correct
(a)	I know no other person here but Ram	I know no other person here than Ram.

Rule 14 :

'The poor' means all poor persons and 'the brave' means all brave persons. So when we want to say all person, just place 'the' before the noun.It will become a plural noun.

This is explained below by some examples :

	Incorrect	Correct
(a)	We should not hate poor.	We should not hate the poor.
(b)	Only brave deserve the fair.	Only the brave deserve the fair.

Rule 15 :

Later and Latest refer to time, while Latter and last refer to position.

This is explained below by some examples :

Incorrect	Correct
(a) He came latter than I.	He come later than I.
(b) Ram sat in latest row.	Ram sat in last row.
(c) Of the three heroes Shahrukh, Salman and Amir the late is my favourite.	Of the three heroes Shahrukh, Salman and Amir, the last is my favourite.

Rule 16 :

'Any' is used in negative sense and **'some'** is used in positive sense.

This is explained below by some examples :

Incorrect	Correct
(a) Ram will not buy some clothes.	Ram will not buy any clothes.
(b) Shyam gave me any books.	Shyam gave me some books.

Rule 17 :

If the first quality of person or subject is in comparative or superlative degree, then the second quality of same person or subject should also be in same degree.

This is explained below by some examples :

Incorrect	Correct
(a) He is ablest and kind person.	He is the ablest and kindest person.
(b) He wants an abler and honest employee.	He wants an abler and more honest employee

Rule 18 :

The comparison is always made between two things of the similiar nature.

This is explained below by an example :

Incorrect	Correct
(a) The streets of chandigarh are wider than Delhi.	The streets of Chandigarh are wider than the streets of Delhi.

In the above sentence we are comparing streets of Chandigarh with the streets of Delhi and not the streets of Chandigarh with Delhi (city). So streets of one place should be compared with streets of second place.

Rule 19 :

When we are comparing the qualities of same person, we should not use comparative degree.

Instead of this 'more' is used. As comparative degree is used to compare the qulities of two different objects or persons.

This is explained below by an example :

Incorrect	Correct
(a) Ram is richer than wise.	Ram is more rich than wise.

MISCELLANEOUS RULES

Rule 20 :

Rather is forced comparative so with rather no other comparative degree is used.

Rule 21 :

Kind and sort must be used in singular form.

Rule 22 :

When whole is used as an adjective it is preceeeded by the 'and' & followed by 'of '.

TEST

	a	b	c	d	e
(A)	They have	less books	than	I have.	No error.
(B)	There is	a little	hope	of his recovery.	No error.
(C)	Of	all the poets	Yeat	is best.	No error.
(D)	My all	friends	helped	me.	No error.
(E)	Your	lovely	friend	Raj.	No error.
(F)	She	is	junior	to me.	No error.
(G)	The	whole India	was shocked at loss	of this learder.	No error.
(H)	He shall	leave by	lastest	plane.	No error.
(I)	It was	much	fine	yestrday.	No error.
(J)	She will	not accept	lesser than	five kilos of sugar.	No error.
(K)	Those flower	smells	sweetly	No error.	
(L)	Pacific ocean is	the most deep	ocean	in the world.	No error.
(M)	Ram is in	most	extreme	difficulty.	No error.
(N)	He	is	becoming	rich.	No error.

Sr.	Word	Meanings
151.	Zenith	Acme
152.	Recompense	Reward
153.	Apoplexy	Loss of feeling
154.	Scotch	To stop, To put an end
155.	Dunno	Do not know

156.	Conscientious	Sincere
157.	Gratifying	Pleasing
158.	Prerogative	Privilege
159.	Cursory	Hurried
160.	Obsolescent	Out of date
161.	Infallible	Never Failing
162.	Lair	Hiding place
163.	Slumber	To sleep
164.	Spick & Span	Neat, clean & tidy
165.	Grain	Nature
166.	Verdant	Fresh
167.	Chagrined	Disappointed
168.	Preposterous	Absurd
169.	Salutary	Beneficial
170.	Merit	To deserve
171.	Sententious	Quick
172.	Ruminate	Ponder
173.	Transient	Brief/Temporary
174.	Transitory	Fleeting
175.	Charisma	Magnetic Appeal
176.	Momentous	Important
177.	Reprieve	Delay
178.	Trice	Very quickly/suddenly
179.	Inception	Beginning
180	Portent	A sign or warning of a future event
181	Verity	Truth, True idea
182	Veritable	Complete, Real
183	Menagerie	Collection of animal
184	Belie	To give a false idea
185	Superannuated	Too old
186	Erroneous	Wrong/Not correct

187	Stint	Tenure
188	Yore	Long ago
189	Strain	Breed or type of
190	Clout	Power/influence
191	Generic	Not specific
192	Farcical	Ridiculous
193	Precipitous	Sudden/Dramatic
194	Unmet	Not satisfied
195	Unfettered	Free
196	Fealty	Loyalty
197	Ramification	Complex consequence
198	Preposterous	Unreasonable/Absurd
199	Revere	Feel great respect for
200	Hubris	Great pride

...

BREAK FOR WORDS REVISION

REVISE THE VOCAB

TEST No- 4
(Words 151-200)

Choose the correct meaning of the given words from amongst their alternatives :

(1) Recompense
(a) rebuke (b) reward
(c) recompensate (d) reconcile

(2) Infallible
(a) never successful (b) never failing
(c) never tired (d) faulty

(3) Lair
(a) ordinary (b) hiding peace
(c) pleasing (d) strong

(4) Conscientious
(a) sincere (b) revolutionary
(c) miserly (d) hateful

(5) Apoplexy
(a) loss of money (b) loss of fame
(c) loss of business (d) loss of feeling

(6) Verdant
(a) stale (b) fresh
(c) prosperous (d) important

(7) Veritable
(a) imaginary (b) real
(c) of variety (d) of same species

(8) Stint
(a) tenure (b) strong
(c) amusing (d) pinching

(9) Trice
(a) lately (b) very quicky
(c) time consuming (d) minute

(10) Charisma
(a) magnetic appeal (b) not appealing
(c) cheerful (d) playful

(11) Superannuated
(a) too big (b) too bulky
(c) too expensive (d) too old

(12) Revere
(a) respect (b) rebuke
(c) scold (d) refer to

(13) Erroneous
(a) wrong (b) imaginary
(c) extraordinary (d) none of these

(14) Precipitous
(a) imaginary (b) hard work
(c) dramatic (d) well thought

(15) Reprieve
(a) delay (b) relax
(c) improve (d) out play

Match the words in the column 'A' with their correct meaning in 'B'

Column 'A'	Column 'B'
(1) Cursory	(1) Beginning
(2) Obsolescent	(2) Hurried
(3) Inception	(3) Long ago
(4) Hubris	(4) Complex consequence
(5) Yore	(5) Neat, clean or tidy
(6) Slumber	(6) Out of date
(7) Ramification	(7) Beneficial
(8) Farcical	(8) Ridiculous
(9) Spick of span	(9) Ponder
(10) Unfettered	(10) Collection of animals
(11) Menagerie	(11) Power/influence
(12) Salutary	(12) Absurd/unreasonable
(13) Ruminate	(13) Free
(14) Clout	(14) To sleep
(15) Preposterous	(15) Great pride

Answer Grammar

(A) a, fewer in place of lesser. (Rule11).

(B) b, little in place of a little. (Rule11).

(C) d, add the before best.

(D) a, All my friends in place of my friends.

(E) b, loving in place of lovely. Since lovely is an adverb.and we are using adjectives.

(F) e.

(G) a, The whole of India (Rule 22).

(H) c, Last in place of Latest (Rule 15).

(I) b, very in much, very is used when we cannot measure the quality mentioned As we cannot measure fineness. Much is used when we can see or measure the quality stated in the sentence.

(J) e.

(K) d, sweet in place of swetly. as sweetly is an adverbs and we are talking about the quality of flower so sweet should be used.

(L) b, the deepest.

(M) b, Remove most (Rule 10).

(N) d, Richer in place of rich.

ANSWERS Vocab List TEST NO.4

(1) b (2) b (3) b (4) a (5) d (6) b (7) b
(8) a (9) b (10) a (11) d (12) a (13) a (14) c
(15) a

Match

(1) 2 (2) 6 (3) 3 (4) 15 (5) 3 (6) 14 (7) 4
(8) 8 (9) 5 (10) 13 (11) 10 (12) 7 (13) 9 (14) 11
(15) 12

Day

6

Verbs & Tenses

Today we will study verbs and the errors in use of the verbs.

Before starting the topic consider the following examples.

(a) Ram came here.

(b) He writes a poem.

(c) He has been singing for two hours.

In sentence	(a)	Came
In sentence	(b)	Writes.
In sentence	(c)	Has been singing.

are the words which show action or help certain words to complete their meaning. For example in (c) **has been** is helping the word **singing** to complete the sentence.

So in English Language **the words by the help of which we can show action or show state of being in action are known as verbs.**

In English Language we have following kinds of verbs.

1. **Transitive verb.**
2. **Intransitive verb.**
3. **Linking verb.**
4. **Auxiliary or helping verbs.**

Now we will define each kind of verb with examples.

1. Transitive verb :

Verbs having object with it are known as Transitive verbs.

For example

Dhanraj played hockey.

In above sentence Dhanraj is subject. 'Played' is verb (action), 'hockey' is object.

2. Intransitive Verb :

Verbs having no object with them.

For example :

(a) Sheela is going.

(b) Ram is playing.

In (a) **'is going'** and in (b) **'is playing'** are intransitive verbs becuse in both the sentences no object is there

As In (a) **Sheela** is subject and **'is going'** is verb.

3. **Linking verb :**

Verbs which join subject to its complement are known as linking verbs. For example

Ram is intelligent.

In above sentence

Ram : subject.

is : linking subject (Ram) to its complement 'intellegent'. Complement means a word which helps in making the sense of sentence complete. Otherwise 'Ram is' incomplete sentence and adding 'intellegent' to this sentence makes its meaning or sense complete.

A few words as **get, go, grow, run, appear, become, look, remain, seen** etc. can also be used as linking verbs.

4. **Auxiliary or helping verbs :**

Words which tell us the time of happening of main action or main verb i.e.whether the action about which we are talking, has happened in past, present or future.

A few examples will make you understand.

(a) Ram has been eating his meals.

(b) Sita is reading a novel.

So in (a) main verb is **'eating'** and auxiliary or helping verb **'is has'** been.

In (b) main verb **'reading'**,

Helping verb **'is'**.

A few helping verbs are : **is, am, are, was, were, can, could, do, does, did, has had, shall, should, will, would.**

The main difference between linking verb and Auxiliary verb is that we can have only one word as linking verb in any sentence and there can be more than one word (normally two) as auxiliary verbs in any given sentence.

So till now we have given you the basic idea about the verbs and their types.

In English we have certain fixed frame of refrences or time on which rules regarding the representation of time are made and in accordance to time, verbs are used.

In English Grammar we call time as tense.Mainly we have three kinds of tenses or frame of refrences with respect to time or situation in which we are writing or speaking english.

These tenses are as follow:

a Present tense.

b Past tense.

c Future tense.

i.e. **(a)** When we are saying or writing anything in or about present, we use present tense.

Similar is the case with Past tense and Furture tense.

Also each tense is divided into four sub-parts. These are:

(a) Indefinite or simple.

(b) Continuous.

(c) Perfect.

(d) Perfect Continuous.

Now without going into the detail of tenses, we will give you the basic idea of each tense and its sub-types. We will give you a few basic rules of sentence construction using each kind of tense.

In sentence construction, using different forms, we will tell you that how verbs are placed in between subject and object. So we will Start with present tense and its four subcategories. Then rest two i.e. Past and Future.

PRESENT TENSE

A. Present indefinite or simple present :

This is used to show that action done or spoken about is in present and also to show daily / routine etc.

For example

He gives, She goes etc.

The construction of sentence using 'simple present' is as follows.

Subject + 1st form of verb +object.

For example

In He goes to school.

He - subject.

goes - 1st form (of go) + es

to - preposition (as per situation).

school - object.

With He, She and It , verb + 's' or 'es' is used .

& You, they, we, are, used with 1st form of verb i.e. without 's' or 'es'.

For example you go, I go etc.

B. Present Continuous :

To show that work is still going on and is not yet finished.

In this we construct sentence as follows.

sub + is/am/are +verb (ing) + object.

With he, she, it - 'is' is used.

With I,- 'am' is used.

With you, we, they - 'are' is used.

Also in this tense 1st form of verb with 'ing' at the end of it is used. In above it is shown as 'verb + ing'.

For example I am eating.

You are eating. etc.

C Present perfect :

It is used to show that work or action has just completed.

In this we speak or write as follows.

Subject + has/have + verb (IIIrd form of verb) +object.

With He, She, It, - 'has' is used .

With You, We, They, I, - 'have' is used.

D Present perfect continuous :

It is used to show that work started some time back and it is still going on and in these situations we have the time period also given to us.

The sentence construction is

Subject + has been/ have been +(V_1+ing) + since/ for +object.

With He, She, It, - 'has been' is used.

With I, We, You, They - 'have been' is used

'Since' is used when the point of time of the start of work is given.

'For' is used when period of time is given.

For example

I have been writing this book since 5'clock.

He has been playing for last two hours.

V_1 means first form of the verbs, V_2 means second form & V_3 means third form.

PAST TENSE

(A) Past indefinite or simple Past tense.

It is used to show that action happend in past but when it started or ended is not given.

Sentence construction is as follows.

Subject + IInd form of verb + object.

For example

I saw, He saw, etc.

(B) Past continuous :

It is used to show that action which started in past, was not completed.

The sentence construction is as follows.

Subject + was/were +(v_1 + ing) + object.

With He, She, It, - 'was' is used.

With I, We, You, They - 'were' is used

For example

I was coming.

You were going.

(C) Past perfect tense :

(1) It is used to show that action started in past was completed.

(2) Some times when two past action are to be told and one of them is over before the start of another. We use past perfect tense.

For Ex. The train had left before I reached the station.

The sentence construction is as follows.

Subject + had +verb (IIIrd form) +object.

In this tense with every subject helping verb **'had'** is used.

(D) Past perfect continuous :

It is used to show that work was started sometime back and was not completed also i.e. it was still going on.

The sentence construction is as follows.

Subject + had been+(v_1 + ing) + Since/for +object.

FUTURE TENSE

(a) Future indefinite :

It is used to show that action will be done in future.

The sentence construction using this tense is as follows.

Subject + will/shall +verb (1st form) +object.

With I and we - 'shall' is used.

With He, She, It, You, They - 'Will' is used

(b) Future continuous tense :

It is used to show that work will go on in future.

The sentence construction using the tense as follows.

Subject + will be/shall be + {verb (1st form) +ing} + object.

(c) Future perfect tense :

It is used to show that work will be finished in future by certain time.

The sentence constrution is as follows.

Subjects + will have/shall have + verb III rd form + object + by/before

With I, We, - 'shall have' is used.

With You, We, They, He, She,It, -'will have' is used.

(d) Future perfect continuous :

It is used to show that work will go on, in future and will not be completed.

The sentence construction is as follows.

Subject + shall have been/ will have been + (verb1st form+ing)+ for + object + when.

ERRORS IN THE USE OF VERBS

Rule 1 : In any sentence when there are words which denote past time like yesterday, ago etc. we have to use past indefinate tense. Examples are given below.

	Incorrect	**Correct.**
(a)	Ram have seen him yesterday.	Ram saw him yesterday.
(b)	I have met him last year.	I met him last year.

Rule 2 : When two nouns connected by **together with, as well as, beside, in addition to**, are followed by verbs in singular, if former of two noun is singular and plural is former of two is plural.

	Incorrect	**Correct**
(a)	The father together with his sons were there.	The father together with his sons was there.

	Incorrect	Correct
(b)	He as well as his friends were winner.	He as well as his friends was winner.

For example

In (c) father and sons are two different noun, joined by 'together with'. And here out of two nouns, the first noun is father, which is singular therefore the verb 'were' has been changed into 'was'.

Rule 3 : When the article is repeated before the nouns, different persons or things are meant and if article is not repeated only one person or thing is meant.

	Incorrect	Correct
(a)	The teacher and the leader is dead.	The teacher and the leader are dead.
(b)	The teacher and novelist are dead.	The teacher and novelist is dead.

Rule 4 : **Each, every, neither, either, nobody, anyone, everyone** is followed by verb in singular.

	Incorrect	Correct
(a)	Neither of these reports are true.	Neither of these report is true.
(b)	Each boy and each girl were given sweets.	Each boy and each girl was given sweets.
(c)	Every one of them have attended the college.	Every one of them has attended college.

As in (a) 'are' has been changed into 'is'.

Rule 5 : When two singular nouns are joined by 'either-or' 'neither-nor' the verb is singular.

	Incorrect	Correct
(a)	Either he or his friend have solution.	Either he or his friend has the solution.

In (a) 'have' is been changed into 'has'.

Rule 6 : When the subjects of 'different persons' are joined by either-or, neither-nor, the verb is placed according to nearest person.

In (a) 'you and I' are different persons i.e. you is second person and I is first person. Both are joined by neither-nor and verb should be as per the nearest person, which is I, therfore 'are' has been changed into 'am'.

	Incorrect	Correct
(a)	Neither you nor I are actor.	Neither you nor I am actor.

Rule 7 : When two different nouns combine to form one idea, the verb is singular.

	Incorrect	Correct
(a)	Bread and butter are his favourite snack.	Bread and butter is his favourite snack.
(b)	Slow and steady win the race.	Slow and steady wins the race.

Rule 8 : The verb used will always be according to subject i.e.if subject is singular then verb is singular and if subject is plural, verb is plural.

	Incorrect	Correct
(a)	Our only hope are promises made by leaders.	Our only hope is promises made by leaders.

(b) The promises made is our only hope. | The promises made are our only hope.

In (a) only hope - is subject which is singular thatswhy 'are' has been changed into 'is'.

In (b) the promises - is subject which is plural thatswhy 'is' has been changed into 'are'.

Rule 9 : 'Many a' is always followed by singular verb.

As below in (a) students (Plural Noun) therefore **were** is **was** replaced by.

But when 'many a' is followed by two different nouns, the verb is plural.

As in (b) after 'many a' two different nouns are boy and girl thatswhy in place of 'was' we have used 'were'. This is shown below by a few examples.

	Incorrect	**Correct**
(a)	Many a students were there.	Many a students was there.
(b)	Many a boy and girl was dancing in the hall.	Many a boy and girl were dancing in the hall.

Rule 10 : In any sentence if main clause is in past tense then dependent clause or part must be in past tense. But if in dependent clause any universal fact is quoted, then it must be present indefinete tense. In examples shown below. We have

in (a) I recognised from his face -main clause (Past tense) & that I knew him - Dependent clause must be in (past tense).

In (b) Ram told me -main part (past tense)

The earth moves around the sun (present). (As it is a universal fact.)

	Incorrect	**Correct**
(a)	I recognised from his face that I know him.	I recognised from his face that I knew him.
(b)	Ram told me that earth moved around the sun.	Ram told me that earth moves around the sun.

Rule 11 : Perfect tenses are used when we are talking about two events and one of events is complete before the start of another.

As in (a) we have two events (i) the train left the station.(ii) Ram arrived late that's why 'had' is used.

	Incorrect	**Correct**
(a)	The train left the station before Ram reached there.	The train had left the station before Ram reached there.

Rule 12 : After 'one of' when noun is in plural number, the verb should also be plural.

In (a) After 'one of' noun is cars which is plural therefore 'Has' changed into 'have'. The same example is given below.

	Incorrect	**Correct**
(a)	This is one of best cars that has ever been built.	This is one of best cars that have ever been built.

Rule 13 : Two future tenses are not used in same sentence and part the sentence after 'if' should be in present indefinite tense. This is shown below.

	Incorrect	**Correct**
(a)	I shall do work if machine will be in good condition.	I shall do work if machine is in good condition.

Rule 14 : 'That' is not used before, when, where, how, what, which who, why & in interrogative sentence verb is placed before the subject.

As in (b) were (verb) is placed before the subject (you). This rule is shown below.

	Incorrect	**Correct**
(a)	I do not know that how to find him.	I do not know how to find him.
(b)	Why you were not present in meeting ?	Why were you not present in the meeting ?

Rule 15: When the sentence starts with never, near, seldom. rarely neither, not only, no sooner, verb is placed before the subject.

As in (a) 'have' is placed before I (subject). This is shown below by an example.

	Incorrect	**Correct**
(a)	Never I have visited such a place.	Never have I visited such a place.

Rule 16 : In indirect question subject comes before the verb.

As in (a) I (subject) is placed before the verb(bought). This is shown below.

	Incorrect	**Correct**
(a)	He asked me that which shirt did I buy.	He asked me which shirt I bought.

Rule 17 : When helping verbs like 'have' and 'will' are used we must complete the sense of sentence.

As in (a) **I have never** is incomplete therfore it is necessary place the verb(see) for which **never** is used. This is shown below.

	Incorrect	**Correct**
(a)	I have never and will never see you.	I have never seen and will never see you.

Rule 18 : Part of the sentence after as, if, as though etc is followed by past tense.

Also 'were' is used after He or I because whatever the subject is speaking or thinking, is only his imagination. This is shown below.

For example **I wish if I were a bird.**

	Incorrect	**Correct.**
(a)	He speaks as if is a leader.	He speaks as if he were a leader.

Rule 19 : When 'worth' is used as an adjective it is generally placed before the verb.

As below in (a) worth is placed before the verb (reading). Example is given.

	Incorrect	**Correct**
(a)	Gitanjali is worth reading book.	Gitanjali is a book worth reading.

Rule 20 : After certain words like avoid, dislike, enjoy, dread help remember, stop succeed etc. we use (verb$_1$ + ing) i.e gerund. This is shown below by an example.

Incorrect	Correct
(a) He dislike to do this.	He dislikes doing this.

Rule 21 : After Had better, Had rather, as soon as 'To' is not used.

Incorrect	Correct
(a) You had better not to read this.	You had better not read this.

Rule 22 : Some nouns like number, plenty, army, brave, variety enemy, pair, dozen are actually plural in meaning though they look like singular noun that is why the verb used after them is always plural. This is shown below by a few examples.

Incorrect	Correct
(a) The brave always deserves the victory.	The brave always deserve the victory.
(b) Our army has all the qualities.	Our army have all the qualities.

Rule 23 : When two nouns or pronouns are joined by 'Not only .... but also' the verb is used as per second noun or pronoun. This is shown by an example.

Incorrect	Correct.
(a) Not only the principal but also the students was playing.	Not only the principal but also the students were playing.

Rule 24 : Generally **'for'** is used to show purpose & **'to'** is used to show the direction but in any sentence if direction is already shown by any other word (not by to)then **'to'** is used to show purpose.

As below in (a) 'here' is showing direction that's why **'to'** is used to show purpose. Example is given below.

Incorrect	Correct
(a) He came here for buying this house.	He came here to buy this house.

Rule 25 : When **'since'** is used as conjunction the verb after **'since'** should be in past indefinite.

Incorrect	Correct
(a) More than a year have passed since I have gone there.	More than a year has passed since I went there.

Rule 26 : When 'neither-nor' is used, the verb comes before the subject.

In the following sentense (a) 'Did' is placed before 'I'.

Incorrect	Correct
(a) He did not go, nor I did .	He did not go nor did I.

Rule 27 : When a plural noun is considered collectively, the verb is a always singular. Examples are given below.

Incorrect	Correct
(a) Ten crores are a big amount.	Ten crore is a big amount.
(b) Fifty kilometers are a long distance.	Fifty kilometers is a long distance.

It is hoped that you have gone through all the rules.

Let us have a simple test to check your understanding.

TEST

(1)	The king as	well as the soliders	are	dancing.	No error.
	a	b	c	d	e
(2)	The Aeroplane	left	before we reached	the airport.	No error.
	a	b	c	d	e
(3)	A week has	passed since	I am going	there.	No error.
	a	b	c	d	e
(4)	Ram asked	me	where did I	live.	No error.
	a	b	c	d	e
(5)	She was	hung	for	murder.	No error.
	a	b	c	d	e
(6)	Ram asked	him	what is	his address.	No error.
	a	b	c	d	
(7)	A variety of	wines were	served	No error.	
	a	b	c	d	
(8)	He need	not worry	for you	No error.	
	a	b	c	d	
(9)	I never	met him	today	No error.	
	a	b	c	d	
(10)	Either Ram	or Shyam have	stolen	my book.	No error.
	a	b	c	d	e
(11)	He	did	no fault	No error.	
	a	b	c	d	
(12)	His desire	was great	his prayers	sincer.	No error.
	a	b	c	d	e

VOCAB LIST

Sr.	*Word*	*Meanings*
201	Brim	To be full of
202	Culminate	Reach the highest point/Conclusion
203	Chum	A good friend
204	Carnival	Revelry
205	Lapse	Error
206	Amenable	Applicable
207	Vicissitudes	Change of fortune
208	Fastidious	Selecting carefully
209	Fussy	Choose only good thing

210	Credulous	Willing to believe easily
211	Glint	Sparkle
212	Obstreperous	Noisy, Difficult to control
213	Lampoon	Criticize publicly
214	Nimiety	Abundance
215	Nimble	Agile
216	Complacent	Satisfied with oneself
217	Bilious	Ill-tempered
218	Preclude	Prevent
219	Precocious	Advanced
220	Restive	Difficult to control
221	Stint	Skimp/Grudge
222	Stolid	Not easily excited
223	Berate	Scold/Rebuke
224	Bequeath	Will
225	Castigate	Criticize Severely
226	Cataclysm	Disaster
227	Amortize	Instalments
228	Vouch	Confidence in a person
229	Moratorium	Temporary stopping of an activity
230	Horrendous	Absolutely terrible
231	Adhere	To obey/follow a set of principle
232	Scrupulous	Extremely careful not to do wrong
233	Throttle	To take a thing that is necessary for survival or function
234	Flummox	To confuse/To make unable to think
235	Paragon	A completely perfect person
236	Rapacious	Greedy
237	Emollient	Soothing
238	Pecuniary	Monetary
239	Impede	Hinder
240	Congruity	Agreement/Consistency
241	Macabre	Gruesome

242	Volition	Will power
243	Iconoclast	Destroyer of images
244	Felicitous	Appropriate
245	Cumulate	Increase
246	Decadent	Moral decay
247	Withered	Shrivel/Lose freshness
248	Atrophy	Wasting away
249	Estrangement	Hostility
250	Gumption	Practical sense/Common sense

. . .

BREAK FOR WORDS REVISION

REVISE THE VOCAB

TEST No- 5
(Words 201-250)

Choose the correct meaning of the given words from amongst their alternatives :

(1) Culminate
(a) to reach the conclusion (b) to squeeze the juicy substance
(c) destroy the harmful substance (d) to bring to an end

(2) Glint
(a) shineless (b) sparkle
(c) sharp (d) blunt

(3) Lampoon
(a) praise publicly (b) criticize publicly
(c) a brook (d) long grass

(4) Obstreperous
(a) silent (b) controlled
(c) noisy (d) transparent

(5) Bilious
(a) ill tempered (b) good natured
(c) praiseworthy (d) of billions

(6) Precocious
(a) precautionary (b) advanced
(c) difficult (d) credulous

(7) Bequeath
(a) mind power (b) will
(c) dumb (d) silent

(8) Cataclysm
(a) miracle (b) disaster
(c) catalogue (d) heavenly

(9) Estrangement
(a) hostility (b) creativity
(c) astonishing (d) credibility

(10) Iconoclast
(a) image-maker (b) image-destroyer
(c) noisy (d) none

(11) Felicitous
(a) inappropriate (b) full
(c) remarkable (d) appropriate

(12) Decadent
(a) health decay (b) moral decay
(c) wealth decay (d) dead

(13) Emollient
(a) hindering (b) soothing
(c) directional (d) practical

(14) Pecuniary
(a) monetary (b) extremely
(c) peculiar (d) imaginary

(15) Congruity

(a) consistency (b) permanence
(c) integrity (d) none

Match the words in the column 'A' with their correct meaning in 'B'

Column 'A'	Column 'B'
(1) Prelude	(1) Choose only good thing
(2) Nimble	(2) Scold
(3) Furry	(3) Practical
(4) Stolid	(4) Not easily excited
(5) Berate	(5) Increase
(6) Horrendous	(6) Prevent
(7) Flummox	(7) To obey a set of principles
(8) Macabre	(8) Agile
(9) Gumption	(9) Hinder
(10) Cumulate	(10) Gruesome
(11) Adhere	(11) To confuse
(12) Atrophy	(12) Appropriate
(13) Rapacious	(13) Greedy
(14) Impede	(14) Wasting away
(15) Felicitous	(15) Absolutely terrible

Answers Grammar

(1) {c} **is** in place of **are.**
(2) {a} had left.
(3) {c} since I went there.
(4) {c} where I lived.
(5) {b} hanged in place of hung.
(6) {c} what his address was.
(7) {c} **were** in place of **was.**
(8) {d}
(9) {a} **did not** in place of **never.**
(10) {b} has in place of have.
(11) {b} committed in place of did.
(12) {d} add were before sincere.

ANSWERS Vocab TEST NO. 5

(1) a (2) b (3) b (4) c (5) a (6) b (7) b
(8) b (9) a (10) b (11) d (12) b (13) b (14) a
(15) a

Match

(1) 6 (2) 8 (3) 1 (4) 4 (5) 2 (6) 15 (7) 11
(8) 10 (9) 3 (10) 5 (11) 7 (12) 14 (13) 13 (14) 9
(15) 12

Day 7

Adverbs

Adverb : Any word used to qualify main verb, an adjective or any other adverb is called an **Adverb**.

For example :

(i) He **walks quickly**.

In this main verb is **walk** and **quickly** is describing the **quality of the action** (walk) in this sentence.

(ii) She **speaks clearly**.

Here also main verb is speak and clearly is qualifying or modifying or describing or telling something about the main verb (speak) .

(iii) He speaks **too** slowly

(iv) This is a **very** sweet mango.

In Ex. (iii) too is an adverb as it is qualifying in another adverb **slowly**

In Ex. (iv) very is an adverb as it is qualifying an adjective **sweet**.

In English language we have following kind of Adverbs.

1. Simple adverbs
2. Interrogative adverbs
3. Relative adverbs

Now we will do each type of adverb one by one.

1. Simple adverbs :

By using these type of adverbs we can tell the time, place, number degree of quantity, manner, affirmation and negation about any action (verb).

So as per use and situation we have following kinds of simple adverbs.

a. Adverb of time
b. Adverb of place
c. Adverb of numbers
d. Adverb of manner
e. Adverb of degree
f. Adverb of affirmation
g. Adverb of negation

Now we will explain each of the above one by one.

(a) Adverbs of time : Words used to tell that when the action (event) has happend or when the action (or event) will happen.

For example :

i He shall go **tommorow.**

ii We go to college **daily.**

iii We go to morning walk **daily.**

iv This will be done **today.**

v I had gone **yesterday**.

Here **tommorow**, **daily**, **today** etc. are telling the **time of the action** or when the **said action** has happened or will happen.

(b) Adverbs of place : It tells the place or direction of an action i.e. where the action has taken place. In this category we use **here, there, everywhere, inside, outside, in, out, up, down, away etc.**

For example :

i. He comes **here**

ii. Come **in**

iii. He looked **up**

(c) Adverbs of number : These words tell us that **how many times** the given action has occurred. In this category we use **often, never, twice, thrice, even, seldom, freq-uently, always** etc.

For example

i I see him **often**.

ii **Always** be punctual.

iii Ravi called him **again**.

(d) Adverbs of manner : Words used to show that how the given action has occurred. In this category we have slowly, fastly, quickly, well, happily, bravely etc.

For example

i They lived **happily** after

ii He jumped **quickly**.

iii **Well** done.

(e) Adverbs of degree : Words which show that to **what extent** or **degree,** the given action has occurred. In this category we use **quite,hardly, too, very, enough, entirely, almost** etc.

For example

i. This work is **almost** complete.

ii The day is **very** cold.

iii He played **pretty** well.

(f) Adverbs of affirmation : Word which show the affirmation of a given action.

For example

i He has **certainly** played.

ii **Surely**, I can do this work.

(g) Adverbs of negation : Words which show the denial.

For example

i I do **not** know.

ii She is **not** coming.

Now we will discuss Relative Adverbs and Interrogative Adverbs.

2. Interrogative adverbs :

Adverbs used for asking questions. They are placed at the start of a sentence. In this category we have **what, where, how etc.**

For example :

i **When** did he woke up ?

ii **When** will you go to Bhopal ?

iii **Where** are you going ?

3 Relative adverbs :

Adverbs which join two sentences and refer to the noun used in given sentences.

For example :

i I know from **where** he is coming.

ii Everybody knows **why** he is a great player.

Generally Relative adverbs are placed in the middle of the sentences.

Now we will study the errors in the use of Adverbs.

Errors in the use of Adverbs

Rule 1 : **Too** can not be used in place of **very** or **much. Very** means **truly**. **Too** means **more than enough**. Also 'too' is used with 'to' This rule is explained below.

	incorrect	**correct**
(a)	It is too cold today.	It is very cold today.
(b)	This movie is too interesting.	This movie is very interesting.
(c)	He is very weak to walk	He is too weak to walk

Rule 2 : Certain Adverbs like, ever, seldomnever, ever, always, sometimes, often, etc. are generally used before the main verbs for which they are used.

	incorrect	**correct**
(a)	He sees me often.	He often sees me.

(**see** is main verb and **often** (adverb) is used before it.)

(b)	I take tea seldom.	I seldom take tea.
(c)	I go there always.	I always go there.

Rule 3 : The adverb **enough** is mostly used after the verb it modifies.

	incorrect	**correct**
(a)	He is enough intelligent to solve this question.	He is intelligent enough to solve this question.

In above example (a) **to solve** is verb and **enough** is used before it.

Rule 4: **Else** is followed by **an Adverb** 'but' and not by **than**. This can be clearly understood by a following example.

	incorrect	**correct**
(a)	It is nothing else than money.	It is nothing else but money.

Rule 5 : Adverbs like **carefully, calmly, quickly, slowly, badly, well, gently, surely** etc.are placed after the verbs.

	incorrect	correct
(a)	He hurriedly caught the train.	He caught the train hurriedly.
(b)	Please carefully do it.	Please do it carefully.
(c)	He gently spoke.	He spoke gently.

Rule 6 : quite can't be used in a sense of very. This is explained below.

	incorrect	correct
(a)	I am quite pleased to see you.	I am very pleased to see you.

Rule7 : In any sentence if there is an **adverb of time** and an **adverb of place** are used then **adverb of place** comes first. Also individually they are placed at end of sentences. This is explained below.

	incorrect	correct
(a)	He last night went to Delhi.	He went to Delhi last night.
(b)	I will go tommorow there.	I will go there tommorow.

Rule 8 : The adverb **only** is used as per context.

	incorrect	correct
(a)	He saw two places only.	He only saw two places
(b)	He ate two pizzas only.	He only ate two pizzas.

Rule 9 :
(i) **Too** is used in negative sense and **very** is used in positive sense.
(ii) Also **Too** shows some kind of excess of anything for which it is used and very is used to show the quality or person is truly great.
(iii) **Too** is always used with **to**.

	incorrect	correct
(a)	It is very hot to go out.	It is too hot to go out.
(b)	He is very tough to break.	He is too tough to break.
(c)	He is very bad.	He is too bad.
(d)	He is too good.	He is very good.

Rule 10 : **Ago** is used if we move from **present time to past**. **Before** is used from **past to further past time**. This is explained by following examples.

	incorrect	correct
(a)	I saw this picture before three weeks.	I saw this picture three weeks ago
(b)	Martin left this place in 1632, he won it ago 10 years.	Martin left this place in 1632, he won it 10 years before.

Rule 11 : **So** can't be used without **as or that** and also it can not be used in sense of **very**. A Few examples are given below.

	incorrect	correct
(a)	He is so kind to me	He is very kind to me.
(b)	He is very kind to me as his brother.	He is so kind to me as his brother.

Rule 12 : **Very** qualifies **adverb or adjective** in **positive degree** and **much** is used in **comparative degree**. An example is given below.

	incorrect	**correct**
(a)	Ritu is very slower than Deepu.	Ritu is much slower than Deepu.

Rule 13 : The adverb **briefly** is always used before the **verb** it qualifies. In the following example **explanation** is supposed to be **brief** not **views** therefore we have placed **briefly** before **explained**.

	incorrect	**correct**
(a)	He explained briefly his views.	He briefly explained his views.

Rule 14 : Certain **adverb** like **fortunately, unfortunately, at length** etc. are meant to **qualify** the **whole sentence** or to **make the sense** of that **situation**. So these **adverbs** are placed at the **start of sentence**. Examples are given below.

	incorrect	**correct**
(a)	I saw that match fortunately.	Fortunately I saw that match.
(b)	He completed this task at length.	At length he completed this task.

Rule 15 : We can't use **quite or too** in place of **very** or in the **sense of very**. An example is given below.

	incorrect	**correct**
(a)	He is quite happy for his new job.	He is very happy for his new job.
(b)	Aadi is too pleased to see her.	Aadi is very pleased to see her.

Rule 16 : We can't say **firstly**, **secondly**, **thirdly** etc. while describing more than one incident at a time. Since it is not allowed in standard English language otherwise also,we can't use so many adverbs at a time or in one sentence. An example is given below.

	incorrect	**correct**
(a)	Firstly we went to movie and secondly we went to picnic.	First we went to movie and secondly we went to picnic.

Rule 17 : For the **events of near future** we use **'presently'** and for **near past or near present** events we use **'just now'**. Examples are given below.

	incorrect	**correct**
(a)	Salman will arrive just now.	Salman will arrive presently.
(b)	We have reached presently.	We have reached just now.

Directions (Questions 1 - 10) :

In each of these questions, a sentence divided into 4 parts a, b, c,d. If there is any error in any of the parts a, b, c, or d then this is your answer, otherwise answer is e.

Test - I

	a	b	c	d	e
(1)	Ram will be	very much	glad to	see you.	No error.
(2)	He is need	of	medicine	badly.	No error.
(3)	We only	should	seek	truth.	No error.
(4)	Hari	behaved	gentlemanly.	No error.	
(5)	We should	speak	the truth	always.	No error.
(6)	Have you	been to	Delhi	ever ?	No error.
(7)	She worked	nobler	than	her brother.	No error.
(8)	The plane	was	an	hour later.	No error.
(9)	He was	very frightened	that he	can't speak.	No error.
(10)	He is	much tall	than	you.	No error.

Answers to the above test are given at the end of this chapter.

Sr.	*Word*	*Meanings*
251	Hinge on	To depend entirely on
252	Evanescence	Disappear/Fading
253	Peruse	To read sth carefully,
254	Peter Out	Decrease or fade gradually
255	Petrify	Frighten sth
256	Phlegmatic	Not easily excited, calm, sluggish
257	Necessitate	To make sth necessary
258	Ordain	Order or Command
259	Dreary	Gloomy/Boring/Dull
260	Fiendishly	Extremely
261	Disservice	Harmful action
262	Intransigence	Stubbornness
263	Amour	Love affair
264	Amour-propre	Self-respect
265	Censure	Disproval/Criticize
266	Grotesque	Ugly/Unnatural

267	Grotly	Unpleasant
268	Penitent	Regretful/Contrite
269	Svelte	Slim in an attractive way
270	Swathe	Wrap in several layers
271	Motif	Theme
272	Doff	Remove/Take off clothing
273	Apogee	Climax
274	Prodigal	Extravagant/Lavish
275	Dolorous	Gloomy
276	Apropos	Appropriate
277	Arbitrary	Capricious/Absolute
278	Arcane	Secret/Mysterious
279	Archaic	Ancient/Very old
280	Archetype	Original
281	Incubus	A constantly worrying problem
282	Finicky	Particular/Fussy
283	Tenuous	So weak that it hardly exists
284	Facets	Particular part or aspect of
285	Perennial	Constantly occurring
286	Embark on	To start new or difficult
287	Propitious	Favourable
288	Galore	In plenty
289	Alibi	Excuse/Plea
290	Agog	Excited
291	Deprecate	Protest/Disapprove
292	Craven	Cowardly
293	Man	Operate
294	Evince	Display
295	Lax	Not strict/severe
296	Charm	To please/Attraction/Fascinate
297	Tangible	Clear & Certain/Definite
298	Headway	Progress
299	Terminus	End Point
300	Innocuous	Harmless

BREAK FOR WORDS REVISION

REVISE THE VOCAB

TEST No-6
(Words 251-300)

Choose the correct meaning of the given words from amongst their alternatives :

(1) Disservice
(a) harmful action (b) beneficial
(c) fruitful (d) out of service

(2) Amour-propre
(a) self-confidence (b) self respect
(c) self-criticism (d) none

(3) Penitent
(a) praise worthy (b) regretful
(c) penniless (d) worthless

(4) Motif
(a) motive (b) thick layer
(c) wrapped (d) theme

(5) Grotly
(a) unpleasant (b) pleasant
(c) unnatural (d) unhealthy

(6) Apogee
(a) beginning (b) middle
(c) climax (d) without end

(7) Arcane
(a) disclosed (b) sharp
(c) original (d) secret

(8) Innocuous
(a) harmful (b) harmless
(c) imaginary (d) intelligent

(9) Agog
(a) excited (b) unpleasant
(c) accumulated (d) plenty

(10) Propitious
(a) unfavourable (b) favourable
(c) prosperous (d) perplexed

(11) Craven
(a) dim (b) cowardly
(c) carved (d) dark

(12) Galore
(a) in plenty (b) in rays
(c) glory (d) shiny

(13) Archetype
(a) fake (b) imaginary
(c) original (d) noisy

(14) Perennial
(a) constantly occurring (b) internepted
(c) unending (d) seasonal

(15) Lax
(a) severe (b) not strict
(c) cowardly (d) gloomy

Match the words in the column 'A' with their correct meaning in 'B'

Column 'A'	Column 'B'
(1) Terminus	(1) Frighten
(2) Tangible	(2) Clear & Certain
(3) Incubus	(3) Criticize
(4) Finicky	(4) To read carefully
(5) Dolorous	(5) Stubbornness
(6) Alibi	(6) Command
(7) Evanescence	(7) Wrap in several layers
(8) Petrify	(8) Gloomy/Boring/Dull
(9) Swathe	(9) End point
(10) Grotesque	(10) Particular/Furry
(11) Intransigence	(11) A constantly worrying problem
(12) Ordain	(12) Ugly
(13) Dreary	(13) Plea
14) Censure	(14) Disappear
(15) Peruse	(15) Gloomy

ANSWER

(1) (b) Remove **much** as **very and much** are not used together.

(2) (d) Place **badly** before **need**.

(3) (a) Place **only** before **truth**.

(4) (c) In **gentlemanly** manner.

(5) (d) Place **always** before **speak**.

(6) (d) Place **ever** before **been**.

(7) (b) **Nobly** in place of **nobler.**

(8) (d) **Late** in place of **later**.

(9) (b) **So** in place of **very**

(10) (b) **Taller** in place of **tall**.

ANSWERS Vocab TEST NO.6

(1) a (2) b (3) b (4) d (5) a (6) c (7) d
(8) b (9) a (10) b (11) b (12) a (13) c (14) a
(15) b

Match

(1) 9 (2) 2 (3) 11 (4) 10 (5) 15 (6) 13 (7) 14
(8) 1 (9) 7 (10) 12 (11) 5 (12) 6 (13) 8 (14) 3
(15) 4

Day

8

Conjunctions

Today we will study **Conjunctions**. Before going into detail of this topic let us consider a few examples which will help you to understand conjunctions in a better way. The examples are as follow.

(a) I went to Agra **and** saw the Taj Mahal.

(b) He was all right **only** he was somewhat tired.

(c) Work hard **if** you want to get good job.

(d) I don't know **if** he is there.

In above examples **and, only, if,** are **conjunctions**. So the words used to join **any two words** or **any two sentences** are called **conjunctions**. Now we will discuss this in detail.

Conjunction : Words used to join two words or two sentences are commonly known as conjunctions. **And**, **but**, **if although** are a few examples of conjunctions.

We have following main types of **conjunctions**.

(1) Co-ordinating conjunction

(2) Subordinating conjunction

We will explain each of them one by one.

(1) Co-ordinating conjunctions :

The words used to join sentences which are independent in nature are called co-ordinating conjunctions. To understand it clearly consider the following examples once again.

(a) I went to Agra **and** saw the Taj Mahal.

In above example I went to Agra is complete in meaning or sense. Also I (understood) saw the Taj Mahal is complete in meaning or sense.

In this type we have **and, but, for, yet, or.**

(2) Subordinating conjunctions :

The words which join dependent and independent sentences are called **subordinating conjunction**. This can be clearly understood by following examples.

(c) **Work hard** if **you want to get good job**.

In above example **work hard** is complete in its meaning while if **you want to get a job** is incomplete in meaning as it depends on the first part i.e. **work hard**. So the conjunction **if** here joins dependent and independent sentences. In this type we have **if, that, though, although, till, before, unless, as, after, when, where, while, lest, until, whence, since.**

Sometimes we have conjunctions used in pairs. These are as follow :

Either --- or, neither --- nor, not only --- but also, although / though --- yet, no --- sooner --- than, hardly --- when, both --- and, whether --- or, scarcely --- when.

Now we will study errors in the use of conjunctions

ERRORS IN THE USE OF CONJUNCTIONS

Rule 1 : Though is always followed by 'yet' not by but. Examples are given below.

	Incorrect	**correct**
(a)	Though he is intelligent but he is not proud.	Though he is intelligent yet he is not proud.

Rule 2 : If **such** is used as an adjective then the conjunction used after such is **as.** In a example given below **(a) such** is telling the **quality of place** and in **(b) such** is telling the **quality of song**. Examples are given below.

	Incorrect	**correct**
(a)	This is such a place that no one likes.	This is such a place as no one likes.
(b)	I like such songs which are melodious.	I like such songs as are melodious.

Rule 3 : When **'not only'** is used, it is followed by **'but also'**. See examples.

	Incorrect	**correct**
(a)	He is not only good in sports but in studies.	He is not only good in sports but also in studies.
(b)	He is not only famous for his speeches but also for his actions.	He is famous not only for his speeches but also for his actions.

Rule 4 : **Other**, is always followed by **than**, if it is used as an adjective. See examples.

	Incorrect	**Correct**
(a)	I had no other plans but to visit there.	I had no other plans than to visit there.

Rule 5 : **'As'** is not followed by **'so'**, except in a few idioms/phrases.

	Incorrect	**Correct**
(a)	As he was tired so he could not go to picnic.	As he was tired, he could not go to picnic.

Rule 6 : **And** is used when both the things in a sentence are to be taken. As in example **(a)** the person **(he)** is interested in going to both Agra and Bhopal. **Or** is used to show the choice between the given alternatives. See examples.

	Incorrect	**Correct**
(a)	He will visit Agra or Bhopal.	He will visit Agra and Bhopal.
(b)	Please do this work and leave the the office.	Please do this work or leave the office.

Rule 7 : **'Without'** should not be used in place or in sense of **'unless'**. See example.

	Incorrect	Correct
(a)	He will not go without being invited.	He will not go unless invited.

Rule 8 : **Both** and **as well as** are not used together. But both is used in **positive sense**. But in negative sense, **'neither --- nor'** is used in place of **both**. See examples.

	Incorrect	Correct
(a)	Both Sita as well as Gita are intelligent students.	Both Sita and Gita are intelligent students.
(b)	Both Sita and Gita are not interested.	Neither Sita nor Gita is interested.

Rule 9 : **But** is used to join the sentences of opposite nature. **'And'** is used to join the sentences of similiar nature. See examples

	Incorrect	Correct
(a)	City life is fast and rural life is slow.	City life is fast but rural life is slow.
(b)	He is intelligent but smart.	He is intelligent and smart.

Rule 10 : **'Neither'** is always followed by **'nor'** and by same form of helping verbs. See examples

	Incorrect	Correct
(a)	Neither did I eat nor he ate.	Neither did I eat nor did he.
(b)	Neither did I speak nor I acted	Neither did I speak nor I act.

Rule 11 : **'As'** is used in positive degree to denote some kind of equality,see example (a). Also **'equally'** is not true conjunction. See examples.

	Incorrect	Correct
(a)	This book is as good if not better than it.	This book is as good as if not better than that.
(b)	His shirt is equally beautiful as that of mine.	His shirt is as beautiful as that of mine.

Rule 12 : **Because, and, therefore** are not used together in same sentence. See example.

	Incorrect	Correct
(a)	Because he is late, therefore he is dismissed.	He is late therefore he is dismissed. **or** Because he is late, he is dismissed.

Rule 13 : Conjunctions like **'neither --- nor', not only --- but also**, should be placed before the words of same sense of speech.

	Incorrect	Correct
(a)	He neither writes English nor Hindi.	He writes neither English nor Hindi.

Rule 14 : **'That'** is not used before **which, when, why, how, where, what** etc.

	Incorrect	Correct
(a)	He asked me that why I was crying.	He asked me why I was crying.

Rule 15 : We can't use double negative. See examples.

	Incorrect	Correct
(a)	I **can't** see train **no**where.	I can't see train anywhere.
(b)	He has **no any** friend.	He has no friend.

Similarly **Unless, untill, lest, deny, forbid** are already negative, they should not be followed by only negative like **not, no** etc. **Lest** is always followed by **should** and not by **may or might**.

TEST
(Conjunctions)

	a	b	c	d	e
(1)	Ram not only	wrote	the poems but	also plays.	No error.
(2)	Hari asked	him	that	how he is.	
(3)	He has	no other	jacket except	this.	No error.
(4)	He is equally	smart	as his	brother.	No error.
(5)	As he is my	friend,therefore	I will	help him.	No error.
(6)	I doubt	that	you will	succed.	No error.
(7)	Both Ram	and	Shyam did not	go there.	No error.
(8)	Guide him	untill	he is with	you.	No error..
(9)	Either the	choice	is right	or wrong.	No error..
(10)	Supposing if	she	fails what will she	do?	No error.
(11)	No sooner he	the train station	the train	started.	No error.
(12)	I asked him	as I would help	him	in.	No error.
(13)	Scarcely had I entered the office		when the	telephone rang.	No error.
(14)	When he reached	Delhi then it	was	raining.	No error.
(15)	Neither you or I	could	do it.	No error.	

Sr.	Word	Meanings
301	Adulatory	Appreciate
302	Pillory	Scorn/To mock publicly
303	Blatant	Too obvious
304	Tantamount	Equal
305	Ignominious	Humiliating
306	Faster	Promote
307	Emasculating	Making weak
308	Rigmarole	Complicated procedure
309	Extant	Existent
310	Restive	Discontent/Difficult to control
311	Ameliorate	Make better
312	Demure	Quiet/Serious/Modest
313	Obsolete	Out of date
314	Cognizance	Knowledge
315	Replica	A close or exact copy of
316	Sundry	Various
317	All & Sundry	Everyone
318	Elated	Very happy/Excited
319	Adversary	Opponent
320	Besmirch	To destroy reputation
321	Passe	Out-dated/Old fashioned
322	Impending	About to happen soon
323	Bicker	To argue about unimportant things
324	Commodious	Ample Spacious/Vast
325	Dote	Adore
326	Prodigious	Huge/Vast
327	Profane	Not sacred/Showing contempt for God
328	Dishevelled	Untidy
329	Disingenuous	Insincere
330	Blandishments	Coax

331	Condescend	Depend on
332	Disposed	Want or prepare to do
333	Censorious	Tending to find faults in people/ things
334	Pew	A seat
335	Proclivity	Natural tendency
336	Detrimental	Harmful
337	Contour	Outline/Map
338	Buckle	Collapse
339	Detente	The Reduction of dangerous tension between two
340	Leverage	Power/Influence
341	Wheedle	Persuade
342	Ferment	Unrest
343	Wangle	Extort
344	Inimical	Hostile/Tending to discourage
345	Contingency	A possibility
346	Lass	Girl/Young lady
347	Stifle	Suppress/Control
348	Fathom	To understand
349	Hails from	Originate from
350	Overt	Openly

...

BREAK FOR WORDS REVISION

TEST No-7
(Words 301-350)

Choose the correct meaning of the given words from amongst their alternatives :

(1) Adulatory

(a) disapprove (b) appreciate
(c) neglect (d) contaminating

(2) Blatant

(a) too obvious (b) hidden
(c) blunt (d) coward

(3) Prodigious

(a) minute (b) vast
(c) saintly (d) smooth

(4) Impending

(a) about to end (b) about to cancel
(c) about to happen (d) none

(5) Sundry

(a) of one type (b) charming
(c) various (d) multipurpose

(6) Elated

(a) raised (b) gloomy
(c) morose (d) very excited

(7) Overt

(a) reverse (b) front
(c) hidden (d) openly

(8) Profane

(a) sacred (b) not sacred
(c) precious (d) hostile

(9) Stifle

(a) suppress (b) persuade
(c) meagre (d) unnecessary

(10) Ferment

(a) unmoved (b) explored
(c) unrest (d) hidden

(11) Blandishment

(a) banned (b) depend on
(c) deserving (d) coax

(12) Leverage

(a) power (b) uninfluencing
(c) lethargic (d) dull

(13) Buckle

(a) to tie (b) to build
(c) collapse (d) outlive

(14) Fathom

(a) to give ears to (b) to understand
(c) to imagine (d) practical

(15) Inimical

(a) hostile (b) fearing
(c) critical (d) obvious

Match the words in the column 'A' with their correct meaning in 'B'

Column 'A'	Column 'B'
(1) Lass	(1) Extort
(2) Disposed	(2) Persuade
(3) Contour	(3) Outline/map
(4) Censonious	(4) A possibility
(5) Wheedle	(5) Untidy
(6) Contingency	(6) Young lady
(7) Detrimental	(7) Harmful
(8) Wangle	(8) To destroy reputation
(9) Proclivity	(9) Opponent
(10) Dishevel	(10) Prepared to do
(11) Disingenuous	(11) Adore
(12) Dote	(12) Tending to find faults
(13) Adversary	(13) Ample spacious/vast
(14) Besmirch	(14) Natural tendency
(15) Commodious	(15) Insincere

ANSWER Grammar

(1) (a) Exchange **wrote** before **not only**, **i.e.** Ram wrote **not only**......
(2) (c) Remove **that**. **'That'** is not used before, **when, which, how, where etc.**
(3) (c) **'Than'** in place of **'except'**.**(Rule 4).**
(4) (a) **'As'** in place of **'equally'**. **(Rule 11).**
(5) (b) Remove **therefore**.
(6) (b) Use **if or whether** in place **of that**.
(7) (a) Use **neither** in place of **both** and **nor** in place of **and.**
(8) (b) Use as **long** as in place of **until**.
(9) (a) Place **either** before **right or wrong**.
(10) (a) Either use **suppose** or **if**.
(11) (a) **No-sooner did he**, Rule- **No-sooner is always followed by did**.

(12) (b) If in place of as.

(13) (e)

(14) (b) Remove then.

(15) (b) Nor in place of or.

ANSWERS Vocab TEST NO. 7

(1) b (2) a (3) b (4) c (5) c (6) d (7) d
(8) b (9) a (10) c (11) d (12) a (13) c (14) b
(15) a

Match

(1) 6 (2) 10 (3) 3 (4) 12 (5) 2 (6) 4 (7) 7
(8) 1 (9) 14 (10) 5 (11) 15 (12) 11 (13) 9 (14) 8
(15) 13

Day

9

Articles

Today we will study **Articles and errors** in the use of Articles. In English languange we have **three** Articles namely **A, An,** and **The**. **A** and **An** are **indefinite articles**. While **The** is **definite Article**. We will discuss indefinite & definite articles.

Indefinite Article : A and An are indefinite articles. The rules to use A and An are explained below.

1. **A** is used before the words which begin with consonant.

   For example : **A** pen, **A** pencil, **A** cat.

2. Sometimes **A** is used before the woıd starting with **U** but it is pronounced like : **Yoo**

   For example : **A** European, **A** Union, **A** University.

3. **An** is used before the words starting with vowels **A, E, I, O, U.**

   For example : **An** elephant, **An** owl, **An** inkpot.

4. **An** is used before words begining with silent H.

   For example : **An** hour, **An** honest.

5. **Also An** is used before the words starting with a Consanants but have the sound of a vowel.

   For example : **An** M.A, **An** L.L.B etc.

   We see that while pronouncing the above words the sound of **A** is coming first(not the sound of the alphabet with which the word is starting).

   No doubt that we can use the word **ONE** in place of **A** and **An** to show that the thing or person about which we are saying something is single in number. But the use of **one** again and again will spoil the beauty of the English language.

Definite Article : **'The'** is **Definite Article**. **The** is used to point out **specific person** or **place** or **object out of given persons** or **objects** or **places**.

For example : i **The Man** in blue shirt.

ii **The place** with beautiful hills.

So in (i) we are referring to particular **Man** who is wearing blue shirt and in (ii) we are referring to a particular **place** which has beautiful hills.

Also **The** is used before certain nouns which are single in kind.

For example : i **The Sun,**

ii **The Taj Mahal,**

iii **The Ganga.**

Till now we have given you the basic idea about the types of Articles and how these Articles are generally used in English language. Now we will study the errors in the use Articles.

ERRORS IN THE USE OF ARTICLES

Rule 1 : Proper and material nouns are not Preceded by article 'a' or 'an'.

	Incorrect	Correct
a.	A uranium is useful metal.	Uranium is useful metal.
b.	A Ram is my friend.	Ram is my friend.

Rule 2 : Generally no article is used before **proper Noun** but if that proper noun is used as common Noun then article is used.

	Incorrect	**Correct**
a.	Ram is Hitler.	Ram is a Hitler.
b.	Raju is Sachin Tendulkar of my team.	Raju is a Sachin Tendulkar of my team.

In above examples Hitler and Sachin are used as common Noun.

Rule 3 : 'The' is used before the names of **holy books, newspaper, rivers, mountains, oceans, lakes, names of season, directions, natural phenomenon, buildings, goups of islands, heavenly bodies and the things single in kind.** Examples are given below.

	Incorrect	**Correct**
a.	Gita is a holy book.	The Gita is a holy book.
b.	I read Hindustan Times daily.	I read the Hindustan Times daily.
c.	He took bath in Yamuna.	He took bath in the Yamuna.

Rule 4 : 'THE' is used to denote nationality or community. In an example given below. The French means persons belonging to France. Also **'THE'** is not used before name of any country unless the name of that country is writen or spoken in abbreviated or short form. As in the example given below it is wrong to write **the America**. While the correct is **America. The U.S.S.R.**, **The U.S.A.** is correct as these are the names of country in short form.

	Incorrect	**Correct**
a.	French have left India for ever.	The French have left India for ever.
b.	Ram has settled in the America.	Ram has settled in America.

Rule 5 : When **'THE'** is used before any common noun it means **all**. In examples given below The rich means all rich. The poor means all poor.

	Incorrect	**Correct**
a.	Rich are happy.	The Rich are happy.
b.	We should help poor.	We should help the poor.
c.	Horse is a faithful animal.	The Horse is a faithful animal.

Rule 6 : 'THE' is always used before superlatives. Examples are given below.

	Incorrect	**Correct**
a.	He is most intelligent boy in this class.	He is the most intelligent boy in this class.
b.	He is tallest man.	He is the tallest man.

Rule 7 : Definite article **'THE'** is not used before the following cases or situation. These are as follows.

i. Before proper nouns unless they are common noun.

ii. Before Abstract noun like Truth, Honesty, Love, Kindness and cruelness.

iii. Before the names of disease sciences, sports and things single in kind. Examples are given below.

	Incorrect	**Correct**
a.	The lucky	lucky
b.	The physics	physics.
c.	The cricket	cricket

iv. The is not used before the plural noun. An example is given below.

	Incorrect	**Correct**
a.	The doctors are next to God.	Doctors are next to God.

v. The is not used before **times of year**, **seasons**, **days of week**. Examples are given below.

	Incorrect	**Correct**
a.	The October	October
b.	The Sunday	Sunday
c.	The Winter	Winter

vi. The is not used before any meal. Examples are given below

	Incorrect	**Correct**
a.	The Lunch	Lunch
b.	The breakfast	Breakfast

vii. The is not used before certain names attached with some kind of honour or post with it. Examples are given below.

	Incorrect	**Correct**
a.	The king Ashoka	King Ashoka
b.	The President Bush	President Bush

viii. The is not used before any philosophical and universal fact. An Example is given below.

	Incorrect	**Correct**
a.	The Man is mortal	Man is a mortal

ix. **'THE'** is not used before any Idiom/ Phrase.

Rule 7 : **'THE'** is used as an adverb with the comparative degree. An example is given below.

	Incorrect	**Correct**
a.	Sooner it is done, better it is.	The sooner it is done, the better it is.

Rule 8 : **'THE'** means every or all. An example is given below.

	Incorrect	**Correct**
a.	Pen is lighter than sword	The pen is lighter than the sword

TEST

Find the error in following senteces.

(1)	Earth	moves	round	the sun.	No error
	a	b	c	d	e
(2)	His morther	went to	college to	see principle.	No error
	a	b	c	d	e
(3)	we	shall start	after	the breakfast.	No error
	a	b	c	d	e
(4)	His friend	speaks	the french	fuently.	No error
	a	b	c	d	e
(5)	His	friend	is	an B.A.	No error
	a	b	c	d	e
(6)	Almighty	will take	care of	us	No error
	a	b	c	d	e
(7)	Mumbai	is New-York	of	India.	No error
	a	b	c	d	e
(8)	He has	read	the Ved Vyas's	the Gita.	No error
	a	b	c	d	e
(9)	Poor are	worst	hit by	cyclone.	No error
	a	b	c	d	e
(10)	Ram want	best	of	everything.	No error
	a	b	c	d	e
(11)	Higher you	go	the cooler	it is	No error
	a	b	c	d	e
(12)	He went to	Delhi	where he stayed	at hotel.	No error
	a	b	c	d	e
(13)	Guilty	must not	be	spared.	No error
	a	b	c	d	e

Sr.	Word	Meanings
351	Relentless	Never ending/Constant/Harsh
352	Relent	Less harsh/Strict
353	Flabbergasted	Astonish completely
354	Unrelenting	Harsh/Cruel
355	Clamour	Loud demand/Protest
356	Keep over	To fall over
357	Deliberate	Carefully done/Intentionally
358	Laudable	Deserving praise
359	Laudatory	Complimentary
360	Mannequin	Dummy
361	Mangy	Shabby
362	Marauder	Raider/Plunderer

363	Defile	Sully/Besmirch
364	Definitive	Explicit/Exact
365	Elucidate	Clarify
366	Emaciated	Thin/Weak/Skinny
367	Paroxysm	Spasm/Fit
368	Abreast	Side by side/Keeping the same face
369	Keep abreast	To be always aware of latest news
370	Exiguous	Meagre
371	Coax	Persuade gently
372	Blase	Bored
373	Modicum	Small amount
374	Dissemble	Conceal/Pretend
375	Profligate	Immoral
376	Bustle	Fuss/Flurry
377	Gratis	Free of charge
378	Gratuitous	Unnecessary
379	In toto	Totally/Completely
380	Intractable	Stubborn
381	Tentative	Provisional
382	Obtuse	Blunt
383	Renegade	Rebel
384	Humbug	Deceit
385	Entangle	Trap
386	Retribution	Compensation
387	Appraisal	Approval
388	Luminary	Famous
389	Stringent	Strict/Rigorous
390	Exotic	Unusual
391	Jeremiad	Trouble
392	Whimper	Cry
393	Gadfly	Nuisance
394	Maim	Disfigure
395	Prognosis	Forecast

396	Outre	Eccentric
397	Cotter	Group
398	Perfidy	Treachery
399	Masticate	Chew
400	Mollify	Appease

. . .

BREAK FOR WORDS REVISION

TEST No- 8 (Words 351-400)

Choose the correct meaning of the given words from amongst their alternatives :

(1) Relentless
(a) never ending (b) restive juicy substance
(c) unnecessary (d) none

(2) Exiguous
(a) fat (b) harmful
(c) untidy (d) meagre

(3) Intractable
(a) stubborn (b) naughty
(c) interchangeable (d) dependable

(4) Flabbergasted
(a) shabby (b) annoy
(c) astonish (d) persuasive

(5) Definitive
(a) definite (b) explicit
(c) longlasting (d) careful

(6) Gratuitous
(a) pretentious (b) necessary
(c) unnecessary (d) great

(7) Modicum

(a) small amount (b) medium
(c) modern (d) monetary

(8) Bustle

(a) flurry (b) weary
(c) needy (d) creative

(9) Mollify

(a) nullify (b) multiply
(c) appease (d) annoy

(10) Prognosis

(a) forecast (b) forerun
(c) foretell (d) forever

(11) Humbug

(a) a type of bug (b) deceit
(c) honest (d) progressive

(12) Appraisal

(a) approval (b) applaud
(c) famous (d) nuisance

(13) Outre

(a) genius (b) intelligent
(c) clever (d) eccentric

(14) Exotic

(a) usual (b) unusual
(c) practical (d) poisonous

(15) Whimper

(a) cry (b) soft
(c) jealous (d) frightful

Match the words in the column 'A' with their correct meaning in 'B'

Column 'A'	Column 'B'
(1) Masticate	(1) Extort
(2) Luminary	(2) Treachery
(3) Perfidy	(3) Trouble
(4) Stringent	(4) Trap
(5) Jeremiad	(5) Chew
(6) Cotter	(6) Conceal
(7) Entangle	(7) Plunderer
(8) Retribution	(8) Protest

(9) Tentative
(10) Dissemble
(11) Blare
(12) Deliberate
(13) Mannequin
(14) Clamour
(15) Marauder

(9) Strict
(10) Dummy
(11) Bored
(12) Famous
(13) Intentionally done
(14) Compensation
(15) Provisional

Answer Grammar :

(1) a, The earth (Rule 3)
(2) c, The college {as she is going to particular college}.
(3) d, Remove The {case when **THE** is not used}.
(4) c, Remove the {Since we are talking about French language not the French persons. As **the** French means all French }.
(5) d, Remove an {as B.A. is starting with consonant and it is not having sound of any vowel while pronouncing}
(6) a, The Almighty {it means God}.
(7) b, The New York (Rule 2).
(8) Remove **The** .
(9) a, add **the** before poor (Rule 5).
(10) b, The best (Rule 6).
(11) a, The higher (Rule 7).
(12) d, **a hotel** here is used to show one hotel.
(13) a, **The Guilty** it means all Guilty persons (Rule 4).

ANSWERS
TEST NO. 8

(1) a (2) d (3) a (4) c (5) b (6) c (7) a
(8) a (9) c (10) a (11) b (12) a (13) d (14) b
(15) a

Match

(1) 4 (2) 12 (3) 1 (4) 9 (5) 2 (6) 6 (7) 3
(8) 14 (9) 15 (10) 5 (11) 11 (12) 13 (13) 10 (14) 8
(15) 7

Day

10

Prepositions

Today we will study Prepositions.

Preposition : A word which is placed before a noun or a pronoun to show what relation it bears to some other words in a sentence is called **preposition**.

Examples : **On, in, at, far, into, after, of, against, with, to, between** etc.

Now we will discuss the rules regarding the error in the use of prepositions.

Errors in the use of prepositions

Rule 1. Never use any preposition after verbs like recommend, attack, reach, accompany, order, lack, percede, obey, combat, afford, reach, joint etc. when these verbs are used in active voice. A few examples are given below.

	Incorrect	**Correct**
(a)	Japneet resembles with her mother.	Japneet resembles her mother.
(b)	He has joined in the school.	He has joined the school.
(c)	India does not lack in able soldiers.	India does not lack able soldiers.
(d)	He attacked upon me.	He attacked me.
(e)	We reached at the college late.	We reached the college late.

Rule 2. **For** is used if actual sum is mentioned and **at** is used if the actual sum is not given. See examples.

	Incorrect	**Correct**
(a)	I bought this book at at 50 rupees.	I bought this book for 50 rupees.
(b)	I can not buy this pen for such a price.	I can not buy this pen at such a price.

Rule 3. **On** is used with the the days of the week or month. **At** is used with the exact time. A Few examples are given below.

	Incorrect	**Correct**
(a)	The train will arrive at Monday.	The train will arrive on Monday.
(b)	He will arrive on 9.30 pm.	He will arrive at 9.30 pm.

Rule 4. **In** denotes position of rest inside something while **into** denotes motion or direction towards inside of something. Examples are given below.

	Incorrect	**Correct**
(a)	He spent all the day into his room.	He spent all the day in his room.
(b)	He came in the room and sat down.	He came into the room and sat down.

Rule 5. When we are speaking of a period of time in future we must use **in** not **after**. An Example is given below.

	Incorrect	Correct
(a)	I may be able to go after a month.	I may be able to go in a month.

Rule 6. **With** is related to the instrument used for doing anything while **by** is used for the doer. Ram was killed **by** Sham **with** a knife.

Rule 7. **Between** is used for two persons while **among** is used for more than two persons. Examples are given below.

	Incorrect	Correct
(a)	Distribute these sweets among two boys.	Distribute these sweets between two boys.
(b)	Distribute these sweets between the class.	Distribute these sweets among the class.

Some more important errors in the use of prepositions are given below. You are to understand them carefully.

	Incorrect	Correct
1.	He did not agree with my proposal.	He did not agree to my proposal.
2.	You should attend your work.	You should attend to your work.
3.	This is different to that.	This is different from that.
4.	Translate this passage word to word.	Translate this passage word for word.
5.	P!ease write with blue ink.	P!ease write in blue ink.
6.	My brother is suffering with fever.	My brother is suffering from fever.
7.	This is a comfortable house to live.	This is a comfortable house to live in.
8.	We arrived to this conclusion.	We arrived at this conclusion.
9.	She lives at America.	She lives in America.
10.	He fears from a snake.	He fears a snake.
11.	You must profit from your experience.	You must profit by your experience.
12.	Anil married with Jyoti.	Anil married Jyoti.
13.	He takes pride of his wealth.	He takes pride in his wealth.
14.	She feels proud from money.	She feels proud of money.
15.	I want to get rid from jaundice.	I want to get rid of jaundice.
16.	You pay for your bill.	You pay your bill.
17.	Hard work is a key for success.	Hard work is a key to success.
18.	The train is running in time.	The train is running on time.
19.	He lost match from his rival.	He lost match to his rival.
20.	Our examination begins from Wednesday.	Our examination begins on Wednesday.
21.	The husband parted with his wife.	The husband parted from his wife.
22.	You carry my orders.	You carry out my orders.
23.	A miser cannot part from money.	A miser cannot part with money.
24.	He applied the Principal for leave.	He applied to the Principal for leave.

	Incorrect	Correct
25.	You must devote some times for studies.	You must devote some times to studies
26.	Translate this passage in Hindi.	Translate this passage into Hindi.
27.	She is pleased on us.	She is pleased with us.
28.	What did he die ?	What did he die of ?
29.	He is searching his dog.	He is searching for his dog.
30.	Have you signed on the agreement.	Have you signed the agreement.
31.	Hard work is key for the success.	Hard work is key to the success.
32.	Do not knock my door.	Do not knock at my door.
33.	I got down from my bicycle.	I got off from my bicycle.
34.	Beware from dogs.	Beware of dogs.
35.	I divided the cake in four parts.	I divided the cake into four parts.
36.	The jug is full with water.	The jug is full of water.
37.	Do not spend money for luxuries.	Do not spend money on luxuries.
38.	The rider fell down his horse.	The rider fell off his horse.
39.	He walked ten miles by foot.	He walked ten miles on foot.
40.	We sat under the feet of our teacher.	We sat at the feet of our teacher.
41.	Your computer is similar with mine.	Your computer is similar to mine.
42.	I killed the rat by one shot.	I killed the rat with one shot.
43.	I subscribe this quarterly magazine.	I subscribe to this quarterly magazine.
44.	She rides on a car.	She rides in a car.
45.	The ceiling fan is on my head.	The ceiling fan is over my head.
46.	I was surprised for his behavior.	I was surprised at his behavior.
47.	I am not satisfied at your progress.	I am not satisfied with your progress.
48.	I am anxious for his health.	I am anxious about his health.
49.	What is the time on your watch ?	What is the time by your watch ?
50.	Pakistan lack in able men.	Pakistan lack able man.

Test

Directions (Questions 1 - 15) :

In each of these questions, a sentence divided into 3 parts A, B and C, if there is some error in any of the parts A, B or C then this is your answer, otherwise answer is D.

1. She did not /(A)/ pity with /(B)/ the labourers/(C)/. /No Error-D.
2. Do you /(A)/ fear from /(B)/ your teacher/(C)/. /No Error-D.
3. I have told /(A)/ to you about /(B)/ this affair/(C)/./(No Error) D.
4. She was /(A)/ waiting for /(B)/ the car /C)/./No Error-D.
5. What is /(A)/ she /(B)/ talking of/(C)/. /No Error-D.
6. She waited /(A)/ me /(B)/ for hours together/(C)/. /(No Error-D).
7. She is /(A)/ angry /(B)/ on you/(C)/. /No Error / D.
8. He asked /(A)/ a /(B)/ holiday /(C)/. /No Error /D.

9. He tore /(A)/ a sheet of /(B)/ paper /(C)/ in pieces. /No Error/
10. He is /(A)/ junior than me/(B)/ in service /(C)/. /No Error/
11. This is /(A)/ inferior/(B)/ than that/(C)/. /No Error (D)/
12. Diwali /(A)/ corresponds /(B)/ with christmas/(C). /No Error(D)/
13. He went /(A)/ near /(B)/ the station/(C)/./No Error(D)/
14. There is /(A)/ no harm/(B)/ in doing this/(C)/./No Error(D)/
15. He /(A)/ rides/(B)/ in a bicycle/(C)/. /No Error (D)/

Answers to the above test are given at the end of this chapter.

VOCAB LIST

401	Imprudent	Rude/Impatient
402	Articulate	Distinct
403	Veer	Shift
404	Supercilious	Haughty
405	Demit	Resign
406	Berserk	Wild
407	Forlorn	Not cared
408	Laze	Rest/Relax
409	Deify	Worship
410	Disparity	Different
411	Gruesome	Frightful
412	Impetuous	Rash
413	Tyranny	Cruelty
414	Nebulous	Vague
415	Bashful	Shy
416	Garner	Collect
417	Berate	Scold
418	Spite	Malice
419	Prolific	Fertile
420	Ostentatious	Showy
421	Exorbitant	Excessive
422	Pivotal	Crucial
423	Obverse	Opposite
424	Compunction	Regret

425	Prune	Reduce/Wane
426	Dilettante	Amateur
427	Spasmodic	Intermittent
428	Paramour	Lover
429	Refectory	Dinning-room
430	Assent	Approval/Agreement
431	Loathe	Detest
432	Vendetta	Revenge
433	Insidious	Slow
434	Convened	Summoned
435	Cosset	Pamper
436	Addle	Confuse
437	Explicit	Clear
438	Animosity	Indifference
439	Teeter	Hesitate
440	Cavort	Jump
441	Exigency	An emergency
442	Concur	To agree
443	Prevaricate	Lie
444	Exude	Ooze
445	Precarious	Critical/dangerous/Not safe
446	Vogue	Fashion
447	Aver	Assert
448	Yaw	Drift
449	Delightful	Delectable
450	Feign	Pretend

...

REVISE THE VOCAB

BREAK FOR WORDS REVISION

TEST 9
Wrods (401-450)

(1) Imputdent
(a) Impatient (b) Impossible
(c) Imposter (d) Prudent.

(2) Tyranny
(a) Cruelty (b) Honesty
(c) Nimble (d) Humble.

(3) Refectory
(a) Retiring- room (b) Dinning-room
(c) Factory (d) Bathroom

(4) Prune
(a) Punctual (b) Loud
(c) Increase (d) Reduce

(5) Nebulous
(a) Vague (b) Important
(c) Precious (d) Shy

(6) Demit
(a) Damn (b) Vague
(c) Resign (d) Rejoin.

(7) Berate
(a) Bold (b) Hold
(c) Scold (d) Fold

(8) Ostentatious
(a) Narrow-minded (b) Showy
(c) Obslute (d) Optimist

(9) Convened
(a) Summoned (b) Conveyed
(c) Convincing (d) Clot

(10) Fegn
(a) faint (b) pretend
(c) agree (d) angry.

(11) Addle
(a) profuse (b) confuse
(c) abuse (d) approve

(12) Aver
(a) assert (b) provoke
(c) secret (d) hesitate

(13) Delightful
(a) delectful (b) delectable
(c) protectable (d) actable.

(14) Vogue
(a) useless (b) fashion
(c) attraction (d) widespread.

(15) Exigency
(a) An emergency (b) irritation
(c) mystery (d) miracle

Match the words in column 'A' with their correct meaning in 'B'.

Column A		Column B	
(1)	Yaw	(1)	Hesitate
(2)	Teeter	(2)	Pamper.
(3)	Exude	(3)	Revenge
(4)	Precarious	(4)	Difference
(5)	Prevaricate	(5)	Drift
(6)	Animosity	(6)	Excessive
(7)	Cosset	(7)	Crucial
(8)	Loathe	(8)	Slow
(9)	Vendetta	(9)	Critical
(10)	Disparity	(10)	Intermittent
(11)	Exorbitant	(11)	Amateur
(12)	Spasmodic	(12)	Indifference.
(13)	Pivotal	(13)	Lie
(14)	Dilettante	(14)	Detest
(15)	Insidous	(15)	Ooze

ANSWER GRAMMAR

1. (d) no error
2. (b) remove **from**
3. (b) remove **to**
4. (d) no error
5. (c) **about** in place of **of**
6. (b) it should be **for me**
7. (c) **with** in place of **on**
8. (b) it should be **for a**
9. (d) no error
10. (b) **to** in place of **than**
11. (c) **to** in place of **than**
12. (c) **to** in place of **with**
13. (b) it should be **to the station**
14. (d) no error
15. (c) **on** in place of **in**

Answer of Test 9

(1) a (2) a (3) b (4) d (5) a (6) c (7) c
(8) b (9) a (10) b (11) b (12) a (13) b (14) b
(15) a

Match

(1) 5 (2) 1 (3) 15 (4) 9 (5) 13 (6) 12 (7) 2
(8) 4 (9) 3 (10) 4 (11) 6 (12) 10 (13) 7 (14) 11
(15) 8

Day

11

Modifiers and Parallelism

Today we shall discuss :

Gerunds, infinitives, participles, modifiers and parallelism.

1. GERUND

Any word (Verb + ing) which is playing the role of noun in the sentence is called gerund. Let us consider two examples to understand more about gerunds.

(i) *He is swimming*

The above sentence has nothing to do with gerunds. In this example "Swimming" is an action performed by the suject (He). So "Swimming" is a verb.

(ii) *Swimming is a good exercise*

In this example "Swimming" (which is actually a verb) is name of an activity. We know that name of anything is noun. So this word "Swimming" is also playing the role of thenoun. These words which are also playing the role of noun are called verbal noun (verb + noun). These verbal nouns are called Gerunds. Gerund can be used in following ways.

(a) As Subject

Dancing is a good exercise

(b) As object to verb

(1) I hate dancing (2) He hates telling lies

(c) As object to preposition.

(1) He is fond of fishing (2) He is addicted to smoking

(d) As the complement of a verb

(1) He is making dinner (2) He is speaking clearly

A few important rules for using gerunds :

(i) After preposition a gerund is used instead of an infinitive for example

(a) Ram is fond of hunting (2) He is good at dancing

(ii) After certain verbs, gerunds are used

These verbs are avoid, dislike, enjoy, propose, consider, keep, admit, escape, risk, practise, forgive, stop, remember etc. For example.

(a) I dislike dancing

(b) He avoids running

(c) I enjoy swimming

(d) He stopped smoking

(e) I enjoy teaching

(f) He escaped Bombay.

(iii) When a noun or pronoun precedes a gerund, then noun or pronoun takes possesive form For example.

(a) He was upset of (me/**my**) getting hurt

In the above example we have used possessive pronoun (my) instead of objective pronoun (me)

2. PARTICIPLES

Consider the following examples to understand participles

(i) *He is running :*

The above sentence is a simple situation in present continuous form in which 'He' is the subject and 'running' is an action done by the subject 'He'. Therefore 'Running' is a verb. Now consider the sentence grow below.

(ii) *He jumped from a running train :*

In example 2 verb 'running' is modifying or telling thequality of the noun 'train'and we know that any word which gives any information about nouns or pronouns is called an adjective. Therefore verb running is also an adjective. These type of words are called verbal adjectives (verb + adjective) these verbal adjectives are called participles

In english language, we have three types of participles. They are:

(a) Present participles (verb + ing forms)

(b) Past participles (verb + d / ed / t forms)

(c) Prefect participles (having + past perfect)

The example which we discussed above was the case of present participles.

A few rules for using participles :

Since participles are verbal adjectives, so there has to be a noun or pronoun in the sentence for which that participle has been used or attached with. When in any sentence that noun or pronoun is missing then that participle is called Dangling participle or unrelated participle or unattached participle.

Let us try to understand the concept of dangling participles by a few examples.

(i) *Walking in the garden a snake bit her.*

In the above sentence it is not clearly stated that who was walking in the garden? i.e. was it a snake? or someone else? But it cannot be a snake so we have to tell clearly that who was walking? Here **walking** is loose or unattached or dangling as the noun or pronoun for which it has been used is not given. Therefore correct sentence or complete sentence will be *while she was walking a snake bit her.*

3. INFINITIVES

Any word which is a combination of 'to' and a verb i.e. to + verb is called an infinitive for example to go, to eat, to watch, etc.

Modifiers and parallelism

Modifier:- it can be a word or a phrase which used to modify other word or a phrase. For eg. Adverbs, Adjective sand participles are modifiers.

A Modifier is generally kept close to word or phrase which it is supposed to qualify or modify. For eg.

(1) He is a good boy

(2) He speaks slowly

(3) I saw theoverloaded truck

In (1) good (an adjective) is placed near to the noun (boy). In (2) slowly (an adverb) is placed near speaks (a verb) In (3) overloaded (a participles) is placed near the noun (truck) when there is any misplacement in using modifier, an error results. This is called misplaced modifiers For eg.

(i) I read that player was injured in the newspaper (incorrect)

In above sentence **in the newspaper** is not at proper place so this is a case of misplaced modifier. hence thecorrect sentence is

I read in the newspaper that player was injured.

Now to correct the misplaced modifiers one does not require indepth knowledge of grammar. One can use common sense to correct the misplaced modifiers. Same is the case with adverbs and adjectives and participles i.e. they should be placed near to those words which they are supposed to qualify.

4. PARALLELISM

In this concept we deal with the sturcture of sentences and alignment of the words in sentences. By structure we mean the placement of subject, object, verb etc in any given sentence. By alignment we mean correct use of parts of speech i.e. noun for names, verbs for action, adjectives for attributes etc.

So if in any sentence these two rules are not followed we say that sentence is not parallel. let us try to understand this concept by a few examples.

(1) He is smart intelligent and has lots of money.

In the above sentence we have described three qualities of the subject (He). We know that in grammar to describe noun or pronoun, adjectives are required/ used. Now first two qualities (smartness/intelligent) have been described by using adjectives. The third quality (richness) has been unnecessarly elaborated. So instead of giving detailed accountof monetary states of subject (He) we could have used an adjective 'rich'. Hence the original structure is a little lengthy and alinhment is not proper i.e. sentence is not parallel. Therefore the correct senence is as follows:

He is smart, intelligent and rich.

Let us look at another example

He likes dancing, running and to climb.

In the above sentence, the first two hobbies have been discribed by gerunds but third hobby (to climb) has been described by an infinitive. This sentence is grammatically acceptable but it is not parallel as third hobby (to climb) has been described by using differentpart of speech (infinitive). The correct sentence is

He likes dancing running and climbing.

5. TENSE BALANCE

In this we check that if the use of tenses is correct in any given sentence. This is generally called tense balance. for eg.

(a) If it will rain, I will not go to market. (incorrect)

If it rains, I will not go to market. (correct)

Rule: We cannot use future tense twice in the conditional sentences. In these sentences, the part which is representing any condition (i.e. starting with if.....) should be simple present or present indefinate.

(b) If he would have helped me, I would have cracked the exam. (incorrect).

If he had helped me, I would have cracked the exam. or Had he helped me, I would have cracked the exam. (correct)

Rule: First we cannot use future tense twice in same sentence. Secondly, when two past activities or action are to be described and one of the actions is complete before the start of other action, we have use part perfect tence. So the correct combination is

had .... would have

or

had ...... could have

SET 1

Directions. Q. 1-90: *(i) In this Section a number of sentences are given. The sentences are divided in three separate parts and each one is labelled (a), (b), (c). Read each sentence to find out whether there is an error in any part. No sentence has more than one error. When you find an error in any one of the parts (a, b, c). If there is no error mark the answer as (d).*

1 . Please try to understand / (a) that the dispute on this issue is between my brother and myself, / (b) and concerns nobody else. / (c) No error /d/

2. Regretfully, profits earned by your company / (a) fell by 20 per cent last year / (b) despite higher sales. / (c) No error. (d)

3. In the interim period, various student groups, in small numbers, / (a) met me and informed that the notice for strike / (b) was issued without proper consultation. / (c) No error. (d)

4. A team of three Indians, two Canadians and three Japanese / (a) was successful in climbing the highest mountain peak on / (b) its third attempt. / (c) No error. (d)

5. He enquired me / (a) why I had not seen him the previous / (b) day as I had promised to do. (c) / No error. (d)

6. She hardly knew how to do that problem, (a) / and so went to her teacher, and asked her, b / "How this problem is to be solved ?" (c) / No error. (d)

7. Samir, who is a close friend of mine, / (a) told me that he was smelling / (b) the rice from a distance of fifty yards while coming to my house. (c) / No error. (d)

8. Most of the members at the meeting felt / (a) that the group appointed for investigating the case / (b) were not competent to do the job efficiently. / (c) No error. (d)

9. It does not matter how you do it; / (a) what I want is that (c) / you should finish the work within a month. / (c) No error. (d)

10. It is time / (a) we should accept all our people as equals / (b) and as partners in the task of building a strong and united nation. / (c) No error. (d)

11. Every motorist knows, / (a) road signs whether symbols or colour codes have an immediacy / (b) that neither the spoken nor, the written word can match. / (c) No error. (d)

12. I had hoped to have met hirn yesterday / (a) to discuss the matter with him / (b) but he was not in his house, and so I could not meet him. / (c) No error. (d)

13. If we'd have heard about the auction in time, / (a) we'd have probably put in a bid / (b) for the exquisite statue. (c) No error. (d)

14. I fail to understand / (a) why he replied in negative / (b) when the proposal was in his favour. / (c) No error. (d)

15. Though he stoutly persisted in denying his involvement in the case, / (a) the facts made it very clear / (b) that he had hand in the cruel murder of his wife. / (c) No error. (d)

16. What we fail to understand / (a) is that the life of a scientist / (b) will always be different from a politician. (c) No error. (d)

17. Unfortunately, in spite of the best efforts of various trade unions, / the factory has been under lockout for the past one month, / to the chagrin of all. / (c) No error. (d)

18. In spi te of my advice to the contrary, / (a) he has been working at a stretch / (b) for four hours. / (c) No error. (d)

19. It is not difficult to understand / (a) why he endeavoured so hard to hide / (b) the traces of the crime which he committed. (c) No error. (d)

20. The managing director along with other members / (a) were accorded a warm welcome / (b) on the plantation. / (c) No error. (d)

21. Neither of these two documents / (a) support your claim / (b) on the property. / (c) No error. (d)

22. Even. on the eve of an inevitable fall, / (a) to everyone's dismay, / (b) their leader seems, to be in their elements / (c) No error. (d)

23. They all met in a room / (a) which was close to the Centre / (b) to discuss about the plan of action. / (c) No error. (d)

24. Two hundred miles / (a) are not a great distance / (b) in these days of fast travel by aeroplanes. / (c) No error. (d)

25. When the police accused him with theft, / (a) nobody believed them, / (b) as he was well-known for his honesty. / (c) No error. (d)

26. This text-book in Physics, which has been / (a) written for under-graduate students, / (b)comprises of fourteen chapters. / (c) No error. (d)

27. He went to England to work as a doctor, / (a) but returned back / (b) as he could not endure the weather there. / No error.

28. The meeting, scheduled to be held / (a) between 2 p.m. to 3 p.m. / (b) was postponed suddenly. / (c) No error. (d)

29. Originally they had planned to buy an air- conditioner, / (a) but finally settled for an air-cooler. / (b) as the cost of the latter was very less. / (c) No error. (d)

30. He was conferred with an Honorary D. Litt. degree / (a) in recognition of his services / (b) to the cause of learning. / (c) No error. (d)

31. Men are apt to / (a) pick up holes / (b) in the views of those whom they do not like. / (c) No error. (d)

32. I am seeing him / (a) this evening / (c) at five. / (c) No error. (d)

33. The myth that some races / (a) are naturally superior than others / (b) has now been fully demolished. / (c) No error. (d)

34. It is truth / (a) that prevails / (b) in long-run. / (c) No error. (d)

35. This particular issue / (a) has been hanging in fire / (b) for a long time. / (c) No error. (d)

36. Summons/was served/on Ram. / (c) No error. (d)

37. The steep rise in the price of petroleum a products / (a) have affected / (b) the economic development of the developing nations. / (c) No error. (d)
No error.

38. Kiran as well as Kamal / (a) are leaving / (b) for Mumbai. / (c) No error. (d)

39. In the past / (a) people travelled / (b) by foot. / (c) No error. (d)

40. Much water / (a) has flown / (b) under the bridge since then. / (c) No error. (d)

41. You should know / (a) that the ultimate decision in the matters / (b) rests upon the board of directors. / (c) No error. (d)

42. Give the book either / (a) to my mother / (b) or my brother. / (c) No error. (d)

43. As a matter of fact / (a) I am not a coward (b) you take me for. / (c) No error. (d)

44. I wish / (a) you learnt / (b) to express better. / (c) No error. (d)

45. I do not wish / (a) to rise / (b) false hopes. / (c) No error. (d)

46. He was not considered for promotion / (a) because his performance was not / (b) as good as the other members of the organisation. / (c) No error. (d)

47. I'd appreciate spending half an hour with you / (a) to discuss about how these and other experience / (b) might be mutually beneficial. / (c) No error. (d)

48. In some tribal areas / (a) people worship snakes / (b) and are not scared from them. / (c) No error. (d)

49. Not only it is our duty / (a) to support our parents / (b) but also to respect them. / (c) No error. (d)

50. After nagging constantly for months / (a) and administering weekly tests / (b) the teacher was at last pleased for the boy's progress. / (c) No error. (d)

51. Don't think you can say unpleasant things / (a) about someone behind his back / (b) and not found out. / (c) No error. (d)

52. When the police approached him / (a) he held up his both hands, / (b) to show that he was surrendering. / (c) No error. (d)

53. This led me to think / (a) that inspiration gradually faded / (b) because the mind is overworked and undernourished. / (c) No error. (d)

54. She insisted to go there / (a) though her husband cautioned her / (b) against it. / (c) No error. (d)

55. As he dived from the spring board / (a) he was terrified to see / (b) that the water was drained from the pool the previous night. / (c) No error. (d)

56. As I am suffering from fever since morning / (a) I shall not be able to attend the function / (b) you are going to organise this evening. / (c) No error. (d)

57. To lead a well-balanced life / (a) you shall have to cultivate other interests / (b) beside your professional ones. / (c) No error. (d)

58. She wishes / (a) that she has studied literature instead of history / (b) when she was in college. / (c) No error. (d)

59. Being a full moon night / (a) the tides were exceptionally high / (b) and the iceberg was mistaken for thick foam. / (c) No error. (d)

60. His new proposal / (a) seems hardly different / (b) than that the one I've just rejected. / (c) No error. (d)

61. The flicker of light from the gas lamps / (a) indicated that the night / (b) was barely passed. / (c) No error. (d)

62. India was committed to keep maintaining peace / (a) and solving all outstanding problems / (b) with her neighbours through dialogue. / (c) No error. (d)

63. Being the second Saturday of the month, / (a) he got up late and spent the whole day at home, / (b) doing his share of the household chores. / (c) No error. (d)

64. As economic restructuring in Central and Eastern Europe progresses, / (a) an estimated 15 million people may be out of work / (b) by the end of the year. / (c) No error. (d)

65. Such of those who have not paid the fees, / (a) the circular says. / (b)will not be permitted to attend classes. / (c) No error. (d)

66. There is a good British Library in the city / (a) and anyone interested in books / (b) can avail of the facility. / (c) No error. (d)

67. Driving a vehicle on the busy roads / (a) require care and skill / (b) to avoid accidents. / (c) No error. (d)

68. He has been away in America / (a) for more than a decade and a half, / (b) and I don't think he will return back to India. / (c) No error. (d)

69. We Indians are / (a) firmly wedded in the / (b) democratic way of life. / (c) No error. (d)or.

70. I am playing football for my school / (a) for the last three years / (b) without ever being dropped for any important match. / (c) No error. (d)

71. The reason why he could not come and attend the meeting was / (a) because his car broke down on the way, / (b) and he had to wait inordinately before it was set right. / (c) No error. (d)

72. They did not want the impression to go round / (a) that they had climbed down over their demand / (b) and had settled for, less. / (c) No error. (d)

73. The two friends walked / (a) besides each other / (b) in silence. / (c) No error. (d)

74. It was so lovely weather / (a) that we spent / (b) the whole day in the garden. / (c) No error. (d)

75. He suggested us / (a) that we should try to, improve our condition / (b) beginning to work hard. / (c) No error. (d)

76. A man jumped / (a) in the river / (b) in a state of depression. / (c) No error. (d)

77. He said he was an employee / (a) of the gas company / (b) and had come to inspect the gas connection. / (c) No error. (d)

78. Over three hundred farmers / (a) marched through the capital / (b) to protest against the new tax. / No error.

79. When a group of teenagers visited the entertainment centre / (a) little did they know / (b) that their outing will lead them to a hospital. / (c) No error. (d)

80. I began to suspect trouble / (a) as soon as one of the boys / (b) threw a stone at the policemen. / (c) No error. (d)

81. It is all the more better / (a) for you to take the examination / (b) than to withdraw your form. / (c) No error. (d)

82. If you had not been so secretive / (a) you had told me all the facts earlier; / (b) I could have helped you. / (c) No error. (d)

83. Although there are some similarities / (a) in the qualifications of both the candidates / (b) the differences among them are considerably pronounced. / (c) No error. (d)

84. The king did not mind / (a) for putting the old people to death / (b) because he was young himself / (c) No error. (d)

85. We went to the zoo / (a) and had spent an enjoyable day / (b) looking at the various creatures there. / (c) No error. (d)

86. It is nothing else than / (a) his stupidity which stands / (b) in the way of his progress. / (c) No error. (d)

87. Now that my children are grown up and gone out into the world, / (a) I would like to spend my old age / (b) in the village I was born. / (c) No error. (d)

88. When he persisted in making the same mistake / (a) despite constant reminders, / (b) I explained him where he had gone wrong. / (c) No error. (d)

89. The teacher asked me / (a) if I had done my home work / (b) and I replied in the negative. / (c) No error. (d)

90. Every group of birds / (a) that fly to the breeding ground / (c) will have an equal number of males and females. / (c) No error. (d)

VOCAB LIST

451	Interim	Temporary
452	Imprecation	Abuse/Curse
453	Jaunty	Cheerfulness
454	Sozzled	Very drunk
455	Leeway	Permissiveness
456	Gawk	Gawp/Stare
457	Rife	Widespread
458	Hegemony	Domination
459	Surreptitious	Secret
460	Encumbrance	Burden
461	Capitulate	Surrender
462	Jaunty	heerfulness
463	Hock	Pledge
464	Heretical	Impious
465	Obdurate	Adamant/tubborn
466	Fractious	Irritable
467	Demise	End
468	Pristine	Original
469	Orotund	Resonant
470	Incense	Angry
471	Incontinent	Unrestrained
472	Nibble	Agile

473	Offal	Refuse
474	Colossus	Towering
475	Helm	Head
476	Occult	Mysterious
477	Pander	Encourage
478	Raucous	Loud/Rough
479	Browse	Examine
480	Prowess	Bravery/Ability/Skill
481	Vulpine	Crafty
482	Imbroglio	Confusion
483	Fiasco	Failure
484	Perky	Buoyant
485	Rancour	Bitter/Angry feelings
486	Cozen	Cheat
487	Schism	Split
488	Disinter	Unearth
489	Terse	Compact
490	Hallowed	Sacred
491	Credence	Credit
492	Empirical	Practical
493	Pastime	Recreation
494	Reprobate	Wicked Person/Scoundrel
495	Skittish	Lively/Playful/Easily excited
496	Sluggard	Idler/Lazy bones
497	Appendage	Accessory/Supplement
498	Clairvoyant	Telepathic
499	Pugilist	Boxer
500	Chary	Cautious/Wary

...

BREAK FOR WORDS REVISION

REVISE THE VOCAB

TEST 10
Words (451-500)

(1) **Interim**
- (a) temporary (b) permanent
- (c) internal (d) external.

(2) **Leeway**
- (a) outspoken (b) clever
- (c) permissiveness (d) cheerful

(3) **Demise**
- (a) Beginning (b) Prevail
- (c) End (d) Revise

(4) **Obdurate**
- (a) Still (b) Stubborn
- (c) Clever (d) Miser

(5) **Colossus**
- (a) Shivering (b) Towering
- (c) Shower (d) Increasing.

(6) **Offal**
- (a) Presume (b) Refuse
- (c) Remit (d) Offense.

(7) **Fiasco**
- (a) Success (b) Fascinating
- (c) Failure (d) Delightful

(8) **Capitulate**
- (a) To make captive (b) To keep secret
- (c) Surrender (d) On the run

(9) **Incontinent**
- (a) Restrained (b) Unrestrained
- (c) Competent (d) Resonant

(10) **Occult**
- (a) Mysterious (b) Natural
- (c) Practical (d) Free-flowing.

(11) **Hallowed**
- (a) Secret (b) Sacred
- (c) Caution (d) Ideal

(12) **Chary**
- (a) Caution (b) Cheerful
- (c) Sullen (d) Angry

(13) Pugilist

(a) Wrestler (b) Magician
(c) Musician (d) Boxer

(14) Reprobate

(a) Wicked person (b) Reprimand
(c) Innocent (d) Intelligent

(15) Empirical

(a) Theoretical (b) Practical
(c) Royal (d) Unpractical

Match the words in column 'A' with their correct meaning in 'B'.

Column A	Column B
(1) Credence	(1) Accessory
(2) Terse	(2) Crafty
(3) Appendage	(3) Examine
(4) Clairvoyant	(4) Resonant
(5) Schism	(5) Credit
(6) Browse	(6) Original
(7) Raucous	(7) Loud/Rough
(8) Vulpine	(8) Bravery
(9) Pristine	(9) Bitter
(10) Orotund	(10) Buoyant
(11) Prowess	(11) Telepathic
(12) Cozen	(12) Secret
(13) Rancour	(13) Spilt
(14) Perky	(14) Cheat
(15) Surreptitious	(15) Compact

ANSWERS

1. (b): After between objective pronouns are used instead of reflexive Pronouns. Therefore **me** in place of **myself**.

2. (a): 'regretfully' should be replaced with 'regretably'.

3. (d): The sentence is correct.

4. (d): The sentence is correct.

5. (a): 'enquired' should be replaced with 'enquired of'

6. (a): We solve the problems and not do the problems. We generally do the activities . Therefore **solve** in place of **do**.

7. (d): The sentence is correct.

8. (c): Here the verb to be used for the group (subject) which is singular therefore **was** inplace of **were** remember subject verb agreement.

9. (d): The sentence is correct.

10. (d): The sentence is correct.

11. (d): The sentence is correct.

12. (a): Had is past tense and have is present therefore have here is wrong. So **to meet** in place of **have met**.

13. (d): The sentence is correct.

14. (a): The sentence is in past tense Therefore **failed** in place of **fail**.

15. (d): The sentence is correct.

16. (c): Here we are comparing live of a Scientist with the life of politician so correct from should be .... that the life of the scientist .... different form that of a politician. Here **'that** ' before a politician has beenused for **life**.

17. (d): The sentence is correct.

18. (d): The sentence is correct.

19. (d): The sentence is correct.

20. (b): Went two different subject are joinent by alongwith then the form of the verb is as per the first subject i.e. if the first subject is singular the following verb is singular and of the first subject is plural, the following verb will be plural. Here 1st subject is (The Managing director) and second subject is 'other members'. Also 1st subject is singular therefore was in place of 'were'.

21. (b): After Neither', singular verb is used. Therefore supports (singular) in place of support (plural)

22. (c): Here leader is singular therefore singular pronoun **his** in place of plural pronoun **their**.

23. (c): With **discuss** no preposition is used.

24. (b): 'are' should be replaced with 'is'. Refer to the chapter on verb.

25. (a): With verb (accused preposition of is used in place with.

26. (c): ‘of' is not used after comprises but 'of' is always used after consists. for example This consist of five chapters. This comprises five chapters.

27. (b): back is not used after return as back and returned have the same meaning i.e. back after returns is redundant.

28. (b): with between ..... and is used and with from ...... to is used.

29. (c): 'much' is used when we are comparing prices of the articles. Also 'much' is used for uncountable nouns. Therefore is very here is wrong.

30. (a): With conferred' the correct preposition is 'on'

31. (b): The correct idiomsis to pick holes which means to find faults so up here is wrong.

32. (a): Verb of sensation is like see smell taste touch, etc. are not used in continuous form (-ing)., also here we are to describe the future activity so the correct form is either 'I will see him' or I am to see him.

33. (b): With -ior ending word like superior junior and senior inferior etc. to is used in place of than in comparison. So superior to in place of superior than.

34. (c): The correct idioms is in thelong run.

35. (b): The correct idioms is hanging fire which means pending or has not been solved yet.

36. (d): The sentence is correct.

37. (b): Here the subject is 'The steep rise' which is singular therefore verb after it has to be singular. So has (singular) in place of have (plurarl)

38. (b): When two different subjects are joined by 'as well as' the following verb is as per the first subject i.e. if 1st subject is singular the verb is singular and if 1st subject is plural the verb will be plural. Here two subjects are kiran (1st) and Kamal (2nd). Kiran is Singular therefore is (singular) in place of are (plural)

39. (c): The correct prepostion is travelled 'on' not travelled by.

40. (b): 'flown' should be replaced with 'flowed'.

41. (c): With rest Preposition with is used and it means lies with. With depend upon is used.

42. (c): In parrallelism same part of speech should be connected to same part of the speech. Here to my mother ...... to my brother. Also when either .... or is used, we have to use same preposition,

43. (c): The correct idioms is as you take me for. Which means 'as you think.'

44. (c): In this to express better is incomplete as it is not showing that what to express. Therefore in place of 'to' it has to be how to express yourself.

45. (b): We raise hopees not rise hopes. So raise in place of rise.

46. (c): 'Here we are comparing performance of pronouns 'He' with rest of members of organization. So that of the in place of the. Here that will represent the performance of the members.

47. (b): No prepostion after discuss'. So 'about' after discuss is wrong.

48. (c): The correct phrase is scaredof.

49. (a): The questions talks about two duties therefore the correct sentence is it is our duty...... not only ...... 1st duty ...... but also .... second duty.

50. (c): The correct structre will be at/by/with boy's progress.

51. (a): To specify the unknown part in the sentence we start that part with 'that' so after don't think that will be used.

52. (b): His both hands is not accepted in standard english so correct structure will be both of his hands.

53. (b): Any general statement or scientific results and proven facts are written in present indefinite tense.

54. (a): After insisted infinitive is not used instead we use gerund. Therefore on going in place of to go.

55. (c): 'was' is not used when we talk about two past activities and one of them is over before the start of another, we use past perfect tense. So had been in place of was.

56.(a): When we are given time (since/for), and activity is in continuous form, we use present perfect tense. So have beenhis place of 'Am'.

57. (c): 'besides' in place of 'beside'.

Besides = in addition to beside = to the side of.

58. (b): The sentence is past tense so has will not go with 'was'. Therefore had in place of 'has'.

59. (a): If we look at 'Being a full moon night'. We do not know that on which day the full moon night was. So we need to specify the day on which full moon night was there. If no day date is mentioned, we used it i.e. it being a full moon is right. Also if we do not put it at the start then it seems that 'the tides' were full moon night. This question is case of Dangling participle. To understand the question in a better way, go through the chapter on modifiers.

60. (c): With different the correct preposition is form.

61. (c): 'Was' is generally used for past continuous form. For the activity which started in past and was over also in past, we used pst perfect tense. Therefore, 'had' in place of was'.

62. (a): 'Keep' before maintaining is unnecessary.

63. (a): Same as Q. 59

64. (d): The sentence is correct.

65. (a): **Such of** before **those** is redudant or not required.

66. (c): We need to specify who wants to avail the facility. Also avail is 'veb' without object in the sentence. So when subject is object, we have to use reflexive pronouns for eg. Jhon killed himself. Therefore in the sentence after avail oneself will be written.

67. (b): Here the subject is Driving a Vehicle. Which is singular therefore verb after it will also be singular (as per subject verb agreement) Therefore requires (singular) in place of require (plural)

68. (c): 'back' after return is redundant or not required.

69. (b): Correct preposition here will be 'to' not 'in'

70. (a): Whenever action starts in past and at the time of speaking if it is in continuous form with time period given we have to use present perfect tense. Here time period is 'for three years' and subject (I) is playing as on today. So we will write have been in place of 'am'.

71. (b): We use past perfect tense when we have to discribed more than one past activity. So correct structure is his car had broke down.

72. (c):

73. (b): 'besides' should be replaced with 'beside'.

74. (a):

75. (a): After suggested 'to is used. Therefore the suggested to us..........

76. (b): When something is in motion inside something the correct preposition is 'into' instad of 'in'.

77. (a): In indirect speech 'that' is used after said. Therefore correct structure is he said that ....

78. (c): The correct phrase is .... in protest against.

79. (c): The sentence is in past tense therefore would in place of will. Would is past from of will.

80. (a):

81. (a): 'all the more' is unnecessary before better. Also before is already in comparative degree so 'more' is not allowed before 'better' in standard english.

82. (b): The proper combination is had .... would have. For i.e. If he had helped we, I would have correct the case. Therefore ' you would have told me' in place of you had to

83. (c): For two persons' between' is used instead of among, which is used for more than two persons.'among' should be replaced with 'between'.

84. (b):

85. (b):

86. (a): 'Else' is followed by 'but' and not by than.

87. (a): The Correct sturcture will be 'Now that all my children are....

88. (c): To after explained.

89. (d): The sentence is correct.

90. (b): 'fly' should be replaced with 'flies'.

Answer of Test 10

(1) a (2) c (3) c (4) b (4) b (6) b (7) c
(8) c (9) b (10) a (11) b (12) a (13) d (14) a
(15) b

Match

(1) 5 (2) 15 (3) 1 (4) 11 (5) 13 (6) 3 (7) 7
(8) 2 (9) 6 (10) 4 (11) 8 (12) 14 (13) 9 (14) 10
(15) 12

Day

12

Common - Errors

We will do second set of important errors today.

SET 2

***Directions (Q. 1–80)** : In this Section a number of sentences are given. The sentences are divided in four separate parts and each one is labelled (a), (b), (c), (d) . Read each sentence to find out whether there is an error in any part. No sentence has more than one error. When you find an error in any one of the parts (a, b, c or d) . If there is no error in the sentence then mark (e) as your answer.*

1. As I reached the hospital (a)/ I had found, a great rush of visitors (b)/ whose relatives had been admitted there (c)/ for one or the other ailment (d)/ No error (e)

2. One should study the history (a)/ of his country because it alone can satisfy (b)/ one's natural curiosity to know (c)/ what happened in the past. (d)/ No error (e)

3. It is interesting to note (a)/ that the greatest lines in poetry are simple (b)/ and yet there is with them some quality, (c)/ which makes them outsandingly great (d)/ No error (e).

4. In order to make human life happy. (a)/ man should live (b)/ as far as possible. (c)/ in perfect harmony with nature. (d)/ No error (e).

5. You have heard (a)/ of Socrates, I suppose, (b)/ Undoubtedly he was one (c)/ of the greatest man of the world. (d)/ No error (e)

6. You may not know it (a)/ but this engine is (b)/ claimed to have twice (c)/ as powerful as the previous one. (d)/ No error (e)

7. Nothing ever becomes real (a)/ till it is experienced. (b)/ Even a proverb is noproverbtoyou (c) / till your life has illustrated with it. (d)/ No error (e).

8. I remember my childhood days (a) / when I was used to go (b) / to the farm with my father (c)/ and help him in his work (d)/ No error (e).

9. I missed the last train (a)/ which I usually catch (b)/ and have to stay at the station (c)/ on my way back home yesterday. (d)/ No error (e).

10. Sureshbabu who is living (a)/ in this own since 1955 (b) / is a well-known scholar of history (c) / and a distinguished musician. (d)/ No error (e).

11. If you had read (a)/ the relevant literature carefully (b)/ you would have answered (c)/ most of the questions correctly. (d)/ No error (e).

12. The house where the dead man was found (a)/ is being guarded by police (b)/ to prevent it from being entered (c)/ and the evidence interfered with (d)/ No error (e).

13. Many animals and plants live 'in water (a)/ but not in the same kind of water (b)/ because not all water is the same. (c)/ Sea water, for instance, contains a lot of salt, fresh water contains very little (d)/ No error (e).
14. A sparrow has made a nest in Kesho's house (a)/ and had laid eggs. Both Kesho and his sister Shyama (b)/ watched the nest for hours every day (c)/ Even meal times were forgotten.(d)/ No error (e).
15. A skillful advertiser may be able to create (a)/ practically a monopoly for himself (b)/ not because his product is superior to (c)/ but because he has succeeded in inducing people to believe that it is. (d)/ No error (e).
16. Whatever may be the origin of speech (a)/ we can be certain that man did not began (b)/ to feel the need to speak (c)/ until he began to live in communities (d)/ No error (e).
17. I am contacting you (a)/ sometime in next week (b)/ to explain, to you (c)/ my problem in detail (d) / No error (e).
18. His speech was (a)/ judged by many (b)/ as one of the most important speech (c)/ given in the function (d)/ No error (e).
19. If you would have (a)/ gone to his house (b) / before 10 a.m. you would have (c)/ got his autograph. (d) / No error (e).
20. The five member committee were (a)/ of the view that the present service conditions (b)/ of the employees of this company (c)/ are quite good (d)/ No error (e).
21. Hardly had I (a)/ entered the compartment (b)/ than I met (c)/ my friend Vishwas. (d)/ No error (e).
22. An anti-extortion cell is opened (a)/ by the district police head quarter (b)/ six months ago (c)/ as a precautionary measure. (d)/ No error (e).
23. Pramod said that (a)/ he prefered a white shirt (b)/ than coloured one (c) / on any festive occasion. (d)/ No error (e).
24. There is just one enough (a)/ timing in my job to sit around (b)/ talking about how we feel (c)/ about each other (d)/. No error (e).
25. When you will pass (a)/ your examination (b)/ with flying colours (c)/ you will get a costly present. (d)/ No error (e).
26. Everyone of the survivers (a)/ of the accident (b)/ have told the same story (c)/ without any difference. (d)/ No error (e).
27. Ramesh said that (a)/ he preferred the (b)/ leather purse (c)/ than the plastic. (d)/ No error (e).
28. The mother as well as (a)/ the children are to be (b)/blamed for (c)/ this sorry state of affairs. (d)/ No error (e).
29. I am one of (a)/ those who believes (b)/ that mathematics need not (c)/ be dull and uninspiring. (d)/No error (e).
30. As he was (a)/ walking down the road (b)/ yesterday a bicycle (c)/ ran into him. (d)/ No error (e).
31. It is a (a)/ well known fact that (b)/ the leopard is faster (c)/ than all animals. (d)/ No error (e).
32. We were happy that (a)/ the audience responded well (b)/ and gave all the speakers (c)/ a patiently listening. (d)/ No error (e).
33. He received timely support (a)/ from his elder brother (b)/ who is working abroad (c)/ for the last six years. (d)/ No error (e).

34. The notorious gang opened (a)/ the door quietly and (b)/ escaped in the dark with (c)/ whatever they would collect. (d)/ No error (e).

35. One of the security men (a)/ rushed forward and asked (b)/ me whether I (c)/ had anything objectionable. (d)/ No error (e).

36. We could not (a)/ believe that one (b)/ of us was (c)/ responsible with the act. (d)/ No error (e).

37. We are now (a)/ reliably learnt that (b)/ he was involved (c)/ in the bank robbery. (d)/ No error (e).

38. I do not know (a)/ what most people feel (b)/ depressed and dejected (c)/ even with the slightest. provocation (d)/ No error (e).

39. She had such pretty (a)/ that she thinks (b)/ she can afford to be (c)/ careless about her clothes. (d)/ No error (e).

40. After carefully examining (a)/ all the medicine bottles (b)/ he submitted a detailed report (c)/ to the higher authorities. (d)/ No error (e).

41. All of you have the liberty (a)/ to come home (b)/ as per the convenient (c)/ and discuss the problems. (d)/ No error (e).

42. He was persuaded (a)/ by his friends (b)/ to end his fast (c)/ because of his condition deteriorated. (d)/ No error (e).

43. I know who (a)/ this job should be (b)/ entrusted to (c)/ for smooth handling. (d)/ No error (e).

44. They have the nasty habit of (a)/ looking down upon people (b)/ and criticized them (c)/ for no reason. (d)/ No error (e).

45. Nowadays, the cost of living (a) is so high that (b)/ people find it difficult (c)/ to make both ends meeting. (d)/ No error (e).

46. Karnavati is (a)/ one of the leading (b)/ business centres (c)/ in our State. (d)/ No error (e).

47.. My secretary is so (a)/ careful of her work that (b)/ none has so far found (c)/ any error in her work. (d)/ No error (e).

48. Our conclusion is that (a)/ between Vinayak and (b)/ Lobo, Vinayak is (c)/ the most honest. (d)/ No error (e).

49. The new project group (a)/ would first look into the tender conditions (b)/ of both basic and value added (c)/ services before submit its bid. (d)/ No error (e).

50. I would have committed (a)/ the same mistake of signing (b)/ the sale deed if my agent (c)/ would not have forewarned me. (d)/ No error (e)

51. The team leaders encourages (a)/ the participants who have (b)/ ditficulty in performing (c)/ the assigned task. (d) No error (e).

52. I live on a top floor (a)/ of an old house. (b)/ When the wind blows (c)/ all the windows rattle. (d)/ No error (e).

53. Had he not reached in time (a)/ he would have missed (b)/ a golden opportunity which comes (c)/ once in a while. (d)/ No error (e).

54. The Ministry of Labour conducts its basic survey (a)/ on trade unions each year (b)/ gathering information with all (c)/ labour unions as of June 30. (d)/ No error (e).

55. Stories have always been used (a)/ as a powerful tool for (b)/ communicating vital information from (c)/ one generation to another. (d)/ No error (e).

56. We all are indebted to him (a)/ for holding not only high moral values (b)/ but also rendering dedicated service (c)/ for the betterment of human race. (d)/ No error (e).

57. We are trying to (a)/ find out the root cause (b)/ of this recurring problem (c)/ since the last four days. (d)/ No error (e).

58. I told him bluntly (a)/ that he is a lazy fellow (b)/ and that he had done (c)/ his work very badly. (d)/ No error. (e).

59. Mumbai is full of tall buildings (a)/ which is at once its (b)/ strength as well as weakness (c)/ depending upon how one look at it. (d)/ No error (e).

60. I am fully aware that (a)/ my boss is one of those (b)/ who is totally dedicated (c)/ to work and proper discipline. (d)/ No error (e).

61. The Director of our Company (a)/ does not believe that (b)/ we are working sincerely (c)/ and with interest for all these years. (d)/ No error (e).

62. I have been (a)/ working for this (b)/ organisatibn for (c)/ the last ten years. (d) I No error (e).

63. The officer along with (a)/ his family members was (b)/ invited at the reception party (c)/ organised by his employer. (d)/ No error (e).

64. On hearing from you (a)/ I will come not only (b)/ to the airport but will (c)/ also help you in customs clearance (4) / No error (5).

65. I always prefer (a)/ working in a (b)/ relaxed atmosphere than (c) one full of tension and anxiety. (d) No error (e).

66. If we had Mohan (a)/ in our tearn we (b)/ would have won the match (c)/ against your teem. (d) /No error (e).

67. My observation is that (a)/ between Ragav and (b)/ Deepe, Ragav is (c)/ the most intelligent. (d) / No error (e).

68. In my opinion (a)/ Balraj is very (b) honest and can (c)/ be depended. (d)/ No error (e).

69. When your father inquired (a)/ about your marks (b)/you lied to him. (c)/ Have you not ? (d)/ No error (e).

70. A nationwide survey has (a)/ brought up an (b)/interesting finding regarding (c)/ infant mortality rate in India. (d)/ No error (e).

71. Yesterday Ramesh got the (a)/ information that his father (b)/ died of accident (c)/ while travelling in a car. (d) / No error (e).

72. No sooner did (a)/ I reach (b)/ Delhi railway station than (c)/ the train departed (d)/ No error (e).

73. As soon as I will (a)/ reach Patna I will (b)/ send you the books (c)/ you have asked for. (d)/ No error (e).

74. One of my good quality (a)/ is that I do not (b)/ take things like (c)/ this very seriously. (d)/ No error (e).

75. Our Housing Society comprises of (a)/ eight blocks and (b)/ forty eight flats in an (c)/ area of about thousand sq. metres. (d)/ No error (e).

76. It being a (a)/ pleasant morning I (b)/ decided to go out (c) /on walking in the garden. (d)/ No error (e).

77. He is (a)/ the greatest (b)/ living cricketer (c)/ today. (d)/ No error (e).

78. These kind (a)/ of cars sold extensively (b)/ here are really (c)/ economical to drive and maintain. (d)/ No error (e).

79. I put the boxes (a)/ of fruits down (b)/ and looked around for (c)/ someone to help me carry them. (d)/ No error (e).

80. My bedroom (a)/ was wide open (b)/ and I leaned out spiritlessly (c)/ to look for night.(d)/ No error (e).

VOCAB LIST

501	Damn	To condemn/To suffer hell
502	Damnation	To condemn/To suffer hell
503	Perdition	Damnation
504	Peremptory	Dictatorial
505	Perfidious	Treacherous/Disloyal
506	Refractory	Difficult to control
507	Penurious	Poor/Very needy
508	Crotchet	Odd notion
509	Derelict	Not cared for
510	Enthral	Capture whole attention of
511	Enthral	Fascinate
512	Anomalous	Abnormal/Atypical
513	Portend	Presage/To be sign of future event
514	Buoyant	Cheerful
515	Buoy	Floating
516	Unprecedented	Never happened or done before
517	Myriad	Many
518	Guise	Appearance
519	Sardonic	Mocking
520	Utopian	Idealistic/ Not realistic
521	Hoary	Very old/Grey with age
522	Jocose	Joyful/Humorous
523	Unctuous	Oily/Greasy
524	Brusque	Rough
525	Wastrel	Good-for-nothing
526	Medicament	Panacea/Cure of all diseases

527	Abjure	Renounce
528	Dwindle	Decrease gradually
529	Visionary	Unpractical
530	Churlish	Ill-tempered/Boorish
531	Repudiate	Refuse
532	Rescind	Cancel/Abrogate/Revoke
533	Mien	Appearance
534	Disconcert	To upset or embarrass
535	Disconsolate	Unhappy
536	Discrete	Separate/Distinct
537	Discrepancy	Difference/Failure to agree
538	Presumptuous	Too bold
539	Over weaning	Showing excessive confidence
540	Forte	A thing that does particularly well
541	Chink	Crack
542	Sissy	Boy lacking the qualities of boy
543	Allude	To mention indirectly
544	Allusion	Indirect reference
545	Infraction	Violation
546	Gorge	Narrow valley with water flowing
547	Pre-eminent	Outstanding
548	Pre-empt	Prevent
549	Preponderance	Greater than others in amount/influence or importance
550	Jingoism	Extreme belief that one's own country is best

REVISE THE VOCAB

BREAK FOR WORDS REVISION

TEST 11
Words (501-550)

(1) Damn
(a) To condemn (b) Praise
(c) Pretty (d) Dull.

(2) Derelict
(a) Not cared for (b) Cared for
(c) Difficult (d) Noisy

(3) Myriad
(a) Many (b) Single
(c) All (d) Couplet

(4) Brusque
(a) Soft (b) Calm
(c) Rough (d) Brutal

(5) Utopian
(a) Realistic (b) Idealistic
(c) Unpractical (d) Practical.

(6) Mien
(a) Appearance (b) Sound of insect
(c) Restlessness (d) Boring

(7) Churlish
(a) Ill- tempered (b) Very old
(c) In rags (d) Oily

(8) Infraction
(a) Violet (b) Violation
(c) Separation (d) Unattractive

(9) Incontinent
(a) Agree (b) To make reputation
(c) Approve (d) Refuse

(10) Abjure
(a) Retry (b) Refuse
(c) Renounce (d) Recreate

(11) Chink
(a) Bold (b) Crack
(c) Wicked (d) Idle

(12) Allusion
(a) Direct reference (b) Indirect reference
(c) Disappearing (d) Appearance

(13) Pre-eminent

(a) Outstanding (b) Familiar

(c) Unknown (d) Careful

(14) Jingoism

(a) Extreme before that one's own country is best

(b) Extreme belief that other country is best

(c) Nation that nothing is everlasting

(d) Notion that nothing can be destroyed

(15) Pre- empt

(a) Prevent (b) Collapse

(c) To empty (d) None of these

Match the words in column 'A' with their correct meaning in 'B'.

Column A	Column B
(1) Gorge	(1) Showing excessive confidence
(2) Allude	(2) Abrogate/ revoke
(3) Over weaning	(3) Unpractical
(4) Presumptuous	(4) Panacea
(5) Rescind	(5) narrow valley with flowing water
(6) Disconsolate	(6) Decrease gradually
(7) Visionary	(7) Joyful
(8) Dwindle	(8) Very old
(9) Jocose	(9) Too bold
(10) Wastrel	(10) Dictatorial
(11) Medicament	(11) To Mention indirectly
(12) Guise	(12) Appearance
(13) Peremptory	(13) Fascinate
(14) Enthral	(14) Unhappy
(15) Hoary	(15) Good- for - nothing

ANSWER 1

1. (b) Whe we have to talk about more than one past activity then 'had' is used with the activity which had happened in the far past. In this sentence event in part (b) had occured before the subject visited the hospital or saw the condition of patients there. Therefore 'had' in part (b) is right but 'had' is part (a) is wrong.

2. (b) The possive pronoun for subjective Pronoun 'one' is one's not 'his'. Therefore 'his' in part (a) should be replaced with one's.

3. (e)

4. (e)

5. (d) 'After one of the' plural noun is used Therefore 'men' in place of 'man'.

6. (a) 'be' in place of 'have' to get the correct sense.

7. (e)

8. (d) The sentence is in past tense therefore help (present) in (d) is wrong and hence helped (past) in place of help.

9. (c) The word 'yesterday' shows that the given event is in past tense so 'have' (present) cannot be used. Hence had (past) in place of have (present)

10. (d) 'a' in (d) is redudant as 'a' in part (c) is sufficient to describe the two qualities of the same subject (Sureshbabu)

11. (e)

12. (b)

13. (e)

14. (a) As the sentence is in past tense therefore 'has' (present perfect) is wrong in (a), Hence 'had' (past perfect) in place of 'Has'

15. (b)

16. (b) After 'did' 1st form of the verb is used therefore 'begin' in (b) in place of 'began'.

17. (a) 'I am contacting you' is wrong in standard english, instead the correct structure will be 'I shall contact you. When we talk about future, we have to use future tense.

18. (c) **Speeches** in place of **speech**

19. (a) The proper combination is if you had ....., you would have. So 'had' in place of 'would have' in (a).

20. (a) **Was** in place of **were,** as five member committee is singular.

21. (c) **When** in place of **than.** Since hardly and scarcely are followed by when.

22. (a) **Was** in place of **is**, as the sentence is in past tense.

23. (c) After 'ior' ending words like superior, senior, junior, and after prefer. 'to' is used for comparisson in place of 'than'.

24. (e)

25. (a) We cannot use future tense twice in the same sentence for e.g.
I will not go to college, if it will rain (wrong)
I will not go to college, if it rains (correct).
So the part of the sentence which is representing any condition/limitation/restriction should always be in simple present tense. Hence we have to Remove 'will' in (a)

26. (c) **has** in place of **have.** Since everyone is followed by verb in singular.

27. (d) **To** in place of **than.**

28. (b) **Is** in place of **are** because of First Subject Rule

29. (e)

30. (a) **While** in place of **as.**

31. (c) Remove **the** as we are not talking about anything specific.

32. (d) **Patient** in place of **patiently.**

33. (c) 'Has been' in place of 'is' as time period (last six years) is mentioned. Whenever in past tense/present tense time is given to us, we have to use present preference/past perfect. Also when since/for will time is given it is understood that we cannot use continuous tense.

34. (d) As the actionis over at the time of speaking so we have to use correct helping verb (past perfect). so 'had collected' in place of 'would collect'.

35. (e)

36. (d) We are 'responsible for; anything and not 'responsible with'.

37. (a) 'Have' in place of 'are' as the action was over at the time of speaking.

38. (b) 'What' here will not make any sense in this sentence. So 'why' in place of 'what'.

39. (a) 'Had' is contextually wrong here. Also wheever we want to represent cause-effect then the proper pair is so .... like. Hence'so' in place of 'that'

40. (e)

41. (c) **Convenience** in place of **convenient.**

42. (d) 'Condition' is a noun therefore verb (deterioted) cannot be used to qualify it. Here we need an adjective (deteriorate) to modify 'condition'. Therefore the correct structure is ..... his deteriorate condition.

43. (a) When ever in any sentence, we are able to insert (him/her) anywhere in the sentence, we have to use whom for eg.

I know (who/whom) this should be entrusted to (him) for smooth handling.

In the above sentence him can be inserted after entrusted therefore whom in place of who is correct in the above example.

To apply this trick do not change the voice/Narration/structure of the sentence.

44. (c) This is related to parrallelism The first habit of the subject (they) is in -ing form therefore their second habit. also should in -ing form. Hence 'criticizing' in place of 'criticized'.

45. (d) This is general statement or truth about today's life so it should in simple present tense and not in continuous tense. Hence 'meet' in place of 'meeting' Also the correct choice is 'to make' both ends meet.

46. (e)

47. (e)

48. (d) When we have to compare two subjects/characters/attributes, we use comparative degree. Here two subjects are Vinayak and lobo so 'more' in place of 'most'

49. (d) Submitting in place of submit

50. (d) If ..... had ..... , would have/could have. Therefore ' had not' in place of would not.

51. (a) The subject here is 'The team leaders (plural) therefore verb also should be plural. Hence Encourage (plural) in place of encourages (singular).

52. (a) 'The' in place of 'a' in part (a), as we are talking about specific floor.

53. (e)

54. (c) 'With' in part (c) is not making any sense so 'about' in its place

55. (e)

56. (b) The correct structure is always not only .... 1st but also 2nd Here we (subject) are indebted for two reasons (1) holding high moral values (2) dedicated service . Therefore the correct structure is not only holding ...... but also rendering dedicated .....

57. (d) When the period of time is given to us, we use 'for' and when point of time/is given to us we use 'since' Hence 'for' in place of 'since'.

58. (b) **Was** in place of **is.**

59. (d) Look (verb) is to used after one (singular) therefore it should also be in singular form. Therefore looks (singular) in place of look (plural)

60. (c) after 'those' ..... 'are'

61. (c) When period of time is given to us, we have to use perfect tense. Also when an action has started in past and is still continuous in present time we have to use present perfect tense.

62. (e)

63. (c) Use reception or party.

64. (b) not only ..... 1st activity/ .... but also 2 activity I will not only ..... 1st...... but will also ......

65. (c) After 'prefer' 'to' is used not 'than'

66. (e)

67. (d) For two subject in comparisson, comparative degree is used. Therefore 'more' in place of 'most'.

68. (d) Add **upon** after **depended.**

69. (e)

70. (b) The correct phrase is brought out means come to picture/light and brought up means to nurture.

71. (c) With completed action in past, we use past perfect. therefore 'had' before died. Also when we talk about two past actions and one of them is over before the start of another we use past perfect for eg. The train left before I reached the station (wrong)

The train had left before I reached the station. (Correct).

72. (e)

73. (a) We cannot use future tense twice in the conditional sentences. the action which occurs at first place should be in simple present. Therefore As soon as I reached Patna. i.e. Remove 'will' from (a)

74. (a) 'One of ....' is followed by noun in plural. Therefore 'qualities in place of quality.

75. (a) 'Of' is not used after comprises. 'of' is used after consists.

76. (d)

77. (e)

78. (b) Add **which are** after **cars.**

79. (a) **Kept** in place of **put.**

80. (d) 'Look for' means searching so it will not make any sense. Therefore 'see the' in place of look for.

Answer of Test 11

(1) a (2) a (3) a (4) c (5) b (6) a (7) a
(8) b (9) d (10) c (11) b (12) b (13) a (14) a
(15) a

Match

(1) 5 (2) 11 (3) 1 (4) 9 (5) 2 (6) 2 (7) 3
(8) 6 (9) 7 (10) 15 (11) 4 (12) 12 (13) 10 (14) 13
(15) 8

Day

13

Sentence Rearrangement

In this section we are given four, five, six jumbled sentences and our task is to arrange these sentences in a proper logical order. We may find questions based on:

(i) Four sentences rearrangement

(ii) Five sentences rearrangement

(iii) When first and last sentences are fixed. You have to rearrange four or five sentences given between first and last sentences.

(iv) Sometimes eight or nine sentences are given and you have to find the redundant sentence (which is not part of given sequence).

Now the most of students attempt these questions with the help of choices only and for them this is the only way. They think that it is the best way for solving these questions. But they are mistaken as we do have a few tricks to deal with these types of questions.

We will discuss each trick one by one.

Tips to solve sentence rearrangement questions

(i) Read all the given sentences very carefully. Try to form the logical sequence (Rough idea) in your mind. i.e. which sentence will come at 1st position or which will come at last position and so on. Now to get the correct answer you will proceed as follows.

(ii) After Reading the given sentences carefully, you will find that there is a sentence which you feel or find that it will be going to open the sequence or likely to come at 1st place. They are called openers or opening sentences or an introductory sentence or likely to introduce the main idea in the sequence.

Now how to recognise openers?

A few hints to identify the openers are

(a) These sentences are independent in nature i.e. if we take out these sentences from the sequence, they can stand alone. You will see that they do not depend upon any of given sentences either to convey the sense or to convey their meaning.

(b) These sentences contain the theme/topic/idea about which the rearrangement is talking.

(c) These sentencess are complete and general in nature.

(iii) There is a possiblity that we may find a sentence, which is likely to conclude the whole sequence i.e. it will come at last position. These are called closers or closing sentences. These sentences generally have conclusion trigger words like 'so' 'therefore' 'thus', 'Hence', 'consequently' etc at the start.

(iv) Also in any rearrangement there can be a possiblity of finding a pair or a trio. These are the sentences which cannot be separated. These are known as Mandatory pairs or trios. Now a few tips to locate Mandatory pairs. These are as follow:-

(a) **Noun-Pronoun Method:** If any sentence has a noun and in any other sentence, there is corresponding pronoun than these two sentences will form a Mandatory pair. The noun containing sentence will come before pronoun containing sentence.

For Example : (1) Amitabh is my friend.

(2) He lives in Mumbai.

Now the above two sentences will be in a pair in the final arrangement. Since Amitabh is a Noun and 'He' (pronoun) has been used for corresponding noun (Amitabh)

(b) **Key-word link Method:** In this we try to link the key-words in any two given sentences.

For Example : If there is a word **Industrilization** in one of the sentences and this same word is there in any of the remaining sentences, then their is a possibility that these two senences will form a pair.

(iv) **Cause-effect Method :** If in any sentence "cause of any event is given. and in any of the reamining sentences, 'effect' is their, then these two sentences will form a Mandatory pair.

(v) **Chrono-pairing or chronological squence :** By Chrono we mean time. So if in any rearrangement we have two or three time frames i.e. past time, present time, future time then order of the placement will be "Past, Present, Future".

Now the Final Step : When you follow the above steps, you are definitely going to find any of the elements like an opener or closure or a mandatory pair. As soon as you find any of them, look at choices. Pick up that choice or those choices in which we have found any of the three elements i.e. opener or Closer or any mandatory pairs. Reject those choices which do not contain any of these elements at proper place. Finally you will see that you are left with two or three choices. Scan and try to match these choices with the given sentences and get the logical or coherent sequences (rearrangement).

Now we will do a few questions and try to learn to apply above tricks or Methods.

(1) *George Bernard Shaw considered*

P a considerable portion of his wealth

Q and in his will left behind

R current English spelling indefensible

S for reforms in spelling

The proper sequence should be:

(a) RSPQ

(b) RQPS

(c) QRPS

(d) QRSP

Explanation: Here opening sentences is already given to us. Actually this is very easy questions and we may not require all the tricks but we will still use a few of them.

Now George Bernard considered what?

Answer to this is sentence (R). So next what did he do to solve the problem?

He left money to be used to solve the problems as per his will.

Therefore after (R), Q will come followed by P and in the last S will come

Hence the answer is choice b.

(2) *Nations of the world*

P as they are fully aware

Q are making efforts in developing

R of the danger of their not coming together

S peaceful international relations

The proper sequence should be:

(a) PRSQ

(b) PSRQ

(c) QSPR

(d) QPRS

Explanation: Here also method will be same, as it was followed in example 1. If we read all the sentences we understand that nations of the world are trying to achieve something. So what is that? That is to develop the cordial or smooth relation among them. Hence after the 'Nation of the world' sentence Q will come. After R, obviously 'S' will come. There is only one choice in which Q & S are together i.e. choice C which is the answer.

Now for your practice, three types of sentence rearrangement questions are given. Do the following questions and learn the application of the tricks discuss above.

ALL THE BEST ....

Type I
(Based on simple sentences)

Directions : In each of the items given below, there is a sentence of which some parts have been jumbled up. You are required to re-arrange these parts which are labelled, P. Q, R and S to produce the correct sentence, Choose the proper sequence and mark in your Answer Sheet accordingly.

1. **George Bernard Shaw considered**

P a considerable portion of his wealth
Q and in his will left behind
R current English spelling indefensible
S for reforms in spelling

The proper sequence should be :

(a) RSPQ (b) RQPS
(c) QRPS (d) QRSP

2. **Psychologists say**

P an innate drive
Q to finish
R that humans have
S what they start

The proper sequence should be

(a) RPQS (b) PQSR
(c) RPSQ (d) PSQR

3. The use of language

P primarily and predominantly involves
Q and receiving other people's speech noises
R making noises with our speech organs
S through our ears

The proper sequence should be :

(a) QSPR (b) PRQS
(c) PSQR (d) QSRP

4. Nations of the world

P as they are fully aware
Q are making efforts in developing
R of the danger of their not coming together
S peaceful international relations

The proper sequence should be :

(a) PRSQ (b) PSRQ
(c) QSPR (d) QPRS

5. The character of upright man

P he takes his stand upon

Q and when all else fails

R shine forth most bright in misfortune

S his integrity and his courage

The proper sequence should be :

(a) RQSP (b) SRQP

(c) RQPS (d) SPQR

6. Men of character are not only the conscience of society

P of a well-governed state

Q but also -the best motive power

R which rule the world

S for it is moral qualities, in the main,

The proper sequence should be :

(a) QPRS (b) SRQP

(c) RPSQ (d) QPSR

7. In a fitting finale to his superb performance

P deservedly drove in an Opel Astra

Q in the Coca-Cola Cup Cricket Tournament at Sharjah

R who lifted his nation up to the pinnacle of glory

S young Tendulkar

The proper sequence should be :

(a) SRPQ (b) RSPQ

(c) SRQP (d) RQSP

8. The fear that conscience would feel guilty

P or disappointing others

Q as it prevents peopie

R exerts a civilising influence

S from cheating

The proper sequence should be:

(a) RQPS (b) RQSP

(c) QSPR (d) SPQR

9. From the high balcony of my flat

P and envied their enthusiasm

Q over the heads of their companions

R as they soared high

S I had noticed the young dare-devil pilots

The proper sequence should be :

(a) RQSP (b) SRPQ

(c) RQPS (d) SPRQ

10. People

P athisdispensary

Q went to him

R of all professions

S for medicine and treatment

The proper sequence should be:

(a) QPRS (b) RPQS

(c) RQSP (d) QRSP

11. If you need help

P promptly and politely

Q ask for attendants

R to'help our customers

S who have instructions

The proper sequence should be:

(a) QSRP (b) PQRS

(c) PRQS (d) QPRS

12. Every afternoon

P the children used to go

Q from school

R and play in the Giant's garden

S as they were coming

The proper sequence should be :

(a) PQRS (b) SPRQ

(c) PSRQ (d) SQPR

13. Fool-proof security arrangements were made

P to prevent the sabotage

Q by the terrorists

R of the railway track

S by the police

The proper sequence should be :

(a) PSRQ (b) SPRQ

(c) RSPQ (d) SRPQ

14. One day when I was busy working in my office

P dressed as a monkey

Q I was startled

R tofindaman

S sitting opposite my table

The proper sequence should be :

(a) QRPS (b) QSRP

(c) SQRP (d) PSQR

15. Feeling flattered by the praise of the fox

P to the piece of cheese

Q the crow began to caw

R it held in its beak

S unmindful of what would happen

The proper sequence should be :

(a) SPRQ (b) QSRP

(c) RSPQ (d) QSPR

16. There is

P that the woman is a kitchen-maid and

Q the traditional belief

R an instrument of man's pleasure,

S a child-bearing machine

The proper sequence should be :

(a) QPRS (b) RQPS

(c) QSPR (d) RSPQ

17. The rapid endangerment and death of many minority languages

P not only among linguists and anthropologists

Q with issues of cultural identity

R is a matter of widespread concern

S but among all concerned

The proper sequence should be :

(a) PSRQ (b) RQPS

(c) RPSQ (d) QRPS

18. Violence

P even before she is born

Q and can happen throughout a woman's life

R against women

S takes many forms

The proper sequence should be :

(a) RPSQ (b) PQSR

(c) RSQP (d) SQRP

19. I saw two roads

P covered with the yellow

Q directions in a forest

R branching in two different

S leaves of autumn

The proper sequence should be :

(a) PSQR (b) PQRS

(c) RQSP (d) RQPS

20. I saw that

P but seeing my host in this mood

Q I deemed it proper to take leave

R as I had frequently done before

S it had been my intention to pass the night there

The proper sequence should be :

(a) QPSR (b) QRPS

(c) SPQR (d) SRPQ

Type II
(When first and last sentence is fixed.)

Directions. : In the following items each passage consists of six sentences. The first and the sixth sentence are given in the beginning. The middle four sentences in each have removed and jumbled up. These are labelled P, Q, R and S. You are required to find out the proper sequence of the four sentences.

1. S_1: There are numerous kinds of superstitions in different parts of the country.

S_6: A dog's howling predicts death this is a typical superstition.

P But people go on respecting it through force of blind custom.

Q Most of them have a bearing on 'luck' - good or bad.

R Superstitions usually have their origin in fear and ignorance.

S Nobody remembers now how a superstition first started in remote ages.

The proper sequence should be :

(a) QPRS

(b) RSPQ

(c) RSQP

(d) QSPR

2. S_I: Society in every country shapes itself out of its initiative.

S_6: And our Indian women are as capable of doing it as any in the world.

P No one can or ought to do this for them.

Q Our part of duty lies in imparting true education to all men and women in society.

R Women must be put in a position to solve their own problems in their own way.

S It will not be then necessary to pull down or set us anything in society by coercion.

The proper sequence should be :

(a) SRQP

(b) QRSP

(c) QSRP

(d) SRPQ

3. S_1: Many people believe that it is cruel to make use of animals for laboratory studies.

S_6: It is in view of these facts that the Government of India has banned the export of monkeys to America.

P They point out that animals too have nervous system~ like us and can feel pain.

Q These people, who have formed the Antivivisection Society, have been pleading for a more humane treatment of animals by scientists.

R Monkeys, rabbits, mice and other mammals are used in large numbers by scientists and many of them are made to suffer diseases artificially produced in them.

S We can avoid such cruelty to animals if we use alternative methods such as tissue culture, gas chromatography and chemical techniques.

The proper sequence should be :

(a) QPRS

(b) PRQS

(c) QRSP

(d) PSQR

4. S_1: A spider's web. after a shower of rain, is a very beautiful thing.

S_6: They are also feared because their bites may have unpleasant effects like a rash on the skin.

P This explains partly why spiders are thoroughly disliked.

Q But no poet has ever sung of the beauty of the spiders, for most spiders are not beautiful.

R On the contrary, most of them are rather unattractive, if not ugly.

S Poets have sung about the beauty of the spider's webs, comparing the water drops on them to ropes of pearls.

The proper sequence should be :

(a) SPQR

(b) QSRP

(c) QRSP

(d) SQRP

5. S_1: We are what our thoughts have . made us,

S_6: If good impressions prevail, the character becomes good, if bad, it becomes bad.

P And so take care of what you think.

Q Every man's character is determined by the sum total of these impressions.

R Every work we do, ew-ry thought that we think, leaves an impression on the mind-stuff

S Thoughts live; they travel far.

The proper sequence should be :

(a) SPRQ

(b) RQSP

(c) SPQR

(d) RQPS

6. S_1: The wise men laughed at Galileo for presuming to differ from the great Aristotle.

S_6: Both struck the ground together, as he had asserted that they would.

P lie then climbed to the top, carrying with him a ten-pound shot and a one-pound shot.

Q So one morning he took some students and teachers to the base of the famous Leaning Tower.

R Ba!ancing them on the edge of the tower, he let them fall together.

S But Galileo said he could prove his statement.

The proper sequence should be:

(a) SQPR
(b) QPSR
(c) PRSQ
(d) RSQP

7. S_1: Trees sustain our lives and ourplanet in a thousand practical ways.

S_6: Well, cocoa beaus and kola nuts are also tree products.

P Do you like chocolate and cola beverages?

Q Both come to us from trees.

R This morning at breakfast you might have enjoyed orange juice or a grape fruit.

S And the morning newspaper was printed on the processed wood pulp we call paper.

The proper sequence should be :

(a) SRPQ
(b) SPQR
(c) RSQP
(d) RQSP

8. S_1: A few light taps upon the pane made him turn to the window.

S_6: Snow was general all over Ireland.

P Yes, the newspapers were right.

Q It had begun to snow again.

R The time had come for him to set out on his journey westwards.

S He watched sleepily the flakes, silver and dark, falling obliquely against the lamplight.

The proper sequence should be :

(a) SQPR
(b) QSRP
(c) SRPQ
(d) QPSR

9. S_1: Closely allied to land management is the plight of the nomadic groups.

S_6: As their grazing lands are gradually being destroyed, these people move with their animals into forested areas, adding to the deforestation problem and showing how easy it is to topple the ecological balance.

P Five per cent of India's population is 34 million.

Q The statistics speak of a mere five per cent.

R It is seldom realised that a large number of eople in this country live a nomadic existence.

S But translate these figures into actual terms and they acquire a new meaning.

The proper sequence should be :

(a) RSQP

(b) PRSQ

(c) PQSR

(d) RQSP

10. S_1: Unlike surface fish, deep-sea fish feed near the bottom of the sea, on sea banks.

S_6: It is quite a big ship, and a powerful one too, as the heavy trawl net has to be dragged over the surface of the sea bank.

P A trawler hauls a large net along the seabed.

Q But today nets are used by specially designed boats called trawlers.

R There was a time when most deep-fish were aught by lines carrying baited hooks.

S These banks are rather like large platforms underneath the sea.

The proper sequence should be:

(a) SRQP

(b) PSRQ

(c) PQSR

(d) SPQR

Type III
(Difficult questions)

Directions: (Q 1 to 5): *Re arrange to form a meaningful paragraph and answers the question below it.*

(A) He was born at Porbunder in Gujarat in a religious minded family.

(B) But by rigorous self-discipline, he rose far above people around him.

(C) Mohandas Karamchand Gandhi, the father of our nation stands prominent and pre-eminent among them all.

(D) In his boyhood, Mohandas was a shy, average type of student.

(E) His father was a Diwan of a princely state and his mother a God-fearing, pious lady.

(F) He showed no promise of future greatness.

(G) The world has produced a number of great men and women from time to time.

1. Which of the following will be the SECOND sentence?
   (1) A (2) B
   (3) E (4) D (5) C
2. Which of the following will be the LAST sentence?
   (1) B (2) C
   (3) D (4) E (5) F
3. Which of the following will be the FIFTH sentence?
   (1) C (2) D
   (3) A (4) B (5) E
4. Which of the following will be the FIRST sentence ?
   (1) E (2) F
   (3) G (4) A (5) B
5. Which of the following will be the FOURTH sentence ?
   (1) D (2) C
   (3) B (4) E (5) A

Directions: (Q 6 to 10): *Re arrange to form a meaningful paragraph and answers the question below it.*

(A) In other words, floods and droughts are built into the countries monsoonal ecology.

(B) "It pours cats and dogs" they said.

(C) In the remaining 8,660 hours there is hardly any precipitation.

(D) If the rain is not caught and stored, it will be impossible to live in this country.

(E) But most of it pours down in a mere hundred hours.

(F) India gets more rain annually 1,100 mm, on an average- than any other part of the world.

(G) When the British came to India, they were struck by the amount it rained here.

6. Which of the following will be the FIRSTsentence?
   (1) G (2) A

(3) C (4) D (5) F

7. Which of the following will be the SECOND sentence?

(1) C (2) D

(3) F (4) G (5) B

8. Which of the following will be the FOURTH sentence?

(1) F (2) C

(3) E (4) F (5) D

9. Which of the following will be the FIFTH sentence?

(1) A (2) C

(3) D (4) F (5) G

10. Which of the following will be the LAST sentence?

(1) D (2) E

(3) F (4) A (5) C

***Directions* (Q 11 to 15):** *Re arrange the following and mark the answers given below each questions.*

11. A. Indian Political life has been dominated by our sentiment of opposition to alien rule.

B. Thus social and moral atmosphere is not suitable for democracy.

C. And the leaders idealised tradition.

D. Even Constitution was not the product of urge for feedom.

E. Consequently democratic aspiralions were relegated into the background.

(1) AEBCD (2) EACBE

(3) AEDCB. (4) AECBD

12. A. It is not possible to say that this is the last word.

B. Its old theories are revised and new tested.

C. Science is not definite body of knowledge.

D. And this mistaken view has led to errors.

E. On the contrary, science is continually expanding.

(1) CABIDE (2) CAEBID

(3) CADBE (4) EACDB

(5) ACBDE

13. A. He did hot believe in theoretical ideologies.

B. So we must keep them.

C. His principles mainly lay in action.

D. Gandhiji hid a way of life.

E. We gave much that suits our tradition.

(1) DACEB (2) DABEC

(3) DAECB (4) DBAEC

(5) ECIDAB

14. A. But there are omissions and commissions in planning.

B. It is true that standard has fallen in general sector.

C. In a period of expansion it is inevitable.

D. Some say that quantitative expansion is achieved at the expense of quality.

E. And the number of substandard institutions has increased.

(1) IDEBCA (2) DBECA

(3) BEDCA (4) BIDECA

(5) ACEDB

15. A. People want that racialism should be wiped out.

B. Our principles are different from our profession.

C. This is the source of main trouble.

D. There has been awakening in this matter.

E. They know that it has become irrelevant.

(1) EDCBA (2) ABCDE

(3) DCEBA (4) ACBED

VOCAB LIST

551	Iniquitous	Unfair and wicked
552	Forestall	Prevent
553	Discreet	Careful/Prudent/Cautious
554	Smidgen	Small amount or bit
555	Snob	Snooty
556	Quiver	Shake or tremble
557	Repast	A meal
558	In fine fettles	Cheerful
559	Defiance	Open refusal
560	Defiant	Openly refusing to obey
561	Hype	Publicity that exaggerates the good quality
562	Codger	Old man
563	Imbibe	To absorb
564	Sop	A thing offered to sb who is angry/ not satisfied in order to calm them
565	Frisson	Sudden strong physical feeling of excitement
566	Grubby	Dirty
567	Assail	To attack
568	Nascent	Beginning to exist
569	Muff	To miss/ Fail to achieve
570	Acclamation	Enthusiastic approval/Welcome

571	Vile	Extremely disgusting/Morally bad
572	Ditty	Song
573	Attune	Become familiar to new environment
574	Tempt	To persuade
575	Brat	Rude child
576	Swoon	To be emotionally affected
577	Forestall	Prevent
578	Dandy	A person who cares too much about his clothes/ Fine/Excellent
579	Nestle	To settle comfortably in warm place/ To hold in sheltered position
580	In-ebriate	Old fashioned/Often drunk
581	Defer	Postpone/Delay
582	Obviate	To remove
583	Arduous	Laborious/Hard
584	Down right	Complete/Total
585	Arrogate	Usurp/Claim
586	Artifice	Ruse/Trick
587	Convoke	Convene
588	Indigent	Penniless
589	Inept	Ill-timed/Having no skill
590	Loath	Unwilling
591	Assiduous	Careful
592	Dint	Using a particular method
593	Picayune	Trivial/Small
594	Cornucopia	A decorative container in the shape of an animal's horn full of fruits
595	Corroborate	Confirm
596	Scabrous	Indecent/Rude/Shocking
597	Smitten	Having become suddenly very fond of
598	Dejure	Right full
599	Parley	Meeting between two/A discussion in which enemies try to achieve piece
600	Duplicity	Deliberate

TEST 12

Words (551-600)

(1) Iniquitous
(a) Unfair & Wicked (b) Unmoved
(c) Unequal (d) Unknown.

(2) Discreet
(a) Prudent (b) Not sacred
(c) Obsolete (d) Cheerful

(3) Defiance
(a) Openly refused (b) Openly accepted
(c) Nullity (d) Neglect

(4) Grubby
(a) Clean (b) Dirty
(c) Thin (d) Trick

(5) Tempt
(a) Persuade (b) Feeling
(c) Begin (d) Try

(6) Corroborate
(a) Concern (b) Confirm
(c) Care of (d) Remove

(7) Assiduous
(a) Careless (b) Careful
(c) Delay (d) Negligent

(8) Loath
(a) Willing (b) Unwilling
(c) Delay (d) Postpone

(9) Artifice
(a) Trick (b) Sacrifice
(c) Prevent (d) Refuse

(10) Arrogate
(a) Unskilled (b) Usurp
(c) Penniless (c) Enthusiastic

(11) In-ebriate
(a) In sense (b) Often drunk
(c) Old people (d) Familiar

(12) Brat
(a) Rude child (b) Happy child
(c) Senseless (d) None

(13) Indigent

(a) Wealthy (b) Reputed
(c) Penniless (d) Miser

(14) Scabrous

(a) Shocking (b) Serene
(c) Noisy (d) Clean

(15) Defer

(a) At the earliest (b) Delay
(c) Deny (d) Attack

Match the words in column 'A' with their correct meaning in 'B'.

Column A	Column B
(1) Smidgen	(1) To remove
(2) Obviate	(2) Tremble
(3) Appendage	(3) Convene
(4) Arduous	(4) Prevent
(5) Convoke	(5) Small amount
(6) IN-ept	(6) Trivial
(7) Picayune	(7) Extremely disgusting
(8) Down	(8) Fail to achieve
(9) Forestall	(9) Become familiar to new environment
(10) Assail	(10) Beginning to exist
(11) Vile	(11) Having
(12) Nascent	(12) Complete/total
(13) Muff	(13) Laborious
(14) Attune	(14) To attack
(15) Quiver	(15) To absorb

ANSWERS (JUMBLED)
(Type I)

1. (b) 2. (a) 3. (b) 4. (c) 5. (c) 6. (d) 7. (c)
8. (b) 9. (d) 10. (c) 11. (a) 12. (a) 13. (b) 14. (a)
15. (d) 16. (a) 17. (c) 18. (c) 19. (d) 20. (d)

(Type II)

1. (b) 2. (c) 3. (a) 4. (d) 5. (b) 6. (a) 7. (d)
8. (c) 9. (d) 10. (a)

(Type III)

1. (5)	2. (1)	3. (2)	4. (3)	5. (4)	6. (5)	7. (4)
8. (3)	9. (2)	10. (1)	11. (4)	12. (2)	13. (3)	14. (2)
15. (2)						

Answer of Test 12

(1) a	(2) a	(3) a	(4) b	(5) a	(6) b	(7) b
(8) b	(9) a	(10) b	(11) b	(12) a	(13) c	(14) a
(15) b						

Match

(1) 5	(2) 15	(3) 1	(4) 13	(5) 3	(6) 11	(7) 6
(8) 12	(9) 4	(10) 114	(11) 7	(12) 10	(13) 8	(14) 9
(15) 2						

Explanation

2. What Pyschologists (Noun) say?
That Humans (Noun) have (What), an innate desire to finish what they (Humans) start. Hence sequence is RPQS.

3. The questions talks about the use of language and what is involves? So after this (P) will come. after this (R) will come as it talks about how to make noise (sound) with our speech organs and then comes the receiving other people's speeches through our ears. Hence the sequence is PRQS

5. The question talks about character of upright (honest) and courageous) man. What will be do in most difficult times? so at first place (R) will come. But when every thing fails, an upright man will take stand based upon his values like integerity and courage. Therefore the correct sequence is RQPS.

6. After 'Not only' .... 'but also' is used. So at firstplace (Q) will come. here we have two choice which start with (Q) i.e. (a) and (d). if you have understood the context then the concluding sentence would be (R). i.e. what if takes to sure the world.

8. The questions talks about the role of conscience (innervoice) which always guides humans in deciding right or wrong and also it prevents a man from cmmitting wrong things. The sentence which shows that how consciences works in any human will come at first place i.e. (R). And what it (conscience) does finally will complete the sequence i.e. it prevetns cheating or disappointing others.

9. If you have understood the sequence then the subject (I) is watching an activity of a few pilots so at 1st place (opener) (S) will come. How 'IU' reacted will come after (I) reacted will come after (S) i.e. (P) after this (R) will come as it is showing what piolots were doing i.e. they soared high. Hence the final sequence is (SPRQ)

10. For medicine and treatment one has to go to dispensary. So the concluding sentence will be (P) For opener, Since Question talks of people of all perfession therefore (R) will open the sequence. therefore the answer choice is (c).

11. If one needs help them he will call somebody. So opener will be (Q). 'who' (Pronoun) (S) has been used in place of attendents (Noun) Hence 'QS' will form a mandatory pair. This is present only in choice (a). If we match the rest of the sequence with choice (a), we find that final sequence will turn out to be correct. Hence the answer is (a).

13. 'Who made fool proof' arrangements? As these were made by police so the sequencw will start with (S). Why did they do so? To prevent (S) terrorish from doing anything wrong. So after (S), (P) will come. Therefore the answer is (b).

14. After going through all the sentence, we find that the subject (I) was startled (surprised) to find something strange, so the opener will be (Q). 'I' was started by what? i.e. to find a man who was dressed like monkey. The correct sequence is QRPS.

15. After going through the question, we find that crow was flatered by praise done by fox. And this made him to do unmindful things like cawing and crow was not able to hold the piece of cheese. So the correst sequence is (QSPR).

16. The quewstion talks about traditional belief held by the world regarding women that women are meant to do household work and to bear child. So the opener would be Q. After (Q) the sentence containing belief will come i.e. P there is only one choice (a) which has [QP] at the start. Hence the answer is (a).

17. The question talks about concern related endangerment and death of many minority languages. So the opening sentence will be R. The sentences containing 'Not only' and but also will form the mandatory pair i.e. PS. hence the answer is choice (c).

18. The question talks about the voilence against women and form of voilence shown against women. So the opener will be R for loved by S. The only choice having this is (c).

19. The questions talks about the two roads bracing in two different direction in forest covered with yellow leaves of autumn. Hence the proper sequence is RQPS.

20. Here the person (I) was interestedin spending night at host's place but mood of the host was not good so person (I) decided to take leave. Hence the sequence SRPQ.

Type 2

2. The sentence S_1 says that every country shakes itself out of its initiative so if we educate all man and women then it is not necessary to use force (coercion) so the opener will be Q. 'Then' in S shows that after educating all, it is not necessary to use force or impose anything by Coercion. 'Them' in P is used form for women in R. So RP will form mandatory pair. Also P gels well with S_6. Hence the sequence is S_1QSRPS_6.

4. Keyword 'Spiders web in S_1 can be linked with 'spider web' in S. So S will open the sequence after S_1. Poet in 'S' can be linked to poets in Q as Q is showing contradiction. 'Them (Pronoun) in R has been used for Noun (Spiders) in Q. Hence QR will form mandatory pair. This is only available in choice (d)/ The final sequence is S_1SQRPS_6.

5. Thoughs in S_1 can be linked to through in R. 'These impression' in Q is in continuation with 'impression' in R 'So' in P thus that it will come at last position (before S_6) The correct sequence is S_1RQSPS_6.

6. The question talks about wise man laughing at Gallieo as he was set to prove one scientific principle, which was against what Aristotle had found. But Galileo was determined to prove himself right and he ultimately proved himself right. After S_1 people 'S' will come as in S_1 people were laughing at Galileo but he had point to prove, his statement. After 'S', 'Q' is obvious choice as one morning he went out to prove himself. After reaching the leaning tower, he climbed to the top carrying with him ...... two articles So after 'S' Q will come. 'Them' in 'R' represents two different shots. So 'PR' will form a mandatory pair. Also 'R' Gelts well with S_6. Hence the sequence of S_1SQPRS$_6$.

7. The questions talks about the importance of trees in our lives.d As per the choice opener is either S or R but 'S' cannot open the sequence. So 'R' will open the sequence. 'Both' in 'Q' has been used for 'orange juice' or grape fruit'. So 'Q' will come after 'R'. Choclate and Cola beverges in 'P' can be linked with S_6, So before S_6 P will come. Therefore the final sequence is S_1RQSPS$_6$.

8. In this question'PQ' will form the mandatory pair. Also 'snow' in 'Q' goes with S_6. 'A few light taps' in S_1 were caused by flakes of snow in 'S'. Therefore S will open the sequence. Hence the answer choice is (c).

9. The questions talks about plight of Nomadic Group. After S_1 'R' is the obvious opener. So SP will form the mandatory pair in Transmlating these figures, it turns out to be 34 million people. Hence the answer is RQSP.

10. 'banks' in S_1 can be linked with these banks is S, so 'S' will open the sequence. After 'S' are will come as it talks about older ways of catching deep sea fish. then question talks about present way of catching deep sea fish using Trawlers. Hence the correct sequence is S_1SRQPS$_6$.

6-10. The question talks about amount of rainfalfl in India and what was the Britishers reaction when they came to India. As the topic is amount of rainfall therefore opener will be F. After this question talks about Britishers. So, G will come after F. 'They in B shows that it will come after G, as 'they' [Pronoun] is used for Noun (Britishers) Hence GB will form the mandatory pair as per Noun pronoun trick. it (pronoun) in E is used for rain (Noun) in contination of B. After 'most of it' in B, E will come as it talks about remaining time and amount of rain. A is concluding what happened in E and C. i.e. first heavy rain (flood) and then no rain (Drought) Finally at last D will come. Therefore the final sequence is FGB.ECAD.

12. These Question talks about the perception and character of science. So here the topic is science andit nature and perception in mind of people. Hence C will be opener. Since it is not definite and hence it is not last workd. So A will come, after C. On contrary and expanding are in contrast with C. So E will come immediately after A. its (pronoun) in B shows that B will come after C, as scientific theories are revised and tested (i.e. continually expanding). Finally D will conclude the sequence. Therefore the choice is 2.

13. The questions talks about Gandhiji's way of life and his idealogy. So the opener will be C. 'He' (Pronoun) in A has been used for Noun (Gandhiji), so DA will form mandatory pair. C shows that what he actually belived in. So it will come after DA. E shows the contribution by Gandhiji. 'So' in B shows that it will finally close the sequence. Hence the answer choice is 1.

Day

14

Reading Comprehension

This section is very important and plays a dominant role in all the competitive exams.

"Reading Comprehension" means reading the given text to understand it, as the word 'Comprehend' stands for 'understand'.

In quantified terms RCs forms upto 50% of English Section in most of the **entrance examinations.** Usually a few pessages are given in the test and our task is to read them carefully, understand them completely and then we have to answer a few questions based on the given passages. Before going into details of this topic, first read the following passage and attempt the questions given after the passage. The passage is as follows:

Passage

Although the number of animals in a given region may fluctuate from year to year, the fluctuations are often temporary and, over long periods, trivial. Scientists have advanced three theories of population control to account for this relative constancy.

The first theory attributes a relatively constant population to periodic climatic catastrophes that decimate populations with such frequency as to prevent them exceeding some particular limit. In the case of small organisms with short life cycles, climatic changes need not be catastrophic: normal seasonal changes in photoperiod (daily amount of sunlight), for example, can govern population growth. The theory - the density - independent view - asserts that climatic factors exert the same regulatory effect on population regardless of the number of individuals in a region.

A second theory argues that population growth is primarily density-dependent - that is, the rate of growth of a population in a region decreases as the number of animals increases. The mechanisms that manage regulation may vary. For example, as numbers increase, the food supply would probably diminish, which would increase mortality. In addition, as Lotka and Volterra have shown, predators can find prey more easily in high-density populations. Other regulators include physiological control mechanisms: for example, Christian and Davis have demonstrated how the crowding that results from a rise in numbers may bring about hormonal changes in the pituitary and adrenal glands that in turn may regulate population by lowering sexual activity and inhibiting sexual maturation. There is evidence that these effects may persist for three generations in the absence of the original provocation. One challenge for density-dependent theorist is to develop models that would allow the precise prediction of the effects of crowding.

A third theory proposed by Wynne-Edwards and termed "epideictic" argues that organisms have evolved a "code" in the form of social or epideictic behaviour displays, such as winter-roosting aggregations or group vocalizing; such codes provide organisms with information on population size in a region so that they can, if necessary, exercise reproductive restraint. However, Wynne-Edwards theory, linking animal social behaviour and population control, has been challenged, with some justification, by several studies.

Questions 1-6 refer to Passage I above

1. The primary purpose of the passage is to

1. provide examples of some of the ways in which animals exercise reproductive restraint to control their own numbers.
2. suggest that theories of population control that concentrate on the social behaviour of animals are more open to debate than are theories that do not
3. summarize a number of scientific theories that attempt to explain why animal populations do not exceed certain limits.
4. compare and contrast the density-dependent and epideictic theories of population control.

2. The challenge posed to the Wynne-Edwards theory by several studies is regarded by the author with

1. skeptical amusement
2. qualified acceptance
3. perplexed astonishment
4. complete indifference

3. It can be inferred from the passage that proponents of the density-dependent theory of population control have not yet been able to —

1. reproduce the results of the study of Christian and Davis.
2. demonstrate how predator populations are themselves regulated.
3. make sufficiently accurate predictions about the effects of crowding.
4. explain adequately why the numbers of a population can increase as the population's rate of growth decreases.

4. Which of the following, if true, would best support the density-dependent theory of population control as it is described in the passage?

1. As the number of elephants in Kaziranga (Assam) decreases, the growth rate of this population of elephants begins to increase
2. As the number of Asiatic lions in Gir Forest (Gujarat) increases, the growth rate of this population of Asiatic lions also begins to increase
3. As the number of white-backed Indian vultures in Delhi decreases, the growth rate of this population of white-backed Indian vultures also begins to decrease
4. After the number of cheetals (spotted deers) in Kanha National Park decreases, the number of predators of these Cheetals begins to increase.

5. Which of the following statements would provide the most logical continuation of the final paragraph of the passage?

1. Because the Wynne-Edwards theory is able to explain more kinds of animal behaviour than the density-dependent theory, epideictic explanations of population regulation are now widely accepted.
2. Some of these studies have, in fact, worked out a systematic and complex code of social behaviour that can regulate population size.
3. Thus Wynne-Edward's theory raises serious questions about the cc .stancy of animal population in a region.
4. The result of one study, for instance, have suggested that group vocalizing is more

often used to defend territory than to provide information about population density.

6. According to Wynne-Edwards theory as it is described in the passage, epideictic behaviour displays serve the function of —

1. attracting predators
2. regulation of sexual activity
3. locating food
4. triggering hormonal changes

Answer Key

1. 3	**2.** 1	**3.** 3	**4.** 1	**5.** 4	**6.** 2

While going through the passage, let us talk about the problems faced by you.

Some of the problems might be as follow:

(i) Length of the RC

(ii) Content of the RC

(iii) Difficult words in RC, leading to less understanding of the given RC.

(iv) Not able to focus completely

(v) Not able to understand the passage

(vi) Partial or no retention.

But most of the above stated problems are apparent except (2) and (3) and can be overcome by a little practice.

A few tips to overcome the above stated problems

(i) Start Reading English Newspaper (Editorials and Business Section)

(ii) Try to read articles/texts/passages that do not lie in your interest area.

(iii) Read anything in English which can generate interest in you for this language.

Also after going through the RC, what you feel regarding

(i) Your reading speed (time taken by you to complete the RC),

(ii) accuracy in getting correct answers (atleast 80% is expected),

(iii) retention etc.

Some of you might have been able to attempt the given passage comfortably but for most of you it was simply a tiresome exercise.

Now we shall discuss the problems which generally reduce your reading speed and can also affect the understanding of the passages. These problems are as follow:

(i) **Regression :** The cause of this problem is retention i.e. while reading you are not able to retain the passage. Now with partial retention when you start attempting questions, you start going back to the passage again and again to search for the answers. The tendency of going back to passage again and again is called **regression**. At times regression is allowed if you want to verify the answers or you know that where in the passage, the right answer is lying. To avoid regression, readers should first read the questions and then come to the passage. Doing so you will know that what to look for while reading the passage. Also while reading the questions try to retain the keywords in the given questions. So as soon as you find the keywords anywhere in the passages, mark that line or paragraph. Hence There will be no waste of time in searching for the answers as you know the locations to find the right answers.

(ii) **Fixation :** This is a problem which can slow down your reading speed and hence you will be spending more time than usual in attempting RCs. By fixation we mean that taking pause after every word you read i.e reading one word at a time. This can be avoided by developing the habbit of reading more than one word at a time. Usually we suggest you to develop the habit of reading 3-4 words at a time.

(iii) Vocalization : It means speaking the text in the RCs while reading. It can hamper your reading speed, break your concentration, and can disturb your time management in the paper. So it is better to read in mind. In order to maintain your focus and concentration Read the passages using horizontal scanning method. In this method, you can use pen pencil or your finger to scan and read the passage. Doing so your eyes and hence focus will remain on the given passage.

Now let us discuss the types of questions and a few tips to deal with them one by one.

Given below are types of questions that we usually come across in RC section in given paper. These are

(i) **Main ideaor Central idea/Primary idea/Theme based Questions :** In order to understand main theme of the passage just ask yourself a very simple question that "why the author has written this passage? What topic or issue has been taken up by the author in the passage. The answer to the question is primary idea or central theme of the passage.

(ii) **Descriptive or direct questions:** These are the easiest questions to deal with, As answer to these questions can be directly found in the given passage. They usually start will "as per the author", Accordingly to the passage" etc. So any body who has read the passage carefully will get 100% accuracy in these questions.

(iii) **Inference based questions:** Before knowing to how to answers these questions, let us first understand the meaning of the word 'inference'. An 'inference' is the conclusion about the unknown on the basis of given fact. Or it is "what can we make out or derive from the lines given in the passage? Let us understand the meaning of inference by an example. Suppose the fact or line in passage is given as "Kriti is devoting at least 10-12 hours to prepare herself for forthcoming I.A.S exams."

Now what conclusion can be drawn about Kriti on the basis of this fact or one of lines in the passage

They can be:

(a) That Kriti is hardworking ambitious, focussed, determined person

(b) That Chances of her clearing the I.A.S exam are very bright

So we are able to draw a few conclusion on the basis of given fact.

Therefore (a) and (b) can be termed as inferences.

Note: *Never try to pick the choice which is directly given in the passage to answer any inference based question. Instead we have to pick up the choice which is based on the given fact in the passage.*

(iv) **Tone based questions :** Before learning, how to answer these question let us understand the meaning of the word 'TONE'

Tone of the author or tone of passage is a way in which the author has presented or written the RC. In other words how the author is looking at the subject / topic / ideas in the passage. Let us try to understand the meaning of TONE by an example. For example if the author has written a few lines about the state of economy of India. The lines are as follow.

(a) The economy is growing at the rate of 6.7% annually. The Next Year projection 8-9%. Almost all the sectors are performing well. The unemployment rate has come down. Exports are all time high etc.

In this passage the author is prasing Indian economy. So the tone or attitude of the author is positive and laudatory (prasing)

(b) "Because of the recession in economy of America and faulty policies of U.P.A. Government, the state of economy of India is in bad shape. The rate of unemployment has increased by 10%. The inflation is all time high. The middle class and the poor have been hit hard. F.D.I is low. The stock market is showing bear run. Economy is likely to collapse.

Now in the above passage the author has listed a few of shortcoming in the Economy of India. He has also given facts to prove his points. The attitude of the author is negative. He is also criticising the govt. So Tones could be

(i) opprobrium (harsh criticism)

(ii) bitter or acrimonious

(iii) negative

(iv) pessimistic

So it is hoped that now you have got the fair idea about the TONE of the passage or attitude of the author. Listed below are a few tones and their implied meaning.

(a) **Didactic :** When the author passage is trying to instruct on any topic.

(b) **Sanguine :** When author is very hopeful about the subject in the passage.

(c) **Pedantic :** When the author is focusing on very very minute things, or on less significant things. Author is worried about normal things / ideas and least bothered about the main aspects related to topic. He is repeating the ideas.

(d) **Rhetoric :** Mere repetition of ideas. Impressive vocabulary used while writing or speaking but generally it is of no use.

(e) **Sardonic :** Making mockery of the subject.

(f) **Pedagogic :** When author has given relevant ideas about the subject. He is talking to the point.

(g) **Factual or informative :** Author tries to inform the reader on any topic. To prove his point, he has also given the facts.

(h) **Jocular :** The author has presented the topic in a very humours way.

(i) **Conjectural :** Author does not know much about the subject so he is just making guesses.

(j) **Critical :** When the author has given positive as well as negative of any subject.

Note: *In order to find out the tone or attitude of the author, you have to read the entire passage. Do not try to base your answer on just a few lines or any particular line or any one of the paragraph.*

(vi) Vocabulary based or based on any line / phrase / idiom in the passage: In these types of questions, either antonyms or synonyms of any specific word from the passage is asked. Sometimes contextual meaning of any ideom/phrase is asked. To answer these questions one should have good vocabulary.

(vii) Title based: This is to be answered keeping the nature of the content of the RC. In the title should be short, catchy and should be able to capture the assence of the passage. Generally it is of 2 or 3 words.

Now for your practice, three types of passages based on the length and difficulty levels have been given below. You have to attempt these passages and answer the questions given at the end of the passages, using the tricks and tips given above.

TYPE I
(Easier paragraphs)

Directions : *Read the following passages carefully and answers the questions given below each passage.*

PASSAGE I

The postmaster's salary was small. He had to cook his own meals, which he used to share with Ratan, an orphan girl of the village, who did odd jobs for him.

When in the evening, the postmaster would light his little lamp, and call out 'Ratan', Ratan would sit outside waiting for this call, and, instead of coming in at once, would reply, 'Did you call me, Sir" ?

'What are you doing'? the postmaster would ask.

I must go and light the kitchen fire', she would reply.

And the postmaster would say: 'Oh, let the kitchen fire wait for a while: light me my pipe first'.

1. The postmaster had to cook his own meals because
- (a) he enjoyed cooking.
- (b) he cultivated this habit from his childhood.
- (c) his salary was small.
- (d) there was no hotel nearb!y.

2. Ratan was the name of
- (a) the postmaster's daughter.
- (b) the postmaster's neighbour.
- (c) the postmaster's cousin.
- (d) the orphan girl who lived with the postmaster.

3. When the lamp was lit, in the evening the ostmaster would call Ratan
- (a) to help her cooking.
- (b) to light his pipe.
- (c) to fetch a pot of water.
- (d) to gossip.

PASSAGE II

If you are caught in an open field, and see the flash of lightning and hear the sound of thunder at practically the same instant, take precautions immediately. Throw away any metallic object you may have. Lie flat on the ground. Do not try to run for shelter until the electrical disturbances have subsided entirely. Remember that poor shelter is worse than none. The big tree standing alone will keep the rain off you, but may draw lightning towards it. If a thunder storm begins when you are swimming or out in a boat, head for the shore at once. There is an old fable that lightning never strikes open water. Many bathers who relied on that belief have lost their lives. Mostly those struck by lightning are iikeiy to be farmers, holiday makers, fishermen or golfers.

4. While sitting in an open field, if one hears the sound of thunder and sees the flash of lightning at the same instant, one should immediately

(a) run for shelter.
(b) grasp a metallic object.
(c) jump into water.
(d) lie flat on the ground.

5. If a thunderstorm begins when one is out in a boat, one should

(a) row fast.
(b) leave the boat.
(c) reach the shore.
(d) remain where one is.

6. What the old fable says about lightning is

(a) wrong.
(b) right.
(c) heresy.
(d) unscientific.

7. Persons most likely to be struck by lightning are those who

(a) go swimming.
(b) walk in the streets.
(c) work indoors.
(d) spend their time outdoors.

8. If there is a flash of lightning in the sky, a tree provides

(a) a poor shelter.
(b) an adequate shelter.
(c) no shelter at all.
(d) a dangerous shelter.

PASSAGE III

Worry is a state of mind based upon fear. It works slowly, but persistently. It is crafty and subtle. Step by step it digs itself in until it paralyses one's reasoning faculty, destroys self-confidence and initiative. Worry is a form of sustained fear caused by indecision; therefore it is a state of mind which can be controlled.

9. The writer's conclusion is that worry

(a) is based upon fear.
(b) can be controlled.
(c) is a form of sustained fear.
(d) works slowly.

10. Worry is a subtle agent that

(a) cripples one's capacity to think.
(b) sustains fear.
(c) leads to indecision.
(d) leads to unhappiness.

11. Worry is ultimately caused by
- (a) sustained fear.
- (b) loss of self-confidence.
- (c) loss of initiative.
- (d) indecision.

12. When the author says that worry destroys 'initiative', he means that it
- (a) destroys marl's strength.
- (b) kills the joy in him.
- (c) kills his capacity to see what is necessary.
- (d) makes him fearful.

13. In this passage the author
- (a) advises us to cast off fear from our minds.
- (b) advises us to be on our guard against worry.
- (c) tells us how to develop selfconfidence.
- (d) gives us useful information about worry.

PASSAGE IV

The dabbawallahs are partly a by-product of Mumbai's overcrowding. There was a time when many men could get home to lunch, but those more comfortable days ended as the city grew. But the conservatism of married men being well-known, they still wanted home-made lunch. An Indian loves his lunch as much as anybody, and feels that only his wife can guarantee the quality and the quantity he requires, that restaurant food is expensive, of poorer quality and is served in meagre portions.

14. According to the author, the dabbawallahs
- (a) are responsible for the overcrowding of Mumbai.
- (b) often create a lot of problems for the city.
- (c) have come mostly from rural areas.
- (d) came into existence as a consequence of Mumbai's overcrowding.

15. The past was more comfortable for the people of Mumbai because
- (a) many of them were rich and could a afford good food.
- (b) they could bring home-made food for lunch.
- (c) many of them could go home to lunch.
- (d) they could eat thier lunch outside.

16. Which of the following best describes the author's attitude to the dabbawallahs ?
- (a) Objective
- (b) Enthusiastic
- (c) Appreciative
- (d) Critical.

PASSAGE V

It seems to me that we cannot learn too early in life to respect the privacy of the individual. When my daughter began to write her memoirs, at the age of four, I decided that she must have a place to keep them, if only a section of a bureau drawer or as it happened, a box with a key. I remembered the agonies of my own childhood when my sister discovered I was writing poems and began to tease me by chanting them in public. I tried desperately to hide the notebook of poems. No place in house seemed secure. For a while I carried it around in the right leg of my trousers until the elastic broke and the book fell out at the feet of my enemy.

17. The author arranged a safe place to keep the memoirs written by her daughter because she

(a) thought that the memoirs would be lost otherwise.

(b) recognised the need for respecting the privacy of her daughter.

(c) decided that the memoirs should not be read by strangers.

(d) knew that the memoirs could fetch a lot of money.

18. The author's sister caused great agony to her by

(a) openly reciting the poems written by the author.

(b) discovering that the author was in the habit of writing poems.

(c) teasing her for the mistakes found in the poems.

(d) warning the author against writing any more poems.

19. No place in the house seemed secure enough to keep the notebook of poems; so the author

(a) kept it in a bureau drawer.

(b) kept it in a box with a key.

(c) carried it inside the -trousers.

(d) threw it at the feet of the enemy.

TYPE II
(Averge but lengthy)

These are a bit tougher and the lengthier than the simple one. A few of these types of comprehension are given below for your practice.

PASSAGE I

Directions : *Read the following passage to answer the given questions. Some words have been printed in bold to help you to locate them-while answering some of the questions.*

Employment exchanges - one of the surviving bastions of babudom - face the prospect of becoming irrelevant in an era of reform. Even in the heart of the nation's capital, the premises are often dilapidated structures with dirty passages and manned by surly staff. Not surprisingly, job seekers hardly throng these exchanges. Paradoxically, when jobs are getting scarce due to pressure of liberalisation, job seekers are spurning an institution intended to help them secure placembnts. The reasons are simple enough. Employment exchanges still concentrate on government and public sector placements which are fast losing ground in the labour market. For most government jobs, the eligibility criterion is still registration with the employment exchanges. But what is the use of going through the formalities of registration when government jobs themselves are dwindling? The placement effected by all the 939-odd exchanges in the country in 2001 was of the order of 1.69 lakh against annual registration levels of 60 lakh. As there are too few jobs when compared to the number of job seekers, the accumulated backlog of registrations is close to 4.16 crore. The latter of course doesn't indicate umemployment levels as those registered with the employment exchanges are not necessarily unemployed.

How can the employment exchanges be revamped ?The thinking in the Union labour ministry is to transform them into employment promotion and guidance centres.The plan includes modernisation, changing the mindset of the staff and making them into an effective instrument for monitoring and coordinating various employment generation schemes. This objective calls for developing a better database on the fast changing employment situation with a comprehensive coverage of new economic establishments. For instance, the various economic censuses are an important source of information on the changing employment profile of say, the nation's capital. Far from being a bureaucrat dominated city, Delhi over the years has become more of an industrial metropolis. According to the fourth economic census, manufacturing accounted for 40 per cent of jobs in the capital. The employment exchanges in the capital thus have their work cut out -, notably, to shift the focus away from government and public sector jobs more towards placements in the private sector, especially in manufacturing and services including the burgeoning retail trade sector. By doing so, they will better reflect the imperatives of economic reform and remain relevant in today's times.

20. Choose the word that is opposite in meaning of the word "spurning" as used in the passage.

(a) thronging (b) evaluating

(c) criticizing (d) following

(e) rejecting

21. Which of the following revamped role can be entrusted to employment exchanges ?

(a) Conducting economic surveys

(b) To conduct vocational training programme for the unemployed

(c) To modernize registration, process through the internet

(d) To reduce the number of exchanges

(e) None of these

22. What can be inferred about the employment exchanges outside Delhi ?

(a) The registration in them would be much less

(b) Their conditions will be worse 13) Their condition will be betterd. They focus more on manufacturing sector

(e) None of these

23. Choose the word that is same in meaning as "Imperatives" as used in the passage.

(a) importance (b) implication

(c) urgency (d) indication

(e) authority

24. Choose the word that is same in meaning as the word "secure" as used in the passage.

(a) fasten (b) safe
(c) obtain (d) re-assure
(e) lock

25. Choose the word that is opposite in meaning of the word "burgeoning" as used in the passage.

(a) flourishing (b) loss-making
(c) expanding (d) distressing
(e) declining

PASSAGE II

Directions : Read the following passage carefully and answer the questions given below it. Crtain words in the passage are printed in bold to help ,you to locate them easily while answering some of the questions.

The University Grants Commission's directive college and university lecturers to spend a minimum of 22 hours a week in direct teaching is the product of budgetary cutbacks rather than pedagogic wisdom. It may seem odd, at first blush, that teachers should protest about teaching a mere 22 hours. However, if one considers the amount of time academics require to prepare lectures of good quality as well as the time they need to spend doing research-it is clear that most conscientious teachers work more than 40 hours a week. In university systems around the world, lecturers rarely spend more than 12 to 15 hours in direct teaching activities a week. The average college lecturer in India does not have any office space. If computers are available, internet connectively is Unlikely. Libraries are poorly stocked. Now the UGC says universities must implement a complete freeze on all permanent recruitment, abolish all posts which have been vacant for more than a year, and cut staff strength by 10 per cent. And it is in order to ensure that these cutbacks do not affect the quantum of teaching that existing lecturers are being asked to work longer. Obviously, the quality of teaching-and academic work in general-woll decline. While it is true that some college teachers do not take their classes regularly, the UGC and the Institutions concerned must find a proper way to hold them accountable. An absentee teacher wilil continue to play truant even if the number of hours he is required to teach goes up.

All of us are well aware of the unsound state that the Indian higher education system is in today. Thanks to years of sustained financial neglect, most Indian universities and colleges do no research worth the name. Even as the number of students entering colleges has increased dramatically, public investment in higher education has actually declined in relative terms. Between 1985 and 1997, when public expenditure on higher education as a percentage of outlays on all levels of education grew by more than 60 per cent in Malaysia and 20 per cent in Thailand, India showed a decline of more than 10 per cent. Thoughout the world, the number of teachers in higher education per million population grow by more than 10 per cent in the same period; in India it fell by one per cent. Instead of transterring the burden of government apathy on to the backs of the teachers, the UGC should insist that the needs of the country's university system are adequately catered for.

26. Why does the UGC want to increase the direct teaching hours of university teachers ?

(a) UGC feels that the duration of contact between teacher and the taught should be more

(b) UGC wants teachers to spend more time in their departments

(c) UGC wants teachers to devote some time to improve university administration
(d) UGC does not have money to I appoint additional teachers
(e) None of these

27. Which of the following is the rea son for the sorry state of affairs of the Indian Universities as mentioned in the passage?
(a) The poor quality of teachers
(b) Involvement of teachers in extra-curricular- activities
(c) Politics within and outside the departments
(d) Heavy burden of teaching hours on the teachers
(e) Not getting enough financial assistance

28. Which of the following statements is/are TRUE in the context of the passage ?
(A) Most colleges do not carry out research worth the name.
(B) UGC wants lecturers to spend minimum 22 hours a week in direct teaching.
(C) Indian higher education system is in unsound state.
(a) Only (A)and (C) (b) All (A), (B) and (C)
(c) Only (C) (d) Only (B)
(e) Only (B) and (C)

29. Besides direct teaching University teachers spend considerable time in/on ....
(a) administrative activities such as admissions
(b) supervising examinations and correction of answer papers
(c) carrying out research in the area of their interest
(d) maintaining research equipment and libraries
(e) developing liaison with the user organizations

30. Which of the following statements is NOT TRUE in the context of the passage.
(a) UGC wants teachers to spend minimum 40 hours in a week in teaching
(b) Some college teachers do not engage their classes regularly
(c) The average college teacher in India does not have any office space
(d) UGC wants universities to abolish all posts which have been vacant for more than a year
(e) All are true

31. Between 1985-1997, the number of teachers in higher education per million population, in India ....
(a) Increased by 60% (b) Increased by 20%
(c) decreased by 22% (d) decreased by 10%
(e) decreased by 1%

32. Which of the following statements is NOT TRUE in the context of the passage ?
(a) Indian universities are financially neglected
(b) All over the world, the university lecturers hardly spend more than 12 to 15 hours a week in direct teaching
(c) Indian Universities are asked to reduce staff trength by 10%
(d) Public investment in higher education has increased in India
(e) Malaysia spends more money on education than Thailand

33. Choose the word which is SIMILAR in meaning as the word 'freeze' as used in the passage.

(a) cold
(b) halt
(c) decay
(d) control
(e) power

PASSAGE III

Directions : Read the following passage carefully and answer the questions given below it. Certain words/ phrases are printed in bold to help you locate them while answering some of the questions.

Since July 1999, the Government of India has effectively put the liberalisation policy into practice.The drastic steps even include some administrative reforms for pruning the Government agencies. Last year Japanese business circles represented by the Shikawa mission called attention of their Indian counterparts to what they considered to be the major impediments in India. However, thanks to the almost revolutionary reforms put into effect by the Indian Government, those impediments either have been removed or now are on their way out. This development gives a new hope for the future of economic cooperation between two countries. At the same time, It should be borne in mind that there is a stiff competition with other countries, notably China and South-East Asian countries, in this regard. The success stories of ASEAN countries welcoming Japanese investments with adequate infrastructure are already known in India but it may be useful it further studies of Japanese joint-ventures in ASEAN countries be made by Indian business circles. The coastal areas of China have initiated a very active campaign to welcome foreign economic participation.

Beyond our bilateral relationship India's more active participation in global economy is needed. India certainly deserves afar bigger share of world trade considering its vast resources. It is strongly hoped that the Indian Government's recently initiated afford of enlarging its export market would bear fruit.

India has steadfastly maintained its parliamentary democracy since independence. Considering its size, its population and its internal complexity, the overall maintenance of national integrity and political stability under parliamentary democracy is remarkable indeed. Here lies the base for the status of India in the world. By effectively implementing its economic reform with the support of public opinion, this democratic polity of India has again demonstrated its viability and resilience. At the same time, it gives hope and inspiration to the whole world which faces the difficult problem of North-South confrontation.

34. How did the Indian Governmentreact to the hurdles in the way of bilateral trade between India and Japan?

(a) The Government, in principle, agreed for removal of these hurdles.
(b) Bureaucracy succeeded in maintaining a status-quo.
(c) Government thought it was against liberalisation policy
(d) The Japanese delegation could not forcefully argue their case.
(e) It failed to remove these hurdles.

35. Which of the following is TRUE about the author's view regarding India's participation in world trade ?

(a) India should actively contribute in a big way as it had tremendous resources.
(b) India sharing global economy has already been very fast and beyond its resources.

(c) Indian should refrain from making efforts in enlarging its export market.

(d) India needs to strengthen its democracy first.

(e) None of these.

36. The Ishikawa Mission during its visit to India emphasized on---

(a) future economic cooperation between Japan and India.

(b) need for removing policy and/ or implementation hurdles.

(c) need for a stiff competition.

(d) striking down revolutionary reforms.

(e) None of these.

37. On India's implemention Liberalisation Policy, the author seems to be

(a) unreasonably critical

(b) sarcastic

(c) appreciative

(d) unconvinced about its effectiveness

(e) None of these

38. What is the result of Japanese investments in ASEAN nations?

(a) It could not gather momentum for want of infrastructure.

(b) The experiment failed because of stiff competition from other countries.

(c) China and South-East Asian countries objected to Japanese investments.

(d) The passage does riot provide complete information.

(e) None of these.

39. Which of the following statements is TRUE in the context of the passage ?

(A) India's successful experi-ment of economic reform has become an inspiration to the world.

(B) Size, population and internal complexity of our country are the barriers in the way of attaining national integrity and political stability.

(C) Few Government agencies were not in favour of liberalisation policy in the beginning.

(a) A only (b) B only

(c) C only (d) All the three

(e) None of these

40. The author feels that India has a better status in the world market because of its ----

(a) success in political stability and national integration in democratic set-up

(b) vast population

(c) giant size

(d) effective bilateral relationship with other countries

(e) foreign economic participation 83. The author seems to appreciate India's national integrity and political stability particularly in view of which of the following ?

41. It can be inferred from the content of the passage that the author is a/an ----

(a) Political analyst (b) Japanese bureaucrat

(c) Economist (d) Japanese politician

(e) Indian Prime Minister

TYPE III
Tough Passages

***Directions** : Read the following passage carefully and answer the questions given below it.*

PASSAGE I

Investing in India is tantamount to investing in democracy. Around 900 million people live together as one political entity under conditions of freedom. It is not surprising that India is badly governed. What is surprising is that it has been possible to govern this mosaic of humanity at all, as a liberal democracy.

Professor Rostow of the Texas University regards the survival of Indian democracy as the most important phenomenon of the post-war era. That survival ought to be a matter of the most vital concern to you; after all, you were our mentor and we turned out to be your greatest pupil-at least in size! To adapt the words of Cecil Rhodes, investing in India would be philanthropy plus twenty-five per cent. To our British friends we say-we have opened doors with hope: you can ensure that we do not close them with despair. This is a critical moment in our history : you can -make-it a harbinger of good times to come. The dynamic and far-seeing section of our society is determined to make India the Mexico of Asia.

Our domestic market is continental in size. The population with buying power is at least 250 million out of the total 900 million. Among the countries of the Third World, India is a safe bet.

Not less than 6,500 companies are listed on the 21 recognised stock exchanges of India. We are next only to the USA which had 6,742 domestic companies listed at the end of 1991. The number of our shareholders is over 14 million. India has now become a major player in the emergingmarkets of the world, second only to Taiwan, Korea and Mexico, in respect of both turnover and market capitalisation.

Again, the high appreciation of most foreign currencies against the Indian rupee offers an excellent opportunity of using India as a manufacturing base.

Giant multinational companies are engaged in worldwide competition for the most scarce resource of all-talent. India has never been charged with an inadequate supply of this resource.

It would be futile to pretend that there are no drawbacks or shortcomings, The New Industrial Polciy does not go far enough. The Government has measured out liberaliscition with coffee spoons Several promises have yet to be implemented. The Indian governmental machinery may be likened to some prehistoric monster; incapable of intelligently controlling itself. This is not because the Government lacks intelligent and capable officials, but because it is so organised that managerial direction on all-India outlook is extremely difficult. The general impression, not very wrong, is that India has one of the most obdurate bureaucraciQs the free world has ever known. But a strong and skillful rider can control an unruly horse. Fotunately, the horse has been in good measure tamed and is less unruly than before

It is highly probable that the sensible New Policy-the one ray of hope for India's fast economic growth-will be implemented in larger doses by the present government and by any government which succeeds it. The change seems irreversible: fruitful egalitarianism has been irrevocably installed inplace of sterile socialism. This is our pledge to the civilised world and the foundation of our belief in a promising future.

42. According to the author, making India the Mexico of Asia means
(a) bringing in more and more Mexicans to India.
(b) encouraging Indians to adopt Mexican life style.
(c) making Indian economy as developed as that of Mexico.
(d) encouraging more and more imports from Mexico.
(e) exporting more and more gocds to Mexico.

43. The author appeals to the
(a) Indian investors to help India realise its dream.
(b) Indian industrialists to seek the help of foreigners.
(c) Indian politicians to amend the constitution to attract foreign investors.
(d) Foreign investors to make profit of not more than 25 per cent.
(e) Foreign investors to help India realise its dream.

44. The author seems to be
(a) pessimistic about the foreign investors' role.
(b) pessimistic about the attitude of the Indian Government.
(c) optimistic about success of [ndian industrialists in the open competition.
(d) optimistic about the oositive role of foreign investors in India.
(e) indifferent to the imminent market fluctuations.

45. According to the author, the credit of survival of Indian democracy goes to
(a) Professor Rostow of Texas University.
(b) the strong bond which is built in democracy,
(c) the situation in the post-war era.
(d) the foreign investors in the country.
(e) None of these.

46. Cecil Rhodes thinks that investing in India would be
(a) a philanthropy plus a loss of 25 per cent.
(b) a service to mankind with a 25 per cent profit.
(c) a service to mankind with a loss of 25 per cent.
(d) a service to mankind with a 75 per cent loss.
(e) None of these

47. The above passage is most probably addressed to
(a) Indian industrialists to invest in the local industries.
(b) Indian industrialists to encourage them to invest in foreign countries.
(c) Foreign investors to encourage them to invest in India.
(d) foreign investors to give loans to Indian companies.
(e) people who have faith in democracy but can't afford any investment.

48. The basis for the author to claim that "India is a safe bet" is
(a) its vast population of 900 million.
(b) its large number of people with buying power.
(c) its strategic position among the Third World Countries.
(d) large number of stock exchanges
(e) its rank among the global countries.

49. The author of the passage seems to believe that the governance of India is

(a) not of the level as it should have been,

(b) too bad for anybody to improve.

(c) Indians do not have faith in liberal democracy.

(d) a matter of utmost surprise to all the foreigners.

(e) not concerned about the economic development of the country.

50. The author thinks that the high appreciation of foreign currencies against the Indian rupee provides

(a) good opportunities for foreigners to export to India.

(b) adverse atmosphere for using India as a manufacturing base.

(c) excellent opportunities for Indian Companies to develop.

(d) good opportunities for Indians to manufacture goods locally.

(d) None of these.

51. Which of the following words is most nearly the SAME in meaning as the world UNRULY, as used in the passage ?

(a) Disorderly (b) Untamed

(c) Controllable (d) Incapable

(e) Amicable

Directions: Each passage In this sectlon followed by questions based on its contents. Read the passages carefully and then answer the questions given below them by choosing the best answer to each questions. Answer the questions on the basis of what is stated or implied in the passages.

PASSAGE II

Academics, activists and the average person-in-the-street seem to have joined together in an outcry against the role given to women in panchayats. Their participation is increasingly being described a rule by 'proxy'. According to the dictionary, this means one person authorising another to act on his/her behalf. The tern, bears insinuations of total passivity on the part of women representatives. Needless to say, this is a sweeping stateme~it about the women who have become elected representatives under the 73rd Amendment and various State Acts. The number of those serving as members and chairpersons of rural councils at various levels is about one million.

Both in the media and elsewhere there is a backlash against women's participation as elected representatives in the panchayat system The allegation of 'proxy' rule follows from the perception that it is the men who are ruling through their wives who are mere mouthpieces. It is true that women do get advice and help from their husbands. But does this in itself constitute 'proxy' rule ? What about the kitchen cabinets of powerful politicians? What about the close kinship and other networks thot leaders here and abroad draw upon for support? Even men politicians function in the context of patrilineal systems where the heads of households and clans exercise significant authority over members. Party policies are another example of their responses as representatives being influenced by others. Why is it that no one calls them I proxy' representatives on these grounds ?

Another means of disparaging newlyelected women representatives is through mischievous allegations regarding sexual conduct. As we do our inter-State study of women and the Panchayat System for the Ministry of Rural Development, we are confronted in case after case with insinvations of women representatives being of loose character. It is alleged but rarely with evidence, that they have an improper 'relationship' with some local official or a friend. It is l.markable here, that male political representatives can have multiple wives, keep mistresses and get away with it. But if women elected to some position happens to be articulate and socially mobile and goes about alone, her morality becomes instantly (even deliberately) suspect. On the other hand if she behaves more acceptably by having her husband accompany her, he is seen as the parti-member or patipradhan who has the real power. Clearly, women are caught in a double bind, between the opposition to their independence and the opposite charge of subservience.

None of the many critics seem to notice that it might be the woman representative who is actually helping her husband : that he might be receiving support and benefit because of her political activity. Further we have evidence of minor but significant shifts in the sexual division of labour, and also of enhancement of family prestige through the involvement of women. These are near invisible yet, but their eventual effect on patriarchal society will be drastic.

52. The central point of information given in para I is that women's participation in panchayats

(a) has reached impressively high levels.

(b) shows that 'proxy' rule can be implemented successfully in India.

(c) is being widely criticised today.

(d) carries insinuations of total passivity on the part of the electorate.

(e) has led to an outcry against diluting the provisions of the 73rd Amendment.

53. Describing women's role in governance as 'rule by proxy' amounts to saying that

(a) rural elections are rigged.

(b) rural voters are still being manipulated through vote banks.

(c) the male dominated style of politics is being replaced by the women's style.

(d) husbands rather than the women representatives have the real power.

(e) women being wives and mothers are better representatives of the people than full time men politicians.

54. In para 2, writer discusses the idea of proxy govern-ance and points out that

(a) all elected representatives function as proxies for the people they represent and whose influence they value.

(b) the influence of party policies, pressCres from clan or caste groups which operates on individuals in real politics is no different from that of husbands on women 'representatives'.

(c) it is unfair to call the effective functioning of a group of women representatives a kitchen cabinet since men in politics also form pressure groups and cliques.

(d) the dictionary meaning of 'proxy' does not cover the wide range of indirect controls that actually exists in practical politics.

(e) most political parties support women's participation in panchayats but they give the highest priority to party policies and discipline.

55. In para 3 the main item of information presented is that

(a) women in rural politics are widely accused of sexual misconduct.

(b) the breakdown of traditional values has led to immorality among both men and women.

(c) the negative side of women entering politics is that men can be accused of having multiple wives or mistresses.

(d) Articulate and socially mobile urban women are still suspect in rural contexts

(e) In a majority of cases women representatives have to be accompanied by their husbands when they leave their neighbourhood for political work.

56. The position of the writers regarding the popular attitude towards women in rural politics is

(a) sympathetic.

(b) critical.

(c) a balanced consensus position.

(d) based on a technical interpretation of the legis-lation.

(e) based on the narrow dictionary meaning of 'proxy'.

57. The writers feel that the role to be played by elected women representatives is such that

(a) most positions are being cornered by urbanised and socially mobile women.

(b) intra-family tensions are more or less unavoidable.

(c) those who can manipulate the proxy system can get away with immorality.

(d) a certain degree of independence and articulateness is needed to do the iob well.

(e) instant and deliberate action against those who are suspected of immorality is needed though difficult to implement.

58. What observers of women in rural politics do not pay sufficient attention to the position of men is

(a) the extent to which male relatives support women socially.

(b) the increasing rate of trickling down of development funds to intended recipients.

(c) the need for more vigilant participation by women to prevent a few from misusing their position to favour their husbands.

(d) the implications for social structure in the subtle changes in the sexual division of labour.

(e) the possibility that husbands in many cases are actually benefiting from this involvement of wives.

59. The 'double bind" referred to in para 3 arises from the

(a) need for women to balance the time and energy needed for public and private affairs.

(b) the conflict between the family role and political role when husband and wife are both elected members.

(c) criticism that is directed against their independence and against their acting conventionally.

(d) the idealistic desire to be honest and pressure to join the existing web of corruption in politics.

(e) the need to encourage women to participate in politics set against the importance of keeping out persons with low morals.

60. Women's political activity leads to changes in the division of labour, in family prestige, etc. These effects

(a) are only subtle and short-term negative features which will disappear soon.

(b) though small are deep rooted and will have a significant impact on society.

(c) are still only subtle tendencies that might not progress for a very long time.

(d) are very likely to lead to another round of backlash to protect the position of women.

(e) show that the 73rd Amendment will become truly effective only after a long struggle by women.

61. The word outcry, in the context of the passage, means

(a) victimisation (b) neutralisation

(c) opposition (d) publicity

(e) scrutiny

VOCAB LIST

601	Reciprocate	To give & receive
602	Xenophobia	Extreme dislike between people of different countries
603	Tangible	Exact/Real that can be felt by touch
604	Plagiarize	Pirate
605	Plaintive	Sorrowful
606	Plebeian	Vulgar/Insulting word
607	Aught	Anything
608	Augur	Foretell
609	Avocation	Hobby/Pastime/Vocation
610	Plethora	Superabundance
611	Poignant feeling	Painful
612	Avow	Admit openly
613	Poltroon	Coward
614	Alacrity	Quickness
615	Alfresco	In open air
616	Cursory	Not through
617	Potentate	Monarch
618	Flout	To disobey a law
619	Foible	Weak points
620	Ferment	Political or Social excitement
621	Brusque	Blunt/Rude
622	Expedite	To dispatch/To free from obstacles

623	Expiate	Atone for
624	Gibberish	Rapid & foolish talk
625	Chicanery	Deceit/Trickery
626	Glean	Collect/To gather
627	Glut	Oversupply/Overload the stomach with food
628	Burnish	Polish by rubbing
629	Cohere	Adhere
630	Coiffure	Style of dressing hair
631	Inordinate	Beyond normal limit
632	Expunge	Remove/Wipe out
633	Expurgate	Censor/To cleanse/To purify
634	Prosaic	Common/Dull/Uninteresting
635	Proscribe	Prohibit
636	Indomitable	Stubborn/Not yielding
637	Industrious	Active/Laborious
638	Inept	Absurd/Unsuitable/Out of place
639	Indolent	Slothful/lazy
640	Herculean	Needing very great strength/efforts
641	Inclement	Severe/Cold/Stormy
642	Incongruous	Improper/Unsuitable
643	Inconsequential	Trivial/Unimportant
644	Replete	Well stocked/Fully filled
645	Charlatan	Fake/A quack
646	Chide	Scold/Rebuke
647	Descry	Perceive/To detect
648	Discern	To judge
649	Desecrate	To deprive of sacred character
650	Consecrate	Sacred/To sanctify

REVISE THE VOCAB

BREAK FOR WORDS REVISION

TEST 13
Words (601-650)

(1) Reciprocate
(a) Opposite (b) To give & receive
(c) Adverse (d) Reverse.

(2) Aught
(a) Nothing (b) All
(c) Many (d) Anything

(3) Potentate
(a) Beggar (b) Monarch
(c) Rich (d) Miser

(4) Avow
(a) Rap publicly (b) Admit openly
(c) Refuse only (d) None

(5) Brusque
(a) Blunt/Rude (b) Soft/Clean
(c) Remove/Wipe out (d) Censor/purity

(6) Industrious
(a) Helpful (b) Laborious
(c) Slothful (d) Absurd

(7) Indolent
(a) Lazy (b) Clever
(c) Calamity (d) Clam

(8) Inclement
(a) Several (b) Severe
(c) Calamity (d) Clam

(9) Replete
(a) Well stocked (b) Empty
(c) Open (d) Closed

(10) Charlatan
(a) Fake (b) Lamp
(c) Rub & Clean (d) To purify

(11) Discern
(a) To judge (b) To detect
(c) To polish (d) To control

(12) Cohere
(a) Collect (b) Remove
(c) Adhere (d) Wipe out

(13) Consecrate
(a) Sacred (b) Not sacred
(c) Contrasting (d) Tear apart

(14) Chide
(a) Scold (b) Little child
(c) Pretty child (d) Stormy

(15) Incongruous
(a) Improper (b) Proper
(c) Not to be concealed (d) Unsuitable

Match the words in column 'A' with their correct meaning in 'B'.

Column A	Column B
(1) Augur	(1) Deceit
(2) Alacrity	(2) Attune for
(3) Chicanery	(3) Needing very great strength
(4) Glut	(4) Prohibit
(5) Expurgate	(5) Coward
(6) Proscribe	(6) Foretell
(7) Herculean	(7) Political or social excitement
(8) Indomitable	(8) Together
(9) Expunge	(9) Quickness
(10) Alfresco	(10) Weak point
(11) Gibberish	(11) Foolish talk
(12) Glean	(12) In open air
(13) Foible	(13) Stubborn
(14) Ferment	(14) Wipe out
(15) Poltroon	(15) Oversupply

Answers : (Comprehension)

1. (c) 2. (d) 3. (b) 4. (d) 5. (c) 6. (a) 7. (a)
8. (d) 9. (a) 10. (a) 11. (d) 12. (c) 13. (a) 14. (d)
15. (c) 16. (a) 17. (b) 18. (a) 19. (c) 20. (a) 21. (a)
22. (b) 23. (b) 24. (c) 25. (e) 26. (e) 27. (e) 28. (b)
29. (a) 30. (a) 31. (e) 32. (d) 33. (b) 34. (a) 35. (a)
36. (b) 37. (c) 38. (d) 39. (a) 40. (a) 41. (a) 42. (c)
43. (e) 44. (b) 45. (e) 46. (b) 47. (c) 48. (a) 49. (a)
50. (e) 51. (a) 52. (c) 53. (d) 54. (b) 55. (a) 56. (e)
57. (d) 58. (e) 59. (c) 60. (b) 61. (c)

Answer of Test 13

(1) b (2) d (3) b (4) b (5) a (6) b (7) a
(8) b (9) a (10) a (11) a (12) c (13) a (14) a
(15) a

Match

(1) 6 (2) 9 (3) 1 (4) 15 (5) 32 (6) 4 (7) 3
(8) 13 (9) 14 (10) 12 (11) 11 (12) 8 (13) 10 (14) 7
(15) 5

EXPLANATIONS
(Passages)

1. As per first line of the first para.
2. Second line of first para
3. Last line of the RC.
4. From the Fourth line of the passage
5. From the Eighth line of the passage
6. Since many bathers had relied on this table and lost there lives so this table has to be wrong.
7. Since Old fable is wrong therefore a person is most likely to be struck by lightining.
8. As per the seventh line of the RC, trees attract lightining and therefore provide dangerous shelter.
9. From the first line of the passage.
10. From the second line of the passage.
11. From the last line of the passage.
12. Initiative means promptness to do any task by exhibiting leadership skills. An this is destroyed by the worry.
13. Last line 'therefore it is state of .... shows that worry is state of mind and can be controled. So we should remove worry from over mind
14. From the first line of the passage.
15. From the second line of the passage.
16. Being critical means taking positive and negative into account but author has not presented poisitive and negative of the working and genesis of dabbawallahs. Therefore (d) is wrong Neither he is appreciative nor he is enthusiastic.
17. As further fifth line author had suffered agonies during childhood therefore he recognised the need for respecting the privacy of her daughter.
18. As per sixth line of the passage.
19. As per the last line of the passage.
21. As per the Eleventh line of the second para.
22. In third line of first para which is even in theheart of the nation's capital, the .... shows that the condition is worse in capital so we can make out that in the rest of the country the condition will be worst
26. As per the second and third lineof the first para.
27. After going to the second para we find that over the years we have not been able to spent enough on education.
28. All the statements are mentioned in the passage.
29. Delete
30. As per the passage teacher has to spent atleast twnety two hours. Therefore choice (a) is not to
31. From the second para, fiftenth line

32. In the paragraph author says that we are not spending enough on higher education so option (d) is not true.

34. As per the seventh, Eighth and Nineth line of the passage.

35. Third line of the second para

36. As per the fifth line of the first para, the mission was created to remove hurdles.

37. First few lines of the passage show that author has praised India's efforts in promoting liberalisation of economy. Therefore option (c) is correct.

38. Since passages does not tell that what exactly happened after japenese investment. Therefore option (d) is correct.

39. As per the last line opation (a) is correct

40. In the last para the line polity of India has again demonstrated its viability and resilience shows that India has got better position in the world market because a political stability and National integration.

41. Here author has talked about government's efforts in executing the policy of liberalisation. Years also talked about democracy, political stability and national integration etc. Therefore there is very high chance that author is Political analyst. Had he been economist, he would have talked about only economics. So option (c) is incorrect. Also from the passage it is not clear that what is nationality of the author. So option (b), (d) and (e) are also incorrect.

42. As per the last line of second para.

43. As per the fourth, fifth, sixth line of first para it is clear that author is requesting foreign investor to come to India and invest in India and also he says that we will not close the door for foreign investors. Therefore option (e) is correct.

44. As per Lines Three, Four and five of Seventh para

45. It is not given in the RC that what are the reason for success of democracy in India. Therefore option (e) is correct.

46. As per the sixth, seventh line of second para

47. Right for the begining the author is insisting on foreign direct investment. and also making them believe that Indian government will do its best to provides conducive environment so as to encourage investments. Therefore option (c) is correct.

48. After reading third para we can definately say that option (b) is correct.

49. As per seventh para option (a) is correct.

50. In fifth para author says that high appreciation of foreign currencies against the Indian rupee provides an opportunity for MNCs to setup their manufacturing base in India. All the options here are wrong. Therefore answer is option (e).

52. From the first few lines it is clear that right option is (c)

53. After reading first para option (d) is correct.

54. After reading para (2) carefully we find that there are various forms of proxy governance. Author has also given the eg. as kinship and kitchen cabinet etc. to prove his point. Therefore option (d) is correct.

58. As per the lines one, two and three of fourth para

59. As per the last few lines of third para.

60. From the last lines of last para.

Day 15

Fill in the Blanks

Today we will learn the tricks to deal with a section, which is called **"Fill in the blanks"** or **"Sentence Completion"**. In this section a few sentences with one, two or three blanks are given. We have to pick up the most appropriate choice that will suitably fill up the given blank / blanks.

Before moving further let us try a few questions and check how much accuracy you can achieve.

1. Many in the crowd whispered, and some even _________ to register there disapproval of remarks of the speaker.

(a) Shouted
(b) rose
(c) protested
(d) criticised

2. A heavy penalty was _________ on the whole village

(a) realised
(b) Imposed
(c) Levied
(d) charged

3. His parents bestowed _________ her all their care and effection.

(a) to
(b) with
(c) in
(d) upon

4. The officier was _________ with immediate effect

(a) prosecuted
(b) charge sheeted
(c) suspended
(d) debarred

5. The great writer _________ art out of facts of life, the segnificant _________ with which pattern of life has been woven.

(a) decides, factors
(b) Selects, element
(c) practices, boundary
(d) creating, disposition
(e) chooses, part

Answers

1. (a) **2.** (b) 3. (d) **4.** (c) **5.** (b)

Now if youhave got all the answers correct then your understanding of english language and vocabulary are good, but if your accuracy is less than 50% then you need to work hard in the areas like vocabulary, comprehension, (understanding of the language/context) usage etc. The problems one faces while attempting this section are

(a) not able to understand context in the given sentence

(b) difficult words in the answer choices.

In order to get the maximum accuracy, you must develop good understanding of this language and for that start reading english from whatever source you are able to find.

A few tips to solve fill in the blanks

(i) *Read the given sentence very carefully and try to understand the context given in the sentence.*

(ii) *Focus on the keywords in the given sentence.*

(iii) *Before looking at the choices, try to anticipate the word/words which you feel, will complete the sentence. Then match this anticipated wor/words with the choices given.*

(iv) *Sometimes choices are very close and it is difficult to select the right answer. So in this situation it is necessary that you must try to understand the context and sense in the given sentence very carefully.*

Besides words in some of the questions, you can come accross, prepositional phrases/ idioms or phrases. So do learn the meaning and usage of some of standard and frequently used prepositional phases. For example

His parents bestored __________ her all their care and affection

(a) to

(b) with

(c) in

(d) upon

Now with 'bestowed', the correction preposition used is 'upon'. so (d) is right answer.

Let us try some questions and then at the end of the chapter an Exercise is given to have more practice.

Examples:

1. Handicrafts constitute an important .... of the decentralized sector of India's economy and .... employment to over six million artisans.

(a) factors, aims

(b) extension, plans

(c) segment, provides

(d) supplier, gives

(e) period, projects

Sol. Here the sense in the question implies that Handicrafts is an important part of decentralized sector. So for first blank best choice would be 'segment' and this sector also helps over six million artisans therefore in 2nd blank the best word would be provides. Hence answer choice is 'C'. Also this sector cannot be 'factor' or extension' or 'period' so choice (a), (b) (e) are rejected. And 1st word in choice (d) is not appropriate as per the context, hence it is also rejected.

2. He was so _________ in the music that he did not hear the door open.

(a) Embroiled
(b) engrossed
(c) engaged
(d) amused.

Sol. The question says that he was so deeply involved in the music than he did not notice anything around. hence as per the context the right word in the blank, woruld be (b) 'Embroiled' means 'Surrounded by' 'amused' means 'surprised' or felt joy 'engaged' means 'involved' only. Therefore they cannot be answer as the person in the question

3. I tried to run away from the police station but I was ______ by my long coat.

(a) arrested
(b) Hampered
(c) Intervened
(d) Saved
(e) escaped

Sol. In the question, the person tried to run away but he was not able to as he was obtsructed or blocked by his long overcoat. So as per the context the best choice would be 'hampered' which also means blocked or obstructed. He was not arrested or saved or escaped by long coat therefore choices (a), (d), and (e) are rejected 'Intervened' mean interfered or distrubed which will not fit in the blank.

Now for your practice three types of sentence completion are given below:

(TYPE I)
(Sentences having single blank space)

Directions : *Each of the following sentences has a blank space and four words given after the sentence. Select whichever word you consider most appropriate for the blank space and indicate your choice on the Answer Sheet.*

1. The campers.....their tent at the base of the mountain.

(a) established (b) grounded
(c) pitched (d) installed

2. The enemy had captured him and his very life was at stake, still he refused to ....the state secrets.

(a) divert (b) divulge
(c) indulge (d) invert

3. If the perceptions of two individuals do not......there are sure to be problems.

(a) match (b) agree
(c) meet (d) tally

4. The scientist......the monkey to get ready for a walk hen it heard a bell.

(a) instructed (b) persuaded
(c) educated (d) conditioned

5. Many in the crowd whispered, and some even......to register their disapproval of the remarks of the speaker.
(a) shouted (b) rose
(c) protested (d) criticised

6. A heavy penalty was......on the whole village.
(a) realised (b) imposed
(c) levied (d) charged

7. The two women looked so alike that it was possible to......between them.
(a) distinguish (b) discriminate
(c) discern (d) identify

8. Her parents bestowed......her all their care and affection.
(a) to (b) with
(c) in (d) upon

9. Vaccination will make people immune ....certain diseases for a given period.
(a) against (b) with
(c) for (d) to

10. He will never......from what he believes to be right.
(a) dissociate (b) distract
(c) separate (d) refrain

11. The completion of the railway line has been held......owing to the workers' strike.
(a) off (b) up
(c) on (d) over

12. It is very.......to miss one's train by half a minute.
(a) annoying (b) exciting
(c) exhausting (d) exasperating

13. The officer was ......with immediate effect.
(a) prosecuted (b) charge-sheeted
(c) suspended (d) debarred

14. For more than a decade now, Indian villages have been ......to television programmes.
(a) accustomed (b) exposed
(c) open (d) attracted

15. The skipper is......that his team would meet any challenge in the forthcoming series.
(a) proud (b) complacent
(c) sure (d) confident

16. Poverty could never......people from becoming great.
(a) hinder (b) prohibit
(c) prevent (d) forbid

17. When the police party arrived on the scene, the rioters fell......and escaped.
(a) out (b) off
(c) through (d) back

18. Thepilot was......injured; he died within half an hour.

(a) seriously (b) fatally

(c) fatefully (d) vitally

19. His......directions misled us; we did not know which road to take.

(a) complex (b) obscure

(c) mingled (d) vague

20. He was very friendly with the press and it really......him even for what he did not achieve.

(a) praised (b) lionized

(c) appreciated (d) highlighted

21. 1 know roughly where the defect is, but Ihave not yet been able to ....it.

(a) see (b) note

(c) discover (d) pinpoint

22. Labour also was very restive, and in some of big industrial centres was becoming aggressive as attempts were made to ....wages.

(a) alter (b) modify

(c) reduce (d) determine

23. The magician.....the man into a rabbit.

(a) transformed (b) made

(c) transfigured (d) converted

24. The ......if not contempt, which many of us have for eligious other than our own, is due to ignorance and incomprehension.

(a) anger (b) opposition

(c) indifference (d) indignation

25. The German force lost no time ......in retreat lest they be cut off and surrounded.

(a) would (b) should

(c) might (d) could

26. Older people usually fear novelty as they subconsciously realise that any......is threat to their established way of life.

(a) action (b) adventure

(c) change (d) movement

27. You must work hard now, to.....for the lost time.

(a) fill (b) pay

(c) compensate (d) recover

28. Efforts to manage the price situation by stepping upproduction need to be met.........effective mand management.

(a) by (b) with

(c) against (d) through

29. Holiness, purity, chastity and charity are not the ....possessions of any religion in the world.

(a) extraordinary (b) exclusive

(c) exceptional (d) invaluable

30. The cost of this journey has........our small store of money.
(a) depleted (b) destroyed
(c) damaged (d) affected

31. They have turned......the water while they were repairing a burst pipe.
(a) out (b) off
(c) down (d) back

32. On the ......Friday, the 30th January, 1948, Gandhiji woke up as usual at 3:30 a.m.
(a) fateful (b) historical
(c) tragic (d) sad

33. He couldn't see himself in the mirror because of the ......rising from the hot bath.
(a) fog (b) mist
(c) smoke (d) steam

34. The television station was ......with letters and hone calls after the announcement.
(a) drowned (b) stormed
(c) deluged (d) absorbed

35. ....,he was there as a butler, although he had come to steal the jewels.
(a) Ostentatiously (b) Obviously
(c) Primarily (d) Ostensibly

36. He was so......in the music that he did not hear the door open.
(a) embroiled (b) engrossed
(c) engaged (d) amused

37. When small minds clash, confrontation becomes ......
(a) imminent (b) expected
(c) essential (d) inevitable

38. He is a famous ......;he has been collecting stamps for the last two decades.
(a) philologist (b) philistine
(c) philatelist (d) philanderer

39. India and Pakistan are geographically ......countries.
(a) contagious (b) contiguous
(c) continuous (d) contentious

40. I have no formal clothes for this occasion perhaps I can get ......in a dark suit.
(a) away (b) into
(c) on (d) by

41. He gave me a......by appearing suddenly in the dark.
(a) scare (b) dash
(c) jolt (d) curse
(e) task

42. People......to see their new representative who was elected recently.
(a) engulfed (b) resumed
(c) thronged (d) flocked
(e) grouped

43. The teacher......the boy's comic which he was reading during the period of Mathematics.

(a) collected (b) criticized
(c) banned (d) possessed
(e) seized

44. He was punished for the......of his duty.

(a) criticism (b) dereliction
(c) immaturity (d) percolation
(e) predestination

45. 1 tried to run away from the police station but I was......by my long coat.

(a) arrested (b) hampered
(c) intervened (d) saved
(e) escaped

46. The old lady.........her' son when he returned triumphantly from the war.

(a) hugged (b) proclaimed
(c) pronounced (d) banged

(TYPE II)
(Sentences having double blank space.)

***Directions** : In each of the following questions, a sentence is given with two blanks in it followed by five pairs of words numbered as (a) , (b) , (c) , (d) and (e) . You have to find which of the five pairs of words can be used in the same sequence to fill up the two blanks to complete the sentence meaningfully. The number of that pair of words is the answer.*

47. In our country, the......use of radio as an instrument of man's education has not yet been......

(a) fullest, exploited
(b) ultimate, used
(c) meaningful, explored
(d) resultant, tried
(e) present, demonstrated

48. The modern world is fast.......it-self into rival camps, armed to the teeth with the sophisticated and deadly......of destruction.

(a) making, sources
(b) changing, factors
(c) developing, procedures
(d) parting, way
(e) resolving, weapons

49. The great writer'........art out of facts of life, the significant........with which the pattern of life has been woven.

(a) decides, factor
(b) selects, element

(c) practises, boundary

(d) creating, disposition

(e) chooses, part

50. We mean by civilization a way of life in which the wilder........of humanity are restrained, the no-bler instructs and inclinations are........and allowed to prevail.

(a) dimensions, created

(b) qualities, discouraged

(c) passions, developed

(d) desires, inhibited

(e) aspects, encouraged

51. We are said to be superstitious when we.......ourselves to fanciful causes for happenings that seem to be.......

(a) bind, unwarranted

(b) project, heavenly

(c) torture, harmful

(d) subject, inexplicable

(e) treat, harrowing

52. The teacher must.......the uniquestyle of a learner in order to ....it to the desired knowledge.

(a) advocate, direct

(b) perpetuate, develop

(c) appreciate, focus

(d) absorb, maintain

(e) discover, harness

53. Not all countries benefit ....from liberalization. The benefits tend to ....first to the advantaged and to those with the right education to be able to benefit from the opportunities presented.

(a) equally, generate

(b) richly , downgrade

(c) suitably, ascribe

(d) uniformaly, percolate

(e) judiciously, facilitate

54. He has.........sense of words. Therefore, the sentence tie constructs are always.........with rich meaning.

(a) profound, pregnant

(b) distinguished, loaded

(c) terrific, tempted

(d) meaningful, full

(e) outstanding, consistent

55. He was an.........musician, had been awarded the George Medal during the second world war and .... with the title of Rai Bahadur.

(a) outstanding, popularized
(b) underestimated, declared
(c) accomplished, honoured
(d) impressive, assigned
(e) obdurate, proclaimed

56. Whether it-be shallow or not, commitment is the.........,the bedrock of any.........loving relationship.

(a) expression, perfunctory
(b) foundation, genuinely
(c) manifestation, deep
(d) key, alarmingly
(e) basis, absorbing

57. Many people take spirituality very seriously.........and about those who don't, worrying about them and.........them to believe.

(a) think, criticizing
(b) pride, appraising
(c) rationalize, enabling
(d) wonder, prodding
(e) ponder, venturing

58. Unless new reserves are found soon, the world's supply of coal is being.........in such a way that with demand continuing to grow at present rates,- reserves will be ....by the year 2050

(a) consumed, completed
(b) depleted, exhausted
(c) reduced, argument
(d) burnt, destroyed
(e) utilized,perished

59. If you are a ....you tend to respond to stressful situations, in a calm, secure, steady and.........way.

(a) resilient, ration a
(b) obdurate, manageable
(c) propitious, stable
(d) delectable, flexible
(e) supportive, positive

60. Management can be defined as the process of ....organizational goals by working with and through human and non-human resources to.........improve value added to the world.

(a) getting, deliberately
(b) managing, purposefully
(c) targeting, critically
(d) realizing, dialectically
(e) reaching, continuously

61. If you are an introvert, you .... to prefer working alone and, if possible, will.........towards projects where you can work by yourself or with as few people as possible.
   (a) like, depart
   (b) advocate, move
   (c) Attend, gravitate
   (d) express, attract
   (e) feel, follow

62. Handicrafts constitute an important.........of the decentralized sector of India's economy and .... employment to over six million artisans.
   (a) factors, aims
   (b) extension, plans
   (c) segment, provides
   (d) supplier, gives
   (e) period, projects

63. Among a number of hobbies that one can......... the hobby of reading is the most useful and.........
   (a) develops, accumulative
   (b) cultivates, enlightened
   (c) nourish, cumulative
   (d) absorbs,durable
   (e) considers, appreciative

64. The quality of......... between individuals and the organization for which they work can be......... to the benefit of both the parties.
   (a) services, evaluated
   (b) interaction, improved
   (c) sophistication, developed
   (d) work, appreciated
   (e) life, conceptualized

65. Part of the confusion in our societies......... from our pursuit of efficiency and economic growth, in the......... that these are the necessary ingredients of progress.
   (a) stems, conviction
   (b) derives, evaluation
   (c) emerges, consideration
   (d) obtains, exploration
   (e) extends, planning

66. The problem of housing shortage......... with the population explosion has also been......... by this policy
   (a) coped, highlighted
   (b) dispensed, acknowledged
   (c) compounded,addressed

(d) threatened, manifested
(e) projected,discussed

67. Nothing is impossible in the world of politics. States which were......... foes and had their deadly missiles pointed at each other find themselves......... in military alliances.
(a) implacable, partners
(b) intense, joining
(c) deadly, approaching
(d) known, soliciting
(e) enviable, grouping

68. .... of whether leaders are born or made, it is......... clear that leaders are not like other people.
(a) Pursuant, manifestly
(b) Sequel, amply
(c) Regardles, sunequivocally
(d) Instead, purely
(e) Inspite , normally

69. There is a common talk today that women have made the .... in many professions; that they have total freedom of opporturlity. But the majority of women are still left......... their goals and ambitions through an almost unbreakable glass ceiling.
(a) entry, inward
(b) grade, gazing
(c) progress, trying
(d) mark, projecting
(e) achievement, wondering

70. Inferring altitudes from expressed opinion has many ....People may......... their attitude and express socially acceptable opinions.
(a) limitation, conceal
(b) advantages, show
(c) drawbacks, support
(d) benefits, avoid
(e) reasons, acknowledge

71. We should move towards a system where the banks can......... capital in the market with......... safeguard so that they continue to be public sector banks.
(a) improve, proper
(b) strengthen, durable
(c) raise, adequate
(d) stimulate, effective
(e) provide, delicate

72. Human Resource Management is an......... of mind rather than a .... of techniques.
(a) organization, quality
(b) attempt, mix

(c) evolution, measure
(d) attitude, set
(e) expertise, collection

73. Statistics is an......... tool for researchers that......... them to make inferences of generalizations about population from their observations of the characteristics of samples.
(a) outstanding, proposes
(b) invaluable, proceeds
(c) invaluable, displays
(d) important, proclaims
(e) indispensable, enables

74. The Dalits have never had a......... of freedom in the suffocating society. They are a wounded people......... and broken.
(a) glimpse, mitigated
(b) sigh, rejected
(c) moment, criticized
(d) satisfaction, prohibited
(e) breath, battered

75. His vision could well be the......... that the policy-makers use to......... the banking sector.
(a) roadmap, restructure
(b) manner, shape
(c) blueprint, plan
(d) remedy, revise
(e) approach, represent

(TYPE III)
(Cloze Test)

Directions: *In the following passage, at certain points you are given a choice of three words / phrases in the blank spaces and marked (a), (b), (c). Choose the best word out of the three and indicate your choice in the relevant column of your Answer Sheet.*

A shop where small colourful bulbs beamed along a magic wire, without being fed by oil or was ... 76 ... Ravi. He had learnt in Ferozpur to ... 77 ... everything he could not understand as English. So he did not pause to... 78 ... but moved on to contemplate, with ... 79 ... eyes, a row of ... 80 ... buildings of which the second storey was supported over the shops by ... 81 ... carved columns and painted in ... 82 ... designs. Beyond this Ravi's eyes were caught by a shop in which a ...83 ... of tailors sat stitching away at ... 84 ... while one of them worked a sewing machine, again, by a shop where jewellers sat ... 85... little bright stones into brown wax. An ... 86 ... with an ash-smeared body and shaggy'... 87 ... naked except for a rag round his waist, glided by Ravi, striking a long ... 88 ... of tongs and swaying his garlands of thick ... 89 ... The crowd became thicker and more ... 90 ... as baggy-trousered young men alternated with saffron-clothed monks and rustic farmers.

76. (a) disappointed (b) puzzled (c) shocked
77. (a) call (b) say (c) label
78. (a) question (b) inquire (c) answer
79. (a) wide (b) narrow (c) slit
80. (a) dusty (b) modern (c) antique
81. (a) intimately (b) innately (c) intricately
82. (a) floral (b) lurid (c) florid
83. (a) bevy (b) group (c) batch
84. (a) cloths (b) needle (c) garments
85. (a) studding (b) driving (c) drilling
86. (a) artist (b) actor (c) ascetic
87. (a) eyes (b) hair (c) cars
88. (a) couple (b) set (c) pair
89. (a) beads (b) buds (c) flowers
90. (a) crowded (b) varied (c) excited

Directions: Q. 76-90: *In the following passage, at certain points, you are given a choice of three words marked (a), (b), (c). Choose the best word out of the three and indicate your choice in the relevant column of your Answer Sheet.*

There was an old penguin, that began to walk slowly towards the sea, and Peterkin took it into his head that he would try to stop it, so he ran ... 91 ... it and the sea and ... 92 ... his stick ... 93 ... its face. But ... 94 ... act proved to be ... 95 ... The old bird would not go ... 96 ... in fact, it would not ... 97 ... to advance, but ... 98 ... with Peterkin bravely, and ... 99 ... him before it ... 100 ... it reached the sea.... 101 ... Peterkin used his stick he could have ... 102 ... killed it, no doubt; but ... 103 ... he had no wish to do so cruel an act ... 104 ... out of sport, he ... 105 ... the bird escape.

91. (a) after (b) between (c) for
92. (a) lifted (b) raised (c) waved
93. (a) over (b) in (c) on
94. (a) its (b) that (c) this
95. (a) determined. (b) crazy (c) foolish
96. (a) back (b) on (c) forth
97. (a) stop (b) stay (c) cease
98. (a) battled (b) struggled (c) threatened
99. (a) pushed (b) forced (c) drove
100. (a) till (b) until (c) when
101. (a) Were (b) Had (c) Would
102. (a) easily (b) instantly (c) certainly
103. (a) if (b) as (c) though
104. (a) only (b) simply (c) merely
105. (a) made (b) let (c) allowed

Directions :In the following passage, there are blanks, each of which has been numbered. These numbers are printed below the passage and against each, five words are suggested, one of which fits the blank appropriately Find out the appropriate word in each case.

In (106) of constitutional guarantees relating to equality of opportunity and various other guarantees of equality before the law, the social and economic (107) of women, especially of poor women in India, is well-known. We are referring mainly to the poor rural women who have little or no assets and who (108) the bulk of the female population in rural areas. It .is not as if only poor rural women get less wages or suffer from social (109) because they belong to a particular community. Even at higher levels of the socio-economic hierarchy among the well-to do groups, women are not(110) to men. Among the economically (111) sections of society, women's proper place is (112) to be the home. In rural areas, women of (113) status families, normally do not go out to work. In the (114) value system, there is a gradation of economic activities, which is (115) in the socio-economic status of the family.

Thus, if the women of the family do manual labour in the fields, it denotes low status. Women earning a living, or supplementing their family income through economic activities like stitching, garmentmaking, or some handicraft work, are also considered low because it clearlyshows that 'their family is poor and they are forced to make ends meet. It is considered right and proper for a women to cook, sew and take up activities like pickle-making for her own family But, if she were to earn a wage through these same activities, it denotes poverty and also, often, low socio-economic status.

106. (1) support (2) spite
(3) contrast (4) wake
(5) view

107. (1) condition (2) prosperity
(3) progress (4) deprivation
(5) value

108. (1) constitute (2) deploy
(3) measure (4) define
(5) exploit

109. (1) status (2) service
(3) indifference (4) ignorance
(5) discrimination

110. (1) dedicated (2) accountable
(3) equal (4) responsible
(5) antagonistic

111. (1) marginal (2) significant
(3) well-off (4) affordable
(5) dependable

112. (1) entitled (2) decided
(3) indicated (4) debated
(5) considered

113. (1) economic (2) appropriate

	(3)	ample	(4)	higher
	(5)	social		
114.	(1)	unequal	(2)	prevailing
	(3)	appropriate	(4)	commendabie
	(5)	deplorable		
115.	(1)	reflected	(2)	exempted
	(3)	barred	(4)	considered
	(5)	neglected		

VOCAB LIST

651	Remiss	Careless
652	Remonstrate	Protest
653	Rend	Tear apart/Split
654	Simulate	Pretend
655	Antithesis	Contrast/Reverse
656	Crevice	Fissure
657	Portly	Plump
658	Potable	Drinkable
659	Flippant	Trivial/Talkative
660	Flippancy	Irreverence/Fluency of speech
661	Sine Quanon	A thing which is very necessary
662	Charm (n)	Attractiveness/Power of pleasing
663	Charm (v)	To attract or fascinate
664	Adduce	Cite/Quote
665	Crotchety	Eccentric/Whimsical
666	Crux	Most vital point of problem issue
667	Cryptic	Mysterious
668	Semblance	Outward appearance/Likeness
669	Munificent	Bountiful/Generous
670	Muse	Meditate/Ponder
671	Concomitant	Contemporary
672	Concoct	Devise/Plot
673	Concede	To admit/To allow
674	Cortege	A line of people/cars etc. that move along slowly in a funeral
675	Protensive	Continuous
676	Hen party	A party for women only
677	Helter-skelter	Quickly & without order

678	Manna	A spiritual food/A purgative medicine
679	Conceal	To hide/Keep secret
680	Specious	Obvious/Showy
681	Exorcism	Freedom/Expelling of evil spirits
682	Toils	Traps/Difficulties
683	Gall	Asperity/Blister/A malignity
684	Galling	Annoying/Making upset
685	Prescient	Knowing about things before they happen/ Prophetic/or knowledge
686	Sphinx-like	Mysterious
687	Guile	Deceit/Clever/Cunning
688	Bandy	Discuss/Exchange
689	Duress	Restraint of liberty/Imprisonment
690	Dupe	To deceive
691	Quack	To boast/To make a harsh sound like duck
692	Perverse	Obstinate/Wicked/Peevish
693	Litany	Supplications for use in a Church
694	Senescent	Becoming old
695	Trample	To tread heavily
696	Nag	To complain/criticize
697	Colloquial	Talks seminar
698	Confabulation	A private conversation
699	Sobering	Serious
700	Phantasm	An illusion

TEST 14
Words (651-700)

(1) Remiss

(a) Careful (b) Careless
(c) Negligent (d) Obstinate.

(2) Galling

(a) Making happy (b) Making upset
(c) Criticizing (d) Peculiar

(3) Sobering

(a) Serious (b) Woofing
(c) Illusive (d) Annoying

(4) Dupe

(a) To make friend (b) To deceive
(c) To complain (d) To exchange

(5) Nag

(a) To criticize (b) To deceives
(c) To deceive (d) To boast

(6) Phantasm

(a) Originality (b) An illusion
(c) Challenge (d) Devise plot

(7) Protensive

(a) Irregular (b) Continues
(c) Protective (d) Quick

(8) Muse

(a) Ponder (b) Wonder
(c) Amuse (d) Charm

(9) Toils

(a) Difficulties (b) Outward
(c) Failure (d) Deceit

(10) Sphinx-like

(a) Fairy-like (b) Mysterious
(c) Kingly (d) Animals-like

(11) Senescent

(a) Becoming old (b) Becoming young
(c) Becoming fresh (d) None

(12) Adduce

(a) Quite (b) Nullify
(c) Revert (d) Agree

(13) Remonstrate

(a) Receive (b) Protest
(c) Fascinate (d) Accept

(14) Crotchety

(a) Whimsical (b) On crutches
(c) Canning (d) Stupid

(15) Cryptic

(a) Mysterious (b) Hidden
(c) Clever (d) Wicked

Day 15— Fill in the Blanks

Match the words in column 'A' with their correct meaning in 'B'.

	Column A		Column B
(1)	Rend	(1)	Very necessary thing
(2)	Flippancy	(2)	Contrast
(3)	Sine Qua non	(3)	A spiritual food
(4)	Pertly	(4)	To boast
(5)	Simulate	(5)	Exchange
(6)	Concede	(6)	Tear apart
(7)	Manna	(7)	Freedom
(8)	Exorcism	(8)	Trivial
(9)	Confabulations	(9)	Plump
(10)	Bandy	(10)	Bountiful
(11)	Munificent	(11)	Irreverence
(12)	Flippant	(12)	Pretend
(13)	Litany	(13)	Supplications for use in a church
(14)	Quack	(14)	To admit
(15)	Antithesis	(15)	A private conversation

ANSWERS (FILL IN THE BLANKS)

1. (c)	2. (b)	3. (b)	4. (a)	5. (a)	6. (b)	7. (a)
8. (d)	9. (d)	10. (d)	11. (b)	12. (d)	13. (c)	14. (b)
15. (d)	16. (c)	17. (d)	18. (b)	19. (d)	20. (a)	21. (d)
22. (c)	23. (a)	24. (b)	25. (d)	26. (c)	27. (c)	28. (d)
29. (b)	30. (a)	31. (b)	32. (a)	33. (d)	34. (c)	35. (d)
36. (b)	37. (d)	38. (c)	39. (b)	40. (a)	41. (c)	42. (c)
43. (e)	43. (b)	45. (b)	46. (a)	47. (a)	48. (e)	49. (b)
50. (d)	51. (b)	52. (c)	53. (a)	54. (a)	55. (c)	56. (b)
57 (d)	58. (b)	59. (a)	60. (e)	61. (c)	62. (c)	63. (c)
64. (b)	65. (c)	66. (c)	67. (a)	68. (c)	69. (b)	70. (a)
71. (c)	72. (e)	73. (e)	74. (e)	75 (a)	76. (b)	77. (c)
78. (d)	79. (a)	80. (c)	81. (c)	82. (c)	83. (b)	84. (c)
85. (c)	86. (c)	87. (b)	88. (c)	89. (a)	90. (c)	91. (a)
92. (c)	93. (a)	94. (c)	95. (c)	96. (c)	97. (c)	98. (a)
99. (b)	100. (a)	101. (b)	102. (a)	103. (b)	104. (b)	105. (c)
106. (b)	107. (a)	108. (a)	10.9 (e)	110. (c)	111. (c)	112. (e)
113. (d)	114. (b)	115. (a)				

Answer of Test 14

(1) b	(2) b	(3) a	(4) b	(5) a	(6) b	(7) b
(8) a	(9) a	(10) b	(11) a	(12) a	(13) b	(14) a
(15) a						

Match

(1) 6	(2) 11	(3) 1	(4) 9	(5) 12	(6) 14	(7) 3
(8) 7	(9) 15	(10) 5	(11) 10	(12) 8	(13) 13	(14) 4
(15) 2						

Day

16

Idioms and Phrases

Today we will study **Idioms & Phrases**. **Idioms** are as vary as life itself. They have different sources. Whereas the vocabulary of the language can be easily mastered, it is hard to master its idioms. Idioms wrongly used is an offence against a language. It is therefore necessary to understand the exact meaning and remember the exact word of the idiom. Seeing the importance of the topic it is divided into two days i.e. day 16 & day 17. On each day nearly two hundred idiom & idiomatic phrases are given. You have to learn them by writing in your notebook & master them so that you may attempt this part accurately. Given below is a list of two hundred idioms. You have to learn them by heart and solve the test given after the list honestly.

Above board (honest)
All and sundry (All irrespective of distinction)
All in all (all powerful)
As a matter of fact (in reality)
At all costs (come what may)
At ones fingures end (having thorough knowledge of)
At a loss (puzzled)
At home in (good at)
At issue (point of discussion)
At all events (in any case)
At daggers drawn (having enmity)
At arm's length (to avoid)
A gentleman at large (a free man)
At large (free)
At random (without order or purpose)
At the eleventh hour (at the last moment)
At stake (in danger)
By virtue of (on account of)
By and by (after some time)
Bag and baggage (completely)
Back and all (At one's command)
Below the mark (below standard)
Beyond question (without doubt)
Between you and me (it is a secret between us)

Day 16— Idioms & Phrases

Fair and square	(fair, honest)
Fair play	(fair competitions)
Few and far between	(Rare)
Fire and sword	(destruction)
Flesh and blood	(Human)
For ever and a day	(for ever)
For good	(permanently)
For good and all	(completely)
Heart and soul	(vigourously)
Hand and glove	(intimate)
Hole and corner	(secret)
In a fix	(in a difficult position)
In black and white	(in writing)
In cold blood	(deliberately)
In eonsequence of	(owing to)
In defiance of	(with no care of)
In favour of	(for)
In favor with	(loved by)
In force	(valid)
In full swing	(busy and blooming)
In name	(not really)
In no way	(by no means)
In no time	(very soon)
In keeping with	(in consistent with)
In good faith	(honesty)
In one`s teens	(immature, young)
In quest of	(in search of)
In round numbers	(approximately)
In season and out of season	(at all times)
Ins and out	(in detail)
In the air	(spread)
In the ascendant	(good)
In the background	(put in obsurity)
In the dark	(ignorant)
In the nick of time	(at the last moment)
In the teeth of	(in the face of)
In the twinking of an eye	(quickly)
In the prime of life	(in the best period of life)
In vogue	(in fashion)
In the wind	(Rumour)

Kith and kin	(relatives)
Null and void	(of on effect)
Odds and ends	(stray articles)
Out of the question	(unworthy of discussion)
Out and out	(completely)
On the wane	(declining)
On the spur of the moment	(when it was fit to)
On the face of it	(obviously)
On the eve of	(at the time of)
Out of enes wits	(puzzled)
With one voice	(unanimously)
Without rhyme and reason	(with out sufficient cause)
Through thick and thin	(in all circumstances)
Sum and substance	(purort)
The three R`s	(Reading writing and arithmetic)
To all intents and purposes	(practically)
To the letter	(strictly)
Stuff and non sense	(rubbish, meaningless)
To one`s heart`s content	(with satisfaction)
On one`s guard	(watchful)
Of the first water	(of the first rate quality)
Of on avail	(useless)
Off and on	(occasionally)
Null and void	(of on effect)
Out of the way	(obscure)
Pros and file	(arguments for and againts)
Rank and file	(common soldiers)
With a high hand	(imperiously, arrogantly)
Weal and woe	(in good and bad plight)
Wear and tear	(the damage caused by the constant use)
Well up in	(proficient)
Of one`s own accord	(voluntarily)
In the nick of time	(just and the right moment)
In the long run	(eventually)
To bring home to	(to make understand)
To bury the hatchet	(to make peace)
To burn the candle at both ends	(to spend recklessly)
To bring to light	(to reval)
To bring to book	(to punish)
To bring to bay	(to bring to a difficult position)

To bring to a stand still	(to stop)
To bear in mind	(to remember)
To bear the brunt of	(to face the fury)
To beat about the bush	(to speak indirectly)
To beat the air	(to struggle in vain)
To break news	(to communicate the bad news with care)
To have an axe to grind	(to serve selfish ends)
To keep up appearance	(to pose)
To give oneself airs	(to be harsh in attitude)
Through fire and water	(through all dificulties)
To add fuel to the fire	(to stimulate fury)
To turn one's back upon	(to leave, to desert)
To breathe one's back upon	(to die)
To break the ice	(To speak)
To blow one's trumpet	(To praise oneself)
To blow hot and cold in the same breath	(To praise and blame)
A Whilte Elephant	(Costly)
At the top of one's voice	(Loudly)
Under lock and key	(Safe)
Un and doing	(Active and engaged)
Tooth and Nail	(Fiercely)
Tit for Tat	(Like for Like)
Worth one's salt	(Efficient)
True to one's salt	(faithful)
The wrong side of sixty	(Above Sixty)
A wild goose chase	(a fruitless chase)
A man of the word	(wordly wise)
Ared letter day	(importent days)
Palmy days	(glorious days)
The sweat of one`s brow	(hard work)
A sleeping partner	(a partner who only invests and does not work)
In a nutshell	(in brief)
Off one`s head	(unbalanced)
With open arms	(to welcome)
An open secret	(A news known to everybody but not published)
The order of the day	(fashion)
Out of sorts	(indisposed)
Out of pocket	(penniless)
The lion's share	(greater share)

The loaves and fishes (the financial gain)
Laughing stock (joker, an object of ridicule)
The long and short of the matter (the substance)
There is no love lost between them (to dislike)
Maiden speech (first speech)
Crocodile tears (false tears)
Cock and bull story (a non sensical story)
Chip of the old block (to be like our farther)
In bad books (not having good opinion)
Greek to one (which is not tangible)
The grapes are sour (which we hate as it is not achieved)
Fair weather friend (false friend)
Curtain lectures (wife's talks at night generally relating to back-bite)
Crying need (greatest need)
Bone of contention (cause of quarrel)
Hard and fast (strict)
Hair breadth escape (to esacpe being hurt)
Blot from the blue (unexpected sad event)
Black sheep (A bad man)
A good hand at (skilful)
Apple of discord (cause of quarrel)
At a low ebb (decreasing)
Apple of ones eyes (dear)
Between the two fires (subject to double attack)

Test -1
Day 16

Match the following :

1.	**Above board**	a	(with no care of)
2.	**All in all**	b	(to face the fury)
3.	**A gentleman at large**	c	(valid)
4.	**At arm's length**	d	(to avoid)
5.	**In favor with**	e	(a free man)
6.	**In force**	f	(honest)
7.	**In defiance of**	g	(all powerful)
8.	**In favour of**	h	(for)
9.	**To bear in mind**	i	(loved by)
10.	**To bear the brunt of**	j	(to remember)

Test - 2

Match the following :

1.	At a low ebb	f	(Costly)
2.	Apple of ones eyes	e	(hard work)
3.	Palmy days	g	(Loudly)
4.	The sweat of one`s brow	c	(glorious days)
5.	A Whilte Elephant	i	(Like for Like)
6.	At the top of one's voice	h	(to dislike)
7.	In the wind	b	(dear)
8.	Tit for Tat	j	(to spend recklessly)
9.	To burn the candle at both ends	a	(decreasing)
10.	There is no love lost	h	(Rumour)

Sr.	Word	Meanings
701	Cartel	A written challenge to duel/An agreement for exchange of Prisoners of war
702	Incise	To engrave/Scribe
703	Bellyache	To complain repeatedly without good reason
704	Riffle	To turn over
705	Rifle	To search/To plunder
706	Mane	Long hair
707	Facile	Easily achieved
708	Shaggy	Rough/Coarse
709	Eatery	Restaurant
710	Nonchalant	Indifferent/Appearing calm
711	Insouciance	Unconcern
712	Adipose	Of fat
713	Narcissism	An abnormal & excessive love
714	Gait	A way of walking
715	Grist to one's mill	A thing that can be used for profit
716	Shop around	Search carefully for services that are most suitable
717	Lunge	Attack
718	Crumple	Crush into folds/To break
719	Efficacious	Effective/Producing desired result
720	Emanate	To come or flow from
721	Siesta	Sleep/rest taken in afternoon
722	Abut	Adjoining
723	Droop	Hanging down
724	Blitz	Concentrated attack

725	Infer	Deduce
726	Histrionic	Very dramatic
727	Pusillanimous	Cowardly/Timid
728	Spurn	Reject/Refuse/To disdain
729	Spunk	Courage/Spirit
730	Marshal	Arrange in proper
731	Riggish	Wanton
732	Embarrass	To perplex/To render intricate
733	Convolute	Curved/Difficult to understand
734	Disinclination	Lack of enthusiasm
735	Odyssey	A long journey full of experiences
736	Odious	Unpleasant/Disgusting
737	Pedant	A person who is too concerned about minor details
738	Inflate	To increase the amount of money in use in a country
739	Ratbag	An unpleasant or disgusting person
740	Rave	To talk wildly
741	Ravel	To separate into threads
742	Ravage	To damage/destroy badly
743	Prance	To move in specified direction in an excited manner
44	Prevaricate	To speak in a misleading way
745	Panorama	A view of a wide area
746	Shambolic	Not organized
747	Senile	Showing the weaknesses & diseases of old age
748	Puddle	A small pool of water
749	Pudgy	Short & fat
750	Spellbinding	Holding the attention completely

BREAK FOR WORDS REVISION

TEST 15
Words (701-750)

(1) Incise
(a) To scribe (b) To supersede
(c) To protect (d) To produce.

(2) Hunge
(a) Praise (b) Pray
(c) Request (d) Attack

(3) Pudgy
(a) Short & fat (b) Thin & short
(c) Thin & fat (d) Obese

(4) Shambolic
(a) Organized (b) Not organized
(c) Damaged (d) Rotten

(5) Infer
(a) Reduce (b) Idea
(c) Deduced (d) Notify

(6) Ravage
(a) To damage (b) To rebuild
(c) To organize (d) None

(7) Panorama
(a) A view of wide area (b) A view of a small area
(c) A view of a book (d) A view of a movie

(8) Riggish
(a) Wanton (b) Wanted
(c) Unpleasant (d) Disgusting

(9) Embarrass
(a) Perplex (b) To cheer up
(c) To Please (d) To complain

(10) Shaggy
(a) Coarse (b) Fine
(c) Pure (d) Curved

(11) Spurn
(a) Reject (b) Spell
(c) Arrange (d) Convey

(12) Pusillanimous
(a) Cowardly (b) Bravely
(c) Tame (d) Sensitive

(13) Abut

(a) Adjoining (b) Next

(c) Previous (d) Related

(14) Odious

(a) Disgusting (b) Pleasant

(c) Oderless (d) Orderless

(15) Efficacious

(a) Effective (b) Not producing desired result

(c) Dull (d) Morose

Match the words in column 'A' with their correct meaning in 'B'.

	Column A		Column B
(1)	Puddle	(1)	Cured
(2)	Convolute	(2)	Speaking in a misleading way
(3)	Rating	(3)	Showing the weakness & disease of old age
(4)	Prevaricate	(4)	Unconcern
(5)	Rave	(5)	To talk wildly
(6)	Senile	(6)	A small pool of water
(7)	Odyssey	(7)	Rest/sleep of afternoon
(8)	Spunk	(8)	Courage
(9)	Droop	(9)	Abnormal &excessive love
(10)	Disinclination	(10)	A disgusting person
(11)	Siesta	(11)	Appealing
(12)	Crumple	(12)	Lack of enthusiasm
(13)	Narcissism	(13)	Hanging down
(14)	Nonchalant	(14)	Crush into folds
(15)	Insouciance	(15)	A long journey full of experience

Solution Test -1
Day 16

Match the following :

1. **Above board** (honest)
2. **All in all** (all powerful)
3. **A gentleman at large** (a free man)
4. **At arm's length** (to avoid)
5. **In favour with** (loved by)
6. **In force** (valid)
7. **In defiance of** (with no care of)
8. **In favour of** (for)

9.	**To bear in mind**	(to remember)
10.	**To bear the brunt of**	(to face the fury)

Solution
Test - 2

Match the following :

1.	**At a low ebb**	(decreasing)
2.	**Apple of ones eyes**	(dear)
3.	**Palmy days**	(glorious days)
4.	**The sweat of one`s brow**	(hard work)
5.	**A White Elephant**	(Costly)
6.	**At the top of one's voice**	(Loudly)
7.	**In the wind**	(Rumour)
8.	**Tit for Tat**	(Like for Like)
9.	**To burn the candle at both ends**	(to spend recklessly)
10.	**There is no love lost**	(to dislike)

Answer of Test 15

(1) a (2) d (3) a (4) b (5) c (6) a (7) a
(8) a (9) a (10) a (11) a (12) a (13) a (14) a
(15) a

Match

(1) 6 (2) 1 (3) 10 (4) 2 (5) 5 (6) 3 (7) 15
(8) 8 (9) 13 (10) 12 (11) 7 (12) 14 (13) 9 (14) 11
(15) 4

Day

17

Idioms and Phrases

Today i.e. on day 17 second list of idioms and idiomatic phrases is given. You have to learn the list by heart & solve the test given after the list honestly.

IDIOMS & PHRASES

Bear away	(to win)
Bear down	(to overthrow)
Bear out	(to confirm)
Bear up	(not to despair)
Bear with	(have patience)
Break down	(to lose balance of mind)
Break down	(to lose health)
Brerak in	(to interrupt)
Break out	(to spread)
Break into	(to enter)
Break off	(to stop)
Bring up	(to rear)
Bring under	(to subdue)
Bring round	(to convert)
Bring over	(to convince)
Bring forth	(to produce)
Bring out	(to cause)
Call for	(to demand)
Call up	(to recall)
Call on	(to recall)
Call off	(withdrawn)
Call forth	(to bring out)
Carry away	(to grow sentimental)
Carry off	(to pass away)
Carry off	(to win)
Carry on	(to go on doing)
Carry out	(to obey)
Carry away	(to grow sentimental)

Carry off	(to pass away)
Carry off	(to win)
Carry on	(to go on doing)
Carry out	(to obey)
Come about	(to happen)
Come by	(to purchase)
Comes of	(to be born)
Comes off	(to take place)
Come out	(to reveal)
Come around	(to recover)
Come round	(to agree)
Cry down	(to deprecate)
Cry up	(to praise much)
Cut down	(to decrease)
Cut in	(to interrupt)
Do away with	(to abloish)
Do up	(to exhaust)
Do for	(to ruin)
Draw on	(to approach)
Draw out	(to unsheathe)
Draw up	(to lengthen)
Drop in	(to visit)
Drop out	(to retire)
Drop off	(to decrease)
Fall back	(to retreat)
Fall back upon	(to rely)
Fall in with	(to acceda)
Fall off	(to leave)
Fall upon	(to attack)
Fall through	(to fail)
Fall in with	(to meet by chance)
Get at	(to reach)
Get along	(make progress)
Get away	(to escape)
Get off	(to escape)
Get on with	(to live)
Get over	(to surmount)
Get through	(to succeed)
Get up	(to be awake)
Give away	(to disburse)

Give in	(to yield)
Given off	(emit)
Given out	(announce)
Go by	(Judge from)
Go back upon	(fail to break)
Go into	(to investigate)
Go up	(to increase)
Go through	(to revise)
Go over	(to examine)
Go of well	(was a success)
Hold on	(to grasp, top grip)
Hold out	(to give)
Hold to	(to ling)
Keep away	(to remain absent)
Keep back	(to conceal)
Keep on	(to continue)
Keep up	(to maintain)
Lay down	(to sacrifice)
Lay out	(to cast)
Lay up	(to confine)
Look for	(to wait)
Look forward to	(to expect)
Look to	(rely on)
Lookin gup	(improving)
Over look	(to ignore)
Look over	(to examine)
Loo to	(care for)
Look down upon	(to hate)
Fall out with	(to quarrel)
Make away	(to take away)
Make for	(conduces to)
Make off	(run away)
Make up	(to settle)
Make over	(to transfer)
Make out	(read)
Pull down	(demolish)
Pull through	(to recover)
Pull toghter	(work toghter)
Put up	(to live)
Put down	(to suppress)

Put forth	(set out)
Put forward	(advance)
Put in	(to make)
Put off	(to postpone)
Put one off	(to evade)
Put off	(to remove)
Put out	(to extinguish)
Put out	(disconcerted, unhinged, confused)
Put out	(annoy)
Put up with	(to tolerate)
Run down	(weakened)
Run down	(to speak ill of)
Run into	(to incur)
Run out	(expire)
Run up	(increase)
Run through	(to spend quickly)
Get on	(make progress)
Set aside	(annul)
Set down	(write down)
Set in.	The rainy season has *set in*.
Set off	(started)
Set off	(added by contrast)
Set on	(attacked)
Set apart	These seats are *set apart* for the guests.
Set up	They *set up* a business.
Set up	(to establish)
Take after	(to resemble)
Take down	(to write)
Take in	(to deceive)
Take up	(to occupy)
Turn off	(to dismiss)
Turn against	(to become hostile)
Trun out	(to prove)
Trun up	(to arrive)
Back up	(to support)
Bear out	(to explain)
Clear up	(to explain)
Close with	(to accept)
Well off	(rich)
Caste down	(depress)

Caste out	(to make)
Stand by	(support)
Throw up	(resign)
Throw out	(solve)
Work up	(to excite)
Work out	(solve)
Pass for	(was regarded)
Pass out	(to allow)
Pass away	(to die)
Keep in	(to stay back)
To compare notes	(to exchange opinion)
To come to head	(to ripen)
To turn one's coat	(to change the party)
To carry the day	(to win)
To hold a candle to anyone	(to compete)
To see eye to eye	(to have the same opinion)
To eat humble pie	(to apologize)
To do yeomen's	(to do good service) service
To do one a good turn	(to show kindness)
To die in harness	(to go in working till death)
To fall flat	(to have no effect)
To play second fiddle	(to be a yes man)
To fight shy of	(to avoid)
To follow suit	(to follow what one has already done)
To gain ground	(to make progress)
To give countenance to	(to support)
To give the lie to	(to prove false)
To give vent to	(to express)
To go a long way	(to help considerably)
To go hard with one	(to trouble one)
To hold one's own	(to contest)
To keep one's head over water	(to avoid bankruptcy)
To turn one's head	(to be vain and proud)
To hang in the balance	(undecided)
To keep an eye on	(to watch)
To throw mud at	(to abuse)
To move heaven and earth	(to make every possible effort)
To leave one in lurch	(to desert in difficulty)
To nip in the bud	(to destroy)
To hold out the olive branch	(to make an offer of peace)

To lead by the nose	(to follow blindly)
To make light of	(not to mind much)
To turn over a new leaf	(to begin afresh)
To keep body and soul together	(to maintain bare existence)
To take a leaf out of another person'book	(to copy the good examples of)
To meet another half way	(to compromise)
To throw cold water on	(to discourage)
To keep the wolf from the door	(to keep hunger away)
To wash one's dirty linen in public	(to speak one's unpleasant private affairs)
To take with a grain of salt	(to believe)
To strain every nerve	(try one's best)
To rise to the occasion	(to act promptly)
To sail in the same boat	(to be alike)
To praise one to the skies	(to over praise one)
To stick at nothing	(to do everthing)
To steal a march upon	(to profit while opponent is negligent)
To stand one in good stead	(to prove of great service)
To save ones skin	(save oneself without any damage)
To put ones shoulder to the wheel	(to work hard)
To give one the cold shoulders	(to treat clodly)
To have an old head on young shoulders	(to be wise though young)
To step into another person's shoes	(to succeed)
To leave no stone unturned	(to try every possible means)

Test -1
Day 17

Match the following :

1.	**In the dark**	a	(common soldiers)
2.	**On the wane**	b	(stray articles)
3.	**To add fuel to the fire**	c	(to stimulate fury)
4.	**Rank and file**	d	(ignorant)
5.	**Fair weather friend**	e	(false friend)
6.	**The wrong side of sixty**	f	(above sixty)
7.	**A Whilte Elephant**	g	(declining)
8.	**Apple of ones eyes**	h	(costly)
9.	**Odds and ends**	i	(to praise oneself)
10.	**To blow one's trumpet**	j	(dear)

Test - 2

Match the following :

1.	**A good hand at**	a	(false friend)
2.	**Fair weather friend**	b	(skilful)
3.	**To rise to the occasion**	c	(save oneself without any damage)
4.	**To give oneself airs**	d	(to copy the good examples of)
5.	**Of the first water**	e	(valid)
6.	**To save ones skin**	f	(to act promptly)
7.	**In keeping with**	g	(to succeed)
8.	**In force**	h	(of the first rate quality)
9.	**To step into another person's shoes**	i	(to be harsh in attitude)
10.	**To take a leaf out of another person'book**	j	(in consistent with)

Sr.	Word	Meanings
751	Stricture	A severe criticism
752	Striated	Marked with lines or ridges
753	Selfsame	Very same
754	Repugnant	Causing a feeling of strong dislike
755	Pursuance	While performing/in the course of
756	Primordial	Existing at or from the beginning
757	Praxis	An accepted way of doing
758	Pilfer	To steal things of little value
759	Half-wit	A foolish/stupid person
760	Gibber	To speak quickly
761	Gamut	The complete range of
762	Denigrate	To criticize
763	Consensus	A general agreement about a matter of opinion
764	Sonorous	Having a full deep sound
765	Unflinching	Not showing fear
766	Unimpaired	Not spoilt or damaged
767	Umbrage	To feel offended
768	Unabated	Without any reduction in intensity
769	Unban	To allow that was previously forbidden
770	Tantrum	A sudden display of anger

771	Onerous	Demanding much efforts
772	Otiose	Serving no useful purpose
773	Picturesque	Forming a pretty scene
774	Maudlin	Foolishly sentimental or full of pity for oneself
775	Mealy-mouthed	Not willing to speak in a direct or open way
776	Crank	A person with fixed ideas
777	Cramp	To delay the movement of
778	Bunion	Painful swelling
779	Biopic	A film about the life of a particular person
780	Bauble	An ornament of little value
781	Badinage	Friendly joking between people
782	Barn	A child
783	Annotate	To add notes to a book
784	Animosity	Strong dislike or hostility
785	Angst	A feeling of anxiety, guilt
786	Constrict	To make tight
787	Conspire	To make secret plans
788	Expunge	To remove words or names completely from a list
789	Famished	Very hungry
790	Fluvial	Found in rivers
791	Gnarled	Twisted & rough
792	Gratis	Without payment/Free of charge
793	Hag	An ugly or evil old woman
794	Hone	To develop & improve for a special purpose over a period of time
795	Impute	To put the responsibility for
796	Intone	To say in a slow level
797	Laid-back	Calm and relaxed
798	Melange	A mixture or variety of different things
799	Resuscitate	To bring back to consciousness
800	Recumbent	Lying down

BREAK FOR WORDS REVISION

REVISE THE VOCAB

TEST 16
Words (751-800)

(1) Stricture

(a) A severe criticism (b) Self structure
(c) Strong but strange structure (d) To attuned to completely

(2) Pilfer

(a) To steal thing of little value
(b) To steal precious things
(c) To steal old things
(d) To steal jewels

(3) Half-wit

(a) Stupid (b) witty
(c) Fearless (d) Penniless

(4) Bunion

(a) Painful swelling (b) Relief
(c) Secretly attacked (d) Reunion

(5) Famished

(a) Very thirsty (b) Very hungry
(c) Ugly (d) Restricted

(6) Recumbent

(a) Lying down (b) Bringing back
(c) Standing back (d) Slow moving

(7) Gnarled

(a) Twisted & rough (b) Bent
(c) Clam & relaxed (d) None

(8) Gratis

(a) With payment (b) Without payment
(c) Greetings (d) Tightly bound

(9) Constrict

(a) To make loose (b) To make tight
(c) To Interrupt (d) To restrict

(10) Hag

(a) An ugly woman (b) Young woman
(c) Pretty woman (d) Beautiful lady

(11) Fluvial

(a) Found in river (b) Found in pound
(c) Found in lakes (d) Found in oceans

(12) Impute

(a) To put the responding for (b) To cause harm

(c) To annoy (d) To pledge

(13) Melange

(a) Mixture or variety of things (b) A weapon

(c) An improved taste (d) A valuable stone

(14) Crank

(a) A person with fixed ideas (b) Flexible

(c) Elastic (d) A person

(15) Umbrage

(a) To feel offended (b) To feel happy

(c) To feel cheated (d) To praise

Match the words in column 'A' with their correct meaning in 'B'.

	Column A		Column B
(1)	Animosity	(1)	Demanding much efforts
(2)	Expunge	(2)	Serving no useful purpose
(3)	Otiose	(3)	Having a full deep sound
(4)	Bauble	(4)	An ornament of little value
(5)	Onerous	(5)	Delay the movement
(6)	Unabated	(6)	A sudden display of anger
(7)	Bauble	(7)	Strong dislike
(8)	Maudlin	(8)	Forming a pretty scene
(9)	Cramp	(9)	To allow that was previously
(10)	Picturesque	(10)	To remove names from a list
(11)	Denigrate	(11)	To criticize
(12)	Unflinching	(12)	Without reduction intensity
(13)	Unban	(13)	Not showing fear
(14)	Tantrum	(14)	Full of pretty for one self
(15)	Sonorous	(15)	A child

Solution Test -1
Day 17

Match the following :

1. **In the dark** (ignorant)
2. **On the wane** (declining)
3. **To add fuel to the fire** (to stimulate fury)
4. **Rank and file** (common soldiers)
5. **Fair weather friend** (false friend)

6. **The wrong side of sixty** (Above Sixty)
7. **A White Elephant** (Costly)
8. **Apple of ones eyes** (dear)
9. **Odds and ends** (stray articles)
10. **To blow one's trumpet** (To praise oneself)

Solution Test - 2

Match the following :

1. **A good hand at** (skilful)
2. **Fair weather friend** (false friend)
3. **To rise to the occasion** (to act promptly)
4. **To give oneself airs** (to be harsh in attitude)
5. **Of the first water** (of the first rate quality)
6. **To save ones skin** (save oneself without any damage)
7. **In keeping with** (in consistent with)
8. **In force** (valid)
9. **To step into another person's shoes** (to succeed)
10. **To take a leaf out of another person's book** (to copy the good examples of)

Answer of Test 15

(1) a (a) a (3) a (4) a (5) b (6) a (7) a
(8) b (9) b (10) a (11) a (12) a (13) a (14) a
(15) a

Match

(1) 7 (2) 10 (3) 2 (4) 15 (5) 1 (6) 12 (7) 4
(8) 14 (9) 5 (10) 8 (11) 11 (12) 13 (13) 9 (14) 6
(15) 3

Day

18

Evaluation

Till now you have covered grammar as well as vocabulary section. Also you have covered jumbled, comprehension, fill in the blanks i.e. nearly all the topics of English language paper from entrance examination's point of view.

If you remember we gave you a full test at the start of this course and here on last day we are again giving you a full length test. Now evaluate yourself and see the difference. All The Best.

TEST

Directions (1-10) :

In the following passage some of the words have been left out. First read the passage over and try to understand what it is about. Then fill in the blanks with the help of the alternatives given.

Mass communication is the delivery of **1**, ideas and entertainment to thousands or millions of **2** simultaneously; it is a force With incalculable **3** on today's world. The **4** of mass communication rests **5** the skills of the communicator to **6** the recipient's thinking, **7** stir emotions, to **8** him or her to **9**. Mass communication is the one-to-one impact of one human intelligence upon **10**, carried on thousand fold simultaneously among individuals who have no direct personal contact.

1. (a) items (b) news
(c) advertisements (d) cartoons

2. (a) People (b) pictures
(c) advertisements (d) items

3. (a) worth (b) impact
(c) force (d) value

4. (a) dynamism (b) force
(c) success (d) power

5. (a) against (b) under
(c) to (d) upon

6. (a) stimulate (b) agitate
(c) understand (d) minimize

7. (a) for (b) to
(c) with (d) from

8. (a) encourage (b) persuade
(c) discourage (d) endanger

9. (a) direction (b) function
(c) action (d) mission

10. (a) Another (b) people
(c) man (d) women

Directions (11–20) : *You have two brief passages with five questions following each passage. Read the passages carefully and choose the best answer to each question out of the four alternatives.*

PASSAGE - 1

The achievement of science in the twentieth century has been very great. Its influence can be felt in every sphere of life. From the small pins and needles to the huge iron sheets and joints, most of the things we require for our- everyday use, come out of factories where scientific principles are utilized for practical ends. Science has enabled man to bring forces of nature under control and to use them for his own advantage. It has brought the distant parts of the world close together. Our knowledge of the universe has been much widened on account of the untiring efforts of the astronomers like Jeans and Eddington. Remarkable cures of human diseases have been possible, owing to the discovery of some wonderful medicines.

11. The main idea of the passage is...........
(a) The impact of science can be felt in every sphere of life
(b) Science is an anathema
(c) Nothing is beyond the purview of science
(d) Science can work miracles

12. The mode of approach is
(a) logical (b) anatomical
(c) descriptive (d) expository

13. What has enabled man to harness the forces of nature to the advantage of mankind?
(a) arts (b) oratory
(c) bravery (d) science

14. Science has proved a great boon for
(a) scientists (b) artists
(c) explorers (d) mankind

15. The most appropriate title for the passage will be
(a) Science is a curse
(b) Science, a great boon
(c) Achievements of science
(d) None of these

PASSAGE - II

"Science cannot reduce the magic of a sunset to arithmetic, nor can it express friendship with a,formula" observed the eminent medical researcher, Dr. Lous Orr. He added, "also beyond science's mastery of nature are love and laughter, pain and loneliness and insights into truth and beauty". This distancing of science from the human condition perhaps explains .why most foreign" tourists visiting Britain flock predictably to see the hallowed homes of playwrights, writers and poets, but choose to ignore the habitatibris where its eminent scientists lived and worked.

16. Why is it that science cannot express friendship with a formula?

(a) Science and friendship cannot co-exist

(b) It is abstract term which cannot be grappled by science

(c) Friendship is beyond science's mastery

(d) Friendship is unknown to scientists

17. The word "magic" refers to.

(a) evening dusk

(b) the sunrise

(c) solar and lunar eclipse

(d) setting of the sun, with all its beauty

18. Which of the following are beyond science's reach, according to the passage?

(a) Love and laughter, pain and loneliness

(b) Derivation of a formula

(c) Complexity of time and tide

(d) Work of the mind

19. The verb 'flock' refers to.........

(a) tourists in Britain

(b) local people

(c) large number of foreign tourists visiting homes of playwrights, writers, poets

(d) Indian tourists

20. Why according to the author do tourists prefer to visit hallowed homes of playwrights writers and poets rather than visiting the habitation of eminent scientists ?

(a) The houses of playwright and writers are well-decorated and are full of splendour

(b) Science cannot explain human emotions hence people have a soft corner for those who produce a splendid display of emotions in their work

(c) Scientists are loathsome,

(d) Houses of scientists are untidy and not well-preserved

Directions (21–30): *Read each of the following sentences to find out if thrre is any error in it. The error, if any, will be in one part of it.,The number of that part is the answer. If there is no error your answer is d. i.e. No error.*

21. When shall we (a) / arrive (b) / to our destination (c) / No error (d)

22. Based on the newspaper reports, (a) / we can conclude that (b) / many accidents caused by reckless driving (c) / No error (d)

23. Females (a) / are not appointed (b) / in our college (c) / No error (d)

24. The officer (a) / is angry, on the clerk (b) / for not attending to the work (c) / No error. (d)

25. No sooner (a) / I had spoken, (b) / than he left. (c) / No error (d)

26. Computer education (a) / in universities and colleges (b) / leaves much to be desired. (c) / No error (d)

27. You will be persecuted (a) / for, bringing seeds (b) / into Australia (c) / No error (d)

28. You must either tell me (a) / the whole story or, at least (b) / the first half of it (c) / No error (d)

29. Our new neighbours (a) / had been living in Arizona (b) / since ten years before moving to their present house (c) / No error (d)

30. The patient a/ was accompanied b/ with his friend c/ No error. d

***Directions 31–35**: Choose the word opposite in meaning to given word.*

31. Conciliation

(a) dispute (b) irritation
(c) separation (d) confrontation

32. Myth

(a) truth (b) fact
(c) falsehood (d) story

33. Reluctantly

(a) pleasingly (b) willingly
(c) satisfactorily (d) happily

34. Mutilate

(a) instruct (b) induct
(c) conduct (d) mend

35. Lament

(a) rejoice (b) rejuvenate
(c) complain (d) cry

Directions (36–40): *Out of the four alternatives, choose the one which expresses the right meaning of the given word.*

36. Grandeur

(a) magnificence (b) admiration
(c) happiness (d) awe

37. Inception

(a) initiative (b) beginning
(c) initial (d) origin

38. Colossal

(a) famous (b) vigorous
(c) energetic (d) enormous

39. Paradox

(a) Paradise (b) question
(c) puzzle (d) challenge

40. Proliferate

(a) proliferate (b) prohibit
(c) stipulate (d) reproduce

Directions (41–50) : *Four alternatives. are given for the idiom/ phrase given in bold. Choose the alternatives which best expresses the meaning of the idiom/phrase given in bold.*

41. The failure of crops in successive years put the farmer **in a tight corner.**

(a) in a closed room (b) in a small field

(c) in a difficult situation (d) in a meadow

42. The effort to trace the culprit was a **wild goose chase**.

(a) fruitful hunting (b) futile search

(c) ideal seeking (d) genuine effort

43. The story **does not hold water.**

(a) does not deserye appreciation (b) does not fulfil the requirements

(c) cannot be believed (d) cannot be valued

44. Raj couldn't pay the bill, so he asked the owner to put it **on the cuff.**

(a) on credit (b) against his credit card

(c) in his bank account (d) in his friend's account

45. His statement is **out and out** a lie.

(a) totally (b) simply

(c) merely (d) slightly

46. The luxury car that they bought turned out to be **a white elephant.**

(a) a rare article

(b) useful mode of transport

(c) costly or troublesome possession

(d) a proud possession

47. **If you are fair and square** in your work you will definitelv prosper.

(a) active (b) honest

(c) business like (d) authoritative

48. There is **no love lost between** any two neighbouring countries in the world.

(a) stop loving (b) not on good terms

(c) forming a group (d) have good understanding

49. The heavy downpour **played havoc** in the coastal area.

(a) caused destruction (b) caused diseases

(c) caused floods (d) caused hardship

50. To have a **green thumb** means

(a) one's nails are painted green

(b) one is artistic

(c) to have a natural interest in gardening

(d) one has a green tattoo on the thumb

Directions (51–55): *Four words have been written out of which three are correctly spelt and one is wrongly spell. Find the wrongly spelt word out of the four responses.*

51. (a) Eminent (b) Iminent

(c) Eloquent (d) Exuberant

52. (a) Tailor (b) Sculpter
(c) Doctor (d) Fitter

53. (a) Mathametician (b) Statistician
(c) Dietician (d) Physician

54. (a) Grotesque (b) Burlesque
(c) Picturesque (d) Piccaresque

55. (a) Indomitable (b) Furmidable
(c) Amicable (d) Admirable

Directions (56–65): *Sentences are given with blanks to be filled in with an appropriate and suitable word. Four alternatives are suggested for each question, Choose the correct alternative out of the four.*

56. Nadheeka was musing..........memories of the past.
(a) over (b) about
(c) on (d) from

57. The lame boy tried to climb up the staircase without ....help.
(a) little (b) any
(c) some (d) many

58. Each school has I its own set of rules......all good pupils should follow them.
(a) but (b) or
(c) so (d) and

59. On my return from a holiday, I had to......with a lot of
(a) catch on (b) catch up
(c) make up (d) take up

60. Only one of the boys......done the home-work gjven yesterday
(a) have (b) has
(c) can (d) could

61. Hopes of a settlement depends on the........of the discussion.
(a) findings (b) outcome
(c) break through (d) resolutions

62. We must avail ourselves........every opportunity that comes........our way.
(a) of; in (b) on; in
(c) against; for (d) to; to

63. It is time we........with determination
(a) act (b) acted
(c) I have acted (d) will act

64. When the thief entered the the inmates........in the hall.
(a) were slept (b) were sleeping
(c) slept (d) had been sleepining

65. 700 men worked for 10 years to ....the Borobudur temple 17 to its former glory.
(a) restore (b) give
(c) create (d) revive

Directions (66–75) : *A part of the sentence is given in bold. Below are given alternatives to the bold part at 1, 2 and 3 which may improve the sentence. Choose the 'correct alternative. In case no improvement is needed, your answer is '4'.*

66. Please report to me when **you return back from** Delhi.

(a) you have returned back from (b) you return from

(c) you returned back from (d) No improvement

67. Ravi has been demanding a lot more marks, **doesn't he?**

(a) hasn't he ? (b) isn't he?

(c) isn't it ? (d) No improvement

68. Exercise is **benevolent** to good health.

(a) beneficial (b) beneficent

(c) bounteous (d) No improvement

69. He parked his vehicle **under** the shade of a tree.

(a) on (b) in

(c) beneath (d) No improvement

70. **In case if** it rains, I shall not visit you.

(a) If so (b) In case of

(c) If (d) No improvement

71. TV sets have become costlier, thanks to the sudden rise in the of imported **compounds.**

(a) tubes (b) components

(c) things (d) No improvement

72. Because the enemy had a nation for engaging in sneak we were **frequently** on the alert

(a) occasionally (b) inevitably

(c) constantly (d) No improvement.

73. **Less** people came to watch cricket matches this year, so the receipts were lesser than last

(a) Many (b) Fewer

(c) Lot of (d) No improvement

74. God has **bestowed man** unsual gifts.

(a) bestowed with man (b) bestowed for man

(c) bestowed on man (d) No improvement

75. Many workers were being **held hostages.**

(a) held to be hostages (b) held as hostages

(c) held like hostages (d) No improvement

Directions (76–80): *The first and the last parts of the sentence are numbered 1 and 6. The rest of the sentence is split into four parts and named P, Q, R and S. These four parts are not given in their proper order. Read the parts and find out which of the four combinations is correct. Then find the correct answer.*

76. **1** A dictionary
P. arranged words
Q. about which information
R. containing alphabetically
S. is a book
6. is given.
(a) RPQS
(b) QRPS
(c) SRPQ
(d) SPRQ

77. **1** Agriculture
P. cotton for our clothes
Q. raw materials like jute
R. and sugarcane for our industries
S. gives us Food
6. and food for cattle.
(a) SRQP
(b) RQPS
(c) QPRS
(d) SPQR

78. **1** Today political freedom
P. and the right
Q. however money and all that money
R. assures people equality before law
S. to elect their Government
6. can buy is not fairly distributed.
(a) SPRQ
(b) RPSQ
(c) QRSP
(d) PSRQ

79. **1** By far the most logical step
P. to relieve the housewife, of routine
Q. which can be programmed
R. to carry out standard operations
S. is to provide a robot
6. when switched by the housewife..
(a) RSPQ
(b) PSQR
(c) QSPR
(d) SRQP

80. **1** During the reign of the Emperor Tiberius

P. called Phaedrus

Q. an Augustan story teller

R. translated Aesop's fables into Latin

S. in ancient Rome

6. and also added some tales of his own.

(a) QRPS

(b) PQRS

(c) SQPR

(d) RSPQ

ANSWERS

1. (b)	**2.** (a)	**3.** (b)	**4.** (c)
5. (d)	**6.** (c)	**7.** (b)	**8.** (a)
9. (c)	**10.** (a)	**11.** (a)	**12.** (b)
13. (d)	**14.** (d)	**15.** (c)	**16.** (c)
17. (d)	**18.** (a)	**19.** (c)	**20.** (b)

21. (c) **at** in place of **to**

22. (c) place **are** after **accidents**

23. (d)

24. (b) **with** in place of **on**

25. (b) **did I** in place of **I had**

26. (d)

27. (a) **prosecuted** in place of **persecuted**

28. (a) It should be **tell me either**

29. (c) **for** in place of **since**

30. (c) **by** in place of **with**

31. (d)	**32.** (b)	**33.** (b)	34. (d)
35. (a)	**36.** (a)	**37.** (c)	38. (d)
39. (c)	**40.** (d)	**41.** (c)	**42.** (b)
43. (b)	**44.** (a)	**45.** (a)	**46.** (c)
47. (b)	**48.** (b)	**49.** (a)	**50.** (c)
51. (b)	**52.** (b)	**53.** (a)	**54.** (d)
55. (b)	**56.** (c)	**57.** (b)	**58.** (d)
59. (b)	**60.** (b)	**61.** (b)	**62.** (a)
63. (b)	**64.** (b)	**65.** (a)	**66.** (b)
67. (a)	**68.** (a)	**69.** (b)	**70.** (c)
71. (b)	**72.** (c)	**73.** (b)	**74.** (c)
75. (d)	**76.** (c)	**77.** (d)	**78.** (b)
79. (b)	**80.** (c)		

TEST YOUR SELF

Question from Latest competitive exams (2007-2009) for the self evaluation.

In this section 30 papers from various competitive exam. (2007-2009) are provided for your practice. These have been divided on the basis of difficulty level of the papers i.e., easy, medium and tough.

So this section is divided into three parts:–

Test Your Section – 1 Easy level papers

Test Your Section – 2 Medium difficulty level papers

Test Your Section – 3 Tough papers

TEST YOUR SELF
SECTION-I

EASY LEVEL PAPERS

1. DENA BANK PO 2008
2. ALLAHABAD BANK CLERK 2008
3. BANK OF BARODA CLERK 2009
4. ANDHRA BANK P.O. 2007
5. BANK OF MAHARASHTRA P.O. 2007
6. B.O.I. CLERK 2008
7. CORPORATION BANK P.O. 2007
8. MAHARASHTRA CET 2009
9. NMAT 2008
10. PNB TRAINEE MANAGEMENT 2008
11. SBI CLERK 2008 – 1ST Shift
12. SBI CLERK 2008 – 2nd Shift
13. SNAP 2008

DENA BANK P.O. 2008

Number of Questions – 50
Time : 25 M.

Directions (Qs. 1 to 15): *Read the following passage carefully and answer these questions.*

Sixty years after independence, India remains one of the unhealthiest places on earth. Millions of people still suffer from diseases that no longer exist almost anywhere else on the planet. What makes the picture even bleaker is the fact that India's economic boom has so far had, little impact on health standards. Between. 2001 and 2006 India's economy grew almost 50%, the country's biggest expansion in decvades. Menatime, its child-malnutrition rate, dropped just a single percentage point, to 46%. This is worse than in most African countries. The incredible economic growth is having an impact in other ways by driving up rates of rich-world diseases such as obesity and encouraging high-end health services, some of which offer world-clkass care but remain far beyond the reach of the vast majority of Indians. The country brags about the skill of India's world -class doctors when its marketers sell India as a medical-tourism destination and an emerging health-service giant. The truth behind the glossy advertising is that: India is the sick man of Asia, malnourished and, baset by epidemics of AIDS and diabetes, and with spending levels on public health that even its Prime Minister has conceded are seriously lagging behind other developing countries in Asia.

Part of the reason for the sorry state of India's medical services is the crumbling public health infrastructure-not fancy hospitals or equipment but basic services such as clean water, a functioning sewage system, power. The World Health Organisation estimates that more than 900,000 Indians die every year from drinking bad water and breathing bad air. Public health experts believe that India's vast population add to the burden, overloading systems where they do exist and aiding the spread of disease in the many places they don't. Moreover for the past decade or so, funding for preventive public-health initiatives such as immunisation derives and programmes to control the spread of communicable diseases has been cut. Experts also blame policies that concentrate on the latest scientific techniques and not enough on basics for the fact that millions of people in India are suffering and dying.

Especially in rural India, health services are poor to nonexistent. Current staff often doesn't turn up for work. Clinics are badly maintained and people end up seeking help from pharmacists who are not sufficiently trained. India needs more than a million more doctors and nurses. the government has also promised more money for rural health through its ambitious National Rural Health Mission. it will increase public-health spending from the current 1% of India's GDP to up to 3% by 2010, but that's still just half the rate at which countries with comparable per capita incomes such as Senegal and Mongolia fund their health sectors. If that is to change, we must realise that the link between wealth and good health isn't clear-cut. Poor states that have made efforts in child immunisation over the past few years now have better coverage than richer states, where immunisation has actually slipped.

India needs to stop being complacent and prepare to spend on health but whenever it is mentioned there is always this debate about cost. Why don't we have the same debate when we spend tens of billions on new arms? It's hard to be an economic superpower if you're too sick to work.

1. Why has the author referred to India 'as one of the unhealthiest places on earth'?

(A) There is no cure available for many of the diseases contracted in India.

(B) The Government has not clearly defined health standards.

(C) A large number of people in India suffer from diseases, which have been wiped out in other countries.

(1) Both (B) & (C)
(2) Only (C)
(3) Both (A) & (C)
(4) All (A), (B) & (C)
(5) None of these

2. What staff-related problems does the rural healthcare system face?

(A) High rate of absenteeism.
(B) Badly maintained clinics
(C) Good maintenance of equipment by staff.

(1) All (A), (B), & (C)
(2) Both (A) & (C)
(3) Only (B)
(4) Both (B) & (C)
(5) None of these

3. What has contributed to the present ill health among Indians?

(1) Disintegration of the public healthcare infrastructure
(2) Healthcare facilities are often monopolished by foreigners.
(3) Doctors in India do not conduct research in areas like diabetes, which are affecting the population.
(4) The current government has taken no interest at all in public health initiatives
(5) Indian economy is not growing

4. What has the impact of high cost of healthcare in India been?

(1) The medical insurance sector is booming
(2) Patients seek care only from those who are adequately qualified.
(3) The National Health Mission Scheme will be discontinued.
(4) The number of poor increases
(5) The healthcare remains beyond the reach of the vast majority.

5. What is the author's main objective in writing the passage?

(1) Comparing India and Africa in terms of economic growth.
(2) Cautioning India to improve its healthcare system
(3) Exhorting India to have higher growth rate which will benefit the healthcare sector.
(4) Criticising medical practitioners for their lack of concern for the health of the weaker sections of society.
(5) Advising India to maintain a lower economic growth and focus on healthcare.

6. Which of the following is true in the context of the passage?

(A) Economic growth leads to provision of better healthcare service, for all
(B) Africa has cheaper and better healthcare facilities than India.
(C) The per capita income of India and Senegal is equivalent.

(1) Only (A)
(2) All (A), (B) & (C)
(3) Only (c)
(4) Both (B) & (C)
(5) Both (A) and (B)

7. Which of the following cannot be seen as a cause for the state of India's healthcare system?

(1) Vast population
(2) Lack of basic services like water, power, etc.
(3) Inadequate waste management facilities
(4) Lack of funding for preventive medical treatmenet like immunisations
(5) Lack of funding from the World Health Organisation

8. What impact has India's economic growth had on the healthcare system?

(1) Economic growth has resulted in higher prices of food and so malnutrition has risen.

(2) India is spending more on healthcare than other developing countries

(3) Excellent healthcare facilities are available at rates unaffordable by most Indians.

(4) Criticising medical practitioners for their lack of concern for the health of the weaker sections of society.

(5) Good healthcare services are available to all

9. What can be inferred from the statistics given for 2001-2006?

(1) India has made strides in reducing its malnutrition rate.

(2) During this period India managed to achieve a growth rate equivalent to that of developed countries.

(3) India managed to achieve high standards both in economic growth and in healthcare.

(4) Though India achieved a high economic growth rate, this did not positively impact the healthcare sector to a great extent.

(5) None of these.

10. How has the Prime Minister reacted to the crisis facing the healthcare sector?

(A) Is concerned about the spending levels on the healthcare system.

(B) Has decided to reduce expenditure on defence.

(C) Has encoraged private sector investment in healthcare.

(1) Both (B) & (C) (2) Only (B)

(3) Only (A) (4) Both (A) & (C)

(5) None of these

Directions (Qs. 11 to 13): *Choose the word / phrase which is most nearly the SAME in meaning as the word printed in bold as used in the passage.*

11. Complacent :

(1) Pleasing (2) Self-satisfied (3) Conforming (4) Willing (5) Rich

12. Sorry :

(1) Forgiveness (2) Apology (3) Repentant (4) Miserable (5) Pity

13. Reach :

(1) Extend (2) Span (3) Grasp (4) Distance (5) Achieve

Directions (Qs. 14 & 15): *Choose the word which is most OPPOSITE in meaning of the word printed in bold as used in the passage.*

14. Bleaker :

(1) Hopeful (2) Warm (3) Cozy (4) Sheltered (5) Protected

15. Non-existent:

(1) Hypothetical (2) Active (3) Realistic (4) Available (5) Fictional

Directions (Qs. 16 to 20): *In each sentence below four words have been printed in bold which are numbered (1), (2), (3) and (4). One of these words may be misspelt or inappropriate in the context of the sentence. Find out the wrongly spelt or inappropriate word. The number of that world is the answer. If all the words are correlctly spelt and are appropriate the answer is (5), i.e. 'All correct.'*

16. An incentive (1) can be as straightforward as praizing (2) an employee publicly (3) for his dedication (4) to the organisation. All correct (5)

17. A company is establissed (1) so that people can accomplish (2) something collectively (3) and make a contribution (4) to society. All correct (5)

18. Naina has made a massive (1) fortune (2) and earned (3) a reputation (4) as a talented stock broker. All correct (5)

19. Industries (1) like software and pharmaceuticals have low production (2) costs and will benefi-cial (3) grately from this initiative (4) All correct (5)

20. We can ensure more business (1) investment in the region (2) if we have laws which guarantee (3) property rites (4) All correct (5)

Directions (Qs. 21 to 25): *Rearrange the following six sentences (A), (B), (c), (D), (E) and (F) in the proper sequence to form a meaningful paragraph; then answer these questions*

(A) However this is too narrow a definition for India.

(B) Most often economic reforms refer to opening the economy in terms of trade and investment and tax cuts.

(C) The sooner action is initiated the faster India will be able to attain its targeted growth rate.

(D) This is a standard definition of economic reform and may be applicable to most countries.

(E) Economic reforms in India have to extend to reforming the public sector, transport, power, agriculture and infrastructure among other sectors.

(F) To identify these sectors and the necessary reforms required, there is a need for new thought leadership.

21. Which of the following should be the FIRST sentence after rearrangement?

(1) (A) (2) (B) (3) (C) (4) (D) (5) (E)

22. Which of the following should be the THIRD sentence after rearrangement?

(1) (A) (2) (B) (3) (C) (4) (D) (5) (E)

23. Which of the following should be the SECOND sentence after rearrangement?

(1) (A) (2) (B) (3) (C) (4) (D) (5) (E)

24. Which of the following should be the SIXTH (LAST) sentence after rearrangtement?

(1) (A) (2) (B) (3) (C) (4) (D) (5) (E)

25. Which of the following should be the FIFTH sentence after rearrangement?

(1) (B) (2) (C) (3) (D) (4) (E) (5) (F)

Direction (Qs: 26 to 30): *Which of the phrases (1), (2), (3) and (4) given below should replace the phrase given in bold in the follwoing sentence to make the sentence grammatically meaningful and correct. if the sentence is correct as it is and no correction is required mark (5) as the answer.*

26. Teaching farmers a few water harvesting techniques will ensure that farmers lack adequate water for irrigation.

(1) do not lack adequate (2) do not have adequate

(3) lacking adequately (4) without adequate

(5) No correction required

27. Awards are important because they recognise and reward individuals who have had a positive impact on society.

(1) of recognition and reward (2) of recognising and rewarding

(3) by recognising rewards (4) it recognise and rewards

(5) No correction required

28. Very often we react to a crisis by pretence that it doesn't exist.

(1) pretending when (2) to pretend that

(3) in pretense (4) by pretending that

(5) No correction required

29. The report stated that countries women are educated have higher economic growth rates.

(1) in countries (2) that countries where

(3) there are countries that (4) countries that

(5) No correction required

30. Economists have predicted that Asia's current economic problems are likely to be temporarily.

(1) likely temporary (2) like being temporary

(3) likely toi be temporary (4) temporarily likely

(5) No correction required

Direction (Qs. 31 to 40): *Read each sentence to find out whether there is any grammatical error in it. The error, if any, will be in one part of the sentence. the number of that part is the answer. if there is no error, the answer is (5) i.e. 'No error.' (ignore the errors of punctuation, if any.*

31. The construction work has (1)/ caused severe inconvenience (2)/ to the two dozen (3)/ families live in this locality. (4)/ No error (5)

32. The government has spent (1)/ several crores of rupees on (2)/ transforming the city before (3)/ the Olympic Games commencement next year. (4)/ No error (5)

33. His speech was very (1)/ though provoking and well appreciated (2)/ by them who attended (3)/ the World Economic Forum held in Davos. (4)/ No error (5)

34. There are several ways (1)/ in that governments (2)/ as well as ordinary citizens (3)/ can spread literacy (4)/ No error (5)

35. One of his suggestions is (1)/ that big corporations do (2)/ give a fixed percentage of (3)/ their earnings to charity. (4)/ No error (5)

36. His first priority on (1)/ being appointed as Chairman is (2)/ to build a rapport (3)/ with his employees. (4)/ No error (5)

37. On account of their forwarded thinking (1)/ leaders Botswana has managed (2)/ to raise over one million (3)/ citizens out of proverty. (4)/ No error (5)

38. Unless the new laws (1)/ to protect the environment (2)/ are enforced pollution (3)/ will reach dangerous levels. (4)/ No error (5)

39. The committee has prescribed (1)/ a code of conduct (2)/ about the recovery agents (3)/ appointed by banks. (4)/ No error (5)

40. This state unemployment rate is (1)/ the highest in the nation (2)/ as many manufacturing units have (3)/ closed down in the last decade. (4)/ No error (5)

Directions (Qs. 41 to 50): *In the following passage there are blanks each of which has been numbered. These numbers are printed below the passage and against each five words are suggested one of which fits the blank appropriately. Find out the appropriate word in each case.*

He helped ....(41).... his country from a system of violence and prejudice. When asked to speak on leadership he would give an analogy. Recollecting his childhood and the time he spent .... (42) .... cattle he would say "You can lead from behind." As a boy he was greatly .... (43) .... by jongintaba, the tribal king who raised him. When jongintaba held meetings of his court the men would gather in a circle and only .... (44) ... all had spoken did the King speak. When Mandela (45) meetings, some of his colleagues would often shout asking him to move faster on various issues. he would simply listen. When he (46) did speak he would slowly and (47) summarise everyone's point of view and then give his own. The (48) in leadership, he believed, was allowing yourself (as a leader) to be led sometimes. In 1993, as President he proposed that the minimum voting age should be (49) to 14. The proposal was not approved. he accepted this setback with great humility (50) how to abandon a failed idea is often the most difficult decision a leader has to make.

41. (1) relive (2) gain (3) freed (4) liberate (5) independent

42. (1) reared (2) flocking (3) caring (4) assembling (5) herding

43. (1) influenced (2) entrusted (3) judged (4) control (5) affected

44. (1) since (2) after (3) then (4) that (5) because

45. (1) hold (2) had (3) presided (4) attend (5) call

46.	1) beginning	(2) intently	(3) finally	(4) decisively	(5) last
47.	(1) methodically	(2) logical	(3) vaguely	(4) order	(5) systematic
48.	(1) purpose	(2) efficiency	(3) trick	(4) message	(5) moral
49.	(1) scaled	(2) made	(3) raised	(4) lowered	(5) change
50.	(1) Realisation	(2) Ability	(3) Wondering	(4) Deliberately	(5) Knowing

Answer Key

1. 2	**2.** 5	**3.** 1	**4.** 5	**5.** 2	**6.** 4	**7.** 3
8. 3	**9.** 4	**10.** 5	**11.** 2	**12.** 4	**13.** 3	**14.** 1
15. 3	**16.** 2	**17.** 1	**18.** 5	**19.** 3	**20.** 4	**21.** 2
22. 4	**23.** 4	**24.** 3	**25.** 5	**26.** 1	**27.** 5	**28.** 4
29 2	**30.** 3	**31.** 4	**32.** 4	**33.** 3	**34.** 2	**35.** 2
36. 2	**37.** 1	**38.** 5	**39.** 3	**40.** 1	**41.** 4	**42.** 5
43. 1	**44.** 2	**45.** 2	**46.** 3	**47.** 1	**48.** 4	**49.** 4
50. 5						

ALLAHABAD BANK CLERK 2008

Number of Questions – 40
Time : 25 M.

Directions (1-10): *Read the following passage carefully and answer the questions given below it. Certain words have been printed in* **bold** *to help you locate them while answering some of the questions.*

In a village in the East, there lived an old couple. They did not have any children and never spent an extra paisa on themselves. They never reparied their house or cooked good food. One day, a family moved into the village. It was their son's second birthday and they sent two delicious laddoos to the old couple. The couple ate the laddoos with great relish. For days after they could talk of nothing else. Finally the old man could take it no more. He said to his wife,"Let's buy the ingredients to make just two laddoos." His wife agreed but said, "If I make the laddoos at home, the neighbours will know and will want a **share**. Let's cook in the woods behind our hut. That way no one will ever know."

The next day the old man purchased the ingredients from the market and they set off to the woods. Having never prepared food like this before, they ended up with three laddoos instead of two. The old couple returned home with the sweets, dying to eat them. But there was a problem."It was my idea and I went to the market, so I ought to get two," said the old man. But his wife refused to give in so easily and said, "Since I prepared the sweets, I ought to have two. "The day wore on and the argument continued.

At last, the old man suggested,"Let us not talk to each other. whoever **breaks** the silence first will get one laddoo and the other person two. "His wife agreed. Hours **passed**, but neither of them spoke and finally they fell asleep with the bowl of sweets between them. That evening one of the neighbours knocked on the door but the couple did not answer for fear of losing the bet. Peering through the window, the man saw the couple lying on the floor with an untouched bowl of food. "They are dead!" He shoulted and alerted the other villagers. Soon the door was broken down and the house was swarming with villagers. they discused everything from the funeral to where the couple had hidden their wealth. but the couple lay **still**.

Finally, the villagers carried them to the cremation ground. As the flames licked his feet, the old man jumped up screaming "You win!" His wife jumped up too, happy that she had won. The two then rushed home leaving the bewildered villagers present there behind. But when they got home .... Alas the door had been left open and they found a stray dog licking the **last** crumbs of the sweets from the bowl.

1. What caused the old couple's sudden longing for laddoos?

(1) They hadn't eaten good food for several days.

(2) They had attended their neighbour's party and enjoyed the ladoos served.

(3) They saw the mouth \watering laddoos being served to guests at the party.

(4) They had tasted the laddoos prepared for their neighbour's son's birthday.

(5) They thought that the laddoos would satisfy their hunger for days to come.

2. Why did the old couple cook in the woods?

(1) It was very convenient to gather firewood.

(2) To avoid the risk of their hut burning down.

(3) To keep the fact that they were preparing laddoos a secret from their neighbours.

(4) To hide the fact that they did not know how to prepare laddoos from their neighbours.

(5) They did not have the ingredients to make enough laddoos for their neighbours as well.

3. Which of the following can be said about the old couple?

(1) They did not have any relatives to look after them in their old age.
(2) They were misers and did not spend even on keeping their house in good condition.
(3) They were not allowed to eat sweets as they were old.
(4) They were fond of animals and sometimes shared their food with stray animals.
(5) They were afraid of the villagers and hid from them.

4. Which of the following is/are **True** in the context of the passage?

(A) The old woman had prepared more laddoos than she had intended.
(B) The family who had recently moved into the village were fond of the old couple.
(C) The villagers were saddened by the death of the old couple and gave them a grand funeral.

(1) Only (A)
(2) Only (B) and (C)
(3) Only (A) and (B)
(4) All (A),(B) and (C)
(5) None of these

5. Why did the neighbour peep into the old couple's house?

(1) To learn what they were being so secretive about
(2) To spy on them and discover where their wealth was hidden
(3) To complain as they had cooked in the forest
(4) To check up on the old couple as he did everyday
(5) Not clearly mentioned in the passage

6. What puzzled the villagers?

(1) The old coupe did not die in the fire.
(2) The sight of the old couple whom they had presumed dead, alive
(3) The fact that the old couple had wasted good food
(4) The lack of concern the old woman had for her husband
(5) The old couple fed the laddoos to the dog

7. Why did the old man scream when surrounded by the villagers?

(1) He was afraid that his wife would get burned
(2) To scare away the villagers who wanted to kill him for his money
(3) His wife refused to allow him to eat more than one laddoo
(4) To indicate to the villagers that he was alive
(5) The fear of being hurt in the fire

8. What did the old couple disagree about?

(1) Where they would cook their meal
(2) Which of them was entitled to the first laddoo
(3) Whether to share the extra laddoo with their neighbours
(4) The quantity of laddoos that they had made
(5) None of these

9. What was the villager's reaction to the old couple's presumed death?

(1) They were upset and allcame to pay their last respects
(2) They were worried about how to pay for the funeral
(3) They could not decide what to do with the couple's wealth

(4) They disliked the old couple and demolished their house

(5) They dutifully arranged the couple's last rites

10. Why did the old couple initially not reveal that they were alive to the villagers?

(1) To learn the villager's true opinion of them

(2) They did not like the villagers and were mocking them

(3) Neither of them wanted to be the first to speak and lost the bet

(4) To test the honesty of the villagers

(5) None of these

Directions (11-13) : *Which of the following is* ***most similar*** *in meaning to the word given in* ***bold*** *as used in the passage.*

11. SHARE

(1) half (2) part (3) participate (4) divide (5) common

12. BREAKS

(1) interupts 2) separates (3) solves (4) defeats (5) escapes

13. PASSED

(1) overtook (2) occupied (3) unnoticed (4) elapsed (5) succeeded

Directions (14-15) : *Which is* ***most opposite*** *in meaning to the word given in* ***bold*** *as used in the passage.*

14. STILL

(1) restless (2) noisly (3) conscious (4) calmly (5) lifeless

15. LAST

(1) new (2) begin (3) constant (4) discontinue (5) first

Directions (16-25): *Read each sentence to find out whether ther is any grammatical mistake error in it. The error, ifany, will be in one part of the sentence. Mark the number of the answer. If there is no error, mark '5'.*

16. The main advantage of (1) / investing such sechemes (2) / is that you will not (3) / have to pay any taxes (4). No error (5)

17. That customer has (1) / written a letter (2) / thanks the manager (3) / for her timely help. (4) . No error (5).

18. Our company was recently (1) / award the contract (2) / to construct two major (3) / bridges in the state. (4) No error (5)

19. Accordingly the circular (1) / that was issued yesterday RBI (2) / has raised the rate at (3) / which it lends to banks. (4). No error (5)

20. Their company is going to incur (1) / heavy losses this year because (2) / of the big discounts they (3) / offers to customers.(4) / No error (5)

21. A large number of policy (1) / have lapsed because many (2)/ people have not paid (3)/their instalments on time.(4).No error (5)

22. The Foreign Investment Promotion Board is (1) /the government body who (2)/regulates investment received (3)/ by Indian factories from foreign countries.(4) No error (5)

23. The final decision can (1) / be taken only after (2)/ we consider all (3)/the panel suggestions. (4).No error (5)

24. If his aim is to (1) / buy a house in the (2) / next three years he all (3)/ should start immediate saving .(4).No error (5)

25. Can you explain why (1) / you were late this morning (2)/ when we had to make (3)/ such an important presentation ? (4). No error (5)

Directions (26-30): *In each question below a sentence with four words printed in* **bold** *type is given. These are numbered as (1),(2),(3) and (4). One of these four words printed in* **bold** *may be either* ***wrongly spelt*** *or* ***inappropriate*** *in the context of the sentence. Find out the word which is* ***wrongly spelt*** *or* ***inappropriate*** *if any. The number of that word is your answer. If all the words printed in* **bold** *are correctly spelt and also appropriate in the context of the sentence mark (5) i.e. 'All correct' as your answer.*

26. He **found** (1) / the company in 1980 to **provide** (2) / electricity to people **living** (3)/ in rural **areas** (4)/ by ten per cent. All correct (5)

27. **Salaries** (1)/ of bank **employees** (2)/ are likely (3) / to go above (4)/ by ten per cent.All correct (5)

28. The Chairman has **promissed** (1) / to **look** (2) /into the **matter** (3)/ and take **necessary** (4)/ action.All correct (5)

29. **Since** (1) / the interest rate on bank deposits is **low** (2)/ at present, people **prefer** (3)/ to deposit their **savings** (4)/ in post office schemes. All correct (5)

30. **Most** (1)/ projects are **delayed** (2)/ because of the **absents** (3)/ or proper **planning** (4)./ All correct (5)

Directions (31-40): *In the following passage there are blanks, each of which has been numbered. These numbers are printed below the passage and against each, five words are suggested, one of which fits the blank appropriately. Find out the appropriate word in each case.*

A rich merchant owned a beautiful horse. Now, one of his neighbours was keen to (**31**) this horse. He offered the merchant gold, (**32**) the merchant refused. This angered the neighbour. He (**33**) to trick the merchant. He disguised himself (**34**) a beggar and lay down at the (**35**) of the road, that the merchant used everyday, he (**36**) at the sad plight of the beggar, he (**37**) from his horse and gently lifted the beggar (**38**) his horse. No sooner did the beggar get into the (**39**) than the he galloped away. But hearing the merchant (**40**) out to him, he stopped when he was a saffe distance away. "Please don't tell anyone how you came to possess this horse. Some day an ill man may be lying by the roadside and people who have heard about your trict, may not want to help, "said the merchant. The merchants' neighbour was deeply ashamed, rode back and returned the horse to the merchant.

31.	(1) sell	(2) buy	(3) steal	(4) free	(5) train
32.	(1) since	(2) so	(3) unless	(4) otherwise	(5) but
33.	(1) deceived	(2) desires	(3) decided	(4) declined	(5) deliberately
34.	(1) similar	(2) being	(3) alike	(4) as	(5) idenitical
35.	(1) side	(2) middle	(3) gutter	(4) ending	(5) distance
36.	(1) unhappily	(2) carefully	(3) distressed	(4) misery	(5) upsetting
37.	(1) climbed	(2) stopped	(3) jump	(4) left	(5) dismounted
38.	(1) onto	(2) with	(3) above	(4) from	(5) off
39.	(1) way	(2) saddle	(3) arms	(4) horse	(5) danger
40.	(1) beg	(2) appeal	(3) shouted	(4) call	(5) cried

Answer Key

1. 4	**2.** 3	**3.** 2	**4.** 1	**5.** 5	**6.** 2	**7.** 5
8. 4	**9.** 5	**10.** 3	**11.** 2	**12.** 1	**13.** 4	**14.** 1
15. 5	**16.** 2	**17.** 3	**18.** 2	**19.** 1	**20.** 4	**21.** 1
22. 2	**23.** 5	**24.** 4	**25.** 2	**26.** 1	**27.** 4	**28.** 1
29 5	**30.** 3	**31.** 2	**32.** 5	**33.** 3	**34.** 4	**35.** 1
36. 3	**37.** 5	**38.** 1	**39.** 2	**40.** 5		

BANK OF BARODA CLERK 2009

Number of Questions – 50
Time : 25 M.

Directions (1–14) : *Read the following passage carefully and answer the questions given below it. Certain words have been printed in **bold** to help you locate them while answering some of the questions.*

During the reign of King Veer, there lived a wise magistrate. Haripant's verdicts were always just and people from all over vast kingdom came to him in order to **settle** their disputes. In the city where Haripant lived, there was a greedy ghee merchant named Niranjan. He always kept twenty barrels of ghee. Of these, fifteen would contain good quality ghee and the remaining would be adulterated. He would mix the two and sell it. This went on for a long time, till finally the people fed up of being **cheated**, complained to Haripant.

Haripant had the ghee examined and found to it be adulterated. He gave Niranjan a choice of punishment - drink the five barrels of adulterated ghee from his shop, or receive a hundred lashings, or pay a thousand gold coins to the treasury. Niranjan thought for a while. Losing a thousand gold coins was too much and a hundred lashings too painful. So he decided to drink the five barrels of ghee. Though Niranjan sold adulterated goods in his shop, he made sure his own food was of the best quality. So after drinking one barrel of ghee he began to feel sick. By the second barrel, he was vomiting. At this point he decided to opt for the lashings in stead. But he was pampered and his body was **unused** to any harsh treatment. After ten lashes, he started trembling and by twenty he was giddy. 'Stop!' he screamed. 'I will pay the thousand gold coins !' And he handed them over.

So he ended up **suffereing** all three punishments, something he did not forget in a hurry and the people of the city got to use only the **best** quality ghee in their food from them on !.

1. Why did Niranjan keep five barrels of adulterated ghee?

(1) To sell to customers who could not aford high quality ghee.

(2) To make a profit by cheating people.

(3) Being a miser he kept the low quality ghee for his family

(4) Demand for this ghee was low so he kept only a small quantity.

(5) None of these

2. Why did the people decide to go to Haripant with their complaint?

(1) He was close to the king and would get justice for them.

(2) They knew Niranjan was afraid of Haripant who punished people severely.

(3) They were confident that he would listen to their complaint and give a fair judgement.

(4) He was the only magistrate in the entire kingdom.

(5) None of these.

3. Why did Haripant allow Niranjan to choose his own punishment?

(1) He felt sorry for Niranjan

(2) Niranjan's offence was minor.

(3) He did not want Niranjan to appeal to the king for leniency.

(4) He did not want to give the wrong punishment

(5) None of these

4. Which of the following can be said about Niranja

(A) He took a lot of time to make any decision.

(B) He only cheated those who would not dare complain against him.

(C) He was allergic to ghee and fell sick whenever he consumed it.

(1) None
(2) Only A
(3) Both A and B
(4) All A,B and C
(5) None of these

5. Why did Niranjan decide to drink adulterated ghee for his punishment?

(1) Since the barrels were from his shop he thought he could substitute the adulterated ghee with good ghee.
(2) He wanted to prove that the quality of ghee he sold was good.
(3) He was greedy and had a big appetite so he thought he would easily drink the ghee.
(4) He considered it the easiest of the punishments as he did not realise what effect the ghee would have on him.
(5) None of these

6. How did Haripant arrive at the conclusion that Niranjan sold adulterated ghee?

(1) Niranjan was ill when he drank the ghee from his shop.
(2) He had the ghee tested to see if it was adulterated.
(3) He trusted the word of those who had eomplained to him.
(4) He too was duped by Niranjan.
(5) Niranjan admitted his guilt when confronted.

7. Which of the following is NOT true in the context of the passage?

(A) Niranjan's customers were so angry that they beat him mercilessly.
(B) King Veer's kingdom was large.
(C) Niranjan had a very good memory.

(1) Only A
(2) Only B
(3) Both A and C
(4) All A,B and C
(5) None of these

8. What made Niranjan opt for paying the fine last of all?

(1) He would be deeply in debt if he paid it.
(2) He knew Haripant would keep the money for himself.
(3) No one was willing to lend him money.
(4) He could not bear to part with such a huge sum.
(5) His business would be ruined if he paid such a large fine.

9. What effect did Niranjan's punishment have?

(1) All the merchants learnt their lesson and supplied only good quality ghee.
(2) Niranjan lost all his customers and had to close down his shop.
(3) People began to fear Haripant because of his severe punishments
(4) Niranjan gave into all his customers demands even if it meant making a loss.
(5) Niranjan improved the quality of the ghee that he sold.

10. Why did Niranjan suffer three punishments?

(1) He had cheapted so many people that his punishment had to be severe.
(2) Haripant had ordered this so that Niranjan would never repeat his offence.

(3) Haripant wanted to make an example of him so that other merchants would not cheat their customers.

(4) Niranjan could not decide which punishment to under-go so Haripant awarded him all three punishments.

(5) None of these

Directions (11-13) : *Choose the word which is **most similar** in meaning to the word printed in **bold** as used in the passage.*

11. SETTLE

(1) Resolve (2) Occupy (3) Compromise (4) Arrange (5) Quiet

12. CHEATED

(1) Unfaithful (2) Blamed (3) Exploited (4) Prevented (5) Dodged

13. SUFFERING

(1) Hardship (2) Distressing (3) Hurting (4) Experiencing (5) Trouble

Directions (14-15): *Choose the word which is **most opposite** in meaning of the word printed in **bold** as used in the passage.*

14. BEST

(1) Damaged (2) Inferior (3) Spoiled (4) Defective (5) Cheap

15. UNUSED

(1) Accustomed (2) Routine (3) Often (4) Normal (5) Repeated

Directions (16-20) : *Which of the phrases (1),(2),(3) and (4) given below each sentence should replace the phrase printed in **bold** in the sentence to make it grammaticallycorrect/ If the sentence is correct as it is given and no correction is required mark (5) as the asnwer.*

16. Since books are quite expensive that many children do not have access to them.

(1) more expensive than (2) so expensive that

(3) very expensive (4) too expensive for

(5) No correction required

17. At the meeting they told us what kind of difficulties we **may likely to face** while establishing a rural branch.

(1) may like to face (2) were being faced

(3) could be likely to face (4) would be likely to face

(5) No correction required

18. What **response you** get to the proposal that you circulated among our investors?

(1) responses have you (2) response did you

(3) were you responses (4) did you respond

(5) No correction required

19. One of our representatives will meet you at the airport **and accompanies you** to our office.

(1) and accompany you (2) to accompany

(3) accompanying you (4) will be accompained by you

(5) No correction required

20. I knew that **because I refused** to accept the old man's gift, It would hurt his feelings.

(1) not to refuse (2) by refusal

(3) if I refused (4) should I refused

(5) No correction required

Directions (21-25) : *In each question below a sentence with four words printed in **bold** type is given. These are numbered as (1),(2),(3) and (4). One of these four words printed in bold may be either wrongly spelt or inappropriate in the context of the sentence. Find out the word which is **wrongly***

***spelt or inappropriate**, if any. The number of that word is your answers. If all the words printed in **bold** are correctly spelt and also appropriate in the context of the sentence, mark (5) i.e. 'All correct' as your answer.*

21. It is better to **seek (1) /advice (2)/** from a financial **consultant (3)/** on how to **safe (4)/** your business. All correct (5).

22. This is the **list (1) /advice (2)/** of people who should be **insisted (3)/** in the **conference (4)/** your All correct (5).

23. The **impact (1)** /of those **schemes (2)/** was **visible (3)/** after a **decade (4)/** All correct (5).

24. Since this offer is **available (1) /** for a **limited (2)/** period **alone (3)/** you should **register (4)/** immediately. All correct (5).

25. **I patently (1)/ explained (2)/** to the customer that it was not **possible (3)/** to fulfill his **request (4)/**.All correct (5).

Directions (26-30): *Rearrange the following six sentences(A),(B),(C),(D),(E),(E)and (F) in the proper sequence to form a meaningful paragraph; then answer the questions given below them.*

(A) Thus they teach us that no matter how insignificant you think you are, you can accomplish extraordinary things.

(B) During the course of its life it was struck by lightning fourteen times.

(C) But one day it was attacked by an army of beetles

(D) The tree stood at the foot of the Himalayas for over four hundred years.

(E) The tiny insects ate their way through the tree and destroyed it.

(F) It even survived innumerable storms and avalanches.

26. Which of the following should be the **FIRST** sentence after rear-rangement?
(1)A (2) B (3) C (4) D (5) E

27. Which of the following should be the **SECOND** sentences after rearrangement?
(1) B (2) C (3) D (4) E (5) F

28. Which of the following should be the **THIRD** sentence after rear-rangement?
(1) B (2) C (3) D (4) E (5) F

29. Which of the following should be the **FIFTH** sentence after rear-rangement?
(1) A (2) B (3) C (4) D (5) E

30. Which of the following should be the **LAST (SIXTH)** sentene after rearrangement?
(1) A (2) B (3) C (4) D (5) E

Directions (31-40): *Read each sentences to find out whether there is any grammatical error or idiomatic error in it. The error, if any, will be in one part of the sentences. The number of that part is the answer. If there is no error, the answer is '5'. (Ignore errors of punctuation, if any).*

31. My cousin's wedding provided (1)/ me with the chance (2)/ to meet which relatives I (3)/ had not met for a long time. (4)/ No error (5).

32. There are floods in this (1)/ region last year but (2)/ many of the victims have (3)/ not yet been compensated. (4)/ Noerror (5)

33. We must ensure that (1)/ all our records (2)/ are computerised (3)/ for next year. (4)/ No error (5)

34. In order to impart (1)/ training to bank employees (2)/ we are setting up (3)/ centres at various location.(4)/ No error (5)

35. When Rahul reached (1)/ the office there was (2)/ nobody there so (3)/ he sat down to wait. (4)/ No error (5)

36. I shall have to check (1)/ my records to find out (2)/ how much cheques (3)/ have been collected so far. (4)/ No error (5)

37. Our first task as (1)/ board members is (2)/ to decide on what we (3)/ should spend these funds. (4) No error (5)

38. She was lucky (1)/ to find a good paying (2)/ job as soon (3)/ as she graducated. (4)/ No error (5)

39. For the last six months (1)/ Seema has been asking them (2)/ to refund the money but (3)/ there is been no action. (4)/ No error (5)

40. He promised to get (1)/ in touch with myself (2)/ as soon as he had (3)/ the information I needed.(4)/ No error (5)

Directions (41-50): *In the following passage there are blanks, each of which has been numbered. These numbers are printed below the passage and aganist each, five words are suggested, one of which fits the blank appropriately. Find out the appropriate word in each case.*

*A profesor was (**41**)the Indian Independence Movement and the idea of non-violence (**42**) by Mahatma Gandhi. "Although others like Nelson Mandela followed this idea and (**43**) the Nobel Prize for Peace Mahatma Gandhi did not." she said. One student spoke up,"It is good that he didn't (**44**) it was an award started by Alfred Nobel who invented dynamite, which causes (**45**)!"*

*The professor (**46**) "In fact the world should be (**47**) to Nobel because he invented dynamite. It was very useful to build tunnels (**48**) mountains for trains to pass. If we choose to use it for war it is not his fault. Furthermore he (**49**) all his wealth into instituting prizes for literature, physics, chemistry, medicine, peace, etc. His (**50**) was that anything which would benefit the human race deserved recognition so that the person who had started it would have no financial diffculties in achieving his goal!"*

41.	(1) lecturing	(2) talking	(3) discussing	(4) speaking	(5) arguing
42.	(1) origniate	(2) spectalised	(3) start	(4) conceived	(5) thought
43.	(1) awarded	(2) given	(3) presented	(4) win	(5) received
44.	(1) that	(2) get	(3) accept	(4) though	(5) since
45.	(1) blast	(2) ruins	(3) destruction	(4) bombs	(5) damages
46.	(1) disagreed	(2) answers	(3) shouted	(4) upset	(5) agreed
47.	(1) dedocated	(2) grateful	(3) appreciated	(4) thanking	(5) cursing
48.	(1) from	(2) through	(3) over	(4) under	(5) within
49.	(1) put	(2) left	(3) gave	(4) donated	(5) contributed
50.	(1) decision	(2) logic	(3) cause	(4) excuse	(5) discovery

Answer Key

1. 2	**2.** 3	**3.** 5	**4.** 5	**5.** 4	**6.** 2	**7.** 3
8. 4	**9.** 1	**10.** 4	**11.** 1	**12.** 5	**13.** 4	**14.** 2
15. 1	**16.** 2	**17.** 4	**18.** 2	**19.** 1	**20.** 3	**21.** 4
22. 2	**23.** 5	**24.** 3	**25.** 1	**26.** 4	**27.** 2	**28.** 5
29 5	**30.** 1	**31.** 3	**32.** 1	**33.** 4	**34.** 4	**35.** 5
36. 3	**37.** 5	**38.** 2	**39.** 4	**40.** 2	**41.** 3	**42.** 4
43. 5	**44.** 5	**45.** 3	**46.** 1	**47.** 2	**48.** 4	**49.** 4
50. 2						

ANDHRA BANK P.O. 2007

Number of Questions – 50
Time : 35 M.

Directions for question 1-10: *Read the following passage carefully and answer the questions given below it. Certain words are printed in bold to help you to locate them while answering some of the questions.*

It is difficult to imagine the **extraordinary** number of controls on Indian industry before 1991. Entrepreneurs needed permission to invest and could be penalised for ex-ceeding production capacity. Even with the given invest-ment capacity they had, entering certain areas was prohib-ited as these were reserved for the public sector. If they had to import anything, they required licences. To get these li-cences was tough. They had to persuade a bureaucrat that the item was required but even so permission was unavail-able if somebody was already producing it m India. The im-pact of the reforms was not instantaneously and permanently wonderful. In India's case it began to show after about a year-and-a-half. After 1993 then came three years of rapid industrial growth of about 8% or so. But, in the second half of the 90s, there was ;i tapering of industrial growth and investment. After 1997 and the East Asian crisis there was global slowdown, which had an impact on the Indian indus-try. But, in the last few years there has been a tremendous upturn. With the **rise** of investment industrial growth has reached double digits or close.

However even during the period when industrial growth was not that rapid, there is a lot of evidence that positive results of the reforms were seen. There were companies that didn't look at all internally but instead performed remarkably in the highly competitive global market. For instance, the software sector's performance was outstanding in an almost totally global market. Reliance built a world-class refinery. Tatas developed an indigenously designed car. The success of the software secto.- has created much higher expectations from and much higher confidence in what Indian industry can do. On the government's side it's a vindication that liberalisation of both domestic and external policies, includ-ing the increased inflow of Foreign Direct Investment, has created an environment in which industry can do well, has done well and is preparing to do even better. What they need is not sops, but good quality infrastructure. For the 1lth Plan an industrial growth rate of around 12% is projected. It will have methods of developing infrastructure, which will close the deficit. This can be done through increased investment in public sector for those infrastructure areas, which cannot **attract** private investment, and through et forts to improve private participation in different ways of public-private par-ticipation.

In the early stages of reforms, the liberalisation of trade policies and a shift to a market-determined exchange rate had the effect of removing constraints on agriculture in terms of depressed prices. The removal of protection on industry helped to produce a more level playing field, because the earlier system was extremely unfair to agriculture. The lesson to be learnt from the reforms process is to **persevere** in **re-**forming the strategic parts of the economy, which will lead to I even higher growth rate. India has to do better than its cur- I rent average growth rate of 8% and ensure that benefits from I this higher growth go beyond industry and urban areas and I extend to agriculture.

1. Which of the following was not a restriction on Indian I industry prior to 1991 ?

A. A private business needed government sanction to invest in any sector.

B. Industrial growth had to be maintained at a certain percentage fixed by the government.

C. It was difficult to obtain licenses.

1. All (A), (B) & (C)
2. Only (B)
3. Only (C)
4. Both (A) & (C)
5. None of these

2. Which of the following factors was responsible for the fall in India's growth rate in the late 1990s?
   1. The implementation of economic reforms was too rapid.
   2. It was expected after achieving a high growth rate of 10%.
   3. There was a slowdown in the global economy.
   4. There were sanctions against East Asian countries by WTO.
   5. The software sector grew but the other sectors were neglected.
3. Which of the following can be said about the reforms of 1991?
   1. They benefited Indian industry immediately.
   2. All Indian companies began to focus on indigenous development instead of looking for opportunities abroad.
   3. They were targeted only at the software sector.
   4. India was among the worst affected countries by the East Asian economic crisis because it had opened up its economy.
   5. They encouraged foreign direct investment in India.
4. What was the impact of the flourishing Indian software sector?
   1. Other companies were unable to be competitive in the global market.
   2. It fuelled expectations of a good performance from the Indian economy.
   3. Growth rate rose to 12%.
   4. It created cut-throat competition among software companies which would hinder the sector in the long
   5. None of these
5. Why was investment by private businesses disallowed in certain sectors?
   1. To ensure proper development in these sectors
   2. To prevent corruption in key sectors like infrastruc-ture
   3. To ensure steady not inconsistent growth in key sec-tors
   4. To protect the interests of the public sector in these sectors
   5. None of these
6. What is the author's opinion about the government's decision to liberalise the economy in 1991 ?
   1. It was beneficial because it created confidence in the Indian economy.
   2. The timing was wrong since the economy experienced a slowdown in growth rate.
   3. It led to a focus on software and other sectors were neglected.
   4. Foreign companies took advantage of the new poli-cies and exploited certain sectors.
   5. None of these
7. How did software companies deal with slow industrial growth in an open Indian economy?
   1. They focused on strengthening their position in the domestic market.
   2. They campaigned for infrastructure development.
   3. They diversified into different sectors.
   4. They entered into partnerships with public sector enterprises in reserved sectors.
   5. They targeted global markets.
8. Which of the following is NOT true in the context of the passage?
   A. India experienced a slowdown in growth during the late 1990s because initially the economic growth rate was too rapid.

B. There were a few stringent regulations on Indian industries which kept economic growth below 12%.

C. Companies did not get import licenses for goods if they were being indigenously produced.

1. Only (A)   2. Both (B) & (C)
3. Both (A) & (B)   4. All (A), (B) & (C)
5. None of these

9. What does the author recommend to ensure that the industrial sector continues to perform better?

1. Subsidies should be provided in infrastructure development.
2. Government should keep control of and monitor all infrastructure projects.
3. Wipe out any infrastructure deficit by transferring responsibility of these projects to the private sector.
4. Ensure a combination of public and private sector involvement in developing infrastructure.
5. None of these

10. How did the economic reform the agriculture sector?

1. A system of market determined exchange rate was introduced.
2. Constraints in agriculture increased.
3. Prices were depressed because there was a removal of protection on the sector.
4. Agriculture growth rate doubled.
5. None of these

Directions for question 11-13: *Choose the word which is most nearly the SAME in meaning as the word given in bold as used in the passage.*

11. extraordinary
(1) unusual (2) wonderfnl (3) rare (4) beautiful (5) strange

12. rise
(1) stand (2) increase (3) slope (4) upward (5) progress

13. projected
(1) discussed (2) needed (3) estimated (4) achieved (5) thrown

Directions for question 14-15: *Choose the word which is most OPPOSITE in meaning of the word given in bold as used in the passage.*

14. persevere
(l) lose (2) hide (3) chase (4) disturb (5) stop

15. attract
(l) ugly (2) offend (3) push (4) sick (5) reject

Directions for question 16-25: *Read each sentence to find out whether there is any error in it the error, if any, will be in one part of the sentence. The number of that part is the answer. It there is no error, the answer is (5). (Ignore errors of punctuation, if any).*

16. (1) Since most of the / (2) employees were in / (3) favour of the merger / (4) it was a success. /(5) No error

17. (1) The Reserve Bank of India are / (2) responsible for en-suring (3)/ that the banking sector / (4) functions effec-tively. /(5) No error

18. (1) There is a shortage / (2) for qualified staff /(3) in many software /(4) companies in India. /(5) No error

19. (1) According to the survey /2) more of forty per cent /3) of Indians do not /4) have access to banks. /(5) No error

20. (1) To improve its efficiency /(2) all income tax officers/(3) will be provided with /4) laptops by next year. /(5) No error

21. (1) He was not a /(2) good manager because /(3) he did not know / (4) what to react in a crisis. (5)/ No error

22. (1) Ram will be suspended /(2) because he opened an account /(3) without obtaining none /(4) of the necessary documents. /(5) No error

23. (1) Mr Bajaj has resigned /(2) from the post of Director/(3) which he holds /(4) for over ten years. /(5) No error

24. (1) In spite of living /(2) in Kerala for two years /(3) he yet does /(4) not speak Malayalam. /(5) No error

25. (1) Mr Patil has approached /(2) the bank for /(3) a loan to finance /(4) his son college education. /(5) No error

DIRECTIONS for questions 26-30: *In each question below a sen-tence with four words printed in bold type is given. These are numbered as (1), (2), (3) and (4). One of these four words printed in bold may be either wrongly spelt or inappropriate in the context of the sentence. Find out the word which is* wrongly spelt or inappropriate if any. The number of that word is your answer. If all the words printed in bold are correctly spelt and also appropriate in the context of the sentence, mark (5), ie 'AH Correct', as your answer.

26. The entire(1) process (2) of assigning (3) projects has undergone (4) a change. All Correct 5)

27. In his speech Mr Leeladhar revealed (1) that banks have to comply (2) with Basel norms (3) last (4) by March next year. All Correct (5)

28. The scheme (1) was launched (2) to allow (3) a customer to know the states (4) of his loan application. All Correct (5)

29. The objective (1) of the seminar was to raise (2) awareness (3) about the consequences (4) of corruption. All Correct (5)

30. The government is **commited** (1) to providing world-class infrastructure to sustain (2) exten-sive (3) growth (4) of industries. All Correct (5)

DIRECTIONS for questions 31-35: *Which of the phrases (1), (2), (3) and (4) given below should replace the phrase given in bold in the following sentences to make the sentence grammatically correct? If the sentence is correct as it is and there is no correction required, mark (5), ie 'No correction required', as the answer.*

31. We have reliably inform that the new branch will not open till next year.

1. reliably to inform
2. reliable information
3. informed reliability
4. to be reliably inform
5. No correction required

32. The appointment to these posts were temporarily so we shall have to apply to other companies.

1. is temporary
2. being temporarily
3. will be temporarily
4. are temporary
5. No correction required

33. In anticipation of the transport strike we have decided for delayed our vacation.

1. to delay
2. on delay
3. in delaying
4. delaying
5. No correction required

34. You cannot dismiss him unless you had a good reason.

1. until having
2. without
3. except you have
4. if there being
5. No correction required

35. In our opinion Mr Dayal's son has carry forward the business well in his absence.

1. carried through
2. been carried out
3. carried on
4. been carrying away
5. No correction required.

DIRECTIONS for questions 36-40: *Rearrange the following six sentences (A), (B), (C), (D), (E) and (F) in the proper se-quence to form a meaningful paragraph; then answer the questions given below them.*

A. He then hid nearby to watch and see who would remove it.

B. He saw a purse full of gold lying in the middle of the road. It was the king's reward to the person who did something about the problem.

C. The king was tired of his subjects only complaining but doing nothing to solve their problems.

D. A youth on his way to market saw the stone, put down his produce and rolled the stone to the side of the road.

E. Many people passed by but dodged their duty of moving the stone instead of blaming the king for not keeping the highways clear.

F. One day he placed a heavy stone in the middle of the road.

36. Which of the following is the **SECOND** sentence after rearrangement?

1. B 2.C 3.D 4.E 5.F

37. Which of the following is the **SIXTH (LAST)** sentence after rearrangement?

1. A 2.B 3.C 4.D 5.E

38. Which of the following is the **FIRST** sentence after rear-rangement?

1. A 2.B 3.C 4.D 5.F

39. Which of the following is the **THIRD** sentence after re-arrangement?

1. A 2. B 3. C 4.D 5.E

40. Which of the following is the **FIFTH** sentence after rearrangement?

1. B 2.C 3.D 4.E 5.F

DIRECTIONS for questions 41-50: *In the following passage there are blanks each of which has been numbered. These numbers are printed below the passage and against each five words are suggested one of which fits the blank appropriately. Find out the appropriate word in each case.*

Our company has set up a foundation which is **41** to spreading literacy. To **42** this cause the foundation has a project called 'A Library for Every School' through **43** the foundation donates books mainly to government school li-braries so that children have easy **44** to books on a variety of sub-jects. In my **45** as Chairperson of the Foundation I travel **46** in rural areas. All this travelling has **47** me to understand what children want to read in different parts of the country. **48** my travels I frequently stay in the houses of people I meet as **49** there are no hotels in small towns and villages that I visit. In India a guest is always treated well; an old Sanskrit saying is Atithi Devo Bhava **50** that God comes in the form of a guest.

41. 1. dedicated 2. responsible 3. trying 4. catered 5. involved

42. 1. awaken 2. further 3. aim 4. contribute 5. perform

43. 1. those 2. which 3. whom 4. where 5. these

44. 1. opportunity 2. admission 3. purchase 4. access 5. contact

45. 1. feeling 2. decision 3. role 4. knowledge 5. order

46.	1. extensively	2. somehow	3. extremely	4. hastily5. sometime	
47.	1. ensured	2. provided	3. enabled	4. deprived	5. made
48.	1. During	2. Since	3. From	4. Through	5. Besides
49.	1. while	2. usual	3. neither	4. often	5. either
50.	1. threatens	2. meaning	3. fearing	4. imply	5. naturally

Answer Key

1. 2	**2.** 3	**3.** 5	**4.** 2	**5.** 4	**6.** 1	**7.** 5
8. 3	**9.** 4	**10.** 5	**11.** 1	**12.** 2	**13.** 3	**14.** 5
15. 5	**16.** 2	**17.** 1	**18.** 2	**19.** 2	**20.** 1	**21.** 4
22. 3	**23.** 3	**24.** 3	**25.** 4	**26.** 3	**27.** 4	**28.** 4
29 4	**30.** 1	**32.** 1	**31** 2	**33** 1	**34.** 2	**35.** 5
33. 3	**37.** 2	**38.** 3	**39.** 1	**40.** 3	**41.** 1	**42.** 2
43. 2	**44.** 4	**45.** 3	**46.** 1	**47.** 3	**48.** 1	**49.** 4
50. 2						

EXPLANATIONS

1. (A) was a restriction because "entre-preneurs needed permission to invest." (C) was also a restriction as "to get these licences was tough."

2. The passage says: "After 1997 and the East Asian crisis there was global slow down, which had an impact on the Indian in-dustry."

3. All other choices can be ruled out.

4. The passage says: "The success of the software sector has created much higher ex-pectations from ... what Indian industry can do."

5. "Entering certain areas was prohib-ited" for the private sector "as these were reserved for the public sector."

6. This is the optimistic tone that runs through the passage.

7. The passage says: "... the software sector's performance was outstanding in an almost totally global market"

8. (A) is not true: the reason lay in global economic slowdown.(B) is not true: 12% is the growth rate pro-jected for the future. The passage doesn't even mention it as a past bench-mark. is true: The passage says: "... permission was unavailable if somebody was already pro-ducing it in India."

9. Read the last sentence of the second para.

10. None of the choices is appropriate.

11. 1 **12.** 2 **13.** 3 **14.** 5 **15.** 5

16. Substitute *had been.* **17.** Substitute *is.* **18.** Substitute *of.*

19. Substitute *than.* **20.** Substitute *their.* **21.** Substitute *how.*

22. Substitute *any.* **23.** Substitute *had held.* **24.** Delete *yet*

25. Substitute *son's.* **26.** Assigning **27.** latest

28. Status **29.** Consequences **30.** Committed

31. 2 **32.** 1 **33.** 1 **34.** 2 **35.** 3

36-40 CFAEDB

36. 5 **37.** 2 **38.** 3 **39.** 1 **40.** 3 **41.** 1

42. 2 **43.** 2 **44.** 4 **45.** 3 **46.** 1 **47.** 3

48. 1 **49.** 4 **50.** 2

BANK OF MAHARASHTRA P.O. 2007

Number of Questions – 50
Time : 35 M.

DIRECTIONS for questions 1-15: *Read the following passage carefully and answer the questions given below it.*

The wakeup call that China represents to India is not limited to its showpiece urban centres or that New Delhi hopes India will experience the benefits that the Olympic games have brought to Beijing. More pertinent is the comparison of the agricultural sectors of the two countries. Why and how has China managed to outstrip India in agriculture when 25 years ago the two countries were on par on most parameters? Both have traditionally been agrarian economies and over half their populations continue to depend on the land for their livelihood. With large populations and histories of famine, India and China share concern on issues such as food security. However, while India's agricultural sector is projected to grow by about 2.5 per cent this year-a slide from the previous year's growth-, China's has been steadily growing at between 4 per cent and 5 per cent over the last fifteen years. The widest divergence between India and China is in the profitable horticultural sector with the production of fruits and vegetables in China leaping from 60 million tonnes in 1980 compared to India's 55 million tonnes at the same time, to 450 million tonnes in 2003 ahead of India's corresponding 135 million tonnes. China's added advantage lies in the more diversified composition of its agricultural sector with animal husbandry and fisheries which account for close to 45 per cent of growth compared to 30 per cent for India.

According to the latest report by the Economic Advisory Council, the traditional excuses for India's substandard performance in the farm sector are inadequate since India is placed favourably when compared to China in terms of quantity of arable land, average farm size, farm mechanisation etc. The reasons for China having outperformed India are threefold: technological improvements accruing from research and development (China has over 1,000 R&D centres devoted to agriculture), investment in rural infrastructure and an increasingly liberalised agricultural policy moving away from self-sufficiency to leveraging the competitive advantage with a focus on "efficiency as much as equity". Investment in rural infrastructure, roads, storage facilities, marketing facilities are also crucial but government support in India has mainly been through subsidies, not investment. There has been much debate about subsidies and their utility; the opposing view being that subsidies are against the market reforms and distort the market as well as reduce resource efficiency. In contrast to the 2,046 applications for the registration of new plant varieties in China over the past few years, data reveals that despite India having the largest number of agricultural scientists in the world India's current research track record is abysmal, equivalent to what China achieved in the 1980s. Far from developing new strains, the number of field crop varieties fell by 50 per cent between 1997 and 2001 despite the fact that there was sharp and sustained increase in funding. One reason is that majority of the budget is eaten up by staff salaries with only 3 per cent being allotted for research. In contrast, most agricultural research centres in China must use Central government funding purely for research. Funds relating to salaries and other administrative incidentals must be generated by the centres themselves. The centres and scientists are thus encouraged to engage in joint ventures with private sector companies to form commercial signoffs from their research. In fact, research staff are now being hired on a contract basis with pay based on performance and salaries raised proportionately for those v/ho perform well. India needs to learn from China's example and adopt a pragmatic approach if it has to meet its targets of the Eleventh Five Year Plan.

1. What has been the major area of difference in the development of the agricultural sectors of India and China?

1. Quantity of arable land in China is far greater than in India.
2. Food security is not a concern for China as the country is basically self-sufficient.

3. China has experienced substantial growth in production in allied agricultural activities like horticulture.
4. India's agricultural sector is too diversified so it is difficult :o channel funds for development.
5. None of these

2. Which of the following is/are area/s in which China has not outdone India?

A. Development of urban infrastructure
B. Activities allied to agriculture like animal husbandry
C. Successful bids for international sporting events se

3. Which of the following is NOT TRUE in the context of the passage?

1. Agricultural status of China and India was equivalent a quarter of a century ago.
2. India's current economic growth rate is half that of China.
3. China is traditionally an agrarian economy.
4. Agricultural research in India is inadequate.
5. India's current agricultural growth rate has fallen from the previous year.

4. How are Chinese agricultural research facilities governed?

1. Salaries of staff are linked to performance and this hampers productive research.
2. Their funding comes from the government alone to prevent private companies from manipulating the di-rection of their research.
3. A fixed proportion of government grants is allotted to be utilised for administrative incidentals which can- not be exceeded.
4. Research staff even those on contract are entitled to increments for good performance.
5. None of these

5. According to the author, which of the following is a legitimate explanation for India's stagnating agricultural sector?

A. (A) India diverts funds that should be spent on agricultural research to urban development.
B. Reforms are hampered because adequate subsidies are not provided by the government.
C. The procedure for registering new plant varieties is very tedious so research is limited.

1. Only (A)
2. Only (B)
3. Only (C)
4. Both (A) & (C)
5. None of these

6. Which of the following is an advantage that India holds over China with respect to the agricultural sector?

1. Lack of diversification of the agricultural sector
2. Superior technology and farming practices
3. Greater prevalence of farm mechanization
4. Provision of fertilizer and power subsidies
5. Abundant research generated by their scientists

7. Why was there a drop in development of new crop varieties for five years from 1997?

1. Government funding for research fell during that period.
2. Funds were diverted during this period to agricultural mechanisation.
3. The private sector was not allowed to fund research.

4. A large number of agricultural scientists left India for better opportunities abroad during this period.
5. None of these

8. What argument has been posed against implementation of subsidies?

A. Subsidies sacrifice equity for efficiency.
B. Subsidies hamper efficient resource utilisation.
C. Subsidies reduce private sector investment and in-volvement in agriculture.

1. Both (A) & (B)
2. Only (B)
3. Both (B) & (C)
4. Only (A)
5. None of these

9. Which of the following cannot be said about Indian agricultural universities?

A. Attendance is poor because of the dwindling funds to carry out research.
B. Enrolments of students and qualified staff have fallen because of the lack of funds for salaries.
C. Allotment for research funding by the government, is non-existent.

1. Only (B)
2. Both (A) & (B)
3. Both (B) & (C)
4. All (A), (B) & (C)
5. None of these

10. Which of the following is not responsible for China's successful transformation of itsagricultural sector?

A. Change in philosophy from self-sufficiency to competitiveness and efficiency
B. Greater allocation for subsidies
C. Increased investment in marketing and distribution networks

1. Only (B)
2. Both (B) & (C)
3. Both (A) & (C)
4. A11 (A), (B) & (C)
5. None of these

DIRECTIONS for questions 11-13: *Choose the word which is most nearly the SAME in meaning as the word printed in bold as used in the passage.*

11. concern

1. importance 2. regret 3. business 4. anxiety 5. emphasis

12. pertinent

1. intense 2. sizeable 3. practical 4. visible 5. significant

13. devoted

1. surrendered 2. dedicated 3. established 4. staunch 5. dependent

DIRECTIONS for questions 14-15: *Choose the word which is most OPPOSITE in meaning of the word printed in bold as used in the passage.*

14. sustained

1. intermittent 2. discouraged 3. habitual 4. defeated 5. restrained

15. pragmatic

1. faithful 2. unwilling 3. idealistic 4. practical 5. inexperienced

DIRECTIONS for questions 16-25: *Read each sentence to find out whether there is any error in it The error, if any, will be in one part of the sentence. The number of that part is the answer. If there is no error, the answer is (5). (Ignore errors of punctuation, if any.)*

16. The ongoing merger among (1)/the two companies will (2) / have an adverse (3) /impact on consumers. (4) No error (5)

17. It is evident that (1)/ the banking sector has underwent (2) / tremendous changes during (1) / the past two decades.(4) No error (5)

18. According to the consultant (1)/ a more detail analysis of (2)/customer needs (3) / and product pricing is required.(4) No error (5)

19. Over the next five years (1)/ the government needs to invest/ (2) at less 350 billion dollars (3) / in rural infrastructure. (4) No error (5)

20. The lack of no funds (1)/ has resulted in several (2)/ delays in launching our (3)/ new product in India. (4) No error (5)

21. The only option is (1)/ for the bank to (2) / modernize its operations (3)/ at all their branches.(4) No error (5)

22. He has a reputation (1) / for acquiring bankrupt companies (2)/restructuring them and sells (3)/ them off for profit. (4) No error (5)

23. If we have to be (1) / competitive we must be (2)/ ready to face/ (3) various technical challenge. No error (5)

24. The government has introduced (1) / a new law who forces (2)/ farmers to sell their produce (3) / only to licensed dealers.(4) No error (5)

25. The company recently opened (1)/ its first branch in Bangalore (2) / and will expand its operations (3)/ to other states sooner. (4) No error (5)

DIRECTIONS for questions 26-30: *In each of the following sentences there are two blank spaces. Below each five words have been denoted by numbers (1), (2), (3), (4) and (5). Find out which pair of words can be filled up in the blanks in the sentence in the same sequence to make the sentence meaningfully complete*

26. Research shows that an organisation's __________to cater to the customers changing needs will ____________its success.

1. intent - realise
2. ability – determine
3. apacity - lead
4. desire – insure
5. flexibility-acquire

27. In many rural areas hospitals are__________equipped because of the__________of funds from the government.

1. well - dearth
2. faulty – lacking
3. ptimally - disparity
4. inadequately - scarcity
5. ill – surplus

28. A company can__________the potential of its employees__________ various training programmes.

1. emphasise - for
2. exploit – from
3. enhance - through
4. appraise - by
5. identify – under

29. The objective of the survey is to____________the impact of the rising rupee on___________ a engineering sector.

1. attribute - profitable
2. establish – tensed
3. intensity - volatile
4. substantiate – reinforced
5. ascertain – thriving

30. The country's economic growth has been achieved___________exports and___________ large amounts of foreign direct investment.

1. on - boosting
2. despite – estimating
3. mostly - soliciting
4. via - attracting
5. substantial-opposing

DIRECTIONS for questions 31-35: *Which of the phrases (1), (2), (3) and (4) given below should replace the phrase given in bold in the following sentence to make the sentence gram-matically meaningful and correct? If the sentence is cor-rect as it is and no correction is required, mark (5) as the answer.*

31. Considering the high demand for flights to Gulf coun-tries airlines can risen prices.

1. should rise
2. could raised
3. may raise
4. will raise up
5. No correction required

32. Without both issue is clarified the Board has kept all other matters before it pending.

1. Unless both issues are
2. Until each issue were
3. Without the issue being
4. Since both issues
5. No correction required

33. The incident has clearly highlighted his knowledge and attentive of detail.

1. attended to detail
2. attentively on details
3. attention to detail
4. attention for detail
5. No correction required

34. The bank's accumulated losses have come up for man-ageable levels this year.

1. come to
2. came into
3. coming from
4. came within
5. No correction required

35. Improving the educational system, which is one of the worst in the world, requires commitment from the country's politicians.

1. among the worse
2. one of the worse
3. become the worse
4. from the worst
5. No correction required

DIRECTIONS for questions 186-190: *Rearrange the following sen-tences (A), (B), (C), (D), (E) and (F) into a meaningful para-graph and then answer the questions given below it.*

(A) Moreover salaries in public sector enterprises are not as competitive as those offered by pri-vate or foreign corporates.

(B) This trend should be a wake-up call for stakeholders to examine why employees are seeking better opportunities with private companies in India and abroad.

(C) Public Sector Enterprises (PSEs) have been experiencing severe challenges in attracting, motivating and retaining their key staff.

(D) Having identified these as the reasons employees leave PSEs, it is important to empower stakeholders to find ways to remedy the situation.

(E) One reason is that young employees lured away by private firms are more willing to undertake professional risks.

(F) Employees in specialist roles especially have become increasingly difficult to retain.

36. Which of the following should be the FIRST sentence after rearrangement?

1. (A) 2. (B) 3. (C) 4. (D) 5. (E)

37. Which of the following should be the SECOND sentence after rearrangement?

1. (B) 2. (C) 3. (D) 4. (E) 5. (F)

38. Which of the following should be the THIRD sentence after rearrangement?

1. (A) 2. (B) 3. (C) 4. (D) 5. (E)

39. Which of the following should be the FOURTH sentence after rearrangement?

1. (A) 2. (B) 3. (C) 4. (D) 5. (E)

40. Which of the following should be the LAST(SIXTH) sentence after rearrangement?

1. (A) 2. (B) 3. (C) 4. (D) 5. (E)

DIRECTIONS for questions 41-50: *In the following passage there are blanks each of which has been numbered. These numbers are printed below the passage and against each five words have been suggested, one of which fills the blanks appropriately. Find out the appropriate word in each case.*

Traditional bank architecture is based on bank branches. These branches ensure the physical **41** of a customer's savings. A customer may go there to deposit and withdraw money, **42** loans and **43** in other financial transactions. In the past two decades banking architecture has changed-the Automated Teller Machine (ATM) has been a big **44** and credit and debit cards have created new financial spaces. **45** the bank branch has remained the bedrock of the banking system-after all a person needs a bank account in a branch before he can operate a debit or ATM card. This may be about to change as technocrats now **46** cell phones as the new architecture of virtual banks. This has the potential to make branches **47**. Cell phone banking looks especially relevant for India since it can penetrate the countryside cheaply and **48**. The world over cell phones are spreading at a **49** rate and in India alone new cell phone connections are growing at the rate of six million a month-a rate of customer **50** that no bank can dream of.

41.	1. knowledge	2. security	3. presence	4. confidentiality	5. guarantee
42.	1. negotiate	2. advance	3. credit	4. disburse	5. sanction
43.	1. pursue	2. interact	3. operate	4. enable	5. engage
44.	1. drawback	2. hurdle	3. consequence	4. luxury	5. innovation
45.	1. Despite	2. Although	3. Even	4. Yet	5. Until
46.	I. view	2. realise	3. display	4. engineer	5. assess
47.	1. essential	2. obsolete	3. extant	4. retreat	5. expired
48.	1. moderately	2. occasionally	3. compulsorily	4. indiscriminately	5. effectively
49.	1. phenomenal	2. gradual	3. proportionate	4. competitive	5. projected
50.	1. discount	2. base	3. expansion	4. satisfaction	5. relationship

Answer Key

1. 3	**2.** 1	**3.** 2	**4.** 5	**5.** 5	**6.** 3	**7.** 5
8. 3	**9.** 4	**10.** 1	**11.** 4	**12.** 5	**13.** 2	**14.** 1
15. 3	**16.** 1	**17.** 2	**18.** 2	**19.** 3	**20.** 1	**21.** 4
22. 3	**23.** 2	**24.** 4	**25.** 2	**26.** 2	**27.** 4	**28.** 3
29. 5	**30.** 4	**31.** 3	**32.** 1	**33.** 3	**34.** 1	**35.** 5
36. 3	**37.** 5	**38.** 2	**39.** 5	**40.** 4	**41.** 3	**42.** 1
43. 5	**44.** 5	**45.** 4	**46.** 1	**47.** 2	**48.** 5	**49.** 1
50. 3						

EXPLANATIONS

1. The widest divergence between India and China is the profitable horticultural sector China's added advantage lies in the more diversified composition of its agricultural sector....

2. In all of these China has outdone India.

3. The passage talks only about agricultural growth rate, not economic growth in general.

4. None of these is fully true.

6. India is placed favourably when compared to china in terms of quantity of arable land, average farm size, farm mechanisation etc.

7. Majority of the budget is eaten up by staff salaries with only 3 per cent being allotted for research.

8. There has been much debate about subsidies and their utility; the opposing view being that subsidies are against the market reforms and distort the market as well as reduce resource efficiency.

9 4

10. China has concentrated on investment rather than on subsidies.

11. 4 **12.** 5 **13.** 2 **14.** 1 **15.** 3

16. Substitute between for among.

17. Substitute undergone.

18. Substitute detailed.

19. Substitute at least.

20. Delete no.

21. Substitute its

22. Substitute selling.

23. Substitute challenges.

24. Substitute which.

25. Substitute soon.

26. 2 **27.** 4 **28.** 3 **29.** 5 **30.** 4 **31.** 3

32. 1 **33.** 3 **34.** 1 **35.** 5

36.-40. C F B E A D

36. 3 **37.** 5 **38.** 2 **39.** 5 **40.** 4 **41.** 3

42. 1 **43.** 5 **44.** 5 **45.** 4 **46.** 1 **47.** 2

48. 5 **49.** 1 **50.** 3

B.O.I. CLERK 2008

Number of Questions – 50
Time : 35 M.

DIRECTIONS—(Q. 1–15): *Read the following passage carefully and answer the questions given below it.*

The King of Kanchi set off to conquer Karnat. He was victorious in batttle. The elephants were laden with sandalwood, ivory, gold and precious stones taken from the conquered kingdom of Karnat. They would be a part of the victory parade for his subjects. On his way back home he stopped at a temple, finished his prayers to the goddess and turned to leave. Around his neck was a garland of scarlet hibiscus and as was the custom for all, his forehead was anointed with red sandal paste. His Minister and the court jester were his only companions. At one spot, in a mango grove by the way-side, they spied some children play. The King said, "Let me go and see what they are playing." The children had lined up two rows of clay dolls and were playing warriors and battles. The King asked, "Who is fighting whom ?" They said, "Karnat is at battle with Kanchi." The King asked, "Who is winning and who is the loser ?" The children puffed their chests up and said, "Karnat will win and Kanchi will lose." The Minister froze in disbelief, the King was furious and the jester burst into laughter. The King was soon joined by his troops and the children were still immersed in their game. The King commanded, "Cane them hard." The children's parents came running from the nearby village and said, "They are naive, it was just a game, please grant them pardon." The King called his commander and ordered, "Teach these children and the village a lesson so that they never forget the King of Kanchi." He went back to his camp. That evening the Commander stood before the King. He bowed low in shame and said, "Your Majesty, with the exception of hyenas and vultures, all lie silent in the village." The Minister said, "His Majesty's honour has been saved." The priest said, "The goddess has blessed our King." The jester said, "Your Highness, please grant me leave to go now." The King asked, "But why ?" The jester said, "I cannot kill, I cannot maim, I can only laugh at God's gift of life." Trembling in the face of the king's anger he bravely continued, "If I stay in your Majesty's court, I shall become like you and I shall forget how to laugh."

1. Why were the elephants carrying loads of gold and other valuables ?

(A) This was what the king had looted from Karnat to distribute among his soldiers as a reward

(B) This was the king's offering to the deity out of gratitude for making him victorious

(C) It was what the king had plundered from Karnat to display to the people of his kingdom as a sign of victory

(D) So that the people of the kingdom of Karnat acknowledged him as their new ruler

(E) None of these

2. Why did the king anoint his head with red sandal paste ?

(A) As a mark of celebration to show he had been victorious

(B) It was the usual practice for all devotees at the temple

(C) To show other devotees that he was king

(D) The priest requested him to do so

(E) To show his soldiers that he had visited the temple

3. Which of the following cannot be said about the jester ?

1. He was not a loyal subject of the king.
2. He was afraid of the king's temper.
3. He did not support the king's war against Karnat.

(A) Both 1 and 3 (B) Only 1

(C) Both 1 and 2 (D) All 1, 2 and 3

(E) None of these

4. What excuse was given for the childrens' behaviour ?

(A) They were disobedient to their parent's wishes

(B) They were unaware of the true facts of the battle

(C) They were upset that their army had lost

(D) They were in the habit of lying

(E) None of these

5. Why did the jester laugh at the children's reply to the king ?

1. They correctly predicted the outcome of the battle.
2. Their reply was cheeky because they knew he was the king.
3. He wanted to show that their reply was a joke to save them from being punished by the king.

(A) Only 1 (B) Both 1 and 2

(C) Only 3 (D) Both 2 and 3

(E) None of these

6. Which of the following is true in the context of the passage ?

(A) The king stopped at the temple to see what else could be plundered

(B) The people of the village to which the children belonged developed great respect for the king

(C) The Commander was ashamed at having obeyed the king's orders to cane the children

(D) The jester was unhappy that the king had defeated the army of Karnat

(E) The children had shown disrespect to the goddess by playing so close to the temple

7. Why did the jester resign from his post ?

(A) He felt that the king was too influenced by the Minister

(B) To show that he disapproved of the king's action of punishing the children

(C) He did not want to accompany the king on his war campaign

(D) He was no longer able to make the king laugh

(E) None of these

8. Which of the following describes the Minister ?

1. He was jealous of the jester.
2. He was the king's most valuable advisor.
3. He did not have a good sense of humour.

(A) Only 1 (B) Only 3

(C) Both 1 and 3 (D) Both 1 and 2

(E) None of these

9. Which of the following was/were the outcome(s) of the soldiers beating the children ?

1. The animals began to howl and wanted to attack the soldiers.
2. The children's parents went to the king to beg for mercy.
3. The priest offered prayers to the goddess of the temple.

(A) Only 1 (B) All 1, 2 and 3

(C) Both 1 and 2 (D) Only 2

(E) None of these

10. Why was the king angry with the children ?

(A) Because the game they were playing was dangerous

(B) They had lied to him

(C) They did not recognize him as king

(D) They had unknowingly insulted him

(E) They were rude to him

DIRECTIONS—(Q. 11–13): *Choose the word which is most nearly the SAME in meaning as the word printed in bold as used in the passage.*

11. froze

(A) cold (B) numb (C) shivered (D) stood still (E) chill

12. leave

(A) holiday (B) transfer (C) exit (D) permission (E) farewell

13. spied

(A) noticed (B) keep watch (C) followed (D) spot (E) caught

DIRECTIONS—(Q. 14–15) Choose the word which is most OPPOSITE in meaning of the word printed in bold as used in the passage.

14. immersed in

(A) safe from (B) distracted from (C) boring (D) drowning in (E) entertained by

15. pardon

(A) punishment (B) excuse (C) convict (D) intolerance (E) imprison

DIRECTIONS—(Q. 16–20): *Which of the phrases (A), (B), (C) and (D) given below should replace the phrase given in bold in the following sentence to make the sentence grammatically meaningful and correct. If the sentence is correct as it is and 'No correction is required', mark (E) as the answer.*

16. Your bonus will dependent the quality of your work.

(A) is dependable (B) depends on

(C) being dependent (D) going to depend

(E) No correction required

17. He did not ask for a raise since he had fear to lose his job.

(A) was fearful of (B) was feared to

(C) was afraid to (D) had been afraid to

(E) No correction required

18. The organizers agreed to shift the conference at some place convenience to all participants.

(A) any of the place convenient (B) at places convenient

(C) from a place of convenience (D) to a place convenient

(E) No correction required

19. As compared to last year there has been a sharp rise in interest rates.

(A) sharper rise of (B) as sharp a rise

(C) sharp rises in (D) sharply rising

(E) No correction required

20. In the 1970s banks required to submit their detailed plans of expansion to RBI.

(A) were required to submit (B) required for submission

(C) are required to submit (D) requirement of submitting

(E) No correction required

DIRECTIONS—(Q. 21–25): *Rearrange the following Six sentences (1), (2), (3), (4), (5) and (6) in the proper sequence to form a meaningful paragraph; then answer the questions given below them—*

1. I had paid a lot of attention during training and could easily answer the questions till I came to the last one. What is the name of the lady who cleans your floor ?

2. 'Yes', he replied. "In your career you will meet many people all of whom are significant even if all you do is greet them."
3. I thought the question was a joke. I had seen her but how would I know her name ?
4. During my internship we were given a quiz to see how much we had learnt.
5. I have never forgotten this lesson.
6. I submitted my paper leaving the last question blank and asked the manager if it would count for assessment.

21. Which of the following will be the SECOND sentence after rearrangement ?

(A) 1 (B) 2 (C) 3 (D) 4 (E) 5

22. Which of the following will be the SIXTH (LAST) sentence after rearrangement ?

(A) 2 (B) 3 (C) 4 (D) 6 (E) 5

23. Which of the following will be the FIFTH sentence after rearrangement ?

(A) 1 (B) 2 (C) 3 (D) 4 (E) 5

24. Which of the following will be the FIRST sentence after rearrangement ?

(A) 1 (B) 2 (C) 3 (D) 4 (E) 5

25. Which of the following will be the THIRD sentence after rearrangement ?

(A) 1 (B) 2 (C) 3 (D) 4 (E) 5

DIRECTIONS—(Q. 26–30): *In each sentence below four words have been printed in bold which are lettered (A), (B), (C) and (D). One of these words may be wrongly spelt or inappropriate in the context of the sentence. Find out the wrongly spelt or inappropriate word. The letter of that word is the answer. If all the words are correctly spelt and are appropriate the answer is (E), i.e. 'All correct'.*

26. My gole (A) is to acquire (B) a position (C) of authority (D) and respect within theorganization. All correct (E)

27. The refusal (A) of the Ministry to clear pending (B) dues is a course (C) for concern (D). All correct (E)

28. He was convinced (A) that discipline (B) and hard work would result (C) in dividends (D) in the long run. All correct (E)

29. This is a company which believes (A) in transparency (B) and appointment is done strictly (C) on merit (D). All correct (E)

30. There will be a decline (A) in the probability (B) of oil companies because of the hike (C) in oil prices (D). All correct (E)

DIRECTIONS—(Q. 31–40): *Read each sentence to find out whether there is any grammatical error in it.The error, if any, will be in one part of the sentence. The letter of that part is the answer. If there is no error, the answer is (E) i.e. 'No error'. (Ignore the errors of punctuation, if any.)*

31. The revised government's (A) /guidelines have reduced (B)/ the number of mergers (C) / taking place among banks. (D) No error (E)

32. I do not know (A) / who of the (B) /new trainees should (C) / be confirmed. (D) No error \ (E)

33. To promote India as (A) / a tourist destination (B)/ the government has organized (C) / many cultural programmes. (D) No error (E)

34. Banks in India (A) / cannot open ATMs (B)/ except obtaining (C) / approval from RBI. (D) No error (E)

35. Today the success of (A) / companies depends on the (B)/ quality of their products and(C) / efficient managing staff. (D) No error (E)

36. Ashok has managed to (A) / achieve his sales targets (B)/ for the quarter very easily (C) / than we expected. (D) No error (E)

37. He did not grant (A) / their request for a loan (B)/ although it would (C) / displease his boss. (D) No error (E)

38. At present oil companies (A) / are making a loss of (B)/ rupees five on all (C) / litre of petrol that they sell. (D) No error (E)

39. The manager's belief that (A) / Ramesh is (B)/ incompetent is not (C) / necessary true. (D) No error (E)

40. Since I was doing (A) / my MBA I initially (B)/ chose to specialize (C) / in marketing management. (D) No error (E)

DIRECTIONS—(Q. 41–50): *In the following passage there are blanks, each of which has been numbered. These numbers are printed below the passage and against each, five words are suggested, one of which fits the blank appropriately. Find out the appropriate word in each case.*

He was a charismatic leader, an entrepreneur and a highly effective manager all rolled into one. As a leader, he ...**41**... the company's growth plan in a dedicated manner and he never ...**42**... focus. The cement industry in those days was doing badly. ...**43**... to everyone's expectations he sanctioned an additional plant in ...**44**... time. He was ...**45**... that since the cement industry was cyclic in nature, by the time the plant was,...**46**... the market would have improved. It did happen and the decision brought rich ...**47**... when the plant was commissioned. Not only was he a great entrepreneur but he also ...**48**... all his senior people to be 'practising entrepreneurs'. I have seen a similar example at the Asian Institute of Management, which allows its professors to ...**49**... their own business. This made their lectures more practical and less theoretical. It is the ...**50**... of the Institute's success.

41. (A) achieved (B) implemented (C) visualised (D) persevered (E) aimed

42. (A) moved (B) shifts (C) missed (D) changes (E) lost

43. (A) Contrary (B) Opposite (C) Yet (D) Obedient (E) Different

44. (A) any (B) mean (C) short (D) no (E) less

45. (A) known (B) calculating (C) certain (D) dreamt (E) surely

46. (A) operational (B) install (C) use (D) produced (E) new

47. (A) supply (B) diversity (C) rewards (D) pay (E) knowledge

48. (A) thought (B) tried (C) wished (D) encourage (E) wanted

49. (A) expand (B) function (C) chose (D) run (E) risk

50. (A) responsibility (B) secret (C) guarantee (D) prize (E) value

Answer Key with Hints

1. (C) 2. (B) 3. (B) 4. (B) 5. (E) 6. (C) 7. (E)
8. (B) 9. (D) 10. (D) 11. (B) 12. (D) 13. (B) 14. (B)
15. (A) 16. (B) 17. (C) 18. (D) 19. (E) 20. (A) 21. (A)
22. (E) 23. (B) 24. (D) 25. (C)

26. (A) Correct spelling is 'goal'.

27. (C) Correct spelling is 'cause'.

Page 152

28. (D) Correct spelling is 'dividends'.

29. (E) 30. (B)

31. (A) Write 'the government's revised'.

32. (B) Write 'which of the'.

33. (C) Write 'the government is organizing'.

34. (C) Write 'without obtaining'.

35. (D) Write 'efficient managerial staff'.

36. (C) Change 'very easily' to 'more easily'.

37. (C) Write 'even though it would'.

38. (C) Write 'each in place of 'all'.

39. (D) Write 'necessarily true'.

40. (B) Delete 'my'.

41. (B) 42. (C) 43. (A) 44. (D) 45. (B)
46. (A) 47. (C) 48. (E) 49. (D) 50.

CORPORATION BANK P.O. 2007

Number of Questions – 50
Time : 35 M.

DIRECTIONS for questions 1-10: *Read the following passage carefully and answer the questions given below it Certain words/phrases are given in bold to help you locate them while answering some of the questions.*

We are well into the 21st century yet half the world's population live in squatter settlements and work in shadow economies, which generate more than one-third of the developing world's GDP. Slums are not caused by the poor but by governments denying people the right to own and exchange property. When people own their own property they have incentives to invest time, money and energy to improve it because they know that they will be able to benefit from any such improvements, i.e. the ability to obtain mortgages etc. In short, property rights beget capital, which begets innovation, which begets wealth. Sadly, the poor typically don't have secure title to their land as there are bureaucratic restrictions on transferring title or there is no clear system for titling. Without legal deeds they live in constant fear of being evicted by landlords or municipal officials. Illiteracy is a major reason poor people often choose not to seek the protection of local courts since in so many countries laws established under colonial rule have never been translated into local languages. When entrepreneurs do set out to legally register business they are discouraged by red tape and costly fees. In Egypt, starting a bakery takes 500 days, compliance with 315 laws and 27 times the monthly minimum wage. The proprietors of such businesses cannot get loans, enforce contracts or expand a personal network of familiar customers and partners. As a result the poor have no choice but to accept insecurity and instability as a way of life.

In India severe restrictions on free transfer of property in most rural areas inhibit investment and encourage urban flight. Planning policies however discourage building homes for these migrants as numerous homes are destroyed if they do not comply with planning rules, essentially forcing people to live in slums and perversely blaming it on population growth. UN Habitat, the UN agency for housing the poor, has implemented more plans to stabilise the unplanned aspects of urban growth but grandiose plans like UN Schemes and government housing projects simply ignore or worsen the underlying problems. It is when governments grant people legal means to control their assets that they empower them to invest and plan ahead. In Buenos Aires, economists studied the experience of two Argentine communities. One had received legal title to its land in the 1980s and surpassed the other group which had not, in a range of social indicators including quality of house construction and education levels. The Commission on Legal Empowerment of the Poor - a UN -affiliated initiative made up of two dozen leaders - is exploring ideas to extend enforceable legal rights to impoverished members of society and is seeking to bring about a consensus on incentives for national and local leaders. As the growth of illegal settlements amply demonstrates, the poor are not helpless, all they need is governments to grant them fundamental human rights of freedom and responsibility.

1. What did the Argentine study indicate?

A. Argentina's economy is booming and the percentage of poor has fallen.

B. When the government gives people the legal means to control their assets they plan for the future.

C. The Government succeeded in widening the gap between the rich and the poor.

1. Only (A)
2. Both (A) & (B)
3. Only (B)
4. All(A),(B) & (C)
5. None of these

2. According to the author, which of the following factors is responsible for the creation of a slum ?

1. Migration of landless labourers to cities
2. Municipal authorities building low-cost housing for the poor

3. Unchecked population growth
4. Government failure to secure property rights for citizens
5. Exorbitant cost of living in cities

3. The author's main objective in writing the passage is to
1. exhort the UN to play a greater role in rehabilitating slum-dwellers.
2. praise government initiatives for migrant slum-dwellers.
3. convince governments to empower the poor.
4. enlist the aid of developed countries to tackle the issue of slums.
5. chastise slum-dwellers for illegal activities that they engage in.

4. What benefit does the author see in providing land ownership rights to the poor?
1. Steady increase in GDP
2. Gaining independence from colonial rulers
3. Municipal services afforded to the poor will improve.
4. It will be an inheritance for future generations.
5. None of these

5. Which of the following is TRUE in the context of the passage?
1. Additional UN projects will exacerbate the plight of slum-dwellers.
2. Although the government allocates land for them the poor choose not to invest in building houses.
3. With the spread of slums populations are drifting back to rural areas.
4. In order to accumulate profit slum-dwellers avoid legally registering their business.
5. UN has declared the right to housing as a fundamental right.

6. What impact do planning policies have on the development of slums?
1. They encourage the poor to invest m land thereby perpetuating slums.
2. They focus on developing rural rather than urban areas so people have to live in slums.
3. They offer alternative practical suggestions for construction of low-cost housing.
4. They advocate demolishing homes which violate planning rules, encouraging slums.
5. None of these

7. What is the objective of the Commission on Legal Empowerment of the Poor?
1. Coerce international leaders to implement housing projects
2. Bring sanctions against countries denying their citizens the right to housing
3. Selecting experts to recommend ideas to do away with poverty
4. Establish practical ways for governments to empower the underprivileged
5. None of these

8. Which of the following difficulties do unregistered businesses face?
A. Banks do not give loans in the absence of security.
B. They are unable to earn the loyalty of any customer.
C. They cannot enforce contracts.

1. Only (A)
2. Both (A) & (C)
3. Both (A) & (B)
4. Only (B)
5. None of these

9. What does the growth of illegal settlements indicate?
1. The Government needs to implement more restrictions on property transfer.
2. Capital earned from underground economies is beneficial to a country's economy.

3. The poor are capable of investing resources in their development.
4. UN housing projects are not properly implemented.
5. None of these

10. Which of the following prevents the poor from obtaining a business license?

1. They do not want to make an effort.
2. Government officials are discourteous.
3. They lack funds to bribe government officials.
4. They do not want to pay taxes.
5. They are intimidated by bureaucratic procedures.

DIRECTIONS for questions 11-13: *Choose the word which is most nearly the SAME in meaning as the word printed in bold as used in the passage.*

11. severe

1. acute 2. dangerous 3. bad 4. flexible 5. demanding

12. beget

1. lead 2. produce 3. happens 4. effect 5. result

13. surpassed

1. excel 2. matched 3. outshone 4. won 5. competed

DIRECTIONS for questions 14-15: *Choose the word which is most OPPOSITE in meaning of the word printed in bold as used in the passage.*

14. perversely

1. treasonably 2. stubbornly 3. conveniently 4. formally 5. helpfully

15. stabilize

1. insecure 2. fixed 3. weaken 4. unsure 5. unreliable

DIRECTIONS for questions 16-20: *Read each sentence to find out if there is any error in it The error, if any, will be in one part of the sentence. The number of that part is the answer. If there is no error the answer is 5). (Ignore errors in punctuation, if any).*

16. The company has launched (1)/ a creative marketing campaign (2) / to reach for (3) / its rural customers.(4) No error (5)

17. After her retiring (1)/ she established many (2) / institutions to train (3)/ underprivileged but talented children. (4) No error (5)

18. Against his family's wishes (1)/ Rajesh plans to (2) / take up a job (3) / as a journalist.(4) No error (5)

19. The candidate has appealed (1) / for donations from younger voters, (2) / who will be used (3) / to defray campaign expenses.(4) No error (5)

20. Most of that country's (1) / hilly land is not only (2) / unsuitable for building (3)/ but also for agriculture. (4) No error (5)

21. It is now (1) / possible for customers (2)/ to handle nearly all (3) / their transactions online. (4) No error (5)

22. The minister has (1) / recently announced (2)/ a detail insurance plan to (3) / meet the needs of the poor. (4) No error (5)

23. In the circumstance (1) / the manager has (2) / no option (3) / except to resign. (4) No error (5)

24. On account of (1) / its new investment rules (2) / more companies are planning (3)/ for open its business in China.(4) None of these (5)

25. He deserves a lot (1) / of praise for all (2) / the records he achieves (3) / during his career. (4) No error. (5)

DIRECTIONS for questions 26-30: *Which of the phrases (1), (2), (3), (4) given below each sentence should replace the phrase printed in bold type to make the sentence grammatically correct? If the sentence is correct, mark (5). i.e. 'No correction required', as the answer.*

26. For honour to the social worker on her tenth death anniversary the government has planned a series of events.

1. In honouring of
2. With honour
3. The honouring of
4. To honour
5. No correction required

27. He is decided to build a luxury hotel for the convenience of tourists visiting the ancient monument.

1. Having decided to
2. He has decided to
3. His decision to
4. Deciding to
5. No correction required

28. Except another restaurants this one offers no discounts.

1. Unlike other
2. Beside other
3. Without another
4. Unless other
5. No correction required

29. He made it a rule to arrive early in order to avoid no delay in the presentation.

1. to no delay
2. not to avoid
3. to avoid any delay
4. without avoiding
5. No correction required

30. The so serious challenge to companies face is to retain its younger staff.

1. more serious of challenge to
2. very serious challenge for
3. most serious challenge
4. quite serious challenge against
5. No correction required

DIRECTIONS for questions 31-35: *In each of the following sentences there are two blank spaces. Below each five words have been denoted by numbers 1), 2), 3), 4) and 5). Find out which pair of words can be filled up in the blanks in the sentence in the same sequence to make the sentence meaningfully complete.*

31. The ____________business trips though____________at times gave the executive a unique chance to meet interesting people.

1. demanding.... memorable
2. frequent.... monotonous
3. crucial ....regular
4. prolonged... .exhausted
5. significant.... influential

32. In order to put an end to the___________that exist regarding the implementation of the policy the company should issue___________guidelines.

1. ambiguities....clear-cut
2. differences....cautious
3. burden——stringent
4. inhibition.... appropriate
5. reservations.... fundamental

33. The government has__________that the infrastructure for the new project must be completed ___________the next six months.

1. stipulated ....for
2. sanction.... by
3. assurance.... in
4. mandated.... within
5. envisage.... during

34. The official not only________the renewal of the contract but also________the information about its status.

1. revealed.... classified
2. withdrawn ....leaked
3. delayed.... withheld
4. interfere.... refused
5. impeded.... excluding

35. To____________any tensions in the minds of the employees and investors alike the company has promised to consider job cuts as a last____________.

1. erase ....effort
2. rid.... hurdle
3. overcome.... decision
4. address ....phase
5. ease.... resort

DIRECTIONS for questions36-40: *Rearrange the following sentences (A), (B), (C), (D), (E) and (F) into a meaningful paragraph and then answer the questions given below it.*

(A) According to conventional wisdom, no amount can suffice.

(B) In the process of seeking it is money which unfortunately gets a bad name.

(C) How much money is enough?

(D) The modern reasoning is that money coming in should cover our basic needs.

(E) The real culprit, however, is a living thing called desire, which although it is difficult to, can be controlled.

(F) However, from the basics of food, clothing and shelter we gradually seek luxury cars and holidays.

36. Which of the following is the FIRST sentence after rearrangement?

1. (A) 2.(B) 3.(C) 4.(D) 5.(E)

37. Which of the following is the SIXTH (LAST) sentence after rearrangement?

1. (A) 2.(B) 3.(C) 4.(D) 5.(E)

38. Which of the following is the FIFTH sentence after rearrangement?

1. (A) 2.(B) 3.(C) 4.(D) 5.(F)

39. Which of the following is the SECOND sentence after rearrangement?

1. (A) 2. (B) 3.(C) 4.(D) 5.(E)

40. Which of the following is the THIRD sentence after rearrangement?

1. (A) 2. (B) 3. (C) 4. (D) 5. (E)

DIRECTIONS for questions 41-50: *In the following passage there are blanks each of which has been numbered. These numbers are printed below the passage and against each five words have been suggested, one of which fills the blanks appropriately. Find out the appropriate word In each case.*

At just **41** midnight on July 1, 1997 in a glittering and poignant ceremony, Hong Kong passed from being a jewel of the British empire to a **42** of a new global power. Hong Kong people **43** their city's handover from the UK to China with **44** feelings: apprehension over the future, joy at a fresh start, sadness at seeing the British go, pride over returning to their motherland. On the eve of the handover, the stock market index, a key barometer of Hong Kong's wealth, **45** at a record 15,200 points and today it **46** near the. 21,000 mark. Being a part of a booming China almost' guarantees that Hong Kong will remain **47**. But mainland China is a **48** as well as a partner. China's new ports, for example, will siphon trade **49** from Hong Kong and its lower labour costs will impact the jobs. However, there is little doubt that Hong Kong is fortunate to have become a part of China at a time when mainland China can provide **50** opportunity.

41. 1. recorded 2. near 3. close 4. past 5. quite

42.	1. component	2. premises	3. captive	4. merger	5. list
43.	1. encounter	2. decided	3. viewed	4.restraine	5. told
44.	1. flexible	2. emotional	3. mixed	4.changed	5. negative
45.	1. plunged	2. rose	3. valued	4. climbed	5. stood
46.	1. follows	2. pauses	3.fell	4. hovers	5. measure
47.	1. marginalised	2. prosperous	3. orderly	4.fiiendly	5. poor
48.	1. competitor	2. representative	3. adversary	4. colleague	5. member
49.	1. against	2. away	3. illegally	4. moving	5. through
50.	1. full	2. risky	3. lucky	4. unfair	5. immense

Answer Key

1. 3	**2.** 4	**3.** 3	**4.** 5	**5.** 2	**6.** 1	**7.** 4
8. 2	**9.** 3	**10.** 5	**11.** 1	**12.** 2	**13.** 3	**14.** 1
15. 1	**16.** 3	**17.** 1	**18.** 1	**19.** 3	**20.** 3	**21.** 5
22. 3	**23.** 4	**24.** 4	**25.** 3	**26.** 4	**27.** 2	**28.** 1
29. 3	**30.** 3	**31.** 2	**32.** 1	**33.** 4	**34.** 3	**35.** 5
36. 3	**37.** 5	**38.** 2	**39.** 1	**40.** 4	**41.** 4	**42.** 1
43. 3	**44.** 3	**45.** 5	**46.** 4	**47.** 2	**48.** 1	**49.** 2
50. 5						

Explanations

1. Refer to the study done by the economists in Buenos Aires.

2. This is what the entire passage dealt with.

3. This is a natural corollary to the question above.

4. It will empower the poor to invest and plan ahead.

5. Since the allocation does not come with a proper title, there is always the fear of eviction.

6. Planning policies discourage building homes.

7. The commission is exploring ideas to extend enforceable legal rights to impoverishedmembers of society and is seeking to bringabout a consensus on incentives for nationaland local leaders.

8. does not follow because of the word *any.*

9. The passage says: "As the growth of illegal settlements amply demonstrates the poor are not helpless...."

10. They are discouraged by red tape.

11. 1 **12.** 2 **13.** 3 **14.** 1 **15.** 1

16. Delete *for.*

17. Substitute retirement.

18. Use singular *wish.*

19. Substitute *which.*

20. Substitute construction for building.

21. 5

22. Substitute detailed

23. Substitute but for except.

24. Substitute to open their business.

25. Substitute achieved or has achieved.

26. 4 **27.** 2 **28.** 1 **29.** 3 **30.** 3 **31.** 2 **32.** 1 **33.** 4

34. 3 **35.** 5

36.-40. C A D F B E

36. 3 **37.** 5 **38.** 2 **39.** 1 **40.** 4 **41.** 4 **42.** 1 **43.** 3

44. 3 **45.** 5 **46.** 4 **47.** 2 **48.** 1 **49.** 2 **50.** 5

MAHARASHTRA CET 2009

Number of Questions – 50
Time : 35 M.

DIRECTION for questions 1-5: *For each statement there are four different sentences given below it. Pick out the one that most appropriately conveys the meaning of the statement. The number of that sentence is the answer. If none of them conveys the meaning of the statement, the answer is (5) i.e. 'None'.*

1. Unlike the tribals who are hardworking, the urbanites cannot withstand physical strain.

1. The tribals do not like to withstand physical strain as the urbanites to
2. The urbanites are hardworking but they do not like to undertake physical do
3. The tribals can withstand physical strain whereas urbanities cannot
4. Because the tribals are hardworking they can tolerate physical strain.
5. None

2. Should you need a Permanent Account Number (PAN) Card, you must submit an application along with a copy of your ration card.

1. Unless you do not submit an application along with a copy of your ration Card.
2. You should require a PAN Card if you want to submit an application along with a copy of your ration card.
3. If you submit your application along with your ration card you do not need a PAN Card
4. If you submit an application along with you ration card you will get only a PAN Card
5. None

3. Despite any kind of hurdles, I shall come.

1. I shall come if there are different kinds of hurdles
2. I shall not be able to come if there are different kinds of hurdles
3. Even though I come, there could be different kinds of hurdles
4. Whether or not there are any kinds of hurdles, I shall come
5. None

4. The Manager would like you to help him locate the conspicuous error.

1. If you help him locate the conspicuous error, the Manager would like you.
2. The Manager desires that you should provide him the necessary assistance to locate the conspicuous error.
3. The Manager feels that if you do not help him, the conspicuous error will not be located
4. The Manager expects that the conspicuous error should be located only with your help
5. None

5. The speaker remarked that not all the politician were really unkind.

1. The speaker remarked that some of the politicians were kind while others were not
2. The speaker remarked that all the politicians were not kind
3. The speaker remarked that all those who are politicians cannot be necessarily kind
4. The speaker remarked that all those who are politicians may hardly include really a group of kind people.
5. None

DIRECTION for questions 6-10: *Given below are six sentences (A), (B), (C), (D), (E) and (F). Rearrange these six sentences in the proper sequence to form a meaningful paragraph; then answer the questions given below them.*

A. But the process does not stop here.

B. In particular by the effects of that small part of society which is our family.

C. As we grow we are constantly and increasingly affected by new forces such as social pressure of our friends and larger world of society.

D. The family and our early life have profound effect on our later life.

E. Psychologists have studied these forces in depth.

F. Much of our adult behavior and our attitude are determined and influenced by our upbringing.

6. Which of the following should be the **FOURTH** sentence after rearrangement?

1. A2. B 3. C 4. 0 5. E

7. Which of the following will be the **SIXTH (LAST)** sentence after rearrangement?

1. A2. B 3. C 4. D 5. E

8. Which of the following should be the **FIFTH** sentence after rearrangement ?

1. F2. E 3. D 4. C 5. B

9. Which of the following should be the **THIRD** sentence after rearrangement?

1. F2. E 3. D 4. C 5. B

10. Which of the following should be the **SECOND** sentence after rearrangement.?

1. B 2. C 3. D 4. E 5. F

DIRECTION for questions 11-15: *In each question below an incomplete sentences, there are parts denoted by A, B, C...........H, I & J. Either none or one/two or maximum three of them can complete the sentence meaningfully. Pick out the correct choice in each case.*

11. As we introduce new risk management systems, perfectly on ethical grounds.

12. With the generalized opening of trade and of capital movement across the world over the past decade and a half.

13. The notion that individual economic agents are ill-equipped to be exposed to exchange rate, interest rates and price risks.

14. The distinguishing feature of the new paradigm is that it does not mean

15. Profound changes have taken place in the economic and financial landscape in India over the past two decades or so.

A. It is important for us to keep in mind the objective conditions that exist in India.

B. Is no longer regarded as tenable.

C. marked by wide ranging reforms in both the real and financial sectors.

D. management products in India must be world class.

E. we must not try to find out any escape routes to avoid risks.

F. prominently maintaining status quo' of the conditions.

G. risk management has become all pervasive across the whole financial sector.

H. cannot be well defended any longer against criticism.

I. should be eliminated by way of insurance-like products that have been known to mankind for a long time.

J. there is a striking need to ensure free trade and movement of capital across the word.

Answer choices for Questions:

11. 1. Only A 2. Only E 3. Either A or E 4. Only B 5. None

12. 1. Only F 2. Only G 3. Either F or G 4. Only J 5. None

13. 1. Only B 2. Only H 3. Only G 4. Either B or H 5. None

14. 1. Only I 2. Only G 3. Only C 4. Either I or C 5. None

15. 1. None 2. Only F 3. Only B 4. Either F or B 5. Only C

DIRECTION for questions 16-20: *In each of the following sentences there are two blank spaces. Below each sentence there are five pairs of words or groups of words denoted by numbers 1, 2, 3, 4 and 5. Find out which pair of words can be filled up in the blanks in the sentence in the same sequence to make the sentence grammatically correct and meaningfully complete.*

16. Preaching__________generally easier than____________it.

1. every ideology has, practice
2. an ideology is, practising
3. ideologies is, experimenting
4. others are, practice
5. None of these

17. While going to the office yesterday I_________that I_________the key of my office room at home.

1. suddenly realized, have forgotten
2. gradually remembered, was forgetting
3. immediately recalled, was left
4. suddenly realized, had forgotten
5. None of these

18. This Physics Laboratory is___________with all the sophisticated ________ but also with most of the recent publications.

1. not only equipped, instruments
2. not equipped, gadgets
3. dumped, old publications
4. equipped not only, instruments
5. None of these

19. If he__________prepared his lecture well in advance it_________the best lecture in the entire conference.

1. would have, would have been
2. would, must be
3. had, would have been
4. should have, would be
5. None of these

20. No other library in town__________so many books belonging to different disciplines as this library

1. has, has
2. having, does
3. have, has
4. possess, have
5. None of these

DIRECTION for questions 21-25: *Find out which one, two, three or none of the given alternatives is/are most nearly the SAME in meaning of the word printed in bold.*

21. Indomitable

A. Feeble B. Unconquerable C. Conspicuous

1. A only
2. B only
3. C only
4. A and B only
5. All the three

22. Melancholy

A. Sad B. Miserable C. Malicious

1. A and B only
2. B and C only
3. A and C only
4. All the three
5. None

23. Versatile

A. Verifiable B. Inflexible C. Multi-talented

1. A only 2. B only
3. C only 4. A and B only 5. A and C only

24. Invigorate

A. Revitalize B. Strengthen C. Rejuvenate

1. A only 2. B only
3. C only 4. A and C only 5. All the three

25. Exasperate

A. Exonerate B. Annoy C. Frustrate

1. A and B only 2. All the three
3. A and C only 4. B and C only 5. B only

What is the sum of the resultants of the two rows ?

1. 23 2. 80
3. 103 4. 138 5. None of these

DIRECTION for questions26-30: *Read the following passage carefully and answer the questions given below it.*

Urbanization and altered lifestyles are indicators of socio-economic, development and lead to risk factors for cardiovascular diseases CVDs. At present, pre-transitional diseases like rheumatic heart disease, mostly the problem of the poor, co-exist as a major cardiovascular disease along with post-transitional diseases such as coronary heart disease and hypertension. In India nearly 2.4 million deaths are caused by cardiovascular disorders. Small-scale community-based studies indicate the prevalence of CVD in adults, ranging from 2-6 per cent in rural and 6-10 per cent in urban areas. The health sector review of the World Bank projects that CVD mortality rates would double between 1985-2015.

26. A country's socio-economic development is generally estimated on the basis of

A. Switchover to urban lifestyle
B. Adaptation of sophisticated lifestyle
C. Number of patients with cardiovascular diseases

1. A and B only 2. B and C only
3. A and C only 4. All the three 5. None of these

27. Which of the following is definitely TRUE in the context of the passage ?

A. CVO adult patients in rural areas outnumber those in urban areas
B. The proportion of the rich and poor CVD patients is almost the same
C. CVD deaths between 1985-2015 would be doubled in respect of rural areas

1. A and B only 2. B and C only
3. A and C only 4. All the three 5. None of these

28. Which of the following is most nearly the SAME as the word PREVALENCE as used in the passage?

1. cure 2. remedy
3. occurrence 4. prevention 5. eradication

29. The passage lays emphasis on which of the following?

A. Association of CVDs with urban lifestyle
B. Diseases of the rich and the poor
C. Diseases prevalent in rural and urban areas

1. All the three
2. A and B only
3. B and C only
4. A only
5. B only

30. Which of the following is most nearly the SAME as the word ALTERED as used in the passage?

1. shifted
2. changed
3. reviewed
4. modern
5. traditional

DIRECTION for questions 31-35: *Read the following passage carefully and answer the questions given below it.*

Marketing communication which comprises services such as advertising, market research and entertainment, depends primarily on the stage of economic development and the nature of the target groups. The Indian economy has been growing at an average rate of 5 percent from 1980-81 resulting in a middle class population of 200-250 million. Though currently 70 percent of the population is rural, by the year 2020 this figure should decline to 55 percent; the literacy rate is expected to rise to 80 percent. Because of these trends there would be major shifts in marketing communication. The strategy now is to focus on innovation and to create new needs.

31. Marketing communication has all of the following as its components EXCEPT —

A. Publicity of the product through various means

B. Exploration of needs, public opinion, etc. of products through surveys

C. Amusement and recreation

1. A only
2. B only
3. C only
4. All the three - A, B & C
5. None of these

32. Which of the following is required as change in strategy for effective marketing communication?

A. To switchover to novel and resourceful methods

B. To generate needs among the public

C. To focus on traditional ways without deviating from them

1. A and B only
2. B and C only
3. A and C only
4. C only
5. None of these

33. Marketing communication will be greatly influenced by which of the following ?

A. Growing rural population

B. Fall in percentage of rural population

C. Decline in literacy rate

1. A only
2. B only
3. C only
4. A and C only
5. None of these

34. Marketing communication nee is to be moulded to suit to which of the following ?

1. Advertising and publicity strategy
2. Composition of the general public and the extent of economic development
3. The strategy adopted for market research
4. Various avenues available for enhancing sales
5. None of these

35. Which of the following is most **OPPOS'TE** of the word **DECLINE** as used in the passage?

1. incline
2. reduce
3. accept
4. increase
5. magnify

DIRECTION for questions 36-40: *Read the following passage carefully and answer the questions given below it.*

The Guided Missile Development Programme envisaged the design and development of our missile systems, Prithvi, Trishul, Akash and Nag, leading to their production. It also established the re-entry technology capability through Agni. The re-entry technology demonstration was completed by 1992, through flight tests of Agni. Prithvi was the first of the four operational missile systems to be inducted into the armed forces.

The technological goal of the programme is to ensure that the systems will be contemporary at the time of their induction into the armed forces. The systems have been designed to be multi-purpose, multi-user and multi-role in nature. The programme has adopted the philosophy of concurrent development and production to reduce the time-cycle from development to induction.

36. What was the technological objective of the programme of guided missile as depicted in the passage?

A. The programme should yield modem gadgets at the time of its induction.

B. The programme should yield gadgets with variety of purposes and facility to use by various users.

C. The programme should be such that it should reduce the time for manufacture.

1. A only
2. A and B only
3. A and C only
4. All the three
5. None of these

37. Which of the following is most OPPOSITE of the word CONTEMPORARY as used in the passage ?

1. regular
2. permanent
3. haphazard
4. prominent
5. old

38. it can be inferred from the passage that the author is most likely to be a/an—

1. Newspaper Reporter
2. Scientist
3. Sociologist
4. Environmentalist
5. Civil Defence Strategist

39. What was the strategy adopted to cut short the time?

1. Starting induction before development
2. Starting development just prior to induction
3. Synchronizing production and development together
4. Starting induction together with development
5. None of these

40. Which of the following is most OPPOSITE of the word CONCURRENT as used in the passage ?

1. flexible
2. sequential
3. modest
4. optimum
5. limited

DIRECTION for questions 41-50: *In the following passage, there are blanks, each of which has been numbered. These numbers are printed below the passage and against each, five words are suggested, one of which fits the blank appropriately. Find out the appropriate word in each case.*

The gross value added to GDP by insurance services increased at the rate of 7.5 per cent during 1980-81 and 1993-94, but only 22 per cent of all insurable persons are covered by life insurance The number of persons covered will increase significantly due to population increase, economic growth and the rise in **41** of risks due to rapid urbanization. **42** less than 1 per cent of the population has any dealings with non-life insurance business, but the demand on these services is **43** to increase as manufacturing, trade and other activities grow. Additionally more and more people will go in for personal accident insurance, medical coverage and other such forms of protection. The business in non-life insurance even currently is increasing at the rate of 20 per cent per annum and is expected to **44** to 30 per cent in the next decade.

45 voluminous growth in the banking and insurance sectors, processing and transactions have been carried out by largely manual means. A national network of banking and the insurance business has to **46**. This lack has **47** affected efficiency and is a major cause of the **48** rates charged for financial services. The introduction of I.T. for various operations at the earliest has become a necessity. This means use of computers for near total electronic data management and the use of telecommunications and multimedia data, **49** a total systems approach. Some modern technologies like Automated Teller Machines (ATM): automatic cheque clearing systems, telephonic banking, credit cards and electronic fund transfers nave been already introduced and will be **50** in most of the banks in the coming years.

41. 1. magnitude 2. form 3. danger 4. perception 5. nature

42. 1. Blissfully 2. Eventually 3. Currently 4. Officially 5. Obviously

43. 1. ceased 2. bound 3. planned 4. decided 5. unlikely

44. 1. make 2. develop 3. promote 4. lead 5. accelerate

45. 1. Assuming 2. Resulting 3. Reversing 4. Despite 5. Poised

46. 1. emerge 2. set 3. found 4. established 5. settle

47. 1. abruptly 2. obviously 3. adversely 4. incidentally 5. finally

48. 1. optimum 2. minimal 3. fluctuating 4. high 5. nominal

49. 1. demanding 2. adopting 3. negating 4. avoiding 5. skipping

50. 1. set up 2. operative 3. engaged 4. functioning 5. prevalent

Answer Key

1. 3	**2.** 5	**3.** 4	**4.** 2	**5.** 1	**6.** 1	**7.** 5
8. 4	**9.** 3	**10** 1	**11.** 3	**12.** 4	**13.** 3	**14.** 1
15. 5	**16.** 2	**17.** 4	**18.** 4	**19.** 3	**20.** 1	**21.** 2
22. 1	**23.** 3	**24** 5	**25.** 4	**26.** 1	**27.** 5	**28.** 3.
29. 4	**30.** 2	**31.** 5	**32.** 1	**33.** 2	**34.** 2	**35.** 4
36. 4	**37.** 5	**38.** 5	**39.** 3	**40.** 2	**41.** 4	**42.** 3
43. 2	**44.** 2	**45.** 4	**46.** 1	**47.** 3	**48.** 4	**49.** 2
50. 2						

EXPLANATIONS

1. Option 1 is conveying the exact opposite meaning, therefore rejected. Option 4th is conveying only half of the meaning; hence rejected.2nd option is grammatically wrong therefore rejected. Only 3rd option is conveying the complete meaning.
2. No option is conveying the same meaning as conveyed by the question statement.
3. Option 1st and 2nd are exactly opposite in sense, compared to question statement hence rejected. 3rd is rejected because cause –effect has been reversed.
4. Option1, 3, 4 are either grammatically wrong or illogical in sense.
5. Options 1 &2 are saying that the entire politician are not kind, which is entirely wrong. As the question statement says that some are kind but some are not. 4th is also way out of track, therefore rejected.
6. The final sequence is FBDACE; the passage is talking about effect of family and early life on one's behavior and attitude. So sentence F WILL open the sequence. It is followed by D as D talks about family can influence one's behavior more in comparison to one's early life

7. E is the concluding sentence as psychologist are trying to study the effect of forces which are mentioned in sentence C.
8. Sentence C will come before sentence E, as C talks about new forces like social pressure of our friends and large world of society.
9. Sentence D will come after sentence B , as it elaborating upon influence of family and also early life.
10. Sentence B as it is talking about effect in particular by family of individual on oneself.
11. As risk management has been introduced, so we should not try to escape risks or it is important for us to keep the conditions that exist in India. Hence the answer is 3
12. Since trade and capital movement have been going across the world, we should ensure the free flow of these. Hence option 4 is correct. Option4
13. Since economic agents are ill-equipped to various risks so risk management is necessary. Option 3
14. We have started adopting new system, it does not mean that these be eliminated like insurance. Option 1
15. Changes are happening in India ranging from reforms in real and financial sectors. Option 5.
16. In the last the sentence has the pronoun 'IT' so 1st blank will have 'an ideology'. Also we have to use verb form of 'practice' which is practice. Option 1, 2 , 3 are either contextually or grammatically wrong.
17. As per the tense in the sentence only option 4 is correct.
18. As per the correct usage of 'not only........ But also' only choice 4 is correct. Because laboratory is equipped with what? With not only ....this but also with .....that.
19. As per the correct use of past perfect tense, only option 3 is correct. The rule is that if we are talking about two past activities and one of them is over before the start of another then we have to use past perfect tense.
20. As per the correct use of tenses if the subject is singular then verb is also singular. here the subject is 'library' which is singular.
21. Refer to oxford advance learner dictionary
22. Refer to oxford advance learner dictionary
23. Refer to oxford advance learner dictionary
24. Refer to oxford advance learner dictionary
25. Refer to oxford advance learner dictionary
26. As per line 1,2,3 of the passage
27. Options 1&2 are factually wrong, hence rejected. Nothing has been said number of deaths in rural area due to CVD , hence it is also rejected.
28. Refer to oxford dictionary.
29. Read the opening sentence of the passage.
30. 2
31. All the attributes of marketing communication are there in lines 1 and 2
32. As per the last line of the passage statement A and B are correct. Nothing has been said about statement C, so it is rejected.
33. Line 4, 5 , 6
34. In the last few lines author says that composition of the population will change in coming years so the marketing communication should take care of changing needs of the population try to create new trends in needs.
35. Refer to oxford advance learner's dictionary
36. As per the last paragraph, statements A, B and C are correct so option 4 is correct.

37. Contemporary means 'of the same period.

38. Option 3 & 4 are ruled out as they have nothing to do with the subject. Option 5 is correct because the author is talking about not only the importance of missile system but also the features to be included in the system. Also he has talked about need to insure the better and faster production of the new missile system. Author cannot be scientist only because scientist will only be interested in methods of developing the system. This passage is not the reporting of any event so option 1 is also ruled out.

39. As per the last line of the passage, only option 3 is correct.

40. Concurrent means 'happening at the same time'.

41. How the people start thinking about the risks in fast paced world leads to 4

42. Passage talks about data so it has to be officially.

43. As other things grow, it will definitely increase the need to insure things as well as life.

44. As business is increasing at the rate of 20% , so in the following blank it is expected to develop.

45. 'Despite' is the obvious choice as in spite of advancement in the field of technology most of things are done manually.

46. As newer methods of doing the things have to be evolved hence 'emerge' is the best choice.

47. Something is affecting something badly or in opposite way so 'adversely' is the best choice.

48. Since things are done manually so high prices are charged for the services.

49. System has to adopt total approach to progress.

50. We will see use of technology in every sector so 'prevalent' is the best choice

NMAT 2008

Number of Questions – 40
Time : 30 M.

PASSAGE – I

Directions for questions 1–7: *Read the following passage and answer the questions.*

Though the last twenty -five years have seen China dazzle the world with its excellent economic performance it has shied away from playing the kind of active role in international affairs that would seem commensurate with its economic weight. This is because traditionally China's politics have been defined by the need for economic development above all else. In the past China's authorities have tended to downplay the country 's international clout, choosing to stress instead its development country status and limited military capabilities. Such modest rhetoric was intended to **allay** the fears that China's rise was causing across its immediate neighborhood. That Beijing is finally acknowledging its status as a major player in the international system is evidenced by the fact that the president has formally development a theory of international relations; the concept of harmonious world .The concept, encompassing broad notions of multilateralism, prosperity for all through common development and tolerance for diversity has left world opinion perplexed. These are **commendable** objectives but the theory is short on specifics regarding the means to achieve them.

China's recent willingness to be a more active player internationally stems from complex factors. The country's economic strength -having acquired the largest foreign exchange reserves in the world - is undeniable and reports favour it to be the largest economy in the next quarter of a century. For sustained double digit economic growth China thus has no choice but to become more active internationally. Moreover as a major proportion of the oil and other natural resources that China needs to feed its growing economy are imported Beijing has to aggressively woo the countries rich in energy resources, which also represent emerging markets for Chinese products .To ensure a stable security environment within the region and thus facilitate economic growth China played an active role in facilitating negotiations with North Korea. Destabilization of a potential flashpoint like the Korean peninsula would lead to a flood of refugees crossing the border, interrupting careful plans economic rejuvenation of China's North - East. China's growing influence has caused a shift in the geopolitical status quo and its influence is beginning to replace that of the United States and European powers in Africa. China 's new diplomacy though has had its share of critics who have expressed their unease at China's military modernization programme and its willingness to deal with regimes widely condemned as corrupt and oppressive Despite this when the Africa was in need of aid and infrastructure or the US needed help in negotiating with Korea they turned to China .By taking a lead in a variety of international and regional forums, initiating bilateral and military exchange and dispensing aid and technical assistance in parts of the world where traditional powers are cautious to tread China has signaled that its days of sitting on the sidelines .content to let other shape world affairs are emphatically over.

1. What has been the fallout of china's increased participation in world affairs?

1. International scrutiny of its economic policies
2. Its influence and prestige grow substantially
3. None of these
4. Growth of corruption among its politicians
5. Its growth rate has stabilized

2. Why has China traditionally been a passive spectator in global affairs?

1. To safeguard its oil resources
2. To conceal its economic predicament
3. Economic dominance of the US

4. To maintain security in its vicinity
5. To focus on domestic economic growth

3. Which of the following best describes China's international status?
1. Cause of insecurity among developing nations
2. Largest economy in the world
3. Largest donor of aid to developing countries
4. Pioneer of implementing a "harmonious world" philosophy
5. None of these

4. The main purpose behind Beijing's intervention in North Korea is to ________
1. Ensure that the US acknowledges China's growing military influence
2. Prevent any hindrances to its domestic economic development programmes
3. Protect its financial investment in neighbouring countries
4. Provide humanitarian assistance to one of its strongest allies Korea
5. None of these

5. Which of the following **CANNOT** be said about China's international relations theory?
1. The theory is ambiguous in nature
2. The theory reflects China's realization that it occupies a vital place in global affairs
3. It promotes the concept of common development for all nations
4. It is a theory which explains China's sustained growth rate
5. It emphasizes achieving prosperity through universal development

6. Which of the following is **TRUE** in the context of the passage?
1. China's current political standing internationally is disproportionate to its financial strength
2. China is a reluctant participant in military dialogues
3. The harmonious world theory is the only utilitarian remedy to the current challenges facing the world
4. The US has recognized and acknowledged China's growing international reputation
5. China has stopped dealing with corrupt countries because of international pressure.

7. Which of the following is an outcome of Beijing's role in Africa?
1. America's influence in the region has reduced.
2. Instability in the region
3. The amount of aid from Europe and other countries has doubled
4. The balance of power in Africa has shifted in favour of Europe over the US
5. None of these

Directions for questions 8–20: *Read the information given below and answer the questions.*

PASSAGE – II

In the debates following the International Day for the Elimination of Violence Against Women observed a few days ago, some critical issues have come to the fore. Is it time to advocate for a completely separate apparatus of courts, law enforcement mechanisms and laws for women? What are the strengths and limits of such a proposal?

The issue of separate courts for women or family disputes has been a subject of debate for many years. A number of states have already set up special courts for women, including Maharashtra, with proposals pending in Karnataka and Delhi. These courts have taken on different incarnations at the state level with the Maharashtra courts designated as family courts to deal with family disputes and matrimonial matters; the Delhi courts are intended to deal exclusively with rape cases. However, the idea behind the special courts is to deal speedily with atrocities against women.

In 2006, a Bill to set up special courts for women was introduced in the Lok Sabha. The courts are intended to deal primarily with offences of rape, criminal assault, mental injury and sexual harassment against women. The courts are to be presided over by a chief judge, with additional judges appointed depending on the requirement in specific cases, and at least half of the judges' posts are to be reserved for women.

The idea behind these special courts is that they will provide speedy justice to women and be women-friendly as well. These courts are also intended to provide a more private space for women, especially to rape victims who are frequently traumatized by the trial process that currently exists.

The idea of separate women police cells has also been mooted from time to time. The Centre has been advising state governments regarding the steps that need to be taken, especially at the level of law enforcement, to afford greater protection to women and in particular to prevent crimes against them. These advisories include gender sensitization of the police, adopting appropriate measures for swift and effective punishment to public servants found guilty of custodial violence against women, minimizing delays in investigations of murder, rape and torture of women and setting up 'crimes against women cells' in districts where **they** do not exist.

The. National Commission for Women has also undertaken, visits to various states to review the status of women and conduct its own investigations in certain cases of serious incidents of crime against women. The Commission's findings indicate that the level of sensitivity and care with which crimes against women are handled is **woefully** inadequate. It has also observed that the filing of FIRs even in **acutely** abusive or violent cases continues to be a problem. The setting up of women police cells is one of the ways in which to alleviate these problems.

While proposals for separate courts, police cells and specific laws for women are demands that women themselves are making, there is a need to be attentive to the ways in which such initiatives might actually **boomerang.** Addressing women's issues of violence in a separate court structure could sequester women's issues into a dark corner, where reports of violence and abuse become **muted,** the role of the media in bringing the spotlight to bear on issues of violence has been crucial.

8. Which of the following was/were the points of debate that followed the celebration of International Day for Elimination of Violence against Women?

A. Propriety of setting up separate courts for dealing with matters related to atrocities against women

B. Whether there should be a separate women police cell

C. Whether there should be a separate set of laws devised exclusively to deal with problems related to women

1. A and B only
2. B and C only
3. A and C only
4. All the three
5. None of these

9. Which of the following is definitely **TRUE** about the courts for women?

A. Family courts in Maharashtra and special courts for women in the other states have a common ideological base.

B. Special courts for women in Delhi have been dealing exclusively with rape cases since 2006.

C. Karnataka State is not in favour of special courts for women.

1. Only B
2. Only C
3. Only A
4. A and B only
5. None of these

10. Which of the following is/are the objective(s) of setting up special courts for women?

A. Hastily disposing of the cases involving women so that the time so saved could be better utilized for settling other disputes.

B. Providing privacy for hearing so that probable embarrassment of women, particularly rape victims, is avoided.

C. Frequently traumatizing the accused of rape victims so that they are duly penalized for their misdeed.

1. Only A
2. Only B
3. Only C
4. A and C only
5. None of these

11. Which of the following is **NOT similar** in meaning to the word **"Boomerang"** as used in the passage?

1. Pull back
2. Bounce back
3. Rebound
4. Ricochet
5. Comeback

12. The word "they" in the last line of the fifth paragraph refers to ______

1. women
2. crimes
3. districts
4. rape and torture
5. none of these

13. The assumption underlying the proposal for reservation of at least fifty percent posts of judges for women is that ______

1. women have better capability to judge criminal cases
2. male judges cannot be impartial in their judgement
3. male judges are likely to tilt their judgement unduly in favour of women victims
4. women judges can easily become duly women friendly and still remain impartial
5. male judges cannot be gender-sensitized easily

14. By establishing separate women police cells, all of the following are likely to be realized **EXCEPT** ______

1. greater protection to women
2. prevention of crimes against women
3. quicker and effective punishment to the guilty of crime against women
4. punitive action against media unduly highlighting the crimes
5. None of these

15. The author of the passage seems to be ______

1. apprehensive about the effectiveness of special courts, laws and separate cells for women
2. in favour of status quo regarding measures to deal with cases against women
3. a strong opponent of the idea of having separate laws and courts for women
4. unduly and irrationally against the male members
5. treating women folk too much vulnerable to crimes

DIRECTIONS for questions 16–18: *Choose the word which is most nearly the SAME in meaning as the word given in bold as used in the passage.*

16. apparatus

1. premises 2. machinery 3. stationery 4. functions 5. regulations

17. acutely

1. highly 2. intentionally 3. primarily 4. mechanically 5. legally

18. muted

1. negligible 2. nullified 3. subdued 4. neutralized 5. empathetic

DIRECTIONS for questions 19 to 20: Choose the word which is most OPPOSITE in meaning of the word given in bold as used in the passage :

19. sequester

1. confiscate 2. hide 3. capture 4. impound 5. restore

20. woefully

1. dolefully 2. rudely 3. significantly 4. cheerfully 5. mercilessly

DIRECTIONS for questions 21–30: *In each question below,* **a** *sentence is given with a part of it printed in* **bold** *type. That part may contain* **a** *grammatical error. Each sentence is followed by phrases 1, 2, 3 and 4.. Find out which phrase should replace the phrase given in* **bold** *to correct the error, if there is any, and to make the sentence grammatically meaningful and correct. If the sentence is correct as it is and no correction is required, mark 5 as the answer.*

21. Many public servants can become **untrustworthy and corruption.**

1. untrustful and corruption
2. untrusting and corruption
3. untrusting and corruptive
4. untrustworthy and corrupt
5. No correction required

22. Systematic and carefully analyses of spoken languages must be done by scholars.

1. Systematic and careful
2. Systematically and careful
3. Systematically and carefully
4. System of carefully
5. No correction required

23. The descriptions of the plight of the miserables **were very touching.**

1. was very touching
2. were very touchy
3. had very touching
4. had been very touchy
5. No correction required

24. Mere being equipped by moral programming does not mean we practice moral behaviour.

1. Mere being equipped with
2. Merely being equipped with
3. Mere equipping by
4. Merely being equipped for
5. No correction required

25. His works of art **rank high in** the appraisal **for** competent critics.

1. are high rank in the appraisal for
2. are ranking high with the appraisal of
3. rank high in the appraisal of
4. rank high by the appraisal of
5. No correction required

26. As **years rolled by,** his name and fame spread all through the country.

1. When years rolled by
2. When years rolled through
3. As years rolled upon
4. After years rolled by
5. No correction required

27. Blessed with much intelligence, he **saw very few meanings** in religious rites that are performed as mere rituals.

1. observes very few meanings
2. saw quite a few meanings
3. looked for very few meanings
4. saw little meaning
5. No correction required

28. He **was devoted his time meticulously** for the good of his people.

1. was meticulous to be devoted his time.
2. devoted his time meticulously

3. was meticulous in his time to devote
4. had been devoted his time meticulously
5. No correction required

29. Many problems that India **faces today are wrought with** the potential for destroying her very integrity as a nation.

1. has faced everyday are wrought with 2. faces today are wrought by
3. faced these days have wrought with 4. faces today have wrought with
5. No correction required

30. Newton states that he could not have made his discoveries **his predecessors had not shown** him the right path.

1. if his predecessors were not shown 2. had his predecessors not been shown
3. had his predecessors not shown 4. if his predecessors had not been shown
5. No correction required

DIRECTIONS for questions 31–40: *In the following passage there are blanks, each of which has been numbered. These numbers are printed below the passage and against each, five words are suggested, one of which fits the blank appropriately. Find out the appropriate word in each case.*

The warning against carbon emissions, which is **31** the Earth, just got more urgent. The UN Human Development Report said on Tuesday that **32** the global community agreed to **33** emissions by half by 2050, the world would face huge economic setbacks and also ecological **34**. "We are on the **35** of seeing human development **36** for the first time in 30 years," Kevin Watkins, the author of the report was **37** as saying. The report said the poor nations would be hit the **38** as they are the least **39** to face nature's **40**, manifest in devastating storms and droughts.

31. 1. depriving 2. entangling 3. warming 4. blackening 5. harassing
32. 1. if 2. because 3. notwithstanding 4. without 5. unless
33. 1. cut 2. aggravate 3. enhance 4. diminish 5. eradicate
34. 1. balances 2. atmosphere 3. concerns 4. catastrophes 5. anxieties
35. 1. step 2. verge 3. top 4. extreme 5. enshrinement
36. 1. shaping 2. nurturing 3. extent 4. reverse 5. annihilation
37. 1. quoted 2. observed 3. found 4. interrogated 5. defined
38. 1. best 2. largest 3. hardest 4. least 5. strongest
39. 1. worried 2. engaged 3. willful 4. struggled 5. equipped
40. 1. boon 2. fury 3. blessing 4. deadline 5. encroachment

Answer Key

1. 2	**2.** 5	**3.** 5	**4.** 2	**5.** 4	**6.** 4	**7.** 1
8. 4	**9.** 1	**10.** 2	**11.** 1	**12.** 5	**13.** 4	**14.** 4
15. 1	**16.** 1	**17.** 1	**18.** 3	**19.** 3	**20.** 1	**21.** 4
22. 1	**23.** 5	**24.** 2	**25.** 3	**26.** 5	**27.** 5	**28.** 2
29. 5	**30.** 3	**31.** 3	**32.** 5	**33.** 3	**34.** 4	**35.** 2
36. 5	**37.** 1	**38.** 3	**39.** 5	**40.** 2		

EXPLANATIONS

1. 2 It cud be inferred from the last para "China's growing influence has caused..."
2. 5 1st para "in the past Chinese...."
3. 5
4. 2 2nd para "to ensure a stable security environment within the region...."
5. 4
6. 4 2nd para - u.s needed help .....
7. 1 2nd para – has caused a shift in the geopolitical status quo
8. 4 1st para
9. 1 2nd para
10. 2 3rd para
11. 1
12. 5
13. 4 Para 3 and para 4
14. 4
15. 1 Last para (last line)
16. 1
17. 1
18. 3
19. 3
20. 1
21. 4 Correction (name of activity) corrupt is an adjective.
22. 1
23. 5
24. 2 Equipped with (standard usage)
25. 3
26. 5
27. 5 Little means nothing (neligible)
28. 2 Past indefinite tense
29. 5
30. 3 Past perfect tense.

31. 3	**32.** 5	**33.** 3	**34.** 4	**35.** 2	**36.** 5
37. 1	**38.** 3	**39.** 5	**40.** 2		

PNB TRAINEE MANAGEMENT 2008

Number of Questions – 50
Time : 30 M.

Directions for questions 1-15: *Read the following passage carefully and answer the questions given below it.*

The current global food situation is very serious and hence, we need to understand the reason for such a dramatic increase in food prices in a short period.

It is argued that increases in energy costs are resulting in cost push inflation but the contribution of energy costs to overall costs in agriculture may not explain the huge increase in food prices.

Related to the current elevated energy prices, there has been a diversion of corn and edible to bio-fuels, which is significantly influenced by policy mandates. Very clearly this diversion to bio' is a policy induced new reality, which coincided with price escalation in precisely those *products* hence, is noteworthy.

The financialisation of commodity trade and current extraordinary conditions in global finance markets could have influenced the spurt in prices. The recent reductions in interest rates in the USA the injection of liquidity have resulted in investors seeking new avenues such as commodity market' view of the turbulence in financial markets and the low returns in treasuries. The relatively easy liquid and low interest rates, by themselves, make holding of inventories attractive and thus inducere volatility in commodity markets. The weakening of the U.S. dollar is also advanced as a reason for t recent volatility in commodity markets, including food items. It is evident that this phenomenon is n. also coinciding with the across the board rise in food prices.

In brief, while there are demand and supply side pressures on food items, there is considerably merit in the argument that the recent extraordinary increases in food prices are closely linked to put policy responses to high energy costs in advanced economies, and the turbulence in financial market and financial institutions. It is said that the impact of such policy induced diversion of food to bio-fuels significant at this juncture and reflects a preference to fill the fuel tanks of automobiles rather than fill *t* empty stomachs of people. Similarly, it is sometimes held that the weight accorded to financial stability in public policy may now be at the expense of stability in real sector - especially of sensitive commodity like food. At the same time, there is a general consensus that public policy in regard to food in man economies around the world has not provided adequate incentive to farmers to increase the supply food and other agricultural products to comfortably match the growing demand over the medium fen

1. The passage lays emphasis on which of the following central theme(s) ?

A. The abysmally throwaway prices offered for food commodities.

B. The worldwide acute shortage of food commodities.

C. Promoting the use of bio-fuel for automobiles.

1. A only
2. B only
3. C only
4. All the three
5. None of these

2. In what way are bio-fuels responsible for the increasing cost of food ?

A. It is a policy mandate to use bio-fuel in place of petroleum products especially in developing countries.

B. Certain essential food commodities are being used for manufacturing alternative fuels.

C. The low cost of bio-fuels has created fluctuation in prices of other agricultural commodities.

1. A only
2. B only
3. C only
4. A and B only
5. None of these

3. Which of the following situation(s) has/have prompted investors to look towards commodity markets ?

A. Dip in rates of interest in the U.S.

B. Easy Liquidity.

C. Volatility in commodity prices.

1. A and B only
2. B and C only
3. A and C only
4. All the three
5. None of these

4. Which of the following shows a cause-effect relationship between its two components?

1. Reduction in interest rates and abundance of food commodities
2. Reduction In energy prices and Increase In food commodity prices
3. Turbulence in financial markets and escalation in production of food commodities
4. Dipping of U.S. dollar value and volatility in commodity markets
5. Injection of liquidity and the drop in investor confidence

5. Which of the following can be inferred from the contents of the passage ?

A. At present the demand for food items exceeds the supply.

B. Fuel production has been given higher priority than caring for the millions who are starving.

C. Farmers have not been motivated to increase their production of food.

1. A and B only
2. B and C only
3. A and C only
4. None of these
5. All A, B & C

6. Which of the following can be thought of as a measure to remedy the global situation mentioned in the passage?

A. Reducing the production of cars and thereby the demand for energy.

B. Inducing farmers to increase their food and other agricultural produce.

C. Increasing the prices of food items to compensate farmers for their losses.

1. A only
2. A and B only
3. B only
4. B and C only
5. None of these

7. Which of the following statements is TRUE in the context of the passage?

1. Commodity markets have become erratic due to easy liquidity and low interest rate
2. Governments of many countries have begun paying better prices for food commodities to ensure their farmers are taken care of
3. Farmers in developing countries have to compulsorily produce a certain quantity of biofuels annually
4. The financialisation of commodity trade has resulted in a dip in prices of food products
5. The weakening of other currencies against the US dollar has resulted in high fuel prices

8. Which of the following statements is FALSE in the context of the passage ?

A. Unusual conditions in global financial markets have aggravated the food price.

B. No government would prefer fueling vehicles to feeding the hungry.

C. Maintenance of financial stability in public policy will be at the cost of stability in the real sector.

1. A and B only 2. B and C only
3. B only 4. C only
5. None of these

9. Which of the following best explains the phrase "this phenomenon" as used in the fourth paragraph of the passage?

1. Volatility in commodity markets which has led to hoarding
2. Escalating food prices caused by high interest rates
3. Easy liquidity because of lack of investment in America
4. Weakening of the US dollar and consequent variability in commodity markets
5. Fluctuation in energy prices and outdated public policy

Directions for questions 110-112: *Choose the word given which is most OPPOSITE in meaning of the word given in bold as used in the passage.*

10. elevated

1. raised 2. stabilised 3. inclined 4. fallen 5. slanted

11. volatility

1. agitation 2. effervescence 3. optimism 4. disparity 5. inactivity

12. consensus

1. deviant 2. disagreement 3. dejection 4. denial 5. dissuasion

Directions for questions 113-115: *Choose the word/group of words which is most nearly the SAME in meaning as the word given in bold as used in the passage.*

13. turbulence

1. tranquility 2. certainty 3. turmoil 4. restless 5. lackluster

14. incentive

1. acceleration 2. surplus 3. baiting 4. inspiration 5. encouragement

15. advanced

1. put forward 2. set aside 3. taken over 4. marched forward
5. escalated further

Directions for questions 116-125: *In each question there is a statement followed by three starters which are denoted by (A), (B) and (C). Each starter is a group of first few words of the sentence which, on proper completion, is supposed to convey the same meaning of the original statement. Find out which one or more starters can form grammatically correct sentence(s) to convey the SAME meaning of the original statement.*

16. It was too dark for us to be able to see anything.

A. We could not see B. Since we could not see
C. For us, it was so dark to

1. Only A 2. Only B
3. Only C 4. Either A or B
5. Either A or C

17. You must act as per my instructions only.

A. Only you act B. My instructions
C. You must do

1. Any one of the three 2. My instructions
3. You must do 4. Either A or C
5. None of these

18. Even if you dislike him you must not be rude to him:

A. you must be polite B. Although you must not be rude
C. Since you don't like

1. Any one of the three 2. A only
3. B only 4. C only
5. None of these

19. However, often I tried my best; I could not succeed in my endeavour.

A. Despite B. In spite of
C. Though I could not succeed

1. Only A 2. Only B
3. Only C 4. Either A or B
5. None of these

20. So terrible was the earthquake that all the skyscrapers in the locality were completely ruined.

A. Owing to the intensityB. None of the skyscrapers in the
C. The intensity of

1. Only A 2. Only B
3. All of these 4. Either A or B
5. Only C

21. If you are diligent, you can master nay skill in a short time span.

A. Unless you master B. If you can be mastering
C. In spite of being diligent.

1. None of three 2. Either A or B
3. Either B or C 4. Either A or C
5. Any one of three

22. Do whatever you think appropriate.

A. Don't do B. Do you think
C. You don't think

1. Any one of the three 2. Only C
3. Either B or C 4. Only B
5. None of these

23. They lost to their opponents although they played most valiantly.

A. Their opponents B. Despite the opponents
C. The opponents played valiantly

1. Any one of the three 2. Only A
3. Only B 4. Only C
5. None of these

24. No sooner did he offer the bouquet to the guest than he left the dais.

A. Hardly had he left the B. As soon as he left
C. He left the dais immediately

1. Only A 2. Only B
3. Either A or B 4. Only C
5. Either B or C

25. That social worker is the most respected person in our district.

A. All other persons B. Most other social workers

C. All the social workers in our

1. None of the three
2. Either A or B
3. Either A or C
4. Either B or C
5. Only A

DIRECTIONS for questions 126-130: *Rearrange the following six sentences (A), (B), (C), (D), (E) and (F) in the proper sequence to form a meaningful paragraph; then answer the questions given below them.*

A. Nobody likes to practise it, no matter how easy and how beneficial it is.

B. An ounce of patience is worth, or at times even better than a pound of brains.

C. Patience, a virtue, is considered to be even better than wisdom.

D. This is the worst drawback in us, in our national character.

E. Every one of us agrees with this fact in principle, without reservation.

F. But, unfortunately, when it comes to practising patience, there is a problem.

26. Which of the following should be the **FIRST** statement after rearrangement ?

1. A 2. B 3. C 4. D 5. E

27. Which of the following should be the **SECOND** statement after rearrangement ?

1. A 2. B 3. C 4. D 5. E

28. Which of the following should be the **THIRD** statement after rearrangement?

1. A 2. B 3. C 4. D 5. E

29. Which of the following should be the **FIFTH** statement after rearrangement ?

1. A 2. B 3. C 4. D 5. E

30. Which of the following should be the **SIXTH** (LAST) statement after rearrangement?

1. A 2. B 3. C 4. D 5. E

DIRECTIONS for questions 31-40: *Which of the phrases (1), (2), (3) and (4) given below each sentence should replace the phrases printed in* ***bold*** *in the following sentences to make the sentence grammatically correct If the sentence is correct as it is and 'No correction is required', mark (5) as the answer.*

31. He didn't want **risking to get** wet as he had only one suit.

1. risking for getting wet
2. risking at getting wet
3. to risk getting wet
4. to get wet at the risk of
5. No correction required

32. He postponed making a decision **until he been given** complete information

1. till he had been given
2. until he will get
3. till he would be giving
4. till he could be giving
5. No correction required

33. They came in **quiet so as not** to wake the others in the dormitory.

1. as quiet as not
2. so quiet as not
3. so quiet that not
4. quietly so as not
5. No correction required

34. If you were rule bound as you claim to be, you **should stop** at the signal.

1. should stop before
2. would have stopped at
3. should be stopped at
4. would have been stopped
5. No correction required

35. He refused to sign till he **would read** the text of the agreement.

1. had read
2. will read

3. would have read
4. should be reading
5. No correction required

36. Kidnappers had telephoned the victim's father from a public booth **to conceal his** identity.
1. for concealing his
2. because of concealing their
3. to conceal their
4. by concealing his
5. No correction required

37. He usually wears a coat but he **is not wearing** it today as it is not cold.
1. has not wearing
2. has not been worn
3. doesn't wear
4. didn't wore
5. No correction required

38. The metal roof was dismantled to be broken up and **sell as scrap.**
1. for selling with scrap
2. for sell as scrap
3. and to sell as scrap
4. and sold as scrap
5. No correction required

39. It **is noteworthy to note that** India had pioneered the use of non-cash based payment systems.
1. is noteworthy that
2. is notably that
3. is worth to note
4. is noted about.
5. No correction required

40. Some social service organizations **are done yeoman service** in empowering the downtrodden women.
1. will be provided yeoman service
2. have been doing yeoman service
3. are doing service of yeoman
4. have been doing services of yeoman
5. No correction required

DIRECTIONS for questions 41-50: *In the following passage there are blanks, each of which has been numbered. These numbers are printed below the passage and against each, "five words are suggested, one of which fits the blank appropriately. Find out the appropriate word in each case.*

Technology **41** lives. But **42** if people want it to. This qualification is important, and **43** to understanding progress. Akio Morita, the founder of Sony, used to make inventions not by writing code but by making minute, detailed studies of **44** people lived their lives. It is observable that when he relinquished direct involvement in product development at the company in the 1980s, Sony seemed to lose its **45** of developing a truly radical invention like the Walkman that the world takes to en masse.

However much it seems that machines are in **46**, they are not, yet the belief that the technology alone holds the key to **47** the way people work, buy, and do business is strong. The rise of dotcoms in the late 1990s was **48** by a belief that technology was changing the rules of marketing and employee relationships. This is not to say there have been no changes in the new economy; but that they **49** to appear where technology makes it **50** for people to communicate with each other, or have been unrelated to the technology. The dynamic is still a human one.

41.	1. ruins	2. changes	3. makes	4. explains	5. shakes
42.	1. not	2. occasionally	3. seldom	4. only	5. never
43.	1. key	2. primarily	3. encouraging	4. supported	5. disastrous
44.	1. why	2. where	3. when	4. whether	5. how
45.	1. share	2. profit	3. knack	4. business	5. plant
46.	1. progress	2. control	3. action	4. operation	5. transition
47.	1. encroaching	2. accomplishing	3. determining	4. highlighting	5. informing
48.	1. govern	2. successful	3. underlying	4. disputed	5. accompanied

49.	1. tend	2. cease	3. fail	4. refuse	5. avoid
50.	1. essential	2. laborious	3. tough	4. easier	5. awkward

Answer Key

1. 2	**2.** 2	**3.** 4	**4.** 5	**5.** 1	**6.** 3	**7.** 1
8. 3	**9.** 4	**10.** 5	**11.** 5	**12.** 2	**13.** 3	**14.** 2
15. 5	**16.** 1	**17.** 3	**18.** 2	**19.** 4	**20.** 1	**21.** 1
22. 5	**23.** 4	**24.** 4	**25.** 5	**26.** 3	**27.** 2	**28.** 5
29. 1	**30.** 4	**31.** 3	**32.** 2	**33.** 4	**34.** 2	**35.** 1
36. 3	**37.** 5	**38.** 3	**39.** 1	**40.** 2	**41.** 2	**42.** 4
43. 1	**44.** 5	**45.** 3	**46.** 2	**47.** 3	**48.** 1	**49.** 1
50. 4						

EXPLANATIONS

1. The passage is discussing only about the acute shortage of food commodities, this is given in option - 2.
2. Answer is option no 2. It is given in 3rd para 1st line related.........mandates.
3. Answer is option - 4 . All three options are given in 4th para .
4. Answer is option - 5. 4th para 2nd line the recent. ....treasuries.
5. Answer is option no 1.first two options can be inferred from the paragraph but last option is directly stated in last para 3rd last line.
6. Answer is none of these as given para is talking about increase in food commodities as these food products are being used in making fuel for the vehicles . But no given option is talking about the solution of this problem.
7. Answer is option no 1. fourth para 2nd line.
8. Answer is option no 3 .Statement B is not true as it is saying that govt has no role in the increase in the prices of food commodities , but in 5th para 4th line it is stated that govt policies are also responsible.
9. Answer is option 4. 3rd para 3rd line.
10. Elevated means to move or raise to a higher place or position and the word which is opposite to it is fallen
11. Volatility changeable; mercurial; flighty and its opposite is option no 5 which is inactivity
12. Consensus is agreement and its opposite is disagreement
13. Turbulence is disorder or confusion and its synonym is option no. 3 turmoil
14. Incentive is motivation or surplus and synonym is option no. 2
15. Advanced means foremost ,higher, further and the option which is same in meaning is option no. 5
16. As it was too dark we were not able to see anything ; and the option which conveys the same meaning is option no 1
17. Either B or C is correct. We can say this statement that my instructions are important and you must act according to them or you must do what I say.
18. The keyword here is must, so you must be polite. So correct ans is option no 2
19. The word however can be replaced by either despite or in spite of. So ans is option no 4
20. Only option no 1 is actually giving the grammatically correct meaning
21. The usage of if in the beginning of the sentence is making it a conditional sentence and no option is providing us the same meaning so ans is option 1

22. Ans is option no 5(which is none of these). Correct ans is statement A which can state that don't do whatever you think is inappropriate. But this is nowhere given as ans choices.

23. Ans is option no 3. The statement can state that despite the opponents' timidity they lost to them

24. Ans is statement c. it can state he left the dias immediately after he offered the bouquet to the guest.

25. Ans is statement a (we can say this given statement in this way also i.e All other persons are not as respected as that social person in our town.)_so ans is option no 5

26-30 Opening sentence is statement C. It is an independent sentence and moreover it is giving an introduction about patience. statement B is further giving as some more information about patience. E is following B as pronoun this(fact) is used for something that is stated in statement B. Then F is following E. F is talking about practicing patience and A is elaborating that concept further. And we are left with statement D which has to come afterwards. So the proper sequence is CBEFAD.

26. Refer to the above explanation

Refer to the above explanation

Refer to the above explanation

29. Refer to the above explanation

30. Refer to the above explanation

31. Risking to is incorrect usage correct answer is option no 3 (to risk)

32. He till he had been given (instead of till he been given) is correct as the sentence is in past tense and according to sequence of tenses past perfect is the required usage here.

33. They came in so quietly is the correct ans as we are talking about the way he came so adverb of manner should be used.

34. If you were rule bound you would (not should) have stopped at the signal

35. Had read is correct usage.

36. Kidnappers are plural so the verb should be used according to the subject. The correct ans is option no 3 (to conceal their).

37. No correction required. Ans is option no 5.

38. Error of parallelism; to be broken, to sell. so correct ans is option 3

39. Noteworthy itself means worthy to be noted so, usage of note that is redundant here. Ans is option no 1.

40. Ans is option 2.

41. Technology can not make, explain or shake life. we are left with changes and ruins , and the best answer is changes.

42. Only if is going with changes

43. Qualification is important and key to is the best answer

44. "The way people lived "so, adverb of manner is required so ans is how.

45. One can lose his/her knack (ability, talent) of doing something.

46. Machines seem to be in control but actually they are not.

47. Key word here is yet, yet people believe that technology determines the way people work.

48. Something can be govern by a belief, no other option is giving the same meaning

49. Tend to is the required usage here.

50. Technology makes it easier for people to communicate.

SBI CLERK 2008 – 1ST Shift

Number of Questions – 40
Time : 30 M.

GENERAL ENGLISH

Directions—(Q. 1–10): *Read the following passage carefully and answer the questions given below it.*

The yearly festival was close at hand. The store room was packed with silk fabrics. Gold ornaments, clay bowls full of sweet curd and platefuls of sweetmeats. The orders had been placed with shops well in advance. The mother was sending out gifts to everyone. The eldest son, a government servant, lived with his wife and children in far off lands. The second son had left home at an early age. As a merchant he travelled all over the world. The other sons had split up over petty squabbles, and they now lived in homes of their own. The relatives were spread all across the world. They rarely visited. The youngest son, left in the company of a servant, was soon ored and stood at the door all day long, waiting and watching. His mother, thrilled and excited, loaded the presents on trays and plates, covered them with colourful kerchiefs, and sent them off with maids and servants. The neighbours looked on. The day came to an end. All the presents had been sent off.The child came back into the house and dejectedly said to his mother, "Maa, you gave a present to everyone, but you didn't give me anything !"His mother laughed, "I have given all the gifts away to everyone, now see what's left for you." She kissed him on the forehead.The child said in a tearful voice, "Don't I get a gift ?""You'll get it when you go far away.""But when I am close to you, don't I get something from your own hands ?" His mother reached out her arms and drew him to her. "This is all I have in my own hands. It is the most precious of all."

1. Why did the woman's second son travel ?
   (A) He was restless by nature
   (B) He did not want to stay at home
   (C) He was rich and could afford to travel
   (D) His job was such that he had to travel
   (E) None of these

2. Why did the woman's eldest son not attend the festival ?
   (A) He was not on good terms with his youngest brother who lived at home
   (B) He had quarrelled with his mother
   (C) His wife did not allow him to return home
   (D) His job prevented him from taking leave
   (E) None of these

3. How did the woman prepare for the festival ?
   1. She bought expensive gifts for her children and neighbours.
   2. She ordered her servants to prepare sweets and food well in advance.
   3. She made sure that her youngest child was looked after so that he wouldn't be bored.

   (A) None (B) Only 1
   (C) Only 2 (D) Both 1 and 2
   (E) All 1, 2 and 3

4. What did the youngest child do while his mother was busy ?
   1. He waited for a chance to steal some sweetmeats.
   2. He pestered his mother to give him a present.

3. He stood at the door with servants.

(A) Only 1 (B) Only 2
(C) Both 1 and 3 (D) Only 3
(E) None of these

5. Which of the following can be said about the woman ?
(A) She was a widow who had brought up her children single handedly
(B) She was not a good mother since her children had left home at an early age
(C) She enjoyed sending her family gifts at festival time
(D) She gave expensive presents to show that she was wealthy
(E) She rarely visited her grand-children because they all lived abroad

6. What did the boy receive from his mother ?
(A) She taught him the value of patience
(B) She encouraged him to grow up and live independently like his brothers
(C) She showed him the importance of giving expensive gifts
(D) She gave him a hug to express her love
(E) None of these

7. Which of the following is TRUE in the context of the passage ?
(A) The woman usually ignored her youngest son
(B) The woman's eldest son lived abroad
(C) The members of the woman's family did not care about her
(D) The woman made all the preparations herself since she did not want to burden the servants
(E) The woman sent gifts to her children to ensure that they visited her

Directions—(Q.8–9) Choose the word which is most nearly the SAME in meaning as the word printed in bold as used in the passage.

8. Left
(A) Gone (B) Quit (C) Remaining (D) Disappeared (E) Forgot

9. Packed
(A) Filled (B) Squeezed (C) Crowd (D) Collected (E) Untidy

10. Choose the word which is most OPPOSITE in meaning of the word **dejectedly** as used in the passage.
(A) Calmly (B) Happily (C) Willingly (D) Fortunately (E) Softly

Directions—(Q. 11–15) Read each sentence to find out whether there is any error in it. The error, if any, will be in one part of the sentence. The letter of that part is the answer. If there is no error, the answer is (E). (Ignore errors of punctuation, if any)

11. Many multinational companies (A) / have not been as (B) /successful in India (C)/than we expected. (D) No error (E)

12. He has ruined (A) /his eyesight (B) /by not using (C) /his spectacles regularly. (D) No error (E)

13. Mostly of the (A) /newly recruited officers (B) /have no experience (C) /in the banking sector. (D) No error (E)

14. The resignation of (A) /one of our directors (B) /have caused the price (C) / of shares to fall. (D) No error (E)

15. There are many (A) /ways of which (B) /inflation can (C) /be measured. (D) No error(E)

Directions—(Q. 16–20) Which of the phrases (A), (B), (C) and (D) given below should replace the phrase given in bold in the following sentence to make the sentence grammatically meaningful and correct. If the sentence is correct as it is and 'No correction is required.' mark (E) as the answer.

16. Each of the loan must be approved by the Branch Manager—

(A) Every loan (B) Each one of the loan

(C) Any of the loan (D) All of the loan

(E) No correction required

17. The issue was taken before the Municipal Corporation meeting last week—

(A) Taking place at (B) Taken after

(C) Being taken in (D) Taken up at

(E) No correction required

18. He has asked for the names of those employees involved in the project.

(A) had asked (B) having asked about

(C) was asked that (D) is asking

(E) no correction required

19. Considerate the traffic, it is better to leave for the airport an hour early—

(A) While considering

(B) Consideration of

(C) Considering

(D) Being considerate to

(E) No correction required

20. He is a good leader, knowing that to motivate his employees to achieve—

(A) That known when (B) Who knows how

(C) Which knows how (D) Knowing what

(E) No correction required

Directions—(Q. 21–25) Rearrange the following six sentences (1), (2), (3), (4), (5) and (6) in the proper sequence to form a meaningful paragraph; then answer the questions given below them.

(1) The able bodied men of the tribe gathered to discuss how to climb the mountain.

(2) As part of their plundering they kidnapped a baby of one of the families.

(3) One day the mountain tribe invaded those living in the valley.

(4) "We couldn't climb the mountain. How could you?", they asked, "It wasn't your baby !" she replied.

(5) There were two tribes in the Andes–one lived in the valley and the other high up in the mountains.

(6) Two days later they noticed the child's mother coming down the mountain that they hadn't yet figured out how to climb.

21. Which of the following should be the SECOND sentence after rearrangement ?

(A) (1) (B) (2) (C) (3) (D) (4) (E) (5)

22. Which of the following should be the FIFTH sentence after rearrangement ?

(A) (6) (B) (5) (C) (4) (D) (3) (E) (2)

23. Which of the following should be the FIRST sentence after rearrangement ?

(A) (1) (B) (2) (C) (3) (D) (4) (E) (5)

24. Which of the following should be the SIXTH (LAST) sentence after rearrangement ?

(A) (1) (B) (2) (C) (3) (D) (4) (E) (5)

25. Which of the following should be the THIRD sentence after rearrangement ?

(A) (1) (B) (2) (C) (3) (D) (4) (E) (5)

Directions—(Q. 26–30) In each question below a sentence with four words printed in bold type is given. These are lettered (A), (B), (C) and (D). One of these four words printed in bold may be either wrongly spelt or inappropriate in the context of the sentence. Find out the word, which is wrongly spelt or inappropriate, if any. The letter of that word is your answer. If all the words printed in bold are correctly spelt and also appropriate in the context of the sentence mark (E) i.e., all correct as your answer.

26. The **income** (A) of many people in **rural** (B) India is **not adequate** (C) to **satisfy** (D) their basic **needs**. All correct (E)

27. He is **always** (A) **prompt** (B) **in caring** (C) out **instructions**. (D) All correct (E)

28. The **revized** (A) **rates** (B) of **interest** will be effective (C) **immediately**. (D) All correct (E)

29. Such **transactions** (A) are **quiet** (B) **expensive** (C) and **time consuming** (D) **for customers**. All correct (E)

30. The **guidelines** (A) of the **new scheme** (B) are **expected** (C) to be **finally** (D) **soon**. All correct (E)

Directions—(Q. 31–40) In the following passage there are blanks each of which has been numbered. These numbers are printed below the passage and against each five words/ phrases are suggested one of which fits the blank appropriately. Find out the appropriate word in each case.

I used to look ...**(31)**... to the holidays. I was usually ...**(32)**... to my uncle's housewhere I ...**(33)**... his children. I did not get paid a salary for ...**(34)**... What I received in return however, was far more ...**(35)**... My uncle was an avid reader. During the time I spent with his family I had an ...**(36)**... to read the vast amount of books and magazines that he possessed. This improved my English to some ...**(37)**... Reading became my new ...**(38–39)**... spending my pocket money on a ticket to the cinema I began to ...**(40)**...books. This has benefited me greatly.

31. (A) forward (B) towards (C) backward (D) up (E) around

32. (A) went (B) sent (C) visited (D) travelled (E) gone

33. (A) cared (B) occupy (C) guarded (D) taught (E) played

34. (A) them (B) whom (C) this (D) now (E) which

35. (A) expensive (B) deserving (C) helping (D) demanding (E) valuable

36. (A) opportunity (B) ability (C) use (D) encouragement (E) achievement

37. (A) distance (B) extent (C) time (D) limits (E) degrees

38. (A) activity (B) hope (C) hobby (D) duty (E) worship

39. (A) despite (B) though (C) by (D) instead of (E) while

40. (A) sell (B) read (C) exchange (D) invest (E) buy

Answer Key

1. (D) **2.** (E) **3.** (A) **4.** (D) **5.** (C) **6.** (D) **7.** (B)
8. (C) **9.** (A) **10.** (C) **11.** (D) Replace 'than' with 'as'.
12. (E) **13.** (A) Change 'Mostly' to 'Most'.
14. (C) Change 'have' to 'has'. **15.** (B) Replace 'of' with 'in'.
16. (A) **17.** (D) **18.** (E) **19.** (C) **20.** (B) **21.** (C) **22.** (A)
23. (E) **24.** (D) **25.** (B) **26.** (E) **27.** (C) **28.** (A) **29.** (E)
30. (D) **31.** (A) **32.** (B) **33.** (D) **34.** (C) **35.** (E) **36.** (A)
37. (B) **38.** (C) **39.** (D) **40.** (E)

SBI CLERK 2008 – 2nd Shift

Number of Questions – 40
Time : 30 M.

Directions—(Q. 1–10): *Read the following passage carefully and answer the questions given below it.*

There was a girl who sang beautifully at the temple every morning. The music master used to happily recall, "One day when I went into the woods to pluck flowers, I found this baby under a pipal tree." He picked her up carefully, raised her lovingly as if she was his daughter and taught her to sing before she spoke her first word. The music master grew old and didn't see too well. The girl tended to him caringly. Many people including young men travelled from far and wide to hear her sing. This made the music master's heart quake with fear. "You will choose one of them as your husband. What is to become of me ?" The girl replied, "I shall not be apart from you." But on a full moon night during the harvest festival, the master's chief disciple touched his feet reverently and said, "Master grant me your permission for your daughter has agreed to marry me." The master's tears flowed freely, "She has chosen well. Go and fetch her, let me hear you sing the first of many melodies that you will sing together." The two began

to sing in harmony. But the song was interrupted by the arrival of the royal messenger. "Your daughter is very fortunate-the king has sent for her," the messenger said. At the palace the Queen summoned the girl to her and said, "I place upon you the honour of making sure my daughter is never unhappy at her husband's home." There wasn't a single tear in the girl's eyes but she thought of the master and her heart was heavy. That very night the princess began her journey to Kambhoj. The princess's royal chariot led the procession and the girl's palanquin followed close behind carrying trunks of silks, jewellry and precious stones. It was covered with a velvet sheet and had soldiers on both sides. As the procession passed, the master and his disciple Kumarsen stood still by the

wayside. A collective sigh escaped the crowd gathered there wishing that the princess wouldn't feel homesick in her faraway home.

1. Which of the following can be said about the girl ?

(1) She was brought up by her father as her mother had died when she was a baby.
(2) She was a talented singer who had learnt to sing at an early age.
(3) She was only allowed to sing with the master's permission.

(A) Only (1) (B) Both (1) and (2)
(C) Only (2) (D) All (1), (2) and (3)
(E) None of these

2. What was the girl's reaction to leaving home ?

(A) She was honoured to be serving the princess
(B) Sadness at leaving the master.
(C) She entrusted the task of looking after the music master to Kumarasen
(D) She was thrilled to be living in luxury
(E) None of these

3. What task was entrusted to the girl by the Queen ?

(A) Seeing that her daughter reached Kambhoj safely
(B) Entertaining the princess on her journey to Kambhoj

(C) Protecting the princess and reporting to the queen if she was unhappy
(D) Ensuring the princess' happiness
(E) None of these

4. What was the master's reaction to the girl's decision to marry his disciple ?
(A) He was upset and cried
(B) He promised to give his permission if the couple sang well together
(C) He was sad because she would be going to Kambhoj which was far away
(D) He was pleased with her choice of husband
(E) None of these

5. Which of the following is not true in the context of the passage ?
(1) The girl was leaving the master and going to Kambhoj once she was married.
(2) The king sent for the girl because she was a good singer.
(3) The master did not let the girl study any other subject except music.

(A) Only (1) (B) Both (1) and (2)
(C) All (1), (2) and (3) (D) Both (1) and (3)
(E) None of these

6. Why was the princess going on a journey ?
(1) She was going to her prospective husband's home to get engaged.
(2) Her parents wanted her to visit the kingdom of which she would be the future queen.
(3) To take expensive gifts for the rulers of the Kambhoj who were well known to her parents.

(A) None (B) Only (2)
(C) Only (1) (D) Both (1) and (2)
(E) Both (2) and (3)

7. Why was the master afraid ?
(A) He felt the princess would treat the young girl unkindly
(B) He would be all alone after the girl's marriage
(C) The girl may not be able to adapt to her new home
(D) He was slowly going blind.
(E) None of these

Directions—(Q. 8–9): *Choose the word which is MOST NEARLY the SAME in MEANING as the word printed in bold as used in the passage.*

68. fortunate
(A) rich (B) liked (C) happy (D) successful (E) lucky

9. raised
(A) nurtured (B) lifted (C) grew (D) built (E) high

10. Choose the word which is most OPPOSITE in meaning of the word Collective as used in the passage—
(A) alone (B) separately (C) united (D) partial (E) single

Directions—(Q. 11–15): *Read each sentence to find out whether there is any error in it. The error, if any, will be in one part of the sentence. The letter of that part is the answer. If there is no error, the answer is (E). (Ignore errors of punctuation, if any.)*

11. In present the (A)/ prices of food grains (B)/ are high all (C)/ over the world. (D) Noerror (E)

12. Majority of the banks (A)/ today uses technology (B)/ to reach out to those (C)/living in rural areas. (D) No error (E)

13. I will give (A)/ you the advance (B)/ if you repay it as (C)/ soon as possibly. (D) No error (E)
14. Though he is very (A)/ wealthy and powerful (B)/ he has any (C)/ concern for the poor. (D) No error (E)
15. Mala has the (A)/ ability t o handle (B)/ many tasks at (C)/ the same time. (D) No error (E)

Directions—(Q. 16–20): *Which of the phrases (A), (B), (C) and (D) given below should replace the phrases given in bold in the following sentences to make the sentence grammatically meaningful and correct. If the Sentence is correct as it is and No correction is required, mark (E) as the answer.*

16. Finding himself in financial difficulty, he came forward me for help and advice—
(A) came across (B) is come upto
(C) came to (D) comes with
(E) No correction required

17. Deepak having been over eighteen years of age, is entitled to vote—
(A) has been of (B) being over
(C) who is having over (D) who is been
(E) No correction required

18. The magazine that we subscribe to is published monthly—
(A) which is subscribed (B) we are subscribed
(C) whom we subscribe (D) whichever we subscribe
(E) No correction required

19. Among of his many good qualities, that I remember is his honesty—
(A) All of his (B) Some of the
(C) Only of his (D) One of his
(E) No correction required

20. Many of our clients have deposit of this foreign bank—
(A) have deposits in (B) had deposited
(C) with deposits (D) have deposited
(E) No correction required

Directions—(Q. 21–25): *Rearrange the following six sentences (1), (2), (3), (4), (5) and (6) in the proper sequence to form a meaningful paragraph; then answer the questions given below them.*

(1) The sailor was told it was placed there as warning signal to sailors to warn them of the danger.
(2) He returned to the spot a few years later as captain of his own ship.
(3) The ship was at sea for many days and finally anchored near the coastline.
(4) The night was stormy and without a warning signal his ship was wrecked on that very rock.
(5) One of the sailors on board saw a bell tied to a dangerous submerged rock.
(6) As a joke the sailor decided to steal the bell and hide it despite being informed of this.

21. Which of the following should be the FIRST sentence after rearrangement ?
(A) (1) (B) (2) (C) (3) (D) (4) (E) (5)

22. Which of the following should be the SECOND sentence after rearrangement ?
(A) (1) (B) (2) (C) (3) (D) (4) (E) (5)

23. Which of the following should be the THIRD sentence after rearrangement ?
(A) (1) (B) (2) (C) (3) (D) (4) (E) (5)

24. Which of the following should be the FIFTH sentence after rearrangement ?
(A) (1) (B) (2) (C) (3) (D) (4) (E) (5)

25. Which of the following should be the SIXTH (LAST) sentence after rearrangement ?
(A) (1) (B) (2) (C) (3) (D) (4) (E) (5)

Directions—(Q. 26–30): *In each question below a sentence with four words printed in bold type is given. These are lettered as (A), (B), (C) and (D). One of these four words printed in bold may be either wrongly spelt or inappropriate in the context of the sentence. Find out the word, which is wrongly spelt or inappropriate, if any. The letter of that word is your answer. If all the words printed in bold are correctly spelt and also appropriate in the context of the sentence, mark (E) i.e. 'All Correct' as your answer.*

26. We have **incurred** (A) an **expense** (B) of over **fifty thousands** (C) this **year alone**. (D) All correct (E)

27. World Earth Day is **celeberated** (A) as a **means** (B) to make people **aware** (C) about **the environment**. (D) All correct (E)

28. The **key issue** (A) **discused** (B) at the meeting was how to **resolve** (C) the **food crisis**. (D) All correct (E)

29. He **deserves** (A) some **recognition** (B) for working **diligently** (C) for the **passed** (D) **five years**. All correct (E)

30. There are many **employment** (A) **opportunities** (B) for **fresh graduates** (C) in the *market* (D) today. All correct (E)

Directions—(Q. 31–40): *In the following passage there are blanks each of which has been numbered. These numbers are printed below the passage and against each five words are suggested one of which fits the blank appropriately. Find out the appropriate word in each case.*

I had ...**(31)**... to become a multipurpose manager. I took three steps to accomplish this. First, I took very ...**(32)**... part in professional associations. I ...**(33)**... the National President of the Indian Society for Training and Development–one of the ...**(34)**... organizations for HR professionals. This helped me to grow professionally. My communication skills ...**(35)**.... It also taught me ...**(36)**... to conduct meetings in an effective manner. My job ...**(37)**... me to different parts of the country and I ...**(38)**... believe that ...**(39)**... provided me with an education. I also wrote a lot. Newspaper editors often approached me with ...**(40)**... to write articles for their publications.

31. (A) achieved (B) aim (C) try (D) dreamed (E) wanted

32. (A) selected (B) active (C) interesting (D) often (E) joint

33. (A) elected (B) voted (C) became (D) applied (E) decided

34. (A) respected (B) status (C) impressed (D) aged (E) common

35. (A) lacked (B) grown (C) learnt (D) improved (E) earned

36. (A) that (B) why (C) how (D) never (E) anyhow

37. (A) saw (B) showed (C) posted (D) discovered (E) took

38. (A) quiet (B) firmly (C) strong (D) first (E) not

39. (A) travelling (B) journey (C) visit (D) migrating (E) shift

40. (A) wish (B) offer (C) appointments (D) requests (E) commands

Answer Key

1. (C) **2.** (B) **3.** (D) **4.** (E) **5.** (B) **6.** (A) **7.** (B)
8. (E) **9.** (B) **10.** (A)

11. (A) Write 'At' in place of 'In'.

12. (B) Write 'use'.

13. (D) Write 'possible'.

14. (C) Write 'no' in place of 'any'.

15. (E) **16.** (C) **17.** (E) **18.** (E) **19.** (D) **20.** (A) **21.** (C)
22. (E) **23.** (A) **24.** (D) **25.** (B)

26. (C) Write change 'thousands' to 'thousand'.

27. (A) Write 'celebrated'.

28. (B) Write 'discussed'.

29. (D) Write 'past'.

30. (E) **31.** (E) **32.** (B) **33.** (C) **34.** (A) **35.** (D) **36.** (C)
37. (E) **38.** (B) **39.** (A) **40.** (D)

SNAP 2008

Number of Questions – 35
Time : 30 M.

For the following 5 questions in this section, correct answers carry 2 marks each.

1. Match the following idiomatic references to parts of the human anatomy

1. palm	5. could not tolerate the insult
2. foot	6. to look at with envy and desire
3. eye	7. to put the blame on someone else
4. stomach	8. forced to pay the bill

1. 1-8, 2-6, 3-5, 4-7 2. 1-5, 2-7, 3-6, 4-8
3. 1-7, 2-8, 3-6, 4-5 4. 1-6, 2-8, 3-5, 4-7

2. Find the maximum number of times any one of the given words fits the set of sentences

RAISE ARISE AROSE RISE

I. Opportunities will __________, and you must grab them.
II. A hot wind __________ from the desert.
III. I __________ at dawn on most days.
IV. A mood of optimism __________ among the people.

1. in all four sentences 2. in 3 sentences
3. in 2 sentences 4. in 1 sentence

3. Which two sentences in the following convey the same idea? Choose from the combinations listed below:

I. He is in a fool's paradise
II. He can't see the wood for the trees
III. He can't distinguish between reality and fancy.
IV. He is unable to separate unimportant details from the really important ones

1. 2, 3 2. 2, 4
3. 1, 4 4. 1, 3

4. Find the correct match of grammatical function with usage of the word THEN.

Function	**Usage**
1. Noun	5. He was the then King of Nepal
2. Adjective	6. I have not heard about him since then.
3. Adverb	7. He is not feeling well, then how can he possibly go for the picnic.
4. Conjunction	8. He was not a graduate then.

1. 1-8, 2-5, 3-7, 4-7 2. 1-6, 2-5, 3-8, 4-7
3. 1-7, 2-5, 3-6, 4-8 4. 1-8, 2-7, 3-6, 4-5

5. We can never make our beliefs regarding the world certain. Even scientific theory of a most rigorous and well-confirmed nature is likely to change over a decade or even tomorrow. If we refuse to even try to understand, then it is like resigning from the human race. Undoubtedly life of an unexamined kind is worth living in other respects –as it is no mean thing to be a vegetable

or an animal. It is also true that a man wishes to see this speculative domain beyond his next dinner.

From the above passage it is clear that the author believes that

1. men would do well not to speculate
2. progress in the scientific field is impossible
3. one should live life with the dictum 'what will be will be'
4. men are different from animals as far as their reasoning abilities are concerned.

For the following questions in this section, correct answers carry 1 mark each.

Directions for the questions 6 – 11: Read the passage and answer within its context.

Rajendra K. Pachauri, head of the Intergovernmental Panel on Climate Change, is getting nightmares because of the Nano, Tata's soon-to-be-launched Rs. One lakh car. Sunita Narain of the Centre for Science and Environment (CSE) says that it isn't the Nano by itself but cars overall that give her nightmares. The villains in my nightmares are neither the Nano nor cars overall, but stupid government policies that subsidize and encourage pollution, adulteration and congestion.

Sanctimonious greens call the Nano disastrous because of its affordability – millions more will now clog roads and consume more fossil fuel. This is elitism parading as virtue. Elite greens own cars, but cannot stand the poorer masses becoming mobile, since the consequent congestion will eat into the time of the elite!

More logical would be a protest against big cars that use more space and fuel, or highly polluting old cars. Instead, green hypocrites aim at a new car with the lowest cost, best mileage and least emissions. The Nano will no burden us with too many cars. India has very few cars per person by world standards. London and New York have ultra-high car densities, yet have clearer aim than Delhi. Our problem is too many bad policies, not too many cars.

We subsidize vehicles on a gargantuan scale invisible to lay folk. Roads and flyovers cost crores to build and maintain, yet road use is free (save on a few toll roads). Traffic police and lights are costly, yet are provided free. These invisible subsidies starve cities of funds to expand roads and public transport.

Land in cities now costs lakhs per square metre. Yet parking is free in the suburbs, and often costs just Rs. 10 day per day in city centres. A single parking space of 23 square metres occupies land worth Rs. 40 lakhs. A car occupies more space than an office desk, yet the desk space pays full commercial rent while parking space costs just about Rs. 10 per day.

Daily parking charges range from $30 (Rs. 630) in Washington to $30 (Rs. 1260) in New York. CSE launched a sensible campaign to raise parking fees in Delhi to Rs. 120 per day, but was foiled. So, parking space now exceeds green space, a scathing comment on priorities.

The world price of crude oil has risen 13 fold since 1998 to over $130 per barrel, but Indian petrol prices have barely doubled. Left Front politicians, who once wanted to soak the rich, now want to subsidize them. Under-recoveries of oil companies' total may be Rs. 2,00,000 crore, even after a recent price hike. This is far more than the cost of Sarva Shiksha Abhiyan (education for all) and the Employment guarantee Scheme put together.

We sanctimoniously lecture rich countries to reduce their green house emissions, yet subsidize our own. Diesel is subsidized to be cheaper than petrol. So, Indian car makers produce the highest proportion of diesel cars in the world. Diesel fumes contain suspended particles that are highly toxic. This subsiy kills.

So does kerosene provided at throwaway prices, ostensibly to benefit poor villagers. One third of all kerosene is used to adulterate petrol and diesel. That causes horrendous pollution even in the greenest of cars.

What's the way forward? We must abolish subsidies and raise taxes on vehicles and fuels to reflect their full social cost. The biggest but least visible subsidy is for parking, and should start there.

Many car owner a in the West take public transport to work since parking space downtown is costly and scarce. We should levy parking fees on an hourly, not daily, basis. Rs. 10 per hour could be a starting point in the metros.

In parts of Tokyo, you cannot own a car useless you own a private parking space. This is too extreme for India, but indicates the future path. If we charge owners the full social cost of parking, people will buy smaller and perhaps fewer vehicles, and fewer still will take them to work. That will slash congestion and pollution.

Cities should levy stiff annual taxes on vehicles, not a one-time tax, and use the revenue to constantly expand public transport and roads. This will create economic synergy: Private transport will finance public transport. London and New York have high density public transport as well as high car density.

Apart from underground rail, cities need elevated roads to ease congestion and pollution, Lata Mangeshkar helped kill a proposal for an elevated road near her Mumbai flat: perhaps she felt her throat and singing would be affected. She did not care that the throats of poor people living on the pavements were far worse affected by fumes, and might get relief if some fumes were diverted to a higher level. What elitism!

Next, some medicine that will be really bitter, politically. The excise duty on all automotive vehicles should be raised to reflect their social costs. Fuel subsidies should be abolished. Price differentials between petrol, diesel and kerosene should be removed, ending incentives for adulteration. Diesel cars should bear a heavy additional cess to finance improved healthcare for those affected by their emission of harmful particulate matter.

That is a long, politically difficult agenda. Only part of it will ever be achieved. Yet that is the way to go, rather than agitate the Nano.

6. By 'Sanctimonious greens' the writer refers to

1. aristocratic environmentalists
2. the rich
3. environmentalists with a 'holier than thou' attitude
4. those who decry deforestation

7. The elite are

1. jealous of Nano owners
2. afraid of traffic jams and depletion of fossil fuel
3. afraid of reaching their destinations late
4. full of disdain that the poor can afford cars

8. The paradox of the situation is that

1. bigger cars mean more fuel, more space and more pollution
2. though India has fewer cars the Nano will bring more pollution
3. London and New York have more cars and less pollution
4. though India is smaller than the US its cars cause more pollution

9. In saying 23 square metres of parking space costs 40 lakhs, the writer is ______

1. caustic
2. exaggerating
3. sarcastic
4. ironical

10. The writer blames India for

1. subsidizing kerosene whereby greenhouse emissions are indirectly subsidized
2. subsidizing diesel
3. for increasing the cost of parking by the hour.
4. for not making it mandatory for car owners to own parking space

11. The most suitable title for this passage is

1. Polluting Politics
2. No No Nano
3. Submerge Subsidies
4. More Cars, Less Pollution

12. The plural of Virus is

1. Viruses
2. Virae
3. Virii
4. Virus

13. If the following segments of a sentence are to be rearranged in logical order as A, B, C, D where would '3' be placed

I. to see that students do not altogether forget to write especially during exam time

II. the education groups are now asking for hand writing classes

III. thanks to mobile testing and computer literacy

IV. writing in long hand is becoming a vanishing art

1. A
2. B
3. C
4. D

14. If leaf is to leaves and knife is to knives, then belief is to ________

1. beliefs
2. believes
3. belief
4. believing

15. Choose the sentence where the underlined word is used correctly.

1. This latest novel is a <u>pedestrian</u> story about spies.
2. The exam paper is not <u>pedestrian</u> but difficult.
3. This is the <u>pedestrian</u> highway.
4. Every week we are forced to listen to a <u>pedestrian</u> lecture.

16. When the fire alarm rang ______________ left the building immediately

1. all
2. everyone
3. all the people
4. every person

17. In the following sentence choose the erroneous segment/s

A B C

He is one of those people / who thinks / he owns the world

1. error in segment A
2. error in segment B
3. error in segment A & C
4. error in segment B & C

18. Choose the correct meaning for the word:

cynic-

1. the person who is selfish
2. the person who is concerned about others
3. the person who isn't misanthropic
4. the person who believes that people always act from selfish motives

19. Choose the word with correct spelling

1. catagories
2. diarrhoea
3. ommission
4. inaugarate

20. Pick out the right sentences.

I. I will go with you.

II. There was nobody I could go with.

III. I have a glass with painting on it.

IV. The curtains do not match with the furniture.

1. I & II
2. II & III
3. I & IV
4. all

21. About the following pair of phrases, choose the correct option.

I. A two days' visit

II. A two day's visit

1. The first phrase is erroneous
2. The second phrase is erroneous
3. Both phrases are erroneous
4. Both phrases are correct

Directions for the question 22 – 24: Read the following passage and answer within its context.

Nearly two thousand years have passed since a census decreed by Caesar Augustus became part of the greatest story ever told. Many things have changed in the intervening years. The hotel industry worries more about overbuilding than overcrowding, and if they had tc meet an unexpected influx, few inns would have managed to accommodate the weary guests. Now it is the census taker that does the traveling in the fond hope that a highly mobile population will stay put long enough to get a good sampling. Methods of gathering, recording and evaluating information have presumably been improved a great deal. And where then it was the modest purpose of Rome to obtain a simple head count as an adequate basis for levying taxes, now batteries of complicated statistical series furnished by governmental agencies and private organizations are eagerly scanned and interpreted by sages and seers to get a clue for future events.

The Bible does not tell us how the Roman census takers made out, and as regards our more immediate concern, the reliability of present-day economic forecasting, there are considerable differences of opinion. They were aired at the celebration of the 125th anniversary of the American Statistical Association. There was the thought that business forecasting might well be on its way from an art to a science, and some speakers talked about new-fangled computers and high-faulting mathematical systems in terms of excitement and endearment, which we, at least in our younger years when these things mattered, would have associated more readily with the description of a fair maiden.

But others pointed to a deplorable record of highly esteemed forecasts and forecasters with a batting average below that of the Mets and the President elect of the Association cautioned that "high-powered statistical methods are usually in order where the facts are crude and inadequate, statisticians assume."

We left his birthday party somewhere between hope and despair and with the conviction, not really newly acquired, that proper statistical methods applied to ascertainable facts have their merits in economic forecasting as long as neither forecaster nor public is deluded into mistaking the delineation of probabilities and trends for a prediction of certainties of mathematical exactitude.

22. According to the passage, taxation in Roman times was based on

1. mobility
2. wealth
3. population
4. census takers

23. The author refers to the Mets primarily in order to

1. show that sports do not depend on statistics
2. contrast verifiable and unverifiable methods of record keeping
3. indicate the changes in attitudes from Roman days to the present
4. illustrate the failure of statistical predictions.

24. The author's tone can best be described as

1. jocular
2. scornful
3. pessimistic
4. humanistic

25. Disinterested is closest in meaning to

1. bored
2. unbiased
3. not interested
4. indifferent

26. Choose the option which is the nearly opposite in meaning to BERATE

1. grant
2. praise
3. refer
4. purchase

27. Arrange the following in the right order to make a complete sentence

I. with interconnected vibrating balls and springs

II. in a naïve sense, a field in physics may be envisioned as if space were filled

III. as the displacement of a ball from its rest position

IV. and the strength of the field can be visualized

1. II, I, IV, III
2. I, II, III, IV
3. IV, III, II, I
4. III, IV, I, II

28. Find the odd one out

1. latent
2. natural
3. inborn
4. inherent

29. He told the teacher that ________________

1. he was liked by the whole class
2. you are liked by the whole class
3. he is liked by the whole class
4. you were liked by the whole class

30. Match the several meanings of the word COMPLEX with their appropriate usages.

Meaning	**Usage**
1. complicated	5. A new sports complex is coming up for the Common Wealth Games.
2. abnormal state of mind	6. Culture is a complex whole of many things
3. group of structures	7. She has a complex about being overweight
4. mixture	8. His motives in carrying out the crime were complex

1. 1-6, 2-8, 3-7, 4-5
2. 1-8, 2-7, 3-5, 4-6
3. 1-5, 2-7, 3-6, 4-8
4. 1-8, 2-5, 3-6, 4-7

31. Which does not make a sensible word/phrase when added to the word?

Honey

1. pot
2. suckle
3. comb
4. taste

Directions for questions 32 – 34: Read the passage carefully and answer within the context.

In September of 1929, traders experienced a lack of confidence in the stock market's ability to continue its phenomenal rise. Prices fell. For many inexperienced investors, the drop produced a panic. They had all their money tied up in the market, and they were pressed to sell before the prices fell even lower. Sell orders were coming in so fast that the ticker tape at the New York Stock Exchange could not accommodate all the transactions.

To try to reestablish confidence in the market, a powerful group of New York bankers agreed to pool their funds and purchase stock above current market values. Although the buy orders were minimal, they were counting on their reputations to restore confidence on the part of the smaller investors, thereby affecting the number of sell orders. On Thursday, October 24, Richard Whitney, the Vice President of the New York Stock Exchange and a broker for the J.P. Morgan Company, made the effort on their behalf. Initially it appeared to have been successful, then on the following Tuesday, the crash began again and accelerated. By 1932, stocks were worth only twenty percent of their value at the 1929 high. The results of the crash had extended into every aspect of the economy, causing a long and painful depression, referred to in American history as the Great Depression.

32. The New York bankers counted on –

1. Current market values
2. The number of sell orders
3. Confidence
4. Their reputation

33. The cause of downfall of share market was –

1. Inexperienced investors
2. Phenomenal decrease
3. Lack of confidence in stock market's ability.
4. Panic amongst investors.

34. Choose the word in the passage that is an antonym of "minimal"

1. negligible
2. minimum
3. maximal
4. significant

35. Identify the correct sentence.

1. The office is opposite to the bank.
2. The office is opposite the bank.
3. The office is opposite from the bank.
4. The office is opposite of the bank

Answer Key

1. 3	**2.** 3	**3.** 4	**4.** 2	**5.** 3	**6.** 3	**7.** 3
8. 3	**9.** 3	**10.** 1	**11.** 3	**12.** 1	**13.** 2	**14.** 1
15. 2	**16.** 2	**17.** 4	**18.** 4	**19.** 2	**20.** 1	**21.** 3
22. 3	**23.** 4	**24.** 2	**25.** 2	**26.** 2	**27.** 1	**28.** 1
29. 1	**30.** 2	**31.** 4	**32.** 4	**33.** 3	**34.** 4	**35.** 1

Answer Key & Explanations

Q. No.	Answer Key	Explanations
1.	3	
2.	3	Word 'arose' can fit (II) & (IV)
3.	4	Tool's Paradise – refer to a state of illusory happiness and hence fits 3.
4.	2	
5.	3	Read the passage properly.
6.	3	Read para 1 and 2.
7.	3	Read para – 2, last line
8.	3	Read para – 3 last line
9.	3	Read para 5
10.	1	Read para 8 and 9.
11.	3	This is the overall idea communicated by the passage that subsidies should be removed to fight the problem of pollution.
12.	1	**13.** 2 **14.** 1
15.	2	Pedestrian – refers to prosaic or dull or commonplace or ordinary.
16.	2	
17.	4	The correct sentence is – He is one of those people who think they own the world.
18.	4	**19.** 2 **20.** 1
21.	3	Correct phrase is – A two day visit.
22.	3	Refer to para – 1.
23.	4	Refer to para – 3.
24.	2	Read the passage carefully.

25. 2 Disinterested means unbiased or unpartial

26. 2 Berate means to belittle, disparage so opposite is 'praise'.

27. 1 (II) is opener, (I) goes with II & then (IV) followed by (III).

28. 1 Latent means hidden', all other are synonyms

29. 1 **30.** 2

31. 4 Honey taste is not a sensible word. **Honey pot** – refers to pot for storing & serving honey **Honey suckle** – refers to a shrub cultivated for its fragrant while, red or yellow tubular flowers. **Honey Comb** – A structure used by honey bees to hold honey and larvae.

32. 4 **33.** 3 **34.** 4 **35.** 1

TEST YOUR SELF
SECTION-II

MEDIUM DIFFICULTY LEVEL PAPERS

1. ATMA 2009
2. IBSAT 2007
3. IRMA 2007
4. JMET 2007
5. JMET 2008
6. MAT – Feb. 2007
7. MAT – MAY 2009
8. MAT –Sept. 2007

ATMA 2009

Number of Questions – 50
Time : 40 M.

Verbal Skills

Directions for questions 1–17: *Each passage I, II and III is followed by questions (Q. 1-17) based on its contents. After reading the passages, choose the* **best** *answer from answer choices numbered (1), (2), (3) and (4) given to each question then darken the corresponding oval in the answer sheet.*

Base your answer on information that is either stated or implied in the passage.

Passage I

Many United States companies have, unfortunately, made the search for legal protection from import competition into a major line of work. Since 1980 the United States International Trade Commission (ITC) has received about 280 complaints alleging damage from imports that benefit from subsidies by foreign governments. Another 340 charge that foreign companies "dumped" their products in the United States at "less than fair value". Even when no unfair practices are alleged, the simple claim that an industry has been injured by imports is sufficient grounds to seek relief.

Contrary to the general impression, this quest for import relief has hurt more companies than it has helped. As corporations begin to function globally, they develop an intricate web of marketing, production, and research relationships. The complexity of these relationships makes it unlikely that a system of import relief laws will meet the strategic needs of all the units under the same parent company.

Internationalization increases the danger that foreign companies will use import relief laws against the very companies the laws were designed to protect. Suppose a United States owned company establishes an overseas plant to manufacture a product while its competitor makes the same product in the United States. If the competitor can prove injury from the imports - and the United States received a subsidy from a foreign government to build its plants abroad - the United States company's products will be uncompetitive in the United States, since they would be subject to duties.

Perhaps the most brazen case occurred when the ITC investigated allegations that Canadian companies were injuring the United States salt industry by dumping rock salt, used to de-ice roads. The bizarre aspect of the complaint was that a foreign conglomerate with United States operations was crying for help a United States company with foreign operations. The "United States" company claiming injury was a subsidiary of a Dutch conglomerate, while the "Canadian" companies included a subsidiary of a Chicago firm that was the second largest domestic producer of rock salt.

Directions for questions 1 – 6: *Refer to the Passage I above.*

1. The last paragraph performs which of the following functions in the passage ?

1. It cites a specific case that illustrates a problem presented more generally in the previous paragraph.
2. It presents a recommendation based on the evidence presented earlier.
3. It aims to refute the necessity of such legal process like ITC against imports of products in the United States.
4. It introduces an additional area of concern not mentioned earlier.

2. The passage is chiefly concerned with ________

1. Advocating the use of trade restrictions for "dumped" products but not for other imports.
2. Indicating the limitations of ITC laws independent of any other considerations.
3. Warning that the application of laws affecting trade frequently has unintended consequences.

4. Arguing against the increased internationalization of United States corporations.

3. The passage warns of which of the following dangers?

1. Companies in the United States that import raw materials may have to pay duties on those materials
2. Companies in the United States may receive no protection from imports unless they actively seek protection from import competition.
3. Companies that are United States owned but operate internationally may not be eligible for protection from import competition under the laws of the countries in which their plants operate
4. Companies that are not United States owned may seek legal protection from import competition under United States import relief laws.

4. It can be inferred from the passage that the author believes which of the following about the complaint mentioned in the last paragraph?

1. The ITC did not have access to appropriate information concerning the case.
2. The complaint violated the intent of import relief laws.
3. The ITC acted unfairly toward the complainant in its investigation
4. The response of the ITC to the complaint provided suitable relief from unfair trade practices to the complainant.

5. It can be inferred from the passage that the minimal basis for a complaint to the International Trade Commission in which of the following?

1. The company requesting import relief has been injured by the sale of imports in the United States.
2. A foreign competitor has substantially increased the volume of products shipped to the United States.
3. A foreign competitor has received a subsidy from a foreign government.
4. A foreign competitor is selling products in the United States at less than fair market value.

6. The passage suggests that which of the following is most likely to be true of United States trade laws?

1. Those that are applied to international companies will accomplish their intended result.
2. Those that help one unit within a parent company will accomplish their intended result.
3. They will eliminate the practice of "dumping" products in the United States
4. They will affect United States trade with Canada more negatively than trade with other nations.

Passage II

Archaeology as a profession faces two major problems. First, it is the poorest of the poor. Only paltry sums are available for excavating and even less are available for publishing the results and preserving the sites once excavated. Yet archaeologists deal with priceless objects every day. Second, there is the problem of illegal excavation, resulting in the museum-quality pieces being sold to the highest bidder.

I would like to make an outrageous suggestion that would at one stroke provide funds for archaeology and reduce the amount of illegal digging. I would propose that scientific archeological expeditions and governmental authorities sell excavated artifacts on the open market. Such sales would provide substantial funds for the excavation and preservation of archaeological sites and publication of results. At the same time, they would break the illegal excavator's grip on the market, thereby decreasing the inducement to engage in illegal activities.

You might object that professionals excavate to acquire knowledge, not money. Moreover, ancient artifact are part of our global cultural heritage, which should be available for all to appreciate, not sold to the highest bidder. I agree sell nothing that has unique artistic merit or scientific value. But you might reply, everything that comes out of the ground has scientific value. Here we part company. Theoretically, you may be correct in claiming that every artifact has potential scientific value. Practically, you are wrong.

I refer to the thousands of pottery vessels and ancient lamps that essentially are duplicates of another. In one small excavation in Cyprus, archaeologists recently uncovered 2,000 virtually indistinguishable small jugs in a single courtyard. Every precious royal seal impressions known as l'melekh handles have been found in abundance – more than 4,000 examples so far.

The basements of museums are simply not large enough to store the artifacts that are likely to be discovered in the future. There is not enough money even to catalog the finds; as a result, they cannot be found again and become as inaccessible as if they had never been discovered, Indeed, with the help of a computer, sold artifacts could be more accessible than are the pieces stored in bulging museum basements.

Prior to sale, each would be photographed and the list of the purchases could be maintained on the computer. A purchaser could even be required to agree to return the piece if it should become needed for scientific purposes.

It would be unrealistic to suggest that illegal digging would stop if artifacts were sold on the open market. But the demand for the clandestine product would be substantially reduced. Who would want an unmarked pot when another was available whose **provenance** was known, and that was dated stratigraphically by the professional archaeologist who excavated it?

Directions for questions 7–10: are based on the Passage II above

7. The word "**provenance**" in the last sentence **(bold)** is used in which of the following sense ?

1. market value
2. historical importance
3. authenticity
4. the place of origin

8. The primary purpose of the passage is to propose ________

1. The governmental regulation of archaeological sites.
2. A way to distinguish artifacts with scientific value from those that have no such value.
3. A way to curb illegal digging while benefiting the archaeological profession.
4. To draw attention of authorities that archaeology – a window showing our glorious past – is neglected due to lack of sufficient funds.

9. The author implies that all of the following statements about duplicate artifacts are true **EXCEPT**–

1. Museums are well supplied with example of such artifacts
2. A market for such artifacts already exists
3. There is likely to be a continuing supply of such artifacts
4. Such artifacts frequently exceed in quality than those already catalogued in museum collections

10. Which of the following is mentioned in the passage as a disadvantage of storing artifacts in museum basements ?

1. Space that could be better used for display is taken up for storage
2. Such artifacts are often damaged by variations in temperature and humidity
3. Artifacts discovered in one excavation often become separated from each other
4. Such artifacts often remain uncataloged and thus cannot be located once they are put in storage.

Passage III

Some observers have attributed the dramatic growth in temporary employment that occurred in the United States during the 1980s to increased participation in the workforce by certain groups, such as first-time or reentering workers, who supposedly prefer such arrangements. However, statistical analyses reveal that demographic changes in the workforce did not correlate with variations in the total number of temporary workers.

Instead, these analyses suggest that **factors affecting employers** account for the rise in temporary employment. One factor is product demand : temporary employment is favoured by employers who are adapting to fluctuating demand for products while at the same time seeking to reduce overall labour costs.

Another factor is labour's reduced bargaining strength, which allows employers more control over the terms of employment. Given the analyses, which reveal that growth in temporary employment now far exceeds the level explainable by recent workforce entry rates groups said to prefer temporary jobs, firms should be discouraged from creating **excessive** numbers of temporary positions.

Government policymakers should consider mandating benefit coverage for temporary and permanent workers, assisting labour unions in organizing temporary workers, and encouraging firms to assign temporary jobs primarily to employees who explicitly indicate that preference.

(This passage was adopted from an article written in 1992; obviously the present situation after global meltdown would be quite different.)

Directions for questions 11 – 17: *are based on Passage III above*

11. The passage suggests which of the following about the workers who took temporary jobs during the 1980s?

1. Their pay declined during the decade in comparison with the pay of permanent employees.
2. Their jobs frequently led to permanent positions within firms
3. They did not necessarily prefer temporary employment to permanent employment
4. They were occasionally involved in actions organized by labour unions.

12. According to the passage, which of the following is true of the **"factors affecting employers"** that are mentioned in the second paragraph?

1. They may account for the increase in the total number of temporary workers during the 1980s
2. They included a sharp increase in the cost of labour during the 1980s
3. Most experts cite them as having initiated the growth in temporary employment that occurred during the 1980s
4. They were less important than demographic change in accounting for the increase of temporary employment during the 1980s

13. The first sentence in the passage suggests that the observers would be most likely to predict which of the following?

1. That employers would have less control over the terms of workers' employment as workers increased their bargaining strength.
2. That the total number of temporary positions would increase as fewer workers were able to find permanent positions.
3. That the number of new temporary positions would decline as fewer workers who preferred temporary employment entered the workforce
4. That more would be hired for temporary positions as product demand increased.

14. The passage suggests which of the following about the use of temporary employment by firms during the 1980s?

1. It increased partly as a result of workers' reduced ability to control the terms of their employment
2. It is discouraged by government-mandated policies
3. It enabled firms to deal with fluctuating product demand far more efficiently than they did before the 1980s
4. It was a response to preferences indicated by certain employees for more flexible working arrangements

15. The passage mentions each of the following as an appropriate kind of governmental action **EXCEPT ——**

1. Encouraging equitable pay for temporary and permanent employees.
2. Ensuring that temporary workers obtain benefits from their employers.
3. Facilitating the organization of temporary workers by labour unions.
4. Establishing guidelines on the proportion of temporally workers that firms should employ.

16. The primary purpose of the passage is to ————

1. Explain a recent development and predict its eventual consequences.
2. Identify the reasons for a trend and recommend measures to address it.
3. Present the results of statistical analyses and propose further studies.
4. Outline several theories about a phenomenon and advocate one of them.

17. In the context of the passage, the word **"excessive"** (last line of paragraph 3) most closely corresponds to which of the following phrases?

1. Far more than can be accounted for by an expanding national economy
2. Far more than can be attributed to increases in the total number of people in the workforce
3. Far more than can be justified by worker by preferences
4. Far more than can be beneficial to the success of the firms themselves

Directions for questions 18 – 19: *For each question, a short passage and four alternative summaries of the passage numbered (1), (2), (3) and (4) are given. Choose the summary that captures the essence of the text of the passage* ***best.*** *Darken the corresponding oval in the answer sheet.*

18. Passage

Try before you buy. We use this memorable saying to urge you to experience the consequences of an alternative before you choose it, whenever this is feasible. If you are considering buying a van after having always owned sedans, rent one for a week or borrow a friend's. By experiencing the consequences first hand, they become more meaningful. In addition, you are likely to identify consequences you had not even thought of before. May be you will discover that it is difficult to park the van in your small parking space at work, but that, on the other hand, your elderly father has a much easier time getting in and out of it.

Summary

1. Before choosing an alternative, experience its consequences, if feasible. If, for example, you want to change from sedans to a van, try one before buying it. You will discover aspects you may have never thought of.
2. We urge you to try products such as vans before buying them. Then you can experience consequences you have not thought of such as parking problems. But your father may find vans more comfortable than cars.

3. If you are planning to buy a van after being used to sedans, borrow a van or rent it and try it before deciding to buy it. Then you may realize that parking a van is difficult while it is easier for you elderly father to get in and out of it.
4. Always try before you buy anything. You are bound to discover many consequences. One of the consequences of going in for a van is that it is more difficult to park than sedans at the office car park.

19. Passage

It is important for shipping companies to be clear about the objectives for maintenance and materials management – as to whether the primary focus is on service level improvement or cost minimization. Often when certain systems are set in place, the cost minimization objective and associated procedure become more important than the flexibility required for service level improvement. The problem really arises since cost minimization tends to focus on out of pocket costs which are visible, while the opportunity costs, often greater in value, are lost sight of.

Summary

1. Shipping companies should focus on quality level improvement rather than cost cutting. Cost cutting will lead to untold opportunity costs. Companies should have systems in place to make the service level flexible.
2. Shipping companies have to either minimize costs or maximize service quality. If they focus on cost minimization, they will reduce quality. They should focus on service level improvement, or else opportunity costs will be lost sight of.
3. Any cost minimization programme in shipping is bound to lower the quality of service. Therefore, shipping companies must be clear about the primary focus of their maintenance and materials management before embarking on cost minimization.
4. Shipping companies should determine the primary focus of their maintenance and materials management. Focus on cost minimization may reduce visible costs, but ignore greater invisible costs and impair service quality.

Directions for questions 20 – 22: *In each question, the word in **CAPITAL** letters is followed by the use of the word in four different ways, numbered (1), (2), (3) and (4). Choose the usage of the word where it is **INCORRECT** or **INAPPROPRIATE.** Darken the corresponding oval in the answer sheet.*

20. BUSINESS

1. How do you spend your money is as much my business as yours
2. I want to do an MBA before going into business
3. My wife runs profitable business in this suburb
4. If we advertise we will get twice as much business as we have now

21. SERVICE

1. I'm not making enough even to service the loan
2. Customers have to service themselves at this canteen
3. It's a service lift; don't get into it
4. Jyoti's husband has been on active service for three months

22. REASON

1. There is little reason in your pompous advice.
2. How do you deal with a friend who doesn't listen to a reason?
3. Has she given you any reason for her resignation?
4. Your stand is beyond all reason

Directions for questions 23 – 25: *Each question presents a sentence, part or all of which is* ***bold.*** *Beneath the sentence, you will find four ways of phrasing the* ***bold*** *sentence. The* ***first*** *answer choice repeats the original; the other* ***three*** *are different. If you think the original phrasing is best, choose the first answer; otherwise choose one of the others numbered (2), (3) and (4).*

This type of question tests your ability to recognize the correctness and effectiveness of expression in standard written English. In choosing your answer, follow the requirements of standard written English; that is, pay attention to grammar, choice of words and sentence construction. Choose the answer that produces the most effective sentence; this answer should be clear and exact, without awkwardness, ambiguity, redundancy, or grammatical error, then darken the corresponding oval in the answer sheet.

23. Galileo was convinced that natural phenomena, as manifestations of the laws of physics, would appear the same to someone on the deck of a ship moving smoothly and uniformly through the **water as a** person standing on land.

1. water as a
2. water; just as it would to a
3. water; just as to the
4. water as to a

24. Paleontologists believe that fragments of a primate jawbone unearthed in Burma and estimated **at 40 to 44 million years old provide evidence of** a crucial step along the evolutionary path that led to human beings.

1. at 40 to 44 million years old provide evidence of
2. to be 40 to 44 million years old provide evidence of
3. that it is 40 to 44 million years old provides evidence of what was
4. as being 40 to 44 million years old provides evidence of

25. In 1527 King Henry VIII sought to have his marriage to Queen Catherine annulled **so as to marry** Anne Boleyan.

1. so as to marry
2. to be married to
3. so that he could marry
4. in order that he would marry

Directions for questions 26 -36:

Passages I and II are followed by questions 26 -36 based on its contents. After reading the passage, choose the ***best*** *answer to each question, then darken the corresponding oval in the answer sheet.*

Base your answer on information that is either stated or implied in the passage.

Passage I

Across the globe, politicians and policy-makers of governments plan to boost government spending to revive flagging economics. Especially popular are big infrastructure projects, widely seen as an excellent way to give a Keynesian boost to economies. Yet this represents a misunderstanding of Keynes. In a recession, many things fall together-production, employment, prices and business profits. Businesses go but, and this can lead to runs on banks and a crisis in the financial system. Keynes emphasized that the root cause of a depression was a vicious downward spiral of consumption. Tackle that, he said, a flagging economy can revive.

Andrew Mellon, US treasury secretary in 1929-33, viewed the Great Depression as moral retribution for wicked over-spenders, and a recipe for increasing prudence and savings. By contrast, Keynes realized that a recession was caused by excess saving, which drove down demand and GDP in a vicious downward spiral. To escape the spiral, Keynes proposed government action to boost consumption and end over-saving. The government could boost its own spending through public works. Or else it could cut taxes to boost private consumption.

Keynes did not advocate building infrastructure. Instead he suggested that governments should pay people to dig ditches and then fill them up again. This would not create infrastructure. But it would put money into the pockets of people, and that was the aim of the exercise.

Why, then is infrastructure creation so widely equated with Keynesian economies ? Because of public misunderstanding of the history of the Great Depression, US President Roosevelt launched the New Deal to combat the 25% unemployment he faced on being elected in 1932. The New Deal created jobs in projects to build roads, dams and electric systems. It was a huge political success, and aided his re-election in 1936 and 1940. Yet economists remain sharply divided on its economic impact.

The economy revived from 1932 to 1936 but then plunged into a fresh depression in 1938, wiping out most earlier gains. So, the New Deal created jobs quickly, but not sustainably. It failed to address the financial collapse and deflation that many economists believe turned a mere recession into a Great Depression. The downturn was finally cured not by the New Deal but by World Was II : the wartime economy needed all manpower available.

In the middle of the Great Depression, Keynes produced his seminal **"General Theory of Employment, Interest and Money",** explaining the interaction of production, wages and employment. During the New Deal, Roosevelt swore by balanced budgets, the ruling economic orthodoxy. But Keyne's **"General Theory"** argued this was a mistake, and that governments should run large fiscal deficits during a recession to pump more demand into the economy Roosevelt's budget-balancing efforts typically failed and he often ended up with budget deficits without meaning to. So he was a Keynesian by accident.

Yet the public remembers Roosevelt as the first leader to try to spend his way out of a recession, exactly what Keynes advocated. After World War II, Keynesian demand management became the new economic orthodoxy. Governments everywhere began pumping money into flagging economies to stimulate growth.

Hubris followed. In the 1970s, constant pumping of money led to many countries to inflation rather than growth. Clearly, Keynesian spending did not boost GDP in all situations. But it retained its reputation as a useful tool, though not a panacea, in recessions. Global experience showed that Keynesian demand management did not require infrastructure spending. The simplest, quickest way to increase purchasing power was to cut taxes. This increased demand instantly.

But, It also had drawbacks. When consumers were given additional purchasing power, they did not necessarily buy domestic goods : they also bought imported goods. Thus the Keynesian stimulus could leak out of the domestic economy through imports, and boost foreign economies instead.

Public spending on infrastructure stood out as a way to minimize such leakages. IN most countries infrastructure utilized mostly domestic equipment and labour. So, stimulus remained mainly within the country and did not leak out through imports. Besides, infrastructure projects were popular with politicians keen to channel projects into their constituencies. Politicians hated Keyne's idea of paying people to dig and fill up ditches. They prefer job creation to build infrastructure, creating a base for future growth.

Some economists think this is the best way to combat the recession, others have reservations.

In Roosevelt's time, road building was labour intensive. But today, It is highly mechanized, using little labour. Dams are no longer built by armies of workers. Power plants, orts and airports are hugely capital intensive. With today's technology, infrastructure is not a massive job creator, unless we insist on obsolete, inefficient techniques. This is exactly what we do in the National Rural Employment Guarantee scheme. This mandates 60% of the cost must be in wages. But such labour-intensive techniques yield low-quality roads that disappear after every monsoon. Decades of rural employment schemes have failed to create permanent assets. This approach cannot create good infrastructure.

Keynes would not have been surprised. He would have said that creating jobs should not be confused with creating infrastructure. He would have opted for digging and filling ditches.

Building infrastructure is time-consuming. Every big project requires a lengthy environmental impact assessment, with public hearings. Land acquisition dispute can hold up projects for years. So infrastructure projects disburse money slowly, and cannot provide a quick Keynesian boost.

Now, India badly needs infrastructure. But this requires massive long-term spending. Don't confuse this worthy aim with providing a rapid Keynesian boost.

The fastest, most effective boost comes from stashing taxes. In the west, cutting income tax is a popular **Keynesian nostrum.** But in India only a tiny fraction of people pay income tax. So the right taxes to slash are excise duty and sales tax. These are paid by everybody, and will immediately boost purchasing power. There will be no time lag, as in project spending. That is the Keynesian way to go.

(**Source:** An authored article-published in a national daily in November 2008. Some minor changes have been made)

Directions for questions 26 – 30: ***refer to the above Passage I***

26. In the last paragraph of the passage **Keynesian nostrum** means –

1. A favourite method for bringing about social or political reforms according to Keyne's theory of economic development
2. Keyne's prophecy
3. Keynesian formulation
4. Keyne's anecdotal economic forecasting

27. The passage is primarily concerned with which of the following issue ?

1. An academic analysis of Keynesian economic theory and its application in economic downturn such as the Great Depression in the US by Roosevelt's New Deal in 1929-34. In the present Indian economic scenario Keynesian economic principles are as well applicable.
2. After the global meltdown, India is experiencing a recession on its own shore, and how India can meet it by Government expenditure through infrastructure development.
3. Across the globe governments plan to boost spending on big infrastructure projects to generate employment that would create demands – the author is questioning this method to boost economy and fight recession.
4. The Indian economy is not so globalized and the recession, if nay, is mild, as such Government of India does not require any hackneyed method to boost economy.

28. Which of the following statements according to the passage, are true **EXCEPT** –

1. Politicians preferred job creation to build infrastructure, creating a base for future growth.
2. According to Keynes a recession was caused by excessive saving which drove down demand and GDP in a vicious downward spiral.
3. Global experience showed t hat Keynesian demand management require infrastructure spending which in t urn create employment and boost economy.
4. The fastest, most effective boost to economy comes from slashing taxes – in India the right taxes to slash are excise duty and sales tax, and this will immediately boost purchasing power.

29. Which of the following is the central theme of the passage ?

I. India badly needs infrastructure which requires massive long-term investment; despite the worthiness of infrastructure development, it is not to be confused with Keynesian theory of employment, interest and money.

II. To extol the grand Keynesian theory of job creation and that government should run even large fiscal deficits during a recession to pump more demand into the economy.

III. Analytically examines the US Great Depression in 1929 and Roosevelt's popular economic measures known as New Deal and the analogous economic recession in India after the global meltdown.

1. I only
2. II only
3. III only
4. I and II only

30. If true, which of the following statement(s) **weaken(s)** the author's conclusion that tax-cuts specially excise duty and sales tax which are paid by everybody will boost the economy ?

I. In may countries across the globe-both developed and developing economies – there is a general trend to reduce interest on corporate borrowing and taxes on goods for public consumption.

II. In BRIC countries – Brazil, Russia, India and China – direct and indirect taxes have been reduced and thus reduced prices of consumer products and inflation.

III. Recent reduction of international price of crude from US$147 to around US$50 at present resulted in reduction of ATF (aviation turbine fuel i.e. Jet fuel) and expected reduction in petroleum products as announced by Government did not directly influence complex interaction of production wages and employment. So also a cut in excise duty and sales tax and other economic factors are more complex than what perhaps is assumed by the author.

IV. It is likely that a reduction in excise duty and sales tax will positively influence the demand which in turn directly influences the economic cycle.

1. I and II only
2. III and IV only
3. III only
4. I, II and III only

Passage II

Milankovitoh proposed in the early twentieth century that the ice ages were caused by variations in the Earth's orbit around the Sun. For some time this theory was considered untestable, largely because there was no sufficiently precise chronology of the ice ages with which the orbital variations could be matched.

To establish such a chronology it is necessary to determine the relative amounts of land ice that existed at various times in the Earth's past. A recent discovery makes such a determination possible : relative land-ice volume for a given period can be deduced from the ratio of two oxygen isotopes, 16 and 18, found in ocean sediments. Almost all the oxygen in water is oxygen 16, but a few molecules out of every thousand incorporate the heavier isotope 18. When an ice age begins the continental ice sheets grow, steadily reducing the amount of water evaporated from the ocean that will eventually return to it. Because heavier isotopes tend to be left behind when water evaporates from the ocean surfaces, the remaining ocean water becomes progressively enriched in oxygen 18. The degree of enrichment can be determined by analyzing ocean sediments of the period, because these sediments are composed of calcium carbonate shells of marine organisms, shells that were constructed with oxygen atoms drawn from the surrounding ocean. The higher the ratio of oxygen 18 to oxygen 16 in a sedimentary specimen, the more land ice there was when the sediment was laid down.

As an indicator of shifts in the Earth's climate, the isotope record has two advantages. First, it is a global record : there is remarkably little variation in isotope ratios in sedimentary specimens taken from different continental locations. Second, it is a more continuous record than that taken from rocks on land. Because of these advantages, sedimentary evidence can be dated with sufficient accuracy by radiometric methods to establish a precise chronology of the ice ages. The dated isotope record shows that the fluctuations in global ice volume over the past several hundred thousand years have a pattern : an ice age occurs roughly every 100,000 years. These data have established a strong connection between variations in the Earth's orbit and the periodicity of the ice ages.

However, it is important to note that other factors, such as volcanic matters or variations in the amount of sunlight received by the Earth, could potentially have affected the climate. The advantage of the Milankovitch theory is that it is testable : changes in the Earth's orbit can be calculated and dated by applying Newton's laws of gravity to progressively earlier configurations of the bodies in the solar system. Yet the lack of information about other possible factors affecting global climate does not make them unimportant.

Directions for questions 31 – 36: *are based on the above Passage II*

31. According to the passage, which of the following is true of the ratios of oxygen isotopes in ocean sediments ?

1. They can be used to deduce the relative volume of land ice that was present when sediment was laid down
2. They are more unpredictable during an ice age than in other climate conditions
3. They can be used to determine atmospheric conditions at various times in the past
4. They are less reliable than the evidence from rocks on land in determining the volume of land ice

32. In the passage, the author is primarily interested in –
1. Initiating a debate about a widely accepted theory
2. Presenting a theory and describing a ne method to test that theory
3. Suggesting an alternative to an outdated research method
4. Emphasizing the instability of data gathered from the application of a new scientific method

33. It can be inferred from the passage that the isotope record taken from ocean sediments would be less useful to researchers if which of the following were true?
1. It stretched back for only a million years
2. It indicated that lighter isotopes of oxygen predominated at certain times
3. It indicated that the ratios of oxygen 16 and oxygen 18 in ocean water were not consistent with those found in fresh water
4. It had far more gaps in its sequence than the record taken from rocks on land

34. It can be inferred from the passage that calcium carbonate shells –
1. Reflect the isotopic composition of the water at the time the shells were formed
2. Reflect a strong connection between variations in Earth's orbit and the periodicity of the ice ages.
3. Reflect variations in amount of sunlight received by the Earth
4. Determine the availability of calcium carbonate in the ocean sediments in different periods of geological time.

35. The author of the passage would be most likely to agree with which of the following statements about the Milankovitch theory?
1. It cannot be tested and confirmed until further research on volcanic activity is done
2. It is the only possible explanation for the ice ages
3. It is too limited to provide a plausible explanation for the ice ages, despite recent research findings
4. It is one plausible explanation, though not the only one, for the ice ages

36. It can be inferred from the passage that precipitation formed from evaporated ocean water has –
1. More oxygen 16 than has precipitation formed from fresh water
2. Less oxygen 18 than does ocean water
3. The same isotope ratio as ocean water
4. Less oxygen 18 than has the ice contained in continental ice sheets

Directions for questions 37 – 41: *These questions test your ability to reorganize correct and effective expression in English. Follow the requirements of standard written English grammar, choice of words and sentence construction.*

In each question below, either part or all of the sentence is printed in bold. The sentence is followed by four ways of writing these **bold** parts. Choose the answer which results in the clearest, most exact sentence. The answer choice (1) repeats the original; the other answer choices numbered (2), (3) and (4) vary.

37. The Internet being an elite organisation when most of the population of the world have not made even a phone call.

1. being an elite organization when most of the population of the world have not made even a phone call.
2. is an elite organization; most of the population of the world has never even made a phone call.
3. being a luxury for rich when most of world population had not made even a phone call.
4. is a facility for rich people; most of population for the world has never even made a phone call.

38. The unleashed power of the atom has changed everything **except our reasons and also our thinking** and we thus drift toward unparalled catastrophe.

1. except our reasons and also our thinking
2. save our modes of thinking
3. except our beliefs and understanding
4. except our philosophy of existence

39. Doctors generally agree that such factors as cigarette smoking, eating rich foods high in fats, and alcohol consumption not only do damage by themselves but also aggravate genetic

1. not only do damage by themselves but also aggravate
2. do damage by themselves but also are aggravating to
3. not only do damage by themselves, they are also aggravating to
4. are damaging by themselves but also are aggravating

40. What's in a name? that which we call a rose / By any other name would smell as sweet.

1. What's in a name? that which we call a rose / By any other name would smell as sweet.
2. A rose would smell as sweet even you call in any other name / so name really doesn't matter.
3. What's in a name? that which we call it a rose / Even if you call it any other name it would smell as sweet as rose.
4. Does a name really matter ? A rose would smell as sweet as the flower / Even if we would call it in any other name.

41. Quasars, at billions of light-years from Earth's most distant observable objects in the Universe, believed to be the cores of galaxies in an early stage of development.

1. believed to be
2. some believe to be
3. are believed to be
4. it is believed that they are

Directions for questions 42 – 45: *For each of these questions, four or five sentences lettered (I) to (IV)/(V) are given. These sentences, if arranged, in a logical sequence, will form a coherent and meaningful paragraph. Choose the most logical order from among the given choices numbered (1), (2), (3) and (4) to construct a coherent paragraph, then darken the corresponding oval in the answer sheet.*

42. I. Financial services are up against tight liquidity and falling markets.

II. More focused action, including fiscal, is needed to stem the worsening of the real economy.

III. Most Indian IT firms are vulnerable to the emerging global recession 70% of India's $40 billion software exports are to the US and 40% of it for financial services which are shrinking rapidly.

IV. Plummeting travel and tourism are slowing down transportation and hospitality sectors.

V. Our manufacturing and construction trade face prospects of further slackening investment.

1. II, V, IV, III, I
2. I, III, IV, V, II
3. III, V, I, IV, II
4. II, IV, I, V, III

43. I. What is the difference between entrepreneurial management and professional management?

II. Entrepreneurialism is moving ahead with a clear vision, often with limited assets.

III. Professional management is mostly about making assets more effective and efficient

IV. An entrepreneur is an owner.

V. We believe entrepreneurial management concentrates on seeking new opportunities and trying to fulfill the needs of others.

1. I, II, IV, III, V
2. I, IV, III, II, V
3. I, II, III, IV, V
4. I, V, III, II, IV

44. I. She is increasingly skeptical in the face of a financial meltdown that it was all worth the effort.

II. Watch cut for a new brand of consumer in 2008 : the middle-aged simplifier.

III. Out will go luxury purchases, conspicuous consumption, and a trophy culture.

IV. She finds herself surrounded by too much stuff acquired.

1. III, I, II, IV
2. II, IV, I, III
3. I, IV, II, III
4. II, I, III, IV

45. I. On October, by which time FIIs had pulled out over $10 billion, the rupee plunged to 49.79 against the dollar

II. India may be one of the least open economies in Asia but its external trade already constitutes over 40% of its GDP.

III. GDP growth had started slowing and it had become obvious that the projected growth at 9% was untenable.

IV. Net investments by FIIs in Indian stock exchanges by January 2008 were $65 billion.

V. In the last four years India has received $50 billion as FDI.

1. II, III, IV, I, V
2. I, III, IV, V, II
3. II, IV, V, I, III
4. II, V, IV, III, I

Directions for questions 46 – 48: *Each sentences below has one or two blanks, each blank indicating that something has been omitted. Beneath the sentences are four numbered words or set of words. Choose the word or set of words for each blank that* ***best*** *fits the meaning of the sentence as a whole. Darken the corresponding oval in the answer sheet.*

46. How could words, confined as they individually are to certain ________ meanings specified in a dictionary, eventually come, when combined in groups, to create obscurity and actually to prevent thought from being ________?

1. precise ________ communicable
2. indefinite ________ articulated
3. unlikely ________ classified
4. conventional ________ conceivable

47. Science advances in ________ spiral in that each new conceptual scheme ________ the phenomena explained by its predecessors and add to those explanations.

1. an explosive ________ question
2. a repetitive ________ vitiates
3. a discontinuous ________ decries
4. a widening ________ embraces

48. Intellectual ________ and flight from boredom have caused him to rush pell-mell into situations that less ________ spirits might hesitate to approach.

1. tranquility ______ versatile
2. resilience ______ quiescent
3. restlessness________ adventurous
4. curiosity _______ lethargic

DIRECTION for questions 49 – 50: *In each of the questions, a related pair of words is followed by four numbered (1), (2), (3) and (4) pairs of words. Select the numbered pair that* **best** *expresses a relationship similar to that expressed in the original pair.*

49. EPITHET : DISPARAGE : :

1. diminutive : respect
2. alias : mislead
3. code : simplify
4. abbreviation : proliferate

50. COGENT : CONVINCE : :

1. dangerous : avoid
2. generous : appreciate
3. eloquent : refine
4. repugnant : repel

Answer Key

1. 1**2.**	3 **3.**	4 **4.**	2 **5.**	1 **6.**	2 **7.**	2 **8.**
3 **9.**	4 **10.**	4 **11.**	3 **12.**	1 **13.**	2 **14.**	1 **15.**
4 **16.**	2 **17.**	3 **18.**	1 **19.**	4 **20.**	4 **21.**	2
22. 2	**23.** 4	**24.** 2	**25.** 3	**26.** 3	**27.** 1	**28.** 3
29. 4	**30.** 3	**31.** 1	**32.** 2	**33.** 4	**34.** 1	**35.** 4
36. 2	**37.** 3	**38.** 1	**39.** 1	**40.** 3	**41.** 3	**42.** 3
43. 4	**44.** 4	**45.** 3	**46.** 1	**47.** 4	**48.** 3	**49.** 2
50. 4						

EXPLANATIONS

1. The last para uses the example of US and Canadian companies to exemplify how foreign companies can misuse relief laws. Hence 1.

2. The passage shows how laws that were made with a good intent can have a flip side too. Hence 3.

3. Refer to the last part of para 3.

4. The author uses the example of the complainant to illustrate how foreign companies can misuse import relief laws. Hence 2.

5. Para 1, last line.

6. The last line of para 2 implies that due to the complexity of the relationships, even the units of the same parent company may have divergent interests. Hence 2.

7. Provenance as used here means the historical origins, as ascertained by archaeologists.

8. The passage tries to bridge the gap between the twin problems archaeology faces- a lack of funds and rampant illegal excavations. Hence 3.

9. Para 4 and para 5 substantiate all the statements except Option 4.

10. Para 5, second sentence.

11. The statistical analyses show that there were factors beyond merely worker preference that led to an upsurge in temporary employment. Hence 3.

12. Except option 1, all other options assume facts that are not substantiated by the passage. Option 1 is general, not too specific and thus defendable.

13. The first sentence suggests that the increase in temporary employment was entirely due to the proclivity of the workers towards the same. Hence 2.

14. Since employers preferred temporary employment(due to the cost advantages) and also since the labour's bargaining strength was reduced, the use of temporary employment by firms gained ground.

15. All the options except 4 are mentioned in para 4.

16. The first three paragraphs elaborate upon the trend of temporary employment and its causes while para 4 provides recommendations that the govt. can make use of. Hence 2.

17. Used as it is in the context of the reduced bargaining power of the labour force, "*excessive*" here contrasts with the workers expectations. Hence 4.

18. Option 1 is the only option to correctly summarize the passage. Option 2 extrapolates a hypothetical example to a real-life one while 3 and 4 are too definite (e.g.the use of the word "*always*").

19. Option 2 and 3 are rejected because of they are too definite (will, bound to). Between 1 and 4, Option 1 is rejected because it implies that cost cutting would *lead to* opportunity costs. Hence 4.

20. The correct usage is "*two times the business*".

21. The correct usage is customers have to "*serve themselves*".

22. The correct usage is "*listen to reason*". The use of "*a*" is redundant.

23. Only option 4 uses the idiomatic and grammatically parallel form.

24. Option.4, the correct choice, correctly follows *estimated* with *to be*. The other choices present structures that are not idiomatic when used with *estimated.*

25. Option 3 is the correct answer. The information generated by the phrase is that the first marriage was annulled for the purpose of getting married a second time. So the phrase portrays reason or purpose, which we find in Option 3.

26. Last para, 1st &2nd line.

27. Last para, 'that is the Keynesian way to go'. Hence option 1

28. Keynes proposed that in the time of depression govt. should even pay the labor for just digging and refilling the holes. So 3rd choice is factually wrong.

29. After reading the passage ,especially 3rd and last para.

30. 2nd and 4th options are supporting the conclusion therefore rejected. Option 1 is out of track choice, hence rejected. Only 3rd choice is weakening the conclusion by stating that even by reducing the duties and taxes did not help in boosting the economy.

31. 2nd para, last line

32. 1st and 2nd para, (line no.2 &3)

33. Whatever conclusion we have by studying the samples from sediments and if these conclusions are not matching with the conclusion (reverse) drawn on the basis of samples taken from rocks on land then the theory would be wrong. This s exactly shown by option 4.

34. After reading para 2. (line 7-8)

35. After reading the passage, we can safely conclude that the given theory is one of the theories to predict about the ice ages. Hence option 4.

36. 'O'18 being heavy, its atoms will not evaporate. Hence option 2

37. Internet cannot be any elite organization therefore 1&2 options rejected. In 4th option preposition is wrong.

38. No change

39. No change

40. In 3rd option the pronoun 'it' is correctly used for rose. This is not there in any of the options

41. The subject is quasars (plural), it needs plural helping verb. Therefore option 3.

42. (iii). will open the sequence and (ii) will close the sequence .iii is followed by v as it is further elaborating the idea in iii.

43. I is opener as it introduces the theme- asking the difference between two styles of managements. it is followed by v. as it is explaining the entrepreneurial management followed by iii ,explaining professional management . iv will close the sequence by defining who can be called an entrepreneur.

44. (ii) Will open the sequence as it is telling about the middle aged simplifier. It is followed by (i), because it is telling that how that consumer is affected by meltdown and how it is going to impact her behavior regarding consumption. I & iii will form the mandatory pair. Finally iv will close the sequence.

45. (ii). Is going to open as it is independent and introducing the topic of Indian economy, GDP etc. it is followed by iv &v in which author is telling positive side of Indian foreign trade. After this (i) will come as some sort of contrast is shown regarding India's foreign trade , and how it affected the fall in Indian currency against dollar .

46. As per the context meanings have to be 'precise' as per the dictionary and if they are not used in proper manner then through words we cannot communicate the thoughts. So answer is 1.

47. The whole context is positive so both words to be filled in blanks have to be positive .this is there only in choice 4

48. Anybody who is adventurous won't hesitate. Restlessness and tendency to run away from the things will push somebody to do some extraordinary things. Hence the answer is 3

49. Epithet is phrase used to disparage similarly alias is to mislead.

50. Cogent means 'to the point.' A precise and cogent argument would convince just as something repugnant (distasteful or objectionable) would repel (ward off or repulse.). ' so it is to convince using to the point arguments. Repugnant things are to be repelled.

IBSAT 2007

Number of Questions – 75
Time : 45 M.

SECTION – I
VOCABULARY & WRITING ABILITY
Number of questions: 50

Directions for questions 1–5: ***Find the SYNONYMS of the given words from among the alternatives under each question.***

1. JINGOISM
1. Excessive patriotism
2. Examining possibilities
3. Evaluation of love for one's country
4. Exhaustion of spirit

2. INDIGENT
1. Indian
2. Native
3. Affluent
4. Poor

3. INCIPIENT
1. Internal
2. Effective
3. Initial
4. Eventual

4. DECIMATE
1. Destroy
2. Delay
3. Desire
4. Construct

5. INGENUOUS
1. Frank
2. Deceitful
3. Ambiguous
4. Amorphous

Directions for questions 6–10: ***Find the ANTONYMS of the given words from among the alternatives under each question.***

6. REVULSION
1. Admiration
2. Disapproval
3. Disparagement
4. Denigration

7. PROFOUND
1. Deep
2. Shallow
3. Hollow
4. Fallow

8. ADULATION
1. Flattery
2. Encomium
3. Confession
4. Condemnation

9. GARRULOUS
1. Vociferous
2. Eloquent
3. Taciturn
4. Vocal

10. INITIAL
1. Terminal
2. Commencing
3. Delayed
4. Disastrous

Directions for questions11to 15: *Choose the ONE-WORD SUBSTITUTE of the given word/ phrase from among the alternatives given under each question.*

11. To be similar
1. Anomalous
2. Analogous
3. Anonymous
4. Amorphous

12. To be present everywhere
1. Inequitable
2. Inadequate
3. Unctuous
4. Ubiquitous

13. Liable to make mistakes
1. Fallible
2. Flexible
3. Erroneous
4. Pliable

14. A state of lawlessness
1. Monarchy
2. Anarchy
3. Diarchy
4. Oligarchy

15. A study of the problems of old age
1. Parentology
2. Anthropology
3. Gerontology
4. Paleontology

Directions for questions 16–20: *For each of the following sections four alternatives are provided. Select the most acceptable and effective of the four options. In considering the alternatives, pay attention to matters of grammar, diction, and syntax as well as clarity, precision and fluency.*

16
1. Many economists are believing that economic recovery is certain
2. Many economists believe that economic recovery is certain
3. Many economists have believed that economic recovery was certain
4. Many economists believe that economic recovery was certain.

17.
1. Many applicants did not turn up for the interview
2. Many applicants did not turn in the interview
3. Many applicants did not turn for the interview
4. Many applicants did not turn away for the interview

18.
1. In some matters Indian students are different to American students
2. In some matters Indian students are different from American students
3. In some matters Indian students are different than American students
4. In some matters Indian students are as well different from American students.

19
1. Lata Mangeshkar sang songs for over five decades; she still sings
2. Lata Mangeshkar is singing songs for over five decades
3. Lata Mangeshkar sings songs for over five decades
4. Lata Mangeshkar has sung songs for over five decades; she still sings.

20.
1. Visiting relatives can cause occasionally troublesome
2. The relatives who visit us can be occasionally troublesome
3. If you visit relatives occasionally can be troublesome
4. Relatives occasionally visiting can be troublesome.

21.
1. The weather man warned that floods were immanent
2. The weather man warned that floods were eminent
3. The weather man warned that floods are imminent
4. The weather man warned that floods were imminent.

22. 1. "The man is mortal", declared the Bhagavat Geetha
2. "Man is mortal", declared Bhagavat Geetha
3. "Man is mortal", declared the Bhagavat Geetha
4. "Man is the mortal", declared the Bhagavat Geetha.

23. 1. Many visitors to India wonder that why India is still backward
2. Many visitors to India wonder as to that India is still backward
3. Many visitors to India wonder so that India is still backward
4. Many visitors to India wonder why India is still backward.

24 1. Indian Airlines flight for Mumbai takes off at 8 a.m. everyday
2. Indian Airlines flight for Mumbai shall take off at 8 a.m. everyday
3. Indian Airlines flight for Mumbai is taking off at 8 a.m. everyday
4. Indian Airlines flight for Mumbai can take off at 8 a.m. everyday.

25. 1. Many Indians are working in the US; isn't it?
2. Many Indians work in the US; isn't it?
3. Many Indians are working in the US; aren't they?
4. Many Indians work in the US; aren't they?

26. 1. The quantum of remittances from NRI's is few in recent times
2. The quantum of remittances from NRI's are less in recent times
3. The quanta of remittances from NRI's are few in recent times
4. The quantum of remittances from NRI's is less in recent times.

27. 1. As many students didn't prepare well, they didn't take the exam
2. As many students didn't prepare well, they didn't give the exam
3. As many students didn't prepare well, they didn't give up the exam
4. As many students didn't prepare well, they didn't take away the exam.

28. 1 By the time I reached Delhi to meet Rajesh, he left for Chennai
2. By the time I reached Delhi to meet Rajesh, he had left for Chennai
3. By the time I had reached Delhi to meet Rajesh, he is left for Chennai
4. By the time I was leaving for Delhi to meet Rajesh, he left for Chennai

29. 1. The High Court of Law is established to dispense with justice
2. The High Court of Law is established to dispense justice
3. The High Court of Law establishes to dispense justice
4. The High Court of Law is established to dispense with the justice

30 1. Relying on indigenous technology, the profits earned from the products made the company a market leader
2. Relying on indigenous technology, the products made profits and the company a market leader
3. Relying on indigenous technology, the company made profits from the products and became a market leader
4. Relying on indigenous technology, the market leader made profits from the products of the company.

Directions for questions 31–35: *Fill in the blanks of the following sentences using the most appropriate word or words from the options given.*

31. Learning is more efficient when it is _____________. It is less efficient when it is ____________

1. fast, slow
2. fun, drudgery
3. rapid, turtle-slow
4. tedious, like a joy ride

32. Physicians may soon have ________ to help paralyzed people move their limbs bypassing the ________ nerves that once controlled their muscles.

1. instruments, detrimental
2. ways, damaged
3. reason, involuntary
4. impediments, complex

33. The Internet is a medium where users have nearly ________ choices and ________ constraints about where to go and what to do.

1. unbalanced, nonexistent
2. embarrassing, no
3. unlimited, minimal
4. choking, shocking

34. Education is central because electronic networks and software-driven technologies are beginning to ________ the economic barriers between nations.

1. break down
2. break
3. crumble
4. dismantle

35. The present Constitution will see ________ amendments but its basic structure will survive.

1. much more
2. too many more
3. quite a few more
4. many more

Directions for questions 36–40: *Each question has a set of 6 sentences marked A to F. Identify the arrangement which makes a logical sequence. A is the 1st sentence and F the last sentence.*

36. A. India, which has two out of every five TB patients, is on the brink of a major health disaster.

B. If untreated a TB patient can die within five years.

C. Unlike AIDS, the great cause of modern sexuality, the TB germ is airborne, which means there are no barriers to its spread.

D. The dreaded infection ranks fourth among major killers worldwide.

E. Every minute, a patient falls prey to the infection in India, which means that over five lakh people die of the disease annually.

F. Anyone, anywhere can be affected by this disease.

1. ADBECF
2. ACBDEF
3. ABCDEF
4. AECBDF

37. A. Until the MBA arrived on the scene, the IIT graduate was king.

B. A degree from one of the five IITs was a passport to a well-paying job, great prospects abroad and, for some, decent dowry to boot.

C. From the day he or she cracked the Joint Entrance Examination, the IIT student commanded the awe of neighbours and close relatives.

D. IIT students had, meanwhile, also developed their own special culture, complete with lingo and attitude, which they passed down.

E. True, the success stories of IIT graduates are legion and they now constitute the concern of the Indian Diaspora.

F. But not many alumni would agree that the IIT undergraduate mindset merits a serious psychological study, let alone an iterative one.

1. ABEDCF
2. ACBDEF
3. ACBEDF
4. ABCDEF

38. A. Good literacy magazines have been good because of their editors.

B. Furthermore, to edit by committee, as it were, would prevent any magazine from finding its own identity.

C. The more quirky and idiosyncratic they have been, the better the magazine is, at least as a general rule.

D. But the number of editors one can have for a magazine should also be determined by the number of contributions to it.

E. To have four editors for an issue that contains only seven contributions, is a bit silly to start with.

F. However, inspite of this anomaly, the magazine does acquire merit in its attempt to give a comprehensive view of the Indian literacy scene as it is today.

1. ABCDEF   2. ACDEBF
3. ABCEDF   4. ADCBEF

39. A. Valmik Thapar traces the cult of the tiger and provides a cache of interesting stories and beliefs connected with this magnificent animal.

B. In all the countries where it is found, the respect in which it is held, owes in large measure to the fear it arouses.

C. "In religion, ritual and art, the tiger holds a place of unmatched eminence because of the sacred status it enjoys."

D. The tiger's immense power and strength give it an aura unmatched in the animal world.

E. The mixture of adoration and fear has led to a wealth of legends and myths.

F. He traces man's relationship with the tiger in a journey from the Siberian forests of Eurasia to the forests of Indonesia.

1. ABDECF   2. ADBECF
3. ABCDEF   4. ABEDCF

40. A. To Krishnamurti, listening was an art, and a miracle.

B. So how you received a question mattered much more than finding an answer.

C. When the brain was absolutely quiet and there was no sound made by the word; that was real listening.

D. Do you feel it, it is there in the room as he once said to his biographer and friends when deep in a meditative conversation.

E. When one listened to it totally and did not translate it nor convert it into an idea, something tremendous happened.

F. Such a dialogue was real meditation, not just sitting and breathing according to a particular system.

1. ABCEDF   2. ADCBEF
3. ADBCEF   4. ACBEDF

DIRECTIONS for questions 91–95: *Each of these questions has a sentence with an idiom which is underlined. Choose the appropriate meaning of the idiom.*

41. Rahul proved to be a <u>wet blanket</u> in the party.

1. good companion   2. warm and friendly
3. kill-joy   4. helpful

42. Do not depend on him, he has <u>an axe to grind</u>.

1. no property   2. personal end to serve
3. no sense   4. no work to do

43. He cannot get that contract, it is a <u>wild goose chase</u>.

1. useless effort   2. baseless effort
3. good effort   4. desperate effort

44. We could finish this work early, only if we <u>cut corners</u>.

1. resort to bribery   2. are brutal
3. take the shortest way   4. are reckless

45. Rima <u>took to her heels</u> and fled from the principal's office.

1. bent down
2. ran off
3. kicked off her shoes
4. cried

DIRECTIONS for questions 46 to 50: *Each of these questions has a pair of words. Identify the option which has a pair of words, which has a relationship which is similar to the pair in the question.*

46. ELUCIDATE :: CLARITY

1. envision : memory
2. aggravate : problem
3. conceal : oblivion
4. illuminate : light
5. mystify enlightenment

47. REPEL :: LURE

1. dismount : devolve
2. abrogate : deny
3. abridge : shorten
4. enervate : weaken
5. miscarry : succeed

48. FURNACE :: SLAG

1. vegetable : garbage
2. factory : goods
3. fire : ashes
4. automobile : gasoline
5. silo : grain

49. PROSAIC :: MUNDANE

1. obdurate : foolish
2. ascetic : austere
3. clamorous : captive
4. loquacious : taciturn
5. peremptory : spontaneous

50. DIVIDEND :: STOCKHOLDER

1. patent : inventor
2. royalty : author
3. wage : employer
4. interest : banker
5. investment : investor

SECTION – II

READING COMPREHENSION

Number of questions: 25

Directions for questions 51 to 75: *Each passage in this section is followed by questions based on its content. After reading a passage, choose the best answer to each question.*

Passage – I

Strategy as a term was coined in Athens around 508-7 B.C., where ten *strategoi* comprised the Athenian war council and controlled both political and military power. Etymologically, the term is associated with "general," "to lead" and "army." So, in the original sense, "strategy" is "the art of leading the army." A commander is expected to be ingenious, energetic, careful, full of stamina and have presence of mind, loving and tough, generous and greedy, trusting and suspicious. An aspiring general should know the business which he proposes to carry out; he is expected not only to plan for battle, but also lead the troops into battle himself.

Parallel developments in Asia included Sun Tzu's *Art of War*, dated to around 5th century BC, which emphasised meticulous planning, the ideal of vanquishing the enemy indirectly without the need to fight, the qualities of effective generals, advice on managing the troops, and general principles and tactics of engaging with the enemy.

While strategy has originated in the military sphere, since the 1960's it has risen to prominence in the business world. Top executives of multidivisional corporations such as Chester Barbard of AT &

T and Alfred Sloan of General Motors were among the firs to draw attention to the needed for strategy within a business context. Peter Drucker argued for an active approach to management which entailed planning and actions intended to shape a firm's environment as opposed to simply reacting passively to it. The Sociologist Philip Selznic proposed the notion of an organization's "distinctive competence" which became a central concept based on the resources of a firm.

51. Chester Barnard was the top executive of
1. AT & T
2. Drucker
3. General Motors
4. None of the above

52. By "meticulous planning" the author of the passage means
1. Planning with attention to details
2. Planning much in advance of action
3. Strategic planning
4. Planning for management

53. The business of a general is
1. To lead the troop to the battle
2. To plan for the battle
3. To plan for and participate in the battle
4. None of these

54. A commander is expected to possess
1. Energy only
2. Carefulness only
3. Contrasting qualities
4. Alertness but not deceptiveness

55. The term "strategy" was first associated with
1. Etymology
2. The generals only
3. Leading the General
4. The Athenian war council

56. Philip Selznick's notion of an organization's "distinctive competence" is based on
1. A central concept
2. The resources of the firm
3. Passive reaction
4. The firm's environment

57. In 1960's strategy has entered the sphere of
1. The military
2. Prominence
3. Origins
4. Business world

58. Sun Tzu's *Art of War* laid emphasis on the ideal of
1. Meticulous planning
2. Vanquishing the enemy
3. The need to fight
4. Management of the troops

59. An essential quality of an aspiring commander is
1. Knowledge of his business
2. Plan for the battle
3. Greed
4. The availability of troops

60. "The art of leading the army" is the meaning of strategy in
1. Greek literature
2. The original sense
3. The British context
4. No context

Passage – II

It's a fight to be selected the most backward of them all. Because on winning the "most backward" tag hinges the amount of money that will be pumped into each state. The amount isn't peanuts, given that the programme lapped up no less than Rs 2000 crores of a total Rs 12000 crore doled out in additional budgetary support three weeks ago.

The government's food-for-work programme in 150 districts, as a result, has run into trouble. At present the Planning Commission and the rural development ministry are reportedly differing on the selection formula while the food ministry is worried about costs.

The issue was slated to come up at the next meeting of the cabinet, but with the food minister away in Mumbai, it was put off. Yojana Bhawan, it would appear, came up with varied criteria to determine the 150 most backward districts, including the SC/ST population, agricultural productivity per worker and prevalent agricultural wages. But this, says a rural development ministry source, wouldn't have passed on the "benefits" to "certain states" considered backward in the common perception – for example, Bihar.

With an RJD leader at the helm of affairs in the rural development ministry, this wouldn't pass without a fight. In came the poverty index and then the ongoing programme aimed at forcing the pace of development, linking aid to reforms. This comprises a special package for Bihar and another for Orissa. All in all, seven formulas were suggested and a mix was being cooked up for the cabinet meeting.

Officially, there is no dispute, but nobody expects this to pass without stiff opposition from some quarter or the other.

61. It is proposed to offer special packages to

1. Two states
2. All states
3. A few backward districts
4. None of the above

62. The statement that an RJD leader is "at the helm of affairs" suggests that he is

1. At the center of a controversy
2. Excessively reasonable
3. In full control of the ministry
4. In favour of crash helmets

63. Agricultural productivity per worker is part of

1. The SC/ST population
2. Varied criteria
3. Backward districts
4. Prevalent agricultural wages

64. The differences between the Planning Commission and the Ministry of Rural Development relate to

1. Amount of the allocation
2. Modalities of allotment
3. Selection formula
4. Quantum of costs involved

65. "The fight" mentioned in the passage is all about

1. Hinges of selection
2. Tag for winning
3. Winning "the most backward" tag
4. Pumping each state

Passage – III

The Indian cooperative sector is celebrating its centenary this year. In the process of completing a century of its presence, this sector has built up a network, which is considered the world's largest. More than five lakh individual cooperative organisations and over 25 crore members make it numerically the largest movement in the world. A paid up capital base of more than 50,000 crore rupees, presence in practically all walks of life and covering almost all villages of the country, makes it economically and socially the most significant set of organisations. But then, the problems too are plenty. The general perception is that the cooperative sector is weak and inactive. Barring exceptions, the sector seems to be ill-equipped to face the challenge of neo-liberal thrust. Even after a hundred years, most cooperatives are dependant on government patronage both for their business and capital requirements. The future does not look bright if some structural changes are not effected to rejuvenate the sector and the movement as a whole.

There are two very important vices that we have inherited and two essential values we have failed to inculcate, which have marred the 'cooperative character' in our setting. The first of the vices is the bureaucratization and government control. When the colonial rulers officially brought the cooperatives to India, they introduced the omnipotent Registrar, a position specially created by the government in order to have the final controlling rights with it and not to allow the cooperative sector to blossom as a people's movement. The government of free India, while championing the cause of cooperatives, not only retained this key position but also further added a long hierarchy of bureaucratic power centres. In fact, a government directed cooperative movement is in itself a contradiction and against the "logic of cooperative movement." The second vice, which we developed by ourselves, is that the politicians are cooperators by default. They are in cooperatives either because they want to move up in the political hierarchy (cooperatives as breeding grounds) or because they have temporarily failed to make headway in that route (cooperatives as rehabilitation centres). There is no harm in cooperators becoming politicians. In fact it would be a welcome development. But the other way round, which is the practice today, would kill the movement.

Our cooperative sector has clearly failed to inculcate two of the very essential cooperative values. The first is that of self-help. Self-help was envisaged as a basic tenet of cooperatives. Both Robert Owen and Charles Fourier had seen cooperation as a process of creating 'self-help communities'. In its very genesis the movement was opposed to Market and State, since both had failed to protect the interest of the common man. Both are, in that sense, forces which the cooperators resist. Drawing support from such sources is essentially a modern day political compromise, and it would be against the cooperative ideology. We need to understand that governments both in centrally planned economies and free market domains were too eager and willing to provide financial and other support to cooperatives and the sector fell prey to this temptation. A cooperative endeavour should necessarily depend on its own resources, energy and time, however small it could turn out to be. Its growth and expansion should be evolutionary.

The second very important missing value is the member centrality. Cooperatives by their very nature are inward looking organisations. They are meant to serve the member community unlike the outward looking organisations such as the corporate which sells to any one so long as there is profit. The focus of all activities of cooperatives should have been members. Business activities are to be developed based on member needs, policies are to be designed according to member views and administration is to be carried out through member participation. Indian cooperatives generally do not stick to this value. It is increasingly felt that the pressures of globalisation will have to be addressed to a large extent through self-help initiatives. The talk of social capital as an input for development and self-help groups as instruments of development is everywhere. This reinforces the need for cooperative endeavours.

There is a definite credibility crisis for the cooperative sector. The process of withdrawal of the state from certain service areas should have in the ordinary course opened up the doors for cooperativisation instead of privatisation. But no one believes that the cooperative sector is competent enough to accept this challenge. Unless the sector moves away from the clutches of government control and comes out with norms for restraining politicians from making use of the sector as a ladder for their personal benefits, the movement is sure to slip down further. It is inevitable that a good number of our cooperative enterprises will disappear in the coming years, since they are not strong enough to stand the trial of time. However, inculcating the values of self-help and member centrality can give rise to cooperatives, which are not just 'enterprises' but instruments of creating 'cooperative communities'. The cooperative ideology is indeed too precious and realistic to discard. Hard introspection and commitment to further the cause is needed during the centenary celebrations.**66.** According to the passage which one of the following statements is not true?

1. The Indian cooperative sector is equipped well to face the challenges of neo-liberal business environment.
2. A definite credibility crisis overshadows the cooperative sector.
3. Cooperators oppose the forces of Market and State.
4. It would be a welcome development if cooperators become politicians.

67. What are the reasons for the cooperative movement to deteriorate?

1. Government control on cooperative sector.
2. Politician's ambition to use cooperative movements for individual gain.
3. Both (1) and (2).
4. None of these.

68. Which is the significant vice that plagues the cooperative system?

1. Bureaucratization
2. Government control
3. Politicians in cooperative movement
4. All the above

69. Which is/are the essential value(s) that the cooperative sector failed to develop?

1. Self help
2. Focus on members
3. Resources
4. Both (1) and (2)

Passage – IV

Man is a social animal, they say. To survive in a society, one must be able to reach out and establish a bond with other people, extending beyond one's family circle. As adults, we tend to take friendships and our ability to form them for granted. But consider a life without friends. In a word, unimaginable. Can you remember the day you made your first friend or even who that person was? Probably not. A child's first friendship could be said to be her first foray into society. This is a whole new ball game for her. Her parents are her guides and protectors, her safety nets. Her siblings are sometimes her teachers and sometimes her tormentors. But a friendship normally begins on an equal footing, a relationship of give-and-take, of two-way traffic, irrespective of what it ultimately evolves into. It is a relationship with a person she has been drawn to, with whom she can explore, experiment, learn about the world and make mistakes with. A friend is a person, like her, who is beginning from square one.

Even though everyone was a child once, as an adult it is difficult to slip into the shoes of a child once again. Parents and siblings can never take the place of friends of the same age and vice versa. Every relationship has a unique place in life and performs a unique function. At what age can you expect your child to be social? Before two years of age, a child is too busy staring wide-eyed at the world around her, trying to take it all in. Her family fills her little world. While her immediate family stays a constant presence, all the time there are new faces and happenings to absorb. She is too young and immature to build a relationship with her peers.

However, once she is two-year-old, she is ready to make her debut in society. When parents put a couple of two-year-olds together to play they may not think so. What they will probably observe is two toddlers pottering about with their respective toys without even acknowledging each other's presence. But parents should not despair, because even though the children seem to engage in parallel play, they are actually learning from each other through imitation. Toddlers can imitate a whole new sequence of actions from their peers and in this way absorb new skills. If parents observe two toddlers 'playing' together closely, they will see one toddler build a tower of blocks in the same manner as the other had without seeming to interact at all. That is about all that you can expect from a relationship between two-year-olds.

Between the ages of three and six, children's ability to relate to their peers takes a tiny step forward. In the case of boys, it is the age to vent their aggression. Parents are most likely to see their little boys locked in combat, rolling around the floor, wrestling with other boys and generally indulging in horseplay. Girls, on the other hand, are more likely to tease and provoke each other and boys and giggle at every opportunity. This is the time when children are initiated into the world of give-and-take. It is important that children should not be isolated for whatever reason. Spoiled and overprotected children will have a difficult time.

Between the ages of six and nine, children begin to form friendships in the conventional sense. Children begin to form small groups. They get attached to particular children and want to spend all their time together with their special friends. They are possessive about their special friends and deeply hurt when a friend shows a preference for another. Group dynamics can be observed. Some children are admired, some bullied and others excluded. This is the time a child will learn the demands of closeness and the need to be sensitive to others' feelings.

When two children get together, it need not necessarily be all sweetness and light. Just like adults, they just may not get on. One child may be particularly aggressive, while the other might cower in response. Given this scenario, most parents tend to jump into the fray, but this could backfire, as they are likely to reinforce their child's imbalanced behavior by their intervention. The parent of the aggressor is likely to reprimand her child with the aim of putting a stop to her aggression. At the same time, she probably resents the parent for expressing her anger. The aggressive child senses her parent's overreaction and increases her aggression.

The parent of the docile child will either angrily exhort her child to fight back at a time when she is not capable, or play the role of the protector. The parent's anger and embarrassment will drive home the docile child's sense of helplessness and inadequacy. Parents should leave their children to hammer out the situation on their own. The minute parents step into the picture, it becomes an adult situation. However, if the children cannot cope even after being left to their own devices, then parents should steer them towards playmates of a similar temperament. Children are more likely to learn from playmates of a similar temperament. If parents of a docile child push her to be more aggressive or gregarious, they are merely giving her the message that they do not approve of her the way she is. Parents of aggressive children will find that when such children are thrown together with other aggressors, they are likely to become bosom buddies as aggression on both sides somehow balances out.

Bullies are insecure children who combat their insecurity through aggression. Bullying behaviour tends to fall into a vicious circle. Children distance themselves from bullies and as the bullies are more and more isolated, their insecurity increases and so do their bullying tactics in an attempt to hide their vulnerability. Parents of bullies should try to bolster their self-image, but at the same time they should make it clear that bullying behaviour is unacceptable. They should try to make their children understand that often children tease each other in an attempt to get to know each other better and that if one can take some ribbing and teasing sportingly, one is likely to make a great deal of friends. Parents should ideally leave their children to find their own feet. The less the adult involvement, the more the children are likely to learn about each other and themselves.

They should be left free to make their own judgements and mistakes. The quantity and quality of a child's friendships is a good indicator of her mental and emotional well-being. In all likelihood, a child who is shunned or ostracized by her peers is sending out a message spelling out anxiety, self-doubt or some kind of turmoil. Sometimes, children can be more sensitive and perceptive than adults. They can tell the difference between a child that is upset by some immediate circumstance and one that is chronically unhappy. In the latter case, children react by staying away because they are threatened by these feelings. When a child cannot establish bonds with her peers, it means that something is fundamentally wrong and needs parental attention.

70. A child's first friendship

1. could be her first move into society.
2. is a bond with her peers.
3. can help her stand on her own feet.
4. All of these.

71. As per the passage,

1. it is incorrect to call man a social animal.
2. parents should never be partial towards any one child.
3. sometimes children can be more sensitive and perceptive than the adults.
4. All the above.

72. Which of the following statement(s) is/are appropriate ?

A. It is difficult for an adult to slip into the shoes of a child once again.

B. Parents and siblings can easily replace friends of the same age and vice versa.

1. Only A
2. Only B
3. Both A and B
4. Neither A nor B

73. The quality of a child's friendships, according to the passage,

1. is a good indicator of her mental and emotional well-being.
2. is something for parents to judge impartially.
3. is sending out a message spelling out anxiety, self doubt or some kind of turmoil.
4. All the above.

74. The writer firmly believes

1. in single parenting.
2. in treating boys and girls differently.
3. in isolating bullies to teach them about self-restraint.
4. that a child who cannot establish bonds with her peer needs parental attention.

75. The passage is __________ in its approach.

1. fastidious
2. captious
3. analytical
4. facetious

Answer Key

1. 1	**2.** 4	**3.** 3	**4.** 1	**5.** 1	**6.** 1	**7.** 2
8. 4	**9.** 3	**10.** 1	**11.** 2	**12.** 4	**13.** 1	**14.** 2
15. 3	**16.** 2	**17.** 1	**18.** 2	**19.** 4	**20.** 2	**21.** 4
22. 3	**23.** 4	**24.** 1	**25.** 3	**26.** 4	**27.** 1	**28.** 2
29. 2	**30.** 3	**31.** 2	**32.** 2	**33.** 3	**34.** 1	**35.** 4
36. 1	**37.** 3	**38.** 2	**39.** 4	**40.** 2	**41.** 3	**42.** 2
43. 1	**44.** 3	**45.** 2	**46.** 4	**47.** 5	**48.** 3	**49.** 2
50. 2	**51.** 1	**52.** 1	**53.** 4	**54.** 3	**55.** 4	**56.** 4
57. 2	**58.** 1	**59.** 1	**60.** 2	**61.** 3	**62.** 3	**63.** 3
64. 3	**65.** 3	**66.** 1	**67.** 3	**68.** 4	**69.** 4	**70.** 1
71. 3	**72.** 1	**73.** 1	**74.** 4	**75.** 3		

EXPLANATIONS

1. 1	**2.** 4	**3.** 3	**4.** 1	**5.** 1
6. 1	**7.** 2	**8.** 4	**9.** 3	**10.** 1
11. 2	**12.** 4	**13.** 1	**14.** 2	**15.** 3

16. "believe" (present) must match with "is".

17. "turn up" is the correct phrase."

18. "are different from..." not "than."

19. "has sung" is past perfect, and fits in this case.

20. This is the only correct sentence.

21. "warned" matches with "were" and the correct word is "imminent" in this case.

22. "Man" should not have "the" but the name of the book should.

23. There should be no "that" in the sentence.

24. "...takes off at 8 a.m. everyday"

25. "they" should come after "many Indians".

26. "quantum" is singular, so should be followed by "is".

27. The correct expression is: "take the exam."

28. "he had left" should be used.

29. "is established to dispense justice."

30. "the company made profits..." is the most direct.

31. The blanks have to be opposites – with the first a positive and the second a negative. Hence 2 fits.

32. You can anticipate the blanks with words like 'help' and 'diseased'. Hence 2.

33. Use common sense to answer this.What are characteristics of the net – mlions of pages and no cost of accessing any of them. Hence 3.

34. You can anticipate the blank with words like 'remove'. Idiomatically only option 1 fits in correctly.

35. This sentence also requires grammar soundness.For count nouns – you use 'many', else you use much.Too many more is incorrect usage. Hence 4.

36. The sentence that follows A can be either D or E.But the sentence preceding F has to be C – because it talks about the spread of the disease. Hence 1.

37. CB is a distinct pair in the set. This is found only in 3.

38. C details out 'the editors' of A – hence AC is a pair.CD is a sequence because of the contrast the word 'but' provides and the continued usage of 'editors'.

39. BE is a pair because of the common word 'fear'.This is only found in 4.

40. The 'it' of E refers to the 'question' of B.Hence BE is a pair.EF is also a pair – because the act of listening to the question without responding is the meditation the author talks of in sentence F. Hence 2.

41.3 **42.** 2 **43.** 1 **44.** 3 **45.** 2

46. The relationship here is of similarity. When you elucidate you make matters clear. In the same way when you illuminate you throw light on.

47. Relationship is of antonyms. Miscarry means a stoppage or a failure. The opposite is succeed.

48. Slag is the waste produced in a furnace.Similarly ashes are the waste after a fire.

49. The relationship is of synonyms.Both prosaic and mundane mean ordinary.Similarly both austere and ascetic mean simple /frugal.

50. Dividend is how a stockholder (share holder) earns on his investment in shares.In the same way Royalty is how an author earns on his investment in writing a book.

51. Stated in the last paragraph.

52. Meticulous: with details.

53. He must plan and lead, as stated in the first paragraph.

54. First paragraph.

55. First line.

56. Second last line.

57. First line of the last paragraph.

58. First line of the second paragraph.

59. Stated in the first paragraph.

60. 2

61. "the most backward of them all."

62. helm – in control.

63. It is the criteria for backward districts.

64. Stated in the second paragraph.

65. Can be inferred from the first line.

66. 1 is not true. Refer the first para –Barring exceptions, the sector seems to be ill-equipped to face the challenge of neo-liberal thrust.

67. The first of the vices is the bureaucratization and government control. The second vice, which we developed by ourselves, is that the politicians are cooperators by default. Hence 3.

68. Refer above answer.

69. The first is that of self-help. *The second very important missing value is the member centrality.* Hence 4.

70. Refer first para. *A child's first friendship could be said to be her first foray into society.* Hence 1.

71. Refer last para.Sometimes, children can be more sensitive and perceptive than adults. They can tell the difference between a child that is upset by some immediate circumstance and one that is chronically unhappy.

72. Refer start of second para.Even though everyone was a child once, as an adult it is difficult to slip into the shoes of a child once again.

73. Refer last para.The quantity and quality of a child's friendships is a good indicator of her mental and emotional well-being.

74. Refer last line of the passage. When a child cannot establish bonds with her peers, it means that something is fundamentally wrong and needs parental attention

75. Here the challenge is of vocabulary. You need to know what each of the options mean. Fastidious means too detailed. Captious means faultfinding. Facetious means frivolous or jocular.

IRMA 2007

Number of Questions – 40
Time : 30 M.

SECTION – I

ENGLISH COMPREHENSION

Number of questions: 40

Directions for questions 1 to 10: *Read the following passage carefully and answer the questions given below it. Certain words have been printed in bold to help you locate them while answering some of the questions.*

Access to schooling, an adequate teaching-teaming environment, an appropriate school curriculum and an empowered and inclusive teaching community are four crucial prerequisites of a school system that seek to enable social transformation. While educational reform since the 1980s was strongly focused on the first two elements, the late 1990s brought the role of the curriculum into national focus. The critical link that binds these four critical elements together - the agency of the teacher continues to be cast aside, by political ideologies of most hues, contemporary curriculum reform efforts and the professional practices of much of the teacher education community.

Radical educational initiatives of both the Left and the Right have recognized the potential power of the agency of the teacher. In multiple experiments.-they have used this latent force to build committed institutions and cadres of teachers dedicated to their particular causes. In many instances this has led to extreme politicization of the schoolteacher. In others it has led to the education of a generation of students in half-truths **underpinned** by the personal beliefs, sectarian concerns and folk pedagogy of teachers who have had little access themselves to education and training in areas outlined by the NCF 2005.

Over the last decade or so, educational reform has included, apart from access, a focus on developing alternative text materials and the training of teachers to transact these materials, without directly engaging with the issue of curriculum redesign. At the turn of the 20th century, a major national curriculum redesign was initiated following the change of political regime at the centre. NCF 2000 and the subsequent development of school textbooks came under wide public scrutiny and debate. Issues of equity, inclusion and exclusion, learner **diversity,** religious identity and communalism gained considerable importance in the curriculum debates that followed. For instance scholars argued that"...the NCF, while loud on rhetoric, fails to address the quality of education that children of poor and marginalized group's experience". Several other critics described the NCF 2000 as a retrogressive step in education that sought to impose the Hindutva agenda in the garb of a national identity.

The subsequent change of national government in 2004, led to the NCERT curriculum review in 2005 underlining a new political interest in the role of education in national development, its role in social mobilization and transformation directed specifically at questions of caste and gender asymmetry and minority empowerment. Deeper than these politically driven initiatives, however, the professional need for curriculum review emerges from the long **ossification** of a national education system that continues to view teachers as "dispensers of information" and children as "passive recipients" of an "education", sought to be "delivered" in four-walled classrooms with little scope to develop critical thinking and understanding.

1. To facilitate social transformation, which of the following factors has been identified by the author?

1. A committed political ideology
2. Support of the well framed curriculum
3. A strong school system
4. Carefully planned education delivery
5. None of these

2. Prior to 1990 what was **NOT** the agenda of the educational reforms?

A. An appropriate curriculum

B. Well trained school teachers

1. Only A
2. Only B
3. Both A and B
4. Either A or B
5. None of these

3. Which of the following best describes the "latent force" as used in the passage?

1. Agency of committed teachers
2. The political ideology of right and left parties
3. Well framed curriculum guiding teaching learning process
4. Free access to school system
5. None of these

4. How did personal beliefs and folk pedagogy entered into educational system?

1. The school acted as an agent of local communities
2. The teachers were not properly trained
3. School teachers started acting as political agents
4. The loop holes in the educational system allowed it to happen
5. None of these

5. Developments of school text books generated public debate on many issues except ______

A. making the curriculum child centered.

B. using teaching community as an agency to bring change.

1. Only A
2. Only B
3. Both A and B
4. Either A or B
5. None of these

6. What hampers the critical thinking ability of school going children?

1. The emphasis on rote memorization and recalling the facts of education
2. Lack of concern of educational planners towards these abilities
3. Absence of focus while designing curriculum framework
4. Ignoring the active role of teacher and the child
5. None of these

7. Which of the following best describes the word **ossification** as used in the passage?

1. hardening
2. flexibility
3. imbibitions
4. assimilation
5. coalescing

8. Alterative development of text material was the main focus in ______

1. early eighties
2. late nineties
3. after year 2000
4. recent curriculum
5. framework

9. Which of the following best describes the meaning of the word underpinned as used in the passage?

1. advocated
2. supported
3. fortified
4. bolstered
5. boasted

10. Which of the following is the **most opposite** in meaning to the word diversity as used in the passage?

1. amalgamate
2. united
3. unity
4. uniformity
5. focusing

Directions for questions 11 to 25: *Read the following passage carefully and answer the questions given below it. Certain words in Ste passage have been printed in bold to help you locate them while answering some of the questions.*

Dairy industry dominates change in India through its **causal** links with factor and product markets. It employs around 20 per cent of the labour force and contributes around 10 per cent of the gross domestic product. In the poorer states, its contribution to the domestic product is close to 40 per cent. Low productivity in dairy sector has led to the concentration of the poor in this sector. Due to the sheer size of the service sector economy and the importance of its products in the diets of the poor, gains in dairy productivity have significant potential impact on poverty. Theoretically, it is possible to reduce poverty as well as expand the domestic market for industry by raising labour productivity in dairy sector and spreading its gains among the low income groups. Modelling of the linkages between dairy sector and industrial growth has shown that a 10 per cent increase in dairy output would increase industrial output by 5 per cent and urban workers would benefit by both increased industrial employment and price **deflation.** However, there is an asymmetry of adjustments in the demand and supply of dairy products. An increase in non-dairy production would lead to an immediate increase in demand for intermediate and final dairy products, whereas supply-side adjustments involving re-allocation of resources and net additional investment for capacity expansion take a much longer period. There is a widely held view that in a large country like India, the demand stimulus for industrialisation would come mainly from dairy industry with less social and economic costs.

Interdependencies in dairy and labour market are important for the development process. An upward shift in the dairy products supply curve would simultaneously result in an upward shift in the labour demand curve. The magnitude of the interdependence depends on the technique of production causing the shifts in the dairy products supply curve. Similarly, an upward shift in the labour supply curve shifts up the dairy products demand curve. The extent of interdependence between the forces of labour supply and dairy products demand depends on the employment-output elasticity and the income elasticity of demand for dairy product. The recent estimate of the employment-output elasticity in dairy sector is around 0.3, income elasticity of dairy product is in the range of 0.35-0.40 and that for cereals is 0.25-0.30. The other important inter-dependency, which plays a crucial role in inducing indirect employment, is that between dairy product and other sectors through demand linkages. Since milk accounts for a sizeable share in the budget of the poor and any reduction in the milk price leaves a significant proportion of income for other items, a lower milk price stimulates employment in industrial and dairy sectors. On the other hand an increase in the milk price would increase the wage costs of industrial products and hence the prices of industrial products. In the absence of adjustments through exports, it would result in demand deficiency. Clearly, the most favourable situation in India is one in which labour demand outpaces its supply and milk supply outpaces its demand.

Wage rates cannot fall below a certain minimum determined by the costs of subsistence living and the labour supply curve turns elastic at the subsistence wage rate. Demographic pressure cannot push the wage rate below the subsistence level. People would be willing to starve rather than work unless the energy expended in physical work is compensated by the energy provided by food. Milk and its product price usually determines the subsistence wage rate in dairy as well as in the urban informal sector since dairy products account for about two-fifth of the calorie intake of the poor.

11. How are dairy product supply and labour demand related?

1. Labour demands more dairy products when supply increases.
2. Higher the dairy product supply lower is the wage rate.
3. The labour demands only if the milk supply decreases.
4. 20% of labour are supplied only 10% of dairy products.
5. None of these

12. What is meant by demand deficiency?

1. The absence of adjustments in dairy product supply and wage cost.
2. The low calorie intake present in dairy products.
3. The increase in dairy production will decrease the industrial production.
4. Lowering of wage structure below subsistence level.
5. None of these

13. Under what conditions people prefer to starve than work?

1. When their legitimate demands are not considered.
2. When social cost supersedes economic cost.
3. When demographic pressures nullify the increased milk production.
4. When milk and its products provides less energy than the required level.
5. None of these

14. The poor are more concentrated in dairy sector because they ____________

1. are socially and economically attached to cattle wealth.
2. feel insecure in urban area.
3. think that their major food product is most secure in dairy sector.
4. are unskilled to take up any industrial jobs.
5. None of these

15. According to the passage, the poverty can be reduced by ____________

A. raising labour productivity in dairy sector.
B. distributing judiciously the dairy sector gain among poor.
C. making the dairy products available to poor at a negligible price.

1. Either A or B
2. Either A or C
3. Both A and B
4. All A, B and C
5. Neither A nor B nor C

16. Supply of dairy products and labour market are interdependent because ____________

1. they help development process in the urban area.
2. lower milk product price will increase labour market.
3. the milk supply curve gets shifted with the production technology.
4. dairy product supply decides calorie intake of the poor.
5. none of these

17. How according to the passage, the dairy sector dominates change process in India?

1. Its contribution to gross domestic product is the maximum.
2. Majority of Indian population depends on dairy sector.
3. The dairy sector is directly linked with factor and product markets.
4. Increase in dairy sector production raises the industrial production.
5. None of these

18. According to the passage, what decides the cost of subsistence living?

1. The author of the passage.
2. The demographic pressures.
3. The social and economic costs of the poor.
4. The dairy product price.
5. None of these

19. Which of the following has the same meaning as the word 'deflation' as used in the passage?

1. reduction
2. manifestation
3. increase
4. air pressure
5. adulation

20. Which of the following is most **opposite** in meaning to the word 'elasticity' as used in the passage?

1. flexibility 2. frailty
3. rigidity 4. adamancy
5. idiosyncrasy

21. In poor States the contribution of dairy sector to gross domestic product is ________

1. higher than its overall contribution. 2. lower than its overall contribution.
3. just the same as in other than poor States. 4. almost 30 %more than overall contribution.
5. None of these

22. According to the passage, the statement "demand stimulus for industrialisation would come mainly from dairy sector..." is applicable for which of the following?

A. All large countries
B. Only India

1. Only A 2. Only B
3. Either A or B 4. Neither A nor B
5. None of these

23. Which of the following is most opposite in meaning to the word/phrase "interdependence" as used in the passage?

1. dependence within 2. reliance
3. self-determination 4. relativity
5. interconnected

24. Which of the following is almost the **same** as the word **"causal"** as used in the passage?

1. casual 2. precursor
3. proficient 4. causing 5. familiarity

25. Which of the following statements is **NOT TRUE** in the context of the passage?

1. In dairy sector as the productivity increases, the concentration of poors in it also increases.
2. Demographic pressures do not lower wage rate below subsistence level.
3. People prefer to starve than to work for less food intake.
4. More than half of the labour force of the country is engaged in dairy sector.
5. Dairy products are one of the major constituents of food of the poor.

Directions for questions 26 to 30: *Rearrange the following six sentences A, B, C, D, E and F in the proper sequence to form a meaningful paragraph. Then answer the questions given below them.*

A. Hence these activities will start getting more emphasis than the production activi ties.
B. This was because of the fact that the former gain popularity sooner than the latter do.
C. The things have now started undergoing drastic changes.
D. The Company's tendency so far had been to give importance to production activities more than the marketing activities.
E. The Company's attention has now been shifted to marketing activities.
F. Also, they are more eye-catching than the former.

26. Which of the following should be the **FIRST** sentence after rearrangement?

1. F 2. E 3. D 4. C 5. B

27. Which of the following should be the **SECOND** sentence after rearrangement?

1. F 2. E 3. D 4. C 5. B

28. Which of the following should be the **THIRD** sentence after rearrangement?

1. F 2. E 3. D 4. C 5. B

29. Which of the following should be the **FOURTH** sentence after rearrangement?

1. A 2. B 3. C 4. D 5. E

30. Which of the following should be the **SIXTH (LAST)** sentence after rearrangement?

1. B 2. A 3. C 4. D 5. E

DIRECTIONS for questions 31 to 40: *In the following passage, there are blanks, each of which has been numbered. These numbers are printed below the passage and against each, five words are suggested, one of which fills the blank appropriately. Find out the appropriate word in each case.*

Electricity is the most important **(31)** for economic development **(32)** a country and **(33)** in the quality of life of its people. Recent advance in the **(34)** of technology have transformed the industrial **(35)** of the country due to which the electricity **(36)** has increased manifold. But these developments also **(37)** a huge quantity of unwanted but **(38)** wastes which are regularly thrown into rivers and the sea. Waste products from thermal power plants, **(39)** fly ash is one of such wastes which has drawn the **(40)** of scientists and policy makers.

31. 1. characteristic 2. ingredient 3. cause 4. substance 5. yield

32. 1. for 2. in 3. about 4. on 5. of

33. 1. improvement 2. refuse 3. descent 4. strength 5. development

34. 1. capacity 2. situate 3. array 4. field 5. value

35. 1. backwardness 2. enlargement 3. condition 4. contribution 5. consumption

36. 1. accretion 2. echelon 3. situation 4. requirement 5. potency

37. 1. preserve 2. maintain 3. generate 4. employ 5. regulate

38. 1. unavoidable 2. useful 3. sustainable 4. marginal 5. needful

39. 1. directly 2. mainly 3. infrequently 4. habitually 5. seldom

40. 1. confidence 2. psyche 3. reflection 4. explore 5. attention

Answer

1. 3	**2.** 3	**3.** 1	**4.** 3	**5.** 5	**6.** 4	**7.** 1
8. 4	**9.** 4	**10.** 4	**11.** 1	**12.** 1	**13.** 4	**14.** 5
15. 3	**16.** 3	**17.** 3	**18.** 3	**19.** 1	**20.** 3	**21.** 4
22. 1	**23.** 5	**24.** 2	**25.** 4	**26.** 4	**27.** 2	**28.** 3
29. 2	**30.** 2	**31.** 3	**32.** 5	**33.** 1	**34.** 4	**35.** 3
36. 4	**37.** 3	**38.** 1	**39.** 2	**40.** 5		

EXPLANATIONS

1. 3 Look at first para.

2. 3 Look at first para, 3rd line.

3. 1 Look at second para, 2nd line.

4. 3 Look at second para, 3rd line.

5. 5

6. 4 Para 4, Read from 3rd line.

7. 1 Para 4, 4th and 5th line.

8. 4

9. 4	**10.** 4	**11.** 1	**12.** 1
13. 4	**14.** 5	**15.** 3	**16.** 3
17. 3	**18.** 3	**19.** 1	**20.** 3
21. 4	**22.** 1	**23.** 5	**24.** 2
25. 4	**26.** 4	**27.** 2	**28.** 3
29. 2	**30.** 2	**31.** 3	**32.** 5
33. 1	**34.** 4	**35.** 3	**36.** 4
37. 3	**38.** 1	**39.** 2	**40.** 5

JMET 2007

Number of Questions – 40
Time : 30 M.

VERBAL COMMUNICATION

Number of questions: 40

Directions for questions 1 to 4: *Relate to the following article.*

Pick up a glossy magazine or newspaper supplement and there will almost certainly be at least one double page spread that looks like a regular editorial page but is headed up either 'promotion' or 'advertisement'. These hybrids - unattractively but aptly called advertorials - are being used with increasing frequency by a growing number of companies. Traditionally the preserve of high-technology clients with a complicated message to get across to potential customers, the use of this technique has now spread to sectors like financial services, alcohol and automobiles.

One major reason why marketing departments are becoming more receptive to ideas for advertorials is that publishers are pursuing them more aggressively at a time of shrinking ad budgets, while they are being treated far more professionally in a bid to persuade clients that this is a creative opportunity to spread their message to their target audiences. Pouring more imagination into them allied with raising production standards has also been a means whereby the commercial executives of magazines and newspapers can try to convince **sceptical** editors who strongly disapprove of blurring the advertising / editorial line of their worth.

What advertorials are about is control - controlling the message in an editorial format. Positive editorial coverage of a company and or its products in credible publications is the best publicity any company can hope for, but often proves **elusive**. A successful advertorial can pinpoint the way the company delivers its message to he heart of its target audience.

High technology was one of the main sources of early advertorials - unsurprisingly, the products are complex and need to be explained with some technical detail to get the story across. That is not so easy with traditional advertising.

Advertorials can also to some degree **circumvent** journalistic indifference to what a company is doing because editorial coverage has already been so extensive. For example, in the case of a company like Compaq, whose swift growth in the computer market attracted many inches of editorial space, that very success can lead to journalists wondering how they can write something different about Compaq There can be diminishing returns from an editorial point of view. So advertorials let the company present things editorially but with bought space. While they should be strongly labeled, information is being given to readers in a format that looks familiar.

1. In the light of your reading of the passage above, identify the option that contains the set of words closest in meaning to the set of words in capitals : SCEPTICAL : CIRCUMVENT : ELUSIVE

1. incredulous : surround : baffling
2. doubtful : avoid : evasive
3. thoughtful : deceit : illustrative
4. philosophical : revolve : deceptive

2. In the above passage, the phrase "blurring the advertising / editorial line of their worth" implies

1. diluting the perceived quality of their editorials
2. hiding the actual value of the paper
3. obscuring the actual facts in the paper
4. devaluing the advertising potential of the editorials

3. The passage <u>DOES NOT</u> discuss

1. attitude of journalists towards advertising
2. advertorials and the publishing industry

3. use of advertorials in industries
4. impact of new technologies on advertorials

4. According to the passage,
1. high technology does not support traditional advertising
2. traditional journalists are indifferent toadvertorials
3. advertorials facilitate advertising of complex products in a professional manner
4. advertorials occupy double-page spreads in magazines

Directions for questions 5 and 6: *Choose from the respective options the CORRECT PASSIVE form of the active sentence:*

5. She resembles a Greek goddess.
1. A Greek goddess resembled her
2. A Greek goddess resembles her
3. She is resembled by a Greek goddess
4. None of the above

6. Mr. Sullivan made a major error in the estimate.
1. A major error was made in the estimate by Mr. Sullivan
2. A major estimate was made m the error by Mr. Sullivan
3. A major error was being made in the estimate by Mr. Sullivan
4. A major error was estimated by Mr. Sullivan

Directions for questions 7 and 8: *Select the set of words from the given options that BEST expresses a relationship SIMILAR to the set in CAPITALS:*

7. LIONS : PRIDE : FOREST
1. geese : gaggle : sky
2. houses : colony : city
3. fish : shoal : ocean
4. paper : ream : press

8. POET : VISION : PROPHET
1. politician : constituency : voter
2. killer : violence : terrorist
3. student : school : principal
4. plant : herbivore : food-chain

Directions for question 9: *Choose the option CLOSEST in meaning to the sentence given below:*

He was convinced that it would take at least fifty years before a few men would understand what he had accomplished: and he feared that even then his teachings would be misinterpreted and misapplied.

9.
1. He was convinced that his teachings would be misinterpreted and misapplied after fifty years.
2. He was convinced that after misinterpreting and misapplying his teachings for fifty years, they would be appreciated
3. He was convinced that understanding his teachings would lead to their misinterpretation and misapplication.
4. He was convinced that understanding and applying his teachings would take at least fifty years.

Directions for questions 10 to 12: *Read the passage carefully and answer the questions.*

I feel that this award was not made to me as a man, but to my work - a life's work in the agony and sweat of the human spirit, not for glory and least of all for profit, but to create out of the materials of the human spirit something which did not exist before. So this award is only mine in trust. It will not be difficult to find a dedication for the money part of it commensurate with the purpose and significance of its origin. But I would like to do the same with the acclaim too. by using this moment as a pinnacle from which I might be listened to by the young men and women already dedicated to the same anguish and travail, among whom is already that one who will some day stand here where I am standing.

Our tragedy today is a general and universal physical fear so long sustained by now that we can even bear it. There are no longer problems of the spirit. There is only the question: When will I be blown up? Because of this, the young man or woman writing today has forgotten the problems of the human heart in conflict with itself which alone can make-good writing because only that is worth writing about, worth the agony and the sweat.

He must learn them again. He must teach himself that the basest of all things is to be afraid: and, teaching himself that, forget it forever, leaving no room in his workshop for anything but the old verities and truths of the heart, the old universal truths tacking which any story is ephemeral and doomed - love and honor and pity and pride and compassion and sacrifice. Until he does so, he labors under a curse. He writes not of love but of lust, of defeats in which nobody loses anything of value, of victories without hope and, worst of all, without pity or compassion. His griefs grieve on no universal bones, leaving no scars. He writes not of the heart but of the glands.

Until he relearns these things, he will write as though he stood among and watched the end of man. I decline to accept the end of man. It is easy enough to say that man is immortal simply because he will endure: that when the last ding-dong of doom has clanged and faded from the last worthless rock hanging tideless in the last red and dying evening, that even then there will still be one more sound: that of his puny inexhaustible voice, still talking. I refuse to accept this. I believe that man will not merely endure: he will prevail. He is immortal, not because he alone among creatures has an inexhaustible voice, but because he has a soul, a spirit capable of compassion and sacrifice and endurance. The poet's, the writer's, duty is to write about these things. It is his privilege to help man endure by lifting his spirit, by reminding him of the courage and honor and hope and pride and compassion and pity and sacrifice which have been the glory of his past. The poet's voice need not merely be the record of man, it can be one of the props, the pillars to help him endure and prevail.

10. The phrase "labors under a curse" in paragraph 3 means that the young writer

1. is under **a** curse, so to speak
2. continues to work though he is cursed
3. is condemned to be abject
4. is given to lusts

11. Which of the following inferences CANNOT be drawn from the passage?

1. Good writing is always about the conflicted human heart
2. A writer should overcome his fear and advocate the universal truths
3. A writer should not seek money or fame
4. A writer should espouse the immortality of the human soul

12. Which of the following is the MOST APT title for this passage?

1. The Tragedy of Mankind
2. Human Heart in Conflict
3. The Writer's Duty
4. The Spirit of Man

Directions for questions 13 to 15: *Identify the grammatically CORRECT AND APPROPRIATE option.*

13.
1. As the boys approached the swamp, frogs could be heard croaking.
2. She put her car in the garage because she never leaves it out when it is bad weather
3. In early colonial villages, you had to depend on wood for fuel.
4. Many students who major in mathematics today find employment with computer companies

14.
1. Because we put a wire fence around the chicken yard, the chickens cannot escape
2. The disadvantages of credit cards can offset the advantages, which merits careful consideration
3. When Madhuri visited her mother, she had a cold
4. These sort of things happen

15.
1. The school is opposite to the township building.
2. In chapter I, she accepts her first job as a kitchen maid, but by chapter 3, she is cooking for an Indian prince.

3. Hold the rifle firmly against your shoulder, and then you should take careful aim.
4. I like an occasional cup of coffee, for they give me an added lift.

Directions for question 16: Identify the option with CORRECT punctuation.

16. 1. The people of this company, have, always been aware of the need, for product's of better quality and lower prices.
2. The new residents of Canada faced still more hardships; loneliness, life in a wilderness, even death.
3. In April 1789 the ship left Ceylon with its cargo.
4. A fairy story as distinct, from a merry tale or an animal story, is a serious tale with a human hero and a happy ending.

Directions for questions 17 and 18: *Relate to the passage given below.*

With each passing day, it is getting easier to believe that the acceleration in India s economic growth from around 6% to 8% is here to stay. The hard part is trying to explain why this has happened. How this is explained is important since it has a bearing on our future policy.

As per conventional wisdom, India's growth accelerated to around 6% in the nineties from the historical rate of 3.5% because reforms" had unleashed the pent-up energies of Indian entrepreneurs long shackled by the socialist raj. It slowed subsequently because 'reforms' had lost momentum. The last three years' spurt in growth is the fortuitous result of a global economic boom. Once the world economy slows down, we will be back to 6% growth - unless we proceed with 'second generation' reforms.

However, each of these propositions bristles with problems. It is not true that economic growth rate accelerated to 6% in the nineties. In fact, research has shown that the 'structural break' in India's economic growth occurred not in the early nineties but in the eighties, when economic growth accelerated to close to 6%. The growth in the first decade after reforms was not significantly different from the growth rate in the eighties. The 'reforms' in the sense of market-oriented or even pro-business policies did not commence overnight in 1991, but had commenced earlier. Economic policies in the nineties merely helped consolidate an underlying trend.

Subsequently, the world economy slowed down in 2001-03, which put the brakes on Indian economy. Then came the crucial change, an acceleration to 8% in 2004-06. This cannot be ascribed to any fresh bout of 'reforms' or even to the global boom. There have been important structural changes in the economy. One is the rise in the savings rate from 23.5% in 2000-01 to 29.1% in 2004-05. Most of this increase has come from the turnaround in public-savings. Thanks to the rise in the savings rate, the economy has moved on to an altogether higher investment rate. The second structural change is enhanced export competitiveness, reflected in the rising share of exports. The total exports (trade plus invisible receipts) / GDP ratio has risen sharply from 16.9% in 2000-01 to 24.6% in 2005-06. A third, less noticed change hi recent years is financial deepening. The bank assets / GDP ratio rose from 48% in 2000-01 to 80% in 2005-06 on the back of a surge in bank credit.

One factor is common, to these three structural changes: lower interest rates. The decline in interest rates has helped fiscal consolidation, it has boosted firms' competitiveness and it has led to a huge increase in retail credit. Lower interest rates have been made possible by the rise in inflows on both current and capital accounts. The rise in inflows, in turn, reflects growing overseas confidence in India's economic potential - confidence created by two decades of economic growth of 6%. The sharp depreciation in the rupee in the nineties undoubtedly helped but it is worth recalling that a trend towards rupee depreciation was under way in the eighties itself.

17. Which of the following statements is INCORRECT according to the passage?

1. Growth rate after reforms was similar to that in the eighties
2. Reforms in economic policies had started prior to the nineties
3. Structural changes in the Indian economy have helped lower interest rates
4. Increase in public savings rate has contributed to higher investment rates

18. The passage <u>DOES NOT</u> discuss

1. factors contributing to lower interest rates
2. the importance of world economy on India's reform rates
3. dimensions of structural changes in India's economic reforms
4. the role of the public sector in India's reforms

Directions for question 19: *Consists of four groups of jumbled phrases, of which only ONE is grammatically correct. Identify the CORRECT option.*

19. 1. those command of the language are poor / other thing being equal / themselves effectively are sure to succeed / more rapidly than / people in any fields who can express.

2. for whatever effects they may create / in analyzing prose rhythms or sentence movement / length, and interrelations of rhythmical units / it is always necessary to take into account not only the number, / but also the patterns of stressed and unstressed words.

3. credence to our own recollections of events / accompanied by vivid compelling details / readily spring to mind and is / than other's when our memories / we are likely to give more.

4. what time is left for living / than to see peoples working from mom till night / in cafes and small-talk / and then proceed to fritter away at card-tables / certainly is common nowdays.

Directions for questions 20 to 22: *Choose the option which is OPPOSITE in mean ing to the CAPITALIZED word.*

20. ANATHEMA

1. Salubrious
2. Feral
3. Benediction
4. Curse

21. FECUND

1. Barren
2. Fertile
3. Auspicious
4. Stolid

22. CONCINNITY

1. Congruity
2. Mismatch
3. Deceit
4. Harmony

Directions for question 23: *Identify the grammatically INCORRECT option.*

23. 1. The meeting has been preponed by a week.

2. Either you or Ram is going to look after it.
3. The argument explains neither what went wrong nor how ii should be put right.
4. Customers want not only good service but also courtesy.

Directions for questions 24 to 26: *Relate to the passage given below.*

As a memory researcher, I have long been intrigued by the phenomenon of memory failures. What are the different ways that memory can gel us inter trouble? Bringing together everything I knew of memory's imperfections, lapses, mistakes and distortions, I hit on a way of thinking that helped to make things fall in place. I propose that memory's malfunctions can be divided into seven fundamental transgressions or "sins", which I call *transience, absent-mindedness. Nocking, misuttribution. suggestibility, bias, and persistence.* Just like the ancient seven deadly sins, the memory sins occur frequently in everyday life and can have serious consequences for all of us.

Transience, absent-mindedness and blocking are sins of omission: we fail to bring to mind a desired fact, event or idea. Transience refers to a weakening or loss of memory over time. It is probably not difficult for you to remember now what you have been doing for the past several hours. But if I ask you about the same activities six weeks, six months, or six years from now, chances are you will remember less and less. Transience is a basic feature of memory, and the culprit in many memory problems.

Absent-mindedness involves a breakdown at the interface between attention and memory. Absent-minded memory errors - misplacing keys or eye-glasses, or forgetting a lunch appointment - typically occur because we are preoccupied with distracting issues or concerns, and do not focus attention on what we need to remember. The desired information is not lost over time; it is either never registered in memory to begin with, or not sought after at the moment it is needed, because attention is focused elsewhere.

The third sin, blocking, entails a thwarted search for information we may be desperately trying to retrieve. We have all failed to produce a name to accompany a familiar face. This frustrating experience happens even though we are attending carefully to the task at hand, and even though the desired name has not faded from our minds - as we become acutely aware when we unexpectedly retrieve the blocked name hours or days later.

In contrast to these three sins of omission, the next four sins of misattribution, suggestibility, bias, and persistence are all sins of commission: some form of memory is present, but it is either incorrect or unwanted. The sin of misattribution involves assigning a memory to the wrong source: mistaking fantasy for reality, or incorrectly remembering that a friend told you a bit of trivia that you actually read about in a newspaper. Misattribution is far more common than people realize, and has potentially profound implications in legal settings. The related sin of suggestibility refers to memories that are implanted as a result of leading questions, comments, or suggestions when a person is trying to call up a past experience. Like misattribution, suggestibility is especially relevant to - and can sometimes create havoc within - the legal system.

The sin of bias reflects the powerful influences of our current knowledge and beliefs on how we remember our pasts. We often unknowingly or unconsciously edit or rewrite our previous experiences in light of what we now know or believe. The result can be a skewed-rendering of a specific incident, or even an extended period of our lives, which says more about how we feel *now* than about what happened *then*.

The seventh sin - persistence - entails repeated recall of disturbing information or events that we would prefer to banish from our minds altogether: remembering what we cannot forget, even though we wish that we could. Everyone is familiar with persistence to some degree: recall the last time that you suddenly awoke at 3:00 AM, unable to keep out of your mind a painful blunder on the job or a disappointing result on an important exam. In more extreme cases of serious depression or traumatic experience, persistence can be disabling and even life-threatening.

24. The above passage <u>DOES NOT</u> mention
1. impact of memory malfunctions on daily lives
2. reasons for memory malfunctions
3. relationship between seven memory sins and seven deadly sins
4. lapses and distortions of memory

25. The above passage implies that
1. sins of commission are more serious memory malfunctions than sins of omission
2. the sin of bias arises as a result of misattribution
3. the sin of persistence most frequently occurs when we are asleep
4. sins of omission involve presence of memory in some form or other

26. In the passage, the term "transience" refers to
1. transference
2. truculence
3. ephemeral
4. epiphanic

Directions for questions 27 and 28: *Select the pair of words from the given options that best expresses a relationship <u>SIMILAR</u> to the pair in <u>CAPITAL</u> letters:*

27. OBJURGATE : OBSECRATE
1. abdicate : abrogate
2. renegade : relegate
3. chide : supplicate
4. obfuscate : obligate

28. RESTLESS : RESTIVE

1. flammable : inflammable
2. imminent : eminent
3. haunted : hunted
4. oculist : occultist

Directions for questions 29 and 30: *Fill in the blanks with the option that has the* ***MOST APPROPRIATE*** *set of words.*

29. Children whose ____________ survives parental discipline and who manage to grow up before they blow up are invited to ____________ the university faculty.

1. inquisitiveness, visit
2. interest, address
3. curiosity, join
4. inquiry, join

30. For years, nuclear-power advocates have claimed that nuclear power is the most ____________ form of energy available; but in light of a few facts, one begins to ____________ this claim.

1. cheap, support
2. useful, question
3. expensive, contest
4. economical, doubt

Directions for questions 31 to 33: *Relate to the passage given below.*

Dear Friend, your letter gently but unmistakably intimates that I am a slacker, a slacker in peace as well as in war. that when the World War was raging bitterly I dawdled my time with subjects tike symbolic logic, and that now when the issues of reconstructing a bleeding world demand the efforts of all who care for the future of the human race. I am shirking ray responsibility and wasting my time with Plato and Cicero. Your sweetly veiled charge is true, but I do not feel ashamed of it. On the contrary, when I look upon my professional colleagues who enlisted their philosophies in the war, who added their shrill voices to the roar of the cannons and their little drops of venom to the torrents of national hatreds, I feel that it is they who should write apologies for their course. For philosophers, I take it, are ordained as priests to keep alive the sacred fires on the altar of impartial truth, and I have but faithfully endeavored to keep my oath of office as well as the circumstances would permit. It is doubtless the height of the unheroic to worship truth in the bombproof shelter of harmless mathematics when men are giving their lives for democracy and for public order which is the basis of civilization. But it would be sad if all the priests deserted their altars and became soldiers, if the Sermon on the Mount were utterly erased to give place to manuals of bayonet practice or instructions on the use of poison gas. What avails it to beat the enemy if the sacred fires which we are sworn to defend meanwhile languish and die for want of attendance?

31. Which of the following is the MOST APPROPRIATE title for the passage?

1. Philosophy in wartime : An Apologia
2. Philosophy versus War
3. In defence of Philosophy
4. Philosophy's quarrels with War

32. According to the passage, a philosopher should

1. always shun action and privilege speculation
2. at all tunes promote the disinterested inquiry of his discourse
3. stay away from ideologues
4. support anti-war activism

33. Which of the following statements CANNOT be directly inferred from the passage?

1. The writer has disagreements with his professional colleagues
2. The writer is aware of the sacrifices made in a war
3. The writer considers philosophy a sacred calling
4. The writer is a pacifist

Directions for question 34: *Sentences in the following passage have been variously combined in the options given below. Choose the* *MOST APPROPRIATE AND CONCISE* *option.*

Keepers of private notebooks are a different breed altogether. They are lonely and resistant rearrangers of things. They are anxious malcontents. They are children afflicted at birth with some presentiment of loss.

34. 1. Keepers of private notebooks are a different breed altogether, lonely and resistant rearrangers of things, anxious malcontents, children afflicted at birth with some presentiment of loss

2. Keepers of private notebooks, who are lonely, resistant rearrangers and anxious malcontents, are children afflicted at birth with some presentiment of loss.

3. Keepers of private notebooks, a different breed in being lonely, resistant rearrangers of things and anxious malcontents, are children afflicted at birth with some presentiment of loss.

4. None of the above.

Directions for question 35: *Choose the option which DOES NOT have a similar meaning to the sentence given below:*

Some of the students reflect a growing confidence in their ability to manage successfully the demands placed upon them by their own ambitions, by their ability to construct intelligent messages, and by their listeners often irascible modes of responding.

35. 1. Listeners' response modes and their own personal ambitions place great demands on students.

2. Students construct intelligent messages to cope with listeners demands

3. Students are becoming increasingly capable of managing multiple demands placed on them

4. Ability to construct intelligent messages helps students cope with increasing demands arising from personal ambitions and listeners' responses.

Directions for questions 36 to 38: *Choose the option that is CLOSEST in meaning to the CAPITALIZED word.*

36. MIRIFIC

1. Marvellous　2. Mundane

3. Mystical　4. Morbid

37. PLEBEIAN

1. Vulgar　2. Aristocratic

3. Prophetic　4. Certainty

38. FIDUCIAL

1. Official　2. Deceit

3. Trustworthy　4. Parochial

Directions for question 39: *Identify the option with INCORRECT spellings.*

39. 1. On the twelfth of every month, the psychiatrist visits the organization

2. Entering the sanctum of South Indian temples dressed in western clothes is considered sacreligeous.

3. We try to accommodate as many students as possible in our hostels.

4. We received the mattress after repeated requests.

DIRECTION for question 40: *The direct speech in question is rewritten as reported speech (indirect form) in the options below. Identify the grammatically CORRECT option.*

40. The President said to the General, "Is your army well supplied? Is it ready for battle?"

1. The President asked the General whether his army was well supplied and whether it was ready for battle.

2. The President asked the General whether his army was well supplied and is it ready for battle.
3. The President asked the General if his army is well supplied and if it is ready for battle.
4. The President asked the General whether his army is well supplied and was it ready for battle.

ANSWER

1. 2	**2.** 1	**3.** 4	**4.** 3	**5.** 4	**6.** 1	**7.** 2
8. 2	**9.** 1	**10.** 3	**11.** 2	**12.** 3	**13.** 1	**14.** 2
15. 1	**16.** 1	**17.** 3	**18.** 4	**19.** 2	**20.** 3	**21.** 1
22. 2	**23.** 3	**24.** 3	**25.** 1	**26.** 3	**27.** 3	**28.** 1
29. 3	**30.** 4	**31.** 3	**32.** 2	**33.** 4	**34.** 1	**35.** 2
36. 1	**37.** 1	**38.** 3	**39.** 2	**40.** 1		

EXPLANATIONS

1. 2 Sceptical – doubtful, Circumvent – Avoid Elusive – Evasive

2. 1 2 & 3 are clearly ruled out as these are out of scope. Editorial don't have advertising potential as 4 lay so 1 is the answer

3. 4 It talks of High Technology as source of advertorials & does not talk of its impact

4. 3 3

5. 4 4

6. 1 1

7. 2 Pride is a group of lions. Pride stays in a forest colony is a group of houses. Colony lies in a city

8. 2 Common to Poet & Prophet – vision Common to killer & Terrorist – Violence

9. 1 2 means that teaching would be appreciated after 50years which is not given in original sentence 3 & 4 are not at all close to the meanings So 1 is the best answer

10. 3

11. 2 The author says in 3rd paragraph that an author needs to be afraid & story on universal truth is ephemeral

12. 3

13. 1 2........ when the weather is bad 3 .... You depended 4........ find employment in

14. 2 1........ the chicken3........ she had cold

15. 1 2........ she cooks 3........ and then take 4........ for it gives me.....

16. 1

17. 3 1, 2, 4, are explicitly given in the passage in 2nd & 3rd paragraphs

18. 4 Nowhere author talks of role of public sector in India's reforms.

19. 2 1 . .....language is poor/........2 ..../people in any field.......3 ....collection of events/.........4 ..../an to see people.......from morn till night

20. 3 Anathema – curse

21. 1 Fecund – Fertile

22. 2 Concinvity – harmony, Congruity

23. 3 The argument explains neither what went wrong nor what should be done to put it right

24. 3 No where passage talks of relationship between seven memory sins and seven deadly sins. The author gives it as a simile.

25. 1 4 – its sins of commission not sins of omission2 – Sins of bias & misattribution are 2 separate sins 3 – Sins of persistence can occur

26. 3 Transicence – Short lived, evanescent

27. 3 Objurgate to reproach vehemently, Obsecrate – to revereChide – to express disapproval of , reproach Supplicate – pray humblyThe words in both pairs have similar corresponding meanings

28. 1 Restive is properly applied to a feeling of impatience or uneasiness induced by external coercion restriction is not a general synonym for restless Similarly, flammable and inflammable means the same things.

29. 3 Visit & address can't fill 2nd blank rubbing out option 1 & 2 curiosity brings out meaning of sentence properly so 3 is the best option.

30. 4 The 2 blanks are to be filled with contrasting words so 1 & 3 are ruled out 2 and 4 are the contenders but 3 is the better option.

31. 3 Read the lines,' On the contrary................apologies for their course.' Options 1,2 and 4 do not gel with the main idea floated in the passage. Read lines, 'For philosophers............would permit.'

32. 2 Option 1, 3 and 4 are against the grain of the psg.

33. 4 Options 1,2 and 3 are clearly mentioned in the psg.

34. 1 The sentence talks of qualities of keepers of Private notebooks which are aptly brought out by option 1

35. 2 The sentences talks of the factors that place demands on the students and how they cope with them 2 is wrong as constructing intelligent message & listeners demands are 2 types of demands.

36. 1 Mirific – Marvellous

37. 1 Plebeian – Vulgar

38. 3 Fiducial – Trustworthy

39. 2 Sacrilegious

40. 1

JMET 2008

Number of Questions – 30
Time : 30 M.

VERBAL COMMUNICATON

Directions for questions 1-4: *Relate to the passage given below:*

Beliefs' soften the hardships, even can make them pleasant. In God, man can find very strong consolation and support. Without Him, man has to depend upon himself. At testing moments, vanity, if any, evaporates and man cannot dare to defy the general beliefs; if he does, then we must conclude that he has got certain other strength than mere vanity. This is exactly the situation now. Judgment is already too well known. Within s week it is to be pronounced. What is the consolation with the exception of the idea that I am going to sacrifice my life for a cause? A God-believing Hindu might be expecting to be reborn as a king, a Muslim or a Christian might dream of the luxuries to be enjoyed in paradise and the reward he is to get for his sufferings and sacrifice. But what am I to expect? I know the moment the rope is fitted round my neck and rafters removed, from under my feet: that will be the final moment. I, or to be more precise, my soul, as interpreted in the metaphysical terminology, shall all be finished there. Nothing further.

A short life of struggle with no such magnificent end shall in itself be the reward if I have the courage to take it in that light. That is all. With no selfish motive or desire to be awarded hear or hereafter, quite disinterestedly have I devoted my life to the cause of independence, because I could not do otherwise. The day we find a great number of men and women with this psychology who cannot devote themselves to anything else than the service of mankind and emancipation of the suffering humanity that day shall inaugurate the era of liberty.

Not to become a king, nor to gain any other rewards here, or in the next birth or after death in paradise, shall they be inspired to challenge the oppressors, exploiters, establish liberty and peace shall they tread this – to their individual selves perilous and to their noble selves the only glorious imaginable path. Is the pride in their in noble cause to be misinterpreted as vanity? Who dares to utter such an abominable epithet? To him, I say either he is a fool or a knave. Let us forgive him for he cannot realize the depth, the emotion, the sentiment and the noble feelings that surge in that heart. His heart is dead as a mere limp of flesh, his eyes are week, the evils of other interpreted as vanity. It is sad and miserable but there is no help.

You go and oppose the prevailing faith, you go and criticize a hero, a great man, who is generally believed to be above criticism because he is thought to be infallible, the strength of your argument shall force the multitude to decry you as vainglorious. This is due to the mental stagnation: criticism and independent thinking are the two indispensable qualities of a revolutionary. Because Mahatmaji is great, therefore none should criticize him. Because he has risen above, therefore everything he says- may be in the field of politics or not you must say, "Yes. That's true". This mentality does not lead towards progress. It is rather too obviously, reactionary.

1. Which one of the following statements can be deduced from the above passage?

1. Individuals who neither believe in God nor in the infallibility of great men are arrogant.
2. Belief is convenient as it even makes a hard reality at present more bearable because of promise of a better future.
3. Only some individuals are able to attain greatness and by following them uncritically the society can make significant progress.
4. If you do not believe in God, then you never hope to achieve anything great in life.

2. Which of the following statements BEST capture the essence of the passage?

1. When we criticize a great man like Mahatmaji, we are motivated by arrogance and a desire to question anything good through meaningless arguments.
2. All human being ought to desist from believing anything in order to be able to achieve something meaningful.

3. The author is trying to present his defense for not believing in the existence of God, even though it is probably more convenient to do so, than going against the generally accepted norms of the society.
4. It is wrong to believe in God for achieving kingship or for rewards in this world, or for paradise after death, and instead, one should believe in God without expecting anything in return.

3. The word 'vainglorious' as used in the passage is EXACTLY OPPOSITE in meaning to:

1. truthful
2. proud.
3. dishonest
4. humble

4. Which of the following statements is NOT TRUE as per the passage?

1. Pride in a noble cause should not be interpreted as vanity.
2. Service to mankind is the ultimate path to freedom.
3. Criticizing heroes and great men can lead to progress.
4. The author is upset because he has nothing to expect in the after life.

Directions for question 5: *Consists of four groups of jumbled phrases, of which only one is grammatically CORRECT. Identify the CORRECT option.*

5.
1. growth and ongoing success/and providing a strong platform for sustainable/the complimentary expertise of/both these companies will create.
2. investment as a money-market account,/although not quite as liquid an/a certificate of deposit is recommended/by financial experts for its high yield.
3. understanding how countries grow rich/but not as the panacea once looks like/the rule of law has reestablished/itself as a cultural concept.
4. a range of skills unique in any age/even present day scholar's who have been able/trace the prominent influence of Leonardo's predecessors on/his scientific theories and designs still credit Da Vinci.

Directions for question 6: *Consists of four groups of jumbled phrases, of which only one is grammatically INCORRECT. Identify the INCORRECT option.*

6.
1. of factors influence diffusion between continents/related to these factors by affecting diffusion/within continents is a third set
2. but historians are nevertheless able/by retrospective tests/to evaluate related hypotheses
3. more starting materials and more/it is just that some environments provide/favorable conditions than do other environments
4. with formation of complex societies/ these correlations suggest that/population density has some- thing to do

Directions for question 7 and 8: *Fill in the blanks with the MOST APPROPRIATE pair given in the options:*

7. Today's __________________ wealth of some nations conceals its long-standing fundamental_______________ in feeding itself.

1. substantial, ability
2. perpetual, belief
3. a martyr, killed
4. ostentatious, urge

8. Because he was ____________________, he __________________ human society.

1. a stereotype, followed
2. a misanthrope, shunned
3. good, represented
4. anthropologist, helped

Directions for question 9 and 10: *The sentences given in the question, when properly sequenced, from a coherent paragraph. Each sentence is labeled with a letter. Choose the most logical order of sentences from among the given options to construct a coherent paragraph.*

9. a. We are to make sure that we do not only see our destination being reached but also see our bodies reaching them.

b. Some of us feel that deep down inside, we lack the enthusiasm for accomplishing what we really desire.

c. If this is the problem, them we are to practice our exercises.

d. This may be a sign that we lack respect for our inner self which results in low self-esteem.

1. a-b-d-c 2. b-d-c-a
3. c-a-d-b 4. a-c-a-b

10. a. Each new encounter with a new culture is fraught with peril.

b. When successful, the feelings really are very much as though a major victory has been won.

c. Then the events occur and you return home either triumphant or defeated.

d. It is preceded by anxiety and information collection and rehearsal.

1. d-c-b-a 2. a-d-c-a
3. c-b-a-d 4. B-a-d-c

Direction for question 11: *Complete the sentence given in Question 11, by replacing the underlined potion with the most suitable phrase from the given options:*

11. Because mobile phones emit signals that can interfere with cockpit-to-control tower trans-missions, airplane passengers' use of these instruments at all time's that the airplane is in motion, even while being on the ground, are prohibited.

1. at all times during which the airplane, even while on the ground, is in motion, are
2. during times of the airplane as being in motion, even while on the ground, is
3. when the airplane is in motion, even while on the ground, is
4. during airplane motion, even when it is on the ground, are

Directions for questions 12-15: *Read the passage given below and answer.*

The starting point for our discussion is the common view expressed in the saying "Necessity is the mother of invention." That is, inventions supposedly arise when a society has an unfulfilled need. Would-be inventors, motivated by the prospect of money or fame, perceive the need and try to meet it. Some inventor finally comes up with a solution superior to an existing, unsatisfactory technology. Society adopts the solution if it is compatible with the society's values and other technologies. Some inventions do conform to this commonsense view of necessity as inventions' mother. Eli Whitney's 1794 invention of a cotton gin to replace laborious hand cleaning of pumping out water out of British coal mines were come such instances. These familiar examples deceive us into assuming that other major inventions were also responses to perceived needs. In fact, many or most inventions were developed by people driven by curiosity or by a love of tinkering, in the absence of any initial demand for the product they 'needed' it. Still other devices, invented to serve one purpose, eventually found most of their use for other, unanticipated purposes. Some inventions in search of an initial use included most of the major technological breakthroughs of modern times, including the airplane, the automobile, internal combustion engine, electric light bulb, the phonograph and transistor. Thus, invention is paten the mother of necessity, rather than vice versa. For example, when Edison built his first phonograph in 1877, he published an article listing ten isles to which his invention might be put. Reproduction of music did not figure high on that list. Only after 20 years did Edison reluctantly concede that the main use of his phonograph was to play and record music. Again, when Nikolas Otto built his first gas engine, in 1866, horses had been supplying people's land transportation needs for nearly 600 years, supplemented increasingly by steam-powered railroads, for several decades. There was no crisis in the availability of horses, no dissatisfaction with railroads. In 1896, Gottfried Daimler built the rich. Public contentment with horses and railroads remained high until World War I, when the military concluded that it really did need trucks. Intensive postwar lobbying by truck manufacturers and armies finally convinced the public of its own needs and enabled trucks to begin to supplant horse drawn wagons in industrialized countries. Thus the commonsense view of invention that served as our starting point reverses the role of invention and need, and probably overstated the importance of rare geniuses such as Watt and Edison. That "heroic theory of invention" is encouraged by patent law, because an applicant for a patent must probably the novelty of the invention submitted. In truth, technology develops cumulatively, and through the inventions and improvements of many predecessors and successors, rather than in isolated heroic acts, and it finds most of its uses after it has been invented, rather than benign invented to meet a foreseen need.

12. The MOST APPROPRIATE title for the passage would be:

1. Mother of Necessity
2. Inventors or Villains?
3. The Heroic Theory of Invention
4. Inventions, not Necessities

13. Which of the following statements is INCORRECT as per the given passage?

1. Patent laws facilitate unnecessary inventions.
2. Inventions give rise to needs in society.
3. Curiosity is the mother of invention.
4. The military helped to popularize the use of trucks.

14. According to the passage:

1. airplanes and automobiles were invented out of curiosity.
2. curiosity and necessity are the main obstacles for invention.
3. the applications of an invention are often not apparent immediately.
4. society helps to fulfill an inventor's need for money and fame.

15. The last sentence of the passage implies that:

1. the author does not believe in the concept of "heroic inventions".
2. an invention does not always have to be in response to some perceived need.
3. isolated heroic acts do not give rise to inventions.
4. initial inventors are never recognized.

Direction for question 16: *From the options given in question 16, choose the sentence which contains an INCORRECT SPELLING:*

16.
1. The dress complements your hair colour.
2. When such adulatory remarks are circulated, we can only despise those who produce them.
3. There are too many dilettantes and not enough serious workers.
4. He has been a mediocre student all his life.

Direction for question 17: *The direct speech in Question 17 is rewritten in the indirect from in the options below. Identify the grammatically CORRECT option.*

17. He said, "I am upset. My boss is not happy with my performance."

1. He said that he was upset since his boss was not happy with his performance.
2. He said his boss is upset because he is unhappy with performance.
3. He said that he is upset as because his boss is not happy with his performance.
4. He said he was upset with his performance since his boss is not happy.

Directions for question 18-20: *Choose the grammatically CORRECT option from the sentences given below:*

18.
1. I requested the principal to remove me from the operation since it was going against my principals.
2. I need to move further away from home in order to continue farther education.
3. Knowledge of economical theories not be helpful in making economic products.
4. I have been working continuously for the last three months while she is continually taking days off.

19.
1. Each of the finalists were exceptionally good and the choice for the best one among all three was very difficult indeed.

2. Each of the finalists was exceptionally good and choosing the best one among the three was very difficult indeed.
3. Each of the finalists was exceptionally good and choosing the best one between the three was very difficult indeed.
4. Each of the finalists was exceptionally good and choices among all three were very difficult indeed.

20. 1. People in this bar often orders foods with beers. Foods hear taste nice and beers are cheap.
2. People in this bar often order foods with beers. Foods hear tastes nice and beers are cheap.
3. People in this bar often orders foods with beers. Foods hear tastes nice and beer is cheap.
4. People in this bar often orders foods with beers. Foods hear taste nice and beers is cheap.

Directions for questions 21 and 22: *Select the pair of words from the given options that best expresses a relationship SIMILAR to the pair in CAPITAL LETTERS.*

21. INDUSTRIOUS : ASSIDUOUS
1. impoverished : poor
2. affluent : impecunious
3. diagnosis : prognosis
4. Impartial : biased

22. SIDEREAL : STARS
1. ethereal : planets
2. chimeral : matter
3. horticultural : plants
4. supernatural : heaven

Directions for questions 23 and 24: *Choose the word which is CLOSEST in meaning to the word given in CAPITAL LETTERS:*

23. DECIMATE
1. reduce
2. destroy
3. bifurcate
4. divide

24. MORIBUND
1. terminal
2. morbid
3. temporary
4. mundane

Directions for questions 25 and 26: *Choose the word is OPPOSITE in meaning to the word given in CAPITAL LETTERS:*

25. FATUOUS
1. stupid
2. obese
3. intelligent
4. sincere

26. TRACTABLE
1. obedient
2. capable
3. corruptible
4. stubborn

Directions for questions 27 – 30: *Relate to the passage given below:*

Can poor countries afford to be green? That is a question which politicians in the developing world have often asked rather pointedly. To them, it seems that the obsession of some rich types with preserving forests and saving cuddly animals like pandas or lemurs, while paying less attention to the human beings living nearby, is both cynical and hypocritical. There is of decades of course plenty of evidence that greenery and growth are not polar opposites. After decades of expansion in China and other fast-emerging economies, some of the negative side-effects and their impact on human welfare, above all the death toll caused by foul air and water, are horribly clear. Yet, the relationship between growth and the state of environment is far from simple. Some experts feel that poor countries have been quite right to challenge the sort of green orthodoxy which rejects the very idea of economic growth. Indeed, the single biggest variable in determining a country's ranking is income per head. But that doesn't imply that economic growth automatically leads to an improvement in the environment. Growth dose offer solutions to the sorts of environmental woes (local air pollution, for example) that directly kill humans. This matters, because about a quarter of all deaths in the world have some link to environmental factors. Most of the victims are poor people who are already vulnerable because of bad living conditions, lack of access to medicine, and malnutrition. Among the killers, especially of children, in which the environment plays a role, are diarrhoea, respiratory infections and malaria. These diseases reinforce a vicious circle of poverty and hopelessness by depressing production. According to the World Bank, the economic burden on society caused by bad environmental health amounts to between 2% and 5% of GDP. As poor countries get richer, they usually invest heavily in environmental improvements, such as cleaning up water supplies and improving sanitation, that boost human health but the link between growth and environmentally benign outcomes is much less clear when it comes to the sort of pollution that fouls up nature (such as acid rain, which poisons lakes and forests) as opposed to directly killing human beings. The key to addressing that sort of pollution is not just money but good governance. Hence, the poor Dominican Republic is much healthier than nearby Haiti, Costa Rica is far ahead of Nicaragua, in spite of broadly similar nature and resources, and wealthy Belgium is the sick man of Western Europe, with an environmental record worse than that of many developing countries.

27. The passage DOES NOT talk about:
1. the impact of environmental health on economic growth.
2. factors determining good governance.
3. the impact of economic growth on environmental health.
4. environmental factors affecting child mortality.

28. The MOST APPROPRIATE title for the passage would be:
1. How Green is their Growth?
2. Green Orthodoxy
3. Growth us Greenery
4. Global Warming

29. Which one of the following can be MOST APPROPRIATELY inferred from the passage?
1. Environmental health should be the single biggest variable in determining a country's ranking.
2. Poor countries cannot afford to save forests or protect cuddly animals.
3. Haiti, Nicaragua and Belgium are the most polluted countries in the word.
4. Economic progress can help to ease environmental woes, as long as the governance is good.

30. Which one of the following statements CANNOT be inferred from the passage?
1. Fast-emerging economies are responsible for polluting their environment.
2. Bad environmental health affects a country's production.
3. Environment can be protected only after economic prosperity has been achieved.
4. The link between the state of the environment and human health is ambiguous.

Explanations

Answer key

1. 2	**2.** 2	**3.** 4	**4.** 3	**5.** 2	**6.** 2	**7.** 1
8. 4	**9.** 2	**10.** 2	**11.** 3	**12.** 1	**13.** 1	**14.** 3
15. 2	**16.** 4	**17.** 1	**18.** 4	**19.** 2	**20.** 3	**21.** 1
22. 3	**23.** 2	**24.** 4	**25.** 3	**26.** 4	**27.** 2	**28** 1
29. 4	**30.** 3					

MAT – Feb. 2007

Number of Questions – 40
Time : 30 M.

Directions for questions 1 to 4: *Fill in the blanks.*

1. Professionals focus their ________ on fulfilling their responsibilities and achieving results, not on ________ a particular image.

1. leadership – attributing
2. planning – devising
3. abilities – contributing
4. energies – portraying

2. When you are living with your ________ values and principles, you can be straightforward, honest and ________.

1. inherited – distinct
2. core – up-front
3. innate – durable
4. cultural – perceptive

3. In the role of a counsellor, you are an authority figure whose objective is to ________ attentively and sensitively to employees who ________ you with their feelings.

1. manage – direct
2. projects – focus
3. listen – trust
4. concentrate – believe

4. If a junior executive neglects his professional development and ________ education, he can easily and quickly become obsolete in a world changing at ________ rates.

1. higher — vulnerable
2. management — voluminous
3. better — supreme
4. continuing — dizzying

Directions for questions 5 to 8: *Each of these questions has an underlined part. Choose the option that best replaces the underlined part.*

5. The political masters of the health care system have not listened to professional health planners because it **has not been profitable for them to do** that thing.

1. has not been profitable for them to do so.
2. has not been profitable for them to do that thing.
3. has been unprofitable for them to do that thing.
4. has been unprofitable for them to do so.

6. Most bacterial population grown in controlled conditions will quickly expand to limit the food supply **produce toxic waste products that inhibit further growth, and reached and equilibrium state within a relatively short time.**

1. will have produce toxic waste products that inhibit further growth and reach equilibrium.
2. will then produce toxic waste products that inhibit further growth and reach equilibrium.
3. will by produce toxic waste products that inhibit further growth and reach equilibrium.
4. produce toxic waste products that inhibit further growth and reach equilibrium.

7. It could be argued that the most significant virtue of a popular democracy is not the right to participate in the selection of leaders, **but rather that it affirms** our importance in the scheme of things.

1. but rather is affirmation of
2. but rather that it affirms
3. but rather it's affirmation in terms of
4. but instead of that, its affirming that

8. Long popular among the connoisseurs of Indian music, Ravi Shankar first impressed western listeners with his phenomenal technical virtuosity, **but they soon came to appreciate his music as an artful** expression of an older culture's musical insight.

1. but it soon occurred that they appreciated his artful music as an
2. but they soon came to appreciate his music as an artful
3. but soon this was surpassed by an appreciation of it as an artful
4. which was soon surpassed by an even deeper appreciation of it as an artful

Directions for questions 9 to 12: *Each question has a group of sentences marked A, B, C, and D. Arrange these to form a logical sequence.*

9. A. We tend to see the similarity within a category as being more important, and the similarity between different categories as being less important, than either actually is.

B. Given a small amount of information about a person, we are ready to classify them as a member of a particular group and then to infer all kinds of additional facts about them, as if all members of the group were the same in most respects.

C. Our tendency to classify and label everything can lead us into the error of seeing the word as made up of only those categories for which we have names.

D. Expecting too much of the descriptive power of languages is itself a serious cause of distorted thinking.

1. DCBA
2. DBAC
3. BDAC
4. BCDA

10. A. Some of us, as a result, gain an overall impression of people as either all good or all bad, making further assumptions on this basis.

B. An example of the assumption some patients make that doctors with a good "bedside manner" are also more technically competent as others who do not relate as well to their patients.

C. This is what the psychologists refer to as halo effect.

D. We have a strong tendency of associate positive attributes with other positive attributes and negative ones with each other.

1. DCBA
2. DABC
3. DBCA
4. DACB

11. A. In the past, the customized tailoring units were localized to the township or city and catered exclusively to domestic demand.

B. Traditionally, Indian preferred custom made clothing and the concept of ready to wear is a relatively recent one,

C. Consumer awareness of styling issues and the convenience afforded by ready to wear helped the RMG industry make small inroads into the domestic market in the 1980s.

D. The customized tailoring outfits have always been a major source of clothing for domestic market.

1. BDAC
2. BCDA
3. CDBA
4. DBAC

12. A. Participation involves more than the formal sharing of decisions.

B. Through anticipation, individuals or organizations consider trends and make plans, shielding institutions from trauma of learning by shock.

C. Innovative learning involves both anticipation and participation.

D. It is an attitude characterized by the co-operation, dialogue and empathy.

1. ABCD
2. BCDA
3. CBAD
4. DABC

Directions for questions 13 to 16: *Each of these questions has a sentence with four alternatives. Choose the alternative which best conveys the content of the given sentence correctly.*

13. No officer had ought to be put into a situation where he has to choose between his love for his family and the responsibilities accompanying his duty.

1. No officer had ought to be put into a situation in which he has to choose between his love for his family and the responsibilities accompanying his duty.
2. No officer had ought to be put into a situation where he has to choose between his love, for his family and the responsibilities accompanying his duty.

3. No officer should be put into a situation where he has to choose between his love for his family and the responsibilities accompanying his duty.
4. No officer ought to be put into a situation in which he has to choose between his love for his family and the responsibilities accompanying his duty.

14. Being a realist, the detective could not accept the statement of the accused that UFOs had caused the disturbance.

1. Since he was a realist, the detective could not accept the statement of the accused that UFOs had caused the disturbance.
2. Being a realist, the detective could not accept the statement of the accused that UFOs had caused the disturbance.
3. Being that he was a realist, the detective could not accept the statement of the accused that UFOs had caused the disturbance.
4. Realist that he was, the detective could not accept the statement of the accused that UFOs had caused the disturbance.

15. Ever since the sting operation, there has been much opposition from they who maintain that it was an unauthorised act.

1. Ever since the sting operation, there has been much opposition from they who maintain that it had been an unauthorised act.
2. Ever since the sting operation, there has been much opposition from they who maintain that it was an unauthorized act.
3. Ever since the sting operation, there has been much opposition from those who maintain that it was an unauthorized act.
4. Ever since the sting operation, there has been much opposition from those maintaining that it was an unauthorised act.

16. The trend toward a decrease in the working hours is already evident in the longer weekend given to employees in many multinational organisations.

1. The trend toward a decrease in the working hours is all ready evident in the longer week-end given to employees in many multinational organisations.
2. The trend toward a decrease in the working hours is already evident in the longer week-end given to employees in many multinational organisations.
3. The trend toward a decrease in the working hours is already evident in the longer week-end given to employees in many multinational organisation.
4. The trend toward a decrease in the working hours is all in already evident in the longer weekend given to employees in many multinational organisations.

Directions for questions 17 to 20: *Attempt these questions independent of each other.*

17. Many of the junk foods on the market today, doughnuts, burgers and pizza, have less nutrients than natural foods, which were dominant a decade or two ago. Many nutritionists claim that pizza and doughnuts give less nourishment than natural foods. A spokesman of a leading junk food company — Pizza House — stated recently that an examination of grade school students shows less nutritional deficiency than in their parents' time. Hence, junk foods are not as bad as made out to be.

Which of the following, if true, would tend to strengthen the view of the spokesman ?

1. Fewer junk foods were available to the parents.
2. Grade school children reported eating no breakfast at all.
3. Adults claim to eat junk foods as well as natural foods.
4. Both (1) and (3)

18. Throughout the first decade of the 21st century, net increases in Indian direct investments in the Far East (funds outflows) exceeded net new Far East direct investment in India.

Each of the following, if true, could help to account for this trend except

1. Labour mobility was higher in India than in the Far East.
2. Land values in the Far East were increasing at a faster rate than in India.
3. The cost of labour (wages) was consistently lower in the Far East than in India.
4. Corporate liquidity was lower in India than in the Far East.

19. Of the world's largest AIDS cases countries in 2010, three had the same share of world AIDS patients as they had in 2000. These three countries may serve as examples of countries that succeeded in holding steady their share of the AIDS disease.

Which of the following, if true, would most seriously undermine the idea that these countries serve as examples as described above ?

1. Countries should strive to reduce their share of the total AIDS patients in the world, rather than try to hold it constant.
2. Of the three countries two had a much larger share of world AIDS incidence in 2000 than in 2010.
3. The three countries have different rates of population growth.
4. None of these

20. The cost of housing in many urban parts of India has become so excessive that many young couples, with above-average salaries, can only afford small apartments. **EMI** and rent commitments are so huge that they cannot consider the possibility of starting a family since a new baby would probably mean either the mother or father giving up a well-paid position — something they can ill afford. The lack of or *great* cost of child-care facilities further precludes the return of both parents to work.

Which of the following adjustments could practically be made to the situation described above which would allow young couples to improve their housing prospects ?

1. Encourage couples to have one child only.
2. Encourage couples to remain childless.
3. Encourage young couples to move to cheaper areas for living.
4. None of these is likely to have an impact on the current situation.

Directions for questions 21 to 36: *Read the passages to answer the questions that follow each passage.*

Passage – I

After President George W. Bush signed the United States — India Nuclear Cooperation Bill, he called up Prime Minister Manmohan Singh to tell him how pleased he was at this development. While welcoming this event, the Prime Minister took the opportunity to tell the President that there remained areas of concern that needed to be addressed during the negotiation of the bilateral agreement (called the 123 agreement, after the relevant clause number in the U.S. Atomic Energy Act, 1954). The U.S. has entered into some twenty-five 123 agreements with various countries, including the one concerning Tarapur. The Tarapur agreement concluded in 1963 was unique in that it guaranteed supplies of enriched uranium fuel from the U.S. for running the Tarapur reactors for their entire life. However, after 1978 the U.S. did not supply fuel saying its domestic legislation (under the Nuclear Non-Proliferation Act) prevented it from doing so. India argued that Tarapur was an inter-governmental agreement and hence it had to be honoured by the U.S. But to no avail. However, later, the U.S. allowed France to supply fuel to India. Subsequently, the USSR (now Russia) and even China supplied fuel for Tarapur. The lesson from the Tarapur episode is that U.S. breached with impunity even a cast-iron guarantee it had furnished. Considerable bitterness grew between the U.S. and India and extended to many other areas beyond the nuclear one. When India agreed, reluctantly, in March 2006 to put imported reactors under "safeguards in perpetuity", the U.S. consented to the Indian insistence on assurances of fuel supply. This meant India could build up a stockpile of fuel to tide over disruption in supply and the U.S. would agree to work with other countries namely Russia, France, and Britain to arrange alternate supplies. The U.S. legislation, based on the Hyde Bill, forbids India building up a stockpile of nuclear fuel. It also obligates the U.S. administration to work with other Nuclear Supplier Group countries to get them to suspend supplies to India, if the U.S. has done so under some provision of the Hyde Bill. It is not evident how the U.S. can address the legitimate concerns of India on continued fuel supply, given the boundaries set by the Hyde Bill. With regard to future nuclear tests, the Prime Minister has said, India is only committed to a voluntary moratorium. A moratorium is only a temporary holding off of an activity, conditioned by specific circumstances that obtained at the time when such a declaration was made. It cannot be construed as a permanent ban. The Hyde Bill has sought to make the moratorium into a permanent ban. However, there is no such restraint imposed on the U.S., China. Pakistan or any other country. In bringing up this issue, I do not wish to suggest that I favour a resumption of tests by India. But India cannot prevent other countries from, carrying out tests. It is, therefore, unacceptable that India forfeits its right to test for all time to come under the agreement with the U.S. Even if the 123 agreement is silent on the issue, Indian negotiators must put this issue on the table. The Hyde Bill calls for suspension of all cooperation and fuel supplies and even calls for return of all equipment and materials supplied earlier in the event of a test. It baffles one how India can return reactor installations that might have been operated a few years, were such a contingency to arise in future. The differences over the definition of "full civilian nuclear cooperation" have been discussed in the media. The Indian understanding was that reprocessing of spent fuel, enrichment of uranium, and production of heavy water also formed part of the term "full civilian nuclear cooperation." In the congressional debate, it has been noted that these were construed by the U.S. to be in the nature of military activities and not civilian. India's future plans for thorium utilisation for civil nuclear power depend crucially or reprocessing. Similarly, civil nuclear power units using natural uranium require heavy water as reactor coolant and moderator. Equally if India were to embark on a sizeable light water reactor programme, it may like to have control on supply of enriched uranium for economic and supply security reasons. India has technologies of its own in these areas and will develop them further in the years ahead. If the Indo-U.S agreement moves ahead in the manner its sponsors have speculated, in a few decades from now some 90 per cent of the nuclear installations in India would be open to International Atomic Energy Agency inspections. In that scenario, how can India reconcile to the embargo from nuclear advanced countries on the export of enrichment, reprocessing, and heavy water technologies ? Even if the issue were to be papered over now, it will then look from India's point of view to have been a very bad bargain.

21. What is the Indian understanding of the definition of "full civilian nuclear cooperation" ?

1. Enrichment of uranium
2. Reprocessing of spent fuel
3. Production of heavy water
4. All the above

22. With reference to the passage, select which of the following statement(s) is/are incorect ?

A. U.S. did not supply fuel to India after 1987.

B. The Hyde Bill calls for suspension of all cooperation and fuel supplies.

C. India can prevent other countries from carrying out the test.

1. A and B
2. B only
3. A and C
4. A, B and C

23. What was the uniqueness of the Tarapur agreement that was concluded in 1963 ?

1. It guaranteed supplies of enriched uranium fuel from the U.S. for running the Tarapur reactors for entire life.
2. It prevented other countries from carrying out nuclear tests.
3. It addresses the legitimate concerns of India on fuel supply.
4. All the above

24. Which of the following countries supplied fuel for Tarapur ?

1. France
2. U.S.A.
3. USSR and France
4. France, USSR and China

Passage – II

Not even a three-day brainstorming session among top psychologists at the Chinese University could unravel one of the world's greatest puzzles — how the Chinese mind ticks. Michael Bond had reason to pace the pavement of the Chinese University campus last week. The psychologist who co-ordinated and moderated a three-day seminar in Chinese psychology and most of the participants came a long way to knock heads. "If a bomb hits this building," muttered Bond, half-seriously," it would wipe out the whole discipline. But the only thing that went-off in the Cho Yiu Conference Hall of Chinese University was the picking of brains, the pouring out of brains and a refrain from an on-going mantra: "more work needs to be done" or "we don't know". Each of the 36 participants was allowed 30 minutes plus use of an over-head projector to condense years of research into data and theories. Their content spilled over from 20 areas of Chinese behaviour, including reading, learning styles, psychopathology, social interaction, personality and modernisation. An over-riding question for observers, however, was why, in this group of 21 Chinese and 15 non-Chinese, weren't there more professionals from mainland China presenting research on the indigenous people ? Michael Philips, a psychiatrist who works in Hubei Province, explained: "The Cultural Revolution silenced and froze the research," said the Canadian-born doctor who has lived and worked in China for more than 10 years. "And 12 years later, research is under way but it is too early to have anything yet. Besides, most of the models being used are from the West anyway." In such a specialised field, how can non-Chinese academics do research without possessing fluency in Chinese ? Those who cannot read, write or speak the language usually team up with Chinese colleagues. "In 10 years, we won't be able to do this. It's a money thing," said William Gabrenya of Florida Institute of Technology, who described himself as an illiterate Gweilo who lacks fluency in Chinese. He said that 93 per cent of the non-Chinese authors in his field cannot read Chinese. Dr. Gabrenya raised questions such as why is research dependent on university students, why is research done on Chinese people in coastal cities (Singapore, Taiwan, Shanghai and Hong Kong) but not inland ? "Chinese psychology is too Confucian, too neat. He's been dead a long time. How about the guy on a motorcycle in Taipei ?" Dr. Gabrenya said, urging that research have a more contemporary outlook. The academics came from Israel, Sweden, Taiwan, Singapore, United States, British Columbia and, of course, Hong Kong. Many of the visual aids they used by way of illustration contained eye-squinting type and cobweb-like graphs. One speaker, a sociologist from Illinois, even warned her colleagues that she would not give anyone enough time to digest the long, skinny columns of numbers. Is Chinese intelligence different from Western ? For half of the audience who are illiterate in Chinese, Professor Jimmy Chan of HKU examined each of the Chinese characters for "intelligence". Phrases such as "a mind as fast as an arrow" and connections between strokes for sun and the moon were made. After his 25-minute speech, Chan and the group lamented that using Western tests are the only measure available to psychologists, who are starving for indigenous studies of Chinese by Chinese. How do Chinese children learn ? David Kember of Hong Kong Polytechnic University zeroed in on deep learning versus surface. Deep is when the student is sincerely interested for his own reasons. Surface is memorising and spitting out facts. It doesn't nurture any deep understanding. If the language of instruction happens to be the children's second language, students in Hong Kong have all sorts of challenges with English-speaking teachers from Australia, Britain and America with accents and colloquialism? Westerners have more self-esteem than Chinese ? Dr. Leung Kwok, chairman of the psychology department of Chinese University, points his finger at belief systems: the collectivist mind-set often stereotypes Chinese unfairly. The philosophy of "yuen" (a concept used to explain good and bad events which are pre-determined and out of the individual's control) does not foster a positive self-concept. Neither do collectivist beliefs, such as sacrifice for the group, compromise and importance of using connections. "If a Chinese loses or fails, he has a stronger sense of responsibility. He tends to blame it on himself. A non-Chinese from the West may blame it on forces outside himself," Dr. Leung said. By the end of the three-day session, there were as many questions raised as answered. It was agreed there was room for further research. To the layman, so much of the discussion was foreign and riddled with jargon and on-going references to studies and researchers. The work of the participants will resurface in a forthcoming Handbook of Chinese Psychology, which will be edited by Dr. Bond and published by Oxford University Press.

25. According to the passage the author suggests that

1. not many people study Chinese psychology.
2. the building is in danger of attack.
3. Chinese psychology is a difficult subject to study.
4. Chinese psychology is a difficult subject to organize.

26. It can be inferred from the passage that

1. the Cultural Revolution was a productive period for Chinese psychology.
2. the Cultural Revolution was a dangerous period for Chinese psychology.
3. the Cultural Revolution was an unproductive period for Chinese psychology.
4. the Cultural Revolution was a new beginning for Chinese psychology.

27. According to the passage, William Gabrenya refers to himself as an 'illiterate gweilo'. This suggests that

1. he feels defensive about not speaking and reading Chinese.
2. he feels secure in his illiteracy.
3. he is representative of other westerners active in this field.
4. he can operate perfectly well without learning Chinese.

28. According to the passage, all of the following are true ***except***

1. the visual aids were not very easy to understand.
2. the conference attracted a very professional standard of presentation.
3. the visual aids were not very tidy.
4. the presenters were under time pressure.

29. According to the passage which of the following is ***not*** true ?

1. Chinese characters are very difficult for westerners to master.
2. It is difficult to come to a conclusion about western and Chinese intelligence.
3. It is difficult to measure Chinese intelligence with western tests.
4. More tests are required that are conducted by the Chinese for the Chinese.

Passage – III

"Since wars begin in the minds of men," so runs the historic UNESCO Preamble, "It is in the minds of men that the defences of peace must be constructed." Wars erupt out when the minds of men are inflamed, when the human mind is blinded and wounded, succumbs to frustration and self-negation. War is the transference of this self-negation into the other-negation. The three Indo-Pak wars and the persisting will to terrorise have emanated from this savage instinct of other-negation that is the legacy of the partition carnage and its still-bleeding and unhealed wound. Truncated from its eastern wing in 1971, Pakistan ever since has suffered from a sense of total existential self-negation. Plus the scars left by the two previously lost wars to India and Kargil fill the Army and the Pakistan psyche with a seething urge to revenge: that India has to be negated, destroyed - in a deep psychological sense, another Hiroshima in the subcontinent is imaginable and possible. Terrorism in Kashmir springs from such deep negating existential grounds. Like the former Soviet Union, Pakistan came into being as a result of a grand delusion and massive perversion of reality - the so called two-nation theory. Like the former Soviet Union, it stands in danger of crumbling unless it modifies its reality perception and comes to terms with its post-Bangladesh ideality within the prevailing subcontinental equation. Failing this, Pakistan is bound to break up, nudging the region to a nuclear nightmare, including possible South Asian Hiroshimas. With 'hot pursuits' and 'surgical operations' freely making rounds among the policy elite and the public at large, the national atmosphere looks ominously charged. "On the brink," headlines The Week adding, "As men and machines are quickly positioned by India and Pakistan, the threat of war looms real." To which Gen. Musharraf counters, "If any war is thrust on Pakistan, Pakistan's aimed forces and the 140 million people of Pakistan are fully prepared to face all consequences with all their might." According to Indian Express, "Pakistan has deployed medium range ballistic missile batteries (MRBBs) along the Line of Control (LoC) near Jammu and Poonch sectors in an action that will further escalate the tension between the two countries." And India's Defence Minister ups the ante, "We could take a (nuclear) strike, survive and then hit back, Pakistan would be finished." (Hindustan Times, December 30, 2001). Mr. Fernandes's formulation is certainly a tactical super shot, even a strategical super hit inasmuch as this is the very logic of India's 'No-first-strike' doctrine. The Defence Minister obviously has no idea of the ethical, phenomenological implications of abandoning chunks of the Indian population to ransom for potential Hiroshimas and then 'finishing' the neighbouring country of 140 million in what could be nothing short of an Armageddon. Forget these horrendous scenarios. But does this hot repudiate the grain of truth for which- India's civilisation stood for and vindicated across the untold millennia of its history ? Yet, Mr. Fernandas, the pacifist and Gandhian, is no warmonger. As Defence Minister he had to react at a level with the Pakistanis, with their proclivity to drop the nuclear speak whenever that suited them, could have Fegistered the message.

30. According to the passage, Pakistan is bound to disintegrate

I. and it will throw the subcontinent into a nuclear backlash.

II. if it refuses to accept its present identity.

III. if it does not stop fuelling terrorism in Kashmir.

1. II and III are correct
2. I, II and III are correct
3. I and II are correct
4. I and III are correct

31. It can be inferred from the passage that

1. Soviet Union crumbled as a result of the grand delusion of the two nation theory.
2. Soviet Union also came into being as a result of the two nation theory.
3. Soviet Union's disintegration was due to her failure to accept the reality.
4. The ideological basis of creation of Soviet Union and Pakistan was the same.

32. According to the passage, the reason for terrorism in Kashmir is

1. Pakistan's perception of two-nation theory.
2. Pakistan's blind faith in terrorism.
3. Pakistan's sense of self-negation.
4. Both (2) and (3)

33. According to the passage, all of the following about the defence minister are ***not*** true, ***except***

1. He is not a Gandhian.
2. He is not logical.
3. He is a pacifist.
4. He is not a warmonger.

Passage – IV

Mobility of capital has given an unprecedented leverage to companies not only to seek low paid, informal wage employees across national boundaries, but the threat of capital flight can also serve to drive down wages and place large numbers of workers in insecure, irregular employment. Informalisation strategies enable employers to draw on the existing pool of labour as and when they require, without having to make a commitment to provide permanent employment or any of the employee-supporting benefits associated with permanent jobs. As far as the working class is concerned, informalisation is in fact, a double-edged sword. For not only is the employee denied the rights associated with permanent employment, but the nature of casual work essentially destroys the foundations of working class organisation. As workmen move from one employer to another, numbers are scattered, everyday interests become divergent, and individualised survival takes precedence over group or collective struggles.

Even workers who have been in sectors with a long tradition of unionisation are difficult to organise once they 'are removed from the arena of permanent employment. About 50,000 textile mill workers in Ahmedabad City were laid off during the late 1980s and early 1990s. The move to obtain compensation and rehabilitation for these workers floundered on the weakness of the struggle, as numbers of workers who were available for pressing their claims and taking to some kind of activism dwindled the motivation of leaders declined and the struggle slowly frittered away. If this is the situation with workers familiar with the concept of unionisation, the task of organising vast masses of casual workers who have never been organised, is obviously much more difficult. The problem, essentially, is not only that of organising workers for struggle, but giver the transitory nature of casual employment, employers are not bound to provide insurance of any kind, and frequently, there is no fixed employer against whom workers' claims can be pressed. In this context, the formation of the National Centre for Labour (NCL) can be seen as a landmark in the history of the working class movement in India. The NCL is an apex body of independent trade unions working in the unorganised sector of labour, registered under the Indian Trade Union Act, 1926. Through its constituent members, the NCL represents the interests of workers in construction, agriculture, fisheries, forests, marble and granite manufacturing, self-employed women, contract workers, anganwadi and domestic workers, as also workers in the ' tiny and small-scale industries. The NCL, launched in 1995, has .about 6,25,000 members spread over 10 states in India. The NCL reflects two tendencies. First, the formation of such a federation highlights that despite the problems in organising workers in the informal sector, there have in fact, been a range of organisations which have sought to address these issues. On a collective plane, their activities represent a marked departure from the traditional way of conceptualising union activities exclusively around organised or formal sector workers. Thus, the unionisation of the hitherto unorganised sector has become inserted into the political universe as a possible and legitimate activity. Second, the formation of the NCL, to an extent, overturns the pessimistic logic that the interests of the unorganised sector — given their diverse and inchoate form — cannot be articulated from a single platform. For the NCL aims precisely, do not only provide an anchoring for these diverse organisations, but more importantly, to articulate the need for institutionalised norms of welfare which can apply to the unorganised sector as a whole. It is in the context of this generalised movement that one needs to view recent efforts to bring in legislative acts which seek to create a new framework of laws and institutions addressing the needs of the unorganised sector. One of the major problems that has dogged this sector has of course been that of implementation. Thus, for example, while there is a stipulated minimum wage for most industries, this is frequently flouted by employers. A central objective of the NCL has been to advocate' legislation to create agencies, which would mediate between the employer and the employee, to institutionalise certain guarantees of welfare and security to the employee. Thus, for example, the State Assisted Scheme of Provident Fund for Unorganised Workers, 2000, proposed by the Labour Department of the Government of West Bengal, introduces the mechanism of a Fund which will be contributed to by the worker (wage-earner or self-employed person), the employer, and the Government and to which the worker would be entitled at the age of 55 or above. By registering a worker to this programme and issuing an identity card, the initial hurdle of identifying a large mass of scattered workers is overcome, and a step is taken towards institutionalising their legitimate claims against the employers and from the State. The Karnataka Unorganised Workers (Regulation of Employment and Conditions of Work) Bill, 2001, offers a more comprehensive framework for addressing the unorganised sector's needs. It envisages the formation of a Fund and a Board, in each sector. The Board, consisting of members from the Government, employers and employees, would be responsible for administering the Fund. Employers must compulsorily pay towards the Fund, a certain fixed percentage of the wages or taxes payable by them, or a certain percentage of the cost of their project, (for example, in construction projects). The concept of the Fund is designed to create the financial viability of social security for workers, and to provide a structure for employers' contribution. Thus, workers would be insured for accident and illness, old age, and unemployment. The Board is designed to provide a mechanism to ensure the working of the Fund, and essentially, to institutionalise workers' claims against employers through an empowered agency. In the broader context of economic liberalisation, recently proposed labour reforms seek to extend the scope of contract employment and to facilitate worker lay-off. As casualisation of labour now seems an irreversible trend, the Bills outlined above would appear to be the only way to ensure workers' interest. To this extent, organisations such as the NCL, which have systematically struggled to push for such legislation, are serving an invaluable historical purpose. As the Karnataka Unorganised Workers Bill awaits endorsement during the Assembly sessions being held currently, for the protagonists of the movement, this would be a watershed, but, nevertheless only a moment in a struggle that needs to be waged at multiple points and to evolve to newer heights.

34. According to the passage, the proposed labour reforms
1. will provide a much needed thrust to liberalization.
2. will encourage the practice of hiring labourers on a contract basis.
3. have resulted in casualisation of labour.
4. seek to extend the scope of employment and to facilitate worker retrenchment.

35. According to the passage, textile mill workers could not obtain compensation because
1. the number of workers available for pressing their claims was not adequate.
2. they were not united.
3. of the weakness of the struggle.
4. the motivation of the leaders was very low.

36. According to the passage, the most important aspect of the NCL is that
1. it has given a voice to the interests of workers in the unorganized sector.
2. it is an apex body of independent trade unions.
3. it has 6,25,000 members spread over 10 states in India.
4. it is the only body of its kind in India.

Directions for questions 37- 40: Each of these questions has four underlined parts. Identify the part which is not correct.

37. No sooner he left the office than it started raining heavily enough to make him completely wet.
1 2 3 4

38. Even after hearing the leader for a long time, the followers could not make out which he was talking about.
1 2 3 4

39. The principal, along with the teachers, were seen boarding a bus to go to a picnic on a national holiday.
1 2 3 4

40. With the introduction of the new syllabus, the number of colleges reporting high results are decreasing
1 2 3 year after year. 4

Answer Key

1. 4	**2.** 2	**3.** 3	**4.** 4	**5.** 1	**6.** 4	**7.** 2
8. 4.	**9.** 1	**10.** 2	**11.** 1	**12.** 3	**13.** 4	**14.** 2
15. 3	**16.** 2	**17.** 1	**18.** 1	**19.** 1	**20.** 3.	**21.** 4
22. 4	**23** 1	**24.** 4	**25.** 3	**26.** 3	**27.** 1	**28.** 2
29. 1	**30.** 3	**31.** 3	**32.** 3	**33.** 3	**34.** 3	**35.** 3
36. 1	**37.** 1	**38.** 4	**39.** 2	**40.** 3		

Answer Key & Explanations

1. 4 Images are not attributed, hence 4 is ruled out as is option 3 due to *devise*. Again option 3 is wrong because of *contributing*, which creates unidiomatic English.

2. 2 The ideas conveyed by *straightforward* and *honest* need to be carried forward with a similar idea. Hence 2.

3. 3 Obviously, a *counsellor* has to be a *good listener*. *Trust* is another desirable quality in a good counsellor.

4. 4 The sentence talks of continuously updating oneself in a changing world. Option 2 creates unidiomatic construction. So is true of option 3.

5. 1 Introducing the word *unprofitable* would change the intended idea, hence ruling out options 3 and 4. We need to economize on the use of words.

6. 4 *Quickly* and *short time* cannot be used together as they are redundant in conjunction with each other.

7. 2

8. 4 There has to be a logically valid comparison between *virtuosity* and another element, which is *appreciation* in this case and the two need to be proximate as far as possible.

9. 1 C-B make a good pair as both talk of classification. A explains it further

10. 2 A is a consequence emanating from D. B-C are well-connected because of generalization-example kind of pairing.

11. 1 D-A make a good pair as they support each other. C is a consequence of A while B is a good opening line.

12. 3 The correct sequence has to be CBA or CAB as C is a brilliant introductory idea. Note the words *more than* in A. It is supported by attitude in D.

13. 4 Options 1 and 2 - *ought* and *had* do not gel.

14. 2 Option 1 and 3 are verbose (compare the opening words) while option 4 is roundabout.

15. 3 Options 1 and 2 and they is misplaced here. In option 4, maintaining is wrong.

16. 2 Note the words all ready in option 1. In option 3, note *organization,* while in option 4 the expression *all in already* is nonsensical.

17. 1 If fewer foods were there in parents' timers, obviously the scope for nutritional deficiency would have been lesser.

18. 1 Lesser liquidity cannot result in more money outflow from India into those countries. The rest three are logical reasons why more should go there as investment.

19. 1 Holding the level of a bad thing constant could be bettered by an example of someone trying to lower or totally eliminate it.

20. 3 This seems to be the only possible way out. Of course, it could pose other problems but this is equally and perhaps more true of other solutions given.

21. 4 It is clearly stated in the passage towards the end./ Read, 'The Indian understanding.........nuclear cooperation.'

22. 4 All three are stated in the passage.

23 1 The sixth line in the passage supports the answer choice.

24. 4 Read 9th and 10th line of the passage.

25. 3 The main idea discussed in the passage points towards option 3.

26. 3 Lines 11 and 12 clearly state the fact.

27. 1 Gwelio defends by saying that 93 percent of the non-Chinese authors in his field cannot read Chinese.

28. 2 Options 1, 3 and 4 are stated in the passage but not option 2.

29. 1 No where in the passage does the writer give an indication to this effect whereas all the others can be easily concluded from the passage.

30. 3 Read 'Like the former............Asian Hiroshimas.'

31. 3 The middle of the passage states that Pakistan will disintegrate like the former Soviet Union.

32. 3 Stated in the passage. Read the 9th line in the passage

33. 3 The 2nd last line of the passage clearly states it.

34. 3 Read the last few lines of 1st paragraph- 'For not only is the employee.......class organisation.'

35. 3 The 3rd line of the 2nd paragraph supports the answer choice.

36. 1 Refer to the 2nd para-'....the NCL represents....small-scale industries.'

37. 1 Insert *had* before *he*.

38. 4 Substitute *what* for *which*.

39. 2 Substitute *was for were*.

40. 3 Substitute is for are.

MAT – MAY 2009

Number of Questions – 40
Time : 30 M.

Directions for questions 1 to 20: *Answer these questions based on the passages.*

Passage I

The Indian steel industry, in line with global trends, is at crossroads, witnessing a resurgent phase of modernization, expansion a consolidation, mainly through mergers and acquisitions. A sector that was moribund just about five years ago because of a worldwide slump, in steel prices, the industry has turned the corner and has in fact been vibrant over the past two years. Domestic steel companies, both public and private, are surging ahead on the strength of an unprecedented buoyancy in the economy and the resultant boom in real estate and various infrastructure sectors such as roads and highways, ports and airports. The official figures speak for themselves. Powered by an increased demand for steel from neighbouring China, which has been clocking a 15 percent sectoral growth annually on account of construction projects in preparation for the Olympics, the steel industry in India has grown by about 10 per cent in the past two years, compared with the global growth rate of about 6 per cent a year. The country's production of crude steel in 2005 — 06 stood at 42.1 million tonnes, reflecting an increase of 7.1 per cent over the previous fiscal. On the other hand, the consumption of steel during the year was pegged at 41.43 million tonnes, a massive growth of 13.88 per cent when compared with the 2004 - 05 figures. - Likewise, the production of sponge iron also increased sharply by 25 per cent, from about 10.3 million tonnes in 2004-05 to 12.9 million tonnes in 2005 - 06. Currently, India is the largest sponge iron producer in the world and ranks seventh among steel-producing countries. The growth in domestic steel consumption is, by and large, in keeping with the International Iron and Steel Institute (IISI) forecast of a 10 per cent increase in steel use in 2006. While the IISI has projected the global demand for steel to grow by 4.9 per cent in the medium term up to 2010, it has pegged its forecast for the 2010 -15 period at 4.2 per cent annually for the entire world. The IISI says India will lead the consumption growth story with an annual demand of 7.7 per cent, followed by China with 6.2 per cent. More heartening is the indication that the exciting phase in the domestic steel industry is expected to continue for the next five to seven years at the least, in terms of both consumption and production. Already, the growth in steel consumption, as projected by the United Progressive Alliance (UPA) government in the National Steel Policy (NSP) formulated in 2005, stands exceeded by a huge margin. The NSP had conservatively estimated the country's steel production to grow by 7.3 per cent, with an annual consumption growth of 6.9 per cent. Considering that the past two years have already witnessed a demand growth of over 10 per cent, the government expects the healthy trend to continue during the Eleventh Plan period (2007-12), provided an annual gross domestic product (GDP) growth of 9 per cent is achieved during the period as projected by the Planning Commission. Clearly, for primary steel producers, India is the place to be in as it has the greatest growth potential. Coupled with this are two other major factors. One, India is bestowed with the largest reserves of high quality iron ore in the world. Secondly, the annual per capita consumption of steel in the country is still one of the lowest in the world, at 35 kilograms against the global benchmark of 250-400 kg. In effect, the growth story in India is here to stay for quite a few decades in view of the sheer disparity in consumption levels. Not surprising, then, that when the three ore-rich states — Jharkhand, Orissa and Chhattisgarh — threw open their doors, steel-makers of all hues jumped into the fray to sign memoranda of understanding (MoUs) with more than one state government. In all, more than 116 MoUs have already been inked, pledging a total investment of a whopping Rs. 3,57,344 crores in the coming years. If all the pledges materialize, the country's installed steel production capacity will surge to anywhere between 150 million and 180 million tones by 2014-15, compared with the conservative NSP target of 110 million tonnes by 2019-20. Orissa signed 43 MoUs to hike its production capacity to 58.04 million tonnes. Not to be left behind, Chhattisgarh entered into 42 MoUs to augment its steel capacity to 19.32 million tonnes, while Jharkhand signed 31 MoUs to increase its capacity to 68.67 million tonnes. The extensive availability of rich iron ore — the basic raw material for steel-making — in the three states has attracted big global names too who, at the outset, made it clear that they would require captive iron ore mines to feed their Greenfield steel projects. Initially, it was the home-grown Tata Steel that signed an MoU with the Orissa government, in November 2004 for setting up a six-million-tonne plant at an estimated cost of Rs. 15,400 crores after the government made a commitment that its ore requirement of 250 million tonnes for a period of 25 years would be met. By the time Pohang Iron and Steel Company (POSCO), the South Korean major and the 3rd largest global steel producer, approached the Orissa government, the terms turned out to be far sweeter. Under the MoU signed in June 2005, POSCO plans to set up a 12-million-tonne plant at Paradeep, with an investment of Rs. 51,000 crores. The initial proposal was for a 10-million-tonne plant. But there is a catch here. The government has committed itself not only to provide 600 million tonnes of ore on a captive basis for a period of 30 years but also allowing POSCO to export the quality domestic ore for use in its steel plants in Korea. It has demanded the raw material from mines in Sundergarh and Keonjhar districts. Lakshmi N. Mittal, the non-resident Indian (NRI) tycoon and the world's biggest steel-maker following the merger of Mittal Steels with the Luxembourg-based Arcelor in June last year, did still better. He put Jharkhand and Orissa in competition by proposing a steel venture in either state, depending upon the terms and incentives and the swiftness in approvals. Jharkhand lost out — owing to litigation over its Chiraia ore mines and for other reasons — to Orissa, which signed an MoU with Mittal-Arcelor in December last year for a 12-million-tonne steel plant at Keonjhar.

The state-owned Steel Authority of India Limited (SAIL) also undertook a major exercise to retain its position as the leading integrated steel producer in the country. The steel behemoth announced its "Corporate Plan-2012,' envisaging an outlay of Rs. 37,000 crores to upgrade its plants and modernize its operations. Under the plan, expansion programmes are under way in various SAIL units to enhance the total production capacity to 22-9 million tonnes of hot metal from the present 12-5 million tonnes by 2011 - 12. Late last year, following the merger of IISCO with SAIL, Prime Minister Manmohan Singh laid the foundation stone for the modernization and expansion of ISP (IISCO Steel Plant) with an investment of Rs. 9,592 crores. Mergers of a few more state-owned units with SAIL are on the cards with a view to consolidating public sector share in the steel market. The other public sector steel enterprise, Rashtriya Ispat Nigam Ltd. (RINL), is already in the process of implementing an ambitious expansion programme for increasing its liquid steel capacity from the current three million tonnes to 6.3 million tonnes at an estimated cost of Rs. 8,692 crores. Launched on May 20, 2006, the project is scheduled for completion by 2008-09. Needless to say, the demand for iron ore has surged in view of the long-term supply commitments being given by the State governments at a time when the international market prices for the raw material are at a high.

This sparked off a debate among domestic steel-makers on whether liberal ore exports should be permitted, as in the past, or the ore should be conserved to the extent possible in view of the projected demand for steel. The government set up a committee under the Planning Commission, headed by Anwarul Hoda, to recommend changes in the National Mineral Policy. The existing policy permits free exports of iron ore with a ferrous content of less than 64 percent. For export of high-grade ore with higher ferrous content, a licence is required and is currently canalized through the Minerals and Metals Trading Corporation (MMTC). The Hoda Committee recommended free exports of iron ore with a ferrous content of less than 65 per cent but advocated discontinuation of the existing regime of canalization and export licensing for the high-grade ore. Instead, the panel suggested free exports of quality ore lumps with ferrous content of more than 65 per cent on payment of an export duty.

1. According to the passage, the steel industry in India has grown by ___________ in the past two years and India ranks ____________ among steel producing countries.

1. 12%, sixth
2. 10%, seventh
3. 8%, first
4. 6%, eighth

2. ___________ per cent is the projected global demand for steel to grow in the medium term up to 2010.

1. 6.9
2. 5.9
3. 4.9
4. 3.9

3. According to the International Iron and Steel Institute, India will lead the' consumption growth with an annual demand of ____________ per cent, followed by China with ____________ per cent.

1. 6.2, 5.7
2. 8.7, 6.7
3. 5.2, 3.2
4. 7.7, 6.2

4. Which one of the following statements is *incorrect* ?

1. The licence for export of high-grade iron ore is being canalized through MMTC.
2. With the merger of Mittal Steels with Arcelor, L.N. Mittal is the world's biggest steel-maker.
3. A South Korean company is the world's third largest steel producer.
4. As per Corporate Plan-2012 of Steel Authority of India Limited, the total production capacity will beenhanced to 12.5 million tonnes by 2011 - 12.

Passage II

P. Chidambaram might have rubbed Corporate India the wrong way by putting the big-bang reforms on the backburner, but he has definitely tried to buy peace with the *aam aadmi* by increasing investment in big ticket projects like Bharat Nirman and National Rural Employment Guarantee Programme (NREG). While the outlay for Bharat Nirman has been hiked by 31.6%, allocations for the education sector and health and family welfare schemes have gone up by 34.2% and by 21.9%, respectively. Chidambaram also surprised many by increasing the education cess to 3%, from 2%, to fund secondary and higher education. The government also proposed to increase funding for the mid-day meal scheme from the primary level to the upper primary classes in 3,427 educationally backward blocks. However, it has pruned allocation for the Sarva Shiksha Abhiyan (SSA) — a scheme started by NDA government. To arrest the drop-out ratio after eighth standard, a means-cum-merit scholarship scheme covering one lakh students has been announced. The first year of the Eleventh Plan period will also see the appointment of two lakh teachers and construction of five lakh classrooms.

As the saying goes, well begun is half done. But how many of these noble intentions will translate into actions ? There are many unanswered questions. One, are the increased outlays enough to achieve the social goals enumerated the UPA government's common minimum programme (CMP) ? Two, is the greater allocation to the flagship programmes in proportion to the GDP growth? And more importantly, will the increased allocation also fix the lacuna in the delivery mechanism? The CMP, for instance, has set a 6% target for education spend (as a proportion of the GDP). However, the spend has hardly touched the halfway mark as the coalition government moves closer to the end of its tenure. The education cess has also been swelling the general pool without any firm commitment from the government on incremental spending to meet specific objectives. Experts also question the success of the Bharat Nirman project touted as "the cornerstone of the UPA government's policies" to fight rural poverty. The IDFC, for instance, raises doubts about the sustainability of the project in its India Infrastructure Report 2007. According to Prof. Jean Dreze, one of the architects of the NREG and member of the Central Employment Guarantee Council, the two big disappointments in the Budgets are the allocations for Integrated Child Development Services (ICDS) and the Rural Employment Scheme.

"Both a virtually unchanged as a proportion of GDP. If anything, they have declined," points out Dreze. The universalisation of ICDS, one of the core commitments of the CMP, assumes importance from another angle. The Supreme Court in a December 2006 directive called for the doubling of operational anganwadis by 2008 and wanted the government to ensure that all ICDS services are extended to all children under six. 'This cannot be done without increasing financial allocations. The absence of any such increase in the Budget is an alarming indication of lack of political commitment to this programme. It is also, in effect, a violation of the court's order," he says.

In the case of Rural Employment Guarantee Schemes, it was estimated by the now defunct National Advisory Council (NAC) that at least around Rs. 20,000 crore would be required for the fair implementation of the NREG Act in the country's 200 poorest districts. However, only Rs. 6,000 crores have been spent as of January 2007 and the implementation is also tardy in many states, says Dreze. "The need of the hour is not only to expand the number of districts covered by NREGA, but also raise expenditure levels much closer to the NAC projections. Instead of this, the government proposes to extend NREGA to 330 districts without any increase in expenditure. This is another sobering indication of lack of commitment to flagship programmes and to the rural poor," says Dreze. TV Mohandas Pai, Director and HR Chief, Infosys, says that the government, instead of so many incremental steps, should have undertaken certain path-breaking initiatives in irrigation and health insurance for the poor. "The government should think of revolutionary steps to catapult the economy into a much higher orbit. For instance, the subsidies for food, fertilizers, kerosene and LPG, which account for about Rs. 75,000 crore, can be done away with, and instead, a direct income transfer of Rs. 1,000 each, to say 10 crore below poverty line families, which the government has already identified, could have been done," he says. This way, at one stroke, nearly 50 crore people (assuming five people in a family) will get a kind of social security, Pai argues.

While it is debatable whether the government would go in for such innovative methods to address social inequalities, a reality check would be in order. Otherwise, the ghost of India Shining would come back to haunt the UPA government as well.

5. Which one of the following statements is *incorrect* ?

1. The implementation National Rural Employment Guarantee Scheme has not been fair.
2. The mid-day meal scheme has been proposed to be extended to upper primary classes in certain educationally backward blocks.
3. During the period 2007-08, it is planned to construct five lakh classrooms.
4. None of these

6. Which one of the following statement(s) is/are true ?

1. The education cess has also been swelling the general pool without any firm commitment from thegovernment on incremental spending to meet specific objectives.
2. The outlay for Bharat Nirman has been hiked by 31.6%.
3. The CMP has set a 6% target for education spend.
4. All are true.

7. Experts question the success of the Bharat Nirman project touted as the cornerstone of the UPA government's policies to

1. develop rural employment scheme.
2. integrate child development.
3. develop rural areas.
4. fight rural poverty.

8. In the case of Rural Employment Guarantee Schemes, it is estimated by the now defunct National Advisory Council (NAC) that at least around ___________ crore would be required for the fair implementation of the NREG Act in the country's 200 poorest districts.

1. Rs. 25,000
2. Rs. 20,000
3. Rs. 10,000
4. Rs. 15,000

Passage III

All men by nature, desire to know. An indication of this is the delight we take in our senses: for even apart from their usefulness they are loved for themselves; and above all others, the sense of sight. For not only with a view to action, but even when we are not going to do anything, we prefer seeing (one might say) to everything else. The reason is that this, most of all the senses, makes us know and brings to light many differences between things. By nature, animals are born with the faculty of sensation, and from sensation, memory is produced in some of them, though not in others. And therefore, the former are more intelligent and apt at learning than those which cannot remember; those which are incapable of hearing sounds are intelligent though they cannot be taught, e.g., the bee and any other race of animals that may be like it; and those which besides memory, have this sense of hearing can be taught. The animals other than man live by appearances and memories, and have but little of connected experience; but the human race lives also by art and reasonings. Now from memory, experience is produced in men; for the several memories of the same thing produce finally the capacity for a single experience. And experience seems pretty much like science and art, but really, science and art come to men through experience; for 'experience made art', as Polus says, 'but inexperience luck.' Now art arises, when from many notions gained by experience, one universal judgement about a class of objects is produced. For to have a judgement that when Callias was ill of this disease that did him good, and similarly, in the case of Socrates and in many individual cases, is a matter of experience; but to judge that it has done good to all persons of a certain constitution, marked off in one class, when they were ill of this disease, e.g., to phlegmatic or bilious people when burning with fevers — this is a matter of art.

With a view to action, experience seems in no respect inferior to art, and men of experience succeed even better than those who have theory without experience. (The reason is that experience is knowledge of individuals, art of universals, and actions and productions are all concerned with the individual; for the physician does not cure man, except in an incidental way, but Callias or Socrates or some other called by some such individual name, who happens to be a man. If, then, a man has the theory without the experience, and recognizes the universal but does not know the individual included in this, he will often fail to cure; for it is the individual that is to be cured.) But yet we think that knowledge and understanding belong to art rather than to experience, and we suppose artists to be wiser than men of experience (which implies that wisdom depends in all cases rather on knowledge); and this because the former know the cause, but the latter do not. For men of experience know that the thing is so, but do not know why, while the others know the 'why* and the cause. Hence we think also that the masterworkers in each craft are more honourable and know in a truer sense and are wiser than the manual workers, because they know the causes of the things that are done (we think the manual workers are like certain lifeless things which act indeed, but act without knowing what they do, as fire burns, but while the lifeless things perform each of their functions by a natural tendency, the labourers perform them through habit); thus we view them as being wiser not in virtue of being able to act, but of having the theory for themselves and knowing the causes. And in general, it is a sign of the man who knows and of the man who does not know, that the former can teach, and therefore, we think art more truly knowledge than experience is; for artists can teach, and men of mere experience cannot.

Again, we do not regard any of the senses as Wisdom; yet surely these give the most authoritative knowledge of particulars. But they do not tell us the 'why' *of* anything e.g., why fire is hot; they only say that it is hot. At first, he who invented any art whatever, that went beyond the common perceptions of man was naturally admired by men, not only because there was something useful in the inventions, but because he was thought wiser and superior to the rest. But as more arts were invented, and some were directed to the necessities of life, others to recreation, the inventors of the latter were naturally always regarded as wiser than the inventors of the former, because their branches of knowledge did not aim at utility.

Hence, when all such inventions were already established, the sciences which do not aim at giving pleasure or at the necessities of life were discovered, and first in the places where men first began to have leisure. This why the mathematical arts were founded in Egypt; for there the priestly caste was allowed to be at leisure. We have said in the Ethics what the difference is between art and science and the other kindred faculties; but the point of our present discussion is this, that all men suppose what is called Wisdom to deal with the first causes and the principles of things; so that, as has been said before, the man of experience is thought to be wiser than the possessors of any sense-perception whatever, the artist wiser than the men of experience. The masterworker than the mechanic, and the theoreticarkinds of knowledge to be more of the nature of Wisdom than the productive. Clearly then, wisdom is knowledge about certain principles and causes.

9. What is the relationship between sensation and memory ?

1. Human beings are intelligent as they can reason, whereas animals do not have the capacity of reasoning.
2. Human beings have sensation and memory both.
3. All animals have sensation but some animals do not have memory.
4. When sensation is remembered, it becomes a memory experience and this leads to connected experience,which in turn gives rise to reasoning.

10. What is the difference between art and experience ?

1. Art does not give the cause and effect of things, whereas experience gives the cause and effect of things.
2. Experience and art give rise to one another and they are complementary and supplementary to each other.
3. Art explains the cause of things together with its effects, whereas experience gives us just the effect of things, not the cause.
4. Both experience and art are views of a contradictory time and space and this is where the difference between the two lies.

11. Why according to the author, were the mathematical arts founded in Egypt ?

1. Because the sciences which do not cater to necessities or pleasures develop only after the previous two havebeen invented and only then, men have time for themselves. So was the case in Egypt where the priestly caste had ample leisure time.
2. Because the inventors of luxuries were considered more important than the inventors of necessities and inEgypt, the kingly and priestly class had developed great standards in luxurious tastes and attitudes.
3. Because they were men of experience and had wisdom and knowledge about certain principles and causes.
4. Because Egyptians were considered to be connoisseurs of art and crafts and had superior civilization asopposed to the other ancient civilizations.

12. Which of the following can be considered to be the central idea of the passage ?

1. Art is superior to experience.
2. What actually is "Wisdom" ?
3. "Experience made art, but inexperience luck".
4. Knowledge is wisdom.

Passage IV

There are a few instances of diseases that have laid waste, huge tracts of forests throughout India. Caused mainly by pathogens and pests, these diseases are deadly and are capable of wiping out entire forests and plantations, causing immense economic as well as ecological loss.

Meanwhile, forest pathologists and entomologists are grappling with new maladies that are surfacing almost every year. But with meagre resources and just a few experts working on the issue, things are heading virtually towards a cul-de-sac.

Moreover, no assessment has been made so far to quantify the devastation. While large chunks of forests fall prey to maladies, it is also an opportunity for some politicians and timber merchants to cash in on it. Research and documentation on forest disease, particularly on forest pathology, began in India way back in 1929, by pioneering pathologists KD Bagchi and BK Bagchi. Although it has been eight decades since then, not much headway has been made in this direction. The forestry sector today in ailing due to its misplaced priorities, resource crunch, and mismanagement. "Forest management lacks scientific approach," says Surendra Kumar, director of the Himalayan Forest Research Institute (HFRI), Shimla.

The scientific community involved with forest diseases is today a dispirited lot. With only a few stalwarts left in this field, forest disease is a neglected area of research. Moreover, bureaucracy in increasingly taking over the scientific institutions and scientists in most of these institutes are a marginalized group.

To top it all, there are no institutions dedicated to forest diseases. Although the ministry of environment and forests is the facilitator for such research, it is not paying enough attention to promote scientific research of forest diseases. In fact, the government's lackadaisical approach came to the fore with the Sal borer epidemic in Madhya Pradesh in 1998. While forest bureaucracy slept, the beetles merrily continued to wipe out entire tracts of precious Sal forests. Eventually, with no solution in sight, thousands of valuable trees were hacked. There were also allegations that the Sal tragedy was a chance for the timber mafia in the state to cash in on timber through the legal loophole, with the nexus of politicians.

Today, things haven't changed one bit. India's forest department and research institutes have yet to formulate contingency plans to face any assault of similar dimensions.

Forest diseases are elusive. Although experts claim that they know quite a lot about forest diseases, there are still aspects of the maladies that are not completely understood. Says R.S. Bhandari, entomologist in the Forest Research Institute (FRI), Dehradun, "We know about all the important pests and insects, their life cycles and their development. But there are a few diseases which remain an enigma." According to Jamaluddin, head of the pathology department in the Tropical Forest Research Institute (TERI), Jabalpur, "Due to micro climatic changes, we are discovering new aspects of the same disease every year. Diseases have also increased manifold." Another FRI scientist points out that although forest diseases are increasing, there is no study to estimate the economic and ecological damage caused by these pests and pathogens.

Varying with different geophysical regions and climatic conditions, pathogens and pests are essentially responsible for the tree maladies and their mortality. When the pristine, natural and mixed forests existed, forest diseases acted as a natural control measure to check the proliferation of a particular species that could threaten the balance of the ecosystem. Perhaps, this is why forest diseases paled into insignificance in the past. But today, with shrinking forests and increasing monoculture plantations, any outbreak of disease takes on a virulent form.

To top this, changed climatic and forest patterns and environmental pollution have given rise to newer forms of forest diseases. While trees are forced to take an additional load of human induced environmental changes, the introduction of monoculture has substantially increased the problems. Whatever little we know about forest diseases today comes primarily through mycology, the study of forest pathogens. Mycology explains that the prime pathological reasons for forest disease are fungi, bacteria and viruses. "Among these, fungi play a major role, while the other two are relatively less significant. There are 150 to 200 major pathological infections in central India. Out of these, only five per cent are bacterial. The rest are fungal," says Jamaluddin.

Most of these pathogens stay close to a tree, waiting for a chance to infiltrate. Their entry points are small openings or wounds in the tree. However, invasion is not always easy. Like human beings, trees also have antibodies that fight anything alien. In case of invasion from the trunk of a tree, the sapwood acts as a shield and secretes enzymes to fight pathogens. But when attacked and conquered, there are tell-tale signs in the form of knotty growths of fruit bodies that are extensions of the fungi in the tree.

13. Which of the following is the author most likely to agree with?

1. The ministry responsible should take a more serious view towards research in forest diseases.
2. There is a likelihood of another forest disease epidemic, similar to the Sal Borer epidemic, spreading in the country.
3. There needs to be a more coordinated effort towards dealing with forest diseases in India.
4. All of these

14. Which of these incidents discourages the government to formulate any kind of concrete plans?

1. India lacks specialists in this area of forestry.
2. The government is not able to work in concomitance with specialists, like entomologists and pathogenists.
3. The prevalence of malpractices such as the alleged nexus of politicians with some of the forest officials.
4. None of these

15. Which of these statements *cannot* be inferred from the passage?

1. With the variation of different climatic conditions, pests responsible for forest tree degradation, disappear.
2. There are hardly any committed institutions in India, for the promotion of research in forest diseases in India.
3. It is possible that the timber mafias could spread their network with help from vested interests in thepolitical and bureaucratic brass.
4. None of these.

16. The discussion on the present condition of forest diseases proves that

1. there must be a cooperative endeavour by scientists, government officials, & politicians to weed out the possibilities of forest diseases.
2. a lot more needs to be done by the government for sustaining the ecological balance.
3. hitherto, forestry has been a neglected area of research.
4. None of these

Passage V

For years, the contents of a child's sandbox have confounded some of the nation's top physicists. Sand and other granular materials, such as powders, seeds, nuts, soils, and detergent, behave in ways that seem to undermine natural laws and cost industries ranging from Pharmaceuticals to agribusiness and mining, billions of dollars.

Just shaking a can of mixed nuts can show you how problematic granular material can be. The nuts do not 'mix'; they 'unmix' and sort themselves out, with the larger Brazil nuts on top and the smaller peanuts at the bottom. In this activity and others, granular matter's behaviour apparently goes counter to the second law of thermodynamics, which states that entropy, or disorder, tends to increase in any natural system.

Mimicking the mixed-nut conundrum with a jar containing many small beads and one large bead, one group of physicists claimed that vibrations causing the beads to percolate open up small gaps rather than larger ones. Thus, when a Brazil nut becomes slightly airborne, the peanuts rush in underneath and gradually nudge it to the top. Another group of physicists colour coded layers of beads to track their circulation in a container and achieved a different result. Vibrations, they found, drive the beads in circles up the centre and down the sides of the container. Yet downward currents, similar to convection currents in air or water, are too narrow to accommodate the larger bead, stranding it on top.

One industrial engineer who has studied the problem says that both the 'percolation' and 'convection current' theories can be right, depending upon the material, and that percolation is the major factor with nuts. Given the inability of scientists to come up with a single equation explaining unmixing, you can see why industrial engineers who must manage granular materials go a little, well, 'nuts'! Take Pharmaceuticals, for instance. There may be six types of powders with different-sized grains in a single medicine tablet. Mixing them at some speeds might sort them, while mixing at other speeds will make them thoroughly amalgamated. One aspirin company still relies on an experienced employee wearing a latex glove who pinches some powder in the giant mixing drum to see if it 'feels right'.

Granular material at rest can be equally frustrating to physicists and engineers. Take a tall cylinder of sand. Unlike a liquid, in which pressure exerted at the bottom increases in direct proportion to the liquid's height, pressure at the base of the sand cylinder doesn't increase indefinitely. Instead, it reaches a maximum value and stays there. This quality allows sand to trickle at a nearly constant rate through the narrow opening separating the two glass bulbs of an hourglass, thus measuring the passage of time.

Physicists have also found that forces are not distributed evenly throughout granular material. It is this characteristic that may account for the frequent rupturing of silos in which grain is stored. In a silo, for instance, the column's weight is carried from grain to grain along jagged chains. As a result the container's walls carry more of the weight than its base, and the force is significantly larger at some points of contact than at others. Coming up with equations to explain, much less, predict the distribution of these force chains" is extremely difficult.

Again, using beads, physicists developed a simple theoretical model in which they assume that a given bead transmits the load it bears unequally and randomly onto the three beads on which it rests. While the model agrees well with experimental results, it does not take into account all of the mechanisms of force transmission between grains of sand or wheat.

In the struggle to understand granular materials, sand-studying physicists have at least one thing in their favour. Unlike particle physicists who must secure billions of dollars in government funding for the building of super-colliders in which to accelerate and view infinitesimal particles, they can conduct experiments using such low-cost, low-tech materials as sand, beads, marbles, and seeds. It is hoped that more low-tech experiments and computer simulations will lead to equations that explain the unwieldy stuff and reduce some of the wastage, guesswork, and accidents that occur in the various industries that handle it.

17. The percolation theory of unmixing is best illustrated by which of the following examples ?

1. Contents settling in a bag of potato chips so that the package appears less full after handling.
2. Currents of small beads blocking the upward movement of large beads in a shaken container.
3. Larger rocks rising to the surface in a garden after a period of frost.
4. Large nuts blocking the upward movement of small nuts in a shaken container.

18. In saying that the percolation and convection current theories may both be right, the industrial engineer means that

1. though the theories have different names, they describe same physical mechanism.
2. both theories are still unproven, as they have not been tested on a variety of materials.
3. neither theory is supported by an adequate mathematical basis.
4. the mechanism causing unmixing varies depending upon the type of granular material.

19. Which of the following appears to be the best solution for combating the 'unmixing" problem faced by pharmaceutical manufacturers that must prepare large quantities of powders?

1. To mix all the powders together at the same speed.
2. To craft' powders in which every grain weighs the same amount.
3. To craft powders so that all the grains have similar sizes and shapes.
4. To hire engineers who have years of experience in powder mixing.

20. The passage implies that if the top bulb of an hourglass were filled with water instead of sand, the pressure pushing the water through the opening would

1. remain constant as water trickles through the opening.
2. decrease as water trickles through the opening.
3. increase as water trickles through the opening.
4. be directed at the walls of the container rather than the base.

Directions for questions 21 to 24: *Choose the correct option for the given blanks.*

21. Pipes are not a safer __________ to cigarettes because, though pipe smokers do not inhale, they are still __________ higher rates of lung and mouth cancers than non-smokers.

1. alternative — subject to
2. answer — responsible for
3. preference — free from
4. rejoinder — involved in

22. Because of its tendency to ____________, most Indian art is ___________ Japanese art, where symbols have been minimized and meaning has been conveyed by using the method of the merest suggestion.

1. overdraw — similar to
2. understate — reminiscent of
3. imitate — superior to
4. sentimentalism — supportive of

23. In the absence of native predators, to stop the spread of their population, the imported goats ___________ to such an inordinate degree that they over-grazed the countryside and ___________ the native vegetation.

1. thrived — threatened
2. suffered — abandoned
3. propagated — cultivated
4. dwindled — eliminated

24. The analysis of the coach's report was anything but ___________, but those of us who have learned to discount such dismal ___________ are optimistic.

1. malicious — benefits
2. sanguinary — traps
3. pessimistic — confusion
4. pleasant — prognostications

Directions for questions 25 to 28: *Each of these questions has a set of four sentences marked A to D. Identify the arrangement of these sentences which makes a logical sequence.*

25. (A) It marks off the beginning of mathematics from what went before.

(B) Ever since this discovery, abstraction has been a major theme in the development of mathematics, as thoseinterested in the field have come up with ideas further and further divorced from their basis in the real world, and then sought ways to bring them back to tell us things about the real world which we might otherwise not have known.

(C) The discoverer of abstraction was the person who first realized that numbers are independent of theobjects being counted, that two oranges and two apples (for instance) share a property, 'twoness', which is independent of what kinds of fruit they are.

(D) Abstraction, the action of divorcing properties of physical objects from the objects themselves, is afundamental concept, perhaps the most fundamental concept, in mathematics.

1. CBAD
2. DBCA
3. DACB
4. DABC

26. (A) The accommodation theory, in linguistics, starts from the premise that speech accommodation takes placewhen people modify their speech so that it conforms more with the way their conversational partner speaks.

(B) For example, the speed at which people talk, the length of both pauses and utterances, the kind ofvocabulary and syntax used, as well as intonation, voice pitch and pronunciation are all subject to theaccommodation process.

(C) A wide range of subtle adaptations have been observed, which tend to occur more or less unconsciously.

(D) This kind of convergence is by no means an automatic feature of all conversations, and we can discerncertain social contexts in which accommodation can be predicted.

1. BDAC
2. DABC
3. ACBD
4. ABCD

27. (A) Fossil evidence suggests that the mammals underwent adaptive radiation to produce the range of mammal types extant today.

(B) Adaptive radiation, in the life sciences, refers to the differentiation (oranagenesis) of one or a few speciesinto many to fill a large number of related ecological niches by adaptation.

(C) Thus the first bird species may have given rise to many more bird species by adaptive radiation.

(D) Typically, a species adapts to colonize a new habitat and, this adaptation opening up a new range ofniches, adapts again to fill the new niches which are presented.

1. CBAD
2. BDCA
3. BADC
4. CBDA

28. (A) When the future date arrives, the bear expects to buy in at a lower price to deliver the stock that had beensold under the future contract at a higher price.

(B) A market in which prices are falling or are expected to fall is called by economists a bear market.

(C) Likewise, the term bear can be applied to a person who expects stock prices to fall and sells stock that heor she does not have for delivery at a future date.

(D) It is a designation commonly used in securities markets and commodity markets and is the opposite of a bull market.

1. BDCA 2. BCAD
3. BACD 4. ACBD

Directions for questions29 to 32: *In each of these questions, a part of the sentence has been underlined. Find the best way of writing the underlined part of the sentence.*

29. To prepare himself, he subjected himself to two weeks of total abstinence and intensive training in the open fields of Panipat, climbing the hills nearby 30 times, spend nights in the open and to test to see how long he could hold out without food.

1. spending nights in the open by climbing the hills nearby 30 times and tested for seeing
2. climbed the hills nearby 30 times, spending nights in the open and tested to see
3. climbing the hills nearby 30 times, spend nights in the open and to test to see
4. climbing the hills nearby 30 times, spending nights in the open and testing to see

30. In rural India, many mango trees are planted at the end of a village or at the border of a district, for providing excellent shade during summer, and shelter during winter.

1. in order to provide excellent shade in summer, and shelter in winter.
2. to provide excellent shade in summer, and shelter in winter.
3. for providing excellent shade during summer, and shelter during winter.
4. so as to excellently provide shade in summer, and shelter in winter.

31. Mental intelligence and common sense are essential for outstanding achievement because they involve your natural ability to comprehend difficult concepts quicker and to analyse them clearly and incisively.

1. your natural ability of comprehension of difficult concepts quickly and clear and incisive analysis of it.
2. one's natural ability for the comprehension of difficult concepts quickly and analysing them clearly and incisively.
3. your natural ability to comprehend difficult concepts quicker and to analyse them clearly and incisively.
4. one's natural ability to comprehend difficult concepts quickly and to analyse them clearly and incisively.

32. Panchayati Raj institutions are now entrusted upon the execution of all rural upliftment schemes and programs in India.

1. entrusted with the execution of all rural upliftment schemes and programs
2. entrusted with the execution of all rural uplift schemes and programs
3. entrusted upon the execution of all rural upliftment schemes and programs
4. entrusted within the execution for all rural uplift programs and schemes

Directions for questions 33 to36: *Each question has a given sentence. Identify the best way of writing the sentence in the context of the correct usage of standard written English. While doing so, ensure that the message being conveyed remains the same in all the cases.*

33. Having bowed our heads, the priest in the temple led us in prayer.

1. After we bowed our heads, the priest in the temple led us to prayer.
2. After we bowed our heads, the priest in the temple led us to prayer.
3. Having bowed our heads, the priest in the temple led us in prayer.
4. After we had bowed our heads, the priest in the temple led us in prayer.

34. Anyone interested in flying planes can learn much if you have access to a flight simulation machine.

1. Anyone interested in flying planes can learn much if access is available to a flight simulation machine.
2. Anyone interested in flying planes can learn much if he has access to a flight simulation machine.
3. Anyone interested in flying planes can learn much if you have access to a flight simulation machine.
4. Anyone interested in flying planes can learn much from access to a flight simulation machine.

35. The moral of the entire story is how money doesn't make you happy.

1. In this novel, the moral of the story is how money doesn't make you happy.
2. The moral of the entire story is that money doesn't make you happy.
3. The moral of the entire story is how money doesn't make you happy.
4. That money does not make you happy, is the entire moral of the story.

36. Ever since the sting operation, there has been much opposition from they who maintain that it was an unauthorised act.

1. Ever since the sting operation, there has been much opposition from those who maintain that it was an unauthorized act.
2. Ever since the sting operation, there has been much opposition from they who maintain that it had been an unauthorised act.
3. Ever since the sting operation, there has been much opposition from they who maintain that it was an unauthorized act.
4. Ever since the sting operation, there has been much opposition from those maintaining that it was an unauthorised act.

Directions for 37 to 40: *Identify the incorrect sentence.*

37.
1. The energy, the faith, the devotion which we bring to this endeavour will light our country and all who serve it.
2. I do not believe that any of us would exchange places with any other people or any other generation.
3. In the long history of the world, only a few generations has been granted the role of defending freedom in its hour of maximum danger.
4. The glow from that fire can truly light the world.

38.
1. It's said without artifice and without care for political correctness.
2. At the most surprising of moments they exactly blurt it out.
3. When they want to, Indians have an amazing way of telling the truth.
4. Unvarnished it no doubt is but it's also refreshingly unalloyed.

39.
1. The second risk lies in the global macroeconomic imbalances, reflected in the twin deficits of the US and rising surpluses of Asia.
2. Therefore, addressing infrastructure gaps needs to doing our topmost priority next year.
3. As the growing economy makes increasing demands on infrastructure inputs, these problems could worsen in the coming year.
4. The longer these imbalances have persisted, the greater has become the risk of a disruptive correction.

40.
1. For years now, pitches have been prepared to suit the home team's strengths and that is fine so long as the pitch is not a lottery.
2. It is here that BCCI needs to show the same will, as they have shown in making players play domestic cricket.
3. The only problem is that the wickets that are on offer for domestic cricket are hardly conducive for batsman.

4. If one goes by the scores in some of the matches, especially Delhi's games, then it is quite obvious that thepitches prepared are sub-standard and not conducive to a fair contest between bat and ball.

Answer Key

1. 2	**2.** 3	**3.** 4	**4.** 4	**5.** 4	**6.** 4	**7.** 4
8. 2	**9.** 4	**10.** 3	**11.** 1	**12.** 1	**13.** 4	**14.** 1
15. 1	**16.** 1	**17.** 4	**18.** 4	**19.** 3	**20.** 2	**21.** 1
22. 2	**23.** 1	**24.** 4	**25.** 3	**26.** 3	**27.** 2	**28.** 1
29. 4	**30.** 1	**31.** 4	**32.** 1	**33.** 1	**34.** 2	**35.** 2
36. 1	**37.**	**38.** 3	**39.** 2	**40.** 3		

Answer Key & Explanations

Q. No.	Answer Key	Explanation
1.	2	Mentioned in lines 8 and 14
2.	3	Read line 17
3.	4	Refer line 18
4.	4	12.5 million tones (mt) is the present capacity. It will be enhanced to 22.9mt by 2011-12
5.	4	1 is an assumption made when the NAC talks about the amount required for the "fair implementation of NREG Act.
6.	4	All are explicitly mentioned in the passage.
7.	4	Refer to the 2nd last sentence of the 2nd para.
8.	2	Read the opening sentence of the penultimate para.
9.	4	Only option 4 talks about a relationship between sensation and memory .
10.	3	Rea lines 7-8 of para 2.
11.	1	Read the first two sentences of the fourth para.
12.	1	The author through out the passage is giving arguments in favor of art and artist being truly knowledgeable.Hence,[1]
13.	4	All are clearly mentioned in the passage. Hence,[4]
14.	1	Refer to para 4 , second sentence. Hence,[1]
15.	1	Option 1 contradicts the information in the passage. Hence, [1]
16.	1	Option 1 clearly sums up the passage . Hence [1]
17.	4	The passage says that "percolation is the major factor with nuts."
18.	4	Hence he qualifies his statement with "depending upon the material"
19.	3	The problem lies with difference in size.
20.	2	The pressure increases in proportion to the liquid's height.
21.	1	The information generated shows that a substitute to pipes is being looked for. Also none of the other three options make sense in the second blank. Hence, [1]
22.	2	Pick up the key words , 'minimized and merest suggestion' which get complemented by 'understate.' Hence,[2]
23.	1	Because their predators were absent goats flourished (thrived) and in turn big nos. of goats endangered (threatened)the vegetation. Hence[1]
24.	4	The first blank would take a positive word as per the structure the sentence-'anything but', hence option 1 and 3 are eliminated. Between 2 and 4 one can not discount traps. Hence, [4]
25.	3	Clearly, the passage is about "abstraction". Hence D must be the first sentence and this rules out 1. Again, "this discovery" should follow what "the discoverer of abstraction" did.

And CB as a sequence rules out 2 and 4.

26. 3 The passage is about “accommodation” theory. Hence A must be the first sentence. Which rules out 1 and 2. And B gives the “examples” of the “subtle adaptation” mentioned in C. CB as a sequence rules out 4.

27. 2 C, starting with “Thus”, can’t be the first sentence. Hence 1 and 3 are ruled out. 2is preferred to 3 because rushing for A, which talks about mammals specifically, leads us to lose the general discussion too soon.

28. 1 “It” in D refers to the “bear market” mentioned in B.BD as a sequence rules out 2 and 3. Again, A is an explanation of C. And CA as a sequence rules out 2 and 3. Again, A is an explanation of C. And CA as a sequence rules out 4.

29. 4 The parallelism of participles needs to be maintained.

30. 1 -The phrase ‘in order to’ signifies that there is a specific purpose for planting mango trees. Hence [1]

31. 4 The pronoun one is preferable to you as an indefinite pronoun. Quicker should be replaced by quickly as we need an adverb. Also, the comparison is unwarranted.

32. 1 If you are entrusted with something, you are given its responsibility.

33. 1 Option 3 carries a dangling modifier. And option 4 has a tense error. Option 2 should read ‘heads’. Hence,[1]

34. 2 Subject ‘anyone’ must be complemented by object ‘he,’ hence option 3 is eliminated. Option contains a dangling modifier. Option 4 distorts information. Hence [2]

35. 2 ‘Moral’ must be qualified with a noun clause. This eliminates options 1 and 3 . Option 2 carries better expression than option 4. Hence,[2]

36. 1 Option is the best option as subject and object complement is correct-‘those ……who’. Hence [1]

37. 3 Replace has with have.

38. 3 It should be written as: “When they want to tell the truth, Indians have an amazing way of doing so”.

39. 2 sMakes no sense at all.

40. 3 Replace for with to.

MAT –Sept. 2007

Number of Questions – 40
Time : 30 M.

Directions for questions 1 to 4: *Each of these questions has a sentence with an underlined part. Choose the best option to replace the underlined part.*

1. Reared in a village where computers and the internet were objects of curiosity, Murty today hardly gives a thought to the immense possibilities that the internet revolution has thrown open to him.

1. Reared in a village where computers and the internet were objects of curiosity
2. Curious to know that computers and the internet were objects of curiosity in the village he was reared up
3. Being reared in the village where the computers and the internet are objects of curiosity
4. Reared in a village where computers and the internet were an object of curiousness

2. An extraordinarily gifted actor and an ingenious criminal;

1. an actor with extraordinary gifts and an ingenious criminal-
2. an ingenious actor and an extraordinarily gifted criminal;
3. a gifted actor and- an ingeniously criminal
4. an extraordinarily gifted actor and an ingenious criminal,

3. In the fall of 1996, the Indian government dispatched samples of the cells of the militants to those four US scientists, who were only the Americans authorized to test them.

1. dispatched samples of the cells of the militants to those four US scientists, who were only the Americans authorized to test them
2. dispatched samples of the militant's cells to those four US scientists, the only Americans authorized to test them
3. dispatched samples of the cells of militants to those four US scientists who were authorized to test them
4. dispatch the samples of the cells of the militants to those four US scientists, who were the only Americans - authorized to test them

4. To prepare himself, he subjected himself to two weeks of total abstinence and intensive training in the open fields of Panipat, climbing the hills nearby 30 times, spend nights in the open and to test to see how long he could hold out without food.

1. climbing the hills nearby 30 times, spend nights in the open and to test to see
2. climbed the hills nearby 30 times, spending nights in the open and tested to see
3. spending nights in the open by climbing the hills nearby 30 times and tested for seeing
4. climbing the hills nearby 30 times, spending nights in the open and testing to see

Directions for questions 5 to 8: *Choose the correct order of the sentences marked A, B, C, D and E to form a logical paragraph.*

5. A. The Naga groups, assuming they are serious about negotiations, should make a realistic reassessment of how far the Indian state can go to meet their demands.

B. The government on its part should show both sincerity and flexibility in crafting a solution that willassure the Naga people a life of peace, dignity, and self-respect recognizing the uniqueness of Naga history.

C. The government should also do everything possible to remove the suspicion that it has been encouraging certain Naga groups.

D. No solution can be found through bloodshed.

E. Growing internecine violence among them is a worry.

1. ACBDE 2. ABDEC
3. DCBEA 4. ABCED

6. A. The latest decline draws attention to a fairly well known fact that stock exchanges in India take theircues as much from developments overseas as from domestic ones.

B. While such reaction is an inevitable consequence of globalisation, it is the magnitude of the reaction that has come as a surprise.

C. The stock indices the world over tumbled on the back of some pessimistic news from the United States credit market, especially its home loan segment.

D. Fears over the failure of risky sub-prime mortgages seem to have spilled over to other closelywatched sectors of the economy such as sales of new homes and consumer durables.

E. Last week the Dow recorded its highest fall since February, dragging the European bourses down.

1. ADEBC 2. ABCDE
3. BEDCA 4. AEDCB

7. A. Moreover, it was felt that leaders elected by villagers themselves would find it easier to implement central government policies regarding taxes and family planning.

B. Since. 1998, elections to village councils, which comprise between three and seven members, have beeninstitutionalized and are now carried out every three years.

C. The council's main responsibilities lie in deciding the allocation and use of communal land, therunning of village enterprises, and the implementation of family planning directives.

D. Councils can also decide local matters like village subscription to newspapers, the renovation of a schoolbuilding, or the. installation of cable television.

E. Following the collapse of the village commune, system after the economic liberalization initiatedin 1978, certain leaders within the Communist Party began pushing for village self-governance as ameans to counter political apathy and violent rebellion by creating mechanisms of participation and conflict resolution.

1. DCBEA 2. CABDE
3. EABCD 4. BACDE

8. A. The U.S. market will continue to be the dominant one in the foreseeable future. The rupee could become even stronger.

B. A greater recourse to hedging as well as striving for multi-currency revenue streams automatically suggests itself.

C. Already one company, TCS, by resorting to these methods extensively has turned in an above averageperformance during the first quarter.

D. Most IT companies have been grappling with more mundane problems such, as a high level of attritionamidst rising wage costs and inability to secure the right type and number of American visas.

E. The BPO industry and many medium-sized software exporters are reportedly operating on thin margins.

1. BCADE 2. ABCDE
3. DCBAE 4. EDABC

Directions for questions 153 to 156: *Choose the pair of words which exhibits the same relationship between each other as the given capitalized pair of words:*

9. WRITING : PLAGIARISM : :

1. confidence : deception

2. money : misappropriation
3. gold : theft
4. germ : disease

10. CONDENSATION : LIQUEFICATION : :

1. evaporation : vaporization
2. consumption : cook
3. oration : listen
4. exhaustion : buy

11. BEWILDERMENT : CONFUSION : :

1. bursa.: sack
2. bewitched : entrance
3. fantod : nervousness
4. coracle : lodestar

12. PREAMBLE : STATUTE : :

1. prologue : novel
2. movement : sympathy
3. sketch : drawing
4. index : book

Directions for questions 157 to 160: *Fill in the blanks.*

13. I am not attracted by the ____________ life of the ____________, always wandering through the countryside, begging for charity.

1. proud, almsgiver
2. noble, philanthropist
3. affluent, mendicant
4. peripatetic, vagabond

14. Her true feelings ______________ themselves in her sarcastic asides; only then was her ____________ revealed.

1. concealed, sweetness
2. manifested, bitterness
3. hid, sarcasm
4. grieved, charm

15. The sugar dissolved in water ___________; finally all that remained was an almost ____________residue on the bottom of the glass.

1. quickly, lumpy
2. immediately, fragrant
3. gradually, imperceptible
4. subsequently, glassy

16. It is foolish to vent your spleen on ____________ object; still, you make ____________ enemies that way.

1. an inanimate, fewer
2. an immobile, bitter
3. an interesting, curious
4. an insipid, dull

Directions for questions 161 to 180: *Read the following passages and answer the questions that follow each passage.*

PASSAGE

The nature of financial integration of developing countries with developed countries has been radically transformed over the last four years. Evidence collated by the World Bank's annual report for 2007 on global development finance reveal a number of features of the new scenario that have far-reaching implications. The first of these is an acceleration of financial flows to developing countries precisely during the years when as a group, they have seen rising surpluses on their current account. Total flows touched a record \$571 billion in 2006, having risen by 19 per cent on top of an average growth of 40 per cent during the three previous years. Relative to the gross domestic product (GDP) of these countries, total flows, at 5:1 per cent, are at levels that they touched at the time of the East Asian financial crisis in 1997. A second feature is the acceleration of the long-term tendency for private flows to dominate over official (bilateral and multilateral) flows. Private debt equity inflows, which had risen by 50 per cent a year over the three years ending 2005 increased by another 17 per cent in 2006 to touch a record $647 billion. On the other hand net official lending has in fact, declined over the past two years. One factor accounting for this is the failure of the Group of Seven (G-7) countries to match promises of a substantial hike in aid disbursements beyond what the retirement of the debt of few heavily indebted poor countries ensures. The other is that the more developed among developing countries have chosen to make advance repayments of debt owed to official creditors, especially the International Monetary Fund (IMF) and the World Bank. Overall, principal repayments to official creditors exceeded disbursements by $70 billion in 2005 and $75 billion in 2006. In the event, there has been a reverse flow of capital to the World Bank and the IMF which is threatening the viability and influence of these institutions, especially the latter. However, the increase in private flows has more than matched the reverse flows to official creditors. The third feature is that the dominance of private flows has meant that both equity and debt flows to developing countries has risen rapidly with the surge being greater in the case of the former. Net private debt and equity flows to developing countries have risen from-a little less than $170 billion in 2002 to close to $647 billion in 2006, an almost fourfold increase over a four year period. While net private equity flows which rose from $163 billion to $ 419 billion, dominated the surge, net private debt flows too increased rapidly. Bond issues rose from $10-4 billion to $49-3 billion and borrowing from international banks increased from $2-3 billion to a huge $112-2 billion. What is more, net short-term debt, outflows of which, tend to trigger financial crises, has risen from around half a billion in 2002 to $72 billion in 2006. The fourth feature, which is a corollary of these developments, is that there is a high degree of concentration of flows to developing countries, implying excess exposure in a few countries. Ten countries (out of 135) accounted for 60 per cent of all borrowing during 2002 - 04 and that proportion has risen subsequently to touch three-fourths in 2006. In the portfolio equity market, flows to developing countries were directed at acquiring a share in equity either through the secondary market or by buying into initial public offers (IPOs). IPOs dominated in 2006 accounting, for $53 billion of the $96 billion in flow. But, here too, there were signs of concentration. Four of the 10 largest IPOs were by Chinese companies,; accounting for two-thirds of the total IPO value. Another three of those 10 were by Russian companies, accounting for an additional 22 per cent of the IPO value. A fifth feature is that despite this rapid rise in developing country exposure, with that exposure being excessively concentrated in a few countries, • the market is still overtly optimistic. Ratings upgrades dominate downgrades in the bond market. And bond market spreads are at unusual lows. This optimism indicates that risk assessments are pro-cyclical, underestimating risk when investments are booming, and overestimating risks when markets turn downwards. But, there are two consequences: the herding of investors in developing country markets and their willingness to invest in a larger volume of money in risky unrated instruments. Finally, the rapid rise in capital flows to developing countries at a time when many of them are recording large current account surpluses has substantially increased their foreign exchange reserves and triggered an outflow of capital; This outflow takes three forms : (i) investment of reserves in safe and low return instruments such as United States Treasury Bills, (ii) financing of asset acquisition to support the growing presence of leading developing country firms in global commodity markets; and (iii) financial investments in and lending to other developing countries, resulting in the South-South flow of capital. These trends together; suggest that developing countries are still largely restricted to the low return or high-risk segments of global capital flow. This is the cost they bear to meet the requirements of ensuring balance in the global balance of payments. These features of the current global financial scenario can be interpreted in two ways. One is in the direction taken by the World Bank. It admits, on the one hand, that "the probability of a turn in the credit cycle" has risen and that a "Key challenge facing developing countries is tib manage the transition by taking pre-emptive measures aimed at lessening the risk of a sharp, unexpected reversal in capital flows". On the other, it downplays the dangers involved by arguing that the surge in capital flow's "speaks well for the resilience of developing economies and for the ability of international financial market to manage risks". An alternative view would be that many emerging market economies that attract a disproportionate share of these capital flows are fast approaching a situation where they are vulnerable to financial crises with the current scenario incorporating features that could make these crises more intense. What is more, it appears that prudential norms, risk management techniques and disclosure requirements that have been put in place as part of the so-called "new international financial architecture" seem inadequate to foreclose a build-up of this kind. This is .not surprising since garnering large and quick profits rather than minimising risks seems to be the dominant requirement of financial institutions from the developed countries. The current situation is the inevitable result of expanding the space for financial capital through dilution or elimination of regulation. Financial liberalisation has ensured that since the late 1970s, the newly discovered "emerging markets". among developing countries have been the new frontier for profiteering by global financial institutions. Awash with the liquidity derived from the surpluses earned by oil exporters and the saving accumulated by the generation of baby-boomers in the West, banks, investment funds and pension funds were looking to new avenues for lucrative investments. The role- of financialntermediaries was one of dressing up developing countries that were hitherto "untouchables" as lucrative destinations for financial capital. And financial innovation consisted in not just identifying, instruments that could carry such investments but derivatives, that could help hedge against the risk associated with rushing into uncharted territory. The process began when developing countries were still reeling under the effects of declining non-fuel commodity prices and rising oil prices which had left gaping holes in the current account of their balance of payments. The new found interest of global finance offered developing country governments an opportunity to finance that gap, even if it meant offering high returns to foreign financial investors. It was this conflation of interests of developing country governments and financial institutions from the developed countries that led up to the debt crisis of the 1980s and the financial crisis of the 1990s, including those that began with the East Asian crisis in 1997. One consequence of the 1997 crisis was a sharp decline in lending to developing countries. But this did not mean a decline in capital flows. Rather, encouraged by the post-crisis deflation in asset prices in emerging markets and the sharp devaluation of their currencies, foreign direct investment kept flowing into developing countries to acquire assets at rock bottom prices when measured in hard currencies. While net debt flows to developing countries declined from $53-1 billion in 1998 to just $1-2 billion in 2000, net FDI flows remained more or less stable at around $170 billion a year. Since 2002 when growth accelerated or remained high in China and India and commodity prices rose sharply in the case of oil and metals and moderately in the case of agriculture, this lull in capital flows has given way to a surge. Besides the features noted above, three kinds of developments have accompanied this surge. First, the growing importance of unregulated hedge funds looking for abnormal returns in portfolio equity markets which renders activity in those markets highly speculative and opaque. Second, the rapid increase in investments by "private equity" firms investing largely in unlisted equity — incorporations in developing countries. The size of each of these investments is such that they identified as foreign "direct 'investments, even though their objective is speculative. The evidence on the controversial role played by these firms in ' the developed countries indicates that their activity too is extremely opaque. Third, the revival once again of the global market for developing country debt, driven this time by private corporate borrowing in the syndicated loan market. Since this new surge in credit rides on a wave of securitisation that transfers the risk associated with such lending to pension and mutual funds among others, accumulating risk does not serve as a deterrent on banks creating such credit. There are a number of implications of these tendencies. To start with, the risk associated - with the current surge in capital flows can be and is much greater than it was true during previous episodes involving a similar surge. Moreover, the surge is accompanied by the growing acquisition of assets in developing countries outside the stock market with objectives that are largely speculative so that a sell-off, if it occurs would be far more widespread. And the persistence of the herd instinct has meant that the surge in fixed and portfolio investment flows has resulted in a revival of credit flows that is unbridled since it is accompanied by risk-mitigation techniques that transfer risk to those who are least equipped to assess them. Unfortunately, all of this occurs in an environment in which the target of both investment and debt flows is the private sector which makes it difficult for governments that have liberalised financial regulation to control such flows. In sum, the risks associated with the current surge in capital flows are far greater than what emerges from the World Bank's rather sanguine assessment of the possible fall-out of the ongoing transformation of global financial flows. A turn in the investment cycle, with far-reaching implications, is real and imminent.

17. According to the passage, which one of the following statement(s) is/are true ?

1. The current situation is the inevitable result of expanding the space for financial capital through dilution or elimination of regulation.
2. The role of financial intermediaries was one of dressing up developing countries that were hithertountouchables as lucrative destinations for financial capital.
3. The new found interest of global finance offered developing country governments an opportunity tofinance that gap, even if it meant offering high returns to foreign financial investors.
4. All of these

18. Total financial flows to developing countries reached a record $571 billion in ________ having risen by nineteen percent on top of an average growth of ________ during the previous three years.

1. 2005, 50%
2. 2006,40%
3. 2004,22%
4. 2002,60%

19. The rapid rise in capital flows to developing countries has substantially increased their foreign exchange reserves and triggered an outflow of capital in the form of

1. financial investments in and lending to other developing countries.
2. financing of asset acquisition to support the growing presence of leading developing country firms in global commodity markets.
3. investment of reserves in safe and low return instruments such as United States Treasury Bills.
4. All of these

20. Ten developing countries out of one hundred and thirty five accounted for sixty percent of all borrowing during 2002-2004 and that proportion has risen subsequently to touch in 2006.

1. sixty per cent
2. fifty per cent
3. seventy five per cent
4. forty percent

PASSAGE

The lithosphere, or outer shell, of the earth is made up of about a dozen rigid plates that move with respect to one another. New lithosphere is created at mid-ocean ridges by the upwelling and cooling of magma from the earth's interior. Since new lithosphere is continuously being created and the earth is not expanding to any appreciable extent, the question arises: What happens to the "old" lithosphere ? The answer came in the late 1960s as the last major link in the theory of sea-floor spreading and plate tectonics that has revolutionized our understanding of tectonic processes, or structural deformations, in the earth and has provided a unifying theme for many diverse observations of the earth sciences. The old lithosphere is subducted, or pushed down, into the earth's mantle (the thick shell of red-hot rock beneath the earth's thin, cooler crust and above its metallic, partly melted core). As the formerly rigid plate descends, it slowly heats up, and over a period of millions of years it is absorbed into the general circulation of the earth's mantle. The subduction of the* lithosphere is perhaps the most significant phenomenon in global tectonics. Subduction not only explains what happens to old lithosphere but also accounts for many of the geologic processes that shape the earth's surface. Most of the world's volcanoes and earthquakes are associated with descending lithospheric plates. The prominent island arcs — chains of islands such as the Aleutians, the Kuriles, the Marianas, and the islands of Japan — are surface expressions of the subduction process. The deepest trenches of the world's oceans, including the Java and Tonga trenches and all others associated with island arcs, mark the seaward boundary of subduction zones. Major mountain belts, such as the Andes and the Himalayas, have resulted from the convergence and subduction of lithospheric plates. To understand the subduction process it is necessary to look at the thermal regime of the earth. The temperatures within the earth at first increase rapidly with depth, reaching about 1,200 degrees Celsius at a depth of 100 kilometers. Then they increase more gradually, approaching 2,000 degrees C at about 500 kilometers. The minerals in peridotite, the major constituent of the upper mantle, start to melt at about 1,200 degrees C, or typically at a depth of 100 kilometers. Under the oceans the upper mantle is fairly soft and may contain some molten material at depths as shallow as 80 kilometers. The soft region of the mantle, over which. the rigid lithospheric plate normally moves, is the asthenosphere. It appears that in certain areas convection currents in the asthenosphere may drive the plates, and that in other regions the plate motions may drive the convection currents. Several factors contribute to the heating of the lithosphere as it descends into the mantle. First, heat simply flows into the cooler lithosphere from the surrounding warmer mantle. Since the conductivity of the rock increases with temperature, the conductive heating becomes more efficient with increasing depth. Second as the lithospheric slab descends it is subjected to increasing pressure, which introduces heat of compression. Third, the slab is heated by the radioactive decay of uranium, thorium and potassium, which are present in the earth's crust and add heat at a constant rate to the descending material. Fourth, heat is provided by the energy released when the minerals in the lithosphere change to denser phases, or more compact crystal structures, as they are subjected to higher pressures during descent. Finally, heat is generated by friction, shear stresses and the dissipation of viscous motions at the boundaries between the moving lithospheric plate and the surrounding mantle. Among all these sources the first and fourth contribute the most toward the heating of the descending lithosphere.

21. Each of the following geological phenomena is mentioned in the passage as being relevant to the subduction of the lithosphere except

1. principal archipelagoes
2. significant rifts in the sea bottom
3. deserts in process of formation
4. prominent mountain ranges

22. The style of the passage can best be described as

1. Oratorical
2. Argumentative
3. Expository
4. Meditative

23. The author is most probably addressing which of the following audiences ?

1. Gepthermal researchers investigating, the asthenosphere as a potential energy source.
2. Historians of science studying the origins of plate tectonic theory.
3. College undergraduates enrolled in an, introductory course on geology.
4. Graduate students engaged in analyzing the rate of sea-floor spreading.

24. Which of the following is **not** true of the heating of the lithosphere as it is described in the passage ?

1. The temperature gradient between the lithosphere and the surrounding mantle enables heat to betransferred from the latter to the former.
2. Minerals in the lithospheric slab release heat in the course of phase changes that occur during their descent into the mantle.
3. The more the temperature of the lithospheric slab increases, the more conductive the rock itself becomes.
4. The further the lithospheric slab descends into the mantle, the faster the radioactive decay of elements within it adds to its heat.

PASSAGE

If religion were not at the root of the Indian psyche, we would not be facing the grim chaos of religious alienation in our country. We are suffering precisely because religion which is supposed to unite man and God has divided us so tragically. Neither secularization nor industrialization has, as yet, sidelined religion in our collective ethos. The religious genius of India, rather than adjust itself to secularism, has brought about its redefinition in our multi-religious context.

Crucial to our national cohesion is the creative co-existence of Hinduism and Islam. The spiritual marriage of Hinduism and Islam, powered by Persian mysticism, gave rise to a philosophy of dissent inspiringly captured, among other, by Kabir. Christianity, which arrived in South India in A.D. 52, long before Europe heard the Gospel, touched and was touched by the soul of India. In other cultures, the arrival of extraneous religious traditions activated negative reations of insecurity and intolerance. It is a sign of the health and wholeness of India's spiritual genius that the advent of religious traditions resulted in spiritual ferments and the revitalization of an already multifarious spiritual heritage. When the western hemisphere was busy coercing conformity and suppressing free-thinking as heresy, the Sufi saints were wandering freely in the garden of truth. To us, the domain of the spirit, as Swami Vivekananda argues, has been a sphere or pure freedom; Indian spirituality is an inspired protect against confining God to places of worship.

The happy co-existence of the most uncompromising from of monotheism and the most varied embodiment of polytheism ever known in human history is a historical paradox that reflects the wonder and the splendour of India.To this must be added the searching self-criticism and searing negations that emerged from the womb of Hinduism, giving birth to Buddhism and Jainism. Reform and self-criticism prove, paradoxically, the hidden vitality of the religious tradition concerned.

The religious, poetic, legal and historical literature of the Hindus could not more different from those of the Indian Muslims, instead, the genius of India transformed incoming religious traditions. In their places of origin, these faiths inhabited distinctive civilizations reigning over designated territories. In India, they became the religious constituents f a single, over –arching civilization, thanks to a host of cementing factors like language, love of the land, cuisine, music, popular art, cothing and a proudly shared history. Islam went to other parts of the world a a conquering faith. It came to India tofind a hom and to become an integral part of the Indo-Gangetic civilization. Islam itself was transformed in this process. While Sunnies and Shias fight in other parts of the world as a conquering faith. It came to India to find a home and to become an integral part of the Indo-Gangetic civilization. Islam itself was transformed in this process. While Sunnies and Shias fight in other parts of the world , and right up to our doorstep, they live together to live in India. History has seen only one Human being – Gandhiji – who said of two radically different religions: Hinduism Islam are like my two eyes. This is the most authentic expression of Indian spirituality.

We are not certain as to how long Hindusm has been in India. By a modest estimate, Hinduism has been the spirtual home for hundreds of millions in this land at least for the last four millennia. Islam has been in India for a thousand years, brought by peaceful traders to the west coast long before the marauding Turks swept into North India discolourig the memory of the Hindis in those regions.

Europe's colonization of India was not confined to the territorial space but went further and deeper. European expansion disrupted the rhythm of Eastern societies, thanks to the invasive and imperialistic nature of European culture. In the Indian context, Muslims and Hindus alike stood paralysed before the onslaught of western materialism. This also bred in them, in due course, a secret admiration; for they realized that although the English were not superior in wisdom, they were irresistibly superior in power. Their knowledge did not result from disembodied contemplation. Nor did it eventuate into aversion to work. Instead, the emphasis on the significance of work bred a dynamic work culture. Western science was action. Nature obeyed the will of man. Not surprisingly, the intellectuals of the East became ambivalent towards the genius of the West.

A century after kabir, the Mighal Emperor Akbar invited Christian missionaries to help him understand their religion. Although Akbar was illiterate- probably history's fsmous dyslexic- his philosophical and intellectual yearning took the form of Din-I-llahi, a synthesis of religious conflict had to be avoided if the social fabric of his kingdom was to endure. Akbar surrounded himself with Hindu advisors, he4 did not bother with quotas.

Going further back, we encounter Emperor Asoka who gave up his religion, we encounter Emperor Asoka who gave up his religion, renounced violence and embraced Buddhism. That was a defining moment in our spiritual history. Hinduism does not condone violence. Gandhiji used the force of truth and non-violence to fight the greatest imperial power of the day. Why have we not learned from his example? The ideology of certain overtly communal political parties is un-Hindu enough to shock us into reckoning the contradictions latent in communal religiosity of every kind. What is the true mandate of Hindu scriptures? Is it to cleanse by killing? Or is it to transcend differences and to respect religious diversities so as to create a culture of peace?

The glorification of communal hate now threatens to rob us of our humaneness. The business of religion is to help Rs. rise above the crudity of history as a chronicle of man's cruelty to man. Preaching hate and romanticizing hurt in the name of God is, hence, an inexcusable sacrilege and an outright insult to the spiritual genius of India. Let us keep the religious boundaries of our great country porous as it has been throughout our history. Unlike in other parts of the world we have unique legacy to protect. Technologically and commercially we may never outstrip other more result oriented countries but spiritually, we cam certainly lead the way.

25. The writer is likely agree with

1. The religious genius of India has rather adjusted itself to secularism.
2. The religious genius genius of India has redefined secularism.
3. The religious genius of India has been redefined in our multi religious content and not adjusted itself to secularism.
4. The religious genius of India is secular and in the multi religious content.

26. According to the author Indian spiritualistic difference from the western as it.

1. Was a sign of the health & wholeness of India's spiritual genius.
2. Inspired protest against confusing god to places of worship.
3. Was touched by a soul of India.
4. Was a sphere of pure freedom.

27. Hindus and Muslims admired the English because

1. of the imperialistic Nature of European culture.
2. They were superior in wisdom.
3. Their knowledge did not result from disembodied contemplation.
4. They were irresistibly superior in power, though not superior in wisdom.

28. The most defining moment in our history ascending to the author

1. Gandhiji using force of truth and nonviolence to fight the greatest comprisal power.
2. Empror Ashoka giving up him rcligion, renouncing violence and embracing.
3. Akbar inviting Christian cristionaries to help him understand their religion.
4. Akbar surrounding himself with Hindu advisors.

PASSAGE

My last growth point offers a chance to bring together the perspectives of Darwin, Marx and Freud. It leads us to the question at the foundations of the human sciences: what is basic, how amenable to change is human nature and how can we bring about more humane human relations ? As I see it, all these matters come together in the problematic Marxist notion of 'second nature'. First, nature is the biologically given domain whose boundaries have themselves never been clearly drawn and are now quite " open as a result of the phenomena of pharmacology, biofeedback (in traditional and modern forms) and genetic engineering (an area in which the future is open in both positive and alarming senses). But without pushing those boundaries between the voluntary and involuntary nervous system' and between mere inheritance. And manipulated inheritance, we have a large scope for deep reflection and serious practice. Historians of the human sciences will know that belief in the extreme plasticity of human behaviour has been held by behaviourists, operant conditioning theorists and those thinking in the related tradition of Pavlovian conditioning. At the other extreme," behavioural geneticists and sociobiologists have held relatively pessimistic views on the potential for change in human behaviour. Moreover, the sociobiologists have made various takeover bids into ethics and the social sciences, although these seem under control for the present. There is a similar continuum on the optimism/pessimism axis among psychoanalysts. Does psychoanalysis or psychoanalytical psychotherapy change the self or merely adapt it to the given of the inner and outer worlds ? Second, nature is history experienced as if it , were unmodifiable — as though it were not amenable to change through practice and enlightenment. Belief in the ability to learn through practical experience is the sine qua non of an enlightened human science, however onerous and slow the process of change.

Those of us in the East and West who reached for rapid change in the nineteen-sixties, have learned a lot about the pace that one can hope for. Neurosis is a perfect example of second nature. On a larger scale, so is racism. On a still larger scale, so are capitalism and East European socialism. . Beyond these in a degree of generality, lie hierarchy and patriarchy. An important desideratum for a human science is the study of the relative refractoriness to change of various aspects and levels of human nature. The writings I have found most helpful in understanding second nature are both Freudo-MJarxist. They are the works of Herbert Marcuse and Russell Jacoby, although other members of the Frankfurt school, as well as the Lukacs of History and Class Consciousness, and various Hungarian philosophers, have also thought about it. Both Marcuse and Jacoby have written widely against various reductionisms — Darwinian, vulgar Marxist arid biologistic Freudian. They have also essayed against extremes of voluntarism and Dionysiac Freudianism. Both have been concerned to pay due respect to the given in biology, economics, culture and therapy, while striving for a better psychic and social order. Both have de-emphasized traditional notions of class struggle as the key to social change and have focused more clearly on cultural and other political processes. Their perspectives are complemented by the writings of Gramsci on the subtle ways in which consent is organized. In addition to his concept of hegemony, I have benefited from Raymond Williams' writings on cultural materialism! His critique of base-superstructure model of vulgar Marxism stresses the complexity of mediation between culture on the one hand, and the production and reproduction of real life on the other. Indeed, he adds the crucial insight that culture is in the base — a material, that is, spiritual need. Raymond Williams died between the delivery and the publication of this talk. His voice — its substance and its tone — are central to my conception of humanity, and I wish to dedicate my remarks to his memory. This brings us back to basics. Look now, Darwin, Marx and Freud are mutually constitutive, Darwin brings historicity to the heart of the sciences, linking life to the earth and our humanity to both. Teleological and anthropomorphic concept lie at the basis of his concept of natural selection. Marx teaches us the historicity of all including scientific concepts, and points out that there is only one science, the science of history. Freud teaches us that all of history and culture continue to be mediated by basic human drives and that no matter how high we reach into abstractions, our thought remains rooted in primitive psychic mechanisms. It would seem,, then, that our conception of human science must always draw on these three dimensions of what Marx calls our species being. The historical, conceptual and practical tasks that follow from this will surely occupy all of us at least to the retiring age. We have in these three thinkers — at first glance — biology, economics and the psyche, but looked at more closely, each takes us to history and historicity, to culture and its roots and to the question of the nature and extent of what is distinctly human — the limits, the realities, the visions, aspirations and achievements now and in the future. As I read them, each offers us a conception of the disciplined study of humanity which always retains a notion of human values in action as the central guiding conception. None will do alone while the task of integrating them in historical studies and in theory has hardly begun. Their writings span the century between about 1840 and 1940. Darwin (1809-82) and Marx (1818-83) were — how easily we forget this — near contemporaries and published their main works almost simultaneously. They died within a year of each other, just over a hundred years ago. Freud was a toddler of three years when The Origin of Species and An Introduction to Political Economy appeared in 1859. The problematic of his life's work makes little sense without seeing both Darwin and Marx as providing the framework of ideas and aspirations about nature and human nature, which he addresses. All three are very much alive today — vivid — providing us with the terms of reference for both a realistic and a cautiously helpful view of our humanity.

29. Which of the following is most helpful in understanding second nature ?

1. Freud and Marx
2. Herbert Marcuse and Russel Jacoby
3. Members of Frankfurt School
4. Both 2. and 3.

30. Which of the following is true according to the passage?

1. Marcuse and Jacoby rejected the role of class struggle as the key to social-change and have laid emphasis on cultural and political processes.
2. Marcuse and Jocob recognized the role of class struggle as the key to social-change.
3. Marcuse and Jacoby saw the cultural and political processes as the only key to social-change.

4. Marcuse and Jacoby recognized a lesser role of class-struggle as the key to social-change than that of the cultural and political processes.

31. According to the passage, all of the following are not true except
1. Freud does not see any meeting point between history and culture.
2. Darwin rejects the centrality of life.
3. Freud, Marx and Darwin are not in contradiction among. themselves, but they do project different perspectives.
4. Darwin and Marx are'unanimous on the role and place of history in linking life to the earth and our humanity to both.

32. Darwin, Marx and Freud all provide us the most important conception of
1. historicity
2. humanity
3. history
4. human sciences

PASSAGE

It goes without saying that Asia matters to the European Union. Europe has a major stake in a stable and prosperous Asia. Our political, security, and economic interests are more intertwined than ever. But our relationship goes far beyond the economic and trade realm : the European Union and Asian -partners contribute actively together to resolving different regional and global problems. We also share an important vision in which a system of global governance, with regional structures as its cornerstones, effectively addresses trans-national problems. It is with this vision that I am once again returning to Asia in early August for the ministerial meeting of the ASEAN Regional Forum (ARF) and bilateral consultations with our ASEAN partners. The progress we have made together over the past year is impressive, perhaps even the most important in our' 30 years of formal ties. And, the EU's early accession to the ASEAN Treaty of Amity and Cooperation can only bring us closer still,. with positive implications for the political and security interests of both groups of countries. We have also agreed to strengthen our political exchanges further and to promote practical cooperation in many areas of mutual interest. One such area, where we work very well together and are set to become closer still, is crisis management. We are, for example, open to sharing more information, boosting technical cooperation and strengthening capacity-building in this field. It was crucial for the EU-led Aceh Monitoring Mission (AMM), which supervised the peace agreement between Indonesia and Aceh rebels from the summer of 2005 to the end of 2006, that ASEAN partners participated in it. This not only helped ensure the success of the mission but also led to the creation of real ties between the two regional organizations. As a result of our joint efforts and, of course, the achievements of the Indonesian government, Aceh was stabilized and is now developing steadily after 30 years of conflict and the devastation wrought by the 2004 tsunami. Its development, which included the elections held last year, was so positive that the Aceh Monitoring Mission was able to complete its work and leave the province.-But the European Union has not left Aceh. On the contrary, we are continuing to give ' active support to the reconstruction efforts of the Indonesian authorities and the local administration in Aceh with a very substantial and visible development programme. Just six weeks ago the EU deployed another mission on Asian soil, a police training mission in Afghanistan, which is also open to Asian partner countries. This mission seeks to help establish sustainable and effective civilian policing arrangements under Afghan ownership and in accordance with international standards. The fact that the mission is to run for at least three years underlines the EU's increased and long-term commitment to security and stability in Asia. We could also envisage cooperating more closely with our Asian partners in future crisis management operations on other continents. We are following with great interest the historic decisions by ASEAN to further develop the South East Asian community and its work on the ASEAN Charter, which includes the development of an appropriate institutional framework. For obvious reasons, the EU appreciates the ambitious integration project of another region. It has also lent, practical support. I myself have met both the Eminent Persons Group and the High-Level Taskforce of Charter drafters and I was very impressed by their vision and commitment and the pertinent questions they asked about the EU's integration process. I wish the region every success in finalizing the new Charter and I give it every encouragement to pursue an ambitious result. In our European experience, far-reaching political and economic integration has not only overcome divisions between former . enemies and ensured stability and prosperity in Europe but it has also proved to be the best solution in tackling regional and global problems that do not stop at national borders. The ARF, which we value greatly as the only political and security dialogue forum in the Asia-Pacific region, is increasingly recognizing the need to find collective solutions to trans-boundary security issues, in particular when it comes to new challenges. Once a year, the ARF meets in a unique forum that brings together the Foreign Ministers of Asian and Pacific countries and their key partners for dialogue on a wide range of issues with a bearing on Asian security. In addition to this fruitful • exchange, the forum is also achieving concrete outcomes at the various seminars and workshops which have made it more result-oriented than in the _ past. The European Union, which attends and contributes to the ARF as a long-standing dialogue partner of the region, is looking forward to the creation of a mechanism that enables the ARF to be active between meetings. This will be a very important and welcome step towards the construction of a regional architecture for Asia. Asia matters to Europe, and it also goes without saying that the European Union matters to Asia. Together, the EU and ASEAN represent two regions, 37 countries, and more than one billion people. In Europe, Asia has a partner in its search, for solutions to global problems such as climate change, energy security' or organized crime. It has, a partner in the economic and trade realm and it has a partner in development issues. Only together can we meet the challenges of the future

33. According to the author, one of the vital mutual interest areas where ASEAN and EU can work together is

1. peace agreement between Indonesia and Aceh rebels.
2. crisis management.
3. civilian policing arrangements.
4. trans-national problems.

34. Deployment of a police training mission in Afghanistan by EU aims at

1. long-term commitment to security and stability in Asia.
2. minimizing terrorism in Asia.
3. drafting of ASEAN Charter.
4. maintaining law and order in Afghanistan.

35. is the only political and security dialogue forum in the Asia-Pacific region.

1. Eminent Persons Group 2. ASEAN
3. ARF 4. None of these

36. The annual ARF meet is attended by foreign ministers of

1. Asian countries 2. EU countries
3. Pacific countries 4. Asian and Pacific countries
5. 4 hour

Directions *for* questions 37 to 41: *Choose the word which is nearly the same in meaning to the word in capital letters.*

37. EMBELLISH

1. Embors 2. design
3. garnish 4. aristocrative

38. ORRORTUNE

1. expected 2. convenient
3. Welcome 4. Chance

39. INDELIBLE

1. uneatable 2. permanent
3. delieate 4. strong

40. CHORE

1. thief
2. relief
3. colour
4. task

41. COPIOUS

1. Vast
2. identical
3. merry
4. plentiful

Answer Key

1. 1	**2.** 4	**3.** 4	**4.** 4	**5.** 4	**6.** 2	**7.** 3
8. 3	**9.** 2	**10.** 1	**11.** 2	**12.** 4	**13.** 4	**14.** 2
15. 3	**16.** 1	**17.** 4	**18.** 2	**19.** 4	**20.** 3	**21.** 3
22. 3	**23.** 3	**24.** 4	**25.** 3	**26.** 2	**27.** 4	**28.** 2
29. 4	**30.** 1	**31.** 4	**32.** 2	**33.** 4	**34.** 1	**35.** 3
36. 4	**37.** 3	**38.** 2	**39.** 4	**40.** 4	**41.** 4	

Explanations

1. 1 The sentence has no error.

2. 4 Error of punctuation. A semi colon is used to introduce an independent clause. Replace the semi colon with a coma.

3. 4 The word 'only' is placed incorrectly distorting the whole information. The author wants to say that they were the 'only Americans' and not 'only the Americans'. Hence, [4]

4. 4 Error of parallelism. Hence, [4]

5. 4 A is clearly the opening statement. C follows B, 'The government should also...', which we find only in option no. 4. Hence [4]

6. 2 A opens the passage. B follows A, 'While such reaction is inevitable.' E is clearly the concluding sentence. Hence [2]

7. 3 E introduces the subject of village self-governance. Hence [3]

8. 3 D introduces the subject of IT companies grappling with problems. Statement D and C link strongly which we find only in 3. Hence [3]

9. 2 Stealing somebody's writings is called plagiarism just as stealing (bungling) of money is called misappropriation. Hence [2]

10.1 Just as condensation leads to turning of vapour into liquid, evaporation leads to turning of liquid into vapour.

11.2 Bewilderment and confusion is a pair of similar meaning words and so is bewitched and entrance.

12.4 Just as there is a preamble in the beginning of a statute, similarly there is an index at the beginning of the book. Hence [4]

13.4 Mark the key word, 'wandering' which gets complimented by peripatetic and vagabond. Hence [4]

14.2 Something would be revealed only if it becomes manifest. Hence [2]

15.3 Keyword, 'almost' gels with imperceptible, completing the sense of the passage. Hence [3]

16.1 If you show your anger to a non-living thing it obviously cannot turn into an enemy. Hence[1]

17.4 All four are mentioned in the passage. Hence [4]

18.2 Refer to the 6-7 line.

19.4 Given in the passage.

20.3 Read the line, 'Ten countries.....in 2006'. Hence [3]

21.3 Deserts are not mentioned to be formed in the process of subduction. Hence, [3] .

22.3 The passage explains the process of subduction of lithosphere. Hence, [3]

23.3 Options 1,2 and 4 are far beyond the passage and only option 3 gels with the central idea of the passage. Hence [3]

24.4 The information is distorted. Hence [4]

25.3 Read the last line of first paragraph. Hence [3]

26.2 Refer to the last lines of the 2nd paragraph. "When western hemisphere… of worship". Hence [2]

27.4 Refer to the 6th paragraph, "This also bred…. In power." Hence [4]

28.2 Refer to the opening lines of the penultimate paragraph. Hence [2]

29.4 Read, "They are the works……. about it". Hence[4]

30.1 Refer to the lines, "Both have… processes". Hence [1]

31.4 Read, "Look now Darwin….to both". Hence [4]

32.2 Read the last line of the passage. Hence [2]

33.4 Mentioned in the 5th line of the passage. Hence [4]

34.1 Mentioned in the 27th line of the passage. Hence [1]

35.3 Read the 38th line of the passage. Hence [3]

36.4 Read the 41st line of the passage. Hence [4]

37.3

38.2

39.4

40.4

41.4

TEST YOUR SELF SECTION-III

TOUGH LEVEL PAPERS

1. ATMA 2008
2. CAT 2008
3. CAT 2007
4. FMS 2008
5. FMS 2009
6. IIFT 2007
7. IIFT 2008
8. XAT 2007
9. XAT 2009

ATMA 2008

Number of Questions – 50
Time :40 M.

Section 1
VERBAL SKILLS

DIRECTIONS for questions 1-15: *Passage I, II and III are followed by questions based on its contents. After reading the passages, choose the best answer to each question then darken the corresponding oval in the answer sheet. Base your answer on information that is either stated or implied in the passage.*

Passage I

Although the number of animals in a given region may fluctuate from year to year, the fluctuations are often temporary and, over long periods, trivial. Scientists have advanced three theories of population control to account for this relative constancy.

The first theory attributes a relatively constant population to periodic climatic catastrophes that decimate populations with such frequency as to prevent them exceeding some particular limit. In the case of small organisms with short life cycles, climatic changes need not be catastrophic: normal seasonal changes in photoperiod (daily amount of sunlight), for example, can govern population growth. The theory - the density - independent view - asserts that climatic factors exert the same regulatory effect on population regardless of the number of individuals in a region.

A second theory argues that population growth is primarily density-dependent - that is, the rate of growth of a population in a region decreases as the number of animals increases. The mechanisms that manage regulation may vary. For example, as numbers increase, the food supply would probably diminish, which would increase mortality. In addition, as Lotka and Volterra have shown, predators can find prey more easily in high-density populations. Other regulators include physiological control mechanisms: for example, Christian and Davis have demonstrated how the crowding that results from a rise in numbers may bring about hormonal changes in the pituitary and adrenal glands that in turn may regulate population by lowering sexual activity and inhibiting sexual maturation. There is evidence that these effects may persist for three generations in the absence of the original provocation. One challenge for density-dependent theorist is to develop models that would allow the precise prediction of the effects of crowding.

A third theory proposed by Wynne-Edwards and termed "epideictic" argues that organisms have evolved a "code" in the form of social or epideictic behaviour displays, such as winter-roosting aggregations or group vocalizing; such codes provide organisms with information on population size in a region so that they can, if necessary, exercise reproductive restraint. However, Wynne-Edwards theory, linking animal social behaviour and population control, has been challenged, with some justification, by several studies.

Questions 1-6 refer to Passage I above

1. The primary purpose of the passage is to

1. provide examples of some of the ways in which animals exercise reproductive restraint to control their own numbers.

2. suggest that theories of population control that concentrate on the social behaviour of animals are more open to debate than are theories that do not
3. summarize a number of scientific theories that attempt to explain why animal populations do not exceed certain limits.
4. compare and contrast the density-dependent and epideictic theories of population control.

2. The challenge posed to the Wynne-Edwards theory by several studies is regarded by the author with

1. skeptical amusement
2. qualified acceptance
3. perplexed astonishment
4. complete indifference

3. It can be inferred from the passage that proponents of the density-dependent theory of population control have not yet been able to —

1. reproduce the results of the study of Christian and Davis.
2. demonstrate how predator populations are themselves regulated.
3. make sufficiently accurate predictions about the effects of crowding.
4. explain adequately why the numbers of a population can increase as the population's rate of growth decreases.

4. Which of the following, if true, would best support the density-dependent theory of population control as it is described in the passage?

1. As the number of elephants in Kaziranga (Assam) decreases, the growth rate of this population of elephants begins to increase
2. As the number of Asiatic lions in Gir Forest (Gujarat) increases, the growth rate of this population of Asiatic lions also begins to increase
3. As the number of white-backed Indian vultures in Delhi decreases, the growth rate of this population of white-backed Indian vultures also begins to decrease
4. After the number of cheetals (spotted deers) in Kanha National Park decreases, the number of predators of these Cheetals begins to increase.

5. Which of the following statements would provide the most logical continuation of the final paragraph of the passage?

1. Because the Wynne-Edwards theory is able to explain more kinds of animal behaviour than the density-dependent theory, epideictic explanations of population regulation are now widely accepted.
2. Some of these studies have, in fact, worked out a systematic and complex code of social behaviour that can regulate population size.
3. Thus Wynne-Edward's theory raises serious questions about the constancy of animal population in a region.
4. The result of one study, for instance, have suggested that group vocalizing is more often used to defend territory than to provide information about population density.

6. According to Wynne-Edwards theory as it is described in the passage, epideictic behaviour displays serve the function of —

1. attracting predators
2. regulation of sexual activity
3. locating food
4. triggering hormonal changes

Passage II

The transplantation of organs from one individual to another normally involves two major problems :

1. organ rejection is less likely unless the transplantation antigens of both individuals are nearly identical, and
2. the introduction of any unmatched transplantation antigens induces the development by the recipient of donor-specific lymphocytes that will produce violent rejection of further transplantations from that donor.

However, we have found that among many strains of rats these "normal" rules of transplantation are not obeyed by liver transplants. Not only are liver transplants never rejected, but they even induce a state of donor-specific unresponsiveness in which subsequent transplants of other organs, such as skin, from that donor are accepted permanently. Our hypothesis is that

1. many strains of rats simply cannot mount a sufficiently vigorous destructive immune-response (using lymphocytes) to outstrip the liver's relatively great capacity to protect itself from immune-response damage and that
2. the systemic unresponsiveness observed is due to concentration of the recipient's donor-specific lymphocytes at the site of the liver transplant.

Questions 7- 10 are based on Passage II above

7. The primary purpose of the passage is to treat the accepted generalizations about organ transplantation in which of the following ways?
1. Criticize the major evidence used to support them
2. Suggest an alternative to them
3. Examine their virtues and limitations
4. Present findings that qualify them

8. According to the hypothesis of the author, after a successful liver transplant, the reason that rats do not reject further transplants of other organs from the same donor is that the —
1. recipient is unable to manufacture the lymphocytes necessary for the immune-response reaction
2. subsequently transplanted organ is able to repair the damage caused by the recipient's immune-response reaction
3. transplantation antigens of the donor and the recipient become matched
4. transplanted liver continues to be the primary locus for the recipient's immune-response reaction

9. Which of the following new findings about strains of rats that do not normally reject liver transplants, if true, would support the author's hypothesis?
I. Stomach transplants are accepted by the recipients in all cases
II. Increasing the strength of the recipient's immune-response reaction can induce liver-transplant rejection
III. Organs from any other donor can be transplanted without rejection after liver transplantation
IV. Preventing lymphocytes from being concentrated at the liver transplant produces acceptance of skin transplants

1. I only
2. II, III and IV only
3. II only
4. IV only

10. It can be inferred from the passage that the author believes that an important difference among the strains of rats is the —

1. strength of their immune-response reactions
2. adaptability of their lymphocytes
3. sensitivity of their antigens
4. size of their livers

Passage III

Corporate earnings growth has begun to slow down, although overall the last quarter's results may not have disappointed too much. But then expectations had been tempered by the sharp strengthening of the rupee and continued rise in prices of commodities. An analysis of results of about 1400 companies, excluding those in the financial services sector, show that more than half of them reported slower growth of PAT (Profit After Tax) in the September quarter ('07-'08) compared to the previous three months. And it is not just the smaller companies that experienced a deceleration in earnings growth.

Several medium-to-large-sized companies across sectors such as information technology, Pharmaceuticals, cement, tyres and metals too experienced a slower quarter. Overall, the topline growth has been showing a slowing trend, with quarterly sales growth (year-on-year) for the sample at a little over 10% compared with almost 30% in the same quarter last financial year fO6-'O7). However, there has been no trend in PAT growth over the last four quarters. The bottomline of the sample rose by 20% in the quarter to September 2007, compared with about 52% in the corresponding quarter last year. However, in the last four quarters the bottomline growth has tended to fluctuate randomly. The days of heady growth rates, though are clearly, over: the corporate sector is unlikely to see 30% growth in sales with 50-60% growth in PAT any time soon.

It is encouraging to note that the order books are still very strong and there is a revival in demand in sectors such as automobiles. More heartening is the finding of an October '07 survey of purchasing managers conducted for ABN Amro Bank by UK based NTC research. The survey reports that the purchasing managers index has risen to its highest reading since April 2005, indicating a recovery and improvement in overall business conditions. Much of this may be triggered by the onset of the festival season in the country but some of the optimism may wane by early next year. That apart, the global conditions are not very encouraging; a slowdown in the US can hurt the Indian economy and the earnings of the corporate sector. The corporate sector and investors need to be mindful of the developments in the global and domestic economy to protect themselves from shocks.

Questions 11 - 15 are based on Passage III above

11. According to the passage, which of the following statement(s) is/are true?

I. Despite the fact that a slowdown in US can hurt the Indian economy, considering the global conditions, the earnings of the corporate sector is not discouraging.

II. Despite the fact that the top-line growth has been showing a slowing trend, there has been no trend in PAT growth over the last four quarters.

III. An analysis of results of about 1400 companies across almost all sectors, shows that more than half of them reported slower growth of PAT In the September quarter ('07-'08) compared to the previous three months.

1. I only
2. II only
3. III only
4. II and III only

12. "Some of the optimism may wane by early next year": The underlined word "wane" here means

1. decline
2. decrease in importance
3. shrink
4. fall off

13. The underlined word "tempered" in the second sentence of the passage means

1. peevishness
2. modulated
3. sang-froid
4. equanimity

14. It can be inferred from the passage that each of the following is a consideration in determining whether the corporate earnings growth in this fiscal and in next year has begun to slow down EXCEPT the –

1. smaller companies as well as several medium-to-large-sized companies across sectors like IT, pharma, etc., experienced a deceleration in earnings growth.
2. corporate sector is unlikely to see 50% growth in sales with 50-60% growth in PAT any time soon.
3. A survey report by a UK based NTC research for ABN-Amro Bank indicates a recovery and improvement in overall business conditions.
4. In an analysis of results of about 1400 companies, the bottomline of the sample rose by 20% in the quarter September 2007, compared with about 52% in the corresponding quarter last year.

15. The primary purpose of the passage is to –

1. provide critical appreciation of the growth of Indian economy in the next fiscal year
2. review the corporate earnings growth in this fiscal year and compare the earnings of the last during the corresponding period
3. provide analytical reasons for the rise of BSE sensex in Indian market recently
4. provide the survey data in support of the principal concern of the author that a recovery and improvement in overall business çonditions in this fiscal which the survey indicated.

DIRECTIONS for questions 16 –20: *Each of the questions below consists of a word in* ***CAPITAL LETTERS,*** *followed by four words or phrases numbered (1), (2), (3), and (4). Choose the numbered word or phrase that is nearly* ***OPPOSITE*** *in meaning to the word in capital letters, then darken the corresponding oval in the answer sheet. Since some of the questions require you to distinguish fine shades of meaning, be sure to consider all the choices before deciding which one is best.*

16. OBDURATE:

1. similar
2. uncommunative
3. transitory
4. Complaisant

17. AVER:

1. condemn unjustly
2. resign indignantly

3. deny
4. Resent

18. PITH:

1. superficial element
2. routine treatment
3. insufficient attention
4. rigid formulation

19. EFFRONTERY:

1. stupidity
2. simplicity
3. deceitfulness
4. Deference

20. SCURVY:

1. above reproach
2. valiant
3. completely centred
4. carefree

DIRECTIONS for questions 21-25: *Each sentence below has one or two blanks, each blank indicating that something has been omitted. Beneath the sentence are four words or sets of words numbered (1), (2), (3), and (4). Choose the word or set of words for each blank that best fits the meaning of the sentence as a whole. Then darken the corresponding oval in the answer sheet.*

21. Although Shakespeare received little formal education, scholars, has in recent years __________ the view that he was __________ the work of classical authors.

1. raised doubts about........fully aware of
2. supported .... scurrilous
3. rejected ....well conversed with
4. undermined ....unfamiliar with

22. Their air of cheerful self-sacrifice and endless complaisance won them undeserved praise, for their seeming gallantry was wholly motivated by a ______________ wish to avoid conflict of any sorts.

1. putative
2. laudable
3. craven
4. poignant

23. Darwin's method did not really __________ the idea of race as an important conceptual category; even the much more central idea of species was little more than a theoretical __________

1. examined.................abstraction
2. require................... convenience
3. used ....speculation
4. subsume .... validation

24. Employees had become so __________ to the caprices of top management's personnel policies that they greeted the announcement of a company-wide dress code with__________

1. inured...............impassivity
2. pleased.................... impassivity
3. inured ....excitement
4. disdainful .... violence

25. The distinction between past, present, and future is only ____________however, __________ (Albert Einstein 1879-1955)

1. man-made .... artificial
2. false...............continuous
3. illusion .... persistent
4. continuous .... discreet

SECTION II
VERBAL SKILLS

DIRECTIONS for questions 26-50: Passages I, II and III are followed by questions based on their contents. After reading the passages, choose the best answer to each question, then darken the corresponding oval in the answer sheet. Base your answer on information that is either stated or implied in the passage.

Passage I

Once upon a time in not-too-distant past there used to *be* economic commentators and analysts galore who would love to preach about the virtues of a strong national currency. It used to be said the strength of a currency reflected the clout of a country's economy, its purchasing power and its position in the comity of nations. As the American greenback progressively weakens against the *"sabse bada rupaiya"*, these learned observers are singing a different tune.

The rise in the value of the Indian currency against the US dollar is double-edged sword that cuts both ways. By making exports more expensive and imports relatively cheaper, the rupee's appreciation vis-a-vis the dollar results in macro-gain and micro-pain. The key question is whether the gains outweigh the losses or vice-versa. The answer is not simple. The gains are not easy to ascertain while it is much easier to quantify the losses.

In March (2007), the Reserve Bank of India almost suddenly stopped intervening in the foreign exchange markets by mopping up dollars to ensure that the value of rupee was artificially low. Consequently, the rupee gained against the dollar by a huge 8.5 per cent in less than 40 working days in March and April (2007). Thereafter, the appreciation was gradual. By October (2007), the rupee had gained roughly 15 per cent against the dollar over a 12-month period and its value had touched a peak over nearly a decade.

The appreciation of the rupee was evidently part of a conscious official policy to contain inflation at a time when rising prices (especially food prices) were threatening to rapidly erode the popularity of that power-that-be and negate whatever benefits that were accruing to the aam admi. Put simply, the RBI was finding it tough and expensive to "sterilize" the rising inflows of foreign currency and prevent these from adding to domestic money supply thus, stoking inflationary fires.

Let's first consider the downside of the rupee's appreciation. Union Commerce Minister Kamal Nath told Parliament on December 4 (2007) that two million people could become jobless in export-oriented industries in different parts of the country. While exports as a whole were growing, there was a net decline in exports in certain sectors like textiles, garments and leather leading to job losses.

An earlier survey conducted by the Commerce Ministry in July (2007) was less alarmist but troubling nonetheless. It said 200,000 jobs would be lost in garments and textiles, 80,000 in Tirupur (Tamil Nadu) alone, famous for its internationally renowned hosiery manufacturing units. In just six leather-making companies surveyed by the Ministry, profitability had crashed three-fourths and nearly 2,000 workers had been rendered unemployed. The other export-oriented industries that have been badly hit include processed agricultural products, handicrafts, sports goods, chemicals, engineering items and marine goods.

The survey, conducted by a senior ministry bureaucrat, pointed out that 70 per cent of India's export are denominated in US dollars and since many export industries operate in buyers' markets that are "elastic" - in other words, demand falls when prices rise even a little - exporters have not been able to change their invoicing patterns to rupees, leave alone euros.

In a country where employment is not easy to come by, such job losses can hardly be justified even if one argues that the Indian economy as a whole has gained on account of a strong rupee.

The complaints of high-profile exporters of computer software and Information Technology (IT) enabled services or firms engaged in business process outsourcing need not be taken as seriously as the loss of jobs of unorganized workers in Tirupur (T.N.) or Moradabad in Uttar Pradesh (well-known for its brass handicrafts). The IT sector has been a beneficiary of generous tax concessions. Today its profit margins have been squeezed. But the industry knows it will have to live with progressively stronger rupee especially since it believes Indians are no longer mere "cyber coolies" but have graduated to become "knowledge workers".

Many Indian exporters have been pampered in the past, which is unusual since the country had to live for decades with acute shortages of hard currency and the government believed in export-promotion and import-substitution. The situation has undergone a sea-change since. At over US$ 260 billion, India's current forex reserves are an embarrassment of riches. We have a real problem of plenty on our hands. Unlike China, the Indian economy is not export-driven. International trade (exports and imports) accounts less than one-third of the country's national income against over three-fourths in China. Hence, China's week yuan policy is predictable. Not so India's policy encouraging a strong rupee.

The other side of the story is that the growing clout of the rupee has cushioned the country from the impact of the sharp rise in world prices of crude oil: up from US$ 53 a barrel in January (2007) and US$ 65 a barrel in May (2007) to kissing the US$ 100 a barrel mark in December (2007) before coming down a bit. The gains from new exchange rate are substantial since India imports three-fourths of its total requirements of crude. At the same time, the benefits of diesel prices not going up sharply are not that easily visible or quantifiable. An unintended result of the appreciation of the rupee is that India has become the 12th country in the world with a one-trillion dollar economy and, of course, the third largest economy in the world in terms of purchasing power parity after the US and China (by overtaking Japan).

Indians are bringing back their dollar stashes in foreign banks. That makes common sense. Indian companies are being told not to borrow abroad. The Government is beginning to discourage non-resident Indians from parking their funds here and encouraging individuals here to buy more dollars - a situation that would have been unthinkable for the first four and a half decades after the country become politically independent. The stock exchanges are booming thanks to unprecedented inflows from foreign institution investors who are sold on India's "growth story". Flows of foreign direct investments are at record levels.

Meanwhile, the American currency continues to decline against most other currencies. The depreciation of US dollars is sending shock waves across the planet. The rest of the world saves so that American citizens can borrow beyond their means - to the tune over US$ 2 billion each day. The US has invested in China and India less than half of what these two countries (accounting 40 per cent of the globe's population) have invested in the world's largest economy. The US accounts for 5 per cent of the world's population and a quarter of its wealth. Economist Joseph Stiglitz has calculated that by investing in American treasury bonds, developing countries end up losing over US$ 300 billion a year - four times the total amount international assistance to all so-called Third World countries. For decades, US governments were able to pressurize Asian countries not to appreciate their currencies. But that is all history.

Should we then feel proud and patriotic about our strong currency because resurgent. muscle-flexing, macho India is no longer being derided as a land of snake-charmers? Not really. Poverty, illiteracy, unemployment, inequality and regional economic imbalances have not disappeared - and will not disappear - in a tearing hurry despite a lot of tall talk about "inclusive" growth

So who is afraid of a strong rupee? Not the new Indian tourist who prefers Bangkok to Bangalore. But do spare a thought for the families of those who have lost their livelihood for no fault of theirs.

(**Source:** an authored article published in a national daily, December 2007)

Questions 26-30 are based on Passage I

26. Which of the following statement(s), according to the passage, is/are true EXCEPT —

I. The fact that the Indian economy, a one-trillion economy, is the third largest economy in the world in terms of purchasing parity after the US and China, and also the fact that the Indian economy is not export-driven unlike China, the hardening of rupee against US dollar will ultimately benefit the domestic market and the Indian economy as a whole.

II. The IT industry prepares itself with a progressively stronger rupee since it believes Indians are no longer mere "cyber coolies" but have graduated to become "knowledge workers".

III. For decades with acute shortages of hard currency, the Government believed in export-promotion and import-substitution, so many Indian exporters have been pampered in the past to earn in hard currency.

1. I only
2. II only
3. III only
4. I and III only

27. Which of the following title could be most suitable for the passage?

1. Hardening of Indian rupee: a boon from heaven for Ind'an economy.
2. Sabse Bada Rupaiya Vs American greenback: India is ahead in the race
3. A double-edged sword: A strong rupee does not spell good news all around.
4. Emerging new India: Who is afraid of a strong rupee?

28. Which of the following statement(s), if true WEAKENS the claim that a strong rupee would cost millions of jobs by making exports more expensive?

I. Export growth in April-September (2007) was 26.9% in dollar terms, and provisional data suggest 35.6% growth in October (2007).

II. The Reserve Bank of India as an official policy so far intervened to mop up dollars to maintain an artificially low rupee-dollar exchange rate to contain inflation within manageable limit. Since March (2007), RBI stopped intervening in the foreign exchange markets.

III. A comparative analysis shows that much stronger rises have been registered by China (10.9%), South Korea (11.1%), Malaysia (12.6%), Thailand (20.2%), and Brazil (25.4%) and so in no way can the rupee's appreciation be called steep or extraordinary. So far these countries have not reported declines in their exports.

1. I only
2. II only
3. III only
4. I and III only

29. Which of the following is the main idea according to the author of the passage?

1. To discuss the decline of the US dollar against the major currency in the world

economy and specially consequent negative fall-outs in Third World countries including India.

2. To discuss post-liberalisation fluctuations of Indian currency *"sabse bada rupaiya"* and its overall effects on imports-exports business in India.
3. To conclude after a persuasive discussion that despite the US government's attempts to pressurize Asian countries not to appreciate their currencies for decades, China's and India's economy grew substantially and are ranked the second and third economy of the world bypassing Japan.
4. To focus on the issue that a strong rupee does not spell good news all around and it results in macro-gain and micro-pain which are not easy to ascertain.

30. Which of the following statement(s) is/are true according to the passage?

I. The rupee appreciated against the US dollar between March and October (2007) because the RBI stopped intervening in the foreign exchange markets by mopping up dollars.

II. The US has invested in India and China less than half of what these two countries invested in the US economy.

III. Although exports as a whole were growing, there was a net decline in exports in certain specific sectors like textile, processed agricultural products, leather, etc., leading to job losses.

1. I only
2. II only
3. III only
4. I, II, III

Passage II

All the cells in a particular plant start out with the same complement of genes. How then can these cells differentiate and form structures as different as roots, stems, leaves, and fruits? The answer is that only a small subset of the genes in a particular kind of cell are expressed, or turned on, at a given time. This is accomplished by a complex system of chemical messengers that in plants include hormones and other regulatory molecules. Five major hormones have been identified: auxin, abscisic acid, cytokinin, ethylene and gibberellin. Studies of plants have identified a new class of regulatory molecules called oligosaccharins.

Unlike the oligosaccharins, the five well-known plant hormones are pleiotropic rather than specific; that is, each has more than one effect on the growth and development of plants. The five have so many simultaneous effects that they are not very useful in artificially controlling the growth of crops. Auxin, for instance, stimulates the rate of cell elongation, causes shoots to grow up and roots to go down, and inhibits that growth of lateral shoots. Auxin also causes the plant to develop a vascular system, to form lateral roots, and to produce ethylene.

The pleiotropy of the five well-studied plant hormones is somewhat analogous to thai of certain hormones in animals. For example, hormones from the hypothalamus in the brain stimulate the anterior lobe of the pituitary gland to synthesize and release many different hormones one of which stimulates the release of hormones from the adrenal cortex. These hormones have specific effects on target organs all over the body. One hormone stimulates the thyroid gland, for example, another the ovarian follicle cells, and so forth. In other words, there is a hierarchy of hormones.

Such a hierarchy may also exist in plants. Oligosaccharins are fragments of the cell wall released by enzymes: different enzymes release different oligosaccharins. There are indications that pleiotropic plant hormones may actually function by activating the enzymes that release these others, more specific chemical messengers from the cell wall.

Questions 31 -36 refer to Passage II

31. The passage suggests that the place of hypothalamic hormones in the hormonal hierarchies of animals in similar to the place of which of the following in plants?

1. The oligosacchrins
2. Plant cell walls
3. The five major hormones
4. The complement of genes in each plant cell

32. The author mentions specific effects that auxin has on plant development in order to illustrate —

1. hierarchical nature of the functioning of plant hormones
2. point that some of the effects of plant hormones can be harmful
3. concept of pleiotropy as it is exhibited by plant hormones
4. way in which hormones are produced by plants

33. The passage suggests which of the following is a function likely to be performed by an oligosaccharin?

1. To stimulate the walls of a particular cell to produce other oligosaccharins
2. To stimulate a particular plant cell to become part of a plant's root system
3. To produce multiple effects on a particular subsystem of plant cells
4. To activate enzymes that release specific chemical messengers from plant cell walls.

34. According to the passage, the five well-known plant hormones are not useful in controlling the growth of crops because

1. each hormone has various effects on plants
2. each hormone has different effects on different kinds of plants
3. each hormone works on only a small subset of a cell's genes at any particular time
4. it is not known exactly what functions the hormones perform

35. According to the passage, which of the following best describes a function performed by oligosaccharin?

1. Releasing specific chemical messengers from a plant's cell walls
2. Influencing the development of a plant's cells by controlling the expression of the cell's genes
3. Interacting with one another to produce different chemicals
4. Producing the hormones that cause plant cells to differentiate to perform different functions.

36. The passage suggests that, unlike the pleiotropic hormones, oligosacchrins could be used effectively to —

1. alter the complement of genes in the cells of plants
2. artificially control specific aspects of the development of crops
3. alter the effects of the five major hormones on plant development
4. pinpoint functions of other plant hormones

Passage III

According to a study by the Indian Council for Research on International Economic Relations (ICRIER), consumers can't get enough of big retail chains. ICRIER was appointed by the Government to study the impact of organized retail on small traders. While the study indicates that organized retail will impact small traders adversely and has indeed already hit sales and profits, the consumer side of the findings indicates that more Indians - as many as 53 percent - want to see western style supermarkets across the country. Any fallout from the introduction of these chains is also likely to be short-term.

Small retailers and Kirana stores are astute businessmen. None of them will shut down. They have survived the onslaught of time and will continue to thrive because of the sheer convenience they provide. They have a special personal rapport with their customers and offer benefits like credit facilities, door delivery and even phone services. India is a huge market. With minor structural benefits, small retailers will be able to coexist with the big ones. If anything **will** change, it will only be for the better.

Organized retailers will push the mom-and-pop stores and small retailers up the value chain to innovate in their offerings. In spite of organized retail growing swiftly in recent years, the unorganized sector accounts for nearly 97 per cent of the total retail in India. According to estimates, the share of organized retail in the $300 billion spent on food and consumer items this year (2007) in India, would be just $12 billion.

Growth of organized retail will benefit everyone across the value chain. It will create huge number of jobs in the country. Farmers will benefit as they will have consistent incomes and would also be able to hedge themselves against crop failure. Consumers will directly profit with retailers passing on cost benefits, accrued through high volume procurements, to them.

(**Source**: an article in the edit page of a national daily, December 2007)

Questions 37-40 refer to Passage III

37. According to the passage, which of the following can be inferred as the main thrust of the author's argument(s)?

I. The organized retail stores would in the long run, have a large adverse effect on large sections of small retail trade.

II. The organized retail stores would help develop a broadbase domestic economy, affordable food prices, farm sector development and inclusive growth; in short, the organized retail stores would improve wide sections of stakeholders concerned in the society - customers, farmers and employment opportunities.

III. The share of organized retail would be insignificant only 4% (approx) of the amount spent on food and consumer products.

1. I only
2. II only
3. III only
4. II and III only

38. Which of the following statement(s), if true, WEAKENS the arguments in favour of the organized retail stores presented in the passage?

I. The organized retail stores with deep pockets can withstand losses for a short-term in order to gain and control the market.

II. In absence of a social security net to help small traders and workers who could lose jobs when and if that happens to tide over the crisis, a public policy that puts a large number of people who are likely to the affected by the organized retail stores, can have disastrous social and economic implications in the long run.

III. The organized retail stores will target rich and wannabes as customers in urban centres with a large disposable income.

1. I only
2. II only
3. III only
4. II and III only

39. Which of the following statement(s), according to the passage, is/are true as per to the author?

1. Across the value chain in retail markets, growth of organized retail will benefit almost all stakeholders
2. The fear among small retailers and traders that they stand to lose their livelihood if mega retail chains enter the market in a big way is more *or* less unreal - according to the ICRIER survey
3. The foreign retail chains like Wal-Mart without any protective clause in an open and free market economy as in India today will kill indigenous entrepreneurship.
4. Organized retailers will push the mom-and-pop stores and small retailers up in the value chain which they can't sustain in the long run.

1. 1 Only
2. 1 and 2 Only
3. 1 and 4 Only
4. 3 Only

40. Which of the following statement(s), if true, will strengthen the argument(s) in favour of the organized retail stores?

I. The organized retail stores - (modern trade) - offer smaller regional brands more shelf-space, better displays and ambience compared to Kirana stores.

II. Regional brands are benefitted by pushing their brands through the organized retail stores with bargains and value deals that are often better and bigger players.

III. The organized retail stores, controlled and invested by big business, Indian and foreign – for example, Reliance, Wal-Mart, and others, offer variety of products at affordable price-tags and better quality.

1. I and II only
2. II and III only
3. I and III only
4. I, II, III

DIRECTIONS for questions 41 -44: *Each sentence or a short passage below has one, two or three blanks, each blank indicating that something has* ***been*** *omitted. Beneath the sentence/passage are four numbered words or set of words. Choose the word or set of words for each blank that best fits the meaning of the sentence/passage as a whole, then darken the corresponding oval in the answer sheet.*

41. Aspartame, a new artificial sugar substitute, is only ___________replacement for saccharin because, unlike saccharin, it breaks down and loses its sweetening characteristics at high temperatures making it _______________for baking.

1. a medically approved ________ unsuitable
2. a significant ____________ problematic
3. a partial ________________ unsuitable
4. a chemical ______________ harmful

42. Arguably the most important document ever to be auctioned goes on sale on Tuesday, 18 December 07, when the Magna Carta, an 800-year-old English royal manuscript goes under the hammer at Sotheby's in New York. The royal charter, dated 1297 and bearing the wax seal of King Edward I _______ the rights of man into English law and is considered________ the of such ________ historical documents as the US Declaration of Independence.

1. recorded________dawn________important
2. evidenced________early attempt________valued
3. enshrined________primordial________benchmarked
4. enshrined________precursor________landmark

43. The manuscript, most likely made of sheepskin, was enshrined at a time of__________between King John' and. the Enlish barons. It was first issued in 1215 and confirmed as English law in 1297.

1. skirmishes
2. closeness
3. bonhomie
4. disagreements

44. The document, which required the king to__________that he was bound by law in the same way as his subjects is described as the first__________on the ladder to freedom and a__________of liberty.

1. accept__________rung__________talisman
2. reject__________step__________early stage
3. accept__________structure__________support
4. accept__________gap__________death knell

DIRECTIONS for questions 45-47: *Each question presents a sentence, part or all of which is underlined. Beneath the sentence, you will find four answer choices numbered (1), (2), (3) and (4); the first answer choice repeats the original; the other three are different ways of phrasing the underlined part. If you think the original phrasing is best, choose the first answer; otherwise choose one of three others; darken the corresponding oval in the answer sheet.*

This type of question tests your ability to recognize the correctness and effectiveness of expression in standard written English. In choosing your answer, follow the requirements of standard written English; that is, pay attention to grammar, choice of words, and sentence construction. Choose the answer that produces the most effective sentence; this answer should be clear and exact, without awkwardness, ambiguity, redundancy, or grammatical error.

45. Like the idolization accorded the Brontes and Browning. James Joyce and Virginia Woolf are often subjected to the kind of veneration that blurs the distinction between the artist and the human being.

1. Like the idolization accorded the Brontes and Brownings
2. Like that accorded to the Brontes end Brownings
3. Like the Brontes and Brownings
4. As it is of the Brontes and Brownings

46. Carnivorous mammals can endure what would otherwise be lethal levels of body heat because they have a heat-exchange network which kept the brain from getting too hot.

1. which kept
2. which has kept
3. that has been keeping
4. that keeps

47. None of the attempts to specify the causes of crime explains why most of the people exposed to the alleged causes do not commit crimes and conversely, why so many of those not so exposed <u>have</u>

1. have
2. could
3. shall
4. do

DIRECTIONS for questions 48-50: *For each of the these questions, four or five sentences lettered (A) to (D)/(E) are given. These sentences, if arranged in a logical sequence, will form a coherent and meaningful paragraph. Choose the most logical order from among the given answer choices numbered (1). (2), (3) and (4) given below the set of these sentences, then darken the corresponding oval in the answer sheet.*

48. A. A major one is that rising costs in India may erode our cost-competitiveness.

B. That is the train on which, in the years ahead, you can expect to see even more corporate leaders in India Inc.

C. Bharat Express

D. As the economy powers ahead at a scorching pace, there are danger signals ahead.

E. But let us start the tale at the beginning today.

1. ABCDE
2. CBEDA
3. CEBAD
4. CADBE

49. A. We are at the threshold of possibly creating an altogether new model of development, based on services-led employment and growth of the tech industry in rural areas.

B. The government's role is crucial.

C. Let us give it a chance at least

D. States need to facilitate and help this process.

E. Technology, the growing worldwide service market, and our dominance in the global IT-BPO marketplace have placed India in a unique position.

1. BCADE
2. BDEAC
3. EABDC
4. CABDE

50. A. Economists see the environment as a subset of the economy

B. Like Ptolemy's view of the solar system, the economists view is confusing efforts to understand our modern world.

C. Ecologists, on the other hand, see the economy as a subset of, the environment.

D. In 1543, Polish astronomer Nicolaus Copernicus published 'On the Revolution of the Celestial Spheres" in which he challenged the view that Sun revolved round the Earth.

E. His alternative to the earlier Ptolemaic model, which placed the Earth at the centre of the universe, led to a revolution in thinking and ultimately to a new world view.

1. DEACB
2. ACEBD
3. DBECA
4. BDECA

Answer Key

1. 3	**2.** 1	**3.** 3	**4.** 1	**5.** 4	**6.** 2	**7.** 1
8. 1	**9.** 3	**10.** 1	**11.** 4	**12.** 1	**13.** 2	**14.** 3
15. 2	**16.** 4	**17.** 3	**18.** 1	**19.** 4	**20.** 3	**21.** 1
22. 1	**23.** 1	**24.** 1	**25.** 3	**26.** 2	**27.** 3	**28.** 3
29. 4	**30.** 4	**31.** 3	**32.** 3	**33.** 4	**34.** 1	**35.** 2
36. 2	**37.** 2	**38.** 2	**39.** 1	**40.** 2	**41.** 3	**42.** 4
43. 1	**44.** 3	**45.** 2	**46.** 4	**47.** 4	**48.** 2	**49.** 3
50. 1						

EXPLANATIONS

1. Central idea question

2. Para 3 last line

3. Para 2

4.

5. Since in the last line author is not supporting the given theory

6. Last para

7. Central idea question

8. Para 2 second line

9 . Last 2 points

10.

11. Para 1

12 . 1st para second line

13.

14. Rest are there in the passage

15.

16. Obdurate means stubborn and complaisant is flexible

17. Aver means to assert so opposite would be to DENY

18. Pith means in depth element

19. Effrontery means disrespect

20. Scurvy mean cursory or superficial

21. Because of key word Although 1st blank will have negative connotation and second blank will be positive

22. Word is putative which means assume, supposed .In this the context is positive

23. The word abstract in answer choice goes with concept category

24. 0 **25.**

26. 1 is true up to china only . 2 in para 8 as it is. Opt. 3 is also stated however the last part i.e to hard currency. Has discrepancy & in addition we know that opt.2 is a fact and the options. Do not combine 2 with any other. Hence it is 2 only.

27.

28. Is the only option which is complete and has both cause (Rs appreciates) and effect…not reported declines .

29.

30. 1 is in para3,2nd is in para1and 3 is in para5.

31. See para 3-first line-pleiotropy Is analogous i.e of hormones in animals..for eg hypothalamus in brain..Hence hypothalamus : five hormones in plants.

32. Refer para 2…Highlights plant hormones are pleitroic….each one has more than one effect..for eg Auxin is taken to highlight this pleiotropy characteristic.

33. Para4 last line: activating…these others…more specific chem. Mess.

34. Para2nd… it has more than 1 effect…

35. Refer para 2—it says unlike the oligosaccharins, 5 hormones are pleiotropic….so many effects that are not useful in controlling growth of plants, so Oligosaccharins help in controlling expression of cell.

36. Dissimilarity is over the specificty

37. Refer Last para.Rest 2 are improper and partially correct

38. 1 supports.3 is hypothetical.2 has both the cause n effect which talks against the organized retail sector hence weakens it.

39. The author talks of positive impact of retail in long run, hence option 1.

40. 1 is only option that weakens the statement.

41. Key words are "unlike saccharin", so first blank should be ..only **Partial** replacemet... Since it breaks down and loses sweetness so makes it **UNSUITABLE** for baking.

42. Precursor is a better option as us follows…..landmark.3rd has primordial and benchmarked unparallel adjectives.

43. The manuscript was issue and then **confirmed..**this could happen only when the relations are friendly**..**hence answer should be BONHOMIE (friendly and affable

44. In First blank..document**..requires** the king so **" accept"**is appropriate here**.** In Second blank key word is ladder so right word should be" rung" (A rod or bar forming a step of a ladder)In 3rd blank we need a word that shows a symbol or a sign of liberty having some power of magic, good) and hence "Talisman" & it is better than deathknell (an omen of death or destruction) which is an antonym

45. There is comparison of two noun phrases so **Like** should be used. Correct idiom is "Accorded to" So option 2 is correct and concise . Like that accorded to… implies "veneration"(respect) accorded to…

46. Can endure in the first part is in the present tense. But **which kept** (underlined) is in past tense.So with **can endure… that keeps** …is the correct tense.

47. Parallel structure a)why most…do not commit….b).why so many….not so exposed do.

48. C is the opening. BC are pairs coz B uses that is the train mentioned in C. DA are pairs as D talks of danger signals ahead and A points out a major danger of rising costs.

49. E introduces a new idea so is the opening. EA are pairs coz "We" used in A refers to noun "India" as given in "E". BD are pairs as B talks of govt's role and D continues with States(refers to state govt) need to help.

50 D is the opening as introduces it the idea. E should follow D. Pronoun "his "in E refers to Nicolaus in "D" . AC are pairs as A talks of Economists and C establishes a contrast by using words ecologists on the other hand. Hence option choice 1.

CAT 2008

Number of Questions – 40
Time :40 M.

SECTION I

DIRECTIONS for questions 1 to 4: *In each question, there are five sentences. Each sentence has a pair of worlds that are italicized and highlighted. From the italicized and highlighted words, select the most appropriate words (A or B) to form correct sentences. The sentences are followed by options that indicate the words, which may be selected to correctly complete the set of sentences. From the options given, choose the* ***most appropriate*** *one.*

1. Anita wore a beautiful ***broach(A)/brooch(B)*** on the lapel of her jacket.

If you want to complain about the amenities in your neighborhood, please meet your ***councilor(A)/counselor(B).***

I would like your ***advice(A)/advise(B)*** on which job I should choose.

The last scene provided a ***climatic(A)/climatic(B)*** ending to the film.

Jeans that ***flair(A)/flare(B)*** at the bottom are in fashion these days.

1. BABAA   2. BABAB
3. BAAAB   4. ABABA
5. BAABA

2. The cake had lots of ***currents(A)/currants(B)*** and nuts in it.

If you engage in such ***exceptional(A)/exceptionable(B)*** behavior, I will be forced to punish you.

He has the same capacity as an adult to ***consent(A)/assent(B)*** to surgical treatment.

The minister is ***obliged(A)/compelled(B)*** to report regularly to a parliamentary board.

His analysis of the situation is far too ***sanguine(A)/genuine(B).***

1. BBABA   2. BBAAA
3. BBBBA   4. ABBAB
5. BABAB

3. She managed to bite back the ***ironic (A)/caustic(B)*** retort on the tip of her tongue.

He gave an impassioned and **valid (A)/cogent(B)** plea for judicial reform.

I am not **adverse (A)/averse(B)** to helping out.

The ***coupe(A)/coup(B)*** broke away as the train climbed the hill.

They heard the bells ***peeling (A)/pealing(B)*** far and wide.

1. BBABA   2. BBBAB
3. BAABB   4. ABBAA
5. BBBBA

4. We were not successful in ***defusing(A)/diffusing(B)*** the Guru's ideas.

The students ***baited(A)/bated(B)*** the instructor with irrelevant questions.

The ***hoard(A)/horde(B)*** rushed into the campus.

The prisoner's ***interment(A)/internment(B)*** came to an end with his early release.

The hockey team could not deal with his ***unsociable(A)/unsocial(B)*** tendencies.

1. BABBA
2. BBABB
3. BABAA
4. ABBAB
5. AABBA

DIRECTIONS ***for questions 55 to 58 :*** *In each of the following questions there are sentences that form a paragraph. Identify the sentence(s) or part(s) of sentence(s) that is/are correct in terms of grammar and usage (including spelling, punctuation and logical consistency). Then, choose the* ***most appropriate*** *option.*

5. A. In 1849, a poor Bavarian imigrant named Levi Strauss
B. landed in San Francisco, California,
C. at the invitation of his brother-in-law David Stern
D. owner of dry goods business.
E. This dry goods business would later became known as Levi Strauss & Company.

1. B only
2. B and C only
3. A and B
4. A only
5. A, B and D

6. A. In response to the allegations and condemnation pouring in,
B. Nike implemented comprehensive changed in their labour policy.
C. Perhaps sensing the rising tide of global labour concerns,
D. From the public would become a prominent media issue,
E. Nike sought to be a industry leader in employee relations.

1. D and E
2. D only
3. A and E
4. A and D
5. B, C and E

7. A. Charges and countercharges mean nothing
B. to the few million who have lost their home.
C. The nightmare is far from over, for the government
D. is still unable to reach hundreds who are marooned.
E. The death count have just begun.

8. A. I did not know what to make of you.
B. Because you'd lived in India, I associate you more with my parents than with me.
C. And yet you were unlike my cousins in Calcutta, who seem so innocent and obedient when I visited them.
D. you were not curious about me in the least.
E. Although you did make effort to meet me.

1. A only
2. A and B
3. A and E
4. D only
5. A and D

DIRECTIONS for questions 59 to 62: *Each of the following questions has a sentence with two blanks. Given below each questions are five pairs of words. Choose the pair that* ***best*** *completes the sentence.*

9. The genocides in Bosnia and Rwanda, apart from being mis-described in the most sinister and ________ manner as 'ethnic cleansing', were also blamed, in further hand-washing rhetoric, on something dark and interior to ________ and perpetrators alike.

1. innovative; communicator
2. Exigent; exploiters
3. enchanting; leaders
4. Tragic; sufferers
5. disingenuous; victims

10. As navigators, calendar makers, and other ____________ of the sky accumulated evidence to the contrary, ancient astronomers were forced to ____________ that certain bodies might move in circles about points, which in turn moved in circles about the earth.

1. scrutinizers; believe2. Observers; concede 3. observers; agree 4. Students; conclude 5. scrutinizers; suggest

11. Every human being, after the first few days of his life, is a product of two factors: on the one hand, there is his ____________ endowment; and on the other hand, there is the effect of environment, including ____________.

1. constitutional; whether2. Economic; learning

3. congenital; education4. Genetic; pedagogy 5. personal; climate

12. Exhaustion of natural resources, destruction of individual initiative by governments, control over men's minds by central ____________ of education and propaganda are some of the major evils which appear to be on the increase as a result of the impact of science upon minds suited by ________ to an earlier kind of world.

1. tenets; fixation
2. Organs; tradition
3. aspects; inhibitions
4. Departments; repulsion
5. institutions; inhibitions

DIRECTIONS ***for questions13 to16 :*** *In each of the questions, a word has been used in sentences in five different ways. Choose the option corresponding to the sentence in which the usage of the word in* ***incorrect or inappropriate.***

13. Run

1. I must run fast to catch up with him.
2. Our team scored a goal against the run of play.
3. You can't run over him like that
4. The newly released book is enjoying a popular run.
5. This film is a run-of-the-mill production.

14. Round

1. The police fired a round of tear gas shells.
2. The shop is located round the corner.
3. We took a ride on the merry-go-round.
4. The doctor is on a hospital round.
5. I shall proceed further only after you come round to admitting it.

15. Buckle

1. After the long hike our knees were beginning to buckle.
2. The horse suddenly broke into a buckle.

3. The accused did not buckle under police interrogation.
4. Sometimes, an earthquake can make a bridge buckle.
5. People should learn to buckle up as soon as they get into a car.

16. File

1. You will find the paper in the file under C.
2. I need to file an insurance claim.
3. The cadets were marching in a single file.
4. File your nails before you apply nail polish.
5. When the parade was on, a soldier broke the file.

DIRECTIONS for questions 17 to20: *Each of the following questions has a paragraph from which the last sentence has been deleted. From the given options, choose the sentence that completes the paragraph in the **most appropriate** way.*

17. Most people at their first consultation take a furtive look at the surgeon's hands in the hope of reassurance. Prospective patients look for delicacy, sensitivity, steadiness, perhaps unblemished pallor. On this basis, Henry Perowne loses a number of cases each year. Generally, he knows it's about to happen before the patient does: the downward glance repeated, the prepared questions beginning to falter, the overemphatic thanks during the retreat to the door.

1. Other people do not communicate due to their poor observation.
2. Other patients don't like what they see but are ignorant of their right to go elsewhere.
3. But Perowne himself is not concerned.
4. But others will take their place, he thought.
5. These hands are steady enough, but they are large.

18. Trade protectionism, disguised as concern for the climate, is raising its head. Citing competitiveness concerns, powerful industrialized countries are holding out threats of a levy on imports of energy-intensive products from developing countries that refuse to accept their imports of energy-intensive products from developing countries that refuse to accept their demands. The actual source of protectionist sentiment in the OECD countries is, of course, their current lackluster economic performance, combined with the challenges posed by the rapid economic rise of China and India – in that order.

1. Climate change is evoked to bring trade protectionism through the back door.
2. OECD countries are taking refuge in climate change issues to erect trade barriers against these two countries.
3. Climate change concerns have come as a convenient stick to beat the rising trade power of China and India.
4. Defenders of the global economic status quo are posing as climate change champions.
5. Today's climate change champions are the perpetrators of global economic inequity.

19. 1. Mattancherry represents, therefore, the perfect picture of peaceful co-existence.

2. India's Jews have almost never suffered discriminations, except for European colonizers and each other.

3. Jews in India were always tolerant.
4. Religious tolerance has always been only a façade and nothing more.
5. The pretty pastel streets are, thus, very popular with the tourists.

20. Given the cultural and intellectual interconnections, the question of what is 'Western' and what is 'Eastern' (or 'Indian') is often hard to decide, and the issue can be discussed only in more dialectical terms. The diagnosis of a thought as 'purely Western' or 'purely Indian' can be very illusory.

1. Thoughts are not the kind of things that can be easily categorized.
2. Though 'occidentalism' and 'orientalism' as dichotomous concepts have found many adherents.
3. 'East is East and West is West' has been a discredited notion for a long time now.
4. compartmentalizing thoughts is often desirable.
5. The origin of a thought is not the kind of thing to which 'purity' happens easily.

DIRECTIONS for questions 21 to 25: *The passage given below is followed by a set of five questions. Choose the* ***most appropriate*** *answer to each questions.*

Language is not a cultural artifact that we learn the way we learn to tell time or how the federal government works. Instead, it is a distinct piece of the biological makeup of our brains. Language is a complex, specialized skill, which develops in the child spontaneously, without conscious effort or formal instruction, is deployed without awareness of its underlying logic, is qualitatively the same in every individual, and is distinct from more general abilities to process information or behave intelligently. For these reasons some cognitive scientists have described language as a psychological faculty, a mental organ, a neural system, and a computational module. But I prefer the admittedly quaint term "instinct". It conveys the idea that people know how to talk in more or less the sense that spiders know how to spin webs. Web-spinning was not invented by some unsung spider genius and does not depend on having had the right education or on having an aptitude for architecture or the construction trades. Rather, spiders spin spider webs because they have spider brains, which give them the urge to spin and the competence to succeed. Although there are differences between webs and words, I will encourage you to see language in this way, for it helps to make sense of the phenomena we will explore.

Thinking of language as an instinct inverts the popular wisdom, especially as it has been passed down in the canon of the humanities and social sciences. Language is no more a cultural invention than is upright posture. It is not a manifestation of a general capacity to use symbols: a three-year-old, we shall see, is a grammatical genius, but is quite incompetent at the visual arts, religious iconography, traffic signs, and the other staples of the semiotics curriculum. Though language is a magnificent ability unique to *Homo sapiens* among living species, it does not call for sequestering the study of humans from the domain of biology, for a magnificent ability unique to a particular living species is far from unique in the animal kingdom. Some kinds of bats home in on flying insects using Doppler sonar. Some kinds of migratory birds navigate thousands of miles by calibrating the positions of the constellations against the time of day and year. In nature's talent show, we are simply a species of primate with our own act, a knack for communicating information about who did what to whom by modulating the sounds we make when we exhale.

Once you begin to look at language not as the ineffable essence of human uniqueness but as t biological adaptation to communicate information, it is no longer as tempting to see language as an insidious shaper of thought, and, we shall see, it is not. Moreover, seeing language as one of nature's engineering marvels – an organ with "that perfection of structure and co-adaptation which justly excites our admiration," in darwin's words – gives us a new respect for your ordinary Joe and the much-maligned English language (or any language). The complexity of language, from the scientist's point of view, is part of our biological birthright; it is not something that parents teach their children or something that must be elaborated in school – as Oscar Wilde said, "Education is an admirable thing, but it is well to remember from time to time that nothing that is worth knowing can be taught." A preschooler's tacit knowledge of grammar is more sophisticated than the thickest style manual or the most state-of-the-art computer language system, and the same applies to all healthy human beings, even the notorious syntax-fracturing professional athlete and the, you know, like, inarticulate teenage skateboarder. Finally, since language is the product of a well-engineered biological instinct, we shall see that it is not the nutty barrel of monkeys that entertainer-columnists make it out to be.

21. According to the passage, which of the following does not stem from popular wisdom on language?

1. Language is a cultural artifact.
2. Language is a cultural invention.
3. Language is learnt as we grow.
4. Language is unique to *Homo sapiens.*
5. Language is a psychological faculty.

22. Which of the following can be used to replace the "spiders know how to spin webs" analogy as used by the author?

1. A kitten learning to jump over a wall.
2. Bees collecting nectar
3. A donkey carrying a load
4. A horse running a Derby
5. A pet dog protecting its owner's property.

23. According to the passage, which of the following is unique to human beings?

1. Ability to use symbols while communicating with one another.
2. Ability to communicate with each other trough voice modulation.
3. Ability to communicate information to other members of the species.
4. Ability to use sound as means of communication.
5. All of the above.

24. According to the passage, complexity of language cannot be taught by parents or at school to children because

1. children instinctively know language.
2. children learn the language on their own.
3. language is not amenable to teaching.
4. children know language better than their teachers or parents.
5. children are born with the knowledge of semiotics.

25. Which of the following best summarizes the passage?

1. Language is unique to Home sapiens.
2. Language is neither learnt nor taught.
3. Language is not a cultural invention or artifact as it is made out.
4. Language is instinctive ability of human beings.
5. Language is use of symbols unique to human beings.

DIRECTIONS for questions 26 to 30: *The passage given below is followed by a set of five questions. Choose the most appropriate answer to each question.*

When I was little, children were bought two kinds of ice cream, sold from those white wagons with canopies made of silvery metal : either the two-cent cone or the four-cent ice-cream pie. The two-cent cone was very small, in fact it could fit comfortably into a child's hand, and it was made by taking the ice cream from its container with a special scoop and piling it on the cone. Granny always suggested I eat only a part of the cone, then throw away the pointed end, because it had been touched by the vendor's hand (though that was the best part, nice and crunchy, and it was regularly eaten in secret, after a pretence of discarding it).

The four-cent pie was made by a special little machine, also silvery, which pressed two disks of sweet biscuit against a cylindrical section of ice cream. First you had to thrust your tongue into the gap between the biscuits until it touched the central nucleus of ice cream; then, gradually, you ate the whole thing, the biscuit surfaces softening as they became soaked in creamy nectar. Granny had no advice to give here: in theory the pies had been touched only by the machine; in practice, the vendor had held them in his hand while giving them to us, but it was impossible to isolate the contaminated area.

I was fascinated, however, by some of my peers, whose parents bought them not a four-cent pie but two two-cent cones. These privileged children advanced proudly with one cone in their right hand and one in their left; and expertly moving their head from side to side, they licked first one, then the other. This liturgy seemed to me so sumptuously enviable, that many times I asked to be allowed to celebrate it. In vain My elders were inflexible: a four-cent ice, yes; but two-cent ones, absolutely no.

As anyone can see, neither mathematics nor economy nor dietetics justified this refusal. Nor did hygiene, assuming that in due course the tips of both cones were discarded. The pathetic, and obviously mendacious, justification was that a boy concerned with turning his eyes from one cone to the other was more inclined to stumble over stones, steps, or cracks in the pavement. I dimly sensed that there was another secret justification, cruelly pedagogical, but I was unable to grasp it.

Today, citizen and victim of a consumer society, a civilization of excess and waste (which the society of the thirties was not), I realize that those dear and now departed elders were right. Two two-cent cones instead of one at four cents did not signify squandering, economically speaking, but symbolically they surely did. It was for this precise reason, that I yearned for them: because two ice creams suggested excess. And this was precisely why they were denied to me : because they looked indecent, an insult to poverty, a display of fictitious privilege, a boast of wealth. Only spoiled children ate two cones at once, those children who in fairy tales were rightly punished, as Pinocchio was when he rejected the skin and the stalk. And parents who encouraged this weakness, appropriate to little parvenus, were bringing up their children in the foolish theatre of "I'd like to but I can't ." They were preparing them to turn up at tourist-class check-in with a fake Gucci bag bought from a street peddler on the beach at Rimini.

Nowadays the moralist risks seeming at odds with morality, in a world where the consumer civilization now wants even adults to be spoiled, and promises them always something more from the wristwatch in the box of detergent to the bonus bangle sheathed, with the magazine it accompanies, in a plastic envelope. Like the parents of those ambidextrous gluttons I so envied, the consumer civilization pretends to give more, but actually gives, for four cents, what is worth four cents. You will throwaway the old transistor radio to purchase the new one, that boasts an alarm clock as well, but some inexplicable defect in the mechanism will guarantee that the radio lasts only a year. The new cheap car will have leather seats, double side mirrors adjustable from inside, and a panelled dashboard, but it will not last nearly so long as the glorious old Fiat 500, which, even when it broke down, could be started again with a kick.

The morality of the old days made Spartans of us all, while today's morality wants all of us to be Sybarites.

26. Which of the following cannot be inferred from the passage?

1. Today's society is more extravagant than the society of the 1930s.
2. The act of eating two ice cream cones is akin to a ceremonial process.
3. Elders rightly suggested that a boy turning eyes from one cone to the other was more likely to fall.
4. Despite seeming to promise more, the consumer civilization gives away exactly what the ting is worth.
5. The consumer civilization attempts to spoil children and adults alike.

27. In the passage, the phrase "little parvenus" refers to

1. naughty midgets.
2. Old hags
3. Arrogant people
4. Young upstarts
5. Foolish kids.

28. The author pined for two two-cent cones instead of one four-cent pie because

1. it made dietetic sense.
2. It suggested intemperance.
3. It was more fun.
4. it had a visual appeal
5. He was a glutton

29. What does the author mean by "nowadays the moralist risks seeming at odds with morality"?

1. The moralists of yesterday have become immoral today.
2. The concept of morality has changed over the years.
3. Consumerism is amoral.
4. The risks associated with immorality have gone up.
5. The purist's view of morality is fast becoming popular.

30. According to the author, the justification for refusal to let him eat two cones was plausibly

1. didactic
2. dietetic
3. dialectic
4. diatonic
5. diastolic

DIRECTIONS for questions 31 to 35: *The passage given below is followed by a set of five questions. Choose the* ***most appropriate*** *answer to each question.*

A remarkable aspect of art of the present century is the range of concepts and ideologies which it embodies. It is almost tempting to see a pattern emerging within the art field – or alternatively imposed upon it *a posteriori* – similar to that which exists under the umbrella of science where the general term covers a whole range of separate, though interconnecting, activities. Any parallelism is however – in this instance at least – misleading. A scientific discipline develops systematically once its bare tenets have been established, named and categorized as conventions. Many of the concepts of modern art, by contrast, have resulted from the almost accidental meetings of groups of talented individuals at certain times and certain places. The ideas generated by these chance meetings had twofold consequences.

Firstly, a corpus of work would be produced which, in great part, remains as a concrete record of the events. Secondly, the ideas would themselves be disseminated through many different channels of communication – seeds that often bore fruit in contexts far removed from their generation. Not all movements were exclusively concerned with innovation. Surrealism, for instance, claimed to embody a kind of insight which can be present in the art of nay period. This claim has been generally accepted so that a sixteenth century painting by Spranger or a mysterious photograph by Atget can legitimately be discussed in surrealist terms. Briefly, then, the concepts of modern art are of many different (often fundamentally different) kinds and resulted from the exposures of painters, sculptors and thinkers to the more complex phenomena of the twentieth century, including our ever increasing knowledge of the thought and products of earlier centuries. Different groups of artists would collaborate in trying to make sense of a rapidly changing world of visual and spiritual experience. We should hardly be surprised if no one group succeeded completely, but achievements, though relative, have been considerable. Landmarks have been established – concrete statements of position which give a pattern to a situation which could easily have degenerated into total chaos. Beyond this, new language tools have been created for those who follow-semantic systems which can provide a springboard for further explorations.

The codifying of art is often criticized. Certainly one can understand that artists are wary of being pigeon-holed since they are apt to think of themselves as individuals – sometimes with good reason. The notion of self-expression, however, no longer carries quite the weight it once did; objectivity has its defenders. There is good reason to accept the ideas codified by artists and critics, over the past sixty years or so, as having attained the status of independent existence – an independence which is not without its own value. The time factor is important here. As an art movement slops into temporal perspective, it ceases to be a living organism – becoming, rather, a fossil. This is not to say that it becomes useless or uninteresting. Just as a scientist can reconstruct the life of a prehistoric environment from the messages codified into the structure of a fossil, so can an artist decipher whole webs of intellectual and creative possibility from the recorded structure of a 'dead' art movement. The artist can match the creative possibility from the recorded structure of a 'dead' art movement. The artist can match the creative patterns crystallized into this structure against the potentials and possibilities of his own time. As T.S. Eliot observed, no one starts anything from scratch; however consciously you may try to live in the present, you are still involved with a nexus of behaviour patterns bequeathed from the part. The original and creative person is not someone who ignores these patterns, but someone who is able to translate and develop them so that they conform move exactly to his – and our – present needs.

31. Many of the concepts of modern art have been the product of

1. ideas generated from planned deliberations between artists, painters and thinkers.
2. the dissemination of ideas through the state and its organizations.
3. accidental interactions among people blessed with creative muse.
4. patronage by the rich and powerful that supported art.
5. systematic investigation, codification and conventions.

32. In the passage, the word 'fossil' can be interpreted as

1. an art movement that has ceased to remain interesting or useful.
2. an analogy from the physical world to indicate a historic art movement.
3. an analogy from the physical world to indicate the barrenness of artistic creations in the past.

4. an embedded codification of pre-historic life.
5. an analogy from the physical world to indicate the passing of an era associated with an art movement.

33. In the passage, which of the following similarities between science and art may lead to erroneous conclusions?

1. Both, in general, include a gamut of distinct but interconnecting activities.
2. Both have movements not necessarily concerned with innovation.
3. Both depend on collaborations between talented individuals.
4. Both involve abstract thought and dissemination of ideas.
5. Both reflect complex priorities of the modern world.

34. The range of concepts and ideologies embodied in the art of the twentieth century is explained by

1. the existence of movements such as surrealism.
2. landmarks which give a pattern to the art history of the twentieth century.
3. new language tools which can be used for further explorations into new areas.
4. the fast changing world of perceptual and transcendental understanding.
5. the quick exchange of ideas and concepts enabled by efficient technology.

35. The passage uses an observation by T.S. Eliot to imply that

1. creative processes are not 'original' because they always borrow from the past.
2. we always carry forward the legacy of the past.
3. past behaviours and thought processes recreate themselves in the present and get labeled as 'original' or 'creative'.
4. 'originality' can only thrive in a 'greenhouse' insulated from the past biases.
5. 'innovations' and 'original thinking' interpret and develop on past thoughts to suit contemporary needs.

DIRECTION for questions 36 to 40: *The passage given below is followed by a set of five questions. Choose the* ***most appropriate*** *answer to each question.*

To summarize the Classic Maya collapse, we can tentatively identify five strands. I acknowledge, however, that Maya archaeologists still disagree vigourously among different parts of the Maya realm; because detailed archaeological studies are available for only some Maya sites; and because it remains puzzling why most of the Maya heartland remained nearly empty of population and failed to recover after the collapse and after re-growth of forests.

With those caveats, it appears to me that one strand consisted of population growth outstripping available resources: a dilemma similar to the one foreseen by Thomas Malthus in 1798 and being played out today in Rwanda, Haiti and elsewhere. As the archaeologist David Webster succinctly puts it, "Too many farmers grew too many crops on too much of landscape." Compounding that mismatch between population and resources was the second strand: the effects of deforestation and hillside erosion, which caused a decrease in the amount of useable farmland at a time when more rather than less farmland was needed, and possibly exacerbated by an anthropogenic drought resulting from deforestation, by soil nutrient depletion and other soil problems, and by the struggle to prevent bracken ferns from overrunning the fields.

The third strand consisted of increased fighting, as more and more people fought over fewer resources. Maya warfare, already endemic, peaked just before the collapse. That is not surprising when one reflects that at least five million people, perhaps many more, were crammed into an area smaller than the US state of Colorado (104,000 square miles). That warfare would have decreased further the amount of land available for agriculture, by creating no-man's land between principalities where it was now unsafe to farm. Bringing matters to a head was the strand of climate change. The drought at the time of the Classic collapse was not the first drought that the Maya had lived through, but it was the most severe. At the time of previous droughts, there were still uninhabited parts of the Maya landscape, and people at a site affected by drought could save themselves by moving to another site. However, by the time of the Classic collapse the landscape was now full, there was no useful unoccupied land in the vicinity on which to begin anew, and the whole population could not be accommodated in the few areas that continued to have reliable water supplies.

As our fifth strand, we have to wonder why the kings and nobles failed to recognize and solve these seemingly obvious problems undermining their society. Their attention was evidently focused on their short-term concerns of enriching themselves, waging wars, erecting monuments, competing with each other, and extracting enough food from the peasants to support all those activities. Like most leaders throughout human history, the Maya kings and nobles did not heed long-term problems, insofar as they perceived them.

Finally, while we still have some other past societies to consider before we switch our attention to the modern world, we must already be struck by some parallels between the Maya and the past societies. As on Mangareva, the Maya environmental and population problems led to increasing warfare and civil strife. Similarly, on Easter Island and at Chaco Canyon, the Maya peak population numbers were followed swiftly by political and social collapse. Paralleling the eventual extension of agriculture from Easter Island's coastal lowlands to its uplands, and from the Mimbres floodplain to the hills, Copan's inhabitants also expanded from the floodplain to the more fragile hill slopes, leaving them with a larger population to feed when the agricultural boom in the hills went bust. Like Easter Island chiefs erecting ever larger statues, eventually crowned by pukao, and like Anasazi elite treating themselves to necklaces of 2,000 turquoise beads, Maya kings sought to outdo each other with more and more impressive temples, covered with thicker and thicker plaster – reminiscent in turn of the extravagant conspicuous consumption by modern American CEOs. The passivity of Easter chiefs and Maya kings in the face of the real big threats to their societies completes our list of disquieting parallels.

36. According to the passage, which of the following best represents the factor that has been cited by the author in the context of Rwanda and Haiti?
1. Various ethnic groups competing for land and other resources
2. Various ethnic groups competing for limited land resources
3. Various ethnic groups fighting with each other.
4. Various ethnic groups competing for political power
5. Various ethnic groups fighting for their identity.

37. By an anthropogenic drought, the author means
1. a drought caused by lack of rains.
2. a drought caused due to deforestation.
3. a drought caused by failure to prevent bracken ferns from overrunning the fields.
4. a drought caused by actions of human beings.
5. a drought caused by climate changes.

38. According to passage, the drought at the time of Maya collapse had a different impact compared to the droughts earlier because

1. the Maya kings continued to be extravagant when common people were suffering.
2. it happened at the time of collapse of leadership among Mayas.
3. it happened when the Maya population had occupied all available land suited for agriculture.
4. it was followed by internecine warfare among Mayans.
5. irreversible environmental degradation led to this drought.

39. According to the author, why is it difficult to explain the reasons for Maya collapse?

1. Copan inhabitants destroyed all records of that period
2. The constant deforestation and hillside erosion have wiped out all traces of the Maya kingdom.
3. Archaeological sites of Mayas do not provide any consistent evidence.
4. It has not been possible to ascertain which of the factors best explains as to why the Maya civilization collapsed.
5. At least five million people were crammed into a small area.

40. Which factor has not been cited as one of the factors causing the collapse of Maya society?

1. Environmental degradation due to excess population
2. Social collapse due to excess population.
3. Increased warfare among Maya people
4. Climate change
5. Obsession of Maya population with their own short-term concerns.

Answer Key

1. 3.	**2.** 2	**3.** 2	**4.** 1	**5.** 1	**6.** 4	**7.** 4
8. 5	**9.** 3	**10.** 4	**11.** 5	**12.** 4	**13.** 3	**14.** 5
15. 2	**16.** 5	**17.** 2	**18.** 4	**19.** 2	**20.** 5	**21.** 1
22. 2	**23.** 2	**24.** 1	**25.** 2	**26.** 2	**27.** 4	**28.** 2
29. 2	**30.** 1	**31.** 3	**32.** 5	**33.** 1	**34.** 4	**35.** 5
36. 2	**37.** 4	**38.** 3	**39.** 4	**40.** 5		

Answer Key & Explanations

1. 3 Brooch - jewellery and item for jewellery, Broach - to think.Councillor – representative of local authority, Counsellor – Advisor.Climactic – constituting a climax, climatic – relating to climate.Flair – aptitude, flare – expanding outward.

2. 2 Currants – fruits.Exceptional – uncommon/extra ordinary, Exceptionable – objectionable.Consent – to accept/give acceptance, Assent – agreement.Obliged – legal obligations, Compel – to force.Sanguine – optimistic, Genuine – real.

3. 2 Caustic – bitter.Cogent plea (idiomatic usage)Adverse – unfavorable, Averse – opposed.Coupé – a small compartment, Coup – a struggle.Peeling – to scrap off, Pealing – a set of bells tuned to each other.

4. 1 Defused – reduce severity of, Diffuse – spread.Bated – to lessen, Bait – to harass.Hoard – to accumulate, Horde – a large group.Internment – to confine.Unsociable – unfriendly.

5. 1 Error in A- spelling of imigrant is immigrantError in C - , (comma) required after in-law & David Stern

6. 4 Error in B- ……changes in "its" labour policyError in C – sensing that….Error in E – an industry leader

7. 4 Error in B – it should be millionsError in E- the death count "has" just begun

8. 5 Error in B & C- of tensesError in E "make an effort"

9. 3 Disingenuous means insincere, Victims is the exact opposite of perpetrators

10. 4 Concede means "to accept/acknowledge reluctantly" hence choice 4

11. 5 Genetic is innate. Clue is "on the other hand" & hence pedagogy (learning).

12. 4 As per the source- RUSSELL ON ETHICS

13. 3 People can't run over rather they run after.

14. 5 Correct usage is "come around"

15. 2 Unidiomatic use.

16. 5 A file refers to a single line/row." Broke the file " is unidiomatic

17. 2 As per the source Medical Journal New Yorker.

18. 4 Sums up the paragraph logically, option 2& 3 look inviting but the author gives eg's of these two countries only to reinforce the main idea which we find in option 4.

19. 2 As per the source – The Economist.

20. 5 As per the source – Article by Amartya Sen.

21. 1 First line of the Paragraph1.

22. 2 Natural Behaviour displayed by bees.

23. 2 Paragraph 2, last line, "In nature's talent….."

24. 1 Paragraph 1, line 3 & 4 "Which child develops spontaneously without conscious effort or formal instruction".

25. 2 The last line of Paragraph 3, reinforces what has been said in 1st line of 2nd para.

26. 2 Rest all the choices are talked about in the passage.

27. 4 Young upstarts- "Seeks attention thinking that he is important but he is not as important". This is confirmed by the passage.

28. 2 Intemperance means not in moderation – hence it is because of his desire to be seen as a person with excess….

29. 2 As per the author we have changed the definition of morality so as to accommodate our excessive consumerist tendency. So it has changed and evolved over the years.(5) & (3) choices are irrelevant.

30. 1 Para (4), last line words like 'pedagogical' gives the hint.

31. 3 Para (1), line 7 "Many of the concepts of modern art, by contrast, have resulted from the almost accidental meeting of groups of talented individual at certain times and certain places.

32. 5 Para (3), line 5 " The Time factor is important here. As an art movement slips into temporal perspective, it ceases to be a living organism – becoming, rather, a fossil. This is not to say that it becomes useless or uninteresting. Just as a scientist can reconstruct the life of a prehistoric environment from the messages codified into the structure of a fossil, so can an artist possibility from the recorded structure of a 'dead' art movement.

33. 1 Para (1), line 2 " It is almost tempting to see a pattern emerging within the art field or alternatively imposed upon it a *posteriori* – similar to that which exists under the umbrella of science where the general term covers a whole range of separate, though interconnecting, activities. Any parallelism is however – in this instance at least – misleading.

34. 4 Para (1), line 20 " Different groups of artists would collaborate in trying to make sense of a rapidly changing world of visual and spiritual experience".

35. 5 Last Para, last line.

36. 2 Para (2), line 1.

37. 4 'anthro' stands for 'mankind'.

38. 3 Para (3), line 9 "However by the time of the classic collapse the landscape was full, there was no useful unoccupied land in the vicinity on which to begin a new, and the whole population could not be accommodated in the few areas that continued to have reliable water supplies.

39. 4

40. 5

CAT 2007

Number of Questions – 25
Time :40 M.

DIRECTIONS ***for questions 1 to 3:*** *The passage given below is followed by a set of three questions. Choose the most appropriate answer to each question.*

Human Biology does nothing to structure human society. Age may enfeeble us all, but cultures vary considerably in the prestige and power they accord to the elderly. Giving birth is a necessary condition for being a mother, but it is not sufficient. We expect mothers to behave in maternal ways and to display appropriately maternal sentiments. We prescribe a clutch of norms or rules that govern the *role* of a mother. That the social role is independent of the biological base can be demonstrated by going back three sentences. Giving birth is certainly not sufficient to be a mother but, as adoption and fostering show, it is not even necessary!

The fine detail of what is expected of a mother or a father or a dutiful son differs from culture to culture, but everywhere behaviour is coordinated by the *reciprocal* nature of roles. Husbands and wives, parents and children, employers and employees, waiters and customers, teachers and pupils, warlords and followers; each makes sense only in its relation to the other. The term [4]role' is an appropriate one, because the metaphor of an actor in a play neatly expresses the rule-governed nature or scripted nature of much of social life and the sense that society is a joint production. Social life occurs only because people play their parts (and that is as true for war and conflicts as for peace and love) and those parts make sense only in the context of the overall show. The drama metaphor also reminds us of the artistic licence available to the players. We can play a part straight or, as the following from J.P. Sartre conveys, we can ham it up.

Let us consider this waiter in the café. His movement is quick and forward, a little too precise, a little too rapid. He comes towards the patrons with a step a little too quick. He bends forward a little too eagerly; his voice, his eyes express an interest a little too solicitous for the order of the customer. Finally there he returns, trying to imitate in his walk the inflexible stiffness of some kind of automaton while carrying his tray with the recklessness of a tightrope-walker....All his behaviour seems to us a game....But what is he playing? We need not watch long before we can explain it: he is playing at being a waiter in a cafe.

The American sociologist Erving Goffman built an influential body of social analysis on elaborations of the metaphor of social life as drama. Perhaps his most telling point was that it is only through acting out a part that we express character. It is not enough to be evil or virtuous; we have to be seen to be evil or virtuous.

There is distinction between the roles we play and some underlying self. Here we might note that some roles are more absorbing than others. We would not be surprised by the waitress who plays the par! m such a way as to signal to us that she is much more than her occupation. We would be surprised and offended by the father who played his part 'tongue in check'. Some roles arc broader and more far-reaching than others. Describing someone as a clergyman or faith healer would say far more about that person than describing someone as a bus driver.

1. What is the thematic highlight of this passage?

1. In the absence of strong biological linkages, reciprocal roles provide the mechanism for coordinating human behaviour.
2. In the absence of reciprocal roles, biological linkages provide the mechanism for coordinating human behaviour.
3. Human behaviour is independent of biological linkages and reciprocal roles.
4. Human behaviour depends on biological linkages and reciprocal roles.
5. Reciprocal roles determine normative human behaviour in society.

2. Which of the following would have been true if biological linkages structured human society?

1. The role of mother would have been defined through her reciprocal relationship with her children.
2. We would not have been offended by the father playing his role 'tongue in cheek'.
3. Women would have adopted and fostered children rather than giving birth to them.
4. Even if warlords were physically weaker than their followers, they would still dominate them.
5. Waiters would have stronger motivation to serve their customers.

3. It has been claimed in the passage that "some roles are more absorbing than others'1. According to the passage, which of the following seem (s) appropriate reason (s) for such a claim?

1. Some roles carry great expectations from the society preventing manifestation of the true self.
2. Society ascribes so much importance to some roles that the conception of self may get aligned with the roles being performed.
3. Some roles require development of skill and expertise leaving little time for manifestation of self

1. A only
2. B only
3. C only
4. A & B
5. B & C

DIRECTIONS ***for questions 4 – 6:*** *In each question, there are five sentences or parts of sentences that form a paragraph. Identify the sentence (s) or part (s) of sentence (s) that is / are correct in terms of grammar and usage. Then, choose the most appropriate option.*

4.
1. When I returned to home, I began to read
2. Everything I could get my hand on about Israel.
3. That same year Israel's Jewish Agency sent
4. A Shaliach a sort of recruiter to Minneapolis.
5. I became one of his most active devotees.

1. C & E
2. C only
3. E only
4. B, C & E
5. C, D & E

5.
1. So once an economy is actually in recession,
2. The authorities can, in principle, move the economy

3. Out of slump assuming hypothetically
4. That they know how to - by a temporary stimuli.
5. In the longer term, however, such policies have no effect on the overall behaviour of the economy.

1. A, B & E 2. B, C & E
3. C & D 4. E only
5. B only

6. 1. It is sometimes told that democratic
2. Government originated in the city-states
3. of ancient Greece. Democratic ideals have been handed to us from that time.
4. In truth, however, this is an unhelpful assertion,
5. The Greeks gave us the word, hence did not provide us with a model.

1. A, B & D 2. B, C & D
3. B & D 4. B only
5. D only

DIRECTIONS for questions 7– 9: *The passage given below is followed by a set of three questions. Choose the most appropriate answer to each question.*

Every civilized society lives and thrives on a silent but profound agreement as to what is to be accepted as the valid mould of experience. Civilization is a complex system of dams, dykes, and canals warding off, directing, and articulating the influx of the surrounding fluid element; a fertile fenland, elaborately drained and protected from the high tides of chaotic, unexercised, and inarticulate experience. In such a culture, stable and sure of itself within the frontiers of 'naturalized' experience, the arts wield their creative power not so much in width as in depth. They do not create new experience, but deepen and purify the old. Their works do not differ from one another like a new horizon from a new horizon, but like a madonna from a madonna.

The periods of art which are most vigorous in creative passion seem to occur when the established pattern of experience loosens its rigidity without as yet losing its force. Such a period was the Renaissance, and Shakespeare its poetic consummation. Then it was as though the discipline of the old order gave depth to the excitement of the breaking away, the depth of job and tragedy, of incomparable conquests arid irredeemable losses. Adventurers of experience set out as though in lifeboats to rescue and bring back to the shore treasures of knowing and feeling which the old order had left floating on the high seas. The works of the early Renaissance and the poetry of Shakespeare vibrate with the compassion for live experience in danger of dying from exposure and neglect. In this compassion was the creative genius of the age. Yet, it was a genius of courage, not of desperate audacity. For, however elusively, it still knew of harbours and anchors, of homes to which to return, and of barns in which to store the harvest. The exploring spirit of art was in the depths of its consciousness still aware of a scheme of things into which to fit its exploits and creations.

But the more this scheme of things loses its stability, the more boundless and uncharted appears the ocean of potential exploration. In the blank confusion of infinite potentialities flotsam of significance gets attached to jetsam of experience; for everything is sea, everything is at sea –

.... The sea is all about us; The sea is the land's edge also, the granite; Into which it reaches, the beaches where it tosses

Its hints of earlier and other creation... - and Rilke tells a story in which, as in T.S. Eliot's poem, it is again the sea and the distance of 'other creation' that becomes the image of the poet's reality. A rowing boat sets out on a difficult passage. The oarsmen labour in exact rhythm. There is no sign yet of the destination. Suddenly a man, seemingly idle, breaks out into song. And if the labour of the oarsmen meaninglessly defeats the real resistance of the real waves, it is the idle single who magically conquers the despair of apparent aimlessness. While the people next to him try to come to grips with the element that is next to them, his voice seems to bind the boat to the farthest distance so that the farthest distance draws it towards itself. 'I don't know why and how,' is Rilke's conclusion, 'but suddenly I understood the situation of the poet, his place and function in this age. It does not matter if one denies him every place - except this one. There one must tolerate him.'

7. In the passage, the expression "like a madonna from a madonna" alludes to
   1. The difference arising as a consequence of artistic license.
   2. The difference between two artistic interpretations.
   3. The difference between 'life' and 'interpretation of life'.
   4. The difference between 'width' and 'depth' of creative power.
   5. The difference between the legendary character and the modern day singer.

8. The sea and 'other creation' leads Rilke to
   1. Define the place of the poet in his culture.
   2. Reflect on the role of the oarsman and the singer.
   3. Muse on artistic labour and its aimlessness.
   4. Understand the elements that one has to deal with.
   5. Delve into natural experience and real waves.

9. According to the passage, the term "adventurers of experience" refers to
   1. Poets and artists who are driven by courage.
   2. Poets and artists who create their own genre.
   3. Poets and artists of the Renaissance.
   4. Poets and artists who revitalize and enrich the past for us.
   5. Poets and artists who delve in flotsam and jetsam in sea.

DIRECTIONS for questions 10 to 12: *Each of the following questions has a paragraph from which the last sentence has been deleted. From the given options, choose the sentence that completes the paragraph in the most appropriate way.*

10. Characters are also part of deep structure. Characters tie events in a story together and provide a thread of continuity and meaning. Stories can be about individuals, groups, projects, or whole organizations, so from an organizational studies perspective, the focal actor(s) determine the level and unit of analysis used in a study. Stories of mergers and acquisitions, for example, are commonplace. In these stories whole organizations are personified as actors. But these macro-level stories usually are not told from the perspective of the macro-level participants, because whole organizations cannot narrate their experiences in the first person.
   1. More generally, data concerning the identities and relationships of the characters in the story are required, if one is to understand role structure and social networks in which that process is embedded.
   2. Personification of a whole Organization abstracts away from the particular actors and from traditional notions of level of analysis.

3. The personification of a whole organization is important because stories differ depending on who is enacting various events.
4. Every story is told from a particular point of view, with a particular narrative voice, which is not regarded as part of the deep structure.
5. The personification of a whole organization is a textual device we use to make macro-level theories more comprehensible.

11. Nevertheless, photographs still retain some of the magical allure that the earliest daguerreotypes inspired. As objects, our photographs have changed; they have become physically flimsier as they have become more technologically sophisticated. Daguerre produced pictures on copper plates; today many of our photographs never become tangible things, but instead remain filed away on computers and cameras, part of the digital ether that envelops the modern world. At the same time, our patience for the creation of images has also eroded. Children today are used to being tracked from birth by digital cameras and video recorders and they expect to see the results of their poses and performances instantly. The space between life as it is being lived and life as it is being displayed shrinks to a mere second.

1. Yet, despite these technical developments, photographs still remain powerful because they are reminders of the people and things we care about.
2. Images, after all, are surrogates carried into battle by a soldier or by a traveller on holiday.
3. Photographs, be they digital or traditional, exist to remind us of the absent, the beloved, and the dead.
4. In the new era of the digital image, the images also have a greater potential for fostering falsehood and trickery, perpetuating fictions that seem so real we cannot tell the difference.
5. Anyway, human nature being what it is, little time has passed after photography's invention became means of living life through images.

12. Mma Ramotswe had a detective agency in Africa, at the foot of Kgale Hill. These were its assets: a tiny white van, two desks, two chairs, a telephone, and an old typewriter. Then there was a teapot, in which Mma Ramotswe - the only private lady detective in Botswana - brewed redbush tea. And three mugs - one for herself, one for her secretary, and one for the client. What else does a detective agency really need? Detective agencies rely on human intuition and intelligence, both of which Mma Ramotswe had in abundance.

1. Bin there was also the view, which again would appear on no inventory.
2. No inventory would ever include those, of course.
3. She had an intelligent secretary too.
4. She was a good detective and a good woman.
5. What she lacked in possessions was more than made up by a natural shrewdness

DIRECTIONS for questions13 to 15: *The passage given below is followed by a set of three questions. Choose the most appropriate answer to each question.*

To discover the relation between rules, paradigms, and normal science, consider first how the historian isolates the particular loci of commitment that have been described as accepted rules. Close historical investigation of a given specialty at a given time discloses a set of recurrent and quasi-standard illustrations of various theories in their conceptual, observational, and instrumental applications. These are the community's paradigms, revealed in its textbooks, lectures, and laboratory exercises. By studying them and by practicing with them, the members of the corresponding community learn their trade. The historian, of course, will discover in addition a penumbral area occupied by achievements whose status is still in doubt, but the core of solved problems and techniques will usually be clear. Despite occasional ambiguities, the paradigms of a mature scientific community can be determined with relative ease.

That demands a second step and one of a somewhat different kind. When undertaking it, the historian must compare the community's paradigms with each other and with its current research reports. In doing so, his object is to discover what isolable elements, explicit or implicit, the members of that community may have abstracted from their more global paradigms and deploy it as rules in their research. Anyone who has attempted to describe or analyze the evolution of a particular scientific tradition will necessarily have sought accepted principles and rules of this sort. Almost certainly, he will have met with at least partial success. But, if his experience has been at all like my own, he will have found the search for rules both more difficult and less satisfying than the search for paradigms. Some of the generalizations he employs to describe the community's shared beliefs will present more problems. Others, however, will seem a shade too strong. Phrased in just that way, or in any other way he can imagine, they would almost certainly have been rejected by some members of the group hc studies. Nevertheless, if the coherence of the research tradition is to be understood in terms of rules, some specification of common ground in the corresponding area is needed. As a result, the search for a body of rules competent to constitute a given normal research tradition becomes a source of continual and deep frustration.

Recognizing that frustration, however, makes it possible to diagnose its source. Scientists can agree that a Newton, Lavoisier, Maxwell, or Einstein has produced an apparently permanent solution to a group of outstanding problems and still disagree, sometimes without being aware of it, about the particular abstract characteristics that make those solutions permanent. They can, that is, agree in their identification of a paradigm without agreeing on, or even attempting to produce, a full interpretation or rationalization of it. Lack of a standard interpretation or of an agreed reduction to rules will not prevent a paradigm from guiding research. Normal science can be determined in part by the direct inspection of paradigms, a process that is often aided by but does not depend upon the formulation of rules and assumption. Indeed, the existence of a paradigm need not even imply that any full set of rules exists.

13. What is the author attempting to illustrate through this passage?

1. Relationships between rules, paradigms, and normal science
2. How a historian would isolate a particular 'loci of commitment'
3. How a set of shared beliefs evolves into a paradigm
4. Ways of understanding a scientific tradition
5. The frustrations of attempting to define a paradigm of a tradition

14. The term 'loci of commitment' as used in the passage would most likely correspond with which of the following?

1. Loyalty between a group of scientists in a research laboratory
2. Loyalty between groups of scientists across research laboratories
3. Loyalty to a certain paradigm of scientific inquiry
4. Loyalty to global patterns of scientific inquiry

5. Loyalty to evolving trends of scientific inquiry

15. The author of this passage is likely to agree with which of the following?

1. Paradigms almost entirely define a scientific tradition.
2. A group of scientists investigating a phenomenon would benefit by defining a set of rules.
3. Acceptance by the giants of a tradition is a sine qua non for a paradigm to emerge.
4. Choice of isolation mechanism determines the type of paradigm that may emerge from a tradition.
5. Paradigms are a general representation of rules and beliefs of a scientific tradition.

DIRECTIONS ***for questions 16 to 18:*** *In each question, there are four sentences. Each sentence has pairs of words / phrases that are italicized and highlighted. From the italicized and highlighted word (s) / phrase (s), select the most appropriate word (s) / phrase (s) to form correct sentences. Then, from the options given, choose the best one.*

16. The cricket council that was [A] I were IB] elected last March is [A] / are [B] at sixes and sevens over new rules.

The critics censored [A] / censured [B] the new movie because of its social unacceptability.

Amit's explanation for missing the meeting was credulous [A] / credible [B].

She coughed discreetly [A] / discretely [B] to announce her presence.

1. BBAAA
2. AAABA
3. BBBBA
4. AABBA
5. BBBAA

17. The further [A] I farther [B] he pushed himself, the more disillusioned he grew.

For the crowds it was more of a historical [A] / historic [B] event; for their leader, it was just another day.

The old man has a healthy distrust [A] / mistrust [B] for all new technology. This film is based on a real [A] / true [B] story.

One suspects that the compliment [A] / complement [B] was backhanded.

1. ABAB
2. ABBBA
3. BAABA
4. BBAAB
5. ABABA

18. *Regrettably* [A] / *Regretfully* [BJ I have to decline your invitation.

I am drawn to the poetic, *sensual* [A] / *sensuous* IB] quality of her paintings.

He was *besides* f A] / *beside* [B] himself with rage when I told him what I had done.

After brushing against a *stationary* [A] *I stationery* [B] truck my car turned turtle.

As the water began to rise *over* [A] *I above* [B] the danger mark, the signs of an imminent flood were clear.

1. BAABA
2. BBAB
3. AAABA
4. BBAAB
5. BABAB

DIRECTIONS ***for questions 19 to21:*** *The passage given below is followed by a set of three questions. Choose the most appropriate answer to each question.*

The difficulties historians face in establishing cause-and-effect relations in the history of human societies are broadly similar to the difficulties facing astronomers, climatologists, ecologists, evolutionary biologists, geologists, and palaeontologists. To varying degrees each of these fields is plagued by the impossibility of performing replicated, controlled experimental interventions, the complexity arising from enormous numbers of variables, the resulting uniqueness of each system, the consequent impossibility of formulating universal laws, and the difficulties of predicting emergent properties and future behaviour. Prediction in history, as in other historical sciences, is most feasible on large spatial scales and over long times, when the unique features of millions of small-scale brief events become averaged out. Just as I could predict the sex ratio of the next 1,000 newborns but not the sexes of my own two children, the historian can recognize factors that made inevitable the broad outcome of the collision between American and Eurasian societies after 13,000 years of separate developments, but not the outcome of the 1960 U.S. presidential election. The details of which candidate said what during a single televised debate in October 1960 could have given the electoral victory to Nixon instead of to Kennedy, but no details of who said what could have blocked the European conquest of Native Americans.

How can students of human history profit from the experience of scientists in other historical sciences? A methodology that has proved useful involves the comparative method and so-called natural experiments. While neither astronomers studying galaxy formation nor human historians can manipulate their systems in controlled laboratory experiments, they both can take advantage of natural experiments, by comparing systems differing in the presence or absence (or in the strong or weak effect) of some putative causative factor. For example, epidemiologists, forbidden to feed large amounts of salt to people experimentally, have still been able to identify effects of high salt intake by comparing groups of humans who already differ greatly in their salt intake; and cultural anthropologists, unable to provide human groups experimentally with varying resource abundances for many centuries, still study long-term effects of resource abundance on human societies by comparing recent Polynesian populations living on islands differing naturally in resource abundance.

The student of human history can draw on many more natural experiments than just comparisons among the five inhabited continents. Comparisons can also utilize large islands that have developed complex societies in a considerable degree of isolation (such as Japan, Madagascar, Native American Hispaniola, New Guinea, Hawaii, and many others), as well as societies on hundreds of smaller islands and regional societies within each of the continents. Natural experiments in any field, whether in ecology or human history, are inherently open to potential methodological criticisms. Those include confounding effects of natural variation in additional variables besides the one of interest, as well as problems in inferring chains of causation from observed correlations between variables. Such methodological problems have been discussed in great detail for some of the historical sciences. In particular, epidemiology, the science of drawing inferences about human diseases by comparing groups of people (often by retrospective historical studies), has for a long time successfully employed formalized procedures for dealing with problems similar to those facing historians of human societies.

In short, I acknowledge that it is much more difficult to understand human history than to understand problems in fields of science where history is unimportant and where fewer individual variables operate. Nevertheless, successful methodologies for analyzing historical problems have been worked out in several fields. As a result, the histories of dinosaurs, nebulae, and glaciers are generally acknowledged to belong to fields of science rather than to the humanities.

19. Why do islands with considerable degree of isolation provide valuable insights into human history?

1. Isolated islands may evolve differently and this difference is of interest to us.
2. Isolated islands increase the number of observations available to historians.
3. Isolated islands, differing in their endowments and size may evolve differently and this difference can be attributed to their endowments and size.
4. Isolated islands, differing in their endowments and size, provide a good comparison to large islands such as Eurasia, Africa, Americas and Australia.
5. Isolated islands, in so far as they are inhabited, arouse curiosity about how human beings evolved there.

20. According to the author, why is prediction difficult in history?

1. Historical explanations are usually broad so that no prediction is possible.
2. Historical outcomes depend upon a large number of factors and hence prediction is difficult for each case.
3. Historical sciences, by their very nature, are not interested in a multitude of minor factors, which might be important in a specific historical outcome.
4. Historians are interested in evolution of human history and hence are only interested in long-term predictions.
5. Historical sciences suffer from the inability to conduct controlled experiments and therefore have explanations based on a few long-term factors.

21. According to the author, which of the following statements would be true?

1. Students of history are missing significant opportunities by not conducting any natural experiments.
2. Complex societies inhabiting large islands provide great opportunities for natural experiments.
3. Students of history are missing significant opportunities by not studying an adequate variety of natural experiments.
4. A unique problem faced by historians is their inability to establish cause and effect relationships.
5. Cultural anthropologists have overcome the problem of confounding variables through natural experiments.

DIRECTIONS ***for questions 22 to 25:*** *In each question, there are five sentences / paragraphs. The sentence / paragraph labelled A is in its correct place. The four that follow are labelled B, C, D and E, and need to be arranged in the logical order to form a coherent paragraph / passage. From the given options, choose the most appropriate option.*

22. A. In America, highly educated women, who are in stronger position in the labour market than less qualified ones, have higher rates of marriage than other groups.

B. Some work supports the Becker thesis, and some appears to contradict it.

C. And, as with crime, it is equally inconclusive.

D. But regardless of the conclusion of any particular piece of work, it is hard to establish convincing connections between family changes and economic factors using conventional approaches.

E. Indeed, just as with crime, an enormous academic literature exists on the validity of the pure economic approach to the evolution of family structures.

1. BCDE
2. DBEC
3. BDCE
4. ECBD
5. EBCD

23. A. Personal experience of mothering and motherhood are largely framed in relation to two discernible or "official" discourses: the "medical discourse and natural child-birth discourse". Both of these tend to focus on the "optimistic stories" of birth and mothering and underpin stereotypes of the "good mother".

B. At the same time, the need for medical expert guidance is also a feature for contemporary reproduction and motherhood. But constructions of good mothering have not always been so conceived - and in different contexts may exist in parallel to other equally dominant discourses.

C. Similarly, historical work has shown how what are now taken-for-granted aspects of reproduction and mothering practices result from contemporary "pseudoscientific directives" and "managed constructs". These changes have led to a refraining of modern discourses that pattern pregnancy and motherhood leading to an acceptance of the need for greater expert management.

D. The contrasting, overlapping, and ambiguous strands within these frameworks focus to varying degrees on a woman's biological tie to her child and predisposition to instinctively know and be able to care for her child.

E. In addition, a third, "unofficial popular discourse" comprising "old wives" tales and based on maternal experiences of childbirth has also been noted. These discourses have also been acknowledged in work exploring the experiences of those who apparently do not "conform" to conventional stereotypes of the "good mother'[1].

1. EDBC
2. BCED
3. DBCE
4. EDCB
5. BCDE

24. A. Indonesia has experienced dramatic shifts in its formal governance arrangements since the fall of President Soeharto and the close of his centralized, authoritarian "New Order" regime in 1997.

B. The political system has taken its place in the nearly 10 years since *Reformasi* began. It has featured the active contest for political office among a proliferation of parties at central, provincial and district levels; direct elections for the presidency (since 2004): and radical changes in centre-local government relations towards administrative, fiscal, and political decentralization.

C. The mass media, once tidily under Soeharto's thumb, has experienced significant liberalization, as has the legal basis for non-governmental organizations, including many dedicated to such controversial issues as corruption control and human rights.

D. Such developments are seen optimistically by a number of donors and some external analysts, who interpret them as signs of Indonesia's political normalization.

E. A different group of analysts paint a picture in which the institutional forms have changed, but power relations have not. Vedi Hadiz argues that Indonesia's "democratic transition" has been anything but linear.

1. BDEC
2. CBDE
3. CEBD
4. DEBC
5. BCDE

25. A. I had six thousand acres of land, and had thus got much spare land besides the coffee plantation. Part of the farm was native forest, and about one thousand acres were squatters' land, what the Kikuyu called their *shambas.*

B. The squatters' land was more intensely alive than the rest of the farm, and was changing with the seasons the year round. The maize grew up higher than your head as you walked on the narrow hard-trampled footpaths in between the tall green rustling regiments.

C. The squatters are Natives, who with their families hold a few acres on a white man's farm, and in return have to work for him a certain number of days in the year. My squatters, I think, saw the relationship in a different light, for many of them were born on the farm, and their fathers before them, and they very likely regarded me as a sort of superior squatter on their estates.

D. The Kikuyu also grew the sweet potatoes that have a vine like leaf and spread over the ground like a dense entangled mat, and many varieties of big yellow and green speckled pumpkins.

E. The beans ripened in the fields, were gathered and thrashed by the women, and the maize stalks and coffee pods were collected and burned, so that in certain seasons thin blue columns of smoke rose here and there all over the farm.

1. CBDE
2. BCDE
3. CBED
4. DBCE
5. EDBC

Answer Key

1. 1	**2.** 2	**3.** 2	**4.** 1	**5.** 5	**6.** 3	**7.** 2
8. 1	**9.** 3	**10.** 5	**11.** 1	**12.** 2	**13.** 1	**14.** 3
15. 5	**16.** 4	**17.** 5	**18.** 2	**19.** 1	**20.** 5	**21.** 2
22. 4	**23.** 1	**24.** 5	**25.** 3			

EXPLANATIONS

1. A clear hint is given in the first line of the passage. ... 'Human biology does nothing to structure human society'. The next para carries the idea forward and talks about reciprocal roles and their role in co coordinating human behavior. Therefore this is the thematic highlight of this passage.

2. Refer to the last paragraph. This clearly shows that a father playing his role "tongue in cheek" would have been acceptable if biological linkages structured human society.

3. The statement tells us that some roles are so absorbing or interesting that the distinction between the role being played and the underlying self gets blurred. Refer to the first line of the fifth para.

4. A – 'returned to home' is a wrong usage.B – It should be 'lay my hands upon'.D – It should be 'a Shaliach, a sort of ………C and E – The right answer.

5. A – 'In recession' is a wrong usage.B – The right answer.C – Usage of words assuming and hypothetically amounts to redundancy.D – It should be 'a temporary stimulus'.E – Instead of verb 'affect'. The usage should be of noun, 'effect'.

6. A – instead of 'told'. It should be 'it is sometimes said.'B & D – The right answers. C – The phrase is 'handed down to us.'D – After 'hence' the subject is missing.

7. Refer to the end of the first paragraph. The writer uses the expression "like a Madonna from a Madonna" to illustrate the fact that the artist does not create anything new but deepens and purifies the old, so the difference in two artistic creations is due to the difference in artistic interpretation.

8. Refer to the last few lines of the passage. The sea and 'other creation' help Rilke to "understand the situation of the poet, his place and function in this age".

9. Refer to the beginning of the 2nd paragraph. "Such a period was the Renaissance ...." The writer goes on to discuss how the poets and artists of this period could break away from the old order and explore the new.

10. The author looks at an organization as a person and takes the example of acquisitions and mergers to explain the importance of characters in an organization. The personification of the organization is thus used as a textual device so that macro level theories are better understood.

11. As the concluding sentence, it talks about what has been said in the whole paragraph. It reiterates what has been stated in the first line....... 'photographs still retain.........' and also talks about the 'technical development' referred to in the rest of the lines.'

12. The writer gives the details of Mma Ramotswe's inventory, her few possessions, and then goes on to add that she had 'human intuition and intelligence' which were 'sufficient to run a detective agency. These two things are obviously never included in an inventory.

13. The attempt to describe a relationship among rules, paradigms and normal science begins from the very first sentence itself and finds manifestation in the second and third paragraphs as well.

14. The term refers to a sense of inherent loyalty - not to something as narrow as a laboratory but to a certain form of scientific inquiry. We also lack information on the trends / patterns.

15. Please refer to the penultimate line of the second paragraph which says ... *if the coherence is to be understood...... some specification of common ground......* Besides, also refer to the succeeding line to get the complete answer. The answer gets more support from these lines in the first paragraph... *quasi-standard illustrations of a given speciality*. The rest of the choices are not supportable in the context of the passage.

16. *Council* is a collective noun and will take a singular verb. The critics can only criticize and not *censor* anything.

17. *Farther* is used for distance while further means to a greater degree. The appropriate word in the second sentence is *historic*, meaning – of great importance. Mistrust means ill placed trust whereas the old man does not seem to believe much in new technology. Films are based on *true* stories. *Compliment* means to praise while *complement* means to complete.

18. *Regretfully* is the best option. It is an expression of disappointment. Sensuous is the appropriate usage. It relates to the pleasure of senses. *Besides* is the correct word, *beside* is a preposition. *Stationary* means immobile, hence the correct option. Water rises *above* the danger mark and not *over* the danger mark.

19. The fourth line of paragraph 3 talks about the "confounding effects of natural variation in additional variables besides the one of interest", thus conveying the differences in the evolution of isolated islands and the potential inherent in studying such differences.
20. Please refer to these lines from the second and third paragraphs, *Prediction in history, as in other historical sciences, ...* . and *While neither astronomers studying galaxy formation nor human historians....*
21. Please refer to the second line of the third paragraph which explicitly talks about this fact.
22. *It* of line C refers to the *validity* being discussed in E. Thus EC is a good combination. BD is also a great combination as D tends to support B.
23. Line A talks of two types of experiences, medical and natural, an idea which is further built on by the last line E which refers to the third discourse. Note the word these in line D which refers to the three frameworks. B gels very well with D, which should lead us to option 1.
24. In a logically sequenced paragraph we should first talk of the overall changes brought about in the political dispensation followed by the changes in mass media. This gives us BC. Note carefully *such developments* which alludes to B and C and also *a different group of analysts* in *E,* which is linked very well with *external analysts in* D. Hence BCDE.
25. C makes the strongest link with A as it elaborates upon the squatters mentioned in A.C also begins to speak about the squatters at the author's farm and this thought is carried forward by B. The "maize" clue then leads us to E.Hence A-C-B-E-D is the answer.

FMS 2008

Number of Questions – 75
Time :50 M.

Section I
READING COMPREHENSION

DIRECTIONS ***for questions 1–8:*** *Read the passage given below and answer the questions.*

Passage – I

How do we go about investigating personologic phenomena? Should we adhere to the time-tested rules of common sense, continuously and painstakingly refining our measures and methods until we are virtually infallible? Or should we explore innovative new concepts that will partition the personological realm in ways that are more theoretically and clinically fruitful? One option would be to anchor personological phenomena directly in the empirical world of observables in a one-to-one fashion, tying each attribute to only one indicator. Each attribute would then be its mode of measurement, possessing no information beyond that contained in the procedure itself, akin to *operational definitions.*

Operational definitions are quite pleasingly precise but considerably limited in scope. Ultimate empirical precision can only be achieved if every defining feature that distinguishes a taxon is anchored to a single observable in the real world; that is, a different datum for every difference observed between personality syndromes. This goal is simply not feasible or desirable: The subject domain of personology is inherently more weakly organized than that of the so-called hard sciences. As one moves from physics and chemistry into biological and psychological arenas, unidirectional causal path-ways give way to feedback and feedforward processes, which in turn give rise to emergent levels of description that are more inferential than the physical substrates that underlie them. Intrapsychic formulations, for example, require that the clinician transcend the level of the merely observable. Owing to their abstract and hypothetical character, these indeterminate and intervening concepts are known as *open concepts.*

The polar distinction between operational definitions (the paradigm of those who prefer to employ data derived from empirical-practical contexts) and open concepts (those whose ideas are derived from a more causal-theoretical stance) represents in part an epistemological continuum of conceptual specificity to conceptual openness. Each end of this polarity embraces a compromise between scope and precision. The virtue of each hides its vices. The advantage of operationism is obvious: Personality syndromes and the attributes of which they are composed are rendered unambiguous. Diagnostic identifications are directly translatable into measurement procedures, maximizing precision. However, the direct mapping of attributes to measurement procedures required ignores the biases incumbent to any one procedure, so that operationism is fatally deficient in scope.

The "open concept" model, likewise, has its own advantage: Open concepts acknowledge the desirability of multiple measurement procedures and encourage their user to move freely in more abstract and inferential realms. Each open concept can be embedded in a theoretical matrix or network from which its meaning is derived through its relations with other open concepts, with only indirect reference to explicit observables. The disadvantage is that open concepts may become so circuitous in their references that they become tautological and completely decoupled from observables. No doubt clarity gets muddled and deductions become tautological in statements such as "in the borderline the mechanisms of the ego disintegrate when libidinous energies overwhelm superego introjections." In such formulations, the scope of a theory overwhelms the testability of its empirical linkages, rendering precision zero.

Due to simple pragmatism, all scientific models, being simplifications of nature, must reach a compromise between scope and precision. We are not yet mystics at the beginning of a science: Unlike the individually borne thinking in a taxonomy which carves nature at its joints, we are acutely conscious that the relations among our naive representations are not those intrinsic to the subject domain itself. No one today would seriously put Hippocrates's humoral theory forward as a model of personality syndromes. Instead, such formulations resemble the more or less unrefined and often self-contradictory knowledge of commonsense than the well-criticized and well-corroborated knowledge of science. As disputable as common sense is, it is nevertheless the point of departure for scientific knowledge and a source of common sense taxonomies.

On an individual level, what distinguishes these two broad approaches? What does each individual scientist do to carry out his or her approach? Evidently, the theoretical approach is driven primarily by taking perspective on sense-near representations in order to discover underlying theoretic-causal relations from which a more coherent, internally corroborating system of constructs might be established. New constructs are generated, "more or less removed from the level of directly observable things and events." Some old ones are discarded, while others have their meaning sharpened or transformed as the system of relations is made more explicit. A process of reflection seems essential. Such representations are referred to as theoretical constructs, to reinforce their abstract origins in the mind of a reflective scientists.

Empiricism, however, tends to keep close to sense-near representations and holds theory as a dubious entity. The empiricist's vocabulary, then, remains "largely observational". As an ideal type, empirical preoccupations tend toward the progressive refinement of methods of observing of preexisting constructs, rather than the generation of new ones, toward ever greater agreement of man-with-man (interrater reliability), man-with-himself (reliability over occasions), and greater purity of observation (internal consistency).

Few members of the modern scientific community are native empiricists, yet "no science embraced empiricism more wholeheartedly than psychology". Moreover, some of the assumptions underlying empiricism are insidious and difficult to escape from, even when one ostensibly believes in the utility of theory. Foremost among criticisms is that the empiricism of common sense, naive realism, believes that the world it takes in is the world as it is. Commensensical empiricism literally believes its constructs are the world. There is no reason to leave the security of immediate perception. Ultimately, this agenda rests on the assumption that theory-neutral data exist; that is, that one can know the world without transforming it. In the world view of radical empiricism, there are no mediating mental constructs to foul things up. If only it were so, then every act of observation would be an act of knowledge. Each small fact would present us with an obectivity, to be plucked from the world like fruit, collected as a hobby, or catalogued like microscope slides. Because naive empiricism remains unconscious of the potentially deceiving role of mental constructs, it believes itself to be carving nature at its joints just as it is. Naive empiricism, then, is really a false mysticism which breaches the gulf between subject and object by denying that any such gulf exists; it is a naive realism which believes that what you see is what you get.

1. The passage discusses two approaches which are used to investigate personologic phenomenon. These are:
   1. "Operational definitions" and "Open concepts"
   2. "Facts" and 'Theory"
   3. "Commonsensical empiricism" and "naive mysticism"
   4. "Personology" and "Hard sciences"
2. Which statement is not an advantage of "operationism"?
   1. Data is derived from empirical-practical content
   2. Direct mapping of personologic attributes to measurement mode, frees them from making inferences
   3. Personality syndromes and attributes become clear and unambiguous
   4. Measurement procedures are maximized and this increases precision
3. Which statement does not describe a characteristic of "open concepts"?
   1. "Open concepts" derive their meaning from theoretical frameworks and models
   2. "Open concepts" allows the researcher to move freely in more abstract and inferential realms
   3. "Open concepts" model allows the researcher to use multiple measurement procedures
   4. "Open concepts" free research from becoming tautological and decoupled from observables
4. Science moves away from commonsense in some essential ways. Which statement reflects one such way?
   1. A scientist introduces new "theoretical terms" which are embedded in theory, and more or less removed from the level of directly observable things and events, while researching.
   2. A scientist ignores biases incumbent in multiple measurement procedures and moves freely in abstractions
   3. A scientist progresses from a "theoretical stage" to the "natural history" stage while researching.
   4. A scientist is acutely conscious of identifying representations that are intrinsic to the subject of inquiry.
5. From the passage what are the characteristics of a researcher who wants to examine personologic phenomenon?
   1. The researcher is adept in clinically and painstakingly refining measures to the point that no information beyond that contained in the procedure is valid.
   2. All the above characteristics.
   3. The researcher should be able to move from empirical to theoretical by discovering underlying theoretic causal relationship existing in the phenomenon that is examined.
   4. The researcher should be a good reflective scientist, who is able to carve nature at its joints.
6. The corner stone of the philosophy of "Empiricism" is:
   1. Empiricism in its pure form is mysticism.
   2. To strive and refine methods of pre-existing constructs, rather than generating new constructs to explain what exists.

3. There is no gulf between "subject" and "object" and all data is theory free.
4. Mediating mental constructs do not affect reality as it exists

7. Which science has adopted "Empiricism" whole heartedly according to the passage?
1. Biology
2. All of these
3. Hard sciences
4. Psychology

8. "Interrater reliability", "Test-retest reliability" and "internal consistency", are terms that will preoccupy a/an:
1. mystic
2. pure empiricist
3. common sense empiricist
4. personologic scientist

DIRECTIONS *for questions 9–16: Read the passage given below and answer the questions.*

Passage – 2

Behaviour therapy has a long and productive history of empirically researched treatments for a wide range of adult and child disorders, but what is *dialectical* behaviour therapy? It is an integration of behaviour therapy with other perspectives and practices that includes, most notably, principles and practice of Zen and an overarching dialectical philosophy that guides the treatment. The treatment, developed by Marsha Linehan (1987) evolved over almost 20 years of work with chronically suicidal women. It is rooted firmly in the principles and practices of behaviour therapy and cognitive therapy, including a strong emphasis on systematic ongoing assessment and data collection during treatment; operational definitions of clearly defined target behaviours; a therapist-patient relationship that emphasizes collaboration, orienting the patient to the treatment, and education of the patient; and the use of any standard cognitive and behavioural treatment strategies. But it also has a number of distinctive characteristics that have emerged partly in response to characteristics of this patient population. One of these is an emphasis on dialectics. The fundamental dialectic with this population is the need for both acceptance and change. The therapist needs to fully accept the patient as he or she is and at the same time to persistently and insistently push for and help the patient to change. The therapist also tries to develop and strengthen an attitude of acceptance towards reality on the part of the patient as well as the motivation and ability to change what can be changed. This dialectic both flows from and is addressed by the integration of behaviour therapy with Zen practice, Rogerian practice, and others. The therapist also needs to think in a dialectical fashion, not becoming polarized but seeing the value of opposing points of view and finding appropriate synthesis.

The treatment rests on the dialectic of two core sets of strategies: validation strategies and problem-solving strategies. Behaviour therapy has emphasized problem solving but has had little to say about validation or acceptance. DBT also involves a dialectic of communication style between a reciprocal, warm, genuine interpersonal style and a more irreverent style and a dialectic in case management between consultation to the patient regarding how to manage his or her environment on the one hand and direct environmental intervention by the therapist on the other. DBT was developed to address the issues that lead therapists of not only behavioural but also other theoretical orientations to frequently get stuck, go down blind alleys, and in some cases even contribute to serious, even fatal, deterioration in the patient's well-being. DBT does not particularly emphasize the role of the patient's motivational factors (e.g., resistance) in understanding the difficulty these patients have in changing. Rather, it recognizes that they almost always are seriously deficient in a wide spectrum of interpersonal, emotion regulation, distress tolerance, and other skills. However, the behaviour therapist who attempts to treat the borderline patient by a relatively structured sequence of skills acquisition and practice, as one might do with some patients who have depressive or anxiety disorders, quickly discovers that the patient's emotional sensitivity necessitates presenting skills, and problem solving in general, within a context in which the patient feels understood and validated, particularly with regard to his or her emotions and motives.

Conducting skills training in individual therapy with borderline patients is frequently almost impossible because of the recurrent chaos and crises of their lives, so that at every session some new behaviour or situation may need to be dealt with. Linehan therefore decided to separate skills training into a separate component of the treatment, typically in a group format, to free up the individual psychotherapist for helping patients manage crises, reinforce the use of skills, and deal with motivational issues that interfere with their using the skills they have. Thus, it is assumed that patients not only have skills deficits but typically also do not use the skills they have. In DBT, the term "motivational" refers to emotions, cognitions, or reinforcement contingencies that interfere with skilled behaviour. The therapist's job therefore becomes one of helping the patient overcome inhibitions, change beliefs and thinking styles, and rearrange reinforcement contigencies for adaptive and maladaptive behaviour, The treatment therefore targets both improvement in skills and adequate attention to these several motivational factors that can interfere with them.

9. What is the corner stone of the philosophy that underlies Dialectical Behaviour Therapy (DBT)?

1. Developing a collaborative relationship between patient-therapist, and standard cognitive and behavioural treatment strategies.
2. On-going and systematic assessment and data collection during treatment, with an emphasis on clearly defined target behaviours of the patient which need to be changed.
3. Accepting the patient for what he or she is; while striving to change the patient so that problems are solved.
4. Integration of behaviour therapy with other perspectives notably Zen and dialectics.

10. DBT has developed because:

1. Traditional models of therapy is didactic and pedogogical rather than being human and realistic.
2. 3 and 4 both
3. Lead therapists found that often patient's health deteriorated totally by the use of traditional methods of therapy.
4. Lead therapists, both behavioural and theoretical, frequently get stuck, and use trial and error while treating patients.

11. The notion of 1 accepting reality as it is and 2 striving to change what can be changed derives from ____________ and ____________ respectively.

1. Behaviour therapy; Cognitive therapy
2. Cognitive therapy; Behaviour therapy
3. Rogerian practice; Zen philosophy
4. Zen philosophy; Rogerian practice

12. An innovation that Linehan introduced in DBT; and which has led to better results with respect to improvements in the patient is:

1. Conducting skills training of patients in a separate component as a group format; allowing the individual psychotherapist help patient with motivational issues.

2. The therapist focuses on helping patient overcome inhibitions, change beliefs and thinking styles, and rearrange reinforcement contingencies for adaptive and maladaptive behaviours.
3. The individual psychotherapist uses both skills training and reduction of motivational deficits to help patients.
4. Borderline patients benefit when they are made to go through relatively structured sequence of skills acquisition and practice.

13. One of the main problems with a DBT therapist could be:
1. Lack of understanding of Zen philosophy.
2. All of the above.
3. Inability to synthesize opposing perspectives and tending to become polarized while treating a patient.
4. To be reverent and irreverent at the same time while treating a patient.

14. In the final analysis the advantages of DBT are numerous. Which statement can be inferred as not to be one of the advantages of DBT?
1. Cultural differences between the patient and the therapist can create complications in the practice of DBT.
2. DBT can be very taxing for the therapist to practice.
3. DBT is an open ended form of treatment, and therapists can choose from a wide repertoire of available techniques.
4. The DBT therapist needs to be a highly skilled and evolved person, which is not possible for many individuals.

15. Marsha Linehan evolved DBT over almost 20 years of work with:
1. women who were deficient in a wide spectrum of interpersonal, emotion regulation, distress tolerance and other skills.
2. all of the above.
3. depressive women.
4. chronically suicidal women.

16. Which social institution practices DBT in its essence, without being conscious of it?
1. Hospitals
2. All of these
3. Schools
4. Families

DIRECTIONS for questions 17–24: *Read the passage given below and answer the questions.*

Passage – 3

A creamy blur of succulent blue sound smells like week-old strawberries dropped onto a tin sieve as mother approaches in a halo of color, chatter, and a perfume like thick golden butterscotch. Newborns ride on intermingling waves of sight, sound, touch, taste, and, especially, smell. As Daphne and Charles Maurer remind us in *The World of the Newborn:*

His world smells to him much as our world smells to us, but he does not perceive odors as coming through his nose alone. He hears odors, and sees odors, and feels them too. His world is a melee of pungent aromas – and pungent sounds, and bitter-smelling sounds, and sweet-smelling sights, and sour-smelling pressures against the skin. If we could visit the newborn's world, we would think ourselves inside a hallucinogenic perfumery.

In time, the newborn learns to sort and tame all its sensory impressions, some of which have names, many of which will remain nameless to the end of its days. Things that elude our verbal grasp are hard to pin down and almost impossible to remember. A cozy blur in the nursery vanishes into the rigorous categories of common sense. But for some people, that sensory blending never quits, and they taste baked beans whenever they hear the word "Francis," as one woman reported, or see yellow on touching a matte surface, or smell the passage of time. The stimulation of one sense stimulates another: *synesthesia* is the technical name, from the Greek *syn* (together) + *aisthanesthai* (to perceive). A thick garment of perception is woven thread by overlapping thread. A similar word is *synthesis,* in which the garment of thought is woven together idea by idea, and which originally referred to the light muslin clothing worn by the ancient Romans.

Daily life is a constant onslaught on one's perceptions, and every-one experiences some intermingling of the senses. According to Gestalt psychologists, when people are asked to relate a list of non-sense words to shapes and colors they identify certain sounds with certain shapes in ways that fall into clear patterns. What's more surprising is that this is true whether they are from the United States, England, the Mahali peninsula, or Lake Tanganyika. People with intense synesthesia tend to respond in predictable ways, too. A survey of two thousand synesthetes from various cultures revealed many similarities in the colors they assigned to sounds. People often associate low sounds with dark colors and high sounds with bright colors, for instance. A certain amount of synesthesia is built into our senses. If one wished to create instant synesthesia, a dose of mescaline or hashish would do nicely by exaggerating the neural connections between the senses. Those who experience intense synesthesia naturally on a regular basis are rare – only about one in every five hundred thousand people – and neurologist Richard Cytowiè traces the phenomenon to the limbic system, the most primitive part of the brain, calling synesthetes "living cognitive fossils," because they may be people whose limbic system is not entirely governed by the much more sophisticated (and more recently evolved) cortex. As he says, "synesthesia .... may be a memory of how early mammals saw, heard, smelled, tasted and touched."

While synesthesia drives some people to distraction, it drives distractions away from others. While it is a small plague to the person who doesn't want all that sensory overload, it invigorates those who are indelibly creative. Some of the most famous synesthetes have been artists. Composers Aleksandr Scriabin and Nikolai Rimski-Korsakov both freely associated colors with music when they wrote. To Rimski-Korsakov, C major was white; to Scriabin it was red. To Rimski-Korsakov, A major was rosy, to Scriabin it was green. More surprising is how closely their music-color synesthesias matched. Both associated E major with blue (for Rimski-Korsakov, it was sapphire blue, for Scriabin blue-white), A-flat major with purple (for Rimski-Korsakov it was grayish-violet, for Scriabin purple-violet), D major with yellow, etc.

Either writers have been especially graced with synesthesia, or they've been keener to describe it. Dr. Johnson once said that scarlet "represented nothing so much as the clangour of a trumpet." Baudelaire took pride in his sensory Esperanto, and his sonnet on the correspondences between perfumes, colors, and sounds greatly influenced the synesthesia-loving Symbolist movement. Symbol comes from the Greek word *symballein,* "to throw together," and, as *The Columbia Dictionary of Modern European Literature* explains, the Symbolists believed that "all arts are parallel translations of one fundamental mystery. Senses correspond to each other; a sound can be translated through a perfume and a perfume through a vision. ....Haunted by these horizontal correspondences" and using suggestion rather than straightforward communication, they sought "the One hidden in Nature behind the Many." Rimbaud, who assigned colors to each of the vowel sounds and once described

A as a "black hairy corset of loud flies," claimed that the only way an artist can arrive at life's truths is by experiencing "every form of love, of suffering, of madness," to be prepared for by "a long immense planned disordering of all the senses." The Symbolists, who were avid drug takers, delighted in the way hallucinogens intensified all their senses simultaneously. They would have loved (for a short time) taking LSD while watching Walt Disney's *Fantasia,* in which pure color dramatizes, melts into, and spurts from classical music. Few artists have written about synesthesia with the all-out precision and charm of Vladimiar Nabokov, who, in *Speak, Memory,* analyses what he calls his "colored hearing":

Perhaps "hearing" is not quite accurate, since the color sensation seems to be produced by the very act of my orally forming a given letter while I imagine its outline. The long *a* of the English alphabet ..... has for me the tint of weathered wood, but a French *a* evokes polished ebony. This black group also includes hard *g* (vulcanized rubber) and *r* (a sooty rag being ripped). Oatmeal *n,* noodle-limp *l*, and the ivory-backed hand mirror of *o* take care of ...."

Synesthesia can be hereditary, so it's not surprising that Nabokov's mother experienced it, nor that it expressed itself slightly differently in her son. However, it's odd to think of Nabokov, Faulkner, Virginia Woolf, Huysmans, Baudelaire, Joyce, Dylan Thomas and other notorious synesthetes as being more primitive than most people, but that may indeed be true. Great artists feel at home in the luminous spill of sensation, to which they add their own complex sensory Niagara. It would certainly have amused Nabokov to imagine himself closer than others to his mammalian ancestors, which he would no doubt have depicted in a fictional hall of mirrors with suave, prankish, Nabokovian finesse.

17. Those who experience intense synesthesia are rare. Which cluster are synesthetes?

1. Some artists, mystics and drug takers
2. Infants and Symbolists and Musicians
3. Some artists, babies and avid drug takers
4. Artists and babies

18. According to Richard Cytowiè the most primitive part of the brain is:

1. Medulla
2. Cerebrum
3. Cortex
4. Limbic system

19. Which statement beat describes the experience of synesthesia?

1. It is a long immense disordering of all the senses.
2. All the sentences are correct.
3. A thick garment of perception is woven thread by overlapping thread.
4. A garment of thought is woven idea by idea, like the light muslin cloth.

20. Which composer/s associated E major with blue, while writing?

1. Alexsandr Scriabin and Rimski-Korsakov
2. Aleksandr Scriabin and Bob Dylan
3. Alek Sandr Scriabin
4. Bob Dylan and Rimski-Korsakov

21. According to synesthesia:

1. "the stimulation of one sense stimulates another"
2. all of the above
3. the brain tries to see "the one hidden in nature behind the many"
4. "all arts are parallel translations of one fundamental mystery. "

22. Non-synesthetes (complete the sentence):

1. can never become artists and reach extraordinary heights.
2. would love to fake LSD (for a short time) while watching Walt Disney's Fantasia.
3. tame all the sensory impressions into rigorous categories of common sense.
4. are living cognitive fossils who use their limbic system more.

23. From the passage, which other category of people (not mentioned in the passage) could be experiencing synesthesia:

1. Mystics
2. Actors
3. Scientists
4. Chefs

24. People with intense synesthesia respond in predictable ways. Which of the following experience is *not, shared* by co-synesthetes?

1. Musical note A Major is green
2. All are not shared by synesthetes
3. Low sounds are associated with dark colours
4. High sounds are associated with bright colours

DIRECTIONS for questions 25–32: *Read the passage given below and answer the questions.*

Passage – 4

How can technology be defined? Technology often is considered a means to a particular end, the means being artificially created, not natural, and something that is not directly necessary for the individual or the end user; it serves, rather, to fulfil the need to produce something that is later to be consumed. However, we use the term in a broader sense. We regard technology as being more than just sum of such artefacts, which are merely the crystallized, concrete manifestations of human behavioral patterns. A method is the how, the way in which a goal is reached and which involves the use of means. A means is a medium in that it mediates between the starting point and the desired result, regardless of what sort of action is involved. Thus one could speak of social technology (e.g., psychotherapy) as a technology and not merely of technology as something used for material production in a society. So technology also includes the know-how involved in the use of the application of the artefacts. In short, technology embraces the ways and means of acting in pursuit of a goal.

How can culture be defined? Using the same analogy of technology, it could be understood to be an equally artefact-based concept, which is not a means to an end, but rather an end in itself. That is to say, it is not in itself an essential of life, but rather something that represents a human desire (i.e., what makes humans distinct from other living beings). Here, too, there is a notion that culture is not only the result of a process but also this very process itself as it moves towards a goal; that is to say, culture is a characteristic of goal-oriented actions (i.e., striving towards goals as well as the goals themselves).

Are there imaginable connections between culture and technology? The two ideal typical extreme positions are well known, each making a single direction of determination.

The first position can be referred to as technological determinism, which postulates the total, or at least dominating, influence of technology on culture. Technology is supposed to develop more or less on its own, pushing social development along as it goes. This may be interpreted positively or negatively. An uncritical opinion of Marxist origin saw social advancement as an inevitable result of technical achievements, just as the ideology of the bourgeoisie justified the progress of technically possible as socially desirable. This view is opposed entirely by fundamentalists who hold technological development responsible for the loss of human values in a society. Neither philosophy accepts the possibility of technological development being influenced in any way. Both ignore the fact that there would be no such development if multinational corporations and national governments were to stop investing in research and development; if there was no political, economic and military interests. The fact that on a micro-level there are countless thousands of engineers constantly involved in technology design, and that on a macro-level managers and politicians decide which technological options are realised, supports the second theory—social constructivism—that technology is constructed deliberately to be a part of a society. According to this view, the interests of those groups that dominate the genesis of technology finally are embodied in the technology, which in itself cannot be neutral. Here again both a critical and an approving variant may be distinguished. While one bemoan the inability of existing technology to pursue ethically justifiable, socially acceptable, and peaceful and environmentally sound objectives, the other sees the existing economic, democratic and human rights structures as the best guarantee of developing optimal technological options. Both approaches neglect the inherent dynamism within technological development.

Do the two theories – technological determinism and social constructivism – together give a realistic view of the relationship between culture and technology? This would mean that two equally matched factors – technical and cultural would not be complete without other. Though as a corollary you may like to add that they are a little independent also of each other. This is a superficial answer. A better explanation can be put forward. Technology is based on cooperation, be it in the application of special methods, the implementation of these in specific social areas, their invention and development or any situation in which skills and knowledge of members of society are required. The same holds true for convictions, value judgements, instructions, standards, behavioural pattern and the like. These are just as much part of content that promote or discourage technological methods. Technology makes every technologically mediated action into a socially determined one, and its use is a human characteristic. Technological development is part of cultural development; this means that technology is part of culture, and their relationship to each other is one of part and whole. Culture is the all embracing factor in this context.

In each part whole relationship, the parts are the necessary precondition for the emergence of the whole but are not the sufficient condition for the complete determination of the result. The whole arises from parts but exerts control over them in the form of downward causation. This means technology has the purpose of solving social problems. Social interests and culture are therefore in the origin of invention of technology – and culture becomes the reason for the existence of technology. But technology is ambivalent, sometimes it fails to do what is wanted, and other times not only fulfills expectations but goes on to do other useful tasks not anticipated. Realizable goals therefore, do not exist at the start of the process, but may be discovered as option made available by technology. However, whether society decides to pursue these goals on grounds they are possible is no longer a question of technology but rather social decision making.

To conclude, the relationship of technology and culture is dialectic. A relationship is usually dialectic if, first, the sides of the relation are opposed to each other; second, both sides depend on each other; and third, they form a relationship that is asymmetrical. A part-whole relationship is dialectic since part and whole represent opposites, the whole depends on parts as well as parts on the whole, and parts and whole build up a hierarchy in which the different levels cannot be replaced by each other. Such is the relationship between technology and culture.

25. With respect to "defining technology" which statement is *true?*

1. Technology is the sum of the artefacts which are crystallized and concrete manifestations of human behavioural patterns.
2. None of the above.
3. Technology is a complex phenomenon and is about the "know how" and "means" to achieve goals that are not natural to human beings.
4. Technology is more than the sum of parts that mediates goals and the realization of goals.

26. Which statement best represents the 'meaning of culture'?

1. Culture is the set of goal oriented activities and their solutions, that are shared by a particular group.
2. All of the above.
3. Culture is the summation of goals that people strive for and the means to achieve them.
4. The trajectory of fulfilling human desires, through chosen ways and the resultant outcomes is culture.

27. Which statement is *true?*

1. Technology and culture shape each other equally.
2. All are wrong.
3. Technology shapes culture.
4. Culture shapes technology.

28. What is common between technology and culture?

1. Both lead to new needs and desired goals.
2. Statement 3 and 4.
3. Both are shared phenomenon.
4. Both are shaped by each other.

29. Which of the following statements is *true?*

1. The Fundamentalists are against technological development.
2. All the statements are correct.
3. The bourgeoisie equate technological growth with socially desirable.
4. The Marxists believe that technology propel social advancement.

30. The passage refers to part-whole relationship. Which of the following statements is correct in this regard?

1. The relationship between part-whole is bidirectional, dynamic and hierarchical.
2. 3 and 4 are correct.
3. In part-whole relationships, the whole is sum of parts.
4. The whole exerts influence on parts, and not the other way round.

31. Which of the following statements is *false?*

1. Realizable goals do not exist, unless technology finds ways to realize them.
2. All goals that are realizable are based on societal decisions.

3. Technology is ambivalent; it both realizes social goals and changes pre- existing goals.
4. Culture defines goals that technology strives to realize.

32. The passage talks of three viewpoints regarding the relationship between technology and culture. Which of the following does not represent a viewpoint?

1. Technological determinism and social constructivism together give a realistic view of the relationship between technology and culture.
2. Technology has the task of functioning as a means for solving social problems, and culture influences the invention, diffusion and application of technology; but sometimes technology also creates new goals.
3. Technology develops more or less on its own, pushing social development.
4. Interests of those groups that dominate the genesis of technology finally are embodied in the technology.

DIRECTIONS for questions 33 to 40: *Read the passage given below and answer the questions.*

Passage – 5

One of the ironies of counterfeiting is that while it reduces demand for authentic products – thus reducing employment that would otherwise be employed in making those products – it also *creates* jobs in the factories, sweatshops, and back-alley operations where counterfeits are made.

"In advanced Western economies, job creation is regarded as a vital imperative for all governments and politicians. This is because unemployment impacts on society in all sorts of ways, in lost tax revenue, unemployment pay, and attendant social costs. In developing countries where counterfeiting is rife, different considerations apply. Counterfeiters are able to tap a vast pool of low cost labor, which has no access to the sort of welfare benefits available in well developed industrialized countries. In addition, taxes are minimal or nonexistent, and counterfeiters can masquerade as Robin Hood figures providing a valuable service for the community at the expense of 'wealthy' rights owners....the message is that (while) counterfeiting does destroy the jobs of victim companies and their suppliers...it does create jobs for those in the counterfeiting industry. This of course may well be one reason why countries that have become well known as havens of counterfeiting have been reluctant to clamp down on this industry too hard." — Peter Lowe, Counterfeiting Intelligence Bureau

In those economies where counterfeiting is an industry itself, jobs are created when counterfeiters employ people to make fake products. In one startling example described by the Counterfeiting Intelligence Bureau, an investigator in China visiting the city of Wenzhou, about 400 kilometres south of Shanghai, uncovered a vast industrial zone, with perhaps as many as a thousand companies engaged in the business of producing counterfeit low-voltage electrical switchgear. The investigator estimated that somewhere between 2,00,000 to 3,00,000 people were employed in these businesses.

Although this type of employment may appear as a benefit to those being employed, it often has other problems associated with it. The same investigator who described the switchgear counterfeiting industry in Wenzhou also described seeing child labor in the various establishments producing fake products. He described unsafe working conditions, with the assembly of finished goods often taking place on the street. Workers are paid by the piece, and unprotected by any insurance, benefits, union representation, or holidays.

Poor working conditions are endemic throughout much of the developing world—where much counterfeiting takes place. But one key difference between being employed by a counterfeiter and being employed by a legitimate industry is obvious: Counterfeiters have little long-term incentive to improve working conditions, and any legislation or change in government policy would not likely affect counterfeiters. When government interference or regulation becomes too onerous—or makes counterfeiting too risky an occupation in a certain location—the counterfeiters simply move to a more conducive locale.

It may not come as a surprise, though, to realize that support in local communities for counterfeiters can be quite high—these establishments, while illegal, create employment. Often this support can overwhelm government attempts to enforce crack downs:

A violent conflict erupted in Xintang Town, Zengcheri City when 5,000 people who were involved in the manufacture of fake jeans and other imitation products confronted a team of government officials who had been sent to crack down on the trade in counterfeits. In what must have been a chilling experience for the enforcers, the local people surrounded the motorcade of more than 60 government officials, reporters and public security officers from Guangzhou who had come to maintain order. The situation turned critical when some of the local people threatened to disarm the public security officials. A "stand off of more than three hours ensued after which negotiations were started which finally diffused the situation.

The costs of hosting counterfeiting to a community are not simply those normally associated with low wages and child labor in unsafe conditions. More far-reaching consequences are being uncovered as the scope of counterfeiting throughout the globe has become more apparent. In the *McKinsey Quarterly* in the spring of 2000, a group of McKinsey consultants looked at the Russian economy's inability to generate growth throughout the 1990s. Among the factors cited as contributing to the poor labor productivity and the disincentive to invest in research and development was counterfeiting:

The software industry, one of the prime creators of jobs and value in healthy modern economies, employs a mere 8,000 workers in Russia, compared with 6,40,000 in the United States. Why is this important industry so small? For starters, 89% of all packaged software in Russia is produced illegally. Russian packaged-software firms, therefore, can't produce sufficient returns to justify investing in new products, or in research and development to improve existing ones. In addition, the software-consuming sectors, whose demand drives the emergence and growth of software firms, are both smaller and less interested in productivity-enhancing software tools than are their Western counterparts. In modern economies, for example, supermarkets – with their complex inventory management systems – are big consumers of software, but Russia has few of them. Similarly, modern banks use software to keep costs low and customer service high, but in Russia, where success in banking depends on relationships with the authorities, the demand for banking software is nearly nonexistent relative to demand in the United States.

This conclusion was echoed in the Counterfeiting Intelligence Bureau's book *Countering Counterfeiting,* which also concluded that "another national consequence resulting from the costs incurred by 'victim' companies is a general decline in R&D, since a company cannot expect the full return from its investment.

In addition, the Organization for Economic Cooperation and Development (OECD) has highlighted the loss of direct foreign investment that can arise as a result of a country becoming known as a haven for counterfeiting. In the OECD's own report on the *Economic Impact of Counterfeiting* (1998), the organization writes that "such countries suffer both tangible and intangible losses...foreign producers of reputable products become reluctant to manufacture their products in countries where counterfeiting is rife as they cannot rely on the enforcement of their intellectual property rights. Hence, such countries not only *lose direct foreign investment but also miss out on foreign know-how*."

While counterfeiting can create jobs, it can also create a series of other problems that ultimately could lead to an economy being less competitive, less integrated into the stream of international commerce, and less productive than economies where governments choose to crack down on counterfeiters.

33. Which one of the following would be a suitable title for the passage?

1. Economic and social consequences of counterfeiting
2. The irony of counterfeiting as a creater of employment
3. Social consequences of counterfeiting
4. Advantages and disadvantages of counterfeiting

34. Based on the arguments presented in the passage which concrete inference can be made regarding counterfeiting:

1. counterfeiting exists because there is a market for it.
2. all of the above.
3. counterfeiting is a necessary evil in developing countries as it generates employment.
4. counterfeiting hurts the economy of developed nations.

35. In Russia the software industry is small because:

1. almost 90% packaged software is illegal and therefore its market also is limited.
2. all of the above.
3. very little money is invested in R&D needed for developing new softwares that can help the industry grow.
4. Russian banks and supermarkets do not need complex software solutions, and so there is no market for software development in this area.

36. What are some of the consequences of counterfeiting in developing countries?

1. perpetuates poor global work ethics.
2. 3 and 4.
3. It encourages exploitation of labour.
4. It discourages investments in research and development.

37. Which statement is *true?*

1. The confrontation between the crackdown team against counterfeiting and thousands of people involved in manufacture of counterfeit goods turned violent in Xintang Town, Zengchen city.
2. All the statements are true.
3. 5,000 people from Wenzhou confronted 60 government officials from Guangzhao.
4. People of Zengchen city were exploited by their employers and worked in poor conditions.

38. In the final analysis who benefits from counterfeiting?

1. Counterfeiting organization and its employees.
2. No one.

3. Developing countries and its people.
4. The counterfeiting organization.

39. What recommendations would you like to make to developing countries which engage in producing counterfeit goods?

1. The passage does not provide information for making recommen-dations.
2. Allow global regulatory agencies to independently handle the counterfeit economy.
3. Clamp down on organizations which produce counterfeit goods.
4. Allow employment through counterfeit but force, such organizations, to provide better work conditions to the employees.

40. Which cluster according to you is the best solution for handling the problem of counter-feiting?

1. Play of market forces; sanctions; allow counterfeiting.
2. None of the above.
3. Allow counterfeiting; regulate work conditions; invest in R&D
4. MOU between original and counterfeiting organization; government regulation; ac-tivism.

SECTION – II

Fill in the blanks with the appropriate allusion from the options given.

41. Her uncle and cousins are reporters, and she, too, hopes to join the ____________

1. juggernaut
2. Armageddon
3. fourth estate
4. fifth column

42. The freedom fighters knew they would be hanged if caught, but they nevertheless decided to:

1. carry coal to Newcastle
2. juggernaut
3. hoist with one's own petard
4. cross the Rubicon

Which pair of words in the options relate to each other in the same way as the capitalized pair?

43. CICCERONE: SIGHTSEER

1. Understudy: actor
2. Audio: video
3. Baedeker: tourist
4. Mentor: guidance

44. QUISLING: TREASON

1. Accomplice: guilt
2. Murderer: homicide
3. Renegade: loyalty
4. Perjurer: arson

45. POLLYANNA: OPTIMISM

1. Diehard: resistance
2. Environmentalist: pollution
3. Malingerer: illness
4. Reactionary: change

46. LARGE: GARGANTUAN

1. Emaciated: thin
2. Wise: Machiavellian
3. Obese: stout
4. Small: tiny

Read each statement, and from the options select the best idiom that describes what is being said in the statement.

47. Reena felt uneasy and slightly unwell in office because of the late night party she had attended the night before:

1. to be off colour
2. to be coloured
3. to be colourless
4. to be under colour

48. Ronald continued to report for work during the strike in defiance of trade union instructions. Ronald is:

1. a black spot
2. in the black
3. a black leg
4. the black sheep

49. A period of great happiness came into Rita, a widow, and Ranjan, a widower's life when they married late in life, after fulfilling the responsibilities towards their respective children. This phase is for them:

1. the autumn of life
2. unexpected rain
3. an Indian summer
4. the spring of their life

50. Which idiom correctly expresses the following: to regret bitterly, either one's own mistakes or success of somebody of whom one is jealous?

1. To grit one's teeth
2. To show one's teeth
3. To grind one's teeth
4. To gnash one's teeth

51. The idiom ________________ refers to a male adult who mentally remains fixated on his childhood.

1. Tommy Atkins
2. Simple Simon
3. Peter Pan
4. Paul Pry

52. A dwelling is a place of residence. Pairs of different types of dwellings are given below. Identify the pair; which is not a dwelling:

1. bungalow – barrack
2. diazo – sappanwood
3. hermitage – hogan
4. prefab – priory

53. Which one is *not* a synonym of 'devil'?

1. Mephisto
2. Velavu
3. Lucifer
4. Beelzebub

54. Calligraphy is to cartooning as gouache is to ______________.

1. baguette
2. chevron
3. scumbling
4. beading

55. Shrewdness of apes is similar to tidings of ______________

1. larks
2. nightingales
3. swallows
4. magpies

56. Autocracy is by an absolute ruler as timocracy is by ______________.

1. property owners
2. rich
3. elected representatives
4. priests

57. One of the options does not contain different types of units of measurement, all others are:

1. radian, lambert, coulomb, kelvin
2. spartan, klang, caslon, sabon
3. acre, month, quintal, pound
4. byte, cubit, furlong, gallon

58. The words given below are all applied to things that are unusual or unfamiliar; they generally also suggest that something is in some way surprising. Which word is the most "neutral" term, and expresses the least of above qualities?

1. Strange
2. Odd
3. Peculiar
4. Curious

59. When a person shake's while experiencing "extreme fear", which of the following words would be the most, appropriate?

1. Shiver
2. Quiver
3. Quake
4. Tremble

60. The following words imply a "mocking attitude". Which one of the following conveys the greatest degree of criticism or rejection?

1. Sardonic
2. Sarcastic
3. Caustic
4. Ironic

61. All the four verbs given below can just mean 'puzzle'; but they also hint at different stages along the road to bewilderment. Select the option in which the verbs are listed from low to the highest level of bewilderment in ascending order.

1. Perplex, mystify, puzzle, baffle
2. Baffle, puzzle, mystify, perplex
3. Mystify, perplex, baffle, puzzle
4. Puzzle, perplex, mystify, baffle

62. These words are all applied to qualities or features that are a central element in something's nature. "______________" refers to a feature of someone or something that is so important to their nature thatwithout it they would not be the same person or thing.

1. innate
2. inherent
3. essential
4. intrinsic

63. "Consistency is contrary to nature, contrary to life. The only completely consistent people are the dead." —Aldous Huxley (1894-1963)

In this quotation the author is talking about:

1. change is natural
2. change is contrary to life
3. consistency is natural
4. life is consistent

64. "Take care to get what you like or you will be forced to like what you get."
—George Bernard Shaw (1856-1950)

In this quotation the author is referring to:

1. choosing what we want
2. all of the above
3. choices we make in life
4. importance of making choices

65. "I must have a prodigious quantity of mind; it takes me as much as a week, sometimes, to make it up." — Mark Twain (1835-1910)

In this quotation the author is referring to:

1. carefully weigh pros and cons
2. how people decide
3. powerful memory
4. inability to decide quickly

DIRECTIONS for questions 66 to 75: *Read the following ten statements and answer the questions.*

(i) During the interview Rakesh answered all the questions in mono syllables like: "yes", "no", and "perhaps".

(ii) Mona advised Sujata, not to end all her business calls with a "feel free to call me" statement, as it was an over used expression. Sujata however disregarded the advice and continued to do so.

(iii) When Shyam was recovering from a severe bout of jaundice, his mother Ramola had no option but to be very strict with Shyam's diet. She called herself a "mean mother" at that time.

(iv) In 1942, Abel Tasman, a Dutch navigator discovered the island of Tasmania off the South-eastern coast of Australia.

(v) When the class, yet again failed to submit the assignment in time, Reena, the class teacher, angrily denounced the class for full fifteen minutes.

(vi) Seema could have very well written WHO, and saved time. By writing the full form World Health Organization, she missed winning the last round of quiz by two seconds.

(vii) "O' Henry", the short story writer was actually William Sydney Porter in real life.

(viii) When Krishna gave the sales figures of the last five years, the client was convinced that the product was "successful" and this was not an exaggeration.

(ix) All the team members were so excited that they rushed to answer first and thus gave many wrong answers in the quiz. Jai, the leader scolded them and said, "Look before you leap".

(x) Sunita was planning a surprise party for her husband. She felt hurt when Bimal, her husband asked, "What are you scheming behind my back."

66. Who used an oxymoron?

1. Sujata
2. Reena
3. Jai
4. Ramola

67. Who had used a Pseudonym?

1. Vivek
2. Ramola
3. William Sydney Porter
4. Abel Tasman

68. Who used a maxim?

1. Jai
2. O' Henry
3. Reena
4. Mona

69. Who spurned an acronym?

1. Ramola
2. Picasso
3. Seema
4. O' Henry

70. Who was inarticulate?

1. Reena
2. Sujata
3. Seema
4. Rakesh

71. Who clung to a cliche?

1. Fred
2. Mona
3. Sujata
4. Jai

72. Who became an eponym?

1. Abel Tasman
2. None of these
3. O' Henry
4. William Sydney Porter

73. Who used a pejorative expression?

1. Ramola
2. Mona
3. Bimal
4. Jai

74. Who made an abstract term concrete?

1. Ramola
2. Krishna
3. Shyam
4. Bimal

75. Who unleashed a diatribe?

1. Anita
2. Fred
3. Mona
4. Reena

Answer Key

1. 1	**2.** 4	**3.** 4	**4.** 1	**5.** 2	**6.** 2	**7.** 4
8. 2	**9.** 3	**10.** 2	**11.** 2	**12.** 3	**13.** 3	**14.** 4
15. 4	**16.** 2	**17.** 3	**18.** 4	**19.** 2	**20.** 1	**21.** 2
22. 3	**23.** 3	**24.** 1	**25.** 3	**26.** 2	**27.** 2	**28.** 2
29. 2	**30.** 2	**31.** 3	**32.** 4	**33.** 1	**34.** 2	**35.** 2
36. 2	**37.** 1	**38.** 4	**39.** 3	**40.** 2	**41.** 3	**42.** 4
43. 3	**44.** 2	**45.** 1	**46.** 4	**47.** 4	**48.** 4	**49.** 1
50. 3	**51.** 2	**52.** 2	**53.** 2	**54.** 3	**55.** 4	**56.** 1
57. 2	**58.** 4	**59.** 4	**60.** 2	**61.** 4	**62.** 1	**63.** 1
64. 2	**65.** 4	**66.** 4	**67.** 3	**68.** 1	**69.** 3	**70.** 4
71. 3	**72.** 1	**73.** 3	**74.** 2	**75.** 4		

EXPLANATIONS

1. Para 2 and Ist sentence of para 3

2. 1 is a feature as well as an advantage 2 and 3 are true (para 3, middle → end)4 is certainly wrong (procedures are 'maximised')Actually, due to direct translation, procedures are a few and precision is maximised.

3. Para 4 (middle) ... The disadvantage is that ...become tautological and ...

4. Para 6 (mid.)... New constraints are generated ... things and events.

5. ... characteristics of various researchers.

6. ... 2nd last para (on Empiricism)...

7. ....Last para, Ist sentence (last word).

8. ...2nd last para... "as an 'ideal' type (pure).

9. Para 1, middle, ...The fundamental... to change.
10. Para 2, ...DBT was developed.
11. Para 1, ending lines.... "This dialectic both..." and Para 1, starting and also Para 3, 2nd sentence *(1) and (2) are close answer choices, be cautious!
12. Last para, last sentences.
13. Zen para 1, starting (could be?)and becoming polarised para 1, end, (main problem).
14. Last para, starting ... Lineman therefore decided to sepatate skills training.
15. Para 1, ... Beginning lines.
16. not directly mentioned but 'features' of DBT are practised to a more or less extent.
17. Para 4... some of the most famous synesthetes (here, 'artists' includes 'musician').Para 3...a dose of mascaline or hashish.and Paras 1 and 2 ...conclusion babies/infants.*(for 'natural' synesthesia, answer would be (4).)
18. —traces the phenomenon to the limbic...(Para 3, 2nd last sentence).
19. 3 is correct (Para2, near the end).4 is correct (Para 2, end).
20. ....Para 4, near the end.
21. (1) ...Para 2 (mid.), (3) ...Para 3rd from last, (4)... (3rd last para)...symblists believed that...
22. Para 2, starting line.
23. Para 4, Ist few lines...while synesthesia denies.... "creative".
24. (1) –not shared...para 4 (mid.).(2) (3) and (4) – true – para 3 (mid).
25. Para 1 – see the beginning and the end.
26. Para 2
27. 3rd last para (Ist line) and last para...both shape each other but culture is "all embracing".Also, Para 4... (starting)...dominating influence of technology.
28. 2nd last para-technology is ambivalent (1) not true.(2) follows from the various contents in the passage.
29. (1) follows – para 3...(after marxist view)..."This view is opposed entirely". (4) follows..para 3.. beginning. (3) follows ... 2nd last and 3rd last paras.
30. 2nd last para... "The whole arises...downward direction."
31. 2nd last para... "fails to do".
32. Para 3, near the end ... "According to this view, ... which in itself connot be neutral."
33. Last para...Economic impact and other paras...Social.
34. Various paras (2,3,4...) General view of passage.
35. Para on Russia... (4th last para.)
36. Paras 4, 5 and 3rde last para (last line).
37. Para 6, ...(on Xintang Town, China).
38. Para 5.
39. (4) is counteracted by the Eg. on Russia (para 7 end, para 8), ...para 3 (last line), last para ((2) is also suitable).
40. Last para.
41. 4th estate journalism.

42. To be harmed by one's own plan to harm others.
43. *(spelling mistake) : cicerone helps sightsee rs and baedeker is a guide book for tourists.
44. quisling = traitor (commits treason) and murderer (commits homicide i.e. murderer)
45. Pollyanna = blindly optimistic,diehard = oppose
46. According to increase in 'degree'.
47. 4
48. 4
49. 1
50. 3
51. 2
52. diazo (related to chemistry)
53. velavu surrounding, circle.
54. gouache opaque (coloured) painting, scumbling using this technique.
55. tidings = information, magpie 'chatter box' bird
57. other are units in physics.
58. 4
59. 4
60. Sarcastic (that wounds).Caustic = corrosive, painful.

62. part of inner nature, inborn and essential characteristic
63. 1
64. 2
65. 4
66. oxymoron contrary epither Ramola
67. pseudonym pen name porter.
68. maxim saying / proverb Jai
69. Acronym = abbreviated form (short form) e.g. WHO Seema
70. Inarticulate = lacking expression Rakesh
71. cliché = stereotype /similar Sujata
72. eponym = base wordThus, Tasman Tasmania
73. pejorative = depreciatory / unfavourable Bimal
74. Krishna, by providing vital statistics
75. diatribe = abuse / exhaustive discussion.

FMS 2009

Number of Questions – 26
Time : 30 M.

SECTION I

DIRECTION for questions 1--5:

The relationship between competition and innovation has been the subject of some debate. Some argue that in a competitive situation any enterprise can earn only normal profit and therefore no enterprise would have the resources for undertaking meaningful research and development. They believe that only an enterprise earning monopoly profit would be able to accumulate the resources needed for it. However, the counter-argument is that though a monopolist may have the resources for innovation, it does not have the motivation to do so in the absence of any competitive pressure. On the other hand, the prospect of monopoly profit is an incentive for innovation. Schumpeter argues that even if existing monopolists earn such profits in the short run, in due course outsiders would enter the market and erode the monopoly. In his view, therefore, short-term monopoly power need not cause concern.

This brings us to the interface between competition law and IPR. A debate rages here as well An IPR, such as a patent or a copyright, confers a monopoly on the IPR holder for a given period of time. Since a monopoly right is prone to abuse, tension arises between the IPR and competition law, one conferring a monopoly, the other wary of it. At the fundamental level, competition law does not challenge the IPR itself; it respects IPR as being necessary for rewarding innovation, for providing an incentive to others, particularly competitors, to innovate or to improve existing innovation and, equally importantly, to bring into the public arena innovations that might otherwise remain only in the private domain. Without the protection offered by IPR, others would be able to free ride on the innovation and the innovator would not be able to secure returns on his investment. The concern that competition authorities have regarding IPR is not in the inherent right itself, but in the manner of the exercise of that right, whether restrictions are being introduced that go beyond the protection of the IPR and result in throttling competition. Usually these concerns arise in the licensing of the IPR by the holder thereof. Thus, the two legal systems at a fundamental level have commonality of goals, but at the operational level, particularly in the short run, the two systems can seem to be pulling in different directions and the interface can become difficult to manage.

In this knowledge era, technological advances are exploding. The quantum of new knowledge or new technology added in the last few decades alone might perhaps be more than in the entire history of mankind. The role of technological advances in our lives and in business is now immense. This is, particularly true of areas like biotechnology, medicine, information technology and communications technology. Correspondingly, the number of patents, copyrights and other forms of IPR has also grown in geometrical progression. This makes the issue of managing the interface more difficult but equally more important and pressing than ever before. In competition law, it has emerged as one of the most important areas demanding attention from competition authorities, governments and regulators.

IPRs have certain special economic characteristics:

1. The fixed costs in producing intellectual property are typically high requiring substantial investment in research facilities and scientific talent.

2. The risk in these investments is also high as many research products may turn out to be unfruitful.
3. Though costly to produce, intellectual property can be easily copied or misappropriated and the marginal costs in doing so are very low.
4. Intellectual property often depends upon other intellectual property for its successful commercial exploitation.

These characteristics explain an IPR holder's special concerns for protecting his right by incorporating conditions and restraints that would ensure his property is not copied. For example, some of the restrictions are cross-licensing agreements, tying, exclusive dealing and exclusive territories. On the other hand, there are practices or constraints which are not directly required for protecting IPR and restrict competition in unjustifiable ways. Some of the objectionable practices are patent pooling, grant back, refusal to deal, payment of royalty after expiry of patent period, condition that the licensee will not challenge the validity of IPR and using tie-in by the IPR holder to gain access in other product markets.

In some merger cases where the merged parties are the only two having IPR over the same product, the competition authority's concern is that this could lead to market power in the hands of the merged parties in that product market. For example, in the merger of Ciba-Geigy with Sandoz, the two were among the very few entities capable of commercially developing a broad range of gene therapy products. The competition authority agreed not to block the merger only after the merging parties agreed to certain compulsory licensing conditions. Similarly with Glaxo and Wellcome : both had products in the US' Food and Drug Administration approval process for treating migraine with an oral dosage; the competition authority had difficulty in agreeing without conditions that would mitigate the merged parties' market power.

1. Which statement alludes to the inherent contradiction between IPR and competition?
   1. IPR confers monopoly to the holder and this encourages others to innovate as they do nothave access to a particular intellectual property
   2. IPR creates monopolies and this reduces competition in the market
   3. IPR inhibits competition in the long term perspective
   4. All are correct

2. For competition authorities which is one of the most difficult responsibility to fulfil:
   1. Encourage small players in the market to innovate
   2. Create suitable regulations so that IPR holder does not abuse market power owned
   3. Create suitable regulatory mechanism to mitigate two merged IPR holders acquired market power
   4. Deal with the malpractice of patent pooling and grant back

3. Some malpractices that are linked to IPR are:
   1. Piracy, Plagiarization, Copyright
   2. Hoarding, Misrepresentation, Trespassing
   3. Piracy, Hoarding, Copyright
   4. Plagiarization, Piracy, Trespassing

4. To which ideological framework does the concept of IPR belong to:
   1. Capitalism
   2. Socialism
   3. Free economy
   4. License Raj

5. GATT/WTO and TRIPS agreement encourages:

1. Biodiversity
2. Biopiracy
3. Genetic engineering
4. All three

The importance of finance and of a productive economic base which created revenues for the state was already clear to Renaissance princes. The rise of the ancient regime monarchies of the eighteenth century, with their large military esta-blishments and fleets of warships, simply increased the government's need to nurture the economy and to create financial institutions which could raise and manage the monies concerned. Moreover, like the First World War, conflicts such as the seven major Anglo-French wars fought between 1689 and 1815 were struggles of endurance. Victory therefore went to the Power—or better, since both Britain and France usually had allies, to the Great Power coalition with the greater capacity to maintain credit and to keep on raising supplies. The mere fact that these were coalition wars increased their duration, since a belligerent whose resources were fading would look to a more powerful ally for loans and reinforcements in order to keep itself in the fight. Given such expensive and exhausting conflicts, what each side desperately required was—to use the old aphorism—"money, money, and yet more money." It was this need which formed the background to what has been termed the "financial revolution" of the late seventeenth and early eighteenth centuries when certain western European states evolved a relatively sophisticated system of banking and credit in order to pay for their wars.

There was, it is true, a second and nonmilitary reason for the financial changes of this time. That was the chronic shortage of specie, particularly in the years before the gold discoveries in Portuguese Brazil in 1693. The more European commerce with the Orient developed in the seventeenth and eighteenth centuries, the greater the outflow of silver to cover the trade imbalances, causing merchants and dealers everywhere complain of the scarcity of coin. In addition, the steady increases in European commerce, especially in essential products such as cloth and naval stores, together with the tendency for the seasonal fairs of medieval Europe to be replaced by permanent centers of exchange, led to a growing regularity and predictability of financial settlements and thus to the greater use of bills of exchange and notes of credit. In Amsterdam especially, but also in London, Lyons, Frankfurt, and other cities, there arose a whole cluster of moneylenders, commodity dealers, goldsmiths (who often dealt in loans), bill merchants, and jobbers in the share of the growing number of joint-stock companies. Adopting banking practices which were already in evidence in Renaissance Italy, these individuals and financial houses steadily created a structure of national and international credit to under-pin the early modern world economy.

Nevertheless, by far the largest and most sustained boost to the "financial revolution" in Europe was given by war. If the difference between the financial burdens of the age of the Philip II and that of Napoleon was one of degree, it still was remarkable enough. The cost of a sixteenth-century war could be measured in millions of pounds; by the late seventeenth century, it had risen to tens of millions of pounds; and at the close of the Napoleonic War the outgoings of the major combatants occasionally reached a hundred million pounds a year. Whether these prolonged and frequent clashes between the Great Powers, when translated into economic terms, were more of a benefit to than a brake upon the commercial and industrial rise of the West can never be satisfactorily resolved. The answer depends, to a great extent, upon whether one is trying to assess the absolute growth of a country as opposed to its relative prosperity and strength before and after a lengthy conflict. What is clear is that even the most thriving and "modern" of the eighteenth-century states could not immediately pay for the wars of this period out of their ordinary revenue. Moreover, vast rises in taxes, even if the machinery existed to collect them, could well provoke domestic unrest, which all regimes feared especially when facing foreign challengers at the same time.

Consequently, the only way a government could finance a war adequately was by borrowing: by selling bonds and offices, or better, negotiable long-term stock paving interest to all who advanced monies to the state. Assured of an inflow of funds, officials could then authorize payments to army contractors, provision merchants, shipbuilders, and the armed services themselves. In many respects, this two-way system of raising and simultaneously spending vast sums of money acted like a bellows, fanning the development of western capitalism and of the nation-state itself.

Yet however natural all this may appear to later eyes, it is important to stress that the success of such a system depended on two critical factors: reasonably efficient machinery for raising loans, and the maintenance of a government's "credit" in the financial markets. In both respects, the United Provinces led the way not surprisingly, since the merchants there were part of the government and desired to see the affairs of state managed according to the same principles of financial rectitude as applied in, say, a joint-stock company. It was therefore appropriate that the States General of the Netherlands, which efficiently and regularly raised the taxes to cover governmental expenditures, was able to set interest rates very low, thus keeping down debt repayments. This system, superbly reinforced by the many financial activities of the city of Amsterdam, soon gave the United Provinces an international reputation for clearing bills, exchanging currency, and providing credit, which naturally created a structure—and an atmosphere within which long-term funded state debt could be regarded as perfectly normal. So successfully did Amsterdam become a center of Dutch "surplus capital" that it soon was able to invest in the stock of foreign companies and, most important of all, to subscribe to a whole variety of loans floated by foreign governments, especially in wartime.

6. During the three decades from sixteenth century to eighteenth century war expenditure increased:

1. Hundredfold
2. Tenfold
3. Twofold
4. Exponentially

7. Which geographical regions are referred to by "United Provinces" in the passage :

1. Spain, Netherland and Italy
2. Prussia, England and France
3. Seven provinces which united in 1579 and formed the basis of Republic of Netherland
4. The treaty of Baltimore united England with Spain and Netherland in 1579

8. Which statement is true with regard to the background to the Financial Revolution in Europe:

1. To mitigate public unrest caused by excessive expenditure on war, the governments in various European countries invented the financial system
2. The need for more and more money to wage enduring, expensive and exhausting wars inEurope gave rise to the financial revolution
3. Borrowing money from the public became an attractive measure for appeasing people andgetting money for wars in the government's coffers
4. All the statements are correct

9. Which set of countries formed the "Great Powers" in Europe during the period from sixteenth century till late eighteenth century:

1. Spain, Netherland, Germany
2. France, Britain, Spain, Germany

3. France, Britain, Russia, Austria and Prussia
4. Britain, France, Prussia and Russia

10. What is the key reason for the growth of Western Capitalism during the reference period in the passage:

1. Expensive wars gave rise to entrepreneur ship in Europe that paved way for the industrial revolution
2. Paying large interest on money borrowed from the public fuelled the capitalist revolution in Europe
3. The reasonably efficient machinery for raising loans and maintenance of government's "credit" inthe financial market fuelled growth The two-way systems of raising and simultaneously spendingvast sums of money fanned the development of Western Capitalism

11. Why was Amsterdam successful in investing in foreign companies during the period when all of Europe was weighed down by excessive expenditure in war ?

1. The United Provinces was efficient in dealing with public and government transactions and thiscreated an atmosphere where long term investments were considered normal
2. Amsterdam per se was never involved in any of the wars the European nations were engaged in,and therefore had surplus capital to invest
3. The merchants in Amsterdam were also government officials and they ensured that alltransactions between people and government were mutually beneficial, as is the case in a joint-venture
4. All statements are correct

12. What is the opinion of experts regarding Europe's economic health during the period of reference in the passage :

1. Experts are still not sure whether the economic health was good or bad in Europe during the period
2. In absolute terms there was definitely a lot of economic loss, but in relative terms there was a gain
3. Keeping a long term perspective, the period of reference led to good economic health in Europe,even though the state did spend a lot on wars
4. None of the statements is true

DIRECTION for questions 13-19:

What do we mean by fear ? Fear of what? There are various types **of fear** and we need not analyse every type. But we can see that fear comes **into** being when our comprehension of relationship is not complete. Relationship is not only between people but between ourselves and nature, between ourselves and property, between ourselves and ideas; as long as that relationship is not fully understood, there must be fear. Life is relationship. To be is to be related and without relationship there is no **life.** Nothing can exist in isolation, so long as the mind is seeking isolation, there must be fear. Fear is not an abstraction; it exists only in relation to something.

The question is, how to be rid of fear ? First of all, anything that is overcome has to be conquered again and again. No problem can be finally overcome, conquered; it can be understood but not conquered. They are two completely different processes and the conquering process leads to further confusion, further fear. To resist, to dominate, to do battle with a problem or to build a defence against it is only to create further conflict, whereas if we can understand fear, go into it fully step by step, explore the whole content of it, then fear will never return in any form.

As I said, fear is not an abstraction; it exists only in relationship. What do we mean by fear ? Ultimately we are afraid, are we not? of not being, of not becoming. Now, when there is fear of not being, of not advancing, or fear of the unknown, of death, can that fear be overcome by determination, by a conclusion, by any choice? Obviously not. Mere suppression, sublimation, or substitution, creates further resistance, does it not? Therefore fear can never be overcome through any form of discipline, through any form of resistance. That fact must be clearly seen, felt and experienced: fear cannot be overcome through any form of defence or resistance nor can there be freedom from fear through the search for an answer or through mere intellectual or verbal explanation.

Now what are we afraid of ? Are we afraid of a fact or of an idea about the fact? Are we afraid of the thing as it is, or are we afraid of what we think it is? Take death, for example. Are we afraid of the fact of death or of the idea of death? The fact is one thing and the idea about the fact is another. Am I afraid of the word 'death' or of the fact itself? Because I-am afraid of the word, of the idea, I never understand the fact, I never look at the fact, I am never in direct relation with the fact. It is only when I am in complete communion with the fact that there is no fear. If I am not in communion with the fact, then there is fear, and there is no communion with the fact so long as I have an idea, an opinion, a theory, about the fact, so I have to be very clear whether I am afraid of the word, the idea or of the fact. If I am face to face with the fact, there is nothing to understand about it: the fact is there, and I can deal with it. If I am afraid of the word, then I must understand the word, go into the whole process of what the word, the term, implies.

For example, one is afraid of loneliness, afraid of the ache, the pain of loneliness. Surely that fear exists because one has never really looked at loneliness, one has never been in complete communion with it. The moment one is completely open to the fact of loneliness one can understand what it is, but one has an idea, an opinion about it, based on previous knowledge; it is this idea, opinion, this previous knowledge about the fact, that creates fear. Fear is obviously the outcome of naming, of terming, of projecting a symbol to represent the fact; that is fear is not independent of the word, of the term have a reaction, say, to loneliness; that is I say I am afraid of being nothing. Am I afraid of the fact itself or is that fear awakened because I have previous knowledge of the fact, knowledge being the word, the symbol, the image ? How can there be fear of a fact? When I am face to face with a fact, in direct communion with it, I can look at it, observe it; therefore there is no fear of the fact. What causes fear is my apprehension about the fact, what the fact might be or do.

It is my opinion, my idea, my experience, my knowledge about the fact, that creates fear. So long as there is verbalization of the fact, giving the fact a name and therefore identifying or condemning it, so long as thought is judging the fact as an observer, there must be-fear. Thought is the product of the past, it can only exist through verbalization, through symbols, through images; so long as thought is regarding or translating the fact, there must be fear.

Thus it is the mind that creates fear, the mind being the process of thinking. Thinking is verbalization. You cannot think without words, without symbols, images; these images, which are the prejudices, the previous knowledge, the apprehensions of the mind, are projected upon the fact, and out of that there arises fear. There is freedom from fear only when the mind is capable of looking at the fact without translating it without giving it a name, a label. This is quite difficult, because the feelings, the reactions, the anxieties that we have, are promptly identified by the mind and given a word. The feeling of jealousy is identified by that word. Is **it** possible not to identify a feeling, to look at that feeling without naming it? It is the naming of the feeling that gives it continuity, that gives it strength. The moment you give a name to that which you call fear, you strengthen it; but if you can look at that feeling without terming it, you will see that it withers away. Therefore if one would be completely free of fear it is essential to understand this whole process of terming, of projecting symbols, images, giving names to facts.

13. Which statement best expresses the meaning of fear as explained in the passage?
1. Fear is experienced because we do not form and understand relationships
2. Fear occurs in the mind and needs to be confronted
3. Fear is caused when we engage more closely with ideas about a fact, than with trying to understand the fact
4. Fear is an act of suppression of an understanding of facts

14. Human beings are victims of...........................because of which they experience fear. (Choose an option to fill the blank)
1. Conditioning
2. Deconditioning
3. Suppression
4. Isolation

15. We can eradicate fear if we do any *one* of the following:
1. Verbalize and think about the fact that causes fear
2. Look at the fact that causes fear and experience it fully

16. Which set of key words, when put to practice will help us overcome fear?
1. Minimise: suppression, sublimation, substitution
2. Avoid: naming, terming, projecting facts
3. Build: relationships, understanding, judgement of facts
4. Engage in: communion, experiencing facts, witholding judgement

17. Which of the following can be concluded from the passage ?
1. As long as there is any relationship, there must be fear of losing it
2. As long as our thoughts can identify and judge a fact as an observer, there would be no fear
3. Previous knowledge about a fact hinders dealing with the fact when it arrives
4. Fear can be best diminished by fighting it and building a defence against it

18. Which of the following can be concluded from the passage ?
1. If one is in complete communion with a fact, there is little chance of fear
2. Ideas of a fact aid us in making a communion with the fact
3. Fear is a feeling that is independent of the tag or the symbol representing the fact
4. None of the above

19. Which of the following can be concluded from the passage ?
1. Fear can be overcome by conquering it once **and for all**
2. Fear of unknown can be overcome **by determined resistance**
3. Freedom of fear can be achieved by a simple intellectual explanation of the phenomenon
4. None of the above

DIRECTION for questions 20-26:

The driving force of evolution, according to the emerging new theory, is not to be found in the chance events of random mutations but in life's inherent tendency to create novelty, in the spontaneous emergence of increasing complexity and order. Once this fundamental new insight has been understood, we can then ask: What are the avenues in which evolution's creativity expresses itself ?

The answer to this question comes not only from molecular biology but also, and even more importantly, from microbiology, from the study of the planetary web of the myriads of micro-organisms that were the only forms of life during the first two billion years of evolution. During those two billion years, bacteria continually transformed the Earth's surface and atmosphere and, in so doing, invented all of life's essential biotechnologies, including fermentation, photosyn-thesis, nitrogen fixation, respiration, and rotary devices for rapid motion.

During the past three decades, extensive research in microbiology has revealed three major avenues of evolution. The first, but least important, is the random mutation of genes, the centrepiece of neo-Darwinian theory. Gene mutation is caused by a chance error in the self-replication of DNA, when the two chains of the DNA's double helix separate and each of them serves as .a template for the construction of a new complementary chain.

It has been estimated that those chance errors occur at a rate of about one per several hundred million cells in each generation. This frequency does not seem to be sufficient to explain the evolution of the great diversity of life forms, given the well-known fact that most mutations are harmful, and only very few result in useful variations.

In the case of bacteria the situation is different, because bacterium divides so rapidly. Fast bacteria can divide about every twenty minutes, so that in principle several billion individual bacteria can be generated from a single cell in less than a day. Because of this enormous rate of reproduction, a single successful bacterial mutant can spread rapidly through its environment, and mutation is indeed an important evolutionary avenue for bacteria.

However, bacteria have developed a second avenue of evolutionary creativity that is vastly more effective than random mutation. They freely pass hereditary traits from one to another in a global exchange network of incredible power and efficiency. Here is how Lynn Margulis and Dorion Sagan describe it:

Over the past fifty years or so, scientists have observed that [bacteria] routinely and rapidly transfer different bits of genetic material to other individuals. Each bacterium at any given time has the use of accessory genes, visiting from sometimes very different strains, which perform functions that its own DNA may not cover. Some of the genetic bits are recombined with the cell's native genes; others are passed on again. As a result of this ability, all the world's bacteria essentially have access to a single gene pool and hence to the adaptive mechanisms of the entire bacterial kingdom.

This global trading of genes, technically known as DNA recombination, must rank as one of the most astonishing discoveries of modern biology. 'If the genetic properties of the microcosm were applied to larger creatures, we would have a science-fiction world,1 write Margulis and Sagan, 'in which green plants could share genes for photosynthesis with nearby mushrooms, or where people could exude perfumes; or grow ivory by picking up genes from a rose or a walrus.1

The speed with which drug resistance spreads among bacterial communities is dramatic proof that the efficiency of their communications network is vastly superior to that of adaptation through mutations. Bacteria are able to adapt to environmental changes in a few years where larger organisms would need thousands of years of evolutionary adaptation.

Thus microbiology teaches us the sobering lesson that technologies like genetic engineering and a global communications network, which we consider to be advanced achievements of our modern civilization, have been used by the planetary web of bacteria for billions of years to regulate life on Earth.

The constant trading of genes among bacteria results in an amazing variety of genetic structures besides their main strand of DNA. These include the formation of viruses, which are not full autopoietic systems but consist merely of a stretch of DNA or RNA in a protein coating. In fact, Canadian bacteriologist Sorin Sonea has argued that bacteria, strictly speaking, should not be classified into species, since all of their strains can potentially share hereditary traits and, typically, change up to fifteen percent of their genetic material on a daily basis. 'A bacterium is not a unicellular organism,' writes Sonea, 'it is an incomplete cell belonging to different chimeras according to circumstances. In other words, all bacteria are part of a single microcosmic web of life'.

20. If all human beings started behaving like bacteria, which of the following would be the most desired outcome by all humanity:

1. Creativity and innovation will increase
2. Greater unity in diversity
3. Population increase
4. We shall become identical to each other and be free of conflict

21. Which three processes are responsible for evolution?

1. Random mutation; Rapid division of genes in bacteria; Genes exchange in bacteria
2. Random exchange of genes in bacteria; Speedy multiplication of bacteria; Creative mutation
3. DNA self replication; Autopoieses; Gene pool theory
4. Chance separation of double helix; Autopoiesis; Random selection

22. Regarding diseases caused by bacteria and virus and their eradication by medical science which conclusion is valid ?

1. Medical science generally remains ahead of bacteria and virus
2. Bacteria and virus are generally ahead of medical science
3. Bacteria and virus are not only ahead, but manage to undo somethings , that medical science have achieved
4. Bacteria and virus, and medical science are equal

23. Which statement is true regarding the work that bacteria do for the cause of humanity?

1. Bacteria invented many essential biotechnologies that sustain life
2. Bacteria challenge human beings to innovate
3. Bacteria can give important lessons to human beings about sharing and communicating
4. All of the above work are important for the cause of humanity

24. Which philosophical paradigm does the model of creativity in evolution as described in the passage derives from:

1. Holistic world view
2. Descartes, Darwin, Newton
3. Ecological framework
4. Deep Ecology

25. What are the reasons given in the passage against the theory of "random mutation", with respect to explaining evolution?

1. Random mutation is a slow process
2. Most of the times random mutation is harmful for the organism
3. Random mutation is not possible in smaller organisms
4. (1) and (2) are correct

26. Which principle described in the passage can become the basis of science fiction:

1. DNA recombination
2. DNA recombination among large organism
3. DNA recombination among very small organism
4. Autopoietic system

Answer Key

1. 2	**2.** 3	**3.** 3	**4.** 3	**5.** 3	**6.** 1	**7.** 3
8. 4	**9.** 3	**10.** 4	**11.** 1	**12.** 3	**13.** 2	**14.** 3
15. 2	**16.** 4	**17.** 3	**18.** 4	**19.** 3	**20.** 1	**21.** 3
22. 3	**23.** 1	**24.** 1	**25.** 2	**26.** 2		

EXPLANATIONS

1. 2 Only option 2 contains a contradiction.

2. 3 The last line of the last para construes the merger issue in the context of IPR as problematic.

3. 3 Point 3 talks about cpied,misapprppiated and marginal cost.Option 2 has mispresentation which is a clear hint in tandem with point 3.

4. 3 A patent holder has an exclusive right or license to share the information that it claims to hold as in its novelty.Yet,it is not associated with License Raj,but free economy.

5. 3 It is the only option which is man-managed and constructive which can fall in the ambit of the international organizations.

6. 1 3rd para-3rd line-the cost of .... War...risen to 10 of millions of pound....hundred million pounds a year.

7. 3 Dutch republic (1581-1795) has its other name UP,Netherland now.Last para.Second line:states general of the Netherlands.

8. 4 First and second para clearly count these three reasons.

9. 3 This is a GK question. And till 18th century,these countries comprised the great power.

10. 4 Fourth para,last line.two way system....fanning the development of....itself.

11. 1 2nd last line of the last para clearly concludes the success of Amsterdam.

12. 3 2nd and 3rd para implies this paradox.

13. 2 Last para in tandem with the rest of the passage brings out this gist.

14. 3 3rd para:mere suppression,sublimation...

15. 2 Last para,last 2 lines.The moment....Therefore.....completely free of fear.

16. 4 These are sread all over the passage,especially in the 4rth,5th and 6th para.

17. 3 Last para,the first line.Thus it is the mind that creates the fear.....

18. 4 none

19. 3 Last line suggests intellectual expansion:Therefore if ne would be completely free of fear it is essential to understand.... facts.

20. 1 Last para- change on a daily basis.Besides the passaes mentios words like .....Great Diversity, genetic engineering and evolutionary activity.Such words are highly suggestive of these characteristics.

21. 3 Three clearly stated processes are in 2nd para,6th and 9th para.

22. 3 Last para :should not be classified into species.It suggests that ot also manages to undo it.

23. 1 Second para,last line.During those....

24. 1 Last line'single microcosmic view of life

25. 2 Fourth para last line.This frewquency does not...

26. 2 8th para,second line:If the ... larger species...

IIFT 2007

Number of Questions – 45
Time : 30 M.

SECTION – A

The questions in this group are based on the content of the passage. After reading the passage, choose the best answer to each question. Answer all questions following the passage on the basis of what is stated or implied in the passage.

PASSAGE – I

From the very beginning TCL (Tata Chemicals Ltd.) has successfully grown by meeting consumer requirements in a mutually beneficial way. To determine its benchmark, it uses its own *'Customer Requirements Determination Process (CRDP)'* wherein it explores present and future customer requirements to enable them to incorporate those in their business offerings. This process starts with listening to end-users by exploring various customer listening information sources. This information captures various expectations of customers. Next step starts with identification of segments and matching of segment wise expectations. Outcome of this exercise gives enough guidelines about new business scopes and grey areas of current business practices. After validation of customer expectations through cross checking, TCL matches its internal resources and skill sets with external opportunities and threats to address attractive business avenues. Launch of Tata Kisan Sansar was an outcome of that to offer all sort of end-to-end agri solutions to farmers.

Agriculture till today contributes a lot for the development of Indian economy with an employment share of around 69 percent of the work force and with a contribution of near about 24 percent of the GDP of the country. Indian agriculture sector has its importance in economic growth but value addition in this sector in terms of earning capacity is decreasing because of greater income streams from industry and services sectors. The continuous expanding of the gap in per capita income between the agricultural and non-agricultural sectors has huge economic and social implications and it is almost necessary to empower the farmers financially by enriching the source of income. In this backdrop, one of the motivations for TCL to start 'Tata Kisan Sansar (TKS)' was to ensure business by empowering agri-product producers. Again TCL felt that due to its business nature of manufacturing and marketing commodities, it developed an image of a purely product centric organization. TCL's internal research substantiated its feeling and it recognized a paradigm shift towards a customer centric organization.

TCL first started 'Tata Kisan Kendra' in 1988, exclusive franchised retail outlets of Tata' with the objective of providing 'one-stop agri input shop' to the farmers. With the marketing function being transferred from Rallis to Tata Chemicals, TCL used the Tata Kisan Kendras (TKKs) more extensively to market their products. It was understood by the company that the range of offerings under the TKKs offered an attractive basket of benefits to the farmers. The business model of the TKKs was based on offering a complete set of inputs to the farmer. Along with this, it also offered extension services and technology inputs to help farmers plan their crops. At that time it dealt more with offering fertilizers and other inputs from those centers. Over the time it realized that the job is half done because requirement of a farmer is multi-layered. To offer a more holistic services it changed "Tata Kisan Kendra' as

'Tata Kisan Sansar' and repositioned it as 'one-stop farmers solution shop' by offering entire range of agri services including quality agri input products. Objective was to empower farmers by providing them information about better agronomic practices, facilitating farm credit and providing quality agri inputs from a single source.

1. Which of the following best describes the purpose of the statement in bold (Agriculture... income)?

1. The emergence of TKS is only because of the rising gap between the income, from the agricultural and non-agricultural sources.
2. The farmers income can be enriched through TKS.
3. The alternate sector growth can only be curtailed through emphasis on TKS.
4. TKS can enhance agriculture's GDP contribution.

2. As a business manager, what ***was not*** a major motivation behind using 'CRDP' model?

1. Ensuring sustainable competitive advantage by knowing customers in a better manner.
2. For segmenting the market into heterogeneous group of customers to serve better.
3 For estimating of gap analysis of what customer expects and TCL delivers.
4. Formulate business offerings and identification of new business scopes.

3. What would have been a ***wrong decision*** as a manager in the context of 'CRDP' programme of TCL?

1. Using external agencies to cross check validity of information.
2. Using information to offer readymade solution for different initiatives of TCL.
3. Identify external opportunities to explore in a strategically profitable manner.
4. Projecting TCL as more customer centric organization.

4. For long term sustainability of TKS as a concept a manager ***should not***?

1. Project TKS as a corporate social responsibility initiative of TCL.
2. Enrich offerings of TKS with value added facilities and services.
3. Position itself as a commodity retailing centre of TCL.
4. Focus on return on investment of TKS initiative.

5. Transition from TKK to TKS was logical for TCL because:

1. Conceptually there was a mismatch between skill sets of TCL and TKK.
2. TKK lost its acceptability as it became older as a concept and could not leverage first mover advantages.
3. Emerging needs sets outmoded existing value proposition of TKK.
4. Changing demographics of farmers forced TCL to add new spark in its offer.

PASSAGE – II

Indian car rental market may be segmented under four broad categories. First, the most popular segment is of a fuel conscious and mileage hungry consumer who prefers a chauffer driven car. To extract maximum benefit from hired car, consumer representing this segment wants to check credibility of car rental agency and chauffer in terms of mileage per liter of fuel that he has paid for. Consumer of this segment is very price sensitive and wants maximum value for money even if he may rent an economy car like a Tata Indica or a top end luxury limousine. This segment is dominated by unorganized players. Branded players are lagging behind to lure this segment because of their stringent service condition in comparison to unorganized players. In Indian market, organized car rental industry is crawling for the last couple of years to position itself as a most sought after option to meet segment requirements. Hertz India is also practicing the same. To position itself perfectly in the mind of the targeted segment, it has gone for multiple strategic routes to win over different segments. The major external influencing factors for the consumer in this segment may be the firm's marketing efforts to establish itself as a service provider with value for money. Due to their association with renowned airlines and hotels, Hertz, to a lot many people means faith. This may help Hertz to create an impression in the mind of this segment that they will definitely not be cheated and get their value, even if it means spending a little extra. Further, it is trying to educate this segment about benefits of self-driven car as a medium of hassle-free journey by projecting a premium value for money image and with a fleet mix of compact and luxury cars (such as Ikon, Accent and Esteem).

Second, a sizable amount of people are there who usually use their own compact or three box mid size car but prefer to enjoy the riding thrill of SUV (Sports Utility Vehicles) like Ford Endeavor/Honda CRV/GM Chevrolet or a Luxury car like a Mercedes/Camry for a shorter time span. Upcoming new generations or urban executives of large corporate in India with a high disposable income and proactive to enjoy all new things in life and to make it more adventurous and eventful represent this segment. To them, renting a self-drive car and driving off to a place of their choice in a Mercedes /SUV gives them an experience similar to that of a foreign holiday. Under this same self-drive segment, another type of consumers are frequent international travelers (including foreign tourists) who prefer their privacy and independence and wish to choose their own routes/car model at the time of exploring destinations. They love their freedom & space in life where-ever they travel without any barrier like being driven by a chauffer. Equipped with their internationally accepted credit cards, an international driving permit or license, they prefer; advance car rental bookings by logging on the car rental company's website and thereafter just picking up the keys of their booked car once they enter a new country/city. They are adventurous, driving enthusiast, belonging to the upper-middle class, have brand loyalty about their car rental agency. In this self-driven segment, Hertz India is trying to position itself as a contemporary service provider by offering both economy cars and SUVs (Scorpio and Tata Safari). To win over occasional self-drivers of SUV type cars and frequent travelers, Hertz uses slogans like "Break free" or "Drive the World's # 1" regularly in travel magazines to portrait the quality of its cars, and the range it offers.

Third segment consists of institutional consumers, mainly hotels in big cities and air service providers. Institutional consumers prefer quality and service assurance to offer maximum possible service-to their customers. In India, all big car rental agencies have contract with star hotels to offer rental service to them. In this segment, Hertz has prominent clienteles like Taj Group of Hotels, Marriott and Jet Airways. Further, they have contract with hotels like Shangrila in Delhi, and Renaissance and JW Mariott in Mumbai to provide all car rental requirements of them. Their other clients are Carlson Wagonlit, BTI Sita, Thomas Cook and online travel sites like Makemytrip, Indiatimes and Travelguru. According to their deal with Jet Airways, it allows Jet Privilege members to earn 'miles' every time they use Hertz car rental service. For every Rs.1000/- spent on Hertz rentals, a Jet privilege member earns 100 JP Miles and special discounts are given to platinum, gold and silver card holders.

In recent past 'fleet management' is coming up as a possible fourth target segment for car rental companies in India. Worldwide cars are not purchased but only leased and this trend is getting its root in Indian market also. It means the management of a fleet of vehicles, using certain tools, to improve operational efficiency and effectiveness. To win over consumers of this segment, services should be professional and a fleet management company should address all the issues a company might deal with pertaining to managing its fleet. In India, LeasePlan Fleet Management India (LPFM), the wholly-owned subsidiary of LeasePlan Corporation, Netherlands is pioneer in this field. Orix Auto and Business Solutions, is also present in this segment. Hertz is focusing more on car rentals than on fleet management. Though it provides chauffeur-driven cars to many companies like IBM, Sony, KPMG, Compaq, there is a huge scope in this segment for future growth. This segment demands customized service in terms of vehicle acquisition, fuel management, vehicle financing and maintenance, resale of the cars at the end of the contract period etc.

6. The primary purpose of this passage is to:
1. Illustrate how Hertz could plan for the Indian market and maximize profits
2. Illustrate buying behavior of unorganized sectors offering car rental services
3. Illustrate segment opportunities for a new entrant in car rental business
4. Illustrate consumer awareness and views about options available in car-rental business in India

7. 'Self-Drive' concept may be a lucrative option to a manager to lure Indian consumers because:
1. Collectivist culture motivates Indian consumers to opt for self drive
2. Indian roads encourage consumers to experience joy of long drive
3. Indians may enjoy driving comfort of SUV as they don't have capacity to own it
4. A sizeable number of Indian consumers aspire to enjoy new things in life

8. As a business manager of a car-rental company, you may popularize 'self-drive' concept to international travelers because:
1. They know Indian roads and want to explore new places by their own
2. They dislike concept of chauffeur as Indian chauffeurs are not very professional
3. Individualistic culture discourages them to travel in group
4. They can easily book their cars through website of car rental agencies

9. As a business manager of a globally recognized 'car-rental' agency if you like to tap institutional consumers of India, you ***<u>should not</u>***:
1. Bank on your globally recognized 'brand name' to ensure sale
2. Make a list of your global clientele to impress your prospective customer
3. Consider offerings of your competitors to formulate your value proposition
4. Accept service assurance not as a major influencer behind buying decision

10. As a business manager you think 'fleet management' a profitable segment for organized sector to explore in India because:
1. Companies want to associate with 'brand name' and unorganized players are lacking here
2. There is a huge scope as competition is low in this field
3. Everywhere in India logistics services are outsourced and companies are focusing on their core business
4. This business demands gamut of customized services and organized professionals may only offer those

11. If you are to tap 'first' segment of 'car rental' business as a manager of a branded company, you ***should not:***

1. Advertise your brand name to communicate with consumers
2. Compare your service conditions vis-a-vis your competitors to influence consumers
3. Match price of your service with your competitors from organized sector
4. Create unique value proposition to position you away from your competition

SECTION – B

DIRECTIONS for questions 12–23: *Read the three passages carefully and answer the questions given at the end of each passage:*

Passage -1

The trouble started on May 4, 2004, only days after Google's celebrated coming-out party. Geico, the giant automobile insurer, filed a lawsuit against the search engine for trademark infringement. The insurer claimed that Google's advertising system unlawfully profited from trademarks that Geico owned. Since all of Google's revenue and growth was from advertising, the disclosure of the lawsuit appeared ominous. "We are, and may be in the future, subject to intellectual property rights clalms, which are costly to defend, could requirc us to pay damages, and could limit our ability to use certain technologies," Google disclosed in a public filing outlining potential risks. Abroad, where Google had promising growth prospects, similar court challenges also arose. "A court in France held us liable for allowing advertisers to select certain trademarked terms as keywords," the company declared. "We have appealed this decision. We were also subject to two lawsuits in Germany on similar matters."

To make matters worse, it turned out that prior to its IPO filing, Google had eased its trademark policy in the U.S., allowing companies to place ads even if they were pegged to terms trademarked and owned by others. That was a significant shift, and one, Google warned could increase the risk of lawsuits against the company. It was also a practice that Yahoo, its search engine rival, did not permit. Google claimed it made the policy change to serve users, but some financial analysts said it appeared designed to pump profits before the IPO.

And there was more. Competition from Yahoo and Microsoft posed a greater challenge to Google following the disclosure about its mammoth profitability. With so much money at stake, the intensity of the competition would heat up. Such competition might be good for computer users searching the Internet, but Google said it posed additional risk for potential shareholders. "If Microsoft or Yahoo are successful in providing similar or better Web search results compared to ours or leverage their platforms to make their Web search services easier to access than ours, we could experience a significant decline in user traffic," the company disclosed. In addition, Google warned that its momentum seemed unsustainable due to competition and "the inevitable decline in growth rates as our revenues increase to a higher level."

Then there was the question of Google's exclusive reliance on advertising, and one particular type of advertising, for all of its revenue. That was potentially quite problematic. If Yahoo or Microsoft gained ground on search, users could flock to their Web sites, and advertisers could follow. "The reduction in spending by; or loss of, advertisers could seriously harm our business," the company disclosed in its SEC filing.

In the beginning, the firm earned all of its money from ads triggered by searches on Google.com. But now, most of its growth and half of its sales were coming primarily from the growing network of Web sites that displayed ads Google provided. This self-reinforcing network had a major stake in Google's successful future. It gave the search engine, operating in the manner of a television network providing ads and programming to network affiliates, a sustainable competitive advantage. But there was a dark side there too, because of the substantial revenue from a handful of Google partners, notably America Online and the search engine Ask Jeeves. If at any point they left Google and cut a deal with Microsoft or Yahoo, the lost revenue would be immense and difficult to replace. "If one or more of these key relationships is terminated or not renewed, and is not replaced with a comparable relationship, our business would be adversely affected," the company stated.

Google's small, nonintrusive text ads were a big hit. But like major television and cable networks, which were hurt by innovations that enabled users to tune out commercials, the company faced the risk that users could simply turn ads off if new technologies emerged.

Going public also posed a potentially grave risk to Google's culture. Life at the Googleplex was informal. Larry and Sergey knew many people by their first names and still signed off on many hires. With rapid growth and an initial public offering, more traditional management and systems would have to be implemented. No more off-the-shelf software to track revenue on the cheap. Now it was time for audits by major accounting firms. As Google's head count and sales increased, keeping it running without destroying its culture was CEO Eric Schmidt's biggest worry.

Google, the noun that became a verb, had built a franchise and a strong brand name with global recognition based entirely on word of mouth. Nothing like it had been done before on this scale. The Internet certainly helped. But Google's profitability would, erode if the company were forced to begin spending the customary sums of money on advertising and marketing to maintain the strength of its brand awareness. Marketing guru Peter Sealey said privately that the advice he gave Google to study consumer perception of the Google brand was rejected by the company and that they were unwilling to spend money on marketing.

12. Which of the following statement is ***true***?

1. Google's growing popularity has been a threat to other players operating in that market segment like Yahoo and Ask Jeeves, as Google eroded their market share.
2. According to Google its decision to considerably relax its industrial design policy in the US was geared to satisfy its clients.
3. One of the major challenges for Peter Sealey has been to expand the Google Empire while keeping its existing internal work culture intact.
4. Google's business potential is likely to be threatened seriously if the capacity, accessibility and quality of the Web search offered by its competitors like Microsoft or Yahoo becomes superior than the same offered by it.

13. Which of the following Statement is ***false***?

1. Google has been potentially vulnerable to external competition owing to its exclusive reliance on advertising for resource generation.
2. By writing the "the noun that became a verb", the author indicates the growing popularity of the search engine.
3. "non-intrusive" in the current passage refers to the advertisement format that does not directly hamper or distract the flow of operation of the person working in the computer.

4. The legal dispute between Google and the automobile giant Geico during May 2004 centered on the advertising system and the trademark policy adopted by the latter.

14. What conclusion can you form about 'Altavista' from the passage?

1. It has been a partner of Google.
2. It has been a Competitor of Google.
3. It can not be concluded from the passage.
4. It was a partner of Google initially, but later merged as a major competitor.

15. Which of the following sentence *is* ***false***?

1. Google has not been keen to undertake any major analysis on the popular impression about the Google brand.
2. Google's resolution to provide the search engine and programming to collaborators like America Online ensured significant revenue for both sides involved.
3. Google's perceived concern over Intellectual Property issues in the passage has been quoted from a confidential company report.
4. With increase in the volume of Google's total annual revenue, it was anticipated by the management that the annual growth rate of their business may decline.

Passage – 2

Around the turn of the century; an interesting trend was slowly becoming prominent in retailing across the globe. Department stores were slowly becoming less and less popular with customers. Large department stores offered a wide range of product categories - from apparel, luggage, toys, crockery, to home furnishing - as well as owned and managed the stock of products they sold inside the store and from their warehouses. Industry analysts started questioning whether this could still be the ideal retail model, and whether the changing retail environment marked the end of large department stores as we knew them.

On one side there were the stores that focussed on a particular category -electronics, toys, women's wear or home appliances. Over the years, these had evolved into giant superstores and had become very popular with customers who went shopping for a particular product. On the other hand, there were discounters, hypermarkets and wholesale clubs that served the bargain-hunting customer very well. Department stores were squeezed in between and the new age shoppers found their ambience to be formal and boring.

To keep pace with these trends, some department stores were steadily reinventing themselves. The most prominent among them was UK based Selfridges chain. In 2003, Selfridges launched a new store in Birmingham, England that completely reinvented the idea of the department store. Brands competed with each other within the store but there was no hierarchy of goods: watches competed with perfume, and luggage with fashion. In addition the store organised various shows, stunts and performances through the day and called it, 'shopping entertainment.' Similar stores had come up in various parts of Southeast Asia, Japan and Europe. For customers, these new-age department stores seemed like a mall, just that they didn't have the walls that separate the different stores within a mall.

While this trend was becoming more and more apparent abroad, within India too, certain consumer patterns were emerging. Our experience showed that a customer visiting a mall typically walks into four or five stores. That includes a large store and a few smaller brand showrooms. After that fatigue sets in and he or she is unwilling to walk into any more stores at the mall. So we asked ourselves, what would happen if we removed the walls between the different stores in a mall? In that case, a customer would be exposed to multiple brands at the same time, without the necessity of walking in and out of different stores. And along with shopping we could also provide her with other entertainment options.

Within the company itself there was a renewed confidence and an urge to play a larger role in shaping the modern retailing space in India. We had completed more than six years in retailing. With Big Bazaar we had tried and tested our skills at offering a wide range of categories while Pantaloons was firmly positioned in the lifestyle segment. We could now create shopping and entertainment landmarks in the cities in which we had already established a strong presence.

These three insights - the metamorphosis of department stores into developed -markets; customer fatigue at the existing shopping malls in India; and the need to create destination malls in Indian cities - formed the genesis of the next format we started working on, Central. The objective was to create a retail format that was much larger and totally different from what India had seen till then. It would offer everything - from multiple brands for shopping, to restaurants, coffee shops, entertainment options and gaming zones - all under one roof. If we were able to deliver on these two fronts, we could attract customers from every part of the city and make it the city's prime shopping destination.

There were a couple of other issues that the Central model addressed quite well. Pantaloons outlets had limited space. We were positioning it as a fashion destination and the business model was based on selling mostly brands that we owned, or what are called private labels. However, with its increasing popularity; we were being approached by multiple foreign and Indian brands to stock these at Pantaloons. Central, being far bigger in size allowed us to open up a lot of space for other brands. However, unlike in any other mall, these brands didn't pay us rent. Instead the brands paid us a certain percentage of their sales in the mall as commission. Based on the performance of these brands, we could decide on which to keep and which to discard.

The first Central mall was launched in Bangalore in May 2004. Measuring 1,20,000 square feet, it was spread over six floors and housed over three hundred brands in categories like apparel, footwear, accessories, home furnishing, music and books. In addition we had coffee shops, food courts, a Food Bazaar, restaurants, pubs and discotheques. A customer could also book tickets for movies and concerts, book travel tickets and make bill payments.

What has primarily made Central the 'destination mall' for Bangalore is its location. It is located in the heart of the city, at M.G. Road, where once Hotel Victoria stood. Moreover, we added a lot of features to further establish it as the focal point of the city. The Central Square located outside the mall building has been made available for art exhibitions, cultural performances, shows and product launches. And in 2005, the vintage car rally was flagged off from the Central flag-point, which has since become the epicenter for many such events. Thus, Central captured in all its glory what we wanted a destination mall to be, and lived up to its tagline of 'Shop, Eat, and Celebrate.'

Soon after the launch of Bangalore Central, we opened the second Central in Hyderabad in November 2004. Once again it was located at the heart of the city on the Punjagutta Cross Road. Here, the roads connecting the city centre with Secunderabad, Jubilee Hills and the old part of the city; converge. It was more than double the size of Bangalore Central. Apart from over hundreds of brands to shop, it had food courts, restaurants, as well as a five-screen multiplex managed by PVR Cinemas. Much like the one in Bangalore, Hyderabad Central didn't take much time to become the nerve centre of the city. With an annual retail turnover of around Rs 200 crore it is presently among the largest retail destinations in the country.

16. Which of the following statement is ***true***?

1. The Central mall in Hyderabad in 2004 occupies more than 2,40,000 square meter in area and currently considered as one of the largest retail destinations in the country with a generated annual retail turnover of around Rs.200 crore.
2. It has been observed during the last decade that the hypermarkets are slowing, failing to retain consumers in competition with the department stores.
3. The market analysis convinced the company referred in the text that the time is ripe to introduce now shopping and entertainment landmarks in cities, where they already enjoy some market presence.
4. While the consumers were able to look for a certain category of products at length in the specialty stores, wholesale clubs allowed them to purchase a number of products at a cheap and negotiable rate.

17. Which of the following statement is ***false***?

1. The recent consumer response towards department stores led to the quest for a new business Model which may replace it in the coming days.
2. Since inauguration the Central Square outside the mall in Hyderabad has been used for various purposes so far including, art exhibitions, cultural shows, product launches etc.
3. When the company mentioned in the passage decided to capitalize on the emerging changes in consumer mindset on the retail sales, they already had an experience of nearly six years of operating in this market segment.
4. The changing structural framework of the new type of malls became very popular in various European and Southeast Asian countries, owing to their boundary-less arrangement of products, coupled with shopping entertainment options.

18. Which of the following terms has not been mentioned in the above passage?

1. Department Stores
2. Hypermarkets
3. Wholesale Clubs
4. Super-specialty stores

19. Which of the following statement is ***true***?

1. The firm discussed here allowed various foreign and Indian garment companies to display their products in their show room on the condition that they will pay them either some rent, or a pre-decided percentage of their sales as commission.
2. Before going for the Central venture, the firm already had the experience of offering a wide range of product categories through Big Bazaar and in specialized segments through Pantaloons.
3. The Central mall in Bangalore provided importance to both goods and services for business development: it displayed around two hundred brands in categories like garments, footwear, music, books etc. on one hand, and ensured eating and entertainment options, ticket-booking for movies and concerts, travel services and bill payments within its premises on the other.
4. The reasons behind the losing out of the specialty stores had been multifarious, covering the traditional and unexciting environment, steep price competition from other rivals, inflexibility in operation etc.

20. Which of the following statements is ***false***?

1. In tune with the changing time, the new store created in Birmingham allowed brand competition within the store without explicit hierarchy of products, and organized

various events to ensure lively amusement for the shoppers.

2. Since visiting different stores even within a mega shopping complex gets monotonous once the initial excitement is over, the exposure to multiple brands simultaneously with removal of the walls has been a consumer-friendly move.
3. The idea behind setting up a mega retail network was to make it city's unique shopping location by ensuring exposure to multiple brands on one hand, and by making it an excellent hang-out option through setting up of entertainment and nourishment options on the other.
4. The market analysis by the company described in the passage revealed that a representative buyer to a shopping center goes to at the most four or five stores, selecting large or small showrooms randomly.

Passage – 3

In the early 1950s, a plague clouded the American landscape. A mysterious virus stalked the nation's youth like a silent, invisible killer. For generations, it had been devouring young lives. But in the previous three decades the number of its victims had increased dramatically. Those it did not kill, it left hopelessly paralyzed and deformed. Newspaper artists sometimes depicted the disease as a dragon. Its common name was infantile paralysis, or poliomyelitis, or simply polio.

Polio struck every summer, turning strong bodies into crumpled ones, leaving in its wake withered limbs in steel braces and straps. It was simply expected when the children returned to school each fall that a friend or classmate would have been lost to polio over the summer. Everyone knew a victim - if not in their own family, it was the boy down the street or one on the next street. By the early 1950s, some 50,000 cases per year were being reported, and 1952 alone saw 59,000 new cases.

But in April of 1955 a miracle occurred. It came in the form of an announcement that a vaccine had been discovered that could actually prevent polio. With completion of a series of research field tests, the news media hailed it as the most dramatic breakthrough in the history of medical research.

The hero of the day; the man who slew the polio dragon, was a shy young doctor named Jonas Salk. Stories of his heroic effort to perfect his vaccine-filled the newspapers. In the months prior to final development of the vaccine, Salk had pushed himself to the limits of human endurance. Realizing he was close to a breakthrough, he worked seven days a week, often up to 20 or 30 hours at a time without sleep. He often skipped meals. The public lionized him for his efforts. But that was not the case among those in the scientific community. Behind the scenes, unknown to the public, Salk was being vilified by his peers. At one point some leading scientists even tried to stop distribution of his life-saving vaccine.

Salk's fellow scientists in biological research considered him an outsider, intruding into their domain. In fact, in order to acquire funds for his research, Salk had to go outside normal channels. When he did so, scientists accused him of being a publicity hound. The research establishment was especially jealous of Salk's relationship with Basil O'Connor, the man who supplied much of his funding. As president of the National Foundation for Infantile Paralysis, O'Connor held the purse strings to millions in research dollars. And he believed in Salk.

Basil O'Connor knew firsthand the devastating effects of the disease. His daughter had been stricken with polio. And when O'Connor was a young man, Franklin Roosevelt had been his best friend and law partner, long before becoming president of the United States.

O'Connor had seen polio turn an athletic young Roosevelt into a man unable to stand without leg braces and walking sticks. In Jonas Salk, O'Connor found someone who shared his outright hatred for the disease.

Viewed in retrospect, one might understand the opposition of biological research scientists to Salk's methods. He made many transgressions against traditional research. For one thing, the very efficacy of his vaccine toppled one of the most universally accepted (though erroneous) tenets of orthodox virology - the notion that an active virus could not be checked by its own dead viral bodies. That was precisely the path Salk chose to develop his vaccine. For decades, traditional biologists had been waging what they considered a deliberate, correct, gentleman's fight against polio with efforts focused on treatment rather than prevention. By contrast, Salk fought the dragon like a man possessed, seeking a final cure. He had grown up on the fringes of poverty and developed an attitude more humanist than scientific, a man unwilling to abide senseless rules in the face of a crisis. He flailed against the disease like a punch-drunk street fighter-and he landed a knockout blow. Finally, his success proved the greatest transgression of all against his fellow scientists. By the 1950s, researching polio was a very big business, and overnight, Salk made further efforts redundant. It was unheard of that an outsider, working independently; could accomplish what the nation's top scientists with their great laboratories and countless millions of dollars could not. They expressed their bitterness in rather petty ways, even refusing to accept Salk into the National Academy of Science. The reason? Salk, they contended, was not really a scientist - only a technician.

The public never knew the depths of his colleagues' resentment. It was almost a decade after his discovery before Salk himself would even discuss it. "The worst tragedy that could have befallen me was my success," he told an interviewer. "I knew right away that I was through, that I would be cast out."

But he was not through. With the polio dragon defeated, he launched a campaign to raise funds to construct the Salk Institute for Biological Studies at Torrey Pines, California. He worked there, surrounded by bright, young scientists until his death at age eighty. Salk later became obsessed with finding a cure for the human immunodeficiency virus (HIV) that causes AIDS. Almost until the day he died, he was trying to catch lightning in a test tube one last time. Perhaps a man is allotted only one miracle in his lifetime. Today, research scientists work in the laboratories Jonas Salk built, searching for new weapons in the fight against dragons that defy destruction: cancer, AIDS, Alzheimer's, cerebral palsy, multiple sclerosis, and Parkinson's. Among those scientists at Torrey Pines, waging gentlemanly wars against the microscopic enemies of man, perhaps a new maverick will emerge - a stubborn street fighter who will defeat the odds and capture the lightning that eluded Jonas Salk.

21. Which of the following statement is ***true***?

1. For a long time the efforts made by traditional biologists in the battle against polio had been a combination of finding cure for the polio patients as well as preventing the newer occurrences.
2. Within three years from the menace of polio reaching a new peak, the antidote for the deadly disease was discovered by a relatively lesser known person.
3. Basil O'Connor had been a good friend of Theodore Roosevelt and his law partner.
4. The scientists at Salk Institute for Biological Studies are currently doing research to invent medicines to ensure permanent cures for diseases like AIDS, cerebral palsy, multiple stenosis etc.

22. Which of the following statement is ***false***?

1. A major proportion of the funds required for the research by Dr. Salk came from National Foundation for Infantile Paralysis, whose president Basil O'Connor ensured the requisite amount for him.
2. The extent of the resentment of the colleagues' of Dr. Salk over his achievement was known to the people almost thirty years after the invention of the vaccine against the disease.
3. The top scientists of the country did not favour the entry of Dr. Salk into National Academy of Science on the ground of his lack of professional qualification with respect to medical and biological science.
4. The driving reason behind the success of Dr. Salk was the fact that he did not accept the framework developed by traditional virology research as foolproof, which was a key factor behind his success.

23. Match the Following:

List I	**List II**
i. Salk	a. Dragon
ii. Polio	b. Breakthrough
iii. Field tests	c. Torrey Pines
iv. HIV Research	d. Vilified

1. ii-c, iii-b, iv-a
2. i-c, iii-c, iv-a
3. i-d, ii-a, iii-b
4. ii-a, iii-c, iv-b

SECTION – C

24. Mark the sentence which used the underlined word *incorrectly*:

1. When Ram started enquiring about the conditions of his business, the *childlike* directness of his approach left Shyam baffled.
2. After the huge loss in the new venture, Amol realized that he had been *childish* in his trust and confidence.
3. The *childlike* gullibility of Bimal has always annoyed Kamal.
4. When the boss demanded an explanation from Amit for not submitting the project report in time, he burst into a *childish* fit of temper.

25. Mark the *correct* sentence in the following:

1. Remember, when we tried to sort out the difference over the new project with Mr. Singh, he spoke to you and I as if we were babies?
2. Was it them who informed you about the music concert yesterday?
3. The picture on the wall, which was taken years back, doesn't look a little like I.
4. Was it she you were talking about during the discussion last week?

DIRECTIONS for questions 102 to 105: *Select the* ***right pair of words*** *to fill in the blanks.*

26. The bell, hung on the door by means of a curved ribbon of steel, was __________ to circumvent. It was hopelessly cracked; but of an evening, at the slightest provocation, it clattered behind the customer with __________ virulence.

1. impossible, melodious
2. effortless, loud
3. difficult, impudent
4. daunting, harmonious

27. A ______________ question caused him to stutter to the point of suffocation. When startled by anything perplexing he used to squint ______________.

1. courteous, palpably
2. brusque, horribly
3. considerate, genially
4. civil, frightfully

28. Vanity and pride are ______________ things, though the words are often used ______________. A person may be proud without being vain. Pride relates more to our ______________ of ourselves, vanity to what we would have others think of us.

1. same, differently, analysis
2. analogous, similarly, evaluation
3. different, synonymously, opinion
4. dissimilar, carelessly, view

29. During the heated discussion the Leader of the group ______________ refuted all the claims brought by his opponents. Later everybody acknowledged that he survived by most ____________ luck.

1. ingeniously, incredible
2. ingeniously, incredulous
3. ingenuously, incredible
4. ingenuously, incredulous

DIRECTIONS for questions 30 to 31: *The following four pairs may have synonymous or antonymous or part-whole relationships or no relationship at all with the pair provided in the question. Select the pair of words which has **the closest relationship** with the numbered pair.*

30. COMMUNICATION : MESSAGE ::

1. Humour : Delight
2. Expression : Words
3. Clarification : Doubt
4. Emission : Cosmic

31. ACTIVATE : DETONATE ::

1. Deaden : Defuse
2. Quicken : Mutilate
3. Connect : Detach
4. Inform : Deform

DIRECTIONS for questions 108: *The following four pairs may have synonymous or antonymous or part-whole relationships or no relationship at all with the pair provided in the question. Select the pair of words which has **no relationship** with the numbered pair.*

32. PLENTITUDE : ABUNDANCE

1. Augury : Divination
2. Indurate : Consolidate
3. Perspicacity : Transparency
4. Mulct: Muzzle

DIRECTIONS for questions 33 to 36: *Select the words from the options below that have the **farthest** meaning to the given word:*

33. REPUDIATE

1. Sanction
2. Afflict
3. Transient
4. Prowl

34. GRANDILOQUENT

1. Immature
2. Innocent
3. Unpleasant
4. Simple

35. VENERATION

1. Congregate
2. Loquacious
3. Consecrate
4. Burlesque

36. PERSPICACIOUS

1. Judicious
2. Obtuse
3. Adroit
4. cerebral

DIRECTIONS for questions 37 to 39: *Mark the* ***wrongly spelt*** *word mentioned among the following options:*

37. 1. Contemporaneous 2. Belligerent 3. Epicurean 4. Recalcitrent

38. 1. Opprobrium 2. Iniquitous 3. Vicisitude 4. Pusillanimous

39. 1. Exonerate 2. Unctuous 3. Flatulant 4. Disencumber

DIRECTIONS for questions 40 to 41: *Mark the* ***correct*** *sentence in the following:*

40. 1. Pele, whom many people consider is the greatest footballer of all times, represented Brazil in four World Cups.

2. When the news about the decline in the quarterly sales' of the product broke out, it was difficult to say who the Company would hold responsible for this disaster.
3. When the tension with the business partners increased, Mr. Singh decided to visit them personally and talk to whomever is willing to sort the discord.
4. Who do you think was supposed to meet Mr. Brown from the news bureau, the well-known author, during his week-long visit to Delhi?

41. 1. Returning home from the dinner, we were annoyed to find that the porch light is broke again.

2. If you keep on losing your composure on minor issues, that isn't going to get you no where.
3. In the meeting, Mr. Mehta informed the executives that they have to fulfill the target regardless of the stringency of the deadline.
4. The call for the assembly was very disappointing, as we haven't hardly initiated our discussion on a new venture outside the main conference bloc.

DIRECTIONS for questions 42 to 43: *Mark the option in the following, which contains a* ***grammatically wrong*** *sentence:*

42. 1. A marvelous stillness pervaded the world, and the stars, together with the serenity of their rays, seemed to shed upon the earth the assurance of everlasting security.

2. We plowed along bravely for a week or more, and without any conflict of jurisdiction among the captains worth mentioning.
3. The tulips, concerning whose cultivation Rosa was taught all the mysteries of the art, formed the principal topic of the conversation; but, interesting as the subject was, people cannot always talking about tulips.
4. She gazed at me as never man's face was scanned yet.

43. 1. Here, a broad, deep, circumvallatory trench, hewn from the solid rock, was defended by a wall of great strength erected upon its inner edge.

2. I might well say now, indeed, that the latter end of job was better than the beginning.
3. I really had not yet been able to make up my mind whether I liked Uriah or detested him;and I was very doubtful about it still, as I stood looking him in the face on the street.

4. The Prior had his own reasons, however, for persevering in the course of temperance which he had adopted.

DIRECTIONS for questions 44 to 45: *Mark the correct option, which puts the parts of the sentence in **right order**:*

44. I. but she gained courage as she went on
II. she was a little nervous about it just at first
III. and opened their eyes and mouths so very wide
IV. the two creatures got so close to her, one on each side

1. IV, III, II, I
2. II, IV, III, I
3. II, I, IV, III
4. None of the above

45. I. it would perhaps be possible for him to be of some use to this brave girl
II. he said to himself, vaguely at first, that
III. without neglecting anything of what was due to his important mission
IV. and this idea pleased him

1. II, III, I, IV
2. III, II, I, IV
3. I, III, II, IV
4. None of the above

Answer Key

1. 2	**2.** 1	**3.** 1	**4.** 3	**5.** 3	**6.** 1	**7.** 3
8. 4	**9.** 4	**10.** 2	**11.** 3	**12.** 4	**13.** 4	**14.** 3
15. 3	**16.** 1	**17.** 3	**18.** 4	**19.** 2	**20.** 3	**21.** 3
22. 2	**23.** 3	**24.** 3	**25.** 4	**26.** 3	**27.** 2	**28.** 3
29. 1	**30.** 2	**31.** 1	**32.** 1	**33.** 1	**34.** 4	**35.** 4
36. 2	**37.** 4	**38.** 3	**39.** 3	**40.** 4	**41.** 3	**42.** 3
43. 2	**44.** 1	**45.** 1				

EXPLANATIONS

1. 2. The purpose of the sentence is describe that the expanding gap in per capita income between agricultural sectors and non-agricultural sectors prompted TCL to form TKS to ensure business by empowering agri-producers and thereby enriching the farmers income.

2. 1. The passage does not talk about ensuring sustainable competitive advantage.

3. 1. The passage clearly states that TCL uses its own Customer Requirement Determination Process. Hence using outside check is invalid.

4. 3. The TKKs were used by TCL to market their products. The TKS was to ensure business by empowering agri-product produces.

5. 3. Because the farmers' requirements were multilayered, the TTK performed only half the job. To offer holistic services it TTK was changed to TKS which offered an entire range of agri-services.

6. 1. The entire passage talks about Hertz and its presence in different markets. It also talks about positioning and profits.

7. 3. Many Indians now have high disposable incomes and hence want to enjoy the new things in life. As they may not be able to buy the car (Honda CRV or Ford Endeavor) , they would still like to rent it for a few days and enjoy that experience.

8. 4. The international travelers do not like chauffeur driven cars does not mean Indian chauffeurs are not very professional. The travelers prefer self drive because they can book their cars through the website of car rental agencies which is clearly mentioned in ". Equipped with their internationally....... they enter a new country/city".

9. 4.The passage clearly states that "Institutional consumers prefer quality and service assurance to offer maximum possible service-to their customers". Hence not accepting service assurance as a major influence would be incorrect.

10. 2. The author clearly states in the last paragraph that there is potential or scope for future growth in this segment.

11. 3. The consumer of the first segment is very price conscious and wants maximum value for money. The passage clearly states that organized players in this segment lag behind because of stringent service conditions. If the manager charges the same price as the organized sector he would be charging higher than those in the unorganised sector. This way he will price himself out.

The passage discusses some of the potential threats faced by Google as it grows into a global giant 1: The article talks of potential threats faced by Google and not how Google is a threat to others.2: Google eased its trade mark policy and not the industrial design policy.3: Peter Sealy is a management advisor and not an executive responsible for running Google.4: This is explicitly stated in the third paragraph.

12.

13. 4.Geico is an insurer and not an automobile giant.

14. 3.Altavista is not mentioned in the passage.

15. 3: The passage clearly states the quotes are from a 'public filing' and an 'SEC filing'This is an extract from 'It Happened in India' a biography of Kishore Biyani of Big Bazaar.

16. 1: From paragraph 8, we get the Bangalore Central is 1,20,000 sq.ft. Since, the Hyderabad Central was 'more than double the size', it is 2,40,000 sq.ft. The rest of the statistics are stated in the tenth para. 4: 'bargain-hunting' in the second paragraph means looking for cheap buys and not negotiating or haggling over prices.

17. 3. 1: See the third paragraph.2: The Central Square is in Bangalore, not Hyderabad.3: Paragraph 5 says 'more than' not 'nearly'.4: The third para only talks of these stores coming up in Europe and SE Asia and no conclusions can be drawn on their degree of popularity

18. 4.All the others are mentioned in the first 2 paras.

19. 2. 1: See the seventh paragraph 'unlike in ..didn't pay us rent. Instead...a certain %ge of their sales'2: See the fifth paragraph.3: The eighth paragraph says 'housed over three hundred brands'.4: This aspect is not covered in the passage.

20. 3. 1: Read the third paragraph2: Read the fourth paragraph3: The sixth paragraph says the option is to make it 'the city's prime shopping destination', not of an 'excellent hang-out option'. The passage discusses the discovery of polio vaccine by Jonas Salk and the reaction of the establishment to it.

21. 3. 1: Read paragraph 7 – 'focused on treatment rather than prevention'2: The second paragraph says '1952 alone saw 59,000 new cases' from which we cannot ascertain if this was a new peak.3: Explicit in the sixth paragraph4: Read paragraph 9 – ' waging gentlemanly wars..searching for new weapons… a new maverick… that eluded Salk' which indicates the author's opinion that the scientists at Torrey Pines were not striving to ensure permanent cures.

22. 2. 1: Explicit in paragraph 52: See paragraph 8: 'the public never knew…It was almost a decade after his discovery…' Hence this statement is wrong.3: See paragraph 7: '..bitterness in rather petty ways….not really a scientist – only a technician. The 4th para qualifies Salk as 'a young doctor'. 4. Stated in the paragraph.

23. 3 Plug options with the relevant link in the passage.

24. **3.Childish**: (*disapproving*): behaving in a stupid or silly way. SYN: immature.**Childlike**: (*usually approving*) : having qualities that children usually have especially innocence.

25. 4. 1: you and me – object clause.2: they not them3: like me not like I

26. 3. Virulent means showing strong negative or bitter feelings. Therefore though 'impossible' or 'difficult' may suit the first blank, 'melodious' does not gel with 'virulent'.

27. 2. We are looking at a person's reaction to stressful stimuli, so actions which cause stress will fit in as the best option.

28. 3.From the context it is clear that vanity and pride are two different things.

29. 1.Ingenious: clever, inventive; ingenuous: naïve.Incredible: impossible or very difficult to believeIncredulous: not able to believe something

30. 2. A communication is the delivery of a message, an expression is a delivery of words.

31. 1.Both the pairs are synonyms

32. 1. They are both synonyms.

33. 1. Sanction

34. 4. Simple

35. 4.Veneration is showing great respect while burlesque is a performance or a piece of writing that tries to make somebody or something ridiculous.

36. 2.Perspicacious means able to understand quickly and accurately, obtuse is slow or willing to understand.

37. 4.Recalcitrant

38. 3.Vicissitude

39. 3.Flatulent

40. 1. 'whom many people consider the greatest' 2. no apostrophe after sales. News broke, not broke out. 3. tension among, sort out the discord 4. Who from the news bureau , do you think was supposed to meet Mr Brown, the well-known author during his weeklong visit to Delhi?

41. 1. '..light was broke' 2. '..isn't going to get you anywhere. '3. correct 4. '..we have hardly initiated'

42. 3. people cannot always talk about tulips.

43. 2. is grammatically incorrect.

44. IV, III and II, I are clearly linked. The 'about it' in II indicates that it will follow III

45. Check options for continuity of coherence.

IIFT 2008

Number of Questions – 35
Time : 30 M.

SECTION - I

DIRECTION for questions 1-12: *Read the three passages carefully and answer the questions given at the end of each passage:*

Passage -1

Turning the business around involved more than segmenting and pulling out of retail. It also meant maximizing every strength we had in order to boost our profit margins. In reexamining the direct model, we realized that inventory management was not just a core strength; it could be an incredible opportunity for us, and one that had not yet been discovered by any of our competitors.

In Version 1.0 of the direct model, we eliminated the reseller, thereby eliminating the markup and the cost of maintaining a store. In Version 1.1, we went one step further to reduce inventory inefficiencies. Traditionally, a long chain of partners was involved in getting a product to the customer. Let's say you have a factory building a PC we'll call model #4000. The system is then sent to the distributor, which sends it to the warehouse, which sends it to the dealer, who eventually pushes it on to the consumer by advertising, "I've got model #4000. Come and buy it." If the consumer says, "But I want model #8000," the dealer replies, "Sorry, I only have model #4000." Meanwhile, the factory keeps building model #4000s and pushing the inventory into the channel.

The result is a glut of model #4000s that nobody warts. Inevitably, someone ends up with too much inventory, and you see big price corrections. The retailer can't sell it at the suggested retail price, so the manufacturer loses money on price protection (a practice common in cur industry of compensating dealers for reductions in suggested selling price). Companies with long, multi-step distribution systems will often fill their distribution channels with products in an attempt to clear out older technologies or meet their financial targets. This dangerous and inefficient practice is called "channel stuffing". Worst of all the customer ends up paying for it by purchasing systems that are already out of date.

Because we were building directly to fill our customers' orders, we didn't have finished goods inventory devaluing on a daily basis. Because we aligned our suppliers to deliver components as we used them, we were able to minimize raw material inventory. Reductions in component costs could be passed on to our customers quickly, which made them happier and improved our competitive advantage. It also allowed us to deliver the latest technology to our customers faster than oar competitors.

The direct model turns conventional manufacturing inside, out. Conventional manufacturing dictates that you should always have a stockpile of raw materials, because if you run out, your plant can't keep going. But if you don't know what you need to build because of dramatic changes in demand, you run the risk of ending up with terrific amounts-, of excess and obsolete inventory. That is not the goal. The concept behind the direct model has nothing to do with stockpiling and everything to do with information. The quality of your information is inversely proportional to the amount of assets required, in this case excess inventory. With less information about customer needs, you need massive amounts of inventory. So, if you have great information - that is, you know exactly what people want and how much - you need that much less inventory. Less inventory, of course, corresponds to less inventory depreciation. In the computer industry, component prices are always falling as suppliers introduce faster chips, bigger disk drives, and modems with ever-greater bandwidth. Let's say that Dell has six days of inventory. Compare that to an indirect competitor who has twenty-five days of inventory with another thirty in their distribution channel. That's a difference of forty-nine days, and in forty-nine days, the cost of materials will decline about 6 percent.

Then there's the threat of getting stuck with obsolete inventory if you're caught in a transition to a next-generation product, as we were with those memory chips in 1989. As the product approaches the end of its life, the manufacturer has to worry about whether it has too much in the channel and whether a competitor will dump products, destroying profit margins for everyone. This is a perpetual problem in the computer industry, but with the direct model, we have virtually eliminated it. We know when our customers are ready to move on technologically, and we can get out of the market before its most precarious time. We don't have to subsidize our losses by charging higher prices for other products.

And ultimately, our customer wins. Optimal inventory management really starts with the design process. You want to design the product so that the entire product supply chain, as well as the manufacturing process, is oriented not just for speed but for what we call velocity. Speed means being fast in the first place. Velocity means squeezing time out of every step in the process.

Inventory velocity has become a passion for us. To achieve maximum velocity, you have to design your products in a way that covers the largest part of the market with the fewest number of parts. For example, you don't need nine different disk drives when you can serve 98 percent of the market with only four. We also learned, to take into account the variability of low-cost and high-cost components. Systems were reconfigured to allow for a greater variety of low-cost parts and a limited variety of expensive parts. The goal was to decrease the number of components to manage, which increased the velocity, which decreased the risk of inventory depreciation, which increased the overall health of our business system.

We were also able to reduce inventory well below the levels anyone thought possible by constantly challenging and surprising ourselves with the results. We had our internal skeptics when we first started pushing for ever-lower levels of inventory. I remember the head of our procurement group telling me that this was like "flying low to the ground 300 knots." He was worried that we wouldn't see the trees.

In 1993, we had $2.9 billion in sales and $220 million in inventory. Four years later, we posted $12.3 billion in sales and had inventory of 33 million. We're now down to six days of inventory and we're starting to measure it in hours instead of days. Once you reduce your inventory while maintaining your growth rate, a significant amount of risk comes from the transition from one generation of product to the next. Without traditional stockpiles of inventory, it is critical to precisely time the discontinuance of the older product line with the ramp-up in customer demand for the newer one. Since we were introducing new products all the time, it became imperative to avoid the huge drag effect from mistakes made during transitions. E&O - short for "excess and obsolete" - became taboo at Dell. We would debate about whether our E&O was 30 or 50 cents per PC. Since anything less than $20 per PC is not bad, when you're down in the cents range, you're approaching stellar performance.

In effect, we got stronger with each transition and more competitive with each turn of the crank. We were increasing our productivity and improving our cash flow in a broader range of products m larger and larger markets. Unlike that period in 1993, when every day the news got a little worse, now, finally, every day the news was better and better.

1. Find out the TRUE statement:

1. According to the passage, the working of the direct model was being heavily exploited by all players in the software business.
2. Analysis of the supply chain of the product reveals that the product is sent to the warehouse by the dealer, and any delay at that stage leads to an obvious increase in cost.
3. The nature of the computer industry is such that the production decision at factory level is usually undertaken after getting the customer demand feedback from the distributors.
4. Whenever the production of some old-fashioned model of a produce by a company exceeds the existing demand, the market forces create a downward pressure on its prices.

2. Find out the FALSE statement:

1. The company mentioned in the passage could attain efficiency on raw material inventory management because they were procuring components only in line with their timely requirement.
2. Generally the more the amount of quality information about the consumer needs and the market a firm possess, the less is its inventory requirement.
3. In order to serve the market more efficiently, the firm mentioned here reconfigured their computers with increased proportion of low-cost parts and a fewer types of high-priced parts.
4. The conventional manufacturing system always ensured that no competitor can lower prices to reduce profit margins for everybody.

3. Choose the option which best matches the following sets:

1. Inventory	i. Precarious
2. Conventional Manufacturing	ii. Warehouse
3. Distributor	iii. Stockpile
4. Market	iv. Velocity

1. 1-iv, 2-ii, 3-i, 4-iii
2. 1-iii, 2-i, 3-iv, 4-ii
3. 1-iv, 2-iii, 3-ii, 4-i
4. 1-iii, 2-ii, 3-iv, 4-i

4. Find out the FALSE Statement:

1. Having less amount of inventory is better in the computer industry as with lime better quality components with enhanced capacity reach the market with lower price.
2. Before improving the inventory management system under the direct model, the firm first removed the reseller from its marketing model, which contributed in its cost-cutting attempt.
3. The efficient inventory management allowed the firm to enhance productivity as well as the flexibility to enter or exit a market.
4. The companies with long distribution network incorporate information- gathering process within their systems which enable them to market products with latest available technologies.

PASSAGE – II

My comrade and I had been quartered in Jamaica, and from there we had been drafted off to the British settlement of Belize, lying away West and North of the Mosquito coast. At Belize there had been great alarm of one cruel gang of pirates (there were always more pirates than enough in those Caribbean Seas), and as they got the better of our English cruisers by running into out-of-the-way creeks and shallows, and taking the land when they were hotly pressed, the governor of Belize had recei'2d orders from home to keep a sharp look-out for them along shore. Now, there was an armed sloop came once a year from Port Royal, Jamaica, to the Island, laden with all manner of necessaries, to eat, and to drink, and to wear, and to use in various ways; and it was aboard of that sloop which had touched at Belize, that I was standing, leaning over the bulwarks.

The Island was occupied by a very small English colony. It had been given the name of Silver-Store. The reason of its being so called, was, that the English colony owned and worked a silver-mine over on the mainland, in Honduras, and used this Island as a safe and convenient place to store their silver in, until it was annually fetched away by the sloop. It was brought down from the mine to the coast on the backs of mules, attended by friendly local people and guarded by white men; from thence it was conveyed over to Silver-Store, when the weather was fair, in the canoes of that country; from Silver-Store, it was carried to Jamaica by the armed sloop once a-year, as I have already mentioned; from Jamaica, it went, of course, all over the world.

How I came to be aboard the armed sloop, is easily told. Four-and-twenty marines under command of a lieutenant - that officer's name was Underwood - had been told off at Belize, to proceed to Silver-Store, in aid of boats and seamen stationed there for the chase of the Pirates. The Island was considered a good post of observation against the pirates. both by land and sea; neither the pirate ship nor yet her boats had been seen by any of us, but they had been so much heard of, that the reinforcement was sent. Of that party, I was one. It included a corporal and a sergeant. Charker was corporal, and the sergeant's name was Drooce. He was the most tyrannical non-commissioned officer in His Majesty's service.

The night came on, soon after I had had the foregoing words with Charker. All the wonderful bright colours went out of the sea and sky in a few minutes, and all the stars in the Heavens seemed to shine out together, and to look down at themselves in the sea, over one another's shoulders, millions deep.

Next morning, we cast anchor off the Island. There was a snug harbour within a little reef; there was a sandy beach; there were cocoa-nut trees with high straight stems, quite bare, and foliage at the top like plumes of magnificent green feathers; there were all the objects that are usually seen in those parts, and I am not going to describe them, having something else to tell about.

Great rejoicings, to be sure, were made on our arrival. All the flags in the place were hoisted, all the guns in the place were fired, and all the people in the place came down to look at us. One of the local people had come off outside the reef, to pilot us in, and remained on board after we had let go our anchor.

My officer, Lieutenant Linderwood, was as ill as the captain of the sloop, and was carried ashore, too. They were both young men of about my age, who had been delicate in the West India climate. I thought I was much fitter for the work than they were, and that if all of us had our deserts, I should be both of them rolled into one. (It may be imagined what sort of an officer of marines I should have made, without the power of reading a written order. And as to any knowledge how to command the sloop—Lord! 1 should have sunk her in a quarter of an hour!)

However, such were my reflections; and when we men were ashore and dismissed, I strolled about the place along with Charker, making my observations in a similar spirit.

It was a pretty place: in all its arrangements partly South American and partly English, and very agreeable to look, at on that account, being like a bit of home that had got chipped off and had floated away to that spot, accommodating itself to circumstances as it drifted along. The huts of the local people, to the number of five-and-twenty, perhaps, were down by the beach to the left of the anchorage. On the right was a sort of barrack, with a South American Flag and the Union Jack, flying from the same staff, where the little English colony could all come together, if they saw occasion. It was a walled square of building, with a sort of pleasure-ground inside, and inside that again a sunken block like a powder magazine, with a little square trench round it, and steps down to the door.

Charker and I were looking in at the gate, which was not guarded; and I bad said to Charker, in reference to the bit like a powder magazine, "That's where they keep the silver you see;" and Charker had said to me, after thinking it over, "And silver ain't gold. Is it, Gill?"

5. Find out the TRUE statement:

1. During the time of the narration, the total number of pirates at Belize was much more than the same in the Caribbean Seas.
2. From the accounts presented here, when the narrator of the passage made the journey he already happened to be an experienced sailor with considerable navigating experiences.
3. The author and his friends used to consider Drooce as the most authoritarian non-commissioned officer in Her Majesty's service.
4. While walking with Charker, the narrator came across a barrack like structure where all the English settlers could assemble and stay together, if there was any necessity for doing so.

6. Find out the FALSE statement:

1. According to the passage, the silver that was being stored in the place where the author went to was being mined in Honduras.
2. The narrator noted that the silver was being transported from the mine to the coast on the backs of mules, after which it was being sent to Jamaica in a sloop, from where it was reaching various destinations.
3. Although the sea-voyage near Belize was being threatened by the presence of one notorious pirate fleet, the captain of the patrolling ship was accompanied by less than thirty soldiers.
4. The Island the author talks here about was considered to be a good point for surveillance against the pirates both by land and sea.

7. Find out the TRUE Statement:

1. The author was initially staying in Jamaica, which is located in the West and North of the Mosquito coast.
2. A casual review of the place by the narrator revealed that the store for keeping the silver was heavily guarded, fearing a possible pirate attack anytime.
3. The narrator and his companion noticed the South American Flag and the Union Jack flying on the port office.
4. When the ship entered the harbour, both it's Captain and Lieutenant Linderwood was unwell as the West Indian climate was not suiting them.

8. Mark the FALSE statement:

1. It was being difficult to capture the pirates because they either used to hide in uncommon waters whenever the patrolling ships were pursuing them or used to disembark and flee whenever severely chased.
2. The local canoes were employed by the miners to bring the silver from the coast to the island during favourable climatic condition.
3. The lifestyle of the island was not exactly British as it had to adjust itself with the local South American culture, but the same seemed quite delightful for the narrator and his company.
4. When Corporal Charker and Sergent Gill were walking around the harbour, they noticed that the size of the settlement of the local people was not very large.

PASSAGE – III

We now come to the second part of our journey under the sea. The first ended with the moving scene in the coral cemetery which left a deep impression on my mind. I could no longer content myself with the theory which satisfied Conseil. That worthy fellow persisted in seeing in the Commander of the Nautilus one of those unknown servants who return mankind contempt for indifference. For him, he was a misunderstood genius who, tired of earth's deceptions, had taken refuge in this inaccessible medium, where he might follow his instincts freely. To my mind, this explains but one side of Captain Nemo's character. Indeed, the mystery of that last night during which we had beer, chained in prison, the sleep, and the precaution so violently taken by the Captain of snatching from my eyes the glass I had raised to sweep the horizon, the mortal wound of the man, due to an unaccountable shock of the Nautilus, all put me on a new track. No; Captain Nemo was not satisfied with shunning man. His formidable apparatus not only suited his instinct of freedom, but perhaps also the design of some terrible retaliation.

That day, at noon, the second officer came to take the altitude of the sun. I mounted the platform, and watched the operation. As he was taking observations with the sextant, one of the sailors of the Nautilus (the strong man who had accompanied us on our first submarine excursion to the Island of Crespo) came to clean the glasses of the lantern. I examined the fittings of the apparatus, the strength of which was increased a hundredfold by lenticular rings, placed similar to those in a lighthouse, and which projected their brilliance in a horizontal plane. The electric lamp was combined in such a way as to give its most powerful light. Indeed, it was produced in vacuo, which insured both its steadiness and its intensity. This vacuum economised the graphite points between which the luminous arc was developed - an important point of economy for Captain Nemo, who could not easily have replaced them; and under these conditions their waste was imperceptible. When the Nautilus was ready to continue its submarine journey, I went down to the saloon. The panel was closed, and the course marked direct west.

We were furrowing the waters of the Indian Ocean, a vast liquid plain, with a surface of 1, 200,000,000 of acres, and whose waters are so clear and transparent that any one leaning over them would turn giddy. The Nautilus usually floated between fifty and a hundred fathoms deep. We went on so for some days. To anyone but myself, who had a great love for the sea, the hours would have seemed long and monotonous; but the daily walks on the platform, when I steeped myself in the reviving air of the ocean, the sight of the rich waters through the windows of the saloon, the books in the library, the compiling of my memoirs, took up all my time, and left me not a moment of ennui or weariness.

From the 21st to the 23rd of January the Nautilus went at the rate of two hundred and fifty leagues in twenty-four hours, being five hundred and forty miles, or twenty-two miles an hour. If we recognized so many different varieties of fish, it was because, attracted by the electric light, they tried to follow us; the greater part, however, were soon distanced by our speed, though some kept their place in the waters of the Nautilus for a time. The morning of the 24th, we observed Keeling Island, a coral formation, planted with magnificent cocos, and which had been visited by Mr. Darwin and Captain Fitzroy. The Nautilus skirted the shores of this desert island for a little distance. Soon Keeling Island disappeared from the horizon, and our course was directed to the north-west in the direction of the Indian Peninsula.

From Keeling Island our course was slower and more variable, often taking us into great depths. Several times they made use of the inclined planes, which certain internal levers placed obliquely to the waterline. I observed that in the upper regions the water was always colder in the high levels than at the surface of the sea. On the 25th of January the ocean was entirely deserted; the Nautilus passed the day on the surface, beating the waves with its powerful screw and making them rebound to a great height. Three parts of this day I spent on the platform. I watched the sea. Nothing on the horizon, till about four o'clock a steamer running west on our counter. Her masts were visible for an instant, but she could not see the Nautilus, being too low in the water. I fancied this steamboat belonged to the P.O. Company, which runs from Ceylon to Sydney, touching at King George's Point and Melbourne.

At five o'clock in the evening, before that fleeting twilight which binds night to day in tropical zones, Conseil and I were astonished by a curious spectacle. It was a shoal of argonauts traveling along on the surface of the ocean. We could count several hundreds. These graceful molluses moved backwards by means of their locomotive tube, through which they propelled the water already drawn in. Of their eight tentacles, six were elongated, and stretched cut floating on the water, whilst the other two, rolled up flat, were spread to the wing like a light sail. I saw their spiral-shaped and fluted shells, which Cuvier justly compares to an elegant skiff. For nearly an hour the Nautilus floated in the midst of this shoal of molluses.

The next day, 26th of January, we cut the equator at the eighty-second meridian and entered the northern hemisphere. During the day a formidable troop of sharks accompanied us. They were "cestracio philippi" sharks, with brown backs and whitish bellies, armed with eleven rows of teeth, their throat being marked with a large black spot surrounded with white like an eye. There were also some Isabella sharks, with rounded snouts marked with dark spots. These powerful creatures often hurled themselves at the windows of the saloon with such violence as to make us feel very insecure. But the Nautilus, accelerating her speed, easily left the most rapid of them behind.

About seven o'clock in the evening, Me Nautilus, half-immersed, was sailing in a sea of milk. At first sight the ocean seemed lactified. Was it the effect of the lunar rays? No; for the moon, scarcely two days old, was still lying hidden under the horizon in the rays of the sun. The whole sky though lit by the sidereal rays, seemed black by contrast with the whiteness of the waters. Conseil could not believe his eyes, and questioned me as to the cause of ibis strange phenomenon. Happily 1 was able to answer him.

"It is called a milk sea," I explained. "A large extent of white wavelets often to be seen on the coasts of Amboyna, and in these parts of the sea."

"But, sir," said Conseil, "can you tell me what causes such an effect? For I suppose the water is not really turned into milk."

"No, my boy; and the whiteness which surprises you is caused only by the presence of myriads of luminous little worm, gelatinous and without colour, of the thickness of a hair, and whose length is not more than seven-thousandths of an inch. These insects adhere to one another sometimes for several leagues."

"Several leagues!" exclaimed Conseil.

"Yes, my boy; and you need not try to compute the number of these infusoria. You will not be able, for, if I am not mistaken, ships have floated on these milk seas for more than forty miles."

Towards midnight the sea suddenly resumed its usual colour; but behind us, even to the limits of the horizon, the sky reflected the whitened waves, and for a long time seemed impregnated with the vague glimmerings of an aurora borealis.

9. Find the TRUE Sentence:

1. According to the narrator, the above-mentioned journey was taking place during full moon period.
2. According to Conseil, the Captain of the Nautilus in which they were traveling was really a brilliant person, a fact which had been corroborated by many people.
3. It is implied from the passage that although the author was witnessing many interesting events during their journey, he was not always having his way.
4. From the chronicle, it is understood that the Nautilus was in the vicinity of the Island of Crespo on the 25th of January.

10. Find the FALSE sentence:

1. After entering the Northern Hemisphere, the narrator witnessed several sea creatures, including several varieties of sharks, who kept bumping on the windows of the submarine.
2. On 25th January, the second officer of Nautilus came to the platform for measuring the altitude of the sun and for that purpose took observations with the sextant.
3. After January 24, Nautilus started traveling at a relatively reduced speed, and some of the time it was going further away from the sea-surface.
4. The course of Nautilus took them near the Keeling Island, which had earlier been visited by Mr. Darwin and Captain Fitzroy.

11.

1.	Molluscs	i.	Colourless
2.	Sharks	ii.	Tentacles
3.	Infusoria	iii.	Coco
4.	Coral	iv.	Snouts

1. 1-ii, 2-iv, 3-i, 4-iii
2. 1-iii, 2-i, 3-iv, 4-ii
3. 1-iv, 2-iii, 3-ii, 4-I
4. 1-iii, 2-ii, 3-iv. 4-i

12. Find the TRUE statement:

1. During 22nd to 24th of January, Nautilus was traveling at the rate of two hundred and fifty leagues in twenty-four hours, which means a speed of twenty-two miles an hour.
2. On 26th January for approximately an hour the narrator witnessed a shoal of mollusks, and he enjoyed watching their spiral-shaped and fluted shells.
3. On the 25th of January the narrator came across a steamboat, which was owned by P.O. Company, which travels between Ceylon to Sydney.
4. The electric lamp of the submarine was an example of efficiency and effective fixture.

SECTION – II

DIRECTION for questions 13–15: *Find the most appropriate word from the given choices which is described by the meaning provided in the question.*

13. Meaning: a bowl-shaped drinking vesse l

1. rumble
2. fracas
3. aquifer
4. chalice

14. Meaning: definition of a substance, especially a strong acid; erosive; mordant.

1. vitriolic
2. briny
3. puerile
4. prophylactic

15. Meaning: an upward slope or grade (as in a road); rise; raise; climb; upgrade.

1. maelstrom
2. acclivity
3. alacrity
4. slighting

DIRECTION for questions 16–19: *Select the most appropriate word(s) from the given choices to fill the blank (s).*

16. Justice Minister Bola Jge, confronted with the general incivility of local police, placed a on the cads. Said the Hon. Bola Ige, "I pray that God will make big holes in their pockets."

1. malediction
2. sanction
3. proscription
4. plea

17. I _________ i _____________ that he will pass his exam and get a good job. I will make a ____________ ii _______________. There will be a new government in less than a year.

1. i. prophecy ii. Prophesy
2. i. prophesy ii. Prophecy
3. i. prophecy ii. Prophecy
4. i. prophesy ii. Prophesy

18. Imagine an ___________ public figure attacked by press and public, who is facing an inquiry into allegations of having obtained money by deception.

1. empowered
2. endangered
3. embattled
4. engrossed

19. His listeners enjoyed his _____________ wit but his, victims often ___________ at its satire.

1. lugubrious, suffered
2. bitter, smarted
3. lugubrious, smiled
4. trenchant, winced

DIRECTIONS for questions 20 –23: *In each of the following sentences, part or all of the sentence is underlined. The answer-choices offer four ways of phrasing the underlined part. If you think the original sentence is better than the alternatives, choose A, which merely repeats the underlined part; otherwise choose one of the alternatives.*

20. Had the President's Administration not lost the vote on the budget reduction package, his first year in office would have been rated an A.

1. Had the President's Administration not lost the vote on the budget reduction package, his first year in office would have been rated an A.

2. Had the President's Administration not lost the vote on the budget reduction package, it would have been rated an A in the first year.
3. If the President had not lost the vote on the budget reduction package, the Administration's first year in office would have been rated an A.
4. Had the President's Administration not lost the vote on its budget reduction package, his first year in office would have been rated an A.

21. The rise in negative attitudes toward foreigners indicate that the country is becoming less tolerant, and therefore that the opportunities are ripe for extremist groups to exploit the illegal immigration problem.

1. indicate that the country is becoming less tolerant, and therefore that
2. indicates that the country is becoming less tolerant, and therefore
3. indicates that the country is becoming less tolerant, and therefore that
4. indicates that the country has become less tolerant, and therefore

22. This century began with war brewing in Europe, the industrial revolution well-established, and a nascent communication age.

1. war brewing in Europe, the industrial revolution well-established, and a nascent communication age.
2. war brewing in Europe, the industrial revolution surging, and a nascent communication age.
3. war brewing in Europe, the industrial revolution well-established, and the communication age beginning.
4. war brewing in Europe, the industrial revolution well-established, and saw the birth of the communication age.

23. Due to the chemical spill, the commute into the city will be delayed by as much as 2 hours.

1. Due to the chemical spill, the commute into the city will be delayed by as much as 2 hours.
2. The chemical spill will be delaying the commute into the city by as much as 2 hours.
3. Due to the chemical spill, the commute into the city had been delayed by as much as 2 hours.
4. Because of the chemical spill, the commute into the city will be delayed by as much as 2 hours.

DIRECTION for questions 24–27: *Select the option which is having similar analogy vis-a-vis the analogy given in the question.*

24. TRAVESTY: PARAGON::

1. autonomy : subordination
2. disqualification : ineptitude
3. sentinel: creed
4. conundrum: accountability

25. CONTRITE : OBDURATE ::

1. grievous: lamentable
2. aphoristic: esoteric
3. sophisticated: cultured
4. favorable: assenting

26. PECCADILLO : FLAW::

1. clandestine : openness
2. nick: score
3. forensics: judiciary
4. invasion: putsch

27. MUTTER: INDISTINCT ::

1. define: easy
2. blunder: polished
3. articulate : well-spoken
4. expedite: completed

DIRECTION for questions 28–30: *Select the most OPPOSITE of the given word from the given choices.*

28. REQUIEM

1. Humility
2. Prerequisite
3. Resolution
4. Reign

29. ASPERSION

1. Infamy
2. Restriction
3. Tradition
4. Obeisance

30. STOLIDITY

1. Posterity
2. Proximity
3. Agility
4. Sobriety

DIRECTIONS for questions 31–33: *A number of sentences are given below which, when properly sequenced, form a COHERENT PARAGRAPH. Choose the most LOGICAL ORDER of sentences from the choices given to construct e COHERENT PARAGRAPH.*

31. I. The economy's performance in expenditure terms was even poorer, with real GDP contracting by 0.6% after a gain of 0.5% in the October-December quarter.

II. On an output basis—the government's preferred measure because it is less volatile than expenditure-based GDP—the economy contracted by 0.3% in real terms from the previous quarter.

III. Data from Statistics New Zealand, a government agency, published on June 27th show an almost uniformly abysmal economic performance in January-March 2008.

IV. This was the first contraction since late 2005, made worse by the fact that the previous quarter's growth rate was revised down from 1% to 0.8%.

1. III, IV, II, I
2. I, II, III, IV
3. III, II, IV, I
4. I, III, II, IV

32. I. Matti Meri, a teacher-trainer at Helsinki University, was a teacher at the time.

II. By the time comprehensives reached the more populous south, teachers were eager to join in what was clearly a rearing success.

III. "Grammar-school teachers were quite afraid of the reforms," he recalls.

IV. "They used to teach only one-third of the students. But the comprehensive schools used almost the same curriculum as the grammar schools had—and we discovered that the two-thirds were mostly able to cope with it."

V. Comprehensive schools **were** introduced in 1972 in the sparsely populated north, and then over the next four years in the rest of the country.

1. V, I, III, IV, II
2. I, II, III, IV, V
3. V, II, IV, I, III
4. I, III, II, IV, V

33. I. "It is a clear illustration of the major role played by diet and culture on your risk of chronic disorders," he says.

II. Little is known about its effects, but changing its levels, possibly through diet or with different gut bacteria, might help to control high blood pressure.

III. Chinese and Japanese people are very similar at a genetic level, but Dr. Nicholson found big differences in the type and variety of metabolites in their blood and urine.

IV. "Metabolomics can provide very specific pointers as to what is going wrong and new ways of intervening."

V. For instance, he found an unexpected metabolic market, called formate that seems to have a role in regulating blood pressure.

1. III, II, IV, I, V
2. III, IV, V, I, II
3. II, III, IV, I, V
4. III, I, IV, V, II

34. There are four sentences S1, S2, S3, S4 where the underlined word is used either correctly or incorrectly. Choose the option which lists the sentences, where the underlined word is used correctly.

S1. Only 22% of the people voted. The rest were totally <u>disinterested</u>.

S2. The management and the union asked a completely <u>disinterested</u> party to mediate between them.

S3. I don't know why he didn't go to the exhibition. Perhaps he was too busy or just <u>disinterested</u>.

S4. France's intervention in the dispute was not entirely <u>disinterested</u>. It gave her increased power and influence in the area.

1. S1, S2, S4.
2. S2, S3, S4.
3. S1, S4.
4. S2, S4

35. There are four sentences S1, S2, S3, S4 where the underlined phrase is used either correctly or incorrectly. Choose the option which lists the sentences, where the underlined phrase is used correctly.

S1. Good Lord, I'm not rich! <u>on the contrary</u>. I'm constantly in debt.

S2. She's very intelligent, but <u>on the contrary</u> she's apt to be impatient.

S3. Yes, it's a very cosmopolitan city. <u>On the contrary</u>. It's very expensive.

S4. I don't think he'll pass the exam. <u>On the contrary</u>, I think he'll almost certainly fail.

1. S1,S2, S4
2. S2,S4
3. S1, S4
4. S2, S3

Answer Key

1. 4	**2.** 4	**3.** 3	**4.** 4	**5.** 2	**6.** 3	**7.** 4
8. 1	**9.** 3	**10.** 2	**11.** 1	**12.** 4	**13.** 4	**14.** 1
15. 2	**16.** 1	**17.** 2	**18.** 3	**19.** 4	**20.** 1	**21.** 2
22. 3	**23** 1	**24.** 1	**25.** 2	**26.** 2	**27.** 3	**28.** 4
29. 4	**30.** 3	**31.** 3	**32.** 1	**33.** 2	**34.** 3	**35.** 3

EXPLANATIONS

1. 4 PARA 3

2. 4 PARA 9

3. 3

4. 4 By choice elimination rest of the options are correct except D

5. 2 para 7

6. 3 By choice elimination rest of the options are correct except C

7. 4 para 7

8. 1 para 1

9. 3 By choice elimination rest of the options are correct except C

10. 2 By choice elimination rest of the options are correct except B

11. 1

12. 4 para 2

13. 4

14. 1

15. 2

16. 1 Clue : "General incivility " & "I pray that……". Hence the correct word is curse or malediction

17. 2 In first blank ,word is a verb & in second as a noun ; hence B

18. 3

19. 4

20. 1

21. 2

22. 3

23 1

24. 1 Both are opposites

25. 2 Obdurate is not contrite & same applies to B

26. 2 Analogy is of intensity

27. 3 Muttering is indistinct. same applies to C

28. 4

29. 4 Aspersion means slander

30. 3 Stolid means lethargic

31. 3

32. 1

33. 2

34. 3 In S2 & S3 , usage should be uninterested

35. 3 In S2, but & on the contrary cannot come together. In S3, the phrase is not required.

XAT 2007

Number of Questions – 36
Time : 35 M.

SECTION - I
VERBAL ABILITY

1. Which of the following choices MOST accurately captures the meaning of *crucible* as used in the sentence below?

General Charles Krulak, the Commandant, introduced "The Crucible" to Marine training—an incredibly grueling fifty-four straight hours of live fire exercises, long marches, and sleep deprivation at the end of basic trailing. After climbing the final hill in this test, ret nuts are presented with the eagle, globe, and anchor emblem.

1. Cauldron
2. Nightmare
3. Albatross
4. Adversity
5. None of the above

2. Which of the following choices will be MOST opposite to the word *juvenile* as used in the sentence below?

Juvenile delinquents and depressive or suicidal psychiatric patients show orphanhood rates similar to those of the eminent public figures.

1. Puerile
2. Naïve
3. Jejune
4. Tyke
5. None of the above

3. "The correlation between technological intensity and diversification may be spurious, as both may be related to selling to the government or to other dominant customers."

In the above sentence, spurious may refer to all of the following but:

1. counterfeit
2. questionable
3. contrived
4. forged
5. misleading

4. The various branches of knowledge complete, correct, and balance each other. This consideration, if well-founded, must be taken into account, not only as regards the attainment of truth, which is their common end, but as regards the influence which they excise upon those whose education consists in the study of them.

The word *excise* in the extract above most nearly means

1. Remove.
2. Cut.
3. Impose.
4. Arrange.
5. Compete.

5. Basic assumptions and beliefs that are shared by members of an organization, that operate unconsciously, and that define in a basic 'taken-for-granted' fashion an organization's view of itself and its environment. These assumptions and beliefs are learned responses to a group's problems. They come to be taken for granted because they solve those problems repeatedly and reliably.

What would be the word that can substitute for *assumptions* in the extract above, WITHOUT changing the extract's meaning?

1. Hunch
2. Conclusion
3. Induction
4. Doctrine
5. None of the above

DIRECTIONS for questions 6 to 9: *Go through the exchange between two poets below and answer the questions that follow.*

I do my thing and you do your thing.
I am not in this world to live up to your expectations...
and you are not in this world to live up to mine.
You are you...
and I am I.
And if, by chance, we find each other...
it's beautiful.
If not, it can't be helped.
~ Poet 1

Beyond Poet 1
~ Poet 2

If I just do my thing and you do yours.
We stand in danger of losing each other
And ourselves.
1 am not in this world to live up to your expectations;
But 1 am in this world to confirm you
as a unique human being.
And to be confirmed by you.
We are fully ourselves only in relation to each other;
The I detached from Thou
Disintegrates.
I do not find you by chance;
I find you by an active life
of reaching out.
Rather than passively letting things happen to me,
I can act intentionally to make them happen.
I must begin within myself, true;
But I must not end with myself:
The truth begins with two.

6. What could the second poem be best characterized as, with respect to the first?

1. Retort
2. Rejoinder
3. Critique
4. criticism
5. Complement

7. Amongst the perspectives listed below, which one would extend Poet 2's argument the most?

1. Human beings these days primarily conceive of themselves as isolated individual selves.
2. Self-exploration is considered the most important pre-occupation by educated individuals.
3. One's active stance towards life does not change fate.
4. Society incorporates multiple simultaneous relationships.
5. Collectivism is considered a virtue in most indigenous societies.

8. What could be the central theme of the second poem?

1. Individualism is debilitating to human existence.
2. Hermits and ascetics stand no chance of reaching their goal.
3. Chance does not play an active role in today's life.
4. One ought to seize the day to make life happen.
5. An individual finds one's individuality only in relation to others.

9. Amongst the following ways of living one's life, which one would the first poet most strongly endorse?

1. The life of a person stranded on an isolated island.
2. The life of a renunciate.
3. The life of a stoic.
4. The life of a person who has no use for anyone else's perspectives.
5. None of the above.

DIRECTIONS for questions 10 to 14: *Go through the passage below and answer the questions that follow.*

This confusion concerns nothing less than the concept of socialism itself. It may mean, and is often used to describe, merely the ideals of social justice, greater equality and security which are the ultimate aims of socialism. But it means also the particular method by which most socialists hope to attain these ends and which many competent people regard as the only methods by which they can be fully and quickly attained. In this sense socialism means the abolition of private enterprise, of private ownership of the means of production, and the creation of a system of "planned economy" in which the entrepreneur working for profit is replaced by a central planning body.

There are many people who call themselves socialists although they care only about the first, who fervently believe in those ultimate aims of socialism but neither care nor understand how they can be achieved, and who are merely certain they must be achieved, whatever the cost. But to nearly all those to whom socialism is not merely a hope but an object of practical politics, the characteristic methods of modem socialism are as essential as the ends themselves. Most people, on the other hand, who value the ultimate ends of socialism no less than the socialists, refuse to support socialism because of the dangers to other values they see in the methods proposed by the socialists. The dispute about socialism has thus become largely a dispute about means and not about ends-although the question whether the different ends of socialism can be simultaneously achieved is also involved.

This would be enough to create confusion. And the confusion has been further increased by the common practice of denying that those who repudiate the means value the ends. But this is not all. The situation is still more complicated by the fact that the same means, the "economic planning" which is the prime instrument for socialist reform, can be used for many other purposes. We must centrally direct economic activity if we want to make the distribution of income conform to current ideas of social justice. "Planning", therefore, is wanted by all those who demand that "production for use" be substituted for production for profit. But such planning is no less indispensable if the distribution of incomes is to be regulated in a way which to us appears to be the opposite of just. Whether we should wish that more of the good things of this world should go to some racial elite, the Nordic men, or the members of a party or an aristocracy, the methods which we shall have to employ-are the same as those which could ensure an equalitarian distribution.

It may, perhaps, seem unfair to use the term socialism to describe its methods rather than its aims, to use for a particular method a term which for many people stand for an ultimate ideal. It is probably preferable to describe the methods which can be used for a great variety of ends as collectivism and to regard socialism as a species of that genus. Yet, although to most socialists only one species of collectivism will represent true socialism, it must always be remembered that socialism is a species of collectivism and that therefore everything which is true for collectivism as such must apply to socialism. Nearly all the points which are disputed between socialists and liberals concerns the methods common to all forms of collectivism and not the particular ends for which the socialists want to use them; and all the consequences with which we shall be concerned in this book follow from the methods of collectivism irrespective of the ends for which they are used. It must also not be forgotten that socialism is not only by far the most important species of collectivism or "planning"; but that it is socialism which has persuaded liberal-minded people to submit once more to that regimentation of economic life which they had overthrown because, in the words of Adam Smith, it puts governments in a position where "to support themselves they are obliged to be oppressive and tyrannical".

10. According to the author, those who agree to the aims of socialism would

1. refuse to support socialism because of possible consequences of the methods advocated to achieve those ends.
2. agree on the collectivisation and centralisation of economic activities since both require strong and powerful governments.
3. have disagreed if only they had known that the only way to achieve the equalitarian ends of socialismrequired centralisation and collectivisation of economic activities.
4. explicitly advocate strict control of economic and social life always since it is a matter of practical politics for them.
5. None of the above.

11. From the passage, it may be inferred that the author is a supporter of

1. the ideals of socialism and does not care much about the means required to achieve them.
2. ends as portrayed by supporters of socialism but is sceptical of the efficacy of the means advocated to reach those ends.
3. the ends of socialism, since the means required to achieve those ends always involve collectivisation and centralization.
4. a strong and powerful government as a means to achieve the ends of socialism, since there is no debateon the desirability of the aforementioned ends.
5. all the possible means of collectivisation as they are the tools which can be used to achieve equalitariandistribution in society.

12. The statement that the author of the passage would support the most is:

1. The development of society, if left to individuals, would be impossible as each individual would exploitopportunities for plundering and exploiting one's fellow citizens.
2. The development of society is best done by individuals working for selfish interests within free economicenvironment that collectively ends up improving the condition of society since the outcomes of each action of individuals are shared by the members of the society.
3. In the absence of a strong government, society would degenerate into anarchy as each individual tries toachieve success at the cost of one's fellow citizens.
4. Individuals would create mechanisms to put a system in place that would have rules and regulations sothat the society does not break down into chaos.
5. In a general environment of chaos, individuals would create clusters of order which would allowand encourage individual clusters' economic development.

13. Amongst the options below, the one that best captures the ideology being advocated by the author is

1. Fascism
2. Democratic socialism
3. Marxism
4. Fabian socialism
5. Capitalism

14. Amongst the options given below, the one most opposite to the ideology being advocated by the author

1. Fascism
2. Democratic socialism
3. Marxism
4. Fabian socialism
5. Capitalism

DIRECTIONS for questions 15 to 20: *Go through the passage below and answer the questions that follow.*

A major problem of Indian industrial and commercial development was the supply of capital. Until 1850, British capital was shy of Indian adventure. The risks and unknown factors were too great, and prospects in other directions too bright. The working capital of the agency houses after 1813 at first consisted mainly of the savings of the Company's servants. Their cries of woe when these houses fell as in the crisis of 1831 were loud and poignant. Indian capital was also shy for different reasons. It needed to acquire confidence in the new regime, and outside the presidency towns, to acquire the habit of investment. Investment for large-scale production for 'enabling' works like railways was an unfamiliar and suspected practice. Thus the first big developments came when European capital was coaxed into the country by government guarantees or went of its own free will to develop industries with which it was already familiar as in the case of jute or coal. Indian capital followed where it was in touch with European practice as in Bombay and dealing with familiar products like cotton. These considerations throw into all the greater relief the achievement of the Tatas in developing iron and steel. Thus the major part of the capital provided was British with a steadily increasing Indian proportion from 1900. As late as 1931-2 the capital of companies registered abroad was nearly four times that of companies registered in India. But this is not an exact guide because it leaves out of account the stock in British companies held by Indians, as well as government stocks. Speaking generally it may be said that the capital of the cotton industry was mainly Indian, that of the iron and steel industry entirely so, that of the jute industry about half and half, while the coal and plantation industries were mainly British, together with that used for the building of railways, irrigation, and other public works. Management in the cotton and steel industries was mainly Indian though European technicians were feely employed, that of the jute, coal, and the plantation industries being European, the jute men in particular being Scotch. Their capital, apart of course from government enterprise, operated through joint-stock companies and managing agencies. The latter arose through the convenience found by bodies of capitalists seeking to develop some new activity and lacking any Indian experience, of operating through local agents. It arose in the period after 1813 when private merchants took over the trade formerly monopolized by the Company. The money would be found in Britain to promote a tea garden, a coal mine, or a jute mill, but the management would be confided to a firm already on the spot. The managing agency was the hyphen connecting capital with experience and local knowledge.

Until 1914 the policy of the government continued in the main to be one of 'enabling' private capital and enterprise to develop the country. Direct promotion was confined to public utilities like canals and railways. The line between enabling and interfering action became distinctly blurred, however, in the case of the cotton industry and there was a tendency for enabling action to pass over into the positive promotion of particular projects. This was most noticeable in the time of Lord Curzon with his establishment of an imperial department of agriculture with a research station at Pusa and a department of commerce and industry presided over by a sixth member of the Viceroy's Council. The first World War began the transition to a new period of active promotion and positive support. As the conflict lengthened there arose a demand for Indian manufactured goods. India failed to take full advantage of this opportunity, partly because of uncertainty as to the future and partly because the means for sudden expansion were lacking. The outcome of this situation was the appointment of an industrial commission in 1916 under pressure from London. The commission criticized the unequal development of Indian industry which had led to the missing of her war opportunity. A much closer co-operation with industry was planned through provincial departments of industry. Increased technical training and technical assistance to industry was proposed while it was suggested that the central government should set up a stores department which should aim at making India self-sufficing in this respect. The commission's report was only partially implemented, but a stores department and provincial industrial departments were created and something was done towards promoting technical assistance. The importance of the report and its aftermath was that it marked the transition from the conception of Indian economy in broadly colonial terms with freedom for private enterprise to the conception of India as an autonomous economic unit.

15. The following can be inferred from the passage:

I. Industrial development of a country requires supply of external capital

II. Investment in uncertain industries is more when government provides guarantees against failure

III. Lack of indigenous technical expertise can be a constraining factor in a country's economic development

IV. Enabling infrastructure like railways would have to be provided necessarily by the government

V. Market development for the final products is an important prerequisite for industrial development.

1. I and II
2. I, III and IV
3. II, III and V
4. III, IV and V
5. I, II, III and V

16. The first capitalists investing in Indian economy were

1. the Indians
2. predominantly the British
3. the Europeans except the British
4. both A and B
5. both A and C

17. After the start of the first World War, all of the following could be likely reasons for the British governmentadopting a proactive stance towards Indian industry except

1. The major investors in Indian enterprises were British and they had missed out on an opportunity.
2. The war had created a huge demand for industrial goods.
3. The British government wanted economic development of the country as India was a strategic economically in the war.
4. The development of Indian economy was required for contributing towards the war effort.
5. The desire to see India as self-sufficient in technical expertise.

18. From this passage, it can be inferred that one of the problem that could have cropped up in the early stages of industrialization might have been

1. government interference in day-to-day operations of business.
2. equitable sharing of risks between domestic and foreign investors.
3. ensuring adequate working capital.
4. regulation of the stock markets to protect investors from dubious enterprises
5. the alignment of interests of the capitalists and the management.

19. From the passage it can be inferred that during the early part of twentieth century, starting a Greenfield project was more difficult for an Indian capitalist than for an European.

1. Definitely true as inferred from the passage.
2. It was true on a selective case by case basis.
3. No trend of discrimination between the two categories of capitalists can be inferred from the passage.
4. Preference was given to British capitalists, buffeted by the fact that the country was under British rule.
5. Preference was given to European capitalists.

20. During the early twentieth century, Indians were restricted to making investment in stocks of companies that were necessarily listed in India. This was done with the aim of confining Indian capital to India so that it could not compete with British capital.

1. Definitely true as inferred from the passage
2. It was true on a selective case by case basis.
3. This was the tact during the early part of the British rule.
4. This was true in the later part of the British rule.
5. No evidence to support the same is given in the passage.

DIRECTIONS for questions 21 to 24: *Go through the passage below and answer the questions that follow.*

Attempting to understand science and scientific reasoning in terms of the subjective beliefs of scientists would seem to be a disappointing departure for those who seek an objective account of science. Howson and Urbach have an answer to that charge. They insist that the Bayesian theory constitutes an *objective* theory of scientific inference. That is, given a set of prior probabilities and some new evidence, Bayes' theorem dictates in an objective way what the new, posterior, probabilities must be in the light of that evidence. There is no difference in this respect between Bayesianism and deductive logic, because logic has nothing to say about the source of the propositions that constitute the premises of a deduction either. It simply dictates what follows from those propositions once they are given. The Bayesian defence can be taken a stage further. It can be argued that the beliefs of individual scientists, however much they might differ at the outset, can be made to converge given the appropriate input of evidence. It is easy to see in an informal way how this can come about. Suppose two scientists start out by disagreeing greatly about the probable truth of hypothesis **h** which predicts otherwise unexpected experimental outcome **e**. The one who attributes a high probability to **h** will regard e as less unlikely than the one who attributes a low probability to **h**. So P(**e**) will be high for the former and low for the latter. Suppose now that **e** is experimentally confirmed. Each scientist will have to adjust the probabilities for **h** by the factor P(**e/h**)/P(**e**). However, since we are assuming that **e** follows from **h**, P(**e/h**) is 1 and the scaling factor is 1/P(**e**). Consequently, the scientist who started with a low probability for **h** will scale up that probability by a larger factor than the scientist who started with a higher probability for **h**. As more positive evidence comes in, the original doubter is forced to scale up the probability in such a way that it eventually approaches that of the already convinced scientist. In this way, argue the Bayesians, widely differing subjective opinions can be brought into conformity in response to evidence in an objective way.

21. Using the idea explicated in the passage above, the only scientific way to deny the validity of a counter-hypothesis put forward to explain a natural phenomenon would be to

1. take the counter-hypothesis and try to find flaws in its components.
2. question the source of alternative hypothesis.
3. question the authority of the scientist stating the alternative hypothesis.
4. Take the alternative explanation and ask for its fullest development in terms of possible ramifications otherthan the already existent outcome (e).
5. None of these.

22. The subjective beliefs of scientists referred to in the passage could be due to

1. multiple scientists studying multiple phenomena and putting forth multiple hypotheses
2. propositions offered by scientists being backed only by one's beliefs about their validity.
3. scientists presenting data selectively in support of their own favourite hypothesis over competing hypotheses.
4. scientists allowing their subjective opinions to bias their testing of hypothesis.
5. none of these

23. Scientists' beliefs which differ at the outset are related to

1. different outcomes only.
2. different hypotheses only.
3. different hypotheses about different outcomes.
4. differences in explanatory power of competing hypotheses.
5. none of these.

24. Strictly following the idea put forward in the article, which one of the following is a logical possibility

1. The idea that astrologers can predict stock market movements better than economists, if astrologers'hypothesis (**h**) is more consistently followed by outcomes (**e**) than that of economists.
2. The fact that stock-market movements are in sync with the movement of the heavenly bodies; both (**h**) and(**e**) contained in the same statement.
3. That certain astrological phenomena can influence thinking of humans (**e**) which is manifested in stock-market booms and crashes (**h**).
4. That certain astrological phenomena (**h**) car influence thinking of humans (e_1) which is manifested instock-market booms and crashes (e_2).
5. None of these.

DIRECTIONS for questions 25 to 28: *Go through the passage below and answer the questions that follow.*

The ignorant man is not the unlearned, but he who does not know himself, and the learned man is stupid when lie relies on books, on knowledge and on authority to give him understanding. Understanding comes only through self-knowledge, which is awareness of one's total psychological process. Thus education, in the true sense, is the understanding of oneself, for it is within each one of us that the whole of existence is gathered.

What we now call education is a matter of accumulating information and knowledge from books, which anyone can do who can read. Such education offers a subtle form of escape from ourselves and, like all escapes, it inevitably creates increasing misery. Conflict and confusion result from our own wrong relationship with people, things and ideas, and until we understand that relationship and alter it, mere learning, the gathering of facts and the acquiring of various skills, can only lead us to engulfing chaos and destruction.

As society is now organized, we send our children to school to learn some technique by which they can eventually earn a livelihood. We want to make the child first and foremost a specialist, hoping thus to give him a secure economic position. But does the cultivation of a technique enable us to understand ourselves?

While it is obviously necessary to know how to read and write, and to learn engineering or some other profession, will technique give us the capacity to understand life? Surely, technique is secondary; and if technique is the only thing we are striving for, we are obviously denying what is by far the greater part of life.

Life is pain, joy, beauty, ugliness, love, and when we understand it as a whole, at every level, that understanding creates its own technique. But the contrary is not true: technique can never bring about creative understanding.

Present-day education is a complete failure because it has overemphasized technique. In overemphasizing technique we destroy man. To cultivate capacity and efficiency without understanding life, without having a comprehensive perception of the ways of thought and desire, will only make us increasingly ruthless, which is to engender wars and jeopardize our physical security. The exclusive cultivation of technique has produced scientists, mathematicians, bridge lwiracrarspace conquerors; but do they understand the total process of life? Can any specialist experience life as a whole? Only when he ceases to be a specialist.

Technological progress does solve certain kinds of problems for some people at one level, but it introduces wider and deeper issues too. To live at one level, disregarding the total process of life, is to invite misery and destruction. The greatest need and most pressing problem for even' individual is to have an integrated comprehension of life, which will enable him to meet its ever-increasing complexities.

Technical knowledge, however necessary, will in no way resolve our inner, psychological pressures and conflict; and it is because we have acquired technical knowledge without understanding the total process of life that technology has become a means of destroying ourselves. The man who knows how to split the atom but has no love in his heart becomes a monster.

We choose a vocation according to our capacities; but will the following of a vocation lead us out of conflict and confusion? Some form of technical training seems necessary; but when we have become engineers, physicians, accountants - then what? Is the practice of a profession the fulfillment of life? Apparently with most of us it is. Our various professions may keep us busy for the greater part of our existence; but the very things that we produce and are so entranced with are causing destruction and misery. Our attitudes and values make of things and occupations the instruments of envy, bitterness and hate.

25. The passage implies that

1. Technique follows creative understanding.
2. A specialist too can enjoy life as a whole.
3. Technology necessarily leads to destruction and misery.
4. An atom-breaker becomes a monster.
5. None of the above.

26. This passage was most likely written in order to

1. persuade readers to shun technology.
2. coax the readers to transcend technological limits.
3. inspire readers to understand life as a whole.
4. rail against present-day education policy.
5. provoke a social movement against present-day education.

27. Which statement would most likely follow the truncated passage above?

1. Throughout the world, engineers are frantically designing machines which do not need men to operate them.
2. Another factor in the cultivation of technique is that it gives us a sense of security, not only economic, butpsychological as well.
3. The right kind of education, while encouraging the learning of a technique, should accomplish somethingwhich is of far greater importance: it should help man to experience the integrated process of life.
4. Without understanding ourselves, mere occupation leads to frustration, with its inevitable escapes throughall kinds of mischievous activities.
5. Life cannot be made to conform to a system, it cannot be forced into a framework, however noblyconceived; and a mind that has merely been trained in factual knowledge is incapable of meeting life with itsvariety, its subtlety, its depths and great heights.

28. What might be the most apposite title for the passage above?

1. Education and the significance of life
2. Life in its wholeness
3. The tragedy of technical education

4. Knowledge and ignorance
5. Technological progress: Is it for real?

29. Choose the option that points out sentence(s) with grammatical error(s).

i. I love the man dancing on the table.

ii. I love the man's dancing on the table.

iii. In 1986 Elie Wiesel was named the Nobel Peace Prize recipient, an honour established by Alfred Nobel.

iv. Neither of the recommendations works as well as we thought they would.

v. Either the Minister or the Minister's wife will have to excuse themselves from the reception to speak to the caterer.

1. iii and v
2. i and iv
3. ii and v
4. iii and iv
5. iv

30. Which revision best combines ideas without losing out on information?

There are still ample physical reminders of the history of the Ao tribe in Meghalaya. Impressive burial mounds, dating back hundreds of years, can be found along many of the rivers, for instance.

1. Impressive burial mounds, dating back hundreds of years, can be found along many of the rivers, forinstance; there are still ample physical reminders of the history of the Ao tribe in Meghalaya.
2. Since there are still ample physical reminders of the history of the Ao tribe in Meghalaya, impressiveburial mounds, dating back hundreds of years, can be found along many of the rivers, for instance.
3. Although impressive burial mounds, dating back hundreds of years, can be found along many of the rivers,for instance, there are still ample physical reminders of the history of the Ao tribe in Meghalaya.
4. I here are still ample physical reminders of the history of the Ao tribe in Meghalaya; impressive burialmounds, dating back hundreds of years, can be found along many of the rivers, for instance.
5. Ample physical reminders - of the history of the Ao tribe in Meghalaya - including impressive burialmounds dating back hundreds of years still exist along many of the rivers.

31. Choose the best revision of the following wordy sentence?

It seems that the library board will meet tomorrow, as a matter of fact.

1. As a matter of fact, the library board will meet tomorrow.
2. In fact, the library board will meet tomorrow.
3. It is apparent that the library board will meet tomorrow.
4. Library board will meet tomorrow.
5. The library board will meet tomorrow.

32. Amongst the options below, choose the one which is correctly punctuated?

1. Last Sunday, we went canoeing on the Brahmaputra river. You could see eagles high in the trees above us.

2. While we were canoeing last Sunday on the Brahmaputra river, high in the trees above us, you could see eagles.
3. We went canoeing last Sunday on the Brahmaputra river, and high in the trees above us, we could see eagles.
4. High in the trees above, the eagles were looking down at you, as we canoed on the Brahmaputra river last Sunday.
5. High above in the trees, eagles were looking at us, as we canoed on the Brahmaputra river last Sunday.

DIRECTIONS for questions 33 to 36: *Choose the option that correctly un-scrambles the paragraphs below:*

33. 1. The same is true for less fraught examples: dispensing with 'Truth' does not mean dispensing withaccuracy and attention to detail, and to suggest for example that the colonization of the New World neverhappened would be equally untenable.

2. To relinquish 'Truth' and the idea of one history does not lead to absolute relativism, where any version ofevents is taken as being equally valid as any other.
3. It does not, for example, give succour to those charlatans and ideologues who seek to deny that theHolocaust ever happened.
4. What I am suggesting here is complex, but its importance demands a careful reading.
5. The evidence for the systematic murder of more than six million people by the Nazis is overwhelming.
6. To try to argue that it never occurred is to violate the voices of the past, to suppress that evidence whichgoes against the twisted thesis.

1. 2-3-5-6-1-4 2. 5-6-1-2-4-3
3. 4-2-3-5-6-1 4. 2-4-5-3-6-1
5. 4-5-1-6-3-2

34. 1. You could try friendly competition, or set yourself team targets and agree that you'll all go out for anevening together if you meet them.

2. Presumably your team members have the same problem, so perhaps you could find collective incentives.
3. Work towards targets of your own, or promise yourself a reward for certain achievements.
4. Or aim towards promotion or earning new responsibilities as an incentive to keep you enthusiastic.
5. Find ways to motivate yourself.
6. Or simply make a point of congratulating each other on good work, even if the boss doesn't join in.

1. 1-4-2-6-3-5 2. 5-2-1-4-3-6
3. 1-4-6-3-2-5 4. 5-3-6-2-1-4
5. 5-3-4-2-1-6

35. 1. Individuals and firms moving into a new and unfamiliar field of activity are increasingly usinginformation resources provided over the Internet.

2. The economic importance of a strong, viable business sector, especially a strong and viable small businesssector with its potential for employment and export gen-

eration, makes it imperative that government agencies provide encouragement, leadership and effective support.

3. Governments undertake a wide variety of initiatives to achieve these ends and online informationprovision is one of many such initiatives.
4. The power of the Internet to deliver information and services online offers an opportunity for governmentsto support businesses and the economies they serve.
5. Many small to medium-size enterprises may turn initially to a government agency for business-relatedinformation, in part because they lack the confidence and financial resources to engage private consultants at the initial stages of the planning process.
6. This is an important issue, both for government economic development strategies and to help them meetthe rising public expectations of online service provision.

1. 1-4-3-6-2-5
2. 4-6-2-3-1-5
3. 3-6-2-1-5-3
4. 2-3-6-5-1-4
5. 5-4-6-2-3-1

36. 1. Employees are seeing organizational leaders who appear to have only their personal interests in sight.

2. All the while, these same leaders appear to be walking away from their failures with multimillion-dollarexit bonuses or millions in forgiven “loans.”
3. They are feeling increasingly expendable and disposable, all for the purpose of enriching CEOs and top leaders.
4. Workers are feeling less and less connected with top management.
5. Some corporate leaders are simply losing touch.
6. Those they lead are, understandably, losing confidence and trust in their leaders.

1. 5-6-1-4-3-2
2. 1-2-4-3-5-6
3. 1-5-6-3-4-2
4. 1-3-4-2-5-6
5. 1-3-5-6-2-4

Answer Key

1. 1	**2.** 1	**3.** 5	**4.** 3	**5.** 1	**6.** 4	**7.** 1
8. 5	**9.** 4	**10.** 5	**11.** 5	**12.** 1	**13.** 2	**14.** 5
15. 3	**16.** 4	**17.** 5	**18.** 3	**19.** 3	**20.** 5	**21.** 2
22. 4	**23.** 1	**24.** 3	**25.** 5	**26.** 3	**27.** 3	**28.** 3
29. 2	**30.** 5	**31.** 3	**32.** 3	**33.** 4	**34.** 5	**35.** 4
36. 1						

Explanations

1. 1 *Crucible* is a container in which metals or other substances may be melted or subjected to very high temperature. In the given question crucible refers to tough exercises. The synonym of crucible is cauldron which means a large cooking pot.

2. 1 *Juvenile* means childish and juvenile delinquency refers to the regular committing of criminal acts by a young person. The antonym of juvenile is puerile which means mature or mellowed.

3. 5 *Spurious* means false or fake. In the given question all the words except questionable means false or fake.

4. 3 *Exercise* in the given question means to use a power right or quality or an effect.

5. 1 *Assumptions* means beliefs or hypothesis. Its synonym is hunch which means something based on a feeling rather than evidence.

6. 4 Criticism is an expression of disapproval.

7. 1

8. 5

9. 4

10. 5 Those who agree to the aims of socialism neither care nor understand how these aims can be achieved.

11. 5

12. 1

13. 2

14. 5

15. 3 The answer should be II, III and IV.

16. 4

17. 5

18. 3

19. 3

20. 5

21. 2

22. 4

23. 1

24. 3

25. 5

26. 3

27. 3

28. 3

29. 2 In sentence I 'man' should be replaced by 'men's'. In sentence IV 'they' should be replaced by 'it'.

30. 5

31. 3

32. 3

33. 4

34. 5

35. 4

36. 1

XAT 2009

Number of Questions – 35
Time : 30 M.

Section - A
VERBAL AND LOGICAL ABILITY

1. Identify the correct sentence from the option given below.

1. The news channel agreed to report that next Sunday the couple had been married for 10 years.
2. The news channel agreed to report that next Sunday the couple will have been married for 10 years.
3. The news channel agreed to report that next Sunday the couple will be married for 10 years.
4. The news channel agreed to report that next Sunday the couple could have been married for 10 years.
5. The news channel agreed to report that next Sunday the couple has been married since 10 years.

DIRECTION for questions 2–4: *Analyse the following passage and provide an appropriate answer for the questions.*

The greens' success has clear policy implications, especially on issue of nuclear power, ecological tax reform, and citizenship rights. But success also has implications for green parties themselves. Greens have always faced a unique 'strategic conundrum' arising from their radical alternative politics with participation in mainstream or 'grey' parliamentary and government structures? Throughout the 1990s most green parties shed their radical cloth in an attempt to capture votes, even at the expense of green party unity and purity. Most were rewarded with electoral success well beyond what had been imaginable in the 1980s. The price to pay has been tortured internal debates about strategy, and new questions about green party identity and purpose. Today the key questions facing green parties revolve around not whether to embrace power, but what to do with it. More specifically, green parties face three new challenges in the new millennium: first how to carve out a policy niche as established parties and governments become wiser to green demands, and as green concerns themselves appear more mainstream. Second, how to take green ideas beyond the confines of rich industrialized states into Eastern Europe and the developing world where green parties remain marginal and environmental problems acute. Third, how to ensure that the broader role of green parties – as consciousness raisers, agitators, conscience of parliament and politics – is not sacrificed on the altar of electoral success. Green parties have come a long way since their emergence and development in the 1970s and 1980s. They have become established players able to shape party competition, government formation, and government policy. But this very 'establishment' carries risks for a party whose core values and identities depend mightily on their ability to challenge the conventional order, to agitate and to annoy. For most green parties, the greatest fear is not electoral decline so much as the prospect of becoming a party with parliamentary platform, ministerial voice, but nothing new to say.

2. Which out of the following is closest in meaning to the first of three challenges mentioned in the paragraph?

1. Niche of green parties is being eroded by mainstream parties.
2. Green parties are finding it difficult to find new strategy.
3. Green Parties have become stronger over a period of time.
4. Some green parties are becoming grey.
5. Non green parties are becoming less relevant than green parties.

3. Which of the following is the most important point that author highlights?

1. Challenges before green parties to change their strategy from green activism to green governance.
2. How should green parties win confidence and support of governments?
3. Transformation of green parties in recent decades.
4. Green movement is not strong in developing countries.
5. Non green parties are becoming less relevant than green parties.

4. How best can mainstream political parties, in India, keep green parties at bay?

1. By imposing green tax
2. By allow carbon trading.
3. By including green agenda in their governance.
4. By hiring Al Gore, the Nobel prize winner, as an ambassador.
5. By not letting green parties fight elections.

DIRECTION for questions 5–7: *Analyse the following passage and provide an appropriate answer for the questions.*

The Sapir-Whorf hypothesis, also known as the linguistic relativity hypothesis, refers to the proposal that the particular language one speaks influences the way one thinks about reality. The linguistic relativity hypothesis focuses on structural differences among natural languages such as Hopi, Chinese, and English, and asks whether the classifications of reality implicit in such structures affect our thinking about reality. Analytically, linguistic relativity as an issue stands between two others: a semiotic-level concern with how speaking any natural language whatsoever might influence the general potential for human thinking (i.e., the general role of natural language in the evolution or development of human intellectual functioning), and a functional or discourse-level concern with how using any given language code in a particular way might influence thinking (i.e., the impact of special discursive practices such as schooling and literacy on formal thought). Although analytically distinct, the three issues are intimately related in both theory and practice. For example, claims about linguistic relativity depend on understanding the general psychological mechanisms linking language to thinking, and on understanding the diverse uses of speech in discourse to accomplish acts of descriptive reference. Hence, the relation of particular linguistic structures to patterns of thinking forms only one part of the broader array of questions about the significance of language for thought. Proposals of linguistic relativity necessarily develop two linked claims among the key terms of the hypothesis (i.e., language, thought, and reality). Fist, languages differ significantly in their *interpretations* of experienced reality – both what they select for representation and how they arrange it. Second, language interpretations have *influences* on thought about reality more generally – whether at the individual or cultural level. Claims for linguistic relativity thus require both articulating the contrasting interpretations of reality latent in the structures of different languages, and assessing their broader influences on, or relationships to, the cognitive interpretation of reality.

5. Which of the following conclusions can be derived based on Sapir-Whorf hypotheses?

1. Americans and Indians would have similar intelligence.
2. South Indians and North Indians would have similar intelligence.
3. Those with same intelligence would speak the same language.
4. Those with similar intelligence may speak the same language.
5. Structure of language does not affect cognition.

6. If Sapir-Whorf hypothesis were to be true, which of the following conclusions would logically follow?

A. To develop vernacular languages, government should promote public debates and discourses.

B. Promote vernacular languages as medium of instruction in school.

C. Cognitive and cultural realities are related.

1. A only
2. B only
3. C only
4. A and B
5. A, B and C

7. Which of the following proverbs may be false, if above passage were to be right?

A. If speech is silver, silence is gold.

B. When you have spoken a word, it reigns over you. When it is unspoken you reign over it.

C. Speech of yourself ought to be seldom and well chosen.

1. A and B
2. B and C
3. C only
4. A only
5. A, B and C

DIRECTION for questions 8–9: *Analyse the following passage and provide an appropriate answer for the questions 8 through 9 that follow.*

In Hume's eyes productive labour was the greatest asset of a country, and foreign trade was valuable because it enabled a nation to use more and more varied labour than would otherwise be possible. But commerce was of mutual advantage to the nations involved, not a benefit to one and injury to other. "The increase of riches and commerce in any one nation," added Hume, "instead of hurting, commonly, promotes the riches and commerce of all its neighbours." "The emulation in rival nations serves…to keep industry alive in all of them."

8. The importance of foreign trade, in eyes of Hume, was due to that:

1. it allowed the employment of surplus labour in a nation.
2. it allowed the diversion of labour to export oriented industries.
3. it allowed the deeper specialization of the same labour force.
4. it allowed varied application of labour force in a nation.
5. it allowed application of varied labour force in a nation.

9. As per Hume, free trade between nations was made advantageous by the outcome of:

1. mutual increase in riches and commerce.
2. emulation of industrial activity by different nations.
3. affable promotion of industrial activity among nations.

4. productive employment of labour in different nations.
5. higher wages received by labour in exporting nations.

DIRECTION for questions 10–13: *Analyse the following passage and provide an appropriate answer for the questions.*

Demography of orgnisations, also called population ecology is an interesting field. It proposes that organisational mortality processes depend upon the age and size of the organizations, as well as on characteristics of populations and environments. Moreover, there is evidence of an imprinting process – meaning that environmental conditions at certain early phases in an organisation's development have long-term consequence. In particular, organizations subject to intense competition have elevated mortality hazards at all ages. A central theme is structural inertia, the tendency for organizations to respond slowly relative to the speed of environmental change. A central argument holds that the inertia derives from the very characteristics that make organizations favoured actors in modern society in terms of reliability and (formal) accountability. It follows that changes in an organisation's core features are disruptive and increase mortality hazards, at least in the short-run. Research on this subject tends to support this view. The concept of niche provides a framework for relating environmental variations and competition to population dynamics and segmentation. Much empirical work examines the niches of organisational populations in terms of dimensions of social, political, and economic environments. Most research in this field builds on theories of resource partition and of density dependence. Resource-partitioning theory concerns the relationship between increasing market concentration and increasing proliferation of specialists in mature industries. The key implication of this theory concerns the effects of concentration on the viability of specialist organizations (those that seek to exploit a narrow range of resources). The theory of density-dependent organisational evolution synthesizes ecological and institutional processes. It holds that growth in the number of organizations in a population (density) drives processes of social legitimatization and competition that, in turn, shape the vital rates.

10. Consider the following: "Tata Steel, one of biggest steel makers in the world, was born in Jamshedpur." If above passage is true, then it can be concluded that location of Tata Steel has been one of the reasons for its success.

A. The conclusion is false.
B. This is a farfetched conclusion.
C. This is a valid conclusion.

1. A only
2. B only
3. C only
4. A and B
5. B and C

11. "Tata Steel, one of biggest steel makers in the world, was born in Jamshedpur. The very success of Tata Steel could lead to its failure in the future and hence the challenge for Tata Steel is to recognize its strengths that made it successful in initial conditions and stick to them."

A. This is a valid conclusion.
B. The conclusion is contrary to the ideas described in the passage.
C. The conclusion is an internally contradictory.

1. A only
2. B only
3. C only
4. A and B
5. B and C

12. Most top-notch business consultants recommend changing the entire configuration of an organisation's strategy, structure and systems. If the ideas contained in the passage are agreed to, then such a recommendation:

1. tends to rejuvenate the organization.
2. tends to make the organization more aligned to the external environment.
3. tends to increase the competitiveness of the organization by redefining its core competence.
4. tends to increase the vulnerability of the organization.
5. tends to make the organization industry leader by reformulating its niche.

13. Recently it was reported that Indian textile sector was not doing well. If the ideas contained in the passage are agreed to, then which of the following could be the possible reason(s)?

A. All Indian firms are as old as international firms.

B. Indian textile firms are dispersed all over the country, with most of them also having international presence.

C. Textile firms in India were subjected to trade union activity in the period from 1960s to 1980s.

1. A
2. B
3. C
4. A and B
5. A, B and C

DIRECTION for questions 14 & 15: *Go through the following passage.*

The Yoga system is divided into two principal parts – Hatha and Raja Yoga. Hatha Yoga deals principally with the physiological part of man with a view to establish his health and train his will. The processes prescribed to arrive at this end are so difficult that only a few resolute souls go through all the stages of its practice. Many have failed and some have died in the attempt. It is therefore strongly denounced by all the philosophers. The most illustrious Shankaracharya has remarked in his treatise called Aparokshanubhuti that "the system of Hatha Yoga was intended for those whose worldly desires are not pacified or uprooted."

14. Which one of the following, if true, most substantially strengthens the idea given in the passage?

1. The percentage of people in a given ashram practicing Raja Yoga is more than the percentage of people practicing Hatha Yoga.
2. The number of people in a given ashram practicing Raja Yoga is more than the number of people practicing Hatha Yoga.
3. The number of Yoga schools teaching Raja Yoga is more than the number of Yoga schools teaching Hatha Yoga.
4. The number of teachers teaching Raja Yoga is more than number of teachers teaching hatha Yoga
5. The percentage of students who have successfully learnt Raja Yoga is more than the percentage of students who have successfully learnt Hatha Yoga.

15. Which of the following option best summarises Shankaracharya's comments on Hatha Yoga?

1. Hatha Yoga is for those whose worldly desires are not placated.
2. Hatha Yoga has disastrous consequences for Yoga practitioners.

3. Practised under the guidance of experts, Hatha Yoga is better than Raja Yoga for some people.
4. Raja Yoga gives better results and in a shorter time period for most people, and therefore it should be encouraged.
5. Hatha Yoga is ill-suited for people with strong worldly desires.

DIRECTION for questions 16–17: *Identify the correct sentences from the options given below.*

16. 1. When kite flying you can always tell when you lose a kite because the string feels loose.
2. When kite flying you can always tell when you loose a kite because the string feels lose.
3. When kite flying you can always tell when you loose a kite because the string feels loose.
4. While flying a kite, you can always tell when you lose a kite because the string feels lose.
5. While flying a kite, you can always tell if you lost a kite when the string felt lose.

17. 1. If XAT aspirants had not taken so long checking each question before attempting the next question they might not have run out of time.
2. If XAT aspirants had taken so long checking each question before attempting the next question they might not have run out of time.
3. Had XAT aspirants not took so long checking every question before attempting the next question they might not have run out of time.
4. If XAT aspirants had took so long checking each and every question before attempting the next question they might not have run out of time.
5. Had XAT aspirants not taken so long checking all questions before attempting the next question they might not have run out of time.

DIRECTION for questions 18–19: *Read the sentences and choose the option that best arranges them in a logical order.*

18. A. The *moral will* arises when, for the reasons we saw earlier, this negation has to be negated; the *individual moral will* understands that it is the existence of the universal will, which is therefore internal to it.
B. This constitutes a negation, because the *individual will* is understood not to be the existence of the universal will.
C. This says that in abstract right, as we have just seen, the *individual will* takes its freedom (the *universal will* that that has being in itself) to exist independent of (that is, in opposition to) itself and its particular contents.
D. Rather, the *universal will* is thought to exist outside any *individual will*, in the contracts that bind a number of property-owning wills together, and in the punishments that enforce breaches of those contracts.

1. A, B, C, D
2. C, B, D, A
3. C, A, B, D
4. A, C, B, D
5. D, C, B, A

19. A. In the concept, universality, particularity, and individuality are understood as being immediately identical to each other.
B. As immediately identical, these "moments of the concept" cannot be separated.

C. This means that they must be thought of as a single unity, that none of three can be understood apart from the others, since in the concept their *identity* is *posited,* each of its moments can only be grasped immediately on the basis of and together with the others.

D. The interrelation of universality, particularity, and individuality is otherwise in judgment.

1. A, B, C, D
2. C, B, D, A
3. D, A, B, C
4. B, C, A, D
5. B, C, D, A

DIRECTION for questions 20–23: *Go through the paragraphs below and answer the questions that follow.*

20. Ram, an economist, and Ramesh, an astrologer, had a debate. Ram said "Astrology does not work. It just cannot predict." "It can predict better than your subject" rebutted Ramesh.

The evidence that best resolves the above debate will be:

1. Conduct a survey among scientists asking which one of the two should be considered as a science.
2. Compare past performance of astrologers and economists in terms of number of predictions, which have come true.
3. Conduct a survey among economists asking their opinion regarding the ability of economic theory to predict economic phenomena.
4. Conduct an experiment where both astrologers and economists would be asked to predict the future. Compare the number of predictions that come true.
5. Conduct an experiment where both astrologers and economists would be asked to predict the future. Compare the percentage of predictions that come true.

21. "There is nothing so stupid as an educated man, if you can get him off the thing he was educated in."

Which of the following, if true, most seriously undermines the author's contention?

1. True education implies a well-rounded exposure to major subjects.
2. An educated man will not discuss things which he does not understand.
3. The cost of a general education has led to the unfortunate fact that a person's education is confined to one field.
4. Stupidity, like intelligence, is relative and therefore depends on the intelligence of the persons' peers.
5. Education is one of the main causes of people recognizing their capabilities and developing them further.

22. In this era of global capital flows, so much money is now flowing throughout the world that no single country can fight the problem of inflation effectively by tightening its monetary policy.

If the above is true, which of the following could be most logically concluded?

1. Changes in cash reserve ratio by Reserve Bank of India will control the rate inflation in India.
2. Countries' finance ministries have sufficient control over their respective economies.
3. Countries' finance ministries have insufficient control over their respective economies.

4. Inflation does not matter as long as incomes increase.
5. Citizens should limit their consumption which will reduce the demand of products, thus reducing inflation.

23. Nature lovers are attracted to forests and nature parks. Just look at the number of people visiting the Corbett National Park. Which of the following exhibits a pattern of reasoning least dissimilar to the one exhibited in the argument above?

1. Defence personnel who are trained in extremely rigorous procedures often end up as dysfunctional members of the society. Hence if an officer is not trained rigorously, such an officer is more likely to be useful to the society.
2. This machinery has increased the work efficiency of the workers. As a result, some of these workers are surplus to the company.
3. Fleas must thrive in a warm environment. During warm whether my dog suffers from fleas more so than during cooler weather.
4. Cigarette smoking is known to cause lung cancer in some people. However, most victims of lung cancer live in region where smoking is uncommon.
5. Alcoholics and teetotalers usually appear at the same restaurant at the same time of the day. Therefore, alcoholics and teetotalers must be hungry at the same time.

DIRECTION for question 24–30: *Go through the questions below and answer them.*

24. *Which sentence includes a euphemism?*

1. Cell phone network signals are weak in the hilly regions.
2. Bottled water is reputed to be safe for drinking under all circumstances.
3. A cemetery is a place where people are buried when they pass away.
4. It is stupid to çry over spilt milk.
5. Criminal court arbitrates between the parties to the case.

25. Which of the following contains a non-sequitur?

1. If statisticians are made judges, they will accept or reject arguments based on probability analyses.
2. Public trust in politicians is at an all time low and we can't insist that the politicians go back to school.
3. Before preparing the annual budget, the CEO of XYZ Steel Limited takes opinion of all the stakeholders.
4. In cricket, the batting average does not always reflect a batsman's ability because it does not reflect how many wins he was instrumental for.
5. Ordinary citizens do not have sufficient grasp of economic indicators to validate published inflation data.

26. Recommence is to suspend as: nonchalant is to:

1. Carefree
2. Beleaguered
3. Tirade
4. Agreement
5. Disagreement

27. Which of the following sentences draws a metaphor?

1. Karl Marx argued that the interests of two classes – the proletariat and the bourgeois – are always in conflict and irreconcilable.

2. Karl Marx labeled the capitalist a parasite on the back of labour because the whole value or produce created by the laboring man was expropriated by the capitalist.
3. Weber held that the protestant ethic was responsible for the rise of capitalism in medieval Europe.
4. Galbraith argued for a better balance between private affluence and public poverty, including measures to protect the environment against the excesses of private companies.
5. Schumpeter argued that changes in economy are brought about by creative destruction.

28. Which sentence includes an example of personification?

1. *Banjaras* of Rajasthan are the human equivalent of an endangered species and have no defence against the encroachment of farmers onto their ancestral lands.
2. Take airline pilots for example: they do not need to be graduates to qualify for this job and most pilots are on a salary of Rs. 300,000 per month or more.
3. Recent research provided stark evidence that in education money still plays an important role; it was found that children from poor households could not perform as well as children from rich households.
4. Girls in the family should have a share in the ancestral property as a matter of right whether the will includes it explicitly or not.
5. Democracy does not help the common citizen and it ultimately degenerates into an oligarchy.

29. As man casts off worn-out garments and puts on others that are new, similarly the embodied soul, casting off worn-out bodies, enters into others, which are new. Of the following, which one best typifies the argument?

1. Inductive generalization
2. Predictive argument
3. Argument from authority
4. Causal argument
5. Argument form analogy

30. Which sentence includes an oxymoron?

1. On weekend we ate and drank a lot.
2. Meena corrected me by pointing out that she wanted pizza instead of burger.
3. Media reported the attack on media-persons.
4. He loved his aunt but found her kindness suffocating.
5. One should not compare apples and oranges.

DIRECTION for questions 31–32: *Analyse the following passage and provide an appropriate answer for the questions.*

Since power is itself a value, forms of influence which include power in their scope usually themselves forms of power. The king's mistress, though she has only influence, not power, over the king, may have power over his subjects to the degree of that influence. Forms of influence based on power are themselves forms of power only if the scope of the influence is included within that of the power in question. The king may exercise influence over standards of morality, say, by virtue of his power position, but he does not necessarily exercise power over morality.

31. Which combination of following statements best summarises the idea expressed in the paragraph?

A. Strength of an influence determines its power.

B. Influence always contributes power to the welder of influence beyond the scope of influence.

C. Proximity to authority is itself a source of power.

D. Forms of influence are power only if they can influence behavior.

1. A, B
2. A, C
3. A, D
4. A, C, D
5. A, B, D

32. Which of the following is similar to ideas expressed in the paragraph?

1. A king can influence what dramas are enacted by artists.
2. A king can influence who acts in dramas in his kingdom.
3. A king can indicate the appropriateness of dramas enacted.
4. A king can influence the prices charged from drama groups by actors.
5. A king can influence on what drama audience spend their money.

DIRECTION for questions 33–34: *Go through the paragraphs below and answer the questions that follow.*

33. Many entrepreneurs try to control the composition of their boards of directions, but more experienced entrepreneurs. Tend to share control, inviting participation from institutional investors and outside directors.

Which option best summarizes the idea that might be guiding experienced entrepreneurs' behavior?

1. The experienced entrepreneurs expect experienced directors to monitor the performance of the enterprise and be a sounding board.
2. The experienced entrepreneurs expect the institutional investors to support the opinion of entrepreneurs on all major decisions.
3. The experienced entrepreneurs expect the institutional investors and outside directors to agree to higher remuneration for the board members.
4. Experienced entrepreneurs expect the experienced directors to engage in day-to-day management of the company.
5. More the number of influential people on board, the easier it is to raise finances.

34. All the parliamentarians whom the reporter interviewed told that they had voted as per their conscience. Therefore, probably all the parliamentarians voted as per their conscience. This argument is an example of:

1. Inductive generalization
2. Predictive argument
3. Generalization based on authority
4. Deduction generalization
5. Argument from analogy

35. Which sentence suffers most from hyperbole?

1. Most collectors of coins would give the Earth to own one of the copper coins issued by Mohammad Bin Tughlaq.
2. It is thought that eating raw tomatoes would greatly reduce the risk of cancer, but tomato sauce can have a greater effect since it is made from many raw tomatoes.
3. Cricket has a great following in India, but the twenty-twenty format took the game to nook and corner of the world.

4. We face an imminent drinking water crisis in India as the population growth is accompanied by a general decrease in rainfall.
5. Nuclear fusion has potential to solve the energy crisis of not only our country, but that of the entire world.

Answer Key

1. 2	**2.** 1	**3.** 1	**4.** 3	**5.** 4	**6.** 3	**7.** 1
8. 5	**9.** 2	**10.** 3	**11.** 1	**12.** 4	**13.** 2	**14.** 5
15. 1	**16.** 1	**17.** 1	**18.** 2	**19.** 1	**20.** 5	**21.** 1
22. 5	**23.** 3	**24.** 3	**25.** 2	**26.** 2	**27.** 2	**28.** 3
29. 5	**30.** 4	**31.** 3	**32.** 3	**33.** 1	**34.** 1	**35.** 1

Explanations

1. 2 The news channel agreed to report something that will be completed at a future date. The present perfecttense (will have been married) is the most appropriate to convey this meaning.

2. 1 The first challenge for the green parties is spelt out in lines 11-12 'how to carve out a policy niche asestablished parties and governments become wiser to green demands'. Option 1 is closest in meaning to this.

3. 1 Choice 1 is the right answer. It is backed by line 1 (the greens' success has clear policy implications . . .),line 10 (. . . not whether to embrace power, but what to do with it') and the concluding lines.

4. 3 The passage says '. . established parties and governments becomes wiser to green demands', 'greenconcerns. . . appear more mainstream' and of green parties having 'nothing new to say'. In view of thischoice 3 is the best answer.

5. 4 The focus of the passage is on how language may influence the way one thinks. Hence only choice 3 and4 are possible answers. Choice 4 is better since it says 'may' whereas C says 'would'.

6. 3 The passage examines a hypothesis on how language may influence people's thinking and the last line refers to 'cognitive interpretation of reality'. Hence only statement C is true. The passage doesn't state or imply the superiority of the vernacular. Hence statements 1 and 2 can be ruled out.

7. 1 The passage discusses the influence of language on cognitive development. Hence proverbs 1 (which says'silence is gold') and proverbs 2 (which says you have power over the unspoken word whereas spoken word has power over you) are both false. Proverb 3 can be true since language has influence over thinking, your speech must be carefully chosen.

8. 5 Refer to line 2 (. . . . foreign trade was valuable because it enabled a nation to use more and more varied labour than would other wise be possible). Choice E is, therefore, the right answer. Choice D is ruled outbecause it is not 'varied application' but 'application of varied labour force'.

9. 2 Refer to the concluding sentence. 'Emulation' means strive to equal or imitate.

10. 3 The conclusion that the location of Tata Steel has been one of the reasons for its success is valid because the passage says '. . . environmental conditions at certain early phases in an organization's development has long-term consequences' (lines 4-5).

11. 1 This is a valid conclusion as per the passage since the passage says '. . . changes in an organisationscore features are disruptive and increase mortality hazards . . . . ' (lines 10-11).

12. 4 Since change is 'disruptive and increases mortality hazards' it follows that 'changing the entireconfiguration of an organisation's strategies, structure and systems' would make it more vulnerable.

13. 2 Since the passage says 'environmental conditions . . . have long-term consequences' (lines 4-5), statement 2 could be the reason. Statement 1 is ruled out since being 'as old as international firms' would means all are affected equally by age or time. Statement 3 is ruled out since nothing is mentioned about trade unions.

14. 5 The passage does not elaborate on Raja Yoga. It only talks about the difficulty in learning it. (. . . only a few resolute souls go through all the stages of its practice). Hence if choice E (which says a greater percentage of students are successful in learning Raja Yoga than Hatha Yoga) were true, it would strengthen the given idea in the passage. The words 'given ashram' makes choices A and B specific. Choices C and D talk of schools and teachers (which are not mentioned) whereas choice E talks of students.

15. 1 Shankarcharya's comment on Hatha Yoga is found in the last sentence. Choices B, C and D can be ruled out. Between A and E, the latter talks of only 'strong worldly desires' whereas the former talks of 'worldly desires not placated'. Hence choice A is more appropriate since Shankracharya also mentions 'worldly desires not pacified or uprooted.'

16. 1 The word 'lose' (form of 'lost') refers to suffering the deprivation of something whereas 'loose' means not rigidly fastened'. Only choice A has both the words in the right places.

17. 1 Choice A is the best sentence - the focus here is on individual questions; hence 'each' is better than 'all' in E. The present perfect (had not taken) in the 'if' clause is rightly matched with 'might not have' in the main clause.

18. 2 None of the sentences appear to be first sentence of a para, so it is clear that they are part of a paragraph.We must, therefore, look for links between the sentences that help us to order them. 'This constitutesa negation . . .' in sentence 2 refers to what has been said in sentence 3 - as seen from the contents of thetwo sentences. Hence 2 follows 3. Sentence 4 follows, as it is an elaboration of what has been said in 3, 2.Sentence 1 concludes with 'this negation has to be negated' which makes it clear that it follows the otherthree.

19. 1 Choice A (1, 2, 3, 4) is the best sequence. Sentences 1 and 2 are linked by the words 'immediately identical' and 'these' in 2 refers to the concepts mentioned in 1. Sentence 3 follows 2 - 'unity' in 3 and 'cannot be separated' in 2. Sentence 4 is conclusive in nature.

20. 5 The para gives an argument between an economist and an astrologer on whose prediction is more reliable.What would resolve their debate is who predicts better and this depends on the 'percentage' of theirpredictions coming true rather than on the 'number'.

21. 1 The author's contention is that an educated man is stupid if you can get him off the things he was educated in. Choice A says' true education implies a well rounded exposure to major subjects'. Hence, if this is true, you can't get an him 'off the thing he was educated in'. So this undermines the author's contention.

22. 5 The given para says 'no single country can fight the problem of inflation effectively; since there is globalcapital flows. Choices A and B negate this. Choice D is irrelevant. Choice C is not right since 'insufficientcontrol' is vague - it still implies some control. Choice E is apt since if all the citizens act in a particular way, they can reduce inflation

23. 3 The given argument has the following reasoning - given the number of people 'visiting a national park, we conclude that nature lovers are attracted to forests. Choice C has similar reasoning - given the number of fleas that afflict the dog (in summer than in winter) the speaker concludes that fleas thrive in a warmenvironment.

24. 3 Choice A is not a euphemism since it talks of weak signals. Choice B only says 'reputed to be safe' (hinting that it may not be safe). Choice D is not a euphemism since it mentions crying and spilt milk. Choice E is a neutral statement. Choice C can be called a euphemism since it refers to death as 'pass away'.

25. 2 A non-sequitur is an inference that does not follow from the premise and statement B is the answer. Theinference' - 'we can't insist that politicians go back to school' is not based on the premise 'public trust inpoliticians is at an all time low'.

26. 2 Recommence is to start again and suspend is to stop. The relationship is antonymous. 'Nonchalant'is 'unworried' or 'indifferent'. Its antonym could be 'beleaguered' (harassed).

27. 2 Sentence B has a metaphor (a figure of speech in which a word for one idea or thing is used in place ofanother to suggest a likeness). Instead of saying that a capitalist is like a parasite the sentence says, 'Karl Marx labelled the capitalist a parasite on the back of labour.

28. 3 A personification is when an inanimate object is presented as a living thing. Sentence C provides anexample when it says 'money . . . plays an important role', money being inanimate cannot 'play'.

29. 5 The given lines use an analogy (comparison) to make an argument. Just as we cast off old clothes and wear new one, so the soul casts off old body to enter a new one.

30. 4 An oxymoron is a combination of contradictory words (like sweet sorrow). Sentence D has an oxymoron in 'kindness suffocating.'

31. 3 Statement 1 and 4 together give the gist of the passage. Statement 2 does not reflect the content of thepassage. Statement 3 is not necessarily true.

32. 3 Choice C echoes the concluding line of the para.

33. 1 The words 'share control' shows that entrepreneurs want experienced directors to monitor the performance of the enterprise'.

34. 1 The word 'inductive' means inference of a generalized conclusion from particular instances. Since the given passage does this, choice A is the answer.

35. 1 A hyperbole is an extravagant exaggeration, and choice A is an example - 'would give the Earth' is a hyperbole. One may want something desperately and be ready to make sacrifices to obtain it but no one can or would 'give the earth'.